UNDERSTANDING MOVIES

FIFTH CANADIAN EDITION

LOUIS GIANNETTI
Case Western
Reserve University

JIM LEACH
Brock University

Pearson Canada
Toronto

Library and Archives Canada Cataloguing in Publication

Giannetti, Louis D

Understanding movies / Louis Giannetti, Jim Leach. — 5th Canadian ed.

Includes index.

ISBN 978-0-13-701036-3

1. Motion pictures — Textbooks. I. Leach, Jim II. Title.

PN1994.G47 2011 791.43 C2010-900201-6

ISBN 978-0-13-701036-3

Vice-President, Editorial Director: Gary Bennett
Editor-in-Chief: Ky Pruesse
Editor, Humanities & Social Sciences: Joel Gladstone
Marketing Manager: Arthur Gee
Developmental Editor: Heather Parker
Production Editor: Richard di Santo
Copy Editor: Barbara Kamienski
Proofreader: Nancy Carroll
Production Coordinator: Avinash Chandra
Composition: MPS Limited, A Macmillan Company
Photo Researchers: Amanda Campbell, Karen Hunter
Art Director: Julia Hall
Interior and Cover Design: Miriam Blier
Cover Image: Patrik Giardino/Corbis

3 4 5 14 13 12 11

Printed and bound in the United States of America.

In Memoriam

Lynn R. Jones
1939–1970
—Louis Giannetti

To Barry, Jeannette, and Joan
—Jim Leach

Contents

Foreword

by Patricia Rozema

Movies have different functions. Some are games of chess, others are calls for justice, others jokes or formal experiments or fashion shows or historical memoirs or defences of the status quo or national anthems or love letters or essays or revenge fantasies (very popular), involuntary *cris du coeur* or, as Jean Renoir liked to say, a ride in a boat with a friend. Many—I might even say most—are fairly bald attempts on the part of the filmmakers to impress and be liked. Another huge percentage are cynical retreads of previous hits intended to make money and advance careers.

Given this huge range in types of cinema, I've never thought it was my place to say what is the *right* kind of movie. I do my kind; everyone else does theirs. But maybe writing a Foreword is the kind of place where one should forego the relativistic there's-room-for-everyone stance and attempt to speak not just about "what is," but also of "what ought to be." A manifesto even.

Especially now, on the eve of seismic change in the filmmaking industry where the old financing and theatrical distribution models just aren't working anymore and the new duplication and transmission technologies are making it pretty much impossible to control or predict profit in any significant way. Some say the sky is falling. Feature-length fiction films other than the "four quadrant tentpole franchise" (giant repeatable spectacles that appeal to young, old, male, female) just won't be made anymore. I'm actually not that worried. People want filmed fiction more than ever. But the business model is making it hard to make money. The ground is shifting under our feet. Filmmakers may end up (unless we're making Harry Potters, etc.) being quite poor, like most painters and singers and entertainers before the Recording Age.

I'm not sure why these industry changes prompt a "manifesto," but it seems like as good an excuse as any. So, this is my first, tentative attempt at a *prescriptive* plan for movies. It is, like most things I do, an experiment.

Film has two jobs: to show us what is inhuman about our world and to show us how we still are or could be human.

So, first, film must show the darkness, namely the sadism, oppression, power mongering, materialism, violence, fear, the people dying in gutters while the other people are walking past gabbing on their cellphones; all the terrible stuff. Many films just stop there. Oh, look how empty we all are, they say. Oh, look how cruel. Oh, look how the entitled ones ignore the tragically poor. Movies are praised for their bracing exposure of various horrors du jour.

Although unsettling the complacent is definitely one of art's functions, it is certainly not enough to shock. In the last few decades, all the restraints have been challenged and removed. There's very little you can't show anymore. We can look at the darkest, direst, most diseased individual or regime with an unflinching gaze.

It's not enough to see clearly any more. Daring to be dark has sort of been done to death.

And we, as a global consciousness, don't need it as much as we once did. Daring is value neutral. It is a knife that can be used for good or ill. Hitler's demonic plan could, in fact, be labelled as "daring." The Armenian genocide could also be described as "daring." Daring can be used for the greatest evils. So, I'm arguing that daring must be used in the service of something greater, like justice or the defence of the vulnerable. For example, I think we've been wrestling with the fact of incest for quite some time now. Dozens upon dozens of movies had the climactic reveal be some horrible incestuous rape, some child being forced to do something awful. And it was good that this terrible secret was revealed and reviled collectively. Women and children have been treated like property for far too long. Fictional portrayals of the trail of psychic wreckage was definitely necessary but we need to move on. We need to say more than "it happens."

Another popular theme these days is "we've moved away from nature." True. But it's getting tired. What's the answer? The "technology could turn on us" story is reaching the end of its usefulness. The "my god, look how materialistic we are" story, even though we are still obscenely so, is also getting a bit long in the tooth. Even "gays are people too" type stories are old news. (I predict a slew of 'respect for the transgendered' stories. The zeitgeist needs to get its head around that one next.)

Just pointing to the darkness side of the moon is a bit too easy. Anyone can do that. That's first-level analysis—if it's analysis at all. It is also great camouflage for the sickos amongst us—people who truly enjoy inflicting pain (though, I don't believe any of it should be censored, just keep it away from the kids). It is subtle work distinguishing between filmmakers who use nightmares to illuminate the violation of something beautiful and sacred and those who just think it's cool.

The great works, the ones that will run deep and last long (even if unrecognized in their time) must go to the next step. They address how it is that we still, sometimes, can feel human. How is it that we can still act out of love sometimes and not just the banal need to be loved?

As soon as I write this I get nervous—movies that are ostensibly extolling happiness, kindness, and good behaviour can be as dangerous and useless as the dark ones. Some of the happiest, general audience "apolitical" movies can be affirmations of disturbing values, like "might makes right" and patriarchal birthright. By replicating the soothing cause-and-effect structures that make us sink contently into our couches, and feeding us enough jokes, enough style, a little conflict but nothing serious, and an endless series of familiar tropes and fantasies, then even the "lightest" entertainment can further the cultural rot that eats at the foundations of our collective personality. Comedies can, like smiling Trojan horses, convince us that "cool" matters more than substance, that money buys peace of mind, that weapons bring safety, that fame is good in and of itself, that sex saves the soul, that the United States of America has more moral authority than any other country, that women should play the supporting role more often than not, that the developed nations are morally superior to the developing ones, that "is" equals "ought," and a big favourite: that buying things will somehow fill us up.

The movie that can see and show *simultaneously* both dark and light is the movie that will fly around the world. Movies that show us our twisted self-serving ways and yet somehow address why we can still connect, feel joy and grace, and engage in heart-stopping generosity. How, in the grotesque world we live in, is it still possible to delight in gentle things? In fruit trees in blossom? How do the viciously victimized learn to forgive? How do cultural scars heal? How, in a world so unfair, where a tiny population owns and runs the whole planet, can we find radical democracy—the kind of radical democracy that treats the plight of the handicapped, AIDS-ravaged child of a whore in deepest Africa with the same alarm and tenderness and public woe as the blond-haired, valedictorian daughter of a US billionaire cultural leader. How, how can we make this love possible?

A movie that accomplishes this is art that is engaged with the essence of things. That is cinema in its highest form.

Canadian filmmaker Patricia Rozema has directed such films as I've Heard the Mermaids Singing *(1987), voted one of the Top Canadian Films Ever;* When Night Is Falling *(1995), which won audience prizes around the world; and Jane Austen's* Mansfield Park *(1999), made with Miramax. Her forays into television include Samuel Beckett's* Happy Days *and her contribution to the Yo-Yo Ma series* Inspired by Bach, *which won her the highest television awards possible in Europe (Golden Rose of Montrose) and North America (Prime Time Emmy) and a Grammy nomination. She did the pilot and first three episodes of the critically acclaimed HBO series* Tell Me You Love Me (2007), *and directed Abigail Breslin in the widely released family film* Kit Kittredge: An American Girl *(2008), which the NYT critic A.O. Scott hailed as featuring one of the top five female performances of the year. Rozema recently co-wrote the Emmy-winning* Grey Gardens *(2009) starring Drew Barrymore and Jessica Lange.*

Preface

The Canadian adaptation of Louis Giannetti's highly successful film studies textbook is intended for use in introductory film courses. In addition to chapters dealing with the basic issues of film language and film criticism, it includes a chapter on Canadian cinema and provides examples from Canadian films throughout.

Movies, like the world in which they are produced and viewed, have changed a great deal since Giannetti's book was first published in 1972. What is more remarkable, however, is the persistence of the movies, despite the proliferation of television channels, the advent of home video, DVDs, personal computers, and the Internet. All these developments have affected how movies are made and how we watch them, and these changes are very important. The end of cinema as we know it has frequently been proclaimed, but, so far at least, movies still provide entertainment and meaningful experiences much as they did in the past. True, we tend to go to the movies less often; rather than watch larger-than-life images projected from celluloid (*film*) onto a screen in a theatre (*cinema*), we increasingly watch them on television in our own homes. Yet, when we do so, something seems to be missing; hence the growing popularity of "home theatre" systems and large-screen, widescreen and high-definition televisions.

Film studies have also changed. There has been a shift away from the promotion of "cineliteracy" (Giannetti's term) to a concern with placing movies in broad historical, political, cultural, and theoretical contexts. The results are often illuminating and exciting, but sometimes the context can replace the texts, as, for example, when a film is denounced for its ideological shortcomings with no attention to the ways in which its aesthetic qualities may complicate the actual experience of viewing it.

Although the movies survive, there is also a sense that they are losing their distinctive qualities in today's media-saturated environment. Indeed, we are now often confronted with an amorphous entity called "the media." Sometimes this is simply a shorthand term for journalists reporting for television, radio, and newspapers, but there is a growing tendency to treat the word "media" as a singular noun, as if all media functioned in the same way.

This introductory text is based on the conviction that understanding movies requires, first of all, an awareness of how film differs from other media, the specific ways in which movies communicate, as well as what they can do and what they have done historically. As Marshall McLuhan once declared, "any understanding of social and cultural change is impossible without a knowledge of the way media work as environments."

The overall goal is not to teach students to change their viewing habits, but to make them more aware of why people respond to movies as they do. In preparing a Canadian edition, my aim has been to make students more aware of their own national cinema and to suggest some of the reasons people respond to Canadian movies in particular ways.

New to the Fifth Canadian Edition

- The chapter on *Canadian Cinema* (Chapter 10) has been updated.
- A chapter on *Writing about Movies* (Chapter 12) has been added.
- The lists of further readings have been updated.
- New film stills have been inserted throughout the book.

Organization

This edition of *Understanding Movies* begins with two chapters designed to introduce the basic properties of the medium and the principles of narrative structure. Chapters 3 through 8 deal with the elements of film language and technique used by filmmakers, and with how these elements affect the spectator's experience. Chapter 9 discusses the specific uses of film language in nonfiction film, because of the importance of the documentary tradition in Canada, while Chapter 10 focuses on Canada as an example of national cinema. Chapter 11 deals with broader issues of film theory. Finally, Chapter 12 discusses how to write about film, using *Citizen Kane* and *Mon oncle Antoine* as examples. The chapters are fairly self-contained and can be read in any sequence to meet the needs of specific courses.

Features

- Chapters begin with brief, often provocative, quotations that can be used as a basis for class discussion.
- Chapter overviews at the beginning of each chapter outline the topics that will be discussed.
- A Glossary of selected terms appears on page 409. Terms are boldfaced the first time they appear in the text, and, where appropriate, in subsequent chapters.
- A list of suggested further readings is included at the end of each chapter.
- A list of weblinks to Internet sites relevant to film studies and a list of print journals are included on pages xvii and xix.

Supplements

- *The Companion Website with Grade Tracker* (www.pearsoned.ca/giannetti) offers students chapter learning objectives, quizzes, and writing activities, as well as animation to illustrate key technical points. This Companion Website includes Grade Tracker functionality. With Grade Tracker, the results from the self-test quizzes you take are preserved in a gradebook. Each time you return to the Companion Website, you can refer back to these results, track your progress, and measure your improvement. Use the access code included with this book to sign on to the Grade Tracker website. Your instructor might also take advantage of the Class Manager function to assign marks for participation or for quiz scores. Ask your instructor if they will be distributing a CourseID that will allow you to enrol in their class.

- *CourseSmart for Students*: CourseSmart goes beyond traditional expectations—providing instant, online access to the textbooks and course materials you need at an average savings of 50%. With instant access from any computer and the ability to search your text, you'll find the content you need quickly, no matter where you are. And with online tools like highlighting and note-taking, you can save time and study efficiently. See all the benefits at www.coursesmart.com/students.

The following instructor supplements are available for download from a password protected section of Pearson Education Canada's online catalogue (vig.pearsoned.ca). Navigate to your book's catalogue page to view a list of the supplements that are available. See your local sales representative for details and access.

- *Instructor's Manual*: This manual offers teaching notes that include an outline summary for each chapter. The outline is followed by a discussion of films appropriate for study with each chapter, along with suggestions for class discussion.
- *Test Item File*: This testing program is comprised of multiple choice, true-false, matching questions, and short-answer topics for each chapter.
- *PowerPoint Presentations*: This instructor's resource contains a variety of material for classroom use.
- *CourseSmart for Instructors*: CourseSmart goes beyond traditional expectations—providing instant, online access to the textbooks and course materials you need at a lower cost for students. And even as students save money, you can save time and hassle with a digital eTextbook that allows you to search for the most relevant content at the very moment you need it. Whether it's evaluating textbooks or creating lecture notes to help students with difficult concepts, CourseSmart can make life a little easier. See how when you visit www.coursesmart.com/instructors.

A Note on Stills

Louis Giannetti prefers to use publicity photos rather than frame enlargements because of their superior quality when reproduced. Frame enlargements are used only when close analysis is required, as in the stills from *The Seven Samurai* (**1-22**) and *Battleship Potemkin* (**6-17**). This edition, somewhat reluctantly, follows Giannetti's lead, partly because of concern for clear reproduction and partly because of the difficulty in obtaining suitable frame enlargements from Canadian films.

Acknowledgments

The following individuals and institutions graciously allowed use of materials under their copyright: Andrew Sarris, for permission to quote from "The Fall and Rise of the Film Director," in *Interviews with Film Directors* (New York: Avon Books, 1967); Kurosawa Productions, Toho International Co., Ltd., and Audio Brandon Films for permission to use the frame enlargements from *The Seven Samurai*; Albert Maysles, in *Documentary Explorations*, edited by G. Roy Levin (Garden City: Doubleday & Company, Inc., 1971); Herbert Read, "Towards a Film Aesthetic," *Film: A Montage of Theories*, edited by Richard Dyer MacCann (New York: E.P. Dutton & Co., Inc. 1966); Vladimir Nilsen, *The Cinema as a Graphic Art* (New York: Hill and Wang, a Division of Farrar, Straus and Giroux); Marcel Carné, from *French Cinema Since 1946, vol. 1*, by Roy Armes (San Diego, Cal.: A. S. Barnes & Co., 1966); Richard Dyer MacCann, "Introduction," *Film: A Montage of Theories* (New York: E. P. Dutton & Co., Inc.) copyright © 1966 by Richard Dyer MacCann, reprinted with permission; V. I. Pudovkin, *Film Technique* (London: Vision, 1954); Akira Kurosawa, from *The Movies as Medium*, edited by Lewis Jacobs (New York: Farrar, Straus and Giroux, 1970); John Grierson, *Grierson on Documentary* (Berkeley: University of California Press, 1966); Margaret Atwood, *Survival: A Thematic Guide to Canadian Literature* (Toronto: Anansi, 1972); Robert Lapsley and Michael Westlake, *Film Theory: An Introduction* (Manchester: Manchester University Press, 1988); Maya Deren, "Cinematography: The Creative Use of Reality," in *The Visual Arts Today*, edited by Gyorgy Kepes (Middletown, Conn: Wesleyan University Press, 1960).

I would like to thank the staff at Pearson Education Canada. Special thanks to the reviewers, whose feedback was extremely valuable in the development of this new edition of *Understanding Movies*. Reviewers included: Stan Beeler, University of Northern British Columbia; Karen Budra, Langara College; Noel Elizabeth Currie, Langara College; Tom Hanrahan, Nipissing University; Scott Henderson, Brock University; Roger Holdstock, Douglas College; Charlie Keil, University of Toronto; Daniel Keyes, UBC Okanagan; Mitchell Parry, University of Victoria.

J.L.

Weblinks and Film Journals

There are thousands of sites on the Internet devoted to movies and other media. They include permanent and growing databases, institutional sites for studios and film organizations, publicity for new releases, fan sites devoted to favourite stars, as well as scholarly journals. The following list is just a selection of some of the most useful addresses.

Information
All Movie Guide:
www.allmovie.com
Internet Movie Database:
www.imdb.com

Archives and research sources
American Film Institute:
www.AFI.com
British Film Institute:
www.bfi.org.uk
Cinematheque Ontario:
www.cinemathequeontario.ca
Cinématheque québécoise:
www.cinematheque.qc.ca
National Film Board of Canada:
www.nfb.ca

Film industry
Academy of Canadian Cinema and Television:
www.academy.ca
Academy of Motion Picture Arts and Sciences:
www.oscars.org
National Screen Institute—Canada:
www.nsi-canada.ca
Telefilm Canada:
www.telefilm.gc.ca

On-line film journals
Bright Lights:
www.brightlightsfilm.com
Film-Philosophy:
www.film-philosophy.com
indieWIRE:
www.indiewire.com
Jump Cut:
www.ejumpcut.org
Rouge:
www.rouge.com.au/espace.html
Scope:
www.nottingham.ac.uk/film/journal
Screening the Past:
www.latrobe.edu.au/screeningthepast
Senses of Cinema:
www.sensesofcinema.com

Film reviews
Eye Weekly:
www.eyeweekly.com/film
Roger Ebert:
rogerebert.suntimes.com
Rotten Tomatoes:
www.rottentomatoes.com
UC Berkeley library film studies resource page:
www.lib.berkeley.edu/MRC/filmstudies/reviewslist.html

Film studies
Film Studies Association of Canada:
www.filmstudies.ca
Society for Cinema and Media Studies:
www.cmstudies.org

University Film and Video Association:
www.ufva.org

Resources for essay writing

Brock University Department of Communication, Popular Culture and Film:
www.brocku.ca/cpcf/cpcf_guide.php#essaystyle

Dartmouth Writing Program:
www.dartmouth.edu/~writing / materials/students/humanities/ film.shtml

George Mason University Writing Program:
www.gmu.edu/departments /writingcenter/handouts/ film.html

Print Journals

Despite the emergence of the Internet as a means of publication, much of the most valuable and exciting work in film studies appears in print journals. These range from publications aimed at a general audience to specialized academic journals. The following lists are only a small sample of what is available.

English-language film journals in Canada

Canadian Journal of Film Studies: The journal of the Film Studies Association of Canada.

Canadian Screenwriter: The journal of the Writers Guild of Canada.

CineAction: A radical journal with articles on Canadian, Hollywood, and international cinema.

Cinema Scope: Lively discussion of Canadian and international films.

French-language film journals in Canada

Cinébulles: International cinema, with an emphasis on Quebec films, published by the Association des cinémas parallèles du Québec.

24 Images: Independent journal of world cinema, with an emphasis on Quebec films.

International film journals in English

Cineaste: U.S. journal with an emphasis on radical and independent cinema.

Cinema Journal: The journal of the Society for Cinema and Media Studies.

Film Comment: Published by The Film Society of Lincoln Center in New York; lively and accessible.

Film Criticism: Scholarly articles on a wide range of film topics.

Film Quarterly: Substantial articles and book and film reviews.

Journal of Popular Film and Television: Film in the context of popular culture.

Literature/Film Quarterly: Adaptation and the relations between film and literature.

Post Script: Scholarly essays on film and the humanities.

Screen: British scholarly journal with an emphasis on theory.

Sight and Sound: Published by the British Film Institute; lively articles and reviews.

PEARSON The Pearson Education Canada COMPANION WEBSITE

A Great Way to Learn and Instruct Online

The Pearson Education Canada Companion Website is easy to navigate and is organized to correspond to the chapters in this textbook. Whether you are a student in the classroom or a distance learner you will discover helpful resources for in-depth study and research that empower you in your quest for greater knowledge and maximize your potential for success in the course.

[www.pearsoned.ca/giannetti]

Enter

PEARSON
Jump to... http://www.pearsoned.ca/giannetti
Home
Search
Help
Profile
Companion Website
Home >
Companion Website
Understanding Movies: Fifth Canadian Edition by Louis Giannetti and Jim Leach
UNDERSTANDING
MOVIES
Student Resources
The modules in this section provide students with tools for learning course material. These modules include:
• Chapter Summaries
• Quizzes
• Film Summaries
• Destinations
• Animations
• Video Interviews
In the quiz modules, students can send answers to the grader and receive instant feedback on their progress through the Results Reporter. Coaching comments and references to the textbook may be available to ensure that students take advantage of all available resources to enhance their learning experience.
Instructor Resources
A link to this book on the Pearson Education Canada online catalogue (vig.pearsoned.ca) provides instructors with additional teaching tools. Downloadable PowerPoint Presentations and an Instructor's Manual are just some of the materials that may be available. The catalogue is password protected. To get a password, simply contact your Pearson Education Canada Representative or call Faculty Sales and Services at 1-800-850-5813.

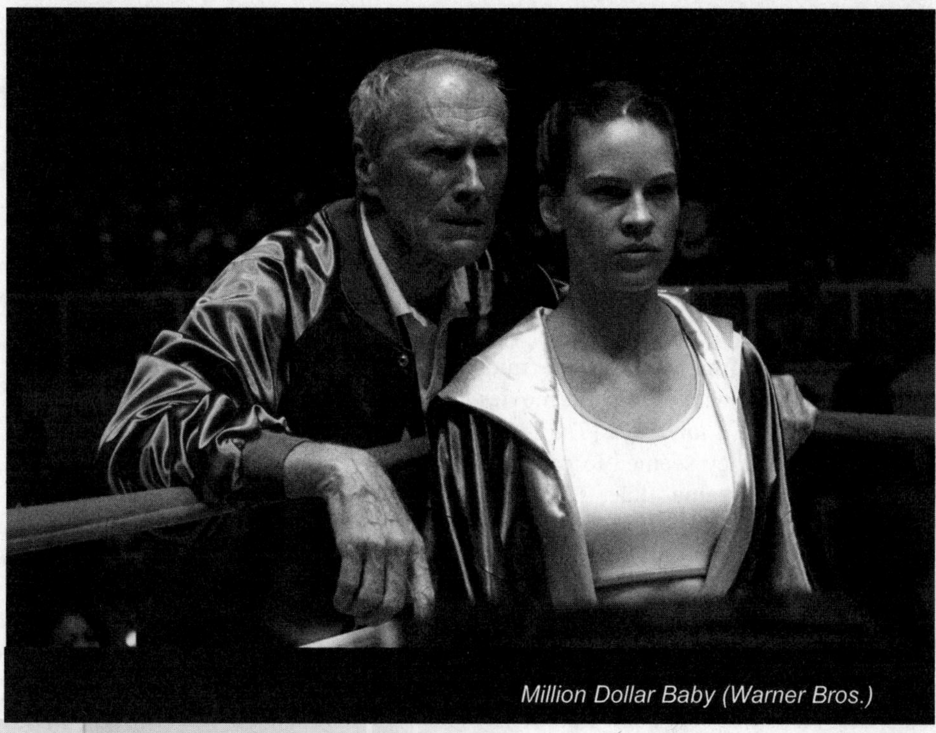

Million Dollar Baby (Warner Bros.)

1 MEDIUM

The film is the art of space-time: It is a space-time continuum.

— HERBERT READ

OVERVIEW

The two major styles of film: realism and formalism. Three modes of cinema: documentaries, fiction films, and avant-garde movies. Form and content, medium and message. Who tells the story? The role of the director: auteurs and metteurs en scène. The role of the screenwriter: words and images. The role of the spectator: co-creator of meaning. The film experience: time and space, the pleasure of looking. Figurative comparisons: motifs, symbols, metaphors, allegories, and allusions. Point of view. Tone.

REALISM AND FORMALISM

Since the early days of the medium, movies have followed two major styles: the realistic and the formalistic. In the mid-1890s in France, the Lumière brothers delighted audiences with their short movies dealing with everyday occurrences. Such films as *L'Arrivée d'un train* [*The Arrival of a Train*] (**6-2**) fascinated viewers precisely because they seemed to capture the flux and spontaneity of events in real life. At about the same time, Georges Méliès was creating fantasy films that emphasized purely imagined events. Such movies as *Le Voyage dans la lune* [*A Trip to the Moon*] (**6-3**) were mixtures of whimsical narrative and trick photography. In many respects, Louis and Auguste Lumière can be regarded as the founders of the realist tradition of cinema, and Méliès of the formalist tradition.

Realism and **formalism** are general rather than absolute terms. When used to suggest a tendency toward either polarity, such labels can be helpful, but most films incorporate elements of both traditions. There is also an important difference between realism and reality, although this distinction is often forgotten: Realism is a particular style (or, rather, a term used to describe a range of different styles), whereas physical reality is the source of all the raw materials of film, both realistic and formalistic. Virtually all movie directors go to the photographable world for their subject matter, but what they do with this material—how they shape and manipulate it—determines their stylistic emphasis.

Realistic films attempt to reproduce the surface of reality with a minimum of distortion. In photographing objects and events, filmmakers try to suggest the copiousness of life itself. Both realist and formalist film directors must select (and, hence, emphasize) certain details from the chaotic sprawl of reality. But the element of selectivity in realistic films is less obvious. Realists, in short, try to preserve the illusion that their film worlds are unmanipulated, objective mirrors of the actual world. Formalists, however, make no such pretence. They deliberately stylize and distort their raw materials so that only the very naive would mistake a manipulated image of an object or event for the real thing.

We rarely notice the style in a realistic movie; the artist tends to be self-effacing. Such filmmakers are more concerned with *what* is being shown than *how* it is being manipulated. The camera is used as a recording mechanism to reproduce the appearance of objects with as little commentary as possible. Some realists aim for a rough look in their images, one that does not prettify the materials with a self-conscious beauty of form. A high premium is placed on simplicity, spontaneity, and directness. This is not to suggest that these movies lack artistry, however, for at its best, the realistic cinema specializes in art that conceals art.

1-1a. *Master and Commander: The Far Side of the World* (U.S.A., 2003), directed by Peter Weir. *(Twentieth Century Fox/Universal Studios/Miramax Films).*

Realism and Formalism. Critics and theorists have championed film as the most realistic of all the arts in capturing how an experience actually looks and sounds, like this thrilling recreation of a ferocious battle at sea during the Napoleonic Wars. A stage director would have to suggest the storm symbolically, with stylized lighting and off-stage sound effects. A novelist would have to recreate the event with words, a painter with pigments brush stroked onto a flat canvas. But a film director can create the event with much greater credibility by plunging the camera (a proxy for us) into the middle of the most terrifying ordeals without actually putting us in harm's way. In short, realism in film is more like "being there" than any other artistic medium or any other style of presentation. Audiences can experience the thrills without facing any of the dangers. As early as 1910, the great Russian novelist Leo Tolstoy realized that this fledgling new art form would surpass the magnificent achievements of nineteenth-century literary realism: "This little clinking contraption with the revolving handle will make a revolution in our life—in the life of writers. It is a direct attack on the old methods of literary art. This swift change of scene, this blending of emotion and experience—it is much better than the heavy, long-drawn-out kind of writing to which we are accustomed. It is closer to life." *Dames* presents us with another type of experience entirely. The choreographies of Busby Berkeley are triumphs of artifice, far removed from the real world. Depression-weary audiences flocked to movies like this precisely to get away from everyday reality. They wanted magic and enchantment, not reminders of their real-life problems. Berkeley's style was the most formalized of all choreographers. He liberated the camera from the narrow confines of the proscenium arch, soaring overhead, even swirling amongst the dancers and juxtaposing shots from a variety of vantage points throughout the musical numbers. He often photographed his dancers from unusual angles, as in this **bird's-eye shot**.

1-1b. *Dames* (U.S.A., 1934), choreographed by Busby Berkeley, directed by Ray Enright. *(Warner Bros.).*

Formalist movies are stylistically self-conscious. Their directors are concerned with expressing their own experience of reality, and, for this reason, they may also be said to belong to a tradition of expressive cinema. Expressive filmmakers are often concerned with spiritual and psychological truths, which they feel can be conveyed best by distorting the appearances of the material world. The camera is used to comment on the subject matter; however, since all films use the camera in this way to some extent, even the most realistic movies use film language in an expressive manner. It is really a question of degree. Formalist movies have a high degree of manipulation, the re-forming of reality. But it is precisely this "distorted" imagery that expresses the director's vision of reality.

Most realists would claim that their major concern is with content rather than form or technique. The subject matter is always supreme, and anything that distracts from the content is viewed with suspicion. In its most extreme form, the realistic cinema tends toward **documentary**, with its emphasis on photographing actual places and people **(1-2, 1-3)**. The formalist cinema, in contrast, tends to emphasize technique and expressiveness **(1-5)**. The most extreme example of this style of

1-2. *Jour après jour* [*Day after Day*] (Canada, 1962), directed by Clément Perron.

Documentary realism uses images as evidence of the way things really are. On the basis of this evidence, the filmmaker constructs an argument and encourages us to see reality in a certain way. According to John Grierson, one of the founders of the documentary movement, documentary style conveys a social message: "Men must accept the environment in which they live, with its smoke and its steel and its mechanical aids, even with its rain." However, documentaries can make powerful arguments for change, as Perron does in *Jour après jour*, a film about the lives of workers in a Quebec paper mill. The rhythms of the editing and a poetic commentary convey the subjective experience of working long hours at repetitive but often dangerous tasks. *(National Film Board of Canada)*

filmmaking is found in **avant-garde** cinema **(1-6)**. Some of these movies are totally abstract; pure forms (that is, nonrepresentational colours, lines, and shapes) constitute the only content. Most fiction films fall somewhere between these two extremes, in a mode critics refer to as **classical cinema (1-4)**.

Realism and *realistic* are overtaxed terms—both in life and in movies. We use these terms to express so many different ideas. For example, people often praise the realism of the boxing matches in *Raging Bull* **(1-7a)**. What they really mean is that these scenes are powerful, intense, and vivid. These traits owe very little to realism as a style. In fact, the boxing matches are extremely stylized. The images are often photographed in dreamy **slow motion**, with lyrical **crane shots**, weird sound effects (like hissing sounds and jungle screams), staccato **editing** in both the images and the sound, and so forth. True, the subject matter is based on actual life—the brief boxing career in the 1940s of American middleweight champion Jake La Motta. But the stylistic treatment of these biographical materials is extravagantly subjective.

Even the terms *form* and *content* are not as clear-cut as they may sometimes seem. The form of a **shot**—the way in which a subject is photographed—is its true content and does not necessarily reproduce the way in which the subject is perceived in reality. Canadian communications theorist Marshall McLuhan pointed out that all media have distinct properties that affect the meanings they convey. For example, the photo of the exhausted boxer in *Raging Bull* **(1-7a)** captures the idea of "crucifixion" expressed

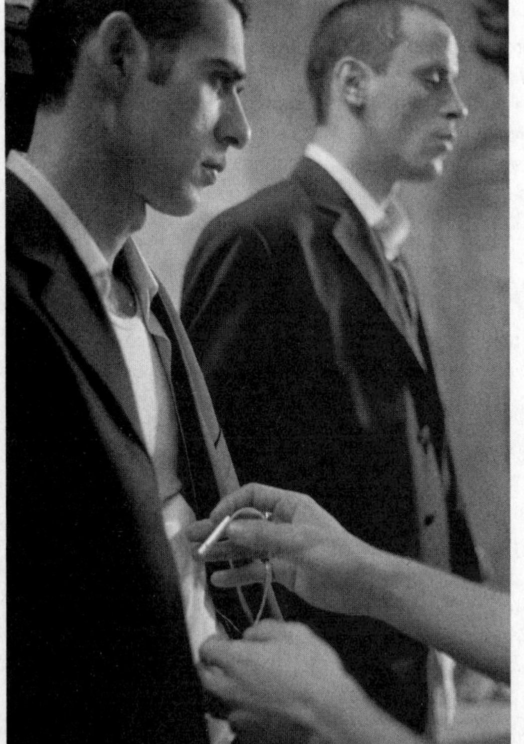

1-3. ***Paradise Now*** **(Palestinian Territories, 2005), with Kais Nashef and Ali Suliman, directed by Hany Abu-Assad.**

In most realistic films, there is a close correspondence of the images to everyday reality. This criterion of value necessarily involves a comparison between the internal world of the movie and the external milieu that the filmmaker has chosen to explore. Realistic cinema tends to deal with people from the lower social echelons and often explores moral issues. The artist rarely intrudes on the subject matter, however, preferring to let it speak for itself. Rather than focusing on extraordinary events, realism tends to emphasize the basic experiences of life. It is a style that excels in making us feel the humanity of others. Beauty of form is often sacrificed to capture the texture of reality as it is ordinarily perceived. Realistic images often seem unmanipulated, haphazard in their design. They frequently convey an intimate snapshot quality—people caught unawares. Generally, the story materials are loosely organized and include many details that do not forward the plot but are offered for their own sake, to heighten the sense of authenticity. *Paradise Now* is about the final hours of two Palestinian auto mechanics, friends since childhood, who have volunteered to be suicide bombers. Here they are being wired up with explosives before crossing over to their target in Israel. Like most realistic movies, the motto of this film might well be: "This is the way things really are." *(Warner Independent Pictures)*

1-4. *Mr. Deeds Goes to Town* (U.S.A., 1936), with Gary Cooper (behind tuba), directed by Frank Capra.
Classical cinema avoids the extremes of realism and formalism in favour of a slightly stylized presentation that has at least a surface plausibility. Movies in this form are often handsomely mounted, but the style rarely calls attention to itself. The images are determined by their relevance to the story and characters, rather than a desire for authenticity or formal beauty alone. The implicit ideal is a functional, invisible style: The pictorial elements are subordinated to the presentation of characters in action. Classical cinema is story oriented. The narrative line is seldom allowed to wander, nor is it broken up by authorial intrusions. A high premium is placed on the entertainment value of the story, which is often shaped to conform to the conventions of a popular genre. Often the characters are played by stars rather than unknown players, and their roles are sometimes tailored to showcase their personal charms. The human materials are paramount in the classical cinema. The characters are generally appealing and slightly romanticized. The audience is encouraged to identify with their values and goals. *(Columbia Pictures)*

verbally in the caption, but the words make this meaning more explicit than the visual arrangement of light and shade. Both the photo and the caption can only approximate the impact of the filmed sequence and draw attention to those meanings that can be captured in a still image or a written description. In each case, the precise information is determined by the medium, although superficially all three have the same content. As McLuhan put it, in his provocative way, "the medium is the message."

In literature, the naive separation of form and content is called "the heresy of paraphrase." For example, the content of Shakespeare's *Hamlet* can be found in a college or university outline, yet no one would seriously suggest that the play and outline are the same "except in form." To paraphrase artistic information is inevitably

1-5. ***The Seventh Seal*** **(Sweden, 1957), with Max von Sydow (right) and Bengt Ekerot, cinematography by Gunnar Fischer, directed by Ingmar Bergman.**

Formalist cinema is largely a director's cinema: Authorial intrusions are common. There is a high degree of manipulation in the narrative materials, and the visual presentation is stylized. The story is exploited as a vehicle for the filmmaker's personal obsessions. Fidelity to objective reality is rarely a relevant criterion of value. The most artificial genres—musicals, sci-fi, fantasy films—are generally classified as formalist. Most movies of this sort deal with extraordinary characters and events—such as this mortal game of chess between a medieval knight and the figure of Death. This style of cinema excels in dealing with ideas—political, religious, philosophical—and is often the chosen medium of propagandistic artists. Its texture is densely symbolic: Feelings are expressed through forms, like the dramatic high-contrast lighting of this shot. Most of the great stylists of the cinema are formalists. *(Janus Films)*

to change its content as well as its form. Artistry can never be gauged by subject matter alone. The manner of their presentation—their forms—is the true content of paintings, literature, and plays. The same applies to movies.

The French film critic and theorist André Bazin noted, "One way of understanding better what a film is trying to say is to know how it is saying it." Bazin was putting forth the theory of organic form—the belief that form and content are mutually interdependent in film and in any other kind of art. American critic Herman G. Weinberg expressed the matter succinctly: "The way a story is told is part of that story. You can tell the same story badly or well; you can also tell it well enough or magnificently. It depends on who is telling the story."

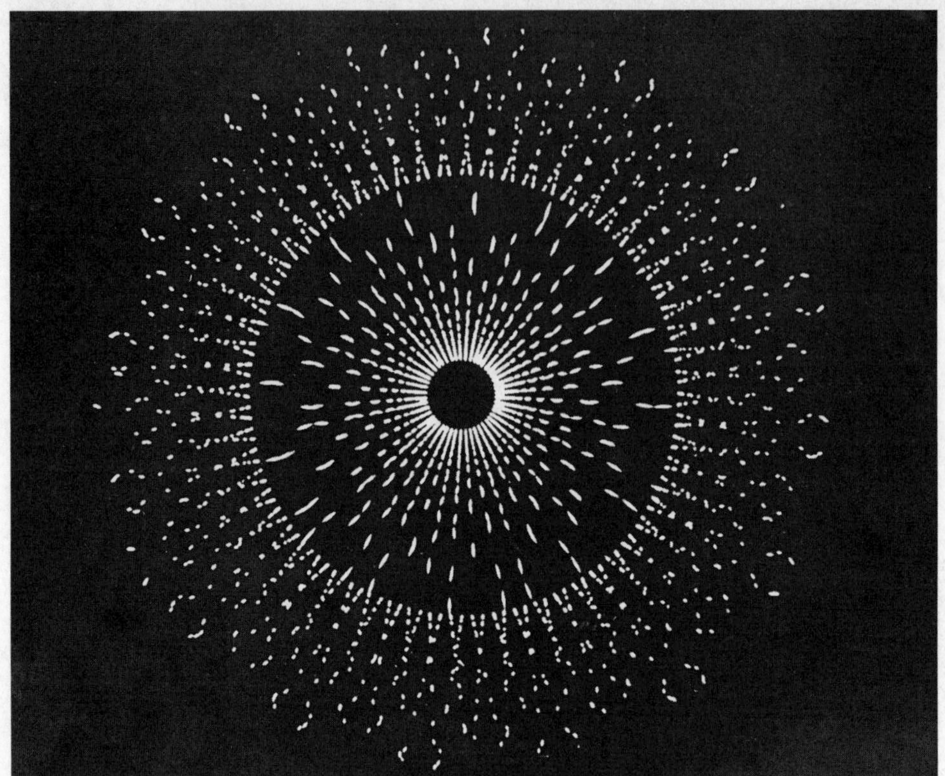

1-6. *Allures* (U.S.A., 1961), directed by Jordan Belson.

In avant-garde cinema, subject matter is often suppressed in favour of abstraction and an emphasis on formal beauty for its own sake. Like many artists in this mode, Belson began as a painter and was attracted to film because of its temporal and kinetic dimensions. He was strongly influenced by such European avant-garde artists as Hans Richter, who championed the "absolute film"—a graphic cinema of pure forms divorced from a recognizable subject matter. Belson's works are inspired by philosophical concepts derived primarily from Oriental religions, but these are essentially private sources and are rarely presented explicitly in the films themselves. Form is the true content of Belson's movies. His animated images are mostly geometrical shapes, dissolving and contracting circles of light, and kinetic swirls. His patterns expand, congeal, flicker, and split off into other shapes, only to reform and explode again. It is a cinema of uncompromising self-expression—personal, often inaccessible, and iconoclastic. (*Pyramid Films*)

It is not always easy to decide exactly who is telling the story in a fiction film. Unlike the more traditional arts, the production of a film involves many people, except in the case of some avant-garde movies. In most production circumstances, the **producer** (or producers) is responsible for providing and overseeing the budget and for ensuring that the whole process is organized efficiently. Especially under the Hollywood studio system, the producer may make decisions that have a major impact on the way the story is told. Actors—especially stars—can influence the treatment of their characters, and the film editor may reorganize the raw footage to change the film's structure. However, the two people who usually have most influence on the way the story is told are the director and the screenwriter.

1-7a. *Raging Bull* (U.S.A., 1980), with Robert De Niro, directed by Martin Scorsese. *(United Artists)*

Realism and formalism are best used as *stylistic* terms rather than terms to describe the nature of the subject matter. For example, although the story of *Raging Bull* is based on actual events, the boxing matches in the film are stylized. In this photo, the badly bruised Jake La Motta resembles an agonized warrior, crucified against the ropes of the ring. The camera floats toward him in lyrical slow motion while the soft focus obliterates his consciousness of the arena.

1-7b. *Constantine* (U.S.A., 2005), with Keanu Reeves, directed by Francis Lawrence. *(Warner Bros.)*

In *Constantine*, on the other hand, the special effects are so realistic they almost convince us that the impossible is possible. Based on the comic book *Hellblazer*, the film contains many scenes of supernatural events. In this episode, for example, the protagonist travels to hell, just beneath the landscape of Los Angeles, a place inhabited by demons and angels. In short, it is quite possible to present fantasy materials in a realistic style. It is equally possible to present reality-based materials in an expressionistic style.

THE DIRECTOR

The director is, at least in principle, responsible for creative decision-making and for the coordination of the work of the other contributors. In many cases, the director is the dominant figure in *pre-production* (preparing the **screenplay** and casting the actors), *production* (the actual shooting of the film), and *post-production* (editing and adding music and other sound effects). Under the Hollywood studio system, which was at its height in the 1930s and 1940s, it was the producer who had ultimate control, and the director was often involved only in the production stage; but, even under these conditions, the director's name usually appeared at the end of the film's opening credits, giving it a special significance.

In the mid-1950s, a group of young critics writing for the French film journal *Cahiers du cinéma* developed the **auteur theory**, a view that stressed the dominance of the director in film art (see Chapter 11, "Theory"). These critics distinguished between two kinds of auteur. On the one hand were directors—mainly in Europe at that time—who exercised complete control over all stages of the production and expressed a personal vision much like artists working in more traditional forms. Jean Renoir, Ingmar Bergman, and Roberto Rossellini were key examples of this kind of director, and the *Cahiers* critics—most notably Jean-Luc Godard and François Truffaut—went on to work in this way when they instigated the French **New Wave** at the end of the 1950s **(1-8)**. On the other hand were certain Hollywood directors, such as John Ford and Howard Hawks, whose films revealed a distinctive personal vision despite the constraints of the studio system.

The auteur theory is less of a theory than a "policy," as Truffaut described it, and it requires the critic to focus on the specific characteristics of film as a medium. Films communicate *primarily* through moving images, and it is the director who determines most of the visual elements: the choice of shots, angles, lighting effects, filters, optical effects, framing, composition, camera movements, and editing. Even in the Hollywood studio system, the director's choices during shooting tend to determine the film's distinctive qualities.

Of course, in many films the director functions simply as a craftsperson, following established conventions and adding little personal vision to the film. According to the *Cahiers du cinéma* critics, these directors are **metteurs en scène** rather than auteurs. Their films are often undistinguished, but we should not assume that only great directors make great films. As in many **genre** films (see Chapter 2, "Story"), following the conventions can produce pleasurable and meaningful films, and some screenplays can generate important films with a merely competent director.

THE SCREENWRITER

According to the auteur theory, great films are made by directors who use film language much as a writer uses written language. Yet, a fiction film usually has its origins in the written words of a screenplay, which includes the dialogue and outlines the action of the film before shooting begins. For this reason, the screenwriter is sometimes regarded as the "author" of a film. But generalizing the writer's contribution in the moviemaking process is an exercise in futility, because the writer's role

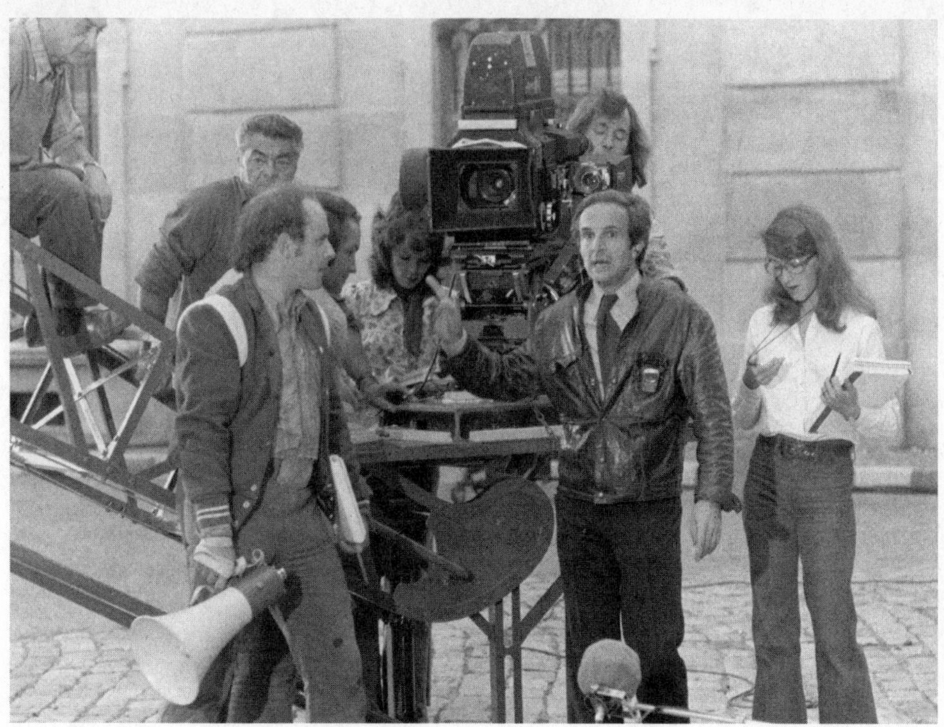

1-8. ***La Nuit américaine*** **[*Day for Night*] (France, 1973), with François Truffaut (leather jacket), directed by Truffaut.**

As a critic in the 1950s, Truffaut attacked conventional French movies that placed more emphasis on the quality of the screenplay than on the vision of the director. His own early films, like other films of the French New Wave, were made on small budgets with minimal crews. In this film, named after the Hollywood studio convention of shooting night scenes in daylight (known as **day-for-night shooting**), Truffaut playfully cast himself as a director making an old-fashioned melodrama and trying desperately to coordinate the efforts of a temperamental cast and crew. (*Warner Bros.*)

varies immensely from film to film and from director to director. Some directors work without scripts; others use only the barest outlines.

Many of the greatest directors have written their own scripts: Jean Cocteau, Sergei Eisenstein, and Ingmar Bergman, to name only a few. In American cinema, many are writer-directors: D.W. Griffith, Erich von Stroheim, Billy Wilder, Preston Sturges, and Woody Allen are among the most famous. The majority of important directors take a major role in writing their scripts, but they bring in other writers to expand on their ideas. Truffaut, Federico Fellini, and Akira Kurosawa all worked in this manner. Although many directors, such as Alfred Hitchcock, Frank Capra, and Ernst Lubitsch, contributed a great deal to the final shape of their scripts, they rarely included their names in the credits, allowing the official writer to take that honour. The final screenplay is often the product of many drafts and many contributors.

Some screenwriters have gone on to become directors: One notable example in the United States is Paul Schrader who has written successfully for several major productions, including Martin Scorsese's *Taxi Driver* **(8-27)** and *Raging Bull*, but

1-9. ***Umberto D*** **(Italy, 1952), with Carlo Battisti (right), written by Cesare Zavattini, directed by Vittorio De Sica.**

Zavattini is the most famous scenarist of the Italian cinema, and one of its most important theorists. (See the section on neorealism in Chapter 11, "Theory.") His best work was done in collaboration with De Sica, including such important works as *Shoeshine* **(1-18)**, *Bicycle Thieves* **(8-26)**, and *Umberto D*. De Sica worked in close collaboration with his scenarists. For example, the protagonist of this film, a retired government employee (Battisti), is a veiled portrait of the director's father, Umberto De Sica, to whom the film is dedicated. *(Audio-Brandon Films)*

who has also directed powerful, and often disturbing, movies such as *Patty Hearst* (1988), *Affliction* (1998), and *AutoFocus* (2002). Others, such as Harold Pinter in Britain, have developed a distinctive style while working for several directors, although, in Pinter's case, most critics feel that his best work was done in collaboration with director Joseph Losey **(11-7)**. Similarly, Cesare Zavattini worked with many Italian directors, writing screenplays that reflected his own theories of realist filmmaking, but he is best known for his collaborations with Vittorio de Sica **(1-9)**. Some major screenwriters have worked almost exclusively for one director **(1-10)**.

Some filmmakers are at their best with "talky" scripts—provided it is scintillating talk, as in the best movies of Lina Wertmüller, Ingmar Bergman, and Woody Allen. The French, Swedish, and British cinemas are also exceptionally literate. Among the important writers who have written for the screen in Britain are George Bernard Shaw, Graham Greene, Alan Sillitoe, John Osborne, Harold Pinter, David Storey, and Hanif Kureishi **(1-12)**.

Despite the enormous importance that the screenplay can have in a film, some directors scoff at the notion that a writer could be the dominant artist in cinema.

1-10. *Howards End* (Britain, 1992), with Sam Wood and Helena Bonham-Carter, directed by James Ivory. The team of director James Ivory, producer Ismail Merchant, and writer Ruth Prawer Jhabvala made movies together for over thirty years. The best of them are adaptations of classic novels, such as E. M. Forster's *A Room With a View* (1985) and Henry James's *The Golden Bowl* (2000). Jhabvala is a respected author in her own right, but she is best known for her literate screenplays for Ivory and Merchant. Nowhere is her artistry more apparent than in this sensitive adaptation of Forster's *Howards End*. Jhabvala's screenplay is beautifully written, in addition to being faithful to the original, funny, and emotionally involving. (*Sony Pictures*)

Michelangelo Antonioni once remarked that Dostoyevsky's *Crime and Punishment* was a rather ordinary crime thriller—the genius of the novel lies in how it is told, not in the subject matter per se. Certainly, the large number of excellent movies based on routine or even mediocre books seems to support this view.

This does not mean that screenwriters must always subordinate their literary talents to the visual demands of the medium. Some screenplays, like those of Joseph L. Mankiewicz, who was one of the most admired writer-directors of the Hollywood big-studio era, revel in the wit and verbal dexterity of highly articulate characters. Mankiewicz's *All About Eve*, for example, features several brilliantly written roles. One of the best is the acid-tongued theatre critic, Addison DeWitt, played with bitchy sang-froid by George Sanders **(1-14)**.

Most of the characters in *All About Eve* are well educated and literate. Those in Elia Kazan's *On the Waterfront* **(8-19)**, which was written by Budd Schulberg, are working-class longshoremen. Such characters usually attempt to conceal their emotions behind a macho façade. But in scenes of intense emotions, the words, though simple, are powerful.

1-11. *Casablanca* (U.S.A., 1940), with Humphrey Bogart and Ingrid Bergman, directed by Michael Curtiz.
Michael Curtiz is a good example of a director who is regarded as a metteur en scène rather than as an auteur. For most of his career, Curtiz was a contract director at Warner Brothers. Known for his speed and efficiency, Curtiz directed dozens of movies in a variety of styles and genres. He often took on several projects at the same time. Curtiz had no personal vision in the sense that the auteur critics define it; he was just getting the job done. He often did it very well and, with the support of the screenwriters and the stars, turned *Casablanca* into one of the best-loved films of the Hollywood studio era. (*Warner Bros.*)

Good dialogue is often the result of having a good ear—for catching the correct rhythms of speech, the right choice of words, the length of people's sentences, the jargon, slang, or swear words people use. The foul-mouthed characters in Quentin Tarantino's *Reservoir Dogs* **(7-29)** speak in torrents of four-letter words, the linguistic equivalent of the violence of their lives. In contexts such as these, polite or laundered prose would constitute bad writing.

THE SPECTATOR

A film's director and its screenwriter are usually the primary (but not the only) creators of the story it tells, but the other major collaborator in the production of meaning is the spectator.

It is impossible to understand a movie without being actively engaged in a dynamic interplay with its images and its narrative logic. Most of us have been

1-12. *My Beautiful Laundrette* (Britain, 1985), with Gordon Warnecke and Daniel Day-Lewis, written by Hanif Kureishi, directed by Stephen Frears.

One of Britain's most outspoken young writers (plays and fiction as well as screenplays for film and television), Hanif Kureishi enjoys shocking the literary establishment. His themes characteristically revolve around conflicts between cultures, races, classes, and sexes. Most of his characters are funny as well as bright. Despite being from different classes and ethnic backgrounds, the two leading characters in this film (pictured) are business partners and lovers. Kureishi, who was born in London with a Pakistani father and British mother, is especially interested in minorities, people outside the mainstream of British culture, which is male, white, and heterosexual. "Gay men and black men have been excluded from history," Kureishi has said: "They're trying to understand themselves. Like women, black people and gay people have been marginalized in society, lacking in power, ridiculed." (*Orion Pictures*)

watching movies and television for so long that we are hardly aware of our instantaneous adjustments to an unfolding **plot**. We absorb auditory and visual stimuli at an incredibly rapid rate. Like a complex computer, our brain processes many language systems simultaneously: photographic, spatial, **kinetic**, vocal, histrionic, musical, sartorial, and so on.

Critic David Bordwell and others have explored how the spectator is constantly interacting with a movie's narrative. Spectators attempt to superimpose their sense of order and coherence on the film's world. In most cases, we bring a set of expectations to a movie even before we have seen it. Our knowledge of a given era or genre leads us to expect a predictable set of variables. For example, most westerns take place in the late nineteenth century and are set in the American western frontier. From books, TV, and other westerns, we have a rough knowledge of how frontier people were supposed to dress and behave (see Chapter 2, "Story").

When narratives fail to act according to tradition, **convention**, or our sense of history, as in Robert Altman's idiosyncratic genre films (see **7-24**) and Don

1-13. ***The Thin Red Line*** **(U.S.A., 1998), with Nick Nolte, written and directed by Terrence Malick.** Successful novelists rarely make good screenwriters because they tend to want the language to carry most of the meaning. But movies communicate primarily through images, and too many words can clutter the eloquence of the visuals. James Jones's famous World War II novel, *The Thin Red Line*, serves almost as an inspiration—rather than a literal source—for Terrence Malick's elliptical, poetic screenplay. The novel emphasizes soldiers in battle and among comrades, but the film is more concerned with philosophical ideas, a melancholy meditation on nature's exquisite beauty and how man defiles it. Like Malick's other movies, this film also explores the mythic idea of a lost paradise and man's corrupt nature, his original sin. (*Twentieth Century Fox*)

McKellar's Canadian take on the disaster movie in *Last Night* **(2-26)**, we are forced to reassess our cognitive methods and our attitude toward the narrative. Either we adjust to the author's presentation, or we reject the offending innovation as inappropriate, crude, or self-indulgent.

Our prior knowledge of a film's star also defines its narrative parameters. We would not expect to see Clint Eastwood in a Shakespearean adaptation, or even in a conventional love story. Eastwood's expertise is in action genres, especially westerns and contemporary urban crime stories. With personality **stars** especially, we can guess the essential nature of a film's narrative in advance. With actor stars like Meryl Streep, however, we are less certain about what to expect, for Streep's range is extraordinarily broad. When Eastwood did star with Streep in *The Bridges of Madison County*, a love story between two middle-aged characters, some viewers had difficulty adjusting their expectations. But Eastwood has frequently challenged his image as an action-movie star and director, as in his depiction in *Million Dollar Baby* of the relationship between an aging ex-boxer and a young woman who sees boxing as the only way out of her dead-end life **(1-15)**.

Audiences also judge a film in advance by the connotations of its title. A movie with a title like *Attack of the Killer Bimbos* is not likely to be chosen as a Gala Presentation at the Toronto International Film Festival. On the other hand, *Lady Windermere's Fan* would probably not play at the local mall theatre because of its somewhat effete, aristocratic-sounding title. Of course, there are always exceptions. *Sammy and Rosie Get Laid* (1987) sounds like a pornographic film, but it is actually a provocative (and sexy) British social comedy, Hanif Kureishi and Stephen Frears's follow-up to their successful collaboration on *My Beautiful Laundrette*. Its title is deliberately aggressive and a bit crude.

An elaborate game is played out between a cinematic narrative and the spectators. While watching a movie, we must sort out irrelevant details, hypothesize, test

1-14. *All About Eve* (U.S.A., 1950), with Bette Davis, Marilyn Monroe, and George Sanders, written and directed by Joseph L. Mankiewicz.

All About Eve is about the New York theatre scene and its fascinatingly neurotic denizens. Its action consists mainly of talk—witty, cynical, and bitchy. Mankiewicz was above all a *verbal* stylist, a master of sophisticated dialogue and repartee. (*Twentieth Century Fox*)

our hypotheses, retreat if necessary, adapt, formulate explanations, and so on. We can analyze the choices made by a film's director and screenwriter to discover how they want the spectator to respond. Their decisions about camera angles or plot construction, for example, provide cues that allow us to envisage an implied spectator. However, spectators do not always react as they are expected to, and interest in finding out how actual spectators respond to films is growing. Historians investigate archives for evidence of what fans thought of stars and how the studios used audience research to plan their publicity campaigns; other researchers use interviews and devise questionnaires to discover how different spectators interpret films to suit their own needs and interests (see Chapter 11, "Theory").

THE FILM EXPERIENCE

The interplay between film and spectator is a complex one shaped by the properties of the medium. Films unfold in time in a linear fashion and, unlike book readers,

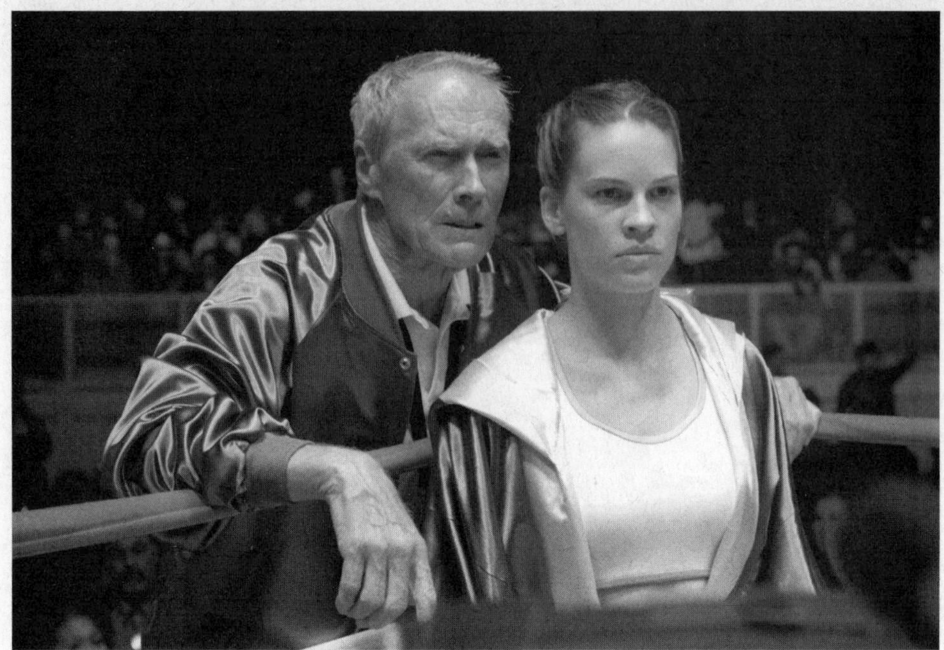

1-15. *Million Dollar Baby* (U.S.A., 2004), with Clint Eastwood and Hillary Swank, directed by Eastwood. Talk is usually kept to a minimum in Eastwood's films. We must infer what the character is thinking: His face is far more expressive than the way he talks, for his words are few, delivered in a matter-of-fact monotone. *(Warner Bros.)*

viewers cannot refer back to earlier stages of the narrative or skip forward to see what is going to happen (at least not before the invention of the video cassette recorder). The treatment of time and space is the basis of a film's style, and it controls the spectator's knowledge of the events and characters depicted.

The basic unit of construction in movies is the shot. The average shot lasts only ten or fifteen seconds, but a shot can be as brief as a fraction of a second or as long as several minutes. A filmmaker can thus lengthen or shorten our experience of time and may introduce temporal dislocations like **flashbacks** and, more rarely, **flash-forwards** (see Chapter 2, "Story").

In cinema, the director converts three-dimensional space into a two-dimensional image of space. Even with **deep-focus** photography, "depth" is not literal **(1-17)**. Each shot represents a new space and, since a camera can be placed virtually anywhere and can be moved during the shot, the director can rearrange the visual space many times for maximum expressiveness with no sacrifice of clarity.

Most movies contain more than a thousand shots. The film director can give us a half-dozen shots of the same object—some emphasizing clarity, others emphasizing expressiveness. A character can enter the frame from below, from above, from any side, and from any angle, and can be shown with his or her back to the camera—the soundtrack guarantees the clarity of the character's speech. A character can be photographed through an obstruction of some kind—a pane of glass or the bars of a prison cell **(1-18)**. By **dollying** or craning, a camera can also take us "into" a set,

1-16. *8½* (Italy, 1963), with Sandra Milo and Marcello Mastroianni, directed by Federico Fellini. Although it is one of the most admired movies in the history of cinema, Fellini's masterpiece features a plot that is diabolically baroque. Most viewers are unable to comprehend it all on first viewing because it is constantly shifting levels of consciousness without warning. Fantasies spill over onto reality, which splashes over memories, which fuse with dreams, which turn into nightmares, which . . . *(Embassy Pictures)*

permitting objects to pass by us. Because the cinematic shot need not be lengthy, clarity can be suspended temporarily in favour of expressiveness.

As film viewers, our primary identification is with the camera. This identification permits us to "move" in any direction and from any distance. An **extreme close-up** allows us to count the lashes on an eyelid; the **extreme long shot** permits us to see several kilometres in each direction. In short, cinema allows the spectator to feel mobile. The pleasures of film viewing are bound up with this capacity to extend and intensify the sense of sight; cinema is thus a voyeuristic medium. In particular, movies make the bodies of actors seem intensely present even though the actors themselves are physically absent **(1-19)**.

In the past, film going was a special event that allowed audiences to escape from the pressures of their everyday lives. Woody Allen's *The Purple Rose of Cairo* (1985), set during the Depression in the 1930s, depicts a woman whose involvement in a movie showing at her local cinema becomes so intense that the handsome star seems to come down off the screen to rescue her from her oppressive home life. When movies were the dominant mass medium, the experience of viewing films in a darkened auditorium with a large audience intensified both the sense of voyeurism and the idea of cinema as

1-17. *Ikiru* [*To Live*] (Japan, 1952), directed by Akira Kurosawa.

In this deep-focus shot, the materials of three depth planes are precisely aligned to produce an ironic contrast. The protagonist (Takashi Shimura, whose picture adorns the Buddhist altar) was a lowly bureaucrat who did something really significant with his existence only in the final months of his life, when he realized he was dying of cancer. In the flashback portions of the movie, his battered hat is a symbol of his humility and dogged perseverance. His funeral wake (pictured) is a rigid, dismal affair, attended primarily by the deceased's fellow bureaucrats. The placement of the camera in this photo implicitly contrasts the unpretentious hat with the chagrined faces of the office workers and with the formal photograph and altar. *(Brandon Films)*

a communal activity. With the emergence of multiplexes, and even more with the growing popularity of home viewing on video or DVD, film has become much more a part of everyday life in a consumer society. Even though movies are now increasingly viewed on television, the development of high-definition and wide-screen televisions points to the enduring appeal of the film experience.

FIGURATIVE COMPARISONS

In his essay "La Caméra-Stylo" ("The Camera-Pen"), Alexandre Astruc observed that film has traditionally been regarded as a medium that has difficulty expressing thought and ideas. The invention of sound, of course, was an enormous advantage to filmmakers, for with spoken language they could express virtually any kind of abstract thought. But film directors also wanted to explore the possibilities of the image as a conveyor of abstract ideas. During the silent era, filmmakers had devised a num-

1-18. ***Shoeshine*** **(Italy, 1946), with Rinaldo Smordoni and Franco Interlenghi, directed by Vittorio De Sica.**

By placing the camera outside the cell, with the bars in front of the boys' faces, the director enforces his theme that children in postwar Italy are trapped in a society that is indifferent to their plight. The spectator must meet the pleading look in their eyes and confront his or her own complicity in the system that created the prison. *(Museum of Modern Art)*

ber of nonverbal figurative techniques that, despite the fears of some critics and filmmakers, were not entirely abandoned in the new "talkies."

A figurative technique is an artistic device that suggests abstract ideas through comparison, either implied or overt. Such devices invite the spectator to go beyond the literal meaning of what is shown, and they are thus more important in formalist than in realist movies. Yet, realist filmmakers cannot avoid using figurative techniques, however discreetly, to express their particular view of reality.

A number of these techniques are used in both literature and cinema, including **motifs**, **symbols**, and **metaphors**. In actual practice, these terms overlap considerably. They are all "symbolic" in the sense that an object or event has meaning beyond its literal significance. Perhaps the most pragmatic method of differentiating these techniques is in their degree of obtrusiveness, but instead of defining each in isolation, we ought to view them as a continuum. Motifs represent the least obtrusive technique, metaphors represent the most conspicuous, symbols represent the middle ground, and each category overlaps with its neighbour.

Motifs are so completely integrated into the realistic texture of a film that we can almost refer to them as submerged or invisible symbols. A motif can be a technique, an object, or anything that is systematically repeated in a movie, yet does not call attention to itself. Even after repeated viewings, a motif is not always apparent, for its symbolic significance is never permitted to emerge or detach itself from its context **(1-21)**.

Symbols can also be palpable things that imply additional meanings that are apparent to the sensitive observer. Furthermore, the symbolic meanings of these things can shift with the dramatic context. A good example of the shifting implications of a symbol can be seen in Kurosawa's *The Seven Samurai* **(1-22)**. In this movie, a young samurai and a peasant girl are attracted to each other, but their class differences present insurmountable barriers. In a scene that takes place late at night, the two accidentally meet. Kurosawa emphasizes their separation by keeping them in separate frames, a raging outdoor fire acting as a kind of barrier **(1-22a, 1-22b)**. But their attraction is too strong, and they then appear in the same shot, the fire between them now suggesting

1-19. ***A Winter Tan*** **(Canada, 1987), with Erando Gonzalez and Jackie Burroughs, directed by Burroughs, Louise Clark, John Walker, Aerlyn Weissman, and John Frizzell.**

Movies make bodies seem intensely present even though the actors are physically absent. Looking at bodies in ways that we normally cannot in real life is one of the pleasures of film-going. But who gets to look at whom? Sexual conventions change over time; nowadays nudity is fairly common in movies, although filmmakers in less permissive times or cultures have created erotic effects with more discreet sexual displays. The naked body can act as a metaphor, as in Burroughs's compelling performance as Maryse Holder, an American woman who died in Mexico, where she had gone in search of sexual adventure. Burroughs's frequently naked body stresses the character's lack of inhibitions and the vulnerability that this brings, while the spectator is left to grapple with the reverse sexism and racism of her treatment of Mexican men as objects. *(John B. Frizzell)*

the only obstacle, yet paradoxically suggesting the sexual passion they both feel **(1-22c)**. They move toward each other, and the fire is now to one side, its sexual symbolism dominating **(1-22d)**. They go inside a hut, and the light from the fire outside emphasizes the eroticism of the scene **(1-22e)**. As they begin to make love in a dark corner of the hut, the shadows cast by the fire's light on the reeds of the hut seem to streak across their bodies **(1-22f)**. Suddenly, the girl's father discovers the lovers, and the billowing flames of the fire suggest his moral outrage **(1-22g)**. He is so incensed that he must be restrained by the samurai chief, both of them almost washed out visually by the intensity of the fire's light **(1-22h)**. It begins to rain, and the sorrowing young samurai walks away despondently **(1-22i)**. At the end of the sequence, Kurosawa offers a close-up of the fire as the rain extinguishes its flames **(1-22j).**

A *metaphor* is defined as a comparison of some kind that cannot be literally true; two terms not ordinarily associated are yoked, producing a sense of literal incongruity. "Poisonous time," "torn with grief," "devoured by love" are all verbal metaphors involving symbolic rather than literal descriptions. Editing is a frequent source of metaphors in film, since two shots can be linked to produce a third, and symbolic, idea. This is the basis of Sergei Eisenstein's theory of **montage** (see Chapter 6, "Editing"). In *October* (1928), for example, he satirized the fears and anxieties of an antirevolutionary politician by **intercutting** shots of a "heavenly choir" of harpists with shots of the politician delivering his cowardly speech. The row of pretty blonde harp players is brought in "from nowhere"; that is, they are certainly not found in the locale (a meeting hall) but are introduced solely for metaphoric purposes. Dissolves and superimpositions can also be used to create

1-20. ***Being at Home with Claude*** **(Canada, 1992), with Jacques Godin, Roy Dupuis, and Gaston Lepage, directed by Jean Beaudin.**

The one-act play by René-Daniel Dubois on which this film is based deals with a murder investigation and takes place in a single one-room set. Filmmakers often "open out" such plays. Much of this film is confined to the same interior as the play, but Beaudin adds a fast-paced prologue in black and white that shows the bloody killing. He thus shifts the focus away from what happened to why it happened. *(Alliance Communications)*

metaphoric ideas. Two or more objects can be yoked in the same frame to create ideas that have no literal existence in reality **(1-23)**. Cinematic metaphors are always somewhat obtrusive; unlike motifs and most symbols, metaphors are less integrated contextually, less "realistic" in terms of our ordinary perceptions.

1-21. ***Cries and Whispers*** **(Sweden, 1972), with Liv Ullmann (a) and Kari Sylwan (b), written and directed by Ingmar Bergman.**

A recurrent motif in this movie is the human face split in two, suggesting self-division, the hidden self, the public versus the private self. *(New World Pictures)*

a

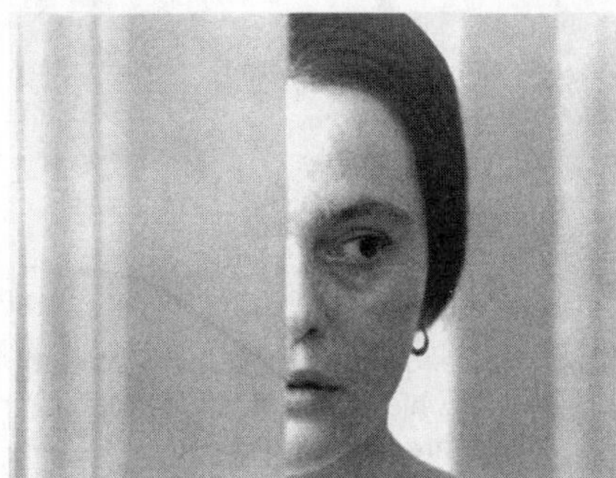

b

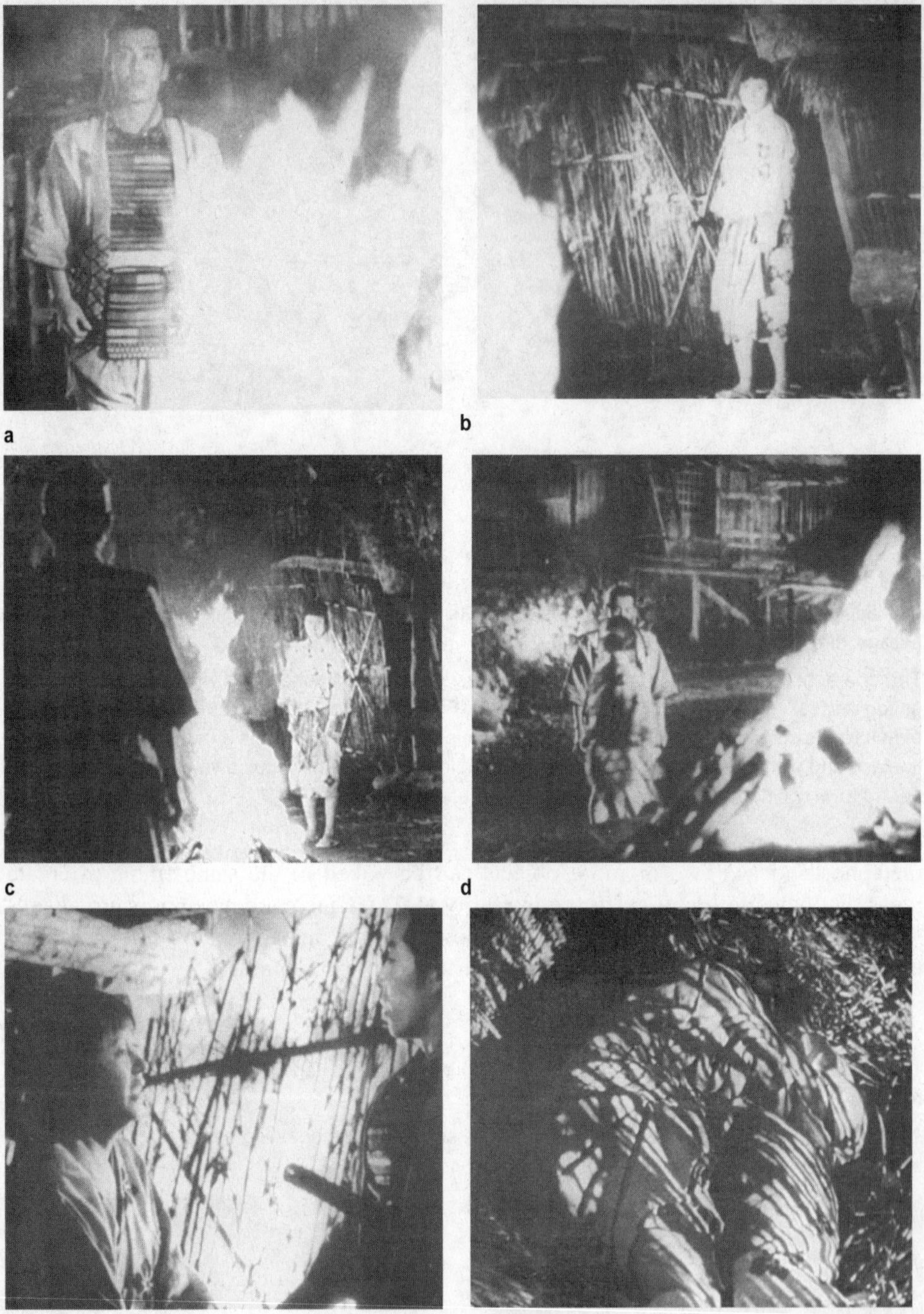

a

b

c

d

e

f

1-22. ***The Seven Samurai*** **(Japan, 1954), directed by Akira Kurosawa.**

Realistic films tend to use symbols less densely than formalist movies, and the symbolism is almost always contextually probable. For example, in addition to being a symbol, the fire in this scene is also a fire. (*Toho International*)

g

h

i

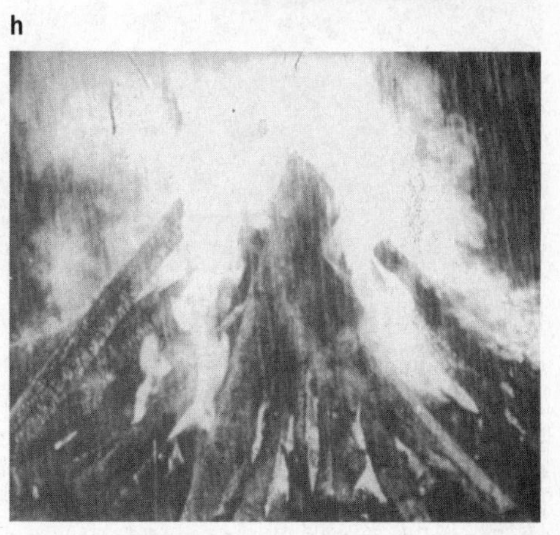

j

Two other kinds of figurative techniques are used in film and literature: **allegory** and **allusions**. The first is seldom used in movies, because it usually involves a total avoidance of realism and probability. A correspondence exists between a character or situation and a symbolic idea or complex of ideas. One of the most famous examples of allegory is the character of Death in Bergman's *The Seventh Seal* **(1-5)**. Little ambiguity is involved in what the character is supposed to symbolize. Allegorical narratives are especially popular in German cinema. For example, virtually all the works of Werner Herzog deal with the idea of life in general and the nature of the human condition in broadly symbolic terms (see **8-15**).

An *allusion* is an implied reference, usually to a well-known event, person, or work of art **(1-24)**. The protagonist of Hawks's *Scarface* (1932) was modelled on the gangster Al Capone (who had a well-publicized scar in the shape of a cross on his cheek), an allusion that was not lost on audiences of the time. In the so-called postmodern age (see Chapter 11, "Theory"), allusion has become a frequent practice in all media, and many films today allude more often to earlier films than to reality outside the cinema. The appeal of a film like *Shrek* **(Colour Plate 13)** consists largely in recognizing the myriad playful allusions to a wide range of cultural texts, past and present. Music videos often pack multiple allusions to other texts into their brief running times, and films such as Wes Craven's *Scream* (1996) and *Not Another Teen Movie* (Joel Gallen, 2001) are made up almost entirely of self-conscious allusions to other films in their respective genres.

1-23. *Psycho* (U.S.A., 1960), directed by Alfred Hitchcock.

Cinematic metaphors can be created through the use of special effects, as in this dissolve which yields the final shot of the film—the dredging up of a car from a swamp. Three images are dissolved: (1) a shot of a catatonic youth (Anthony Perkins) looking directly at us; (2) a duplicate shot of his mother's skeleton, whose skull flickers briefly beneath her son's features, and whose personality he has now assumed; and (3) a heavy chain, which seems anchored to his/her heart, hauling up the murder victim's car that contains her corpse. *(Paramount Pictures)*

In cinema, an overt reference or allusion to another movie, director, or memorable shot is sometimes called a **homage**. The cinematic homage is a kind of acknowledgment, the director's graceful tribute to a colleague or established master. The homage was popularized by the French New Wave filmmakers, whose movies are profuse in such tributes. In Godard's *Une Femme est une femme* [*A Woman Is a Woman*] (1961), for example, two decidedly nonmusical characters burst out in spontaneous song and dance while expressing their desire to appear in an MGM musical by Gene Kelly, choreographed by Bob Fosse. Fosse's *All That Jazz* (1979) contains more than one homage to his idol Fellini, and especially to *81/2*, while Léa Pool's *Emporte-moi* [*Set Me Free*] (1998) pays homage to the French New Wave through its depiction of a young woman, growing up in 1960s Montreal, who identifies with the beauty and vitality of Anna Karina in Godard's *Vivre sa vie* [*My Life to Live*] (1962). Steven Spielberg often pays tribute to his three idols, Walt Disney, Alfred Hitchcock, and Stanley Kubrick.

POINT OF VIEW

The techniques chosen by the filmmakers constitute the film's style and establish its point of view. Of course, in films—unlike in novels—we actually see the characters

1-24. *Hot Shots! Part Deux* (U.S.A., 1993), with Charlie Sheen and Valeria Golino, directed by Jim Abrahams.

An allusion is an indirect reference, sometimes respectful, other times scornful, to an artist or work of art. This movie is filled with comical film allusions, some of which are recognizable only to the cognoscenti, hard-core film fans. For example, this shot is a playful allusion to a scene from the Disney animated romance, *The Lady and the Tramp* (1955), in which two moonstruck canines share a platter of spaghetti. *(Twentieth Century Fox)*

and events depicted, and point of view is thus literally a matter of the angle and distance from which we see them. As in the novel, how we see things may also be affected by the ways in which they are presented by a narrator, who should not be confused with the director or the screenwriter **(1-25)**.

The first-person narrator tells his or her own story. Many films use first-person narrative techniques, but only sporadically. The cinematic equivalent to the "voice" of literary narrator is the "eye" of the camera, but the differences are important. In literature, the distinction between the narrator and the reader is clear: It is as if the reader were listening to a friend telling a story. In film, however, the viewer identifies with the camera and thus tends to fuse with the narrator. To produce first-person narration in film, the camera would have to record all the action through the eyes of the character, which, in effect, would also make the viewer the protagonist.

In *The Lady in the Lake* (1946), Robert Montgomery attempted to use the first-person camera throughout the film. It was a provocative experiment but a failure, for several reasons. In the first place, the director was forced into a number of absurdities. Having the characters address the camera was not much of a problem since **point-of-view shots** are common in most movies. However, for several actions the device simply broke down. When a woman walked up to the hero and kissed him, for example, she had to slink toward the camera and begin to embrace it while her face came closer to the lens. Similarly, when the hero was involved in a fistfight,

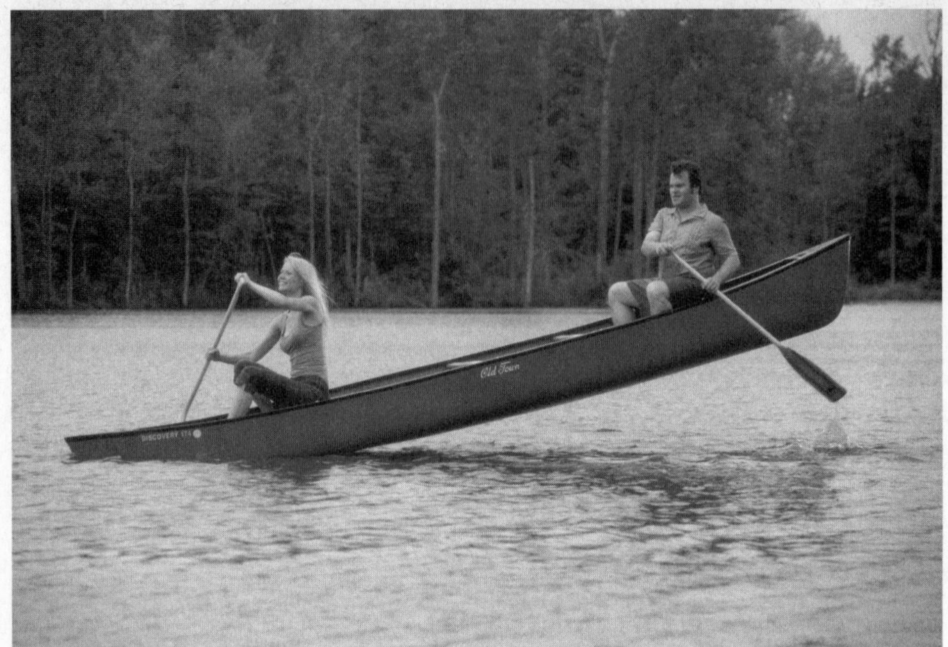

1-25. ***Shallow Hal*** **(U.S.A., 2001), with Gwyneth Paltrow and Jack Black, directed by Bobby and Peter Farrelly.** Formerly a superficial jerk who valued women solely for their looks, the callow protagonist of this comedy (Black) is hypnotized into seeing a woman's inner beauty rather than her actual physical appearance. Thus, we are given two points of view at the same time, one objective, the other subjective—the source of much of the humour in the film. In this shot, for example, we see his 300-pound girlfriend through his adoring eyes; but in the canoe's precarious tilt, we also see the physical effects of her actual obesity. *(Twentieth Century Fox)*

the antagonist literally had to attack the camera, which jarred appropriately whenever the "narrator" was dealt a blow. The problem with the exclusive use of the first-person camera, then, is its literalness. Furthermore, it tends to create a sense of frustration in the viewer, who wants to see the hero. In fiction, we get to know people through their words and through their judgments and values, which are reflected in their language. But in movies, we get to know a character by seeing how he or she reacts to people and events. Unless the director breaks the first-person camera convention, we can never see the hero and can see only what he or she sees.

The **omniscient point of view** is often associated with the nineteenth-century novel. Generally, the narrators of such novels are not participants in the story but are all-knowing observers who supply readers with all the facts they need to appreciate the story. Omniscient narration is almost inevitable in film. Each time the director moves the camera—either within a shot or between shots—we are offered a new point of view from which to evaluate the scene. The filmmaker can cut easily from a subjective point-of-view shot (first person) to a variety of objective shots. He or she can concentrate on a single reaction (close-up) or the simultaneous reactions of several characters (long shot). Within a matter of seconds, the director can show us a cause and an effect, an action and a reaction. He or she can connect various times and

1-26. *The Magnificent Ambersons* (U.S.A., 1942), with Dolores Costello, Agnes Moorehead, Joseph Cotten, and Ray Collins, directed by Orson Welles.

Like most of Welles's movies, this, his favourite work, deals with the theme of a lost paradise. In his previous film, *Citizen Kane,* Welles established himself as a youthful phenomenon with his depiction, as director and actor, of a newspaper tycoon whose story is told after his death by the testimony of those who knew him. The virtuoso play with points of view in that film is replaced in *The Magnificent Ambersons* with a more warm and nostalgic vision of a time that is no more. The leisurely pace was too much for the studio who recut the ending in a much more conventional style. Welles does not appear in the film, though he does narrate the story off screen. He concludes with a shot of a microphone on a swinging boom, accompanied by his spoken credit: "I wrote the picture and directed it. My name is Orson Welles." *(RKO)*

locations almost instantaneously (**parallel editing**) or superimpose different times (**dissolve** or **multiple exposure**). The omniscient camera can be a dispassionate observer, as it is in many of Chaplin's films, or it can be a witty commentator—an evaluator of events—as it often is in Hitchcock's films or those of Atom Egoyan.

Although the point of view of the camera is of prime importance in film, many films do use **voice-over** narrators who provide information and commentary. Some critics regard this technique as uncinematic, and it is usually avoided in classical cinema because it supposedly violates the rule that style should not call attention to itself. Voice-over narration can be first person or omniscient and is often much more than an easy device for providing essential information about the story. In *The Lady from Shanghai* (1948), Orson Welles uses a first-person narrator who reflects on the naive mistakes that led to his involvement in a web of mystery and intrigue. Since Welles, who directed and wrote the film, plays the main character and thus speaks

1-27. *Tilai* (Burkina Faso, 1990), with Rasmane Ouedraogo (holding water jug) and Ina Cisse (collapsed), directed by Idrissa Ouedraogo.

Winner of the Special Jury Prize at the Cannes Film Festival, *Tilai* is the story of a love triangle that tears a family apart in a remote African village. The tone is dedramatized, simple, and ultimately tragic. The film is complemented by a spare and poignant score by the great jazz musician Abdullah Ibrahim. *(New Yorker Films)*

the narration, this is an especially complex case of film authorship. Welles also acts as voice-over narrator in *The Magnificent Ambersons*, but in this film he provides an omniscient and detached perspective on the decline of an aristocratic family **(1-26)**.

TONE

A movie's **tone** refers to its manner of presentation and the general atmosphere that a filmmaker creates through his or her attitude toward the story. Tone can strongly affect our responses to the values presented by the narrative. Tone can also be elusive in movies, especially in those works in which it deliberately shifts from scene to scene.

In movies like David Lynch's *Blue Velvet* (1986), for example, we can never be sure what to make of the events, because Lynch's tone is sometimes mocking, other times bizarre, and occasionally terrifying. In one scene, an innocent high school girl (Laura Dern) recounts to her boyfriend (Kyle MacLachlan) a dream she had about a perfect world. With her blonde hair radiating with halo lighting, she seems almost angelic. In the background we hear organ music emanating from a church. The music and lighting subtly mock her *naiveté* as a form of stupidity.

1-28. ***Careful*** **(Canada, 1992), with Jackie Burroughs, Kyle McCulloch, and Brent Neale, directed by Guy Maddin.**

Winnipeg-based Maddin creates films that seem far removed from the Canadian tradition of regional cinema. The convoluted plot of his third feature takes place in the shadow of the Alps, in a community where people are constantly being warned to be "careful" lest their raised voices cause an avalanche. Nevertheless, it is difficult not to see this zany depiction of an inhibited community, living on the edge and toppling into absurdly tangled relationships, as a perverse parable about the conservative tendencies in Canadian culture. *(Photo by Jeff Solylo)*

A film's tone can be orchestrated in a number of ways. Acting styles strongly affect our response to a given scene. In Idrissa Ouedraogo's *Tilai* **(1-27)**, for example, the tone is objective, matter of fact. The acting style by the largely nonprofessional cast is scrupulously realistic. They do not exaggerate the desperation of their situation with heightened emotional fervour. At the opposite extreme, in Guy Maddin's *Careful* **(1-28)**, an exaggerated silent-movie acting style sets the bizarre comic tone.

A voice-over narrator can be used to set a tone that is different from an objective presentation of a scene, creating a double perspective on the events. Voice-overs can be ironic, as in *Sunset Boulevard* **(8-8)**; sympathetic, as in *Dances With Wolves* **(11-12)**; paranoid, as in *Taxi Driver* **(8-27)**; or cynical as in Stanley Kubrick's *A Clockwork Orange* (1972), which is narrated by a thug. The unexpected use of a fish as the voice-over narrator in Denis Villeneuve's *Maelström* creates a novel perception of a familiar melodramatic story **(2-6)**. Music is a common way to establish a movie's tone. A music track consisting primarily of rock and roll will create a very different tone from a picture accompanied by Mozart or Ray Charles. In Spike Lee's *Jungle Fever* (1991), the Italian-American scenes are accompanied by the ballads of Frank Sinatra; the African-American scenes are underscored by gospel and soul music.

Without considering a film's tone, a mechanistic analysis of its ideological values can be misleading. For example, Hawks's *Bringing Up Baby* (1938) might be interpreted as a leftist critique of a decadent society. Set in the final years of the Great Depression, the movie deals with the desperate schemes of an idle society woman (Katharine Hepburn) to lure a dedicated scientist (Cary Grant) away from his work—to join her in amorous frolic (see **2-10**). This is hardly a goal that would be applauded by most leftists.

But the movie's tone says otherwise. In the first place, the Grant character is engaged to a prim, sexless associate who is utterly devoid of humour. She regards their work as all-important—even to the exclusion of considering taking a honeymoon or eventually having children. She is the Work Ethic incarnate. Enter the Hepburn character—flighty, beautiful, and rich. Once she discovers that Grant is about to be married, she determines that only she must have him, and she contrives a series of ruses to lure him away from his fiancée. Hepburn's character is exciting and exasperating—but fun. Grant is forced to shed his stodgy demeanour merely to keep up with her desperate antics. She proves to be his salvation, and they are united at the film's conclusion. Clearly, they are made for each other.

In short, the charm of Hawks's **screwball comedy** lies precisely in what critic Robin Wood described as "the lure of irresponsibility." The middle-class work ethic is portrayed as joyless—as dry as the fossil bones that Grant and his fiancée have devoted their lives to.

During the 1930s many American movies dealt with the style and glamour of the rich, who were often portrayed as eccentric and good-hearted. Hawks's film is very much in this tradition. The hardships of the Depression are not even alluded to in the movie, and the film's settings—expensive nightclubs, swanky apartments, gracious country homes—are precisely what audiences of that era craved in order to forget about the Depression.

The emphasis is on the charisma of the leading players and the madcap adventures they pursue. The luxurious lifestyle of the heroine enhances her appeal, and the fact that she does not have a job (nor seem to want one) is simply irrelevant. *Bringing Up Baby* is a comedy and a love story, not a social critique.

The properties of film as a medium affect the ways in which production is organized, both as a business and as an art form, as well as the meanings and effects that movies create for audiences. In the most familiar kinds of film, film language is used to tell a story and—as the discussion of narration has already shown—it is difficult to separate film language from storytelling in these films. Before looking more closely at the specific technical processes that go into the making of a film, we need to discuss the different forms that film stories can take.

FURTHER READING

Armstrong, Richard, *Understanding Realism* (London: British Film Institute, 2005). Introduction to developments in realism in the age of digital technology and Reality TV.

Bazin, André, *What Is Cinema?* vols. 1 and 2, trans. Hugh Gray (Berkeley: University of California Press, 1967/1971). A selection of essays exploring the properties of the medium.

Bordwell, David, *On the History of Film Style* (Cambridge, Mass.: Harvard University Press, 1997). Exploration of changing approaches to film style.

Branston, Gillian, *Cinema and Cultural Modernity* (Buckingham: Open University Press, 2000). The cultural politics of contemporary popular cinema.

Enticknap, Leo, *Moving Image Technology: From Zoetrope to Digital* (London: Wallflower Press, 2005). The history and theory of film and related technologies.

Hallam, Julia, with Margaret Marshment, *Realism and Popular Cinema* (Manchester: Manchester University Press, 2000). How popular films use realism to address social and political issues.

Loiselle, André, *Stage-Bound: Feature Film Adaptations of Canadian and Québécois Drama* (Montreal: McGill-Queen's University Press, 2003). The relations of theatre and film in the context of Canadian cinema.

Mayne, Judith, *Cinema and Spectatorship* (London: Routledge, 1993). Examination of issues about how spectators interpret films.

Nowell-Smith, Geoffrey, ed., *The Oxford History of World Cinema* (Oxford: Oxford University Press, 1996). Exhaustive collection of essays on the history of the medium.

Toles, George, *A House Made of Light: Essays on the Art of Film* (Detroit: Wayne State University Press, 2001). Close readings of films by a noted Canadian screenwriter.

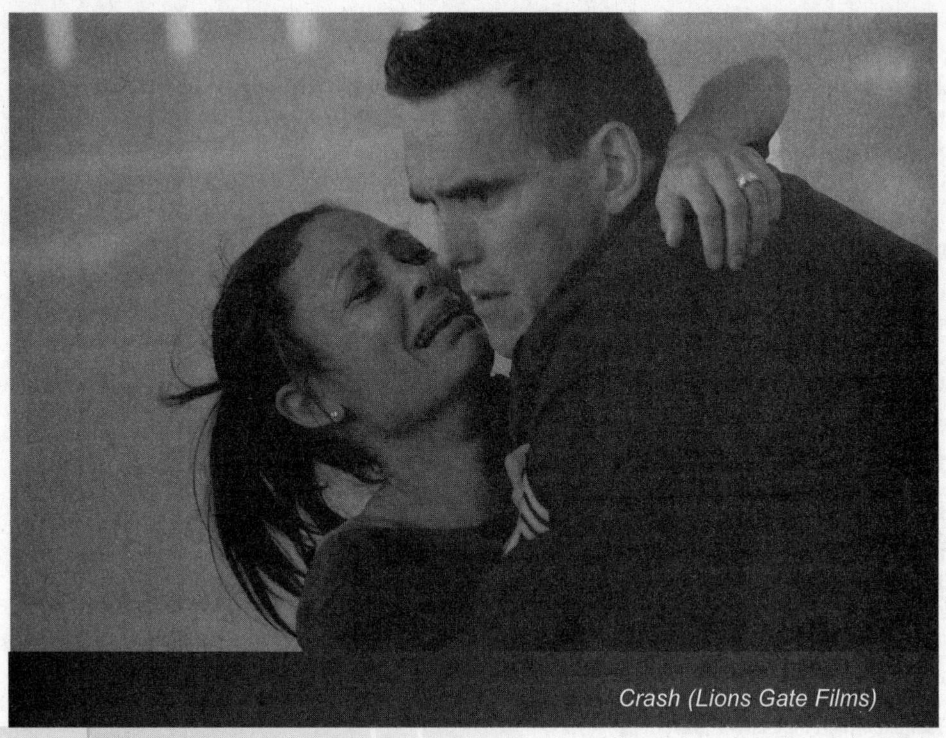
Crash (Lions Gate Films)

STORY

2

Narratives are composed in order to reward, modify, frustrate, or defeat the perceiver's search for coherence.

—David Bordwell

OVERVIEW

Stories: showing and telling. Story and plot. Time and narrative structure. Narration. The classical paradigm: Syd Field's three-act model. Realistic narratives. Realism as a style: the illusion of being "lifelike." Slice-of-life, open-ended stories. The pretence of authorial neutrality. Formalistic narratives: the importance of pattern and design as values in themselves. Intrusive narrators: overt manipulation of the storytelling apparatus. Adaptations: loose, faithful, literal. Genre films: iconography. Genres and gender. Overlap and hybridity. Genre and auteur. Myth and binary oppositions. Formative, classical, revisionist, and reflexive phases of a genre's evolution.

Not all movies tell stories. Most documentaries and avant-garde films do not (see Chapter 9, "Nonfiction Films"). In the early days of cinema, theatres offered programs consisting of a variety of shorts, including *actualitiés*, travelogues, and trick films, that catered to the audience's fascination with the novelty of moving pictures. After the first ten years or so, story films gradually took over and inspired a trend toward longer movies. The fiction feature film soon became dominant and continues to be so.

Not all stories are told in the same way. In a feature film, how the story is told involves all the other elements that combine to create the final effect: photography, mise en scène, editing, sound, and acting. Movies, after all, not only tell stories, they show them. Yet, basic to all narrative cinema is the art of narration, the construction of a self-contained fictional world (or **diegesis**) within which the story is told **(2-1)**.

2-1. *Sunshine* (Hungary/Germany/Canada/Austria, 1999), with James Frain, Jennifer Ehle, and Ralph Fiennes, directed by Istvan Szabo.

Epic stories are usually concerned with important themes, in heroic proportions. The protagonist is generally an ideal representative of a culture—national, religious, or ethnic. The title of this epic saga is bitterly ironic. The Sonnenschein (sunshine) family is Jewish, trying to survive in the bleak climate of anti-Semitic Hungary during three convulsive epochs—the Austro-Hungarian Empire, the Nazi occupation, and the Communist era. They work hard. They bring honour to their family and their country. They downplay their religion. But it is never enough. The family is degraded, their wealth confiscated, their religious identity almost obliterated. *(Paramount Classics)*

NARRATIVE

Theorists have offered several different models of how narratives work. One of the most straightforward distinguishes between **story** and **plot**. The story consists of all the events that we learn about in the course of a narrative, in the order in which they supposedly actually happened; the plot refers to the reshaping and organization of this raw material by the narrator. This is an important distinction because it is extremely rare that the story will be told in strict chronological order. As the ancient Greek philosopher Aristotle recommended, most narratives begin in media res (in the middle of things) and then provide background information once we are caught up in the action. The spectator infers the story on the basis of the information that the plot dispenses.

According to French New Wave director Jean-Luc Godard, narratives must have a beginning, a middle and an end, "but not necessarily in that order" **(2-2)**. Realist

2-2. *Masculin-Féminin* (France, 1966), with Jean-Pierre Léaud and Chantal Goya, directed by Jean-Luc Godard.

"The Americans are good at storytelling," Godard noted, "the French are not. Flaubert and Proust can't tell stories. They do something else. So does the cinema. I prefer to use a kind of tapestry, a background on which I can embroider on my own ideas." Instead of using scripts, Godard set up dramatic situations, then asked his actors to improvise their dialogue, as in this interview scene—a technique he derived from the documentary movement called *cinéma vérité* (see Chapter 9, "Nonfiction Films"). He intersperses these scenes with digressions, opinions, and jokes. Above all, he wanted to capture the spontaneity of the moment, which he believed was more authentic when he and his actors had to fend for themselves, without the security of a script. "If you know in advance everything you are going to do, it is not worth doing," Godard insisted, "If a show is all written down, what is the point of filming it? What use is cinema if it trails after literature?" *(Columbia Pictures)*

narratives usually rearrange story events in fairly unobtrusive ways, providing information about the past only when we need it to understand what is happening on screen at the moment. Formalist filmmakers are more likely to distort chronology and to call attention to what they are doing.

The most obvious way that movies provide information about the past is through **flashbacks**. From the very earliest days, filmmakers used conventional signals to cue the audience that a flashback was about to begin, an **iris** or a **dissolve**, for example. The same conventions were often used to introduce dream sequences, and, indeed, flashbacks were usually motivated as the subjective memory of a character. In a daring move that he later regretted, Alfred Hitchcock presented a murder in *Stage Fright* (1950) in a flashback from the point of view of a character who, as the ending reveals, was not telling the truth. Hitchcock attributed the film's failure to his violation of the trust of the spectator, who assumes that the events shown in a flashback, however subjective its origin, will be true.

If there is no clear transition to a flashback, the audience may be confused, but some directors may omit the usual cues on purpose to call attention to the relativity of our experience of time itself. Almost all the films of the French director Alain Resnais have narrative structures that disorient the viewer and call into question the idea of time as a linear progression. In *L'Année dernière à Marienbad* [*Last Year at Marienbad*] (1961), Resnais and writer Alain Robbe-Grillet created a highly enigmatic narrative in which a man tries to convince a woman that they had an affair a year ago. She denies ever having met him, but, as the characters wander through a *château* that may or may not be in Marienbad, images from the past seem to confirm some aspects of his story. These images are often contradictory, and may be imaginary, and it becomes difficult to distinguish the present from the so-called past. At the end, we are no closer to knowing what, if anything, happened last year at Marienbad.

The films of the Canadian director Atom Egoyan also often juxtapose past and present events and create doubts about whether the past is being remembered or imagined. *Exotica* (1994) and *The Sweet Hereafter* (1997), for example, both cut back and forth between a traumatic event—the murder of a schoolgirl in the former and the crash of a school bus in the latter—and sequences depicting the effect that it has had on the lives of those who experienced it. In such films, the juxtaposition of the sequences becomes more important than their chronological relations: Plot time takes precedence over story time.

Of course, most films tell their stories in more straightforward ways, but they almost always depend on some form of temporal rearrangement. Flashbacks may be used to narrate past events that help to explain present situations, but the past also affects the present in less obvious ways. Crime films, for example, often begin with a murder or the discovery of a corpse and then depict the process by which a detective uncovers evidence about what led to the crime and who committed it **(2-3)**.

Contemporary Canadian films often adopt "mosaic" rather than linear narrative structures, a feature that contrasts strongly with the dynamic and action-oriented approach found in much U.S. popular culture **(2-4)**. Yet, several recent Hollywood movies also disorient their audiences with unusual time schemes. In Quentin Tarantino's *Pulp Fiction* (1994), for example, a character who died earlier in the film reappears in the final sequence, surprising the audience, who must adjust their sense

2-3. *The Maltese Falcon* (U.S.A., 1941), with Humphrey Bogart, Peter Lorre, Mary Astor, and Sydney Greenstreet, directed by John Huston.

Huston's classic crime thriller, based on a hard-boiled novel by Dashiell Hammett, begins when a private detective is gunned down by an unseen assailant. His partner, Sam Spade (Bogart), is then hired by a beautiful woman (Astor) to investigate the disappearance of the old and valuable statue that gives the film its title. The plot gradually reveals a complex web of blackmail and double-crosses among rival criminals. Spade's investigation in the present leads him into many dangerous situations, but he gradually uncovers the story of events that occurred before the opening sequence, including the relations among the criminals, the historical origins of the statue, and the identity of his partner's killer. *(Warner Bros.)*

of the cause-and-effect structure by recognizing that the plot has unexpectedly rearranged story time. Christopher Nolan's *Memento* (2000) even tells its story backward. Such films suggest that many filmmakers and viewers are no longer satisfied with traditional narrative conventions in a media-saturated environment in which the experience of time and space becomes increasingly fragmented and unpredictable. Of course, many films continue to be made using these conventions.

The process by which a story is told is called narration, and the telling of the story is usually attributed to a narrator. Literary critics insist that the narrator in a novel should not be confused with the author, who uses the narrator to establish a perspective that may well prove to be selective or unreliable. Film theorists are divided over whether fiction films have a narrator in this sense, but the problem of the elusive film author is complicated when a movie has a voice-over narration **(2-6)**.

2-4. *Rude* (Canada, 1996), with Sharon M. Lewis, directed by Clement Virgo.

The plot of this film interweaves three separate stories linked only by the voice of Rude (Lewis), a pirate radio announcer broadcasting on the Easter weekend to the black community. She speaks to people who have been brought from "the land of the Zulu" to "the land of the Ojibway," and her poetic utterances are matched by the atmospheric and dream-like images. The three stories thus become elements of the collective consciousness of people's longing for freedom. *(The Feature Film Project)*

Usually, this off-screen narrator is also a character in the story and hence has a stake in "helping" us interpret the events. Sometimes the narrator—as in the first-person novel—is the main character of a movie. (For a fuller discussion of these ideas, see "Point of View" in Chapter 1 and the "Speech" section in Chapter 7, "Sound").

Narration also differs according to a movie's style. Realistic films often create the impression that the events speak for themselves. The story seems to unfold automatically, usually in chronological sequence. In **classical** narrative structures, we are vaguely aware of a shaping hand in the storyline, editing out the uninteresting or inessential parts of story time and ensuring that we have a clear point of view on the action. The storyteller keeps the action on track, moving toward a specific destination—the resolution of the story's central conflict—but usually maintains a low profile, except when filmmakers—Hitchcock is the prime example—want to make us aware of our willingness to be taken in even while we know we are being taken in. In **formalistic** narratives, the author is more overtly manipulative, sometimes scrambling the chronology of the story or heightening or restructuring events to maximize a thematic idea. The story is told from a subjective perspective, as in Oliver Stone's polemical *JFK* **(11-3)**.

2-5. *Crash* (U.S.A., 2005), with Thandie Newton and Matt Dillon, screenplay by Paul Haggis and Bobby Moresco, directed by Haggis.

"Character-driven" stories tend to downplay narrative in favour of exploring people's psychological complexities. In this ensemble drama, for example, we get to see many of the characters in two different contexts. The movie is set in the sprawling city of Los Angeles, where the chances of meeting the same people twice in a short period are very unlikely. In a sense, the doubled narrative structure of this film is deliberately artificial, despite the realism of the visual style, the acting, and the individual scenes. We first meet the Dillon character early in the movie. He is a police officer who is rudely brushed off by a female African-American municipal bureaucrat when he tries to get some help for his invalid father. Later in the story, he stops an auto containing an upscale black couple (Newton and Terrence Howard). The cop deliberately humiliates them by pretending to body search the woman in front of her helpless husband. Later in the movie, the officer comes to the rescue of the same woman, who is trapped inside her crashed auto. Initially repelled by his presence at the accident site, she reluctantly yields to his commands in getting her out of harm's way. In fact, he saves her life. Which is the real police officer—the sadistic racist or the heroic saviour? *(Lions Gate Films)*

Once a movie begins, we start to define its narrative limits. The style of the credits and the accompanying score help us to determine the tone of the picture, while the opening sequences suggest how the narrative will be developed and where it is likely to end up. These opening expository sequences also establish the **diegetic** "world" of the narrative—what is possible, what is probable, what is not very likely, and so on. The opening scenes of most movies establish the time frame of the narrative—whether it will unfold in flashbacks, in the present, or in some combination. The exposition also establishes the ground rules about fantasy scenes, dreams, and the stylistic variables associated with these levels of the narrative **(2-7)**.

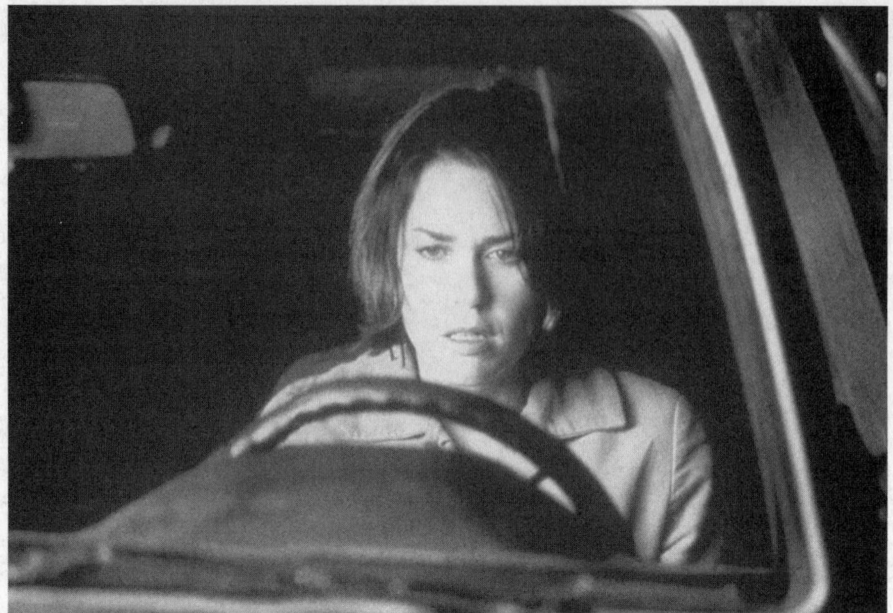

2-6. *Maelström* (2000), with Marie-Josée Croze, directed by Denis Villeneuve.

Maelström is narrated by a fish—or, more accurately, by a succession of fish—who continue the story as they are gutted and beheaded by a monstrous fishmonger. In the story itself, Bibiane (Croze) has an abortion and then kills an old Norwegian man in a car accident. This man is also a fishmonger, and the motifs of fish and water recur throughout the film, giving the otherwise realist narrative an unsettling tone that is both mythic and very strange. *(Max Films/Photographer Michel Tramblay)*

THE CLASSICAL PARADIGM

The **classical paradigm** is a term invented by scholars to describe a certain kind of narrative structure that has dominated fiction film production since the 1920s. It is by far the most popular type of story organization, especially in the United States, where it has, until recently, reigned virtually unchallenged.

The classical paradigm is a set of conventions, not rules. Most films in this form begin with an implied dramatic question. We want to know how the protagonist will get what he or she wants, or solve a mystery, in the face of considerable opposition. The opening sets up the situation, and the scenes that follow intensify the conflict in a rising pattern of action. This escalation is treated in terms of cause and effect, with each scene implying a link to the next. After the conflict builds to its maximum tension in the climax, in which the protagonist defeats the antagonist and resolves the tensions, the narrative ends with some kind of formal closure—traditionally, a wedding or a dance in comedies, a death in tragedies, and a reunion or return to normal in dramas. The final shot—because of its privileged position—is often meant to be a philosophical overview of some kind, a summing up of the significance of the previous material. The classical paradigm emphasizes dramatic unity, plausible motivation, and coherence of its constituent parts. Each shot is seamlessly linked to the

2-7. *eXistenZ* (Canada, 1999), with Jennifer Jason Leigh, directed by David Cronenberg.

Many recent films explore the fragmentation of identity in a society saturated with media images. In these films, the plot often refers to story events that take place on different levels of reality. Modern teenagers find themselves in a 1950s sitcom in *Pleasantville* (Gary Ross, 1998); a man grows up inside a TV show in *The Truman Show* (Peter Weir, 1998); characters travel through computer programs in *The Matrix* (Andy and Larry Wachowski, 1999); and in Cronenberg's playful science-fiction film, a game designer (Leigh) uses her "bio-port" to enter the simulated worlds that she has created. We are often unsure whether events are taking place inside or outside the game as she seeks to evade the traps laid by her enemies, referred to as "realists." *(Alliance Atlantis)*

next in an effort to produce a smooth flow of action and often a sense of inevitability. To add urgency to the conflict, filmmakers may include some kind of deadline, thus intensifying the emotion. During the Hollywood **studio** era especially, classical structures often featured double plot lines, in which a romantic love story was developed to parallel the main line of action. In love stories, a comic second couple often paralleled the main lovers.

Classical plot structures are linear and often take the form of a journey, a chase, or a search. Even characters are defined primarily in terms of what they do. "Action is character," insists Syd Field, the author of several handbooks on screenwriting. "What a person does is what he is, not what he says." Field and other advocates of the classical paradigm are not very interested in passive characters—people to whom things are done. (These types of characters are more typical in other national cinemas, including Canadian cinema.) Classicists favour characters who are goal-oriented, so that we can take an interest in their plans of action.

Field's conceptual model is expressed in traditional theatrical terms **(2-9)**. A screenplay comprises three acts. Act I, "The **Setup**," occupies the first quarter of the **script**. It establishes the dramatic premise: What is the main character's goal, and what obstacles are likely to get in the way of its attainment? Act II, "The Confrontation," consists of the middle two quarters of the story, with a major reversal of fortune at the midpoint. This portion of the screenplay complicates the conflict with plot twists and an increasing sense of urgency, showing the main character fighting against obstacles. Act III, "The Resolution," constitutes the final quarter of the story. This section dramatizes what happens as a result of the climactic confrontation.

REALISTIC NARRATIVES

Both realistic and formalistic narratives are patterned and manipulated, but the realistic storyteller attempts to submerge the pattern, to bury it beneath the surface

2-8. *E.T.: The Extra-Terrestrial* (U.S.A., 1982), with Henry Thomas and E.T., directed by Steven Spielberg.
In the opening sequences of his blockbuster family film, Spielberg prepares us for the supernatural events that occur in the middle and later portions of the movie by showing us how E.T. was left behind by his spaceship and by establishing supernaturalism as a narrative variable. *(Universal Pictures)*

"clutter" and apparent randomness of the dramatic events. In other words, the pretence that a realistic narrative is "unmanipulated" or "lifelike" is precisely that—a pretence, an aesthetic deception.

Realists generally prefer loose, discursive plots, with no clearly defined beginning, middle, or end. We dip into the story at an arbitrary point. Usually we are not presented with a clear-cut conflict, as in classical narratives. Rather, the conflict emerges unobtrusively from the unforced events of the exposition. The story itself is presented as a "slice of life," as a poetic fragment, not a neatly structured tale. Rarely is reality neatly structured; realistic art must follow suit. Life goes on, even after the final reel.

Realists often borrow their structures from the cycles of nature. For example, many of the movies of Yasujiro Ozu are given seasonal titles that symbolize an appropriate human counterpart—*Early Summer* (1951), *Late Autumn* (1960), *Early Spring* (1956), *The End of Summer* (1961), *Late Spring* **(2-11)**. Other realistic films are structured around a limited time, like summer vacation or a school semester. Such movies sometimes centre on rites of passage, such as birth, puberty, first love, first job, marriage, painful separations, death.

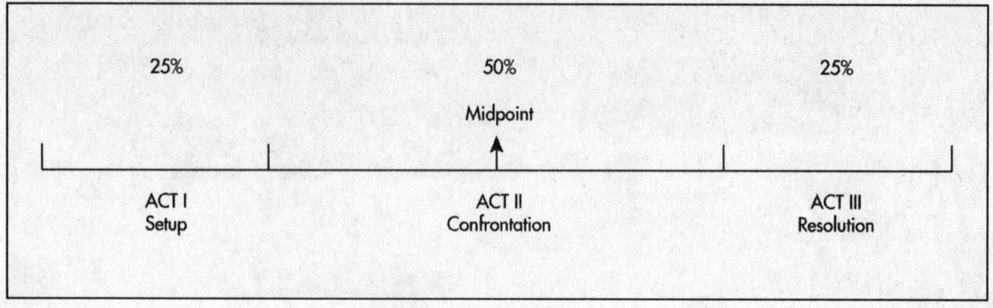

2-9. According to Syd Field, the narrative structure of a movie can be broken down into three acts. The story should contain about ten to twenty "plot points," major twists or key events in the action. At the midpoint of the second act, there is usually a big reversal of expectations, sending the action spinning in a new direction. In a reassessment of Field's model, Kristin Thompson has pointed out that the central portion is rather vaguely defined and usually much longer than the first and last acts. She suggests instead a four-part model that consists of the setup, the complicating action, the development, and the climax.

Often we cannot guess the principle of narrative coherence until the end of the movie, especially if it has a circular or cyclical structure, as many realistic films do. For example, Robert Altman's *M*A*S*H* (1970) opens with the arrival of two soldier-surgeons, Hawkeye Pierce and Duke Forrest. The movie ends when their tour of duty is over. Yet the M*A*S*H unit will continue saving lives, even after these two excellent surgeons have left.

The episodic structure of *M*A*S*H* is what appealed to those who adapted it as a television series. Realistic film narratives frequently seem episodic, the sequence of events almost interchangeable. The plot does not "build" inexorably but seems to drift into surprising scenes that do not necessarily propel the story forward. These are offered for their own sake, as examples of real-life oddities.

Spectators who like fast-moving stories are often impatient with realistic films, which frequently move slowly. This is especially true in the earlier scenes, while we wait for the main narrative strand to emerge. Digressions often turn out to be parallels to the central plotline, but this parallelism must be inferred; it is rarely pointed out explicitly. Other traits of realistic narratives include the following:

- A nonintrusive implied author who "reports" objectively and avoids making judgments
- A rejection of *clichés*, stale conventions, and stock situations and characters in favour of the individual, the concrete, the specific
- A fondness for *exposé*, with shocking or "low" subject matter that is often criticized for its grittiness and bad taste **(2-12)**
- An antisentimental point of view that rejects glib happy endings, wishful thinking, miraculous cures, and other forms of phony optimism
- An avoidance of melodrama and exaggeration in favour of understatement and dedramatization
- A scientific view of causality and motivation, with a corresponding rejection of such romantic concepts as destiny and fate

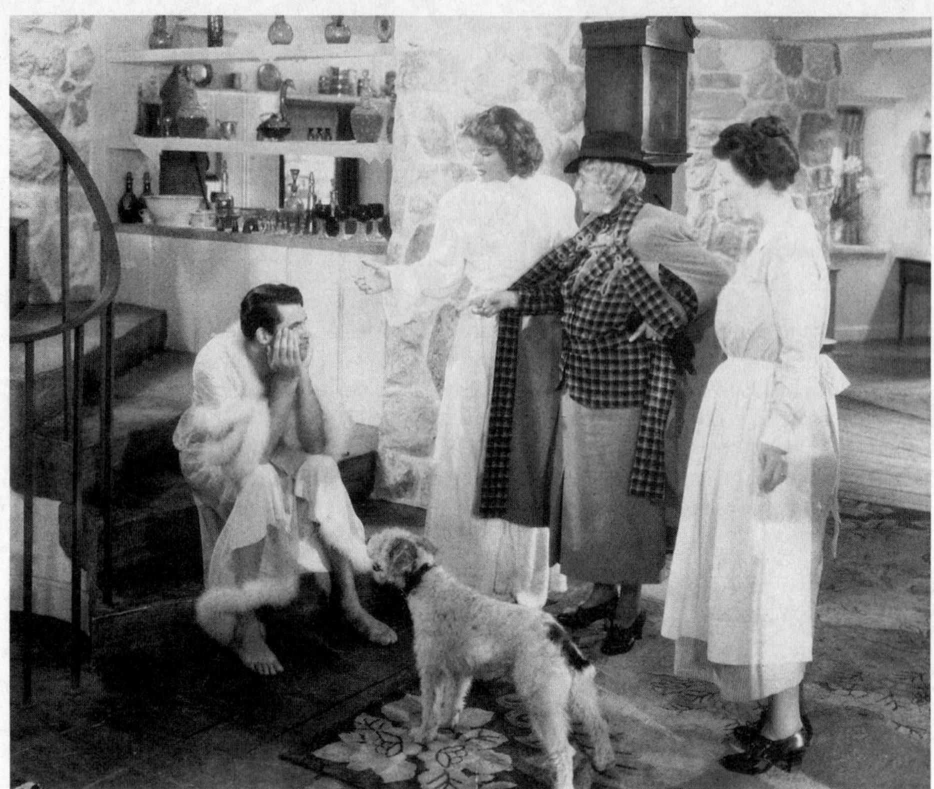

2-10. *Bringing Up Baby* (U.S.A., 1938), with Cary Grant and Katharine Hepburn, directed by Howard Hawks.

The popular Hollywood **screwball comedies** of the 1930s demonstrate the capacity of the classical paradigm to impose order on chaos. Essentially love stories, these films feature zany but glamorous lovers, often from different social classes, whose snappy dialogue crackles with wit and speed. The narrative premises are absurdly improbable, and the plots, which are intricate and filled with preposterous twists and turns, tend to snowball out of control. Yet the classical structure ensures that all the complications are worked out happily in the conclusion, with no loose ends showing. *(Columbia Pictures)*

- An avoidance of the **lyrical** impulse in favour of a plain, straightforward presentation

Few realist films incorporate all these qualities. Italian neorealist films (see Chapter 11, "Theory") are often melodramatic or lyrical in the narrative style, while Canadian direct cinema films (see Chapter 10, "Canadian Cinema") often question the objectivity of the implied author.

FORMALISTIC NARRATIVES

In formalistic narratives, time is often scrambled and rearranged to hammer home a thematic point more forcefully. The design of the plot is not concealed but height-

2-11. *Late Spring* (Japan, 1949), with Chishu Ryu (seated) and Setsuko Hara (centre), directed by Yasujiro Ozu.

One of the most common genres in Japan is the home drama. It is the only genre Ozu worked in, and he was one of its most popular practitioners. This type of film deals with the day-to-day routines of domestic life. Although Ozu was a profoundly philosophical artist, his movies consist almost entirely of "little things"—the bitter pills of self-denial that ultimately render life disappointing. Many of Ozu's films have seasonal titles that symbolically evoke appropriate human analogues. *Late Spring*, for example, deals with the attempts of a decent widower (Ryu) to marry off his only daughter (Hara) because he fears she will grow old looking after him. *(New Yorker Films)*

ened. Formalistic plots come in a wide assortment, but usually they are structured according to the filmmaker's theme. For example, Alfred Hitchcock was obsessed by themes dealing with "doubles" and "the wrong man"—a technically innocent man who is accused of a crime committed by an undetected counterpart.

Hitchcock's *The Wrong Man* (1957) is his most explicit treatment of these narrative motifs. The entire plot is doubled, structured in twos. There are two imprisonments, two handwriting tests, two conversations in the kitchen, two legal hearings, two visits to a clinic, two visits to the lawyer. The hero is arrested twice by two policemen. He is identified (wrongly) by two witnesses at two different shops. There are two transfers of guilt: The main character (Henry Fonda) is accused of a crime he did not commit, and midway through the movie, his emotionally disturbed wife (Vera Miles) takes on the guilt and has to be committed to an asylum.

Many formalistic narratives are intruded on by the author. For example, it is virtually impossible to ignore the personality of Buñuel in his films. He slyly interjects his sardonic black humour into his narratives. He loves to undermine his charac-

2-12. *City of God* (Brazil, 2003), with Alexandre Rodrigues, directed by Fernando Meirelles.
Ever since the late nineteenth century, when it became a dominant international style in the arts, realism has provoked controversy for its "sordid" or "shocking" subject matter, its preoccupation with details that the conventional majority finds repulsive but fascinating. This story is set in a vicious slum of Rio de Janeiro, ironically nicknamed City of God. Many of the youngsters in the cast were actually street children of the neighborhood. "Some of them worked for drug dealers," Meirelles said. "They knew much more than me about the film I was doing." Violent, brutal, and bloody, the movie offers very little hope for these lost children. Most of them will never reach adulthood. Viewers are likely to ask themselves: How did the world get this way? *(Miramax Films)*

ters—their pomposity, their self-deception, their mean little souls **(2-13)**. Godard's personality is also highly intrusive, especially in his nontraditional narratives, which he called "cinematic essays" **(2-2)**.

Formalistic narratives are often interrupted by lyrical interludes, exercises in pure style—like the exhilarating dance numbers in the Fred Astaire and Ginger Rogers musicals made by RKO Studio in the 1930s. In fact, stylized genre films such as musicals, science fiction, and fantasies offer the richest potential for displays of stylistic rapture and bravura effects. These lyrical interludes interrupt the forward momentum of the plot, which is often a mere pretext anyway.

The films of David Lynch frequently defy the rules of logic and causality that underpin conventional narratives as well as our sense of everyday reality. *Blue Velvet* (1986), for example, juxtaposes life in an excessively "normal" small town and the dark world of sexual obsession and obscenity into which a young man is drawn as he investigates the mystery associated with a beautiful newcomer to his neighbourhood. At the beginning of *Lost Highway* (1997), a man receives a strange message over his apartment intercom that seems to set in motion a whole series of bizarre happenings. After he is jailed for murdering his wife, the police find in his cell an apparently different man, who becomes obsessed with a woman who looks like the wife except for the colour of her hair (both women are played by Patricia Arquette). At the end, it is this man who delivers the message that was heard by his former self. Lynch's *Mulholland*

2-13. *Le Charme discret de la bourgeoisie* [*The Discreet Charm of the Bourgeoisie*] (France, 1972), directed by Luis Buñuel.

Most of Buñuel's movies feature bizarre scenes that are left unexplained, as though they were the most natural thing in the world. He delighted in satirizing middle-class hypocrisies, treating them with a kind of affectionate bemusement mingled with contempt. In this film, he presents us with a series of loosely connected episodes dealing with the inane rituals of a group of well-heeled semi-zombies. Interspersing these episodes are shots of the main characters walking on an empty road (pictured). No one questions why they are there. No one seems to know where they are going. Buñuel does not say. *(Twentieth Century Fox)*

Drive also has a bifurcated narrative structure in which actors change roles and names in the middle and seem to enter into a different dimension of reality **(2-14)**.

ADAPTATION

A great many movies are **adaptations** of literary sources. In some respects, adapting a novel or play requires more skill and originality than working with an original screenplay. Furthermore, the better the literary work, the more difficult the adaptation. For this reason, many film adaptations are based on mediocre sources. There are many adaptations that are superior to their originals: D.W. Griffith's *The Birth of a Nation* (see **6-4**), for instance, was based on Thomas Dixon's sensationalist novel *The Klansman*. Some commentators believe that if a work of art has reached its fullest artistic expression in one form, an adaptation will inevitably be inferior.

2-14. *Mulholland Drive* (U.S.A., 2001), with Naomi Watts and Laura Elena Harring, written and directed by David Lynch.

Almost from the inception of the cinema, filmmakers and critics have noted the similarity of movies to dreams. Perhaps no one is more in touch with this irrational, trancelike state than David Lynch. This movie was originally conceived as a pilot for a TV series. Unable to market it, Lynch added a new second half and released it as a movie. *(Universal Pictures)*

According to this argument, no film adaptation of Jane Austen's *Pride and Prejudice* could equal the original, nor could any novel hope to capture the richness of Ingmar Bergman's *Persona* (see **4-30**). There is a good deal of sense in this view because the true content of each medium is organically governed by its forms.

The real problem of the adapter is not how to reproduce the *content* of a literary work (an impossibility), but how close he or she should remain to the raw data of the *subject matter*. This degree of fidelity is what determines the three types of adaptations: the loose, the faithful, and the literal. Of course, these classifications are for convenience only; in actual practice, most movies fall somewhere between these classifications.

The loose adaptation is barely that. Generally, only an idea, a situation, or a character is taken from a literary source and then developed independently. A film that falls into this class is Akira Kurosawa's *Ran* (1985), which transforms Shakespeare's *King Lear* into a quite different tale set in medieval Japan, though the filmmaker retains several plot elements from Shakespeare's original (see also **2-16**). In a similar spirit, but with very different results, Gurinder Chadha's *Bride and Prejudice* (2004) translates Jane Austen's nineteenth-century novel into a high-spirited Bollywood musical set in contemporary India, Britain, and the United States.

Faithful adaptations, as the phrase implies, attempt to re-create the literary source in filmic terms, keeping as close to the spirit of the original as possible. Critic André Bazin likened the faithful adapter to a translator who tries to find equivalents to the original. Of course, Bazin realized that fundamental differences exist between the two media: The translator's problem in converting the word *road* to *strada* or *Strasse* is not as acute as a filmmaker's problem in transforming the word into a picture. An example of a faithful adaptation is Joe Wright's *Pride and Prejudice* (2005). The narrative preserves much of the novel's plot structure, its major events, and most of the important characters **(2-15)**. As in most Jane Austen adaptations, the witty omniscient narrator is not retained, and so the film has to find cinematic equivalents for the ironic perspective that characterizes the novel. It frequently reminds us of the larger social context within which affairs of the Bennett family are conducted. The contrast between the country gathering, at which Darcy first displays his pride, and the elegant ball given by the Bingleys situates the family as belonging to an interme-

2-15. *Pride and Prejudice* (Britain, 2005), with Keira Knightly and Matthew Macfadyen, directed by Joe Wright. Jane Austen's novels have proved highly attractive to adapters for movies and television. Deborah Moggach's adaptation of Jane Austen's most famous novel preserves much of the book's 1813 literary style. To modern ears, the dialogue sounds rather formal and polite. Stylized period dialogue requires first-rate performers like these, actors who can infuse the language with a sense of suppressed passion. *(Focus Features)*

diate social class. At times, the camera wanders away from the main action to follow a servant and thus reminds us of the life of leisure and privilege that makes the story possible. The film also respects the reticence of the social manners of the time, in which kissing—or even touching—was frowned upon, and sexual attraction was restrained by concerns about status and property. These constraints are emphasized by several close-ups of hands reaching out but not touching, a motif that proved too much for the U.S. distributors, who demanded a more passionate ending.

Literal adaptations are usually restricted to plays. The two basic modes of drama—action and dialogue—are also found in films, but the major problem with adaptations from the stage is in the handling of space and time. If the film adapter were to leave the camera at long shot and restrict the editing to scene shifts only, the result would be similar to the original. But few filmmakers would be willing merely to record a play, nor indeed should they, for in doing so they would lose much of the excitement of the original and contribute none of the advantages of the adapting medium, particularly its greater freedom in the treatment of space and time (see **1-20**).

The differences among loose, faithful, and literal adaptations, then, are essentially matters of degree. In each case, the cinematic form inevitably alters the content of the literary original. There is thus little point in studying adaptation merely to castigate movies for not doing what literature does better; rather the goal should be to throw light on how the different media respond to the same underlying narrative structure.

2-16. *Throne of Blood* (Japan, 1957), based on Shakespeare's *Macbeth*, directed by Akira Kurosawa. The loose adaptation takes a few general ideas from an original source, then develops them independently. Kurosawa's film is one of the greatest of all Shakespearean adaptations precisely because the filmmaker doesn't attempt to compete with *Macbeth*. Kurosawa's samurai movie is a *cinematic* masterpiece, owing relatively little to language for its power. Its similarities to Shakespeare's literary masterpiece are superficial, just as the play's similarities to Holingshed's *Chronicles* (Shakespeare's primary source) are of no great artistic significance.
(Audio-Brandon Films)

GENRE

The concept of genre has its roots in literary theory, where it is often traced back to Aristotle's *The Poetics*, in which the Greek philosopher distinguished between different narrative forms (such as epic, tragedy, comedy). Film theorists tend to define genres more specifically, but a genre film is still a type of movie—a war picture, a gangster film, a science-fiction movie, and so on. Genres thus denote groups of films that share distinctive and recurring themes, narrative structures, and images. Some genres are more realistic than others, but in all of them, the credibility of the narrative depends less on its correspondence to a reality outside the film than on its appropriateness within the established framework of the genre.

Genres are immediately recognizable through their **iconography**, motifs that become associated with a specific genre through repetition. Whereas a motif accrues meaning in the course of a single film (see Chapter 1, "Medium"), an icon recurs in many films and carries meanings developed through previous use (although its actual meaning will also depend on its specific context in a movie). A film establishes itself

2-17. *The Searchers* (U.S.A., 1956), with John Wayne, directed by John Ford.

The lone cowboy, mounted on his horse, overlooking a wilderness landscape, is a basic iconic image in the western genre. Wayne's sturdy, sometimes lumbering, figure was closely identified with the genre, although he also appeared in other action genres, most notably the war movie. In this later western, Ford uses the iconography he had helped establish to critique the values of the classical western. Ethan (Wayne) sets out to rescue his niece who has been kidnapped by Indians but becomes increasingly obsessive, exposing the dark side of the western hero. His long journey through the wilderness seems to take him round in circles and turns him into an isolated and bitter racist whose goal is to kill the young woman he thinks of as contaminated by her captors. *(Warner Bros.)*

as a western, for example, as soon as we see wide open spaces, cowboys driving cattle, a dusty street with a saloon and a sheriff's office, Indians attacking a wagon train, and so on. A gangster film includes seedy urban settings, dark shadowy locations, machine guns, violent men who dress in fancy suits and often wear dark glasses. Not all the possible iconic elements will appear in every film, of course, but those that do construct a diegetic world in which all the others exist in off-screen space and in the spectator's memory.

The word "genre" comes from the same root as "gender," a term that refers to the cultural codes that define and regulate human sexuality. Genres are deeply implicated in the construction and circulation of gender codes: This involves both the ways in which men and women (and the relations between them) are represented in specific genres and the distinction between genres that appeal primarily to men (mainly action genres) and those supposedly addressed to women (musicals, domes-

2-18. *GoodFellas* (U.S.A., 1990), with Lorraine Bracco and Ray Liotta, directed by Martin Scorsese.

Gangster films depict criminal environments in which the gangster figure often has intense relationships with other men (his "gang") and enjoys the sexual attentions of his "moll." Yet, many gangsters also have a strong sense of "family" and the rituals of domestic life also play a part in the iconography of the genre. In this wedding dance scene, Scorsese conveys the couple's euphoria by swirling the camera along with the dancers. These spontaneous eruptions destabilize the visual materials, infusing the action with a surge of energy, almost a kinetic high that matches the young gangster's euphoria at having become one of the "wise guys." As in many earlier gangster films, the narrative charts the tension between his criminal life and his desire to settle down. *(Warner Bros.)*

tic melodramas). While genres thus seek to define "proper" gender identities, the treatment of gender is often the source of underlying tensions and contradictions. In the western, for example, women usually have relatively marginal roles, and the most intense relationships are among men; the stories stress the importance of marriage and the family, and the homoerotic implications are rarely acknowledged, although they do finally surface in the updated western *Brokeback Mountain* (Ang Lee, 2005) set in Wyoming and Texas during the 1960s **(2-19)**.

Assigning films to particular genres serves a number of purposes in different contexts. Genre is thus (1) a critical tool (enabling critics to map the vast territory of movie production); (2) an aspect of the film industry (a way of organizing production and exhibition); and (3) a guide to spectators (helping them to decide what films to see and providing cues that shape their interpretation of what they do see).

Genre filmmaking is usually associated with Hollywood, although all national cinemas produce genre films. The origins of the genre system coincided with the Hollywood studios' achievement of a dominant position in world cinema, and genre is thus closely related to the star system, mass-production techniques, and the classical paradigm. According to Hollywood's critics, the production of genre films was a symptom of the poverty of mass culture, encouraging the use of easily digested formulas rather than the creation of original works of art. They regarded genre as a defining feature of popular cinema as opposed to "art cinema," which supposedly consisted of nongeneric movies (although more recent critics often discuss art cinema as a genre in itself).

It is certainly true that genre is a conservative cultural force, which is not the same as saying that all genre films are conservative. Genres are restrictive in that

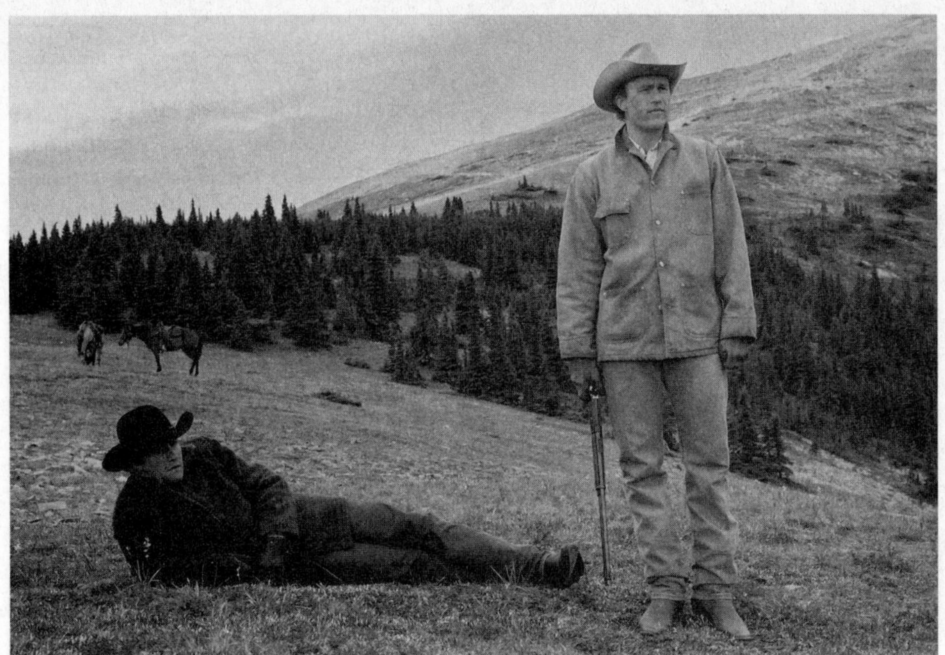

2-19. *Brokeback Mountain* (U.S.A., 2005), with Jake Gyllenhaal and Heath Ledger, directed by Ang Lee.
The story is about two young westerners—one a ranch hand (Ledger), the other an aspiring rodeo rider (Gyllenhaal). A drunken night of revelry morphs into a passionate sexual encounter, which soon becomes a furtive love affair in the isolated, pristine mountains of Wyoming in 1963. Over the next 20 years, they marry women and father children, but the men's love affair continues sporadically, urgently, secretly. The toxic homophobia of their culture ultimately destroys the relationship, and the story ends on a note of poignant loss, missed opportunities, and wasted lives. *(Focus Features)*

their conventions limit the choices of the filmmaker and the spectator, although the conventions should not be treated as rules. Rather they create a paradigm, a set of norms, which the filmmaker can reinforce, call into question, or even reject—as long as the deviation does not go so far as to alienate the audience. Generic plots are predictable, but the pleasure comes from *how* the film treats the story materials rather than from the outcome; because of the constraints, small variations will produce large meanings. Filmmakers are attracted to genres because they automatically synthesize a vast amount of cultural information, reducing the amount of screen time needed to establish the characters and the situation.

Although the genre system depends on defining, and sometimes policing, boundaries between genres, in practice there is a great deal of overlap and instability. This is partly because genres are defined in different ways: Some refer to a specific content (westerns or science-fiction movies, for example), others are named after a stylistic feature (musicals, melodramas), while still others are distinguished by the effect they have on audiences (thrillers, horror films). Genre terms may also be used differently by critics, the industry, and spectators. Some genres are defined so broadly that they have given rise to numerous sub-genres (slapstick, screwball, and

2-20. *Seven Brides for Seven Brothers* (U.S.A., 1954), with Jacques D'Amboise (flying aloft), choreography by Michael Kidd, directed by Stanley Donen.

Set on a ranch in Oregon during pioneer days, this classical musical displays much of the iconography of the western. When the oldest rancher gets married, his six brothers kidnap brides from a nearby town, and they spend the winter isolated on the ranch. Despite their rustic manners, the men treat the women with respect, and, by the time the snows melt, the women have tamed them and fallen in love. The musical conventions win out, but the western influence is apparent in Kidd's choreography, which highlights the athletic male body. *(MGM)*

romantic comedies, for example), while gangster films, detective films, heist films, police procedurals, and so on overlap to such an extent that they are often grouped together as "crime films."

There is also a long tradition of hybrid genre films, in which two or more genres are combined to increase the potential audience. Many films combine elements of science fiction and horror so that it becomes difficult to categorize them satisfactorily, and the musical often draws on the iconography of other genres. *The Harvey Girls* (George Sidney, 1946) and *Calamity Jane* (David Butler, 1953) both provide the lyrical and exuberant singing and dancing (featuring Judy Garland and Doris Day, respectively) expected of the genre, but their visual iconography is borrowed from the western (see also **2-20**). These films are classified as musicals, but "singing cowboys" such as Gene Autry and Roy Rogers starred in many westerns from the 1930s to the 1950s.

The genre system allowed the Hollywood studios, and many smaller production companies, to turn out a steady stream of movies to meet the voracious public demand during the 1930s and 1940s, recycling plots, settings, costumes, even actors who

2-21. *Some Like It Hot* (U.S.A., 1959), with Jack Lemmon and Tony Curtis, directed by Billy Wilder.

Two musicians from Chicago witness a gangland killing in 1929 and fear for their own lives. They try to escape by dressing as women and joining an all-girl band whose banjoist and lead singer is Sugar Kane, played by Marilyn Monroe. Their clumsy efforts to maintain their disguise are juxtaposed with Monroe's excessive feminine masquerade. Joe/Josephine (Curtis) ends up with Sugar, while Jerry/Daphne (Lemmon) finds him/herself engaged to an eccentric millionaire (Joe E. Brown). The gender-bending predicaments provide most of the hilarious comedy, but the situation is given a darker edge by the film's serious treatment of the gangster film elements. *(United Artists)*

played essentially the same role in one film after another. Many of these films were undistinguished, but the low-budget sector, whose films were often supporting features on double bills, frequently outdid the more prestigious productions. The *Cahiers du cinéma* critics of the 1950s, who were campaigning for the *politique des auteurs* (see Chapter 1, "Medium"), often admired directors working for small studios: Godard dedicated his own first feature, *À bout de souffle* [*Breathless*] (1959) to one such studio, Monogram. André Bazin reminded his young acolytes that the presence of an auteur does not automatically lead to a great film and that "the tradition of genres is the base of operations for creative freedom." They needed little reminding, and the idea of the creative tension between personal vision and generic conventions has flourished in much subsequent genre criticism. By exploiting the broad outlines of a well-known tale or story type, the storyteller can play off its main features, creating provocative tensions between the genre's conventions and the artist's inventions, between the familiar and the original, the general and the particular.

A rather different approach to genre emerged from critics in the 1960s, who were influenced by the movement known as "structuralism" (see Chapter 11, "Theory"). These critics argued that the conventional language of genre films enabled them to embody the myths of the culture that produced them. According to the cultural theorist Roland Barthes, a myth is not untrue but selective: It heightens selected aspects of a situation and makes them stand for the whole, thereby translating a complex and contradictory reality into simple structures that seem to be rooted in a natural order. The stylized conventions and **archetypal** story patterns of genres are ideal vehicles for myth, encouraging viewers to participate ritualistically in the basic beliefs, fears, and anxieties of their age **(2-22)**. As social conditions change, genres often change with them, challenging some cultural myths, reaffirming or creating others.

2-22. *Invasion of the Body Snatchers* (U.S.A., 1956), directed by Don Siegel.
Genre films often appeal to subconscious anxieties in the audience. A number of cultural commentators have remarked on the "paranoid style" of many American science-fiction movies of the 1950s, when the "Red Scare" intensified the Cold War atmosphere between the United States and the Soviet Union. Siegel's low-budget classic deals with how some alien pod-people insidiously invade human bodies, reducing their owners to anonymous zombies, incapable of feelings. The movie used genre conventions to powerful, but highly ambiguous, effect: The zombies might represent the supposedly dehumanizing ideology of communism but could equally be seen as a critique of the conformism in U.S. society promoted by those who were fighting communism. *(Allied Artists)*

Myths depend on binary oppositions (see Chapter 11, "Theory"): the conflict between good and bad, self and other, male and female, for example. The narrative structures in genre films depend on these basic oppositions, but they interact with each other in ways that can be morally quite complex. In many routine westerns, the hero wore a white hat and the villain, a black one, but the central opposition between civilization and wilderness is inherently ambivalent. The western deals with the Myth of the Frontier and the introduction of law and order to the new western territories during the nineteenth century. Yet civilization is associated with the east and the often dubious authority of politicians and business men. The security it offers is also less exciting than the open spaces and gunfights that attract audiences to the genre. Typically, the western hero paves the way for civilization but does not settle down himself. Similarly, in the gangster film, audiences may identify with the cause of law and order, but the aggression and self-assurance of the gangster figure are vital to the appeal of the genre, as the censors were often well aware.

One of the key issues in genre theory is why certain genres flourish at certain times and go into decline at other times. The western was one of the most popular genres until the 1960s but has made only sporadic comebacks since then. Perhaps its vision of American history no longer seemed relevant, although the genre continued to thrive on television for a while, and its iconography is still a potent force in popular culture. It seems, by contrast, that gangster films are especially popular during periods of social breakdown.

Some critics and scholars also argue that genres have their own internal history and have identified four main phases: (1) formative, (2) classical, (3) revisionist, and (4) reflexive. These phases occur in different periods for different genres, although they do correspond roughly to the history of Hollywood in general and to broader cultural and historical changes. It is important to note that, apart from the first of these (when the genre proper has not yet emerged), a new phase may become dominant but does not eliminate its predecessor, and films continue to be produced that seem to belong to earlier phases.

The formative phase is often termed "primitive," but this can lead to the misleading implication that each phase is an improvement on the last. During this phase, films may be naive but powerful in their emotional impact, in part because of the novelty of the form. The conventions and iconography of the genre are established in this phase. For example, the formative phase of the western is exemplified by Edwin S. Porter's *The Great Train Robbery* (1903), the first western ever made (even if it was shot in New Jersey and regarded as a crime film at the time). While the film genre did not really emerge until a number of movies had been made in the same vein, the western, like other genres, could draw on earlier forms: dime novels, the paintings of Frederic Remington and other artists, and the popular "wild west" shows of the late nineteenth century. The origins of the gangster film were more contempo-

2-23. *Unforgiven* (U.S.A., 1992), with Gene Hackman and Clint Eastwood, directed by Eastwood.

Genres in their classical phase tend to portray a world where right and wrong are fairly clear-cut, where the moral values of the movie are widely shared by the audience, and where justice eventually triumphs over evil. The contemporary cinema tends to favour genres that are more critical—less idealistic, more morally ambiguous, and far from reassuring in their presentation of the human condition. For example, *Unforgiven* is a revisionist western whose grim protagonist, William Munny (Eastwood), is a hired killer, so lost in violence that he has doomed his soul. When a youthful crony remarks that their victim "had it coming," Munny replies, "We all got it coming, kid." *(Warner Bros.)*

rary, as the genre had its roots in the rise of organized crime during the Prohibition era (1920–1933). Crime was a staple of popular cinema from early on in films like D.W. Griffith's short *The Musketeers of Pig Alley* (1912), but the gangster film began to emerge as a distinct genre in Joseph von Sternberg's *Underworld* (1927).

The classical phase is the period during which the genre is most assured and its conventions and iconography fully worked out. During this phase, the consensus-building function of the genre system is at the forefront: The genre's values are widely shared by the audience, who acts as what literary theorist Stanley Fish calls an "interpretive community." In its classical phase, the western constructs an idealized myth of nation-building that affirms the dominant values of American society even as it points to some of the contradictions within those values. John Ford directed many westerns now accepted as among the greatest achievements in the genre: *Stagecoach* (1939) established John Wayne, who had already appeared in numerous low-budget westerns, as a major star, indelibly associated with the genre; the sequence in *My Darling Clementine* (1946) in which Wyatt Earp (Henry Fonda) dances with a schoolteacher on the floor of an unfinished church, surrounded by the mesas of Ford's beloved Monument Valley, is often cited as the most perfect expression of western iconography.

Unlike the western, the classical gangster film is often a covert critique of American capitalism, which means that the classical phase already contains a strong critical element. The protagonists—usually played by small men—are likened to ruthless businessmen, their climb to power a sardonic parody of the Horatio Alger myth. The genre entered its classical phase during the early years of the sound film, at the height of the Depression, when *Little Caesar* (Mervyn Leroy, 1931), *The Public Enemy* (William Wellman, 1931), and *Scarface* (Howard Hawks, 1932) reflected the country's shaken confidence in authority and traditional social institutions. The consensus-building function of these films is grounded in a desire for social order, but the fragility of this consensus is apparent in the initial attractiveness of the gangster figure.

2-24. *Fargo* (U.S.A., 1996), with Frances McDormand, written and directed by Joel and Ethan Coen.

Fargo is a revisionist detective film loosely based on an actual police case. The protagonist is Marge Gunderson (McDormand), the very pregnant police chief of Brainerd, Minnesota. The movie is often funny, interspersed with unsettling scenes of brutality and gore. Though the chief finally solves the case, the film's "happy ending" is considerably undercut by its tone of sadness and pessimism concerning the human condition. *(Gramercy Pictures)*

During the revisionist or "critical" phase, the values of the classical genre are called into question or revised. These films still work broadly within the established framework of the genre but question the moral assumptions that had sustained it. Consensus is replaced by irony and uncertainty, community by individual differences. In Howard Hawks's *Red River* (1948), for example, John Wayne's status as an iconic hero is undermined when he plays a deeply divided man, embittered by the death of his fiançée in an Indian raid and driven to the verge of madness during a desperate cattle drive (see also **2-17**). Fred Zinnemann's *High Noon* (1952) used the genre to develop a parable about conformism in Cold War America in which the marshal of a small western town (Gary Cooper) tries to avoid violence in a showdown with a band of outlaws but is gradually abandoned by the citizens he is trying to protect **(6-10)**. Throughout the two decades that followed, most westerns remained in this skeptical mode, including such major works as Sam Peckinpah's *The Wild Bunch* (1969) and Robert Altman's *McCabe and Mrs. Miller* (1971) **(7-24)**.

The revisionist gangster film builds on the instability already apparent in the egocentric gangster figure. Gangsters of all periods tend to suffer from an inability to relate to women, but during the 1940s gangster films such as *White Heat* (Raoul Walsh, 1949) featured protagonists who were outright sexual neurotics. In the period after World War II, a period of anxiety in American society gave rise to the *film noir*, sometimes referred to as a genre but actually a particular tone, emphasizing deep shadows and unusual camera angles, that affected many genres (see **3-10**). Gangster movies were deeply influenced, and nowhere more so than in the corrupt underworlds depicted in the films of Samuel Fuller, notably *Pickup on South Street* (1952) and *Underworld USA* (1960).

The reflexive phase is often associated with genre parodies, but "reflexive" simply means that a film makes the audience aware of its own production conditions and conventions. What characterizes a reflexive genre film is a self-conscious awareness that it belongs to a specific genre. The title often gives the game away: *The Rocky*

2-25. *Pulp Fiction* (U.S.A., 1994), with John Travolta, written and directed by Quentin Tarantino.

Tarantino used to work as a clerk in a video store, and *Pulp Fiction* is a black comedy based on pulp magazines and old movies, not real life. In the first of the film's three stories—told out of chronological order—Travolta plays Vincent Vega, a junkie/hit man who has been asked to take his gangster boss's wife to dinner while the boss is out of town. Wary of her flaky, unpredictable behaviour, and fully conscious that a careless slip-up could cost him his life, the Travolta character "keeps his distance" from her—an aloofness that intrigues her. *(Miramax Films)*

2-26. *Last Night* (Canada, 1998), with Sandra Oh, directed by Don McKellar.

According to Rick Altman in *Film/Genre*, "today's genres have increasingly taken on what we might call a pseudo-memorial function. That is, they count on spectator memory to work their magic, but . . . they themselves implant in spectators the necessary memories, in the form of other genre films. . . . Genre film spectators have become the true twentieth-century cyborgs." McKellar's Canadian disaster film activates spectator memories of recent Hollywood blockbusters such as *Armageddon* (Michael Bay, 1998) and *Deep Impact* (Mimi Leder, 1998). The Canadian film distinguishes itself by resolutely avoiding all forms of spectacle and heroic action; it eschews special effects, offers no explanation for the imminent catastrophe, and nobody even suggests the possibility of averting it. Instead the characters wander the streets of Toronto caught between their old routines and the desire to experience something significant before the end. *(Rhombus Media)*

Horror Picture Show, *The Last Action Hero*, *Scary Movie*. In the case of the western, the reflexive phase includes parodies such as *Cat Ballou* (Elliot Silverstein, 1965) and Mel Brooks's *Blazing Saddles* (1973), as well as the "spaghetti" westerns of Sergio Leone and other Italian filmmakers. As Leone's fable-like title suggests, *Once Upon a Time in America* (1984) is a reflexive but also frankly mythic gangster film, treating the traditional rise-and-fall structure of the genre in an almost ritualistic manner. Tarantino's *Pulp Fiction* is a witty send-up of the genre, parodying many of its conventions, but also providing the graphic violence that contemporary audiences associate with the genre **(2-25)**. Such films reflect a culture in which even the fragile consensus that operated in the classical gangster film is a thing of the past (perhaps only of past genre films) and all that remains is the sense of style that has always been a major attraction of the gangster figure.

Whereas the classical paradigm assumed that showing is telling, reflexive effects constantly remind us that we are being told a story. Since all genre films are

2-27. *Ginger Snaps* (Canada, 2000), with Katharine Isabelle (left) and Emily Perkins, directed by John Fawcett.

Ginger (Isabelle) and her sister Brigitte (Perkins) live in a middle-class suburb and play gruesome "death" games to combat the boredom of their everyday lives. When Ginger begins to menstruate, she is suddenly attacked by a werewolf and begins to both turn into one herself and infect those around her. The sisters are plunged into a nightmare world that embodies their sexual fears but also their resentment of the roles that society expects them to play.
(Lions Gate/Courtesy of the Everett Collection and Canadian Press)

reflexive—after all, they depend on audience awareness of previous films in the genre—this phase perhaps is better seen as a product of the ways in which films are viewed by contemporary audiences. In today's media-saturated environment, spectators may have become so aware of the icons and conventions of genre films that even earlier films cannot be viewed other than reflexively.

Nowhere is this development more apparent than in the contemporary sub-genre of the teen comedy in which the characters define themselves through their knowledge of media culture (film, television, music) and which depends on a similar awareness on the part of the audience. The comic tone carries over into the teen horror film, which achieved enormous popularity with Wes Craven's *Scream* (1996) and its sequels. As in the equally popular television series *Buffy the Vampire Slayer* (1997–2003) and its spin-offs, the genre retains its traditional concern with anxieties about the body and sexuality, but the characters now know all the conventions of the genre in which they find themselves. The tension between this knowingness and the horror that nevertheless engulfs them heightens the dynamic that has always been central to the genre film in the pull between a known formula and the thrill of the cinematic spectacle.

A story can be many things. To a producer it is a **property** that has a box-office value. To a writer it is a screenplay. To a film star it is a vehicle. To a director it is an artistic medium. To a genre critic it is a classifiable narrative form. To a sociologist it is an index of public sentiment. To a psychologist it is an instinctive exploration of hidden fears or communal ideas. To a moviegoer it can be all these and more.

FURTHER READING

Altman, Rick, *Film/Genre* (London: British Film Institute, 1999). Thorough account of the industrial and critical uses of genre.

Bordwell, David, Janet Staiger, and Kristin Thompson, *The Classical Hollywood Cinema: Film Style and Mode of Production to 1960* (New York: Columbia University Press, 1985). The most thorough account of the classical style.

Fell, John L., *Film and the Narrative Tradition* (Berkeley: University of California Press, 1974). Historical influences on early film narrative, covering stage melodramas, comic strips, dime novels, and other forms of pop culture.

Grant, Barry Keith. *Film Genre: From Iconography to Ideology* (London: Wallflower Press, 2007). A concise introduction to genre theory and cririicism.

Grant, Barry Keith, ed., *Film Genre Reader III* (Austin: University of Texas Press, 2003). A collection of important critical discussions of genre.

Kitses, Jim. *Horizons West: The Western from John Ford to Clint Eastwood* (London: British Film Institute, 2004). Revised and updated edition.

Kozloff, Sarah. *Invisible Storytellers* (Berkeley: University of California Press, 1988). Voice-over narration in American fiction films.

Neupert, Richard, *The End: Narration and Closure in the Cinema* (Detroit: Wayne State University Press, 1995). The importance of endings in interpreting narrative structures.

Thompson, Kristin, *Storytelling in the New Hollywood: Understanding Classical Narrative Technique* (Cambridge, Mass.: Harvard University Press, 1999). Close reading of films from the 1980s and 1990s.

Turim, Maureen, *Flashbacks in Film: Memory and History* (New York: Routledge, 1989). The history of the flashback and its narrative functions.

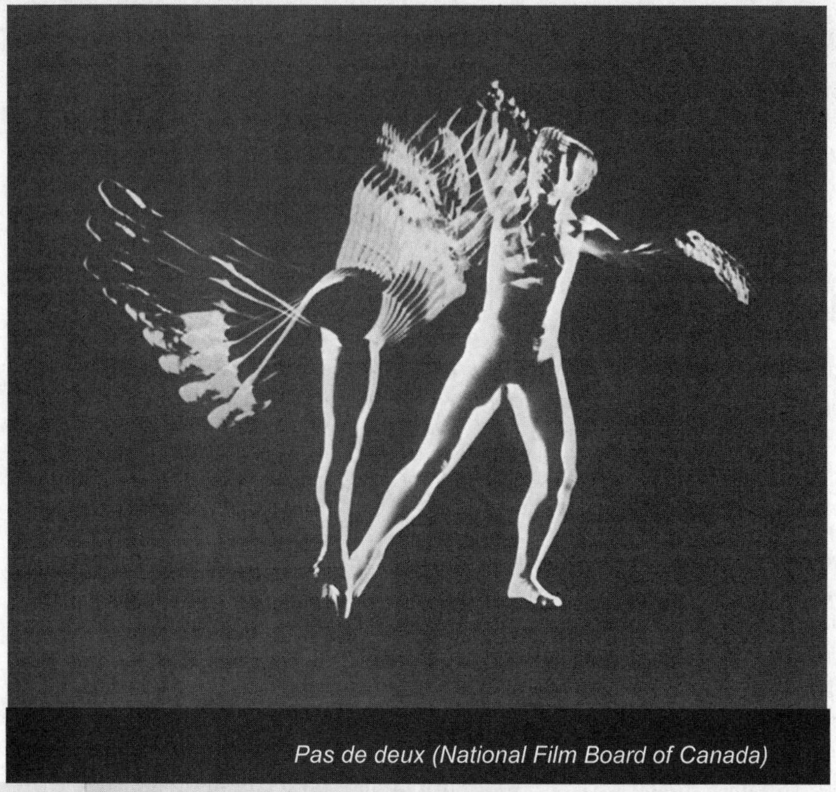

Pas de deux (National Film Board of Canada)

PHOTOGRAPHY

3

A photograph is by no means a complete and whole reflection of reality: The photographic picture represents only one or another selection from the sum of physical attributes of the object photographed.

—VLADIMIR NILSEN

OVERVIEW

The cinematographer: the film director's main visual collaborator. The shots: apparent distance of the camera from the subject. The angles: looking up, down, or at eye level. Lighting styles: high key, low key, high contrast. The symbolism of light and darkness. Colour symbolism. How lenses distort the subject matter: telephoto, wide-angle, and standard lenses. Filtered reality: more distortions. Special effects and digital imaging.

THE CINEMATOGRAPHER

The rich and compelling stories that movies tell are a major source of their fascination, but film is a visual medium that not only tells stories but also shows them happening. Their appeal also comes from the vivid images that convey the story to us and sometimes become even more important to the final effect. The look of a film, and its relation to the story, depend on the collaboration between the director and the **cinematographer**.

It is impossible to make generalizations about the role of the cinematographer, for it varies widely from film to film and from director to director. In actual practice, virtually all cinematographers agree that the style of the photography should be geared to the story, theme, and mood of the film. William Daniels had a prestigious reputation as a glamour photographer at MGM and for many years was known as "Greta Garbo's cameraman." Yet Daniels also shot Erich von Stroheim's harshly realistic *Greed* **(4-15)**, and the cinematographer won an Academy Award for his work in Jules Dassin's *Naked City* (1948), a thriller shot on location on the streets of New York in the style of a **documentary**.

During the big-studio era, most cinematographers believed that the aesthetic elements of a film should be maximized—making beautiful pictures with beautiful people was the goal. After World War II, the Italian neorealist filmmakers—Luchino Visconti, Roberto Rossellini, Vittorio de Sica—challenged this attitude with their location shooting amid the ruins and rubble of war-torn cities. Their raw depiction of suffering and poverty moved audiences around the world, but some Italian politicians castigated them for making the country look ugly **(1-18, 8-26, 11-1)**. Today, images are often coarsened if such a technique is considered appropriate to the dramatic materials. In *21 Grams* (2003), for example, Mexican director Alejandro Gonzalez Inarritu and his cinematographer, Rodrigo Prieto, used grainy, murky, high contrast images, further degraded during the development of the negative. As in the case of the **neorealist** films, the visual style enhances the **realist** effect, but, coupled with the fragmented narrative structure, it also expresses the nightmare logic of the traumatic events that entangle the lives of three strangers.

"You don't make beautiful compositions just for the sake of making compositions," insists Hungarian-born cinematographer Laszlo Kovacs, whose credits range from *Easy Rider* (Dennis Hopper, 1969) to *Miss Congeniality* (Donald Petrie, 2000). Some critics complained that Walter Lassally did just this in his cinematography for Tony Richardson's *A Taste of Honey* (1961) and *The Loneliness of the Long Distance Runner* (1962). These films were part of the British New Wave that depicted working-class life in northern industrial cities, but the critics objected that their realism was compromised by images that made the slums look beautiful.

3-1. ***Twentieth Century Fox* publicity photo of Marilyn Monroe (1953).**

Cinematographers often comment that the camera "likes" certain individuals and "doesn't like" others, even though these others might be good-looking people in real life. Highly photogenic performers like Marilyn Monroe are rarely uncomfortable in front of the camera. Indeed, they often play to it, ensnaring our attention. Photographer Richard Avedon said of Marilyn, "She understood photography, and she also understood what makes a great photograph—not the technique, but the content. She was more comfortable in front of the camera than away from it." *(Twentieth Century Fox)*

Yet, a visual style that counterpoints the meaning of the narrative can have ironic or disturbing effects, and critics proved much more accepting of Michelangelo Antonioni's *Red Desert* (1964). In this film, Carlo di Palma's camera draws attention to the formal beauty of colours and shapes in the industrial environment that oppresses the film's heroine **(4-28)**.

"Many times, what you don't see is much more effective than what you do see," Gordon Willis once noted. Willis was a specialist in **low-key** lighting styles (see **4-1**). He photographed all three of Francis Ford Coppola's *Godfather* films—which many traditionalists considered too dark. But Willis was aiming for poetry, not realism. Most of the interior scenes were very dark, to suggest an atmosphere of evil and secrecy. Darkness was also used to suggest entrapment and claustrophobia in Claude Jutra's *Kamouraska* **(6-13)**, in which Canadian cinematographer Michel Brault, who had established an international reputation as a pioneer in the use of the handheld camera in documentary, explored the possibilities of using **available light** to re-create the visual impression of domestic life before the advent of electricity.

Some great movies are photographed competently but without distinction. Realist directors are especially likely to prefer an unobtrusive style, and many of the works of surrealist filmmaker Luis Buñuel can only be described as "professional" in their cinematography. Buñuel was rarely interested in formal beauty—except occasionally to mock it. Rollie Totheroh, who photographed most of Charlie Chaplin's films, merely set up his camera and let Chaplin the actor take over. Photographically speaking, his films have few memorable shots. What makes the images compelling is

3-2. ***The Emigrants*** **(Sweden, 1972), with Liv Ullmann and Max von Sydow, photographed and directed by Jan Troell.**

If we were to view a scene similar to this in real life, we would probably concentrate most of our attention on the people in the wagon. But there are considerable differences between reality and cinematic realism. In selecting materials from the chaotic sprawl of reality, the realist filmmaker necessarily eliminates some details and emphasizes others into a structured hierarchy of visual significance. For example, the stone wall in the foreground of this **shot** occupies more space than the humans. Visually, this dominance suggests that the rocks are more important than the people. The unyielding stone wall symbolizes divisiveness and exclusion—ideas that are appropriate to the dramatic context. If the wall were irrelevant to the theme, Troell would have eliminated it and selected other details from the copiousness of reality—details that would be more pertinent to the dramatic context. *(Warner Bros.)*

the genius of Chaplin's acting. This photographic austerity—some would consider it poverty—is especially apparent in those rare scenes when Chaplin is off-screen.

THE SHOTS

The different cinematic shots are defined by the amount of subject matter included within the frame of the screen. In actual practice, however, shot designations vary considerably. A medium shot for one director might be considered a close-up by another. Furthermore, the longer the shot, the less precise are the designations. In general, shots are determined on the basis of how much of the human figure is in view. The shot is not necessarily defined by the distance between the camera and the object photographed, since certain lenses distort distances. For example, a **telephoto lens** can produce a close-up on the screen, yet the camera in such shots is generally quite distant from the subject matter.

Although many different kinds of shots are used in the cinema, most of them are subsumed under the six basic categories: (1) the extreme long shot, (2) the long shot, (3) the full shot, (4) the medium shot, (5) the close-up, and (6) the extreme close-up.

The **extreme long shot** is taken from a great distance, sometimes almost half a kilometre away. It is usually an exterior shot and shows much of the locale. Extreme long shots also serve as spatial frames of reference for the closer shots and for this reason are often placed at the beginning of sequences; they are then called **establishing shots**. If people are included in extreme long shots, they usually appear as mere specks on the screen **(3-3)**. These shots are often found in epic films, where locale plays an important role: westerns, war films, samurai films, and historical movies. Not surprisingly, the greatest masters of the extreme long shot are those directors associated with epic genres: D.W. Griffith, Sergei Eisenstein, John Ford, Akira Kurosawa, and Steven Spielberg.

The **long shot** is perhaps the most complex in cinema, and the term itself one of the most imprecise **(3-4)**. The closest range within this category is the **full shot**, which just barely includes the human body in full, with the head near the top of the frame and the feet near the bottom. Chaplin and other slapstick comedians favoured the full shot because it was best suited to the art of pantomime yet was close enough to capture at least gross facial expressions.

3-3. *Days of Heaven* (U.S.A., 1978), written and directed by Terrence Malick.

The setting dominates most extreme long shots. Humans are dwarfed into visual insignificance, making them appear unimportant and vulnerable. Malick's film is set in the early twentieth century in a lonely wheat-growing region of Texas. The extreme long shot of the wheat fields at dusk brings out the idyllic beauty of the setting but also the vulnerability of the people who will soon be evicted from it. *(Paramount Pictures)*

3-4. ***Mary Shelley's Frankenstein*** **(U.S.A., 1994), with Robert De Niro (under wraps) and Kenneth Branagh, directed by Branagh.**

At its most distant range, the long shot encompasses roughly the same amount of space as the staging area of a large theatre. Setting can dominate characters unless they are located near the foreground. Lighting a long shot is usually costly, time-consuming, and labour-intensive. The laboratory in this movie had to be moody and scary, yet still sufficiently clear to enable us to see back into the "depth" of the set. Note how the lighting in this shot is layered, punctuated with patches of gloom and accusatory shafts of light from above. *(TriStar Pictures)*

The **medium shot** contains a figure from the knees or waist up. A functional shot, it is useful for shooting exposition scenes, for carrying movement, and for dialogue. For this reason, the medium shot suits the needs of classical cinema, and it was so dominant during the studio era in Hollywood that French writers call it "*le plan Américain*" (the American shot). The medium shot has several variations. The two shot contains two figures from the waist up **(3-5)**. The **three shot** contains three figures; beyond three, the shot tends to become a full shot, unless the other figures are in the background. The over-the-shoulder shot usually contains two figures, one with part of his or her back to the camera, the other facing the camera.

The **close-up** shows very little if any locale and concentrates on a relatively small object—the human face, for example. Because the close-up magnifies the size of an object, it tends to elevate the importance of things, often suggesting a symbolic significance. The **extreme close-up** is a variation of this shot. Instead of a face, the extreme close-up might show only a person's eyes or mouth.

The **deep-focus** shot is usually a long shot, consisting of several focal distances and photographed in depth **(12-14)**. Sometimes called a wide-angle shot because it requires a **wide-angle lens** to photograph, this type of shot captures objects at close,

3-5. *Almost Famous* (U.S.A., 2000), with Patrick Fugit and Kate Hudson, directed by Cameron Crowe.

Above all, the medium shot is the shot of the couple, romantic or otherwise. Generally, two shots have a split focus rather than a single dominant: The bifurcated composition usually emphasizes equality, two people sharing the same intimate space. The medium two shot reigns supreme in such genres as romantic comedies, love stories, and buddy films. *(DreamWorks Pictures)*

medium, and long ranges simultaneously, all in sharp focus. The objects in a deep-focus shot are carefully arranged in a succession of planes. By using this layering technique, the director can guide the viewer's eye from one distance to another. Generally, the eye travels from a close range to a medium to a long.

THE ANGLES

The **angle** from which an object is photographed can often serve as an expressive commentary on the subject matter. If the angle is slight, it can serve as a subtle form of emotional colouration. If the angle is extreme, it can represent the major meaning of an image. The angle is determined by where the camera is placed, not what subject is photographed. A picture of a person photographed from a high angle suggests an opposite interpretation from an image of the same person photographed from a low angle. The subject matter can be identical in the two images, yet the information we derive from both clearly shows that the form is the content, the content the form.

Filmmakers in the realistic tradition tend to avoid extreme angles. Most of their shots are photographed from eye level, roughly one and a half metres to two metres off the ground—the way an actual observer might view a scene. Usually, these directors attempt to capture the clearest view of an object. Eye-level shots are seldom intrinsically dramatic because they tend to be the norm. Virtually all directors use some eye-level shots, particularly in routine expository scenes.

Formalist directors are not always concerned with the clearest image of an object, but with the image that best conveys the emotional or symbolic qualities associated with an object. Extreme angles involve distortions. Yet many filmmakers feel that by distorting the appearance of an object, a greater truth is achieved—a symbolic truth. Both realist and formalist directors know that the viewer tends to identify with the camera. The realist wants to make the audience forget that there is a camera at all. The formalist is constantly calling attention to it.

There are five basic angles in cinema: (1) the bird's-eye view, (2) the high angle, (3) the eye-level shot, (4) the low angle, and (5) the oblique angle. As in the case of shot designations, there are many intermediate kinds of angles. For example, there can be a considerable difference between a low and extreme-low angle—although usually, of course, such differences tend to be matters of degree. Generally, the more extreme the angle, the more conspicuous it is in terms of the subject matter being photographed.

3-6. *Bonnie and Clyde* (U.S.A., 1967), with Faye Dunaway and Warren Beatty, directed by Arthur Penn.
High angles tend to suggest entrapment, powerlessness, or vulnerability. The higher the angle, the more it tends to imply fatality. The camera's angle can be inferred from the background of a shot: High angles usually show the ground or floor; low angles the sky or ceiling. Because we tend to associate light with safety, high-key lighting is generally nonthreatening and reassuring, but not always. We have been socially conditioned to believe that danger lurks in darkness, so when a traumatic assault takes place in broad daylight, as in this scene, the effect is doubly scary because it is so unexpected. *(Warner Bros.)*

The **bird's-eye view** is perhaps the most disorienting angle of all, for it involves photographing a scene from directly overhead. Because we seldom view events from this perspective, the subject matter of such shots might initially seem unrecognizable and abstract, like the kaleidoscopic arrangements of choreographer Busby Berkeley **(1-1b)**. In effect, bird's-eye shots permit us to hover above a scene like all-powerful gods. The people photographed seem ant-like and insignificant. In Alfred Hitchcock's *The Birds* (1963), for example, the director includes a literal bird's-eye view, looking down on the California town devastated by the unexplained bird attacks.

Ordinary **high-angle shots** are not as extreme and are therefore not as disorienting. The camera is placed on a **crane**, or some natural high promontory, but the sense of audience omnipotence is not overwhelming. High angles reduce the height of the objects photographed and usually include the ground or floor as background. Movement is slowed down: This angle tends to be ineffective for conveying a sense of speed, but it is useful for suggesting tediousness. The importance of the setting or environment is increased: The locale often seems to swallow people. High angles reduce the importance of a subject. A person seems harmless and insignificant when photographed from above **(3-6)**. This angle can also be used to convey a character's self-contempt.

Some filmmakers avoid angles because they are too manipulative and judgmental. Instead, they use **eye-level shots**. In the movies of the Japanese director Yasujiro Ozu, the camera is usually placed about a metre from the floor—as if an observer were viewing the events while seated Japanese style **(11-11)**. Ozu treated his characters as equals; his approach discourages us from viewing them either condescendingly or sentimentally. For the most part, they are ordinary people, decent and conscientious. But Ozu lets them reveal themselves. He believed that value judgments are implied through the use of angles, and he kept his camera neutral and dispassionate. Eye-level shots permit us to make up our own minds about what kinds of people are being presented.

Low-angle shots have the opposite effect of high-angle shots. They increase height and thus are useful for suggesting verticality. More practically, they increase a short actor's height. Motion is speeded up, and in scenes of violence especially, low angles capture a sense of confusion. The environment is usually minimized in low angles, and often the sky or a ceiling is the only background. Psychologically, low angles heighten the importance of a subject. The figure looms threateningly over the spectator, who is made to feel insecure and dominated **(3-7)**. A person photographed from below inspires fear, awe, and respect. For this reason, low angles are often used in propaganda films or in scenes depicting heroism.

An **oblique angle** or **canted shot** involves tipping the camera to one side. When the image is projected, the horizon is skewed. A man photographed at an oblique angle will look as though he is about to fall to one side. This angle is sometimes used for point-of-view shots (or **pov shots**)—to suggest the imbalance of a drunk, for example. Psychologically, oblique angles suggest tension, transition, and impending movement. The natural horizontal and vertical lines of a scene are converted into unstable diagonals. Oblique angles are not used often, for they can disorient a viewer. In scenes depicting violence, however, they can be effective in capturing precisely this sense of visual anxiety.

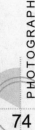

3-7. *Halloween: The Curse of Michael Myers* (U.S.A., 1995), with George Wilbur, directed by Joe Chappelle.

Extreme low angles can make characters seem threatening and powerful, for they loom above the camera—and us—like towering giants. We are collapsed in a position of maximum vulnerability—pinned to the ground, dominated. *(Dimension Films)*

LIGHT AND DARK

Generally, the cinematographer is responsible for arranging and controlling the lighting of a film and the quality of the photography. Usually the cinematographer executes the specific or general instructions of the director. The illumination of most movies is seldom a casual matter, for lights can be used with pinpoint accuracy. By using spotlights, which are highly selective in their **focus** and intensity, a director can guide the viewer's eyes to any area of the photographed image. Motion-picture lighting is seldom static, since even the slightest movement of the camera or the subject can cause the lighting to shift. Movies take so long to complete, in part, because of the enormous complexities involved in lighting each new shot. The cinematographer must make allowances for every movement within a continuous take. Each different colour, shape, and texture reflects or absorbs differing amounts of light. If an image is photographed in depth, an even greater complication is involved, for the lighting must also be in depth. In a colour film, the subtle effects of lights and darks are often obscured, since colour tends to obliterate shadings and flatten images: Depth is negated.

3-8. *Trois couleurs: rouge* [*Three Colours: Red*] (France/Poland/Switzerland, 1994), with Irene Jacob and Jean-Louis Trintignant, cinematography by Piotr Sobocinski, directed by Krzysztof Kieslowski.

During the Hollywood big studio era, cinematographers developed the technique of three-point lighting, which is still widely practised throughout the world. With three-point lighting, the **key light** is the primary source of illumination. This light creates the **dominant** of an image—that area that first attracts our eye because it contains the most compelling contrast, usually of light and shadow. Generally, the dominant is also the area of greatest dramatic interest, the shot's focal point of action, either physical or psychological. Fill lights, which are less intense than the key, soften the harshness of the main light source, revealing subsidiary details that would otherwise be hidden by shadow. The backlights separate the foreground figures from their setting, heightening the illusion of three-dimensional depth in the image. Three-point methods tend to be most expressive with low-key lighting such as this. On the other hand, when a shot is bathed with high-key illumination, the three sources of light are more equally distributed over the surface of the image, and hence are more bland photographically. *(Miramax Films)*

There are several different styles of lighting. Usually designated as a lighting key, the style is geared to the theme and mood of a film, as well as its genre. Comedies and musicals, for example, tend to be lit in **high key**, with bright, even illumination and few conspicuous shadows. Tragedies and melodramas are usually lit in **high contrast**, with harsh shafts of lights and dramatic streaks of blackness **(3-9)**. Mysteries and thrillers are generally in low key, with diffused shadows and atmospheric pools of light **(3-10)**. Each lighting key is only an approximation, and some images consist of a combination of lighting styles—a low-key background with a few high-contrast elements in the foreground, for example. Movies shot in studios are generally more stylized and theatrical, whereas location photography tends to use available illumination, with a more natural style of lighting.

Lights and darks have had symbolic connotations since the dawn of humanity. The Bible is filled with light and dark symbolism. Painters like Rembrandt and Caravaggio used light and dark contrasts for psychological purposes as well. In general, artists have used darkness to suggest fear, evil, the unknown. Light usually suggests security, virtue, truth, joy. Because of these conventional symbolic associations, some filmmakers deliberately reverse light-dark expectations **(3-6)**. Hitchcock's movies attempt to jolt the viewers by exposing their shallow sense of security. He staged many of his most violent scenes in the glaring light.

3-9. *The Return of the Jedi Special Edition* (U.S.A., 1997), directed by Richard Marquand.

High-contrast lighting is aggressively theatrical, infusing the photographed materials with a sense of tension and visual anguish. This dueling sequence is rendered more dynamic by the jagged knife blades of light that pierce the pervasive darkness. In the background, a desperate cosmic search is tearing up the sky. High-contrast lighting is typical of such genres as crime films, melodramas, thrillers, and mysteries. The lack of light in such movies symbolizes the unknown, deceptive surfaces, evil itself. *(LucasFilm, Ltd.)*

➤ **Colour Plate 1. *The Age of Innocence* (U.S.A., 1993), with Michelle Pfeiffer and Daniel Day-Lewis, directed by Martin Scorsese.**

Based on the great American novel by Edith Wharton, this movie explores a forbidden love among New York's upper crust in the 1870s. The film's colours—reflecting the conservative values of the society itself—are tastefully subdued, correct, almost repressed. *(Columbia Pictures)*

➤ **Colour Plate 2. *When Night is Falling* (Canada, 1994), with Rachael Crawford (left) and Pascale Bussières, directed by Patricia Rozema.**

The life of a professor of mythology at a theological college is turned upside down when she becomes attracted to a performer in a fantastic circus, where myths come to life. The warm colours of this close-up emphasize the moment that she realizes her true feelings. *(Patricia Rozema/Caroline Benjo)*

➤ Colour Plate 3. ***The Royal Tenenbaums*** **(U.S.A., 2001), with Luke Wilson, Gwyneth Paltrow, Ben Stiller, and Gene Hackman, directed by Wes Anderson.**

The tensions in the dysfunctional Tenenbaum family contrast with the controlled environment that the parents have created. Here, the unexpected return of the prodigal father (Hackman) stuns his children, who seem to blend in with the reds, pinks, and browns of the well-lit room. *(Touchstone Pictures)*

➤ Colour Plate 4. ***Aliens*** **(U.S.A., 1986), with Sigourney Weaver and Carrie Henn, directed by James Cameron.**

The futuristic setting in this science-fiction film uses colour in a rigorously realistic manner. *Aliens* takes place in a world of cold, hard surfaces, heavy-metal technology, and blue-gray fluorescence. The colours are radically muted, mostly military tans and drab earth colours. Only the red filter adds a note of alarm and urgency. *(Twentieth Century Fox)*

➤ Colour Plate 5. ***Lulu*** **(Canada, 1996), with Kim Lieu and Michael Rhoades, directed by Srinivas Krishna.**

The lack of light and the dominant browns of the apartment, in which Steven/Lucky (Rhoades) and Khuyen/Lulu (Lieu) live, emphasize their feelings of entrapment despite their need for a refuge from the threatening reality of the world outside. *(Alliance Communications)*

➤ Colour Plate 6. ***Black Hawk Down*** **(U.S.A., 2001), directed by Ridley Scott.**

The extreme contrast between the blue night sky outside, punctuated with flashes of light, and the yellow walls inside captures the fear of the isolated U.S. soldier under attack in Somalia. *(Revolution Studios)*

➤ Colour Plate 7. ***American Beauty* (U.S.A., 1999), with Kevin Spacey and Mena Suvari, directed by Sam Mendes.**

Red is a colour that is often linked with sex, but the dramatic context determines whether the red (and the sex) is seductive or repellent. In this film, the unhappily married protagonist (Spacey) escapes the banality of his suburban hell by fantasizing about a flirtatious teenager (Suvari), a friend of his daughter. He often imagines her nude, covered with red rose petals—a symbol of his fiercely aroused sexuality, his reawakening manhood. *(DreamWorks Pictures)*

➤ Colour Plate 8. ***Les Nuits fauves* [*Savage Nights*] (France, 1993), with Cyril Collard and Romane Bohringer, directed by Collard.**

Red is also the colour of danger, violence, and blood. This movie explores the sado-masochistic behaviour of an HIV-positive bisexual (Collard) who has unprotected sex with two lovers, including Bohringer. The intense colours evoke those of the Fauvist painters of the early twentieth century, so named because they reminded critics of "wild beasts," and the film's French title is a homage to these artists. *(Gramercy Pictures)*

➤ **Colour Plate 9. *Eternal Sunshine of the Spotless Mind* (U.S.A., 2004), with Kate Winslet and Jim Carrey, directed by Michel Gondry.**

The fantastic world of this film is expressed through its non-linear narrative structure, but also through its use of colour. Joel (Carrey) submits to a new procedure to erase his memories of Clementine (Winslet). When he meets her, apparently for the first time, at the beginning of the film, she has dyed her hair blue; when he remembers their real first meeting, her hair is green. As he regresses into his past, her hair becomes a brilliant red, contrasting with the colour of the beach that figures prominently in their relationship and whose sand is indistinguishable from the snow that often covers it. *(Focus Features)*

➤ **Colour Plate 10. *Le Vent du Wyoming* [*A Wind from Wyoming*] (Canada, 1994), with Sarah-Jeanne Salvy (left), Léo Munger (centre), and France Castel, directed by André Forcier.**

Forcier uses filters and colour to give each location in this "magic realist" film a specific symbolic atmosphere. In the womb-like motel bar, a woman confronts her mother, surrounded by customers, some of whom are wax dummies. *(TRANSFILM/EGM Productions/Eiffel Productions)*

➤ Colour Plate 11. ***Edward Scissorhands* (U.S.A., 1990), with Johnny Depp, directed by Tim Burton.**

Burton is one of the foremost expressionists of contemporary cinema, a conjuror of magical worlds of colour and light, and myth and imagination. His worlds are created in the sealed-off confines of the studio, far removed from the contaminations of prosaic reality. *(Twentieth Century Fox)*

➤ Colour Plate 12. ***Crash* (Canada, 1996), with James Spader and Deborah Unger, directed by David Cronenberg.**

Much of Cronenberg's bizarre fable was shot on location in Toronto. The colour scheme is dominated by the contrast between flesh and the glossy surface of metal and plastic, with the natural world relegated to the strips of grass beside urban highways. *(Alliance Communications)*

➤ Colour Plate 13. ***Shrek*** **(U.S.A., 2001), special effects by Pacific Data Images, directed by Andrew Adamson and Vicky Jenson.**

Animated films have always been able to create imaginative fantasy worlds, but computer animation can enhance the realism of these worlds. Shrek is a rather appealing ogre who sets out to rescue a princess, with the help of his donkey sidekick. The settings are created digitally with vivid attention to detail, while the ogre himself is almost human, except for being yellow—and the ears. *(DreamWorks Pictures)*

➤ Colour Plate 14. ***Fido*** **(Canada, 2006), with K'Sun Ray (foreground), Dylan Baker and Carrie-Anne Moss (father and mother) and Billy Connolly (Fido the zombie), directed by Andrew Currie.**

Set apparently in the future, this film depicts suburban life much like that in 1950s melodramas (and TV sitcoms), except that the families that live there keep zombies as pets. As in the films of Douglas Sirk (see Chapter 7), the vivid colours accentuate the cosy complacency of the neighbourhood but also create an ironic contrast with the creatures from another genre (who are in fact more human than most of the living characters). *(Lion's Gate/The Kobal Collection)*

➤ Colour Plate 15. ***The Lord of the Rings: The Fellowship of the Ring* (New Zealand / U.S.A., 2001), with Ian McKellen and Elijah Wood, directed by Peter Jackson.**

The light on the faces of the characters, surrounded by a mysterious darkness, emphasizes the humanity of the other-worldly creatures at the centre of this epic adaptation of Tolkein's fantastic story. Gandalf (McKellen) is a wizard and Frodo (Wood) a hobbit on a dangerous quest, and this is a contemplative moment amid spectacular adventures that stretch the resources of digital special effects. *(New Line Home Entertainment)*

➤ Colour Plate 16. ***The Sweet Hereafter* (Canada, 1997), with Sarah Polley and Tom McCamus, directed by Atom Egoyan.**

The colourful but deserted fairground behind the couple gives this early moment in the film a sense of carefree normality that will soon be shattered not only by the bus accident, but by the gradual revelation that this is an incestuous relationship. *(Ego Film Arts/Johnnie Eisen)*

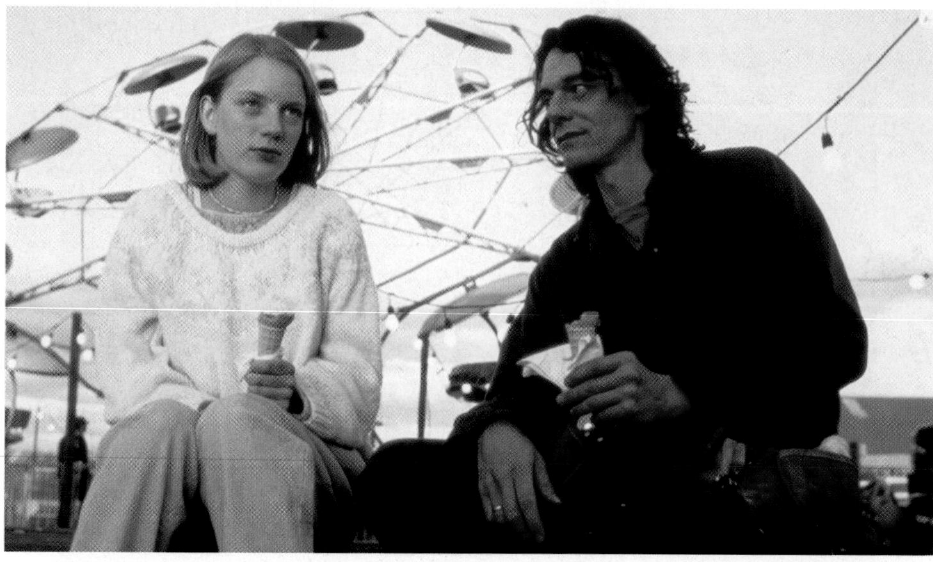

Lighting can be used realistically or expressionistically. The realist tends to favour **available light**, at least in exterior scenes. Even out of doors, however, most filmmakers use some lamps and reflectors, either to augment the natural light or, on bright days, to soften the harsh contrasts produced by the sun. With the aid of special **lenses** and more light-sensitive film stocks, some directors have managed to dispense with artificial lighting completely. Available light tends to produce a documentary look in the film image, a hard-edged quality and an absence of smooth modelling. For interior shots, realists tend to prefer images with an obvious light source—a window or a lamp. Or they often use a diffused kind of lighting with no artificial, strong contrasts. In short, the realist avoids conspicuous lighting unless its source is dictated by the context.

Formalists use light less literally. They are guided by its symbolic implications and will often stress these qualities by deliberately distorting natural light patterns. A face lighted from below almost always appears sinister, even if the actor assumes a totally neutral expression. Similarly, an obstruction placed in front of a light source can assume frightening implications, for it tends to threaten our sense of safety. Conversely, in some contexts, especially in exterior shots, a silhouette effect can be soft and romantic.

3-10. *Double Indemnity* (U.S.A., 1944), with Barbara Stanwyck and Fred MacMurray, directed by Billy Wilder.

Film noir (literally, black cinema) is a style defined primarily in terms of light—or the lack of it. This style typified a variety of American genres in the 1940s and early 1950s. *Noir* is a world of night and shadows. Its milieu is almost exclusively urban. The style is profuse in images of dark streets, cigarette smoke swirling in dimly lit cocktail lounges, and symbols of fragility, such as windowpanes, sheer clothing, glasses, and mirrors. Motifs of entrapment abound: alleys, tunnels, subways, elevators, and train cars. Often the settings are locations of transience, like cheap rented rooms, piers, bus terminals, and railroad yards. The images are rich in sensuous textures, like neon-lit streets, windshields streaked with mud, and shafts of light streaming through windows of lonely rooms. Characters are imprisoned behind ornate lattices, grillwork, drifting fog, and smoke. Visual designs emphasize harsh lighting contrasts, jagged shapes, and violated surfaces. The tone of *film noir* is fatalistic and paranoid. It is suffused with pessimism, emphasizing the darker aspects of the human condition. Its themes characteristically revolve around violence, lust, greed, betrayal, and depravity. *(Paramount Pictures)*

3-11. *The Man Who Wasn't There* (U.S.A., 2001), with James Gandolfini, directed by Joel and Ethan Coen.

Set in 1949, this movie is in black and white rather than colour, a tribute to the post–World War II style of *film noir*. As the Coen brothers pointed out, the setting and story are indebted to the world of James M. Cain, the author of the novel *Double Indemnity*. Cinematographer Roger Deakins said: "I love black and white—it can be very expressive. Colour can sometimes make things too pretty." Usually Deakins used only a few large light sources, sometimes from unusual positions, to heighten the sleazy milieu of crime, sexual infidelity, and mendacity. Note how the lighting from below in this shot produces a creepy effect: This is not a man you would want to do business with. *(USA Films)*

Lighting a face from above produces a certain angelic quality, known as the halo effect. "Spiritual" lighting of this type tends to border on the cliché, however. **Backlighting**, which is a kind of semi-silhouetting, is soft and ethereal. Love scenes are often photographed with a halo effect around the heads of the lovers to give them a romantic aura. Backlighting is especially evocative when used to highlight blonde hair **(3-15)**.

The use of spotlights makes it possible to compose images with violent contrasts of lights and darks. The surface of such images seems disfigured, torn up. The formalist director uses such severe contrasts for psychological and thematic purposes.

By deliberately permitting too much light to enter the aperture of the camera, a filmmaker can overexpose an image—producing a blanching flood of light over the entire surface of the picture. **Overexposure** has been most effectively used in nightmare and fantasy sequences. Sometimes this technique can suggest a kind of horrible glaring publicity, a sense of emotional exaggeration.

COLOUR

Colour in film did not become commercially widespread until the 1940s. There were many experiments in colour before this period, however. Some of Georges Méliès's movies, for example, were painted by hand in assembly-line fashion, with each painter responsible for colouring a minute area of the filmstrip. The original version of D.W. Griffith's *The Birth of a Nation* (1915) was printed on various tinted stocks to suggest different moods: The burning of Atlanta was tinted red, the night scenes blue, the exterior love scenes pale yellow. Many silent filmmakers used this tinting technique to suggest different moods.

Sophisticated film colour was developed in the 1930s, but for many years, a major problem was its tendency to prettify everything. If colour enhanced a sense of beauty—in a musical or a historical extravaganza—the effects were often appropriate. Thus, the best feature films of the early years of colour were usually those with artificial or exotic settings. Realistic dramas were thought to be unsuitable vehicles for colour. The earliest colour processes tended also to emphasize garishness, and often special consultants had to be called in to harmonize the colour schemes of costumes, makeup, and décor.

Furthermore, each colour process tended to specialize in a certain base hue—usually red, blue, or yellow—whereas other colours of the spectrum were somewhat distorted. It was well into the 1950s before these problems were resolved. Compared with the subtle colour perceptions of the human eye, however, and despite the apparent precision of most present-day colour processing, cinematic colour is still a relatively crude approximation.

The most famous colour films tend to be **expressionistic**. Antonioni's attitude is typical: "It is necessary to intervene in a colour film, to take away the usual reality and replace it with the reality of the moment." In *Red Desert*, Antonioni spray-painted natural locales to emphasize internal, psychological states **(4-28)**. Industrial wastes, river pollution, marshes, and large stretches of terrain were painted grey. Whenever red appears in the movie, it suggests sexual passion. Yet the red—like the loveless sexuality—is an ineffective coverup of the pervasive grey.

Colour tends to be a subconscious element in film. It is strongly emotional in its appeal, expressive and atmospheric rather than conspicuous or intellectual. Psychologists have discovered that most people actively attempt to interpret the lines of a composition, but they tend to accept colour passively, permitting it to suggest moods rather than objects. However, there are many ways in which film-makers can encourage a more active response. In the opening sequence of Jim Jarmusch's *Broken Flowers* (2005), for example, a pink envelope stands out in shots of letters moving through the postal system. When it is delivered to an aging womanizer (Bill Murray), he finds that it contains an anonymous letter informing him that he has a child about whom he knows nothing. He does not know which of the many women from his past has sent the letter, and, when he sets out to visit them one by one, his friend urges him to look for pink objects that may give him a clue. Of course, we cannot avoid noticing pink associated with each of the women he visits, and the film ends without revealing the secret, suggesting that the quest was less to solve the mystery than to confront him (and us) with some insights into his relationships with these idiosyncratic women.

3-12a. *Braveheart* (U.S.A., 1995), with Sophie Marceau and Mel Gibson, directed by Gibson.

Art historians often distinguish between a "painterly" and a "linear" style, a distinction that is also useful in the photographic arts. A painterly style is soft-edged, sensuous, and romantic, best typified by the Impressionist landscapes of Claude Monet and the voluptuous figure paintings of Pierre Auguste Renoir. Line is de-emphasized: Colours and textures shimmer in a hazily defined, radiantly illuminated environment. On the other hand, a linear style emphasizes drawing, sharply defined edges, and the supremacy of line over colour and texture.

Movies can also be photographed in a painterly or linear style, depending on the lighting, the lenses, and filters. The shot from *Braveheart* might almost have been painted by Renoir. Cinematographer John Toll used soft focus lenses and warm "natural" back-lighting (creating a halo effect around the characters' heads) to produce an intensely romantic lyricism. *The Best Years of Our Lives* was photographed by Gregg Toland. In contrast to the flamboyant use of deep-focus and camera angles in Toland's work with Orson Welles on *Citizen Kane*, five years earlier, the style in this film is austere, deglamourized. It was a style suited to the theme of service men struggling to adjust to civilian life after World War II. The postwar era was a period of disillusionment, sober re-evaluations, and very few sentimental illusions. The high-key cinematography is polished, to be sure, but it is also simple, matter-of-fact, the invisible servant of a serious subject matter. *(Paramount Pictures)*

3-12b. *The Best Years of Our Lives* (U.S.A., 1946), with Harold Russell, Teresa Wright, Dana Andrews, Myrna Loy, Hoagy Carmichael (standing), and Fredric March, directed by William Wyler. *(RKO)*

Since earliest times, visual artists have used colour for symbolic purposes. Colour symbolism is probably culturally acquired, though its implications are surprisingly similar in otherwise differing societies. In general, cool colours (blue, green, violet) tend to suggest tranquility, aloofness, and serenity. Cool colours also have a tendency to recede in an image. Warm colours (red, yellow, orange) suggest aggressiveness, violence, and stimulation. They tend to come forward in most images.

Some filmmakers deliberately exploit colour's natural tendency to garishness. Federico Fellini's *Juliet of the Spirits* (1965) features many bizarre costumes and settings to suggest the tawdry but fascinating glamour of the world of show business. Bob Fosse's *Cabaret* is set in Germany and shows the early rise of the Nazi party **(5-13)**. The colours are somewhat neurotic, with emphasis on such 1930s favourites as plum, acid green, and purple, and florid combinations, like gold, black, and pink.

Black-and-white photography in a colour film is sometimes used for symbolic purposes. Some filmmakers alternate whole episodes in black and white with entire sequences in colour. This technique calls attention to itself and is thus most often used by expressionist filmmakers, although realist directors may incorporate black-and-white newsreel footage as flashbacks in films in which the present action is in colour. A more subtle variation is simply not to use too much colour, to let black and white predominate. In Vittorio De Sica's *The Garden of the Finzi-Continis* (1970), which is set in fascist Italy, the early portions of the movie are richly resplendent in shimmering golds, reds, and almost every shade of green. As political repression becomes more brutal, these colours almost imperceptibly begin to wash out, until near the end of the film, whites, blacks, and blue-greys dominate the images. A similar technique is used in Roberto Benigni's *Life is Beautiful* (1998).

In the colour photo section, we can see that film colour functions in a variety of ways. In *When Night Is Falling* **(Colour Plate 2)**, a circus performer's colourful costumes suggest both the love and the risk she brings into the life of a teacher at a theological college. In stories dealing with the darker side of the human condition,

3.13. *Four Weddings and a Funeral* (Britain, 1994), with Andie MacDowell and Hugh Grant, directed by Mike Newell.

This romantic comedy goes to extreme lengths to avoid being sentimental. Hence its concluding sequence of love triumphant at last takes place in a cold London downpour, all light and colour drained from the image. The lovers are too wrapped up in each other to notice, but the audience enjoys the contrast with the brightly lit endings associated with the genre, an effect completely suited to a film whose comedy depends on the clash between romance and cynicism. *(Gramercy Pictures)*

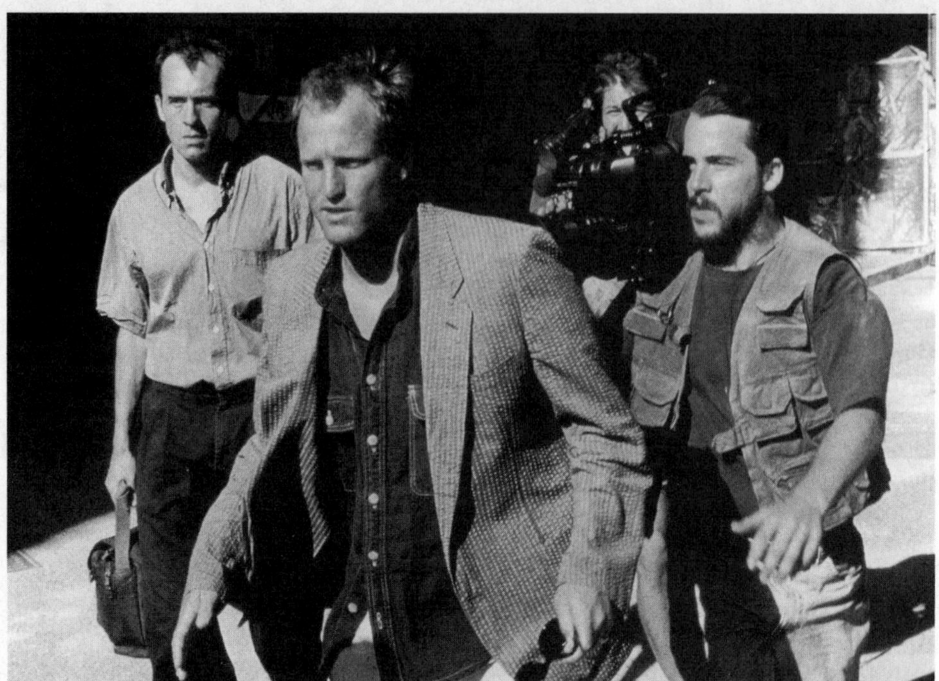

3.14. *Welcome to Sarajevo* (Britain, 1997), with Stephen Dillane (left) and Woody Harrelson (centre), directed by Michael Winterbottom.

A journalist (Dillane) covering the war in Bosnia is so appalled by the suffering of children in the conflict that he decides to take one of them illegally back to Britain. Like many other films based on true stories, *Welcome to Sarajevo* incorporates newsreel footage to convey a sense of authenticity. In earlier films such footage would have been in black-and-white, and the film indeed opens with black-and-white newsreel footage of the devastation, but now the reality effect is mainly created by the graininess and instability of the colour video images shot by the television reporters. Although the fiction sequences were shot on film in 35mm, they also make use of handheld documentary techniques during the frequent outbreaks of violence. *(Miramax Films)*

filmmakers generally avoid bright colours, which are incongruously cheerful. In the *Alien* series, for example, Ripley (Sigourney Weaver) pursues the monstrous force unleashed in the first film through dark and shadowy environments that symbolize the threat and fear of an unspeakable evil **(Colour Plate 4)**.

In the 1980s, new computer technology was developed that allowed black-and-white movies to be "colourized"—a process that provoked a howl of protest from most film artists and critics. This technique is especially unfortunate when applied to carefully photographed black-and-white films. In the colourized version of *Dark Victory*, for example, the man's blue suit, which is irrelevant to the dramatic context, becomes the dominant. In the original black-and-white version **(7-19)**, Davis is the dominant, her dark outfit contrasting with the white fireplace that frames her figure.

3-15. *Starman* (U.S.A., 1984), with Karen Allen and Jeff Bridges, directed by John Carpenter.
Many of the earlier portions of this science-fiction film are photographed in a plain, functional style. After the earthling protagonist (Allen) falls in love with an attractive alien (Bridges), the photographic style becomes more romantic. The city's lights are etherealized by the shimmering, **soft-focus** photography. The halo effect around the lovers' heads reinforces the air of enchantment. The gently falling snowflakes conspire to enhance the magical moment. These are not just lovers; these are soulmates. *(Columbia Pictures)*

LENSES, FILTERS, AND STOCKS

Because the camera's lens is a crude mechanism when compared with the human eye, some of the most striking effects in a movie image can be achieved through the distortions of the photographic process itself. Particularly with regard to size and distance, the lens does not make mental adjustments but records things literally. For example, whatever is placed closest to the lens will appear larger than an object at a greater distance. Hence, a coffee cup can totally obliterate a human being if the cup is in front of the lens and the human is standing at long-shot range.

Realist filmmakers tend to use normal, or standard, lenses to produce a minimum of distortion. These lenses photograph subjects more or less as the human eye perceives them, or as the system of perspective developed by Italian Renaissance painters has trained us to perceive them. Formalist filmmakers often prefer lenses and **filters** that intensify given qualities and suppress others. Cloud formations, for example, can be exaggerated threateningly or softly diffused, depending on what kind of lens or filter is used. Different shapes, colours, and lighting intensities can be radically altered by using specific optical modifiers. There are literally dozens of different lenses, but most of them are subsumed under three major categories: those in the standard (non-distorted) range, the telephoto lenses, and the wide angles.

The telephoto lens is often used to get close-ups of objects from extreme distances. For example, no cinematographer is likely to want to get close enough to a lion to photograph a close-up with a standard lens. In cases such as these, the telephoto is used, thus guaranteeing the safety of the cinematographer while still producing the necessary close-up. Telephotos also allow cinematographers to work discreetly. In crowded city locations, for example, passersby are likely to stare at a movie camera. The telephoto permits the cinematographer to remain hidden—in a truck, for example—while shooting close shots through the windshield or back window of the truck. In effect, the lens works like a telescope, and because of its long focal length, it is sometimes called a long lens.

Telephoto lenses produce a number of side effects that are sometimes exploited by directors for symbolic purposes. Most long lenses are in sharp focus on one distance plane only. Objects placed before or beyond that distance blur, go out of focus—an expressive technique, especially to the formalist filmmaker **(3-16a)**. The longer the lens, the more sensitive it is to distances; in the case of extremely long lenses, objects placed a mere few centimetres away from the selected focal plane can be out of focus. This deliberate blurring of planes in the background, foreground, or both can produce striking photographic and atmospheric effects.

The focal distance of long lenses can usually be adjusted while actually shooting, and thus the director is able to neutralize planes and guide the viewer's eye to various distances in a sequence—a technique called **rack focusing**, or **selective focusing**. In *The Graduate* (1967), director Mike Nichols used a slight focus shift instead of a cut when he wanted the viewer to look first at the young heroine, who then blurs out of focus, then at her mother, who is standing in a doorway nearby. The focus-shifting technique suggests a cause-and-effect relationship and parallels the heroine's sudden realization that her boyfriend's secret mistress is her own mother. In *The French Connection* (1971), William Friedkin used selective focus in a sequence showing a criminal under surveillance. He remains in sharp focus while the city crowds of his environment are an undifferentiated blur. At strategic moments in the sequence, Friedkin shifted the focus plane from the criminal to the dogged detective who is tailing him in the crowd.

Long lenses also flatten images, decreasing the sense of distance between depth planes. Two people standing metres apart might look much closer when photographed with a telephoto lens. With very long lenses, distance planes are so compressed that the image can resemble a flat surface of abstract patterns. When anything moves toward or away from the camera in such shots, the mobile object seems not to be moving at all. In *The Graduate*, the hero (Dustin Hoffman) runs desperately toward the camera, but because of the flattening effect of the long lens, he seems almost to be running in place rather than moving toward his destination.

3-16. Four Degrees of Exaggeration.

The lens of each of these four shots provides a subtle commentary on the relationship of the characters to their settings.

3-16a. *Assault on Precinct 13* (U.S.A., 2004), with Ja Rule, directed by Jean-François Richet.

Some telephoto lenses are so precise they can focus on a thin slice of action that is only a few inches deep. Note how the gun and Ja Rule's hands are radically blurred. So is the background behind him. Our eyes are forced to concentrate on the face of the character during a decisive moment of his life. *(Rogue Pictures)*

3-16b. *Cinderella Man* (U.S.A., 2005), with Russell Crowe and Renée Zellweger, directed by Ron Howard.

Telephoto lenses are often used to enhance the lyrical potential of an image. In this shot, the blurry background renders it supremely irrelevant to what matters most to these characters—each other. The telephoto lens, in effect, is a silent declaration of their total devotion. *(Universal Studios)*

3-16c. *Dark Blue* (U.S.A., 2003), with Michael Michele and Ving Rhames, directed by Ron Shelton.

A high-ranking police officer must break off his adulterous affair with his lover, a policewoman who is his subordinate. The lens forces us to focus on his feelings, while she is nearly obliterated by the soft focus, hardly worthy of our notice. If Shelton wanted to emphasize her feelings, Rhames would be in soft focus, and she in sharp. If the director wanted to stress the equality of their emotions, he would have used a wide-angle lens, thus rendering them both in sharp focus. *(United Artists)*

3-16d. *Schindler's List* (U.S.A., 1993), with Liam Neeson (outstretched arms), directed by Steven Spielberg.

Wide-angle lenses are used whenever deep-focus photography is called for. Objects a few feet from the lens as well as those in the "depth" of the background are in equal focus, reinforcing the interconnectedness of the visual planes. This movie deals with a German industrialist (Neeson) who saved the lives of hundreds of Jews during the Nazi Holocaust. Because deep focus allows for the repetition of visual motifs into infinity, Spielberg is able to suggest that Jews all over Europe were being herded in a similar manner, but they were not as lucky as Schindler's Jews. *(Universal Pictures)*

The wide-angle lenses, also called **short lenses**, have short focal lengths and wide angles of view. These lenses are used in deep-focus shots as they preserve a sharpness of focus on virtually all distance planes. The distortions involved in short lenses are both linear and spatial. The wider the angle, the more lines and shapes tend to warp, especially at the edges of the image. Distances between various depth planes are also exaggerated with these lenses: Two people standing very close to each other can appear metres apart in a wide-angle image. Orson Welles's films are filled with wide-angle shots. In *The Trial* (1962), for example, he used such lenses to emphasize the vast, vacuous distance between people. In close-up ranges, wide-angle lenses tend to make huge bulbs of people's noses and slanting, sinister slits of their eyes. Welles used several such shots in *Touch of Evil* (1958).

Movement toward or away from the camera is exaggerated when photographed with a short lens. Two or three ordinary steps can seem like inhumanly lengthy strides—an effective technique when a director wants to emphasize a character's strength, dominance, or ruthlessness. The fish-eye lens is the most extreme wide-angle modifier; it creates such severe distortions that the lateral portions of the screen seem reflected in a sphere, as though we were looking through a crystal ball.

Lenses and filters can be used for purely cosmetic purposes—to make an actor taller, slimmer, younger, or older. Josef von Sternberg sometimes covered his lens with a translucent silk stocking to give his images a gauzy, romantic aura. A few glamour actresses during the Hollywood studio era even had clauses in their contracts stipulating that only beautifying **soft-focus** lenses could be used for their close-ups. These optical modifiers eliminate small facial wrinkles and skin blemishes.

Filters are even more numerous than lenses. Some trap light and refract it in such a way as to produce a diamond-like sparkle in the image. Many filters are used to suppress or heighten certain colours. Colour filters can be especially striking in exterior scenes. Robert Altman's *McCabe and Mrs. Miller* (1971), photographed by

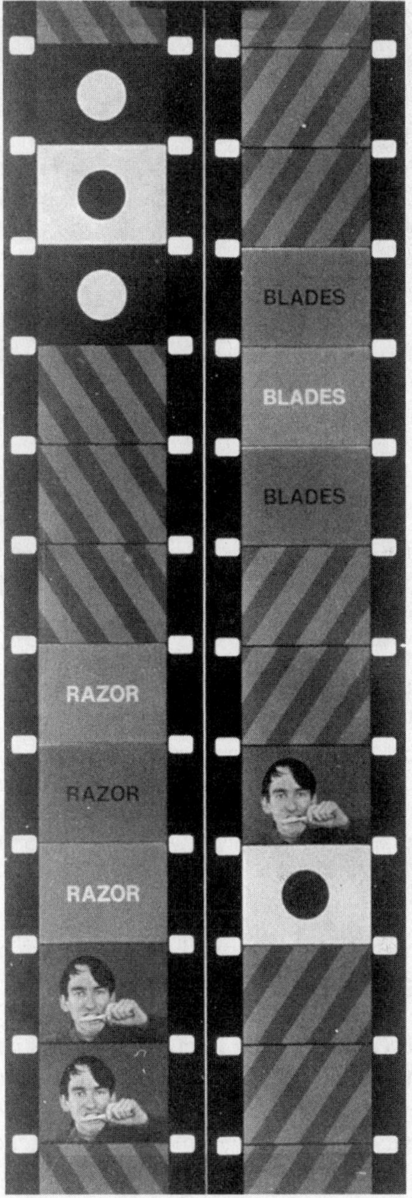

3-17. ***Razor Blades*** **(U.S.A., 1968), directed by Paul Sharits.**

Avant-garde filmmakers are often anti-illusionist—they attempt to break down the realism of an image by calling attention to its artificiality and its material properties. A movie image is printed on a strip of celluloid, which can be manipulated, even violated. In Sharits's flicker film, two images (requiring separate screens and projectors) are simultaneously juxtaposed. Each filmstrip consists of irregularly recurring images—two or three frames in duration, interspersed by blank or colour frames—or purely abstract designs, like coloured stripes or circular shapes. The rapid flickering of images creates a mesmerizing stroboscopic effect, testing the audience's psychological and physiological tolerance. The content of the film is its structural form rather than the subject matter of the images as images. *(Anthology Film Archives)*

Vilmos Zsigmond, used green and blue filters for many of the exterior scenes, yellow and orange for interiors. These filters emphasize the bitter cold of the winter setting and the communal warmth of the rooms inside the primitive buildings.

Though there are several different kinds of film **stocks**, most of them fall within the two basic categories: fast and slow. **Fast stocks** are highly sensitive to light and, in some cases, can register images with no illumination except what is available on **location**, even in nighttime sequences. **Slow stocks** are relatively insensitive to light and require as much as ten times more illumination than fast stocks. Traditionally,

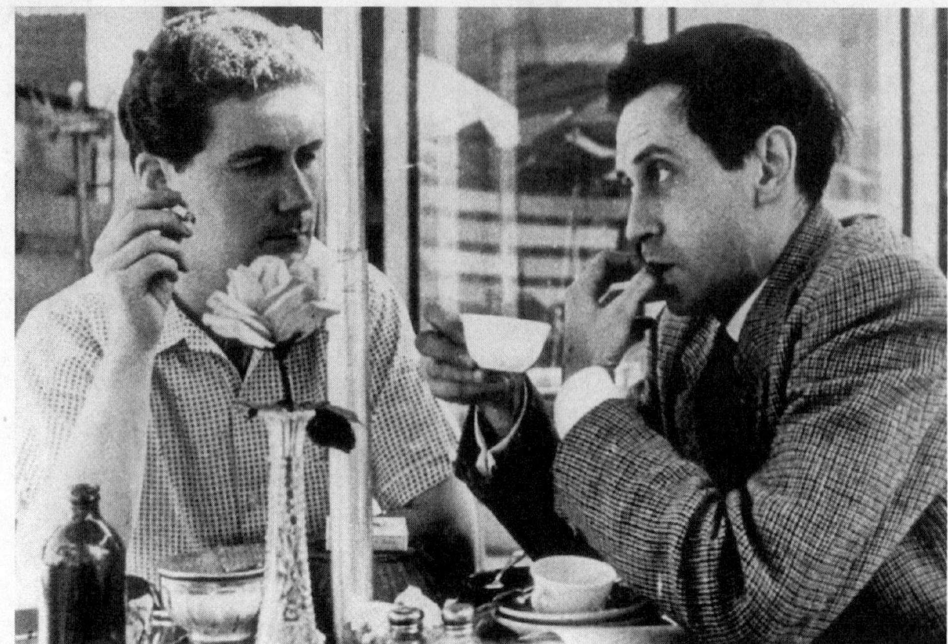

3-18. *A tout prendre* [*The Way It Goes*] (Canada, 1963), with Claude Jutra and Victor Désy, directed by Jutra.

Small-budget independent films often have grainy images as a result of using fast stocks that allow filming with available light. Many, like Jutra's pioneering Canadian feature film, were also originally shot on 16 mm and "blown up" to 35 mm for commercial distribution. The effect often evokes the authenticity of documentary realism and has frequently been imitated by filmmakers with much larger budgets. *(The Claude Jutra Estate)*

slow stocks are capable of capturing colours with precision, without washing them out.

Fast stocks are commonly associated with documentary movies, since with their great sensitivity to light, these stocks can reproduce images of events while they are actually occurring. The filmmakers are able to photograph people and places without having to set up cumbersome lights. Because of this light sensitivity, fast stocks produce a grainy image in which lines tend to be fuzzy and colours tend to be washed out. In a black-and-white film, lights and darks contrast sharply and many variations of grey can be lost **(3-18).**

Ordinarily, technical considerations such as these would have no place in a book of this sort, but the choice of stock can produce considerable psychological and aesthetic differences in a movie. Since the early 1960s, many fiction filmmakers have switched to fast stocks to give their images a documentary sense of urgency.

DIGITAL IMAGING

Not everything we see on the screen was actually present in front of the camera at the time a film was shot. From Georges Méliès on, filmmakers have sought ways to trick

3-19. *Pas de deux* (Canada, 1968), directed by Norman McLaren.

The optical printer was an invaluable piece of equipment, particularly to the formalist filmmaker, because, among other things, it allowed the superimposition of two or more realities within a unified space. This film uses a technique called chronophotography, in which the movements of two dancers are staggered and overlayed by the optical printer to produce a stroboscopic effect: As the dancers move, they leave a ghostly imprint on the screen. *(National Film Board of Canada)*

the eye in the search for greater illusion or to overcome budgetary constraints. Through the use of such devices as models, **matte shots**, and rear projection, literal space could be transformed into a more impressive (or expressive) virtual space. The **optical printer** was an elaborate machine that produced many special effects in cinema before the introduction of computers. It included a camera and projector precisely aligned, and it permitted the operator to rephotograph all or a portion of an existing frame of a film. **Double exposure**, or the superimposition of two images, allowed the director to portray two levels of reality simultaneously. For this reason, the technique was often used in fantasy and dream sequences, as well as in scenes dealing with the supernatural. The optical printer could also produce multiple exposures, or the superimposition of many images simultaneously **(3-19)**. Multiple exposures were useful for suggesting mood, time lapses, and any sense of mixture—of time, places, objects, and events. The optical printer could combine one actor with moving images of others in a different time and place.

Today the optical printer has been rendered virtually obsolete by computer-generated imagery (CGI). Digital technology, perfected in the 1990s, has revolutionized special effects, allowing filmmakers to generate whole armies by computer, as in the trilogy *The Lord of the Rings* (Peter Jackson, 2001–2003), or to depict characters performing physically impossible feats **(3-20)**.

In the past, whole scenes often had to be reshot because of technical glitches. For example, if a modern building or car appeared in a period film, the scene had to be recut or even rephotographed. Today, such details can be removed individually. Conversely, this technology allowed George Lucas, whose company Industrial Light & Magic was a pioneer in this field, to insert even more elaborate special effects into the 1997 Special Edition of the *Star Wars* trilogy.

3-20. *The Matrix* (U.S.A., 1999), with Keanu Reeves and Hugo Weaving, directed by Andy and Larry Wachowski.

The Matrix Trilogy is a veritable cornucopia of influences, including comic books, Hong Kong kung fu films, western action films, Eastern mysticism, fairy tales, video games, Japanese anime (animation), cyberpunk, computer games, and traditional science-fiction movies like *Blade Runner* (see **4-21**). The trilogy is profuse in gravity-defying stunts, like people floating and hovering in the air, running up walls, moving in **slow motion**, and levitation fighting. In one scene, a battle is "frozen" while the camera swings around it. The F/X team also devised a technique called "bullet time," in which characters dodge gunfire in super-slow-motion vacuums. *(Warner Bros.)*

In addition, CGI technology is beginning to make film distribution and exhibition cheaper. Today, film prints can cost up to $2000 each. A mainstream American movie may be shown simultaneously on 2000 screens, costing $4 million just for the prints. In the future, movies will be stored on digital discs, like a DVD, and will cost only a few dollars to manufacture. Distributors will also save on shipping fees. Instead of the heavy reels of traditional movies, costing thousands of dollars to ship by bus, plane, or rail, in the future, a lightweight disc will be sent to movie theatres for only a few dollars. Projection equipment will basically consist of commercial DVD machines, not the cumbersome, expensive mechanical projectors that have dominated film exhibition for over 100 years. The replacement of celluloid by digital projection will also bring the public viewing of movies closer to the home theatre experience, which has also benefitted from the development of larger television screens, high-definition images, and sophisticated digital sound systems (see Chapter 1, "Medium").

Alongside its economic benefits for the industry and its use to create stunning special effects in blockbuster movies, the digital revolution has also created new possibilities for small-budget production. In this way, digital video (DV) is the contemporary equivalent to the lightweight equipment developed for documentary production in the 1950s (see Chapter 9, "Nonfiction Films") that made possible the emergence of the French **New Wave** and the Canadian direct cinema feature films. The impact of this development was made vividly apparent with the commercial success of *The Blair Witch Project* **(5-20)**. Digitally shot and edited for about $25 000, the film was publicized through a website that claimed it was a true story consisting of footage taken by film students who mysteriously disappeared while shooting a documentary about witchcraft.

Digital video is also at the heart of the project of the Danish filmmakers who formed the group Dogme 95, whose manifesto set out a list of rules designed to bring their films closer to reality (see **11-5**). Thomas Vinterberg's *The Celebration* (1998), for example, was shot on video and blown up to 35mm, producing grainy and shaky images that capture the tensions at a family gathering where a son accuses his father of sexual abuse. It was the development of digital technology that made possible the shooting of *Atanarjuat: The Fast Runner*, recreating an Inuit legend in the Arctic, where the bitter cold would have frozen conventional film cameras **(10-27)**.

Even before video became digital, it transformed our lives by creating an environment in which cameras are everywhere. Security cameras allow us to watch crimes as they are committed, and camcorders capture the events in our personal lives from weddings and graduation ceremonies to natural disasters and terrorist attacks. While such images push the voyeurism of image-making to new levels in so-called Reality Television, the technology also offers the potential for new ways of understanding the world in which we live. In *ABC Africa* (2001), the Iranian director Abbas Kiarostami investigated the AIDS crisis in Uganda using two handheld video

3-21. *Speaking Parts* (Canada, 1989), with Gabrielle Rose, directed by Atom Egoyan.

Cameras are an increasingly visible part of everyday reality, and are frequently seen on our movie screens. More often than not these cameras are video cameras—surveillance cameras or camcorders. Egoyan's films explore the impact on our lives of this new image technology. In this film, a couple makes love long-distance by means of a teleconferencing link, and Clara (Rose) communes with her dead brother in a video mausoleum where funeral urns have been replaced by video monitors. *(Ego Film Arts/Johnny Eisen)*

cameras. As the enormity of the situation emerges, we see the filmmakers engaging with the people, holding a camera in one hand so that it becomes part of the environment it is filming. In the past, the camera was excluded from the image; in the future, for better or worse, cameras will be an increasingly visible presence in films, as they are in the reality that movies represent.

In this chapter, we have been concerned with visual images largely as they relate to the art and technology of cinematography. But the camera must have materials to photograph—objects, people, settings. Through the manipulation of these materials, the director is able to convey a multitude of ideas and emotions spatially. This arrangement of objects in space is referred to as a director's mise en scène—the subject of the following chapter.

FURTHER READING (AND VIEWING)

Brown, Blain, *Cinematography Theory and Practice: Image Making for Cinematographers, Directors and Videographers* (Burlington MA: Focal Press, 2002). The aesthetics and practice of image-making.

Cameron, Ian, ed. *The Movie Book of Film Noir* (London: Studio Vista, 1992). Collection of essays on the style and meanings of film noir.

Dalle Vacche, Angela, *Cinema and Painting: How Art is Used in Film* (Austin: University of Texas Press, 1996). Analysis of films that incorporate paintings in their visual imagery.

Dalle Vacche, Angela, and Brian Price, ed., *Color: The Film Reader* (London: Routledge, 2006). Anthology of essays dealing with the history and effect of colour in film.

Darley, Andrew, *Visual Digital Culture: Surface Play and Spectacle in New Media Genres* (London: Routledge, 2000). Suggestive account of the impact of digital imaging techniques.

Figgis, Mike, *Digital Filmmaking* (London: Faber and Faber, 2007). A leading film director assesses the possibilities of digital production.

Enticknap, Leo, *Moving Image Technology: From Zoetrope to Digital* (London: Wallflower Press, 2005). The history and theory of image technologies.

Graham, Gerald G., *Canadian Film Technology, 1896–1986* (Newark: University of Delaware Press, 1989). History of filmmaking technology in Canada.

McCarthy, Todd, *Visions of Light* (American Film Institute, 1992). Film (and now DVD) history of cinematography with many interviews and examples.

Willis, Holly, *New Digital Cinema: Reinventing the Moving Image* (London: Wallflower Press, 2005). The impact of digital technology on feature films, video art, music videos, animation.

Unleashed (Rogue Pictures)

MISE EN SCÈNE

4

One must compose images as the old masters did their canvases, with the same preoccupation with effect and expression.

—MARCEL CARNÉ

OVERVIEW

Mise en scène: How the visual materials are staged, framed, and photographed. The frame's aspect ratio: dimensions of the screen's height and width. Functions of the frame: excluding the irrelevant, pinpointing the particular, symbolizing other enclosures. The symbolic implications of the geography of the frame: top, bottom, centre, and edges. Off-screen space. How images are structured: composition and design. Where we look first: the dominant. Settings: realist and expressionist. Art directors and the studio system. Analyzing sets. The territorial imperative: How space can be used to communicate ideas about power. Staging positions vis-à-vis the camera and what they suggest. Room for movement: tight and loose framing. Proxemic patterns and how they define the relationships between people. Camera proxemics and the shots. Open and closed forms. The elements of a mise en scène analysis.

Mise en scène was originally a French theatrical term, meaning "placing on stage." The phrase refers to the arrangement of all the visual elements of a theatrical production within a given playing area—the stage. This area can be defined by the proscenium arch, which encloses the stage in a kind of picture frame, or the acting area can be more fluid, extending even into the auditorium. No matter what the confines of the stage may be, its mise en scène is always in three dimensions. Objects and people are arranged in actual space, which has depth as well as height and width. This space is also a continuation of the same space that the audience occupies, no matter how much a theatre director tries to suggest a separate "world" on the stage.

In movies, mise en scène is somewhat more complicated, a blend of the visual conventions of live theatre with those of the plastic arts. Like the stage director, the filmmaker arranges objects and people within a given three-dimensional space. But once this arrangement is photographed, it is converted into a two-dimensional image of the real thing. The space in the "world" of the movie is not the same as that occupied by the audience. Only the image exists in the same physical area, like a picture in an art gallery. Mise en scène in the movies resembles the art of painting in that an image of formal patterns and shapes is presented on a flat surface and is enclosed within a **frame**. But cinematic mise en scène is also a fluid choreographing of visual elements that correspond to a dramatic idea or complex of ideas **(4-1)**.

THE FRAME

Each movie image is enclosed by the frame of the screen, which defines the world of the film, separating it from the actual world of the darkened auditorium. Unlike the painter or still photographer, the filmmaker does not conceive of the framed compositions as self-sufficient statements. Film is a temporal as well as spatial art, and consequently the visuals are constantly in flux. The compositions are broken down, redefined, and reassembled before our eyes. A single-frame image from a movie, then, is necessarily an artificially frozen moment that was never intended to be yanked from its context in time and motion. For critical purposes, it is sometimes necessary to analyze a still frame in isolation, but the viewer ought to make due allowances for the dramatic context **(4-2)**.

4-1. *Manhattan* (U.S.A., 1979), with Woody Allen and Diane Keaton, directed by Allen.

Mise en scène is a complex analytical term, encompassing four distinct formal elements: (1) the staging of the action, (2) the physical setting and décor, (3) the manner in which these materials are framed, and (4) the manner in which they are photographed. The art of mise en scène is indissolubly linked with the art of cinematography. In this shot, for example, the story content is simple: The characters are conversing, getting to know each other, becoming attracted. Gordon Willis's tender, low-key lighting, combined with the beauty of the setting—the sculpture garden of the Museum of Modern Art—provides the scene with an intensely romantic atmosphere. *(United Artists)*

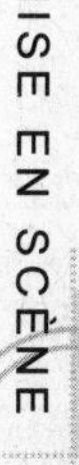

The frame functions as the basis of composition in a movie image. Unlike the painter or still photographer, however, the filmmaker fits not the frame to the compositions, but the compositions to a single-sized frame. The ratio of the frame's horizontal and vertical dimensions—known as the **aspect ratio**—remains constant throughout the movie. Screens come in a variety of aspect ratios, especially since the introduction of **widescreen** in the early 1950s. Before this time, most movies were shot in a 1.33:1 aspect ratio (approximately the shape of a regular television screen), though even in the silent era filmmakers were constantly experimenting with different-sized screens **(4-3)**.

Today, most movies are projected in one of two aspect ratios: the 1.85:1 (standard) and the 2.35:1 (widescreen) **(4-4)**. Some films originally photographed in widescreen are cropped down to a conventional aspect ratio after their initial theatrical release, when they are shown on television or transferred to video. The more imaginatively the widescreen is used, the more a movie is likely to suffer when its

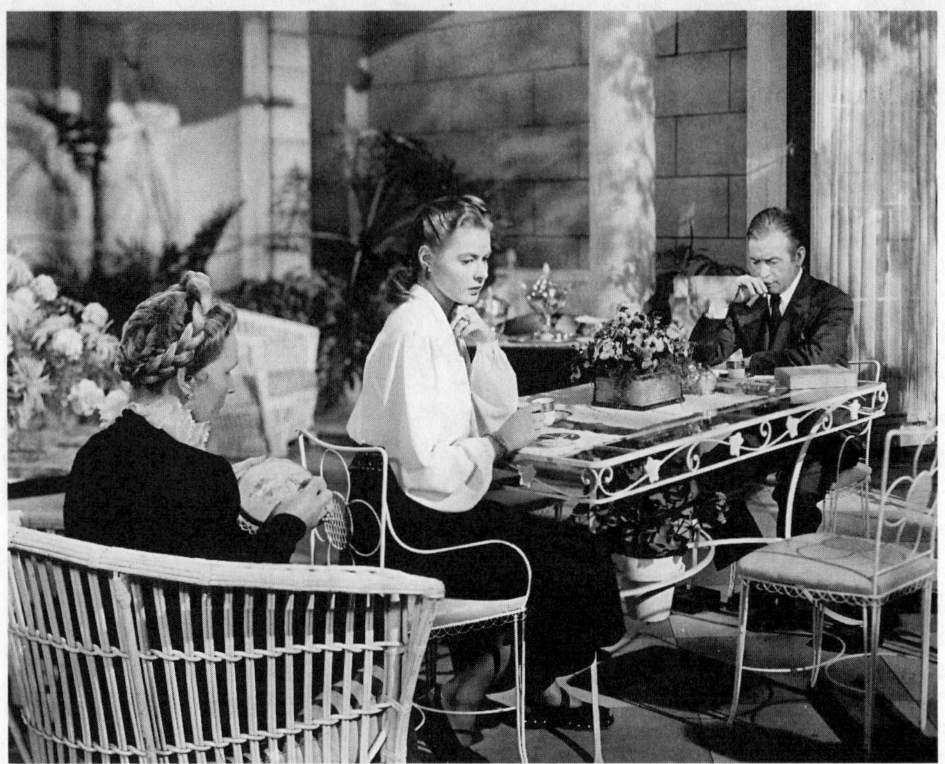

4-2. *Notorious* (U.S.A., 1946), with Ingrid Bergman, Claude Rains, and Leopoldine Konstantine, directed by Alfred Hitchcock.

Hitchcock always regarded himself as a formalist, calculating his effects with an extraordinary degree of precision. He believed that an unmanipulated reality is filled with irrelevancies: "I do not follow the geography of a set, I follow the geography of the screen," he said. The space around actors must be orchestrated from shot to shot. "I think only of that white screen that has to be filled up the way you fill up a canvas. That's why I draw rough setups for the cameraman." Here, the mise en scène is a perfect analogue of the heroine's sense of entrapment, without violating the civilized veneer demanded by the dramatic context. The dialogue in such instances can be perfectly neutral, for the psychological tensions are conveyed by the placement of the camera and the way the characters are arranged in space. *(RKO)*

aspect ratio is violated in this manner. Generally, at least a third of the image is hacked away by lopping off the edges of the frame. This kind of cropping can result in many visual absurdities: A speaker at the edge of the frame might be totally absent in the "revised" composition, or an actor might react in horror at something that never even comes into view. When shown on television—which has an aspect ratio of approximately 1.33:1—some of the greatest widescreen films can actually seem clumsy and poorly composed **(4-5)**. The advent of DVDs (which usually, but not always, present films in their original aspect ratios) and widescreen televisions is changing this situation, enabling home viewers to experience the film as the filmmakers intended.

4-3. *Napoléon* (France, 1927), directed by Abel Gance.

Napoléon is the most famous widescreen experiment of the silent era. Its triptych sequences—such as the French army's march into Italy (pictured)—were shot in what Gance called "Polyvision." The process involved the coordination of three cameras so as to photograph a 160° panorama—three times wider than the conventional aspect ratio. *(Universal Pictures)*

a

b

4-4. *2001: A Space Odyssey* (U.S.A. / Britain, 1968), directed by Stanley Kubrick.

The wide screen is particularly suited to capturing the vastness of a locale. If this image were cropped to a conventional aspect ratio **(b),** much of the feel of the infinity of space would be sacrificed. We tend to scan an image from left to right, and therefore, in Kubrick's composition **(a),** the astronaut seems to be in danger of slipping off into the endlessness of space. If the composition is turned upside down, however **(c)**, the astronaut seems to be coming home into the safety of the spacecraft. *(MGM)*

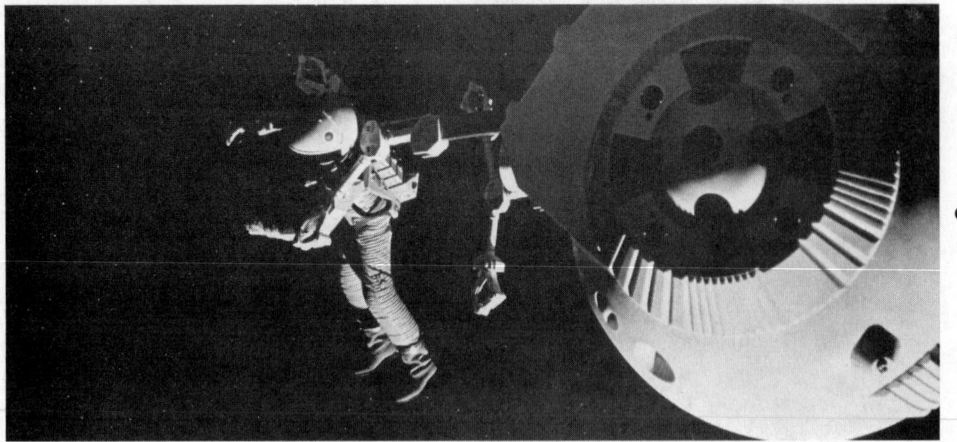

c

4-5. ***Unleashed*** **(France/U.S.A./Britain, 2005), with Jet Li (centre), martial arts choreography by Yuan Wo Ping, directed by Louis Letterrier.**

The widescreen is especially effective in scenes that require elaborately choreographed movements, like a dance number, or shown here, a kung fu fight sequence. Most action scenes are edited in quick cuts, to suggest a sense of fragmentation and events that are out of control. When such scenes are shot in lengthier takes, with the action coordinated within the confines of the frame, the impression is that the protagonist is totally in control, flipping off his adversaries like pesky flies. *(Rogue Pictures)*

In the traditional visual arts, frame dimensions are governed by the nature of the subject matter. Thus, a painting of a skyscraper is likely to be vertical and would be framed accordingly. A vast panoramic scene would probably be horizontal. But in movies the frame ratio is imposed from without and is not necessarily governed by the nature of the materials being photographed.

The constant size of the movie frame is especially hard to overcome in vertical compositions. A sense of height must be conveyed in spite of the dominantly horizontal shape of the screen. One method of overcoming the problem is through **masking**. In his 1916 epic, *Intolerance*, D.W. Griffith blocked out portions of his images by using black masks, which in effect connected the darkened portions of the screen with the darkness of the auditorium. To emphasize the steep fall of a soldier from a wall, the sides of the image were masked out. To stress the vast horizon of a location, Griffith masked out the lower third of the image—thus creating a widescreen effect. Many kinds of masks are used in this movie, including diagonal, circular, and oval shapes.

In the silent-movie era, the **iris** (a circular or oval mask that can open up or close in on a subject) was rather overused, and it was largely discontinued after the coming of sound. As a device that called attention to itself, the iris did not suit the trend toward brisk and straightforward storytelling during the studio era. When used by later filmmakers, the iris can have powerful dramatic effects, but it also evokes the visual language of silent cinema. It was revived by the French **New Wave** filmmakers. In *L'Enfant sauvage* [*The Wild Child*] (1969), for example, François Truffaut uses an iris to suggest the intense concentration of a young boy: The surrounding blackness is a metaphor of how the youngster "blocks out" his social environment while focusing on an object immediately in front of him.

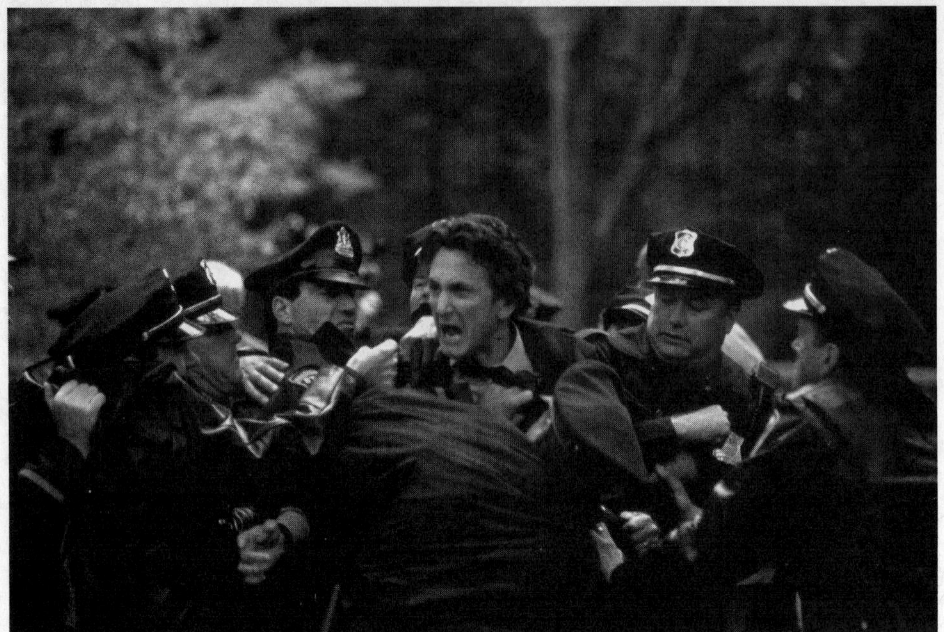

4-6. *Mystic River* (U.S.A., 2003), with Sean Penn, directed by Clint Eastwood.

All the compositional elements of this shot contribute to a sense of entrapment. The Penn character has just learned that his daughter's body has been found in the woods, and he tries frantically to go to her. But he is totally surrounded by a double ring of police officers who try to restrain him, lest he destroy possible evidence around the corpse. The action is tightly framed, and the camera is at a slightly high angle, further reinforcing the sense of confinement. The image might almost be entitled No Exit. (*Warner Bros.)*

As an aesthetic device, the frame performs in several ways. The sensitive director is just as concerned with what is left out of the frame as with what is included. The frame selects and delimits the subject, excluding all irrelevancies and presenting us with only a "piece" of reality. The materials included within a shot are unified by the frame, which in effect imposes an order on them—the order that art carves out of the chaos of reality. The frame is thus essentially an isolating device, a technique that permits the director to confer special attention on what might be overlooked in a wider context.

The movie frame can function as a metaphor for other types of enclosures. Some directors use the frame voyeuristically. In many of the films of Alfred Hitchcock, for example, the frame is likened to a window through which the audience may satisfy its impulse to pry into the intimate details of the characters' lives. In fact, *Rear Window* uses this peeping technique literally **(11-9)**. Other directors use the frame to bring out the theatricality of the actions depicted in the film. In Jean Renoir's *Le Carosse d'or* [*The Golden Coach*] (1953), for instance, the frame suggests the proscenium arch of the live theatre and appropriately so, since the controlling symbol of the movie centres on the idea of life as a stage.

Certain areas within the frame can suggest symbolic ideas. By placing an object or actor within a particular section of the frame, the filmmaker can radically alter his

4-7. *Bend It Like Beckham* (Britain, 2003), with Parminder K. Nagra, written and directed by Gurinder Chadha.

The top of the frame is often associated with power, prestige, and people with godlike qualities—like David Beckham, Britain's most famous football (i.e., soccer) player. Beckham is almost worshipped by the main character of this ethnic comedy about an Anglo-Indian girl (Nagra) who wants to play professional soccer like her hero. Her traditional Indian parents have other ideas. As her mum says: "Who'd want a girl who plays football all day but can't make *chapati*s?" *(Fox Searchlight Pictures)*

or her comment on that object or character. Placement within the frame is another instance of how form is actually content. Each of the major sections of the frame—centre, top, bottom, and sides—can be exploited for such symbolic purposes.

The central portions of the screen are generally reserved for the most important visual elements. This area is instinctively regarded by most people as the intrinsic centre of interest. When we take a snapshot of a friend, we generally centre his or her figure within the confines of the **viewfinder**. Since childhood, we have been taught that a drawing must be balanced, with the middle serving as the focal point. The centre, then, is a kind of norm: We *expect* dominant visual elements to be placed there. Precisely because of this expectation, objects placed in the centre tend to be visually undramatic. Central dominance is generally favoured when the subject matter is intrinsically compelling. Realist filmmakers prefer central dominance because, formally, it is the most unobtrusive kind of framing. The viewer is allowed to concentrate on the subject matter without being distracted by visual elements that seem off centre. However, even formalists use the middle of the screen for dominance in routine expository shots.

4-8. ***Women on the Verge of a Nervous Breakdown*** **(Spain, 1988), with Carmen Maura, directed by Pedro Almodóvar.**

What is wrong with this photo? For one thing, the character is not centred in the composition. The image is asymmetrical, apparently off balance, because the "empty" space on the right takes up over half the viewing area. Visual artists often use "negative space" such as this to create a vacuum in the image, a sense of something missing, something left unsaid. In this case, the pregnant protagonist (Maura) has just been dumped by her lover. He is an unworthy swine, but inexplicably, perversely, she still loves him. His abandonment has left a painful empty place in her life. *(Orion Pictures)*

The area near the top of the frame can suggest ideas dealing with power, authority, and aspiration. A person placed here seems to control all the visual elements below, and for this reason, authority figures are often photographed in this manner. In images suggesting spirituality, often the top of the frame is exploited to convey a god-like splendour **(4-7)**. This grandeur can also apply to objects—a palace, the top of a mountain. If an unattractive character is placed near the top of the screen, he or she can seem threatening and dangerous, superior to the other figures within the frame. However, these generalizations are true only when the other figures are approximately the same size or smaller than the dominating figure.

The top of the frame is not always used in this symbolic manner. In some instances, this is simply the most sensible area to place an object. In a medium shot of a figure, for example, the person's head is logically going to be near the top of the screen, but obviously this kind of framing is not meant to be symbolic. It is merely reasonable, since that is where we *expect* the head to appear in medium shots. Indeed, mise en scène is essentially an art of the long and extreme long shot, for when the subject matter is detailed in a closer shot, the director has fewer choices concerning the distribution of visual elements.

The areas near the bottom of the frame tend to suggest opposite meanings from the top: subservience, vulnerability, and powerlessness. Objects and figures placed in these positions seem to be in danger of slipping out of the frame entirely. For this reason, these areas are often exploited symbolically to suggest danger. When there are two or more figures in the frame and they are approximately the same size, the figure nearer the bottom of the screen tends to be dominated by those above.

The left and right edges of the frame tend to suggest insignificance because these are the areas farthest removed from the centre of the screen. Objects and figures placed near the edges are literally close to the darkness outside the frame. Many directors use this darkness to suggest those symbolic ideas traditionally associated with the lack of light—the unknown, the unseen, and the feared. In some instances, the blackness outside the frame can symbolize oblivion or even death. In movies about people who want to remain anonymous and unnoticed, the director sometimes deliberately places them off centre, near the "insignificant" edges of the screen **(4-8)**.

Finally, in some instances a director places the most important visual elements completely off screen. Especially when a character is associated with darkness, mystery, or death, this technique can be highly effective, for the audience is most fearful

4-9. *Family Viewing* (Canada, 1986), with David Hemblen and Gabrielle Rose, directed by Atom Egoyan. Egoyan's films deal with the impact of modern communications technology on human relations. Interweaving film and video images, as well as sequences made in a television studio, this film explores the image and reality of modern family life. At the root of the problem is the father, Stan (Hemblen), who is unable to make love to his wife (Rose) without the aid of a video camera and a telephone sex worker. The placement of the telephone in this shot provides a wry comment on Stan's impotence when the expected call fails to come through on time. *(Ego Film Arts/Johnny Eisen)*

of what it cannot see. In the early portions of Fritz Lang's *M* (1931), for example, the psychotic child-killer is never seen directly. We can only sense his presence as he lurks in the darkness outside the light of the frame. Occasionally, we catch a glimpse of his shadow streaking across the **set**, and we are aware of his presence by the eerie tune he whistles when he is emotionally excited or upset.

Two other off-screen areas can be exploited for symbolic purposes: the space behind the set and the space in front of the camera. By not showing us what is happening behind a closed door, the filmmaker can provoke the viewer's curiosity, creating an unsettling effect, for we tend to fill in such vacuums with vivid imaginings. The final shot from Hitchcock's *Notorious* is a good example. The hero helps the groggy heroine past a group of Nazi agents to a waiting vehicle. The rather sympathetic villain (Claude Rains) escorts the two, hoping his colleagues will not become suspicious. In a deep-focus long shot, we see the three principals in the foreground while the Nazi agents remain near the open door of the house in the upper background—watching, wondering. The hero maliciously locks the villain out of the car, then drives out of frame, leaving the villain stranded without an explanation. His colleagues call out his name, and he is forced to return to the house, dreading the worst. He climbs the stairs and reenters the house with the suspicious agents, who then close the door behind them. Hitchcock never does show us what happens behind the door.

The area in front of the camera can also create unsettling effects of this sort. In John Huston's *The Maltese Falcon* (1941), for example, we witness a murder without ever seeing the killer. The victim is photographed in a **medium shot** as a gun enters the frame just in front of the camera. Not until the end of the movie do we discover the identity of the off-screen killer.

COMPOSITION AND DESIGN

Although the photographable materials of movies exist in three dimensions, one of the primary problems facing the filmmaker is much like that confronting the painter: the arrangement of shapes, colours, lines, and textures on a flat, rectangular surface. In classical cinema, this arrangement is generally held in some kind of balance, or harmonious equilibrium. The desire for balance is analogous to people balancing on their feet, and indeed to most manufactured structures, which are balanced on the surface of the earth. Instinctively, we assume that balance is the norm in most human enterprises.

In movies, however, there are some important exceptions to this rule. When a visual artist wants to stress a *lack* of equilibrium, many of the standard conventions of composition are deliberately violated. The dramatic context is usually the determining factor, and what is superficially a bad composition might actually be highly effective, depending on its psychological context.

There are no set rules about these matters. A classical filmmaker like Buster Keaton used mostly balanced compositions. Other filmmakers are more likely to use compositions that are asymmetrical or off centre. In movies, a variety of techniques can be used to convey the same ideas and emotions. Some filmmakers favour visual methods, others favour dialogue, still others editing or acting **(4-10)**.

4-10a. *Macbeth* (U.S.A. / Britain, 1971), with Francesca Annis and Jon Finch, directed by Roman Polanski. Movie images are generally scanned in a structured sequence of eye-stops. The eye is first attracted to a dominant contrast that compels our most immediate attention by virtue of its conspicuousness, and then travels to the subsidiary areas of interest within the frame. In this photo, for example, the eye is initially attracted to the face of Lady Macbeth, which is lit in high contrast and is surrounded by darkness. We then scan the brightly lit "empty" space between her and her husband. The third area of interest is Macbeth's thoughtful face, which is lit in a more subdued manner. The visual interest of this photo corresponds to the dramatic context of the film, for Lady Macbeth is slowly descending into madness and feels spiritually alienated and isolated from her husband. *(Columbia Pictures)*

4-10b. *Macbeth* (U.S.A., 1948), with Peggy Webber, directed by Orson Welles. Realists and formalists solve problems in different ways, with different visual techniques. Polanski's presentation of Lady Macbeth's madness is conveyed in a relatively realistic manner, with emphasis on acting and subtle lighting effects. Welles took a more formalistic approach, using physical correlatives to convey interior states, such as the iron fence's knifelike blades, which almost seem to pierce Webber's body. The fence is not particularly realistic or even functional: Welles exploited it primarily as a symbolic analogue of her inner torment. *(Republic Pictures)*

The human eye automatically attempts to harmonize the formal elements of a composition into a unified whole. The eye can detect as many as seven or eight major elements of a composition simultaneously. In most cases, however, the eye does not wander promiscuously over the surface of an image but is guided to specific areas in sequence. The director accomplishes this through the use of a **dominant contrast**, also known as the **dominant**. The dominant is that area of an image that immediately attracts our attention because of a conspicuous and compelling contrast. It stands out in some kind of isolation from the other elements within the image. In black-and-white movies, the dominant contrast is generally achieved through a juxtaposition of lights and darks. For example, if the director wants the viewer to look first at an actor's hand rather than his face, the lighting of the hand would be harsher than that of the face, which would be lit in a more subdued manner. In colour films, the dominant is often achieved by having one colour stand out from the others.

After we take in the dominant, our eye then scans the **subsidiary contrasts** that the artist has arranged to act as counterbalancing devices. Our eyes are seldom at rest with visual compositions, even with paintings or still photographs. We look somewhere first, then we look at those areas of diminishing interest. None of this is accidental; visual artists deliberately structure their images so that a specific sequence is followed. In short, movement in film is not confined only to objects and people that are literally in motion.

In most cases, the visual interest of the dominant corresponds with the dramatic interest of the image. Because films have temporal and dramatic contexts, however, the dominant is often movement itself, and what some aestheticians call **intrinsic interest**. Intrinsic interest simply means that the audience, through the context of a story, knows that an object is more important dramatically than it appears to be visually. Thus, even though a gun might occupy only a small portion of the surface of an

4-11. *Caffé Italia Montréal* (Canada, 1985), directed by Paul Tana.

This film combines documentary and theatrical conventions to tell the story of Italians in Quebec. In this shot, Italian workers, during the early years of immigration, angrily gather outside the window of the café while their "godfather" holds court inside, taking bribes to secure them jobs on the Canadian Pacific Railroad. The camera is on the inside with the bosses, and the crown in the window that partly obscures our view of the workers underlines the archaic power relations that lead to their exclusion and frustration. *(ACPAV)*

image, if we know that the gun is *dramatically* important, it will assume dominance in the picture despite its visual insignificance.

Movement is usually an automatic dominant contrast, if the other elements in the image are stationary. For this reason, some filmmakers rely solely on movement as a means of capturing the viewer's attention. However, most directors will vary their dominants, sometimes emphasizing motion, other times using movement as a subsidiary contrast only. The importance of motion varies with the kind of shot used. Movement tends to be less distracting in the longer shots and highly conspicuous in the closer ranges.

Unless the viewer has time to explore the surface of an image at leisure, visual confusion can result when there are more than eight or nine major compositional elements. If visual confusion is the deliberate intention of an image—as in a battle scene, for example—the director will sometimes overload the composition to produce this effect. In general, the eye struggles to unify various elements into an ordered pattern. For example, even in a complex design, the eye will connect similar shapes, colours, textures, and so on. The very repetition of a formal element can suggest the repetition of an experience. These connections form a visual rhythm,

4-12. *Deux actrices* [*Two Can Play*] (Canada, 1993), with Pascale Bussières (left) and Pascale Paroissien, directed by Micheline Lanctôt.

Often the context of a scene does not permit a director to express emotions dramatically. In this film, Solange (Bussières) finds her life turned upside down by the arrival of Fabienne (Paroissien), a sister she never knew she had. Their story is punctuated by sequences in which the actresses discuss their roles with the director (played by Lanctôt herself). It is often unclear whether the actresses are talking about themselves or the characters they play. Here the two sisters peer through the wire fence of a school after Fabienne has belatedly revealed that she has a daughter. Their inward agitation is conveyed by the diagonal lines of the fence, which separates them from the children but also implies their entrapment in their fraught relationship. *(Stopfilm Inc./Antoine Saito)*

4-13. *Le Déclin de l'empire américain* [*The Decline of the American Empire*] (Canada, 1986), with (clockwise from upper left) Louise Portal, Dominique Michel, Dorothée Berryman, and Geneviève Rioux, directed by Denys Arcand.

A group of women work out, talk, and laugh in a health club while the men in their lives prepare a gourmet meal in a lakeside cottage. The circular design in this shot reinforces the air of camaraderie among the women. The shot's design embodies their shared experiences and interconnectedness: literally, a relaxed circle of friends. *(Cineplex Odeon Films)*

forcing the eye to leap over the surface of the design to perceive the overall balance. Visual artists often refer to compositional elements as *weights*. In most cases, especially in classical cinema, the artist distributes these weights harmoniously over the surface of the image. In a totally symmetrical design—almost never found in fiction movies—the visual weights are distributed evenly, with the centre of the composition as the axis point. Because most compositions are asymmetrical, however, the weight of one element is counterpoised with another. A shape, for example, counteracts the weight of a colour. Psychologists and art theorists have discovered that certain portions of a composition are intrinsically weighted. The Swiss art historian Heinrich Wölfflin, for instance, pointed out that we tend to scan pictures from left to right, all other compositional elements being equal. Spectators from non-Western cultures read images differently, but, in classical compositions, the image is often more heavily weighted on the left to counteract the intrinsic heaviness of the right.

The upper part of the composition is heavier than the lower. For this reason, skyscrapers, columns, and obelisks taper upward or they would appear top-heavy. Images seem more balanced when the centre of gravity is kept low, with most of the weights in the lower portions of the screen. A landscape is seldom divided horizontally at the midpoint of a composition, or the sky would appear to oppress the earth. Epic filmmakers like Eisenstein and Ford create some of their most disquieting effects with precisely this technique: They let the sky dominate through its intrinsic heaviness. The terrain and its inhabitants seem overwhelmed from above **(3-3)**.

Isolated figures and objects tend to be heavier than those in a cluster. Sometimes one object—merely by virtue of its isolation—can balance a whole group of otherwise equal objects. In many movies, the protagonist is shown apart from a hostile group, yet the two seem evenly matched despite the arithmetical differences. This effect is conveyed through the visual weight of the hero in isolation **(5-10)**.

Psychological experiments have revealed that certain lines suggest directional movements. Although vertical and horizontal lines seem to be visually at rest, if movement is perceived, horizontal lines tend to move from left to right, vertical lines, from bottom to top. Diagonal or oblique lines are more dynamic—that is, in transition. They tend to sweep upward. These psychological phenomena are important to the visual artist, especially the filmmaker, for the dramatic context is not always conducive to an overt expression of emotion **(4-12)**. For example, if a director wants to show a character's inward agitation within a calm context, this quality can be conveyed through the dynamic use of line: An image comprising tense diagonals can

4-14. *Jules et Jim* (France, 1961), with Henri Serre, Jeanne Moreau, and Oskar Werner, directed by François Truffaut.

Compositions grouped into units of three, five, and seven tend to suggest dynamic, unstable relationships. Those organized in units of two, four, or six, on the other hand, tend to imply fixed, harmonious relationships. This triangular composition is organically related to the theme of the movie, which deals with the shifting love relationships between the three characters. The woman is almost invariably at the apex of the triangle: She likes it that way. *(Janus Films)*

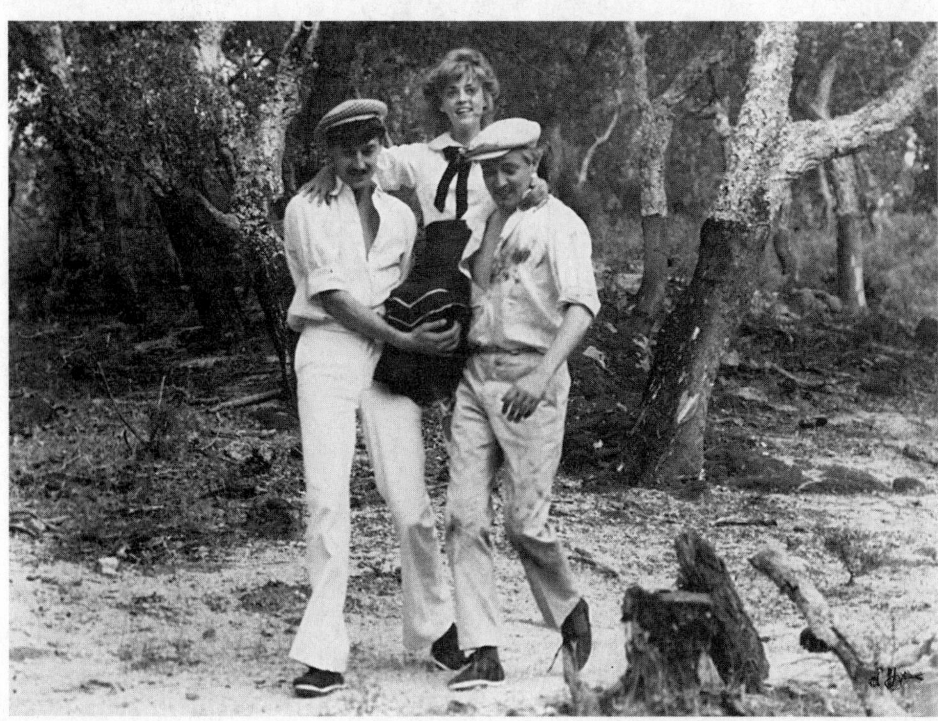

suggest the character's inner turmoil, despite the apparent lack of drama in the action. Some of the most expressive cinematic effects can be achieved precisely through this tension between the compositional elements of an image and its dramatic context.

A skeletal structure underlies most visual compositions. Throughout the ages, artists have especially favoured S and X shapes, triangular designs, and circles. These designs are often used simply because they are thought to be inherently beautiful. Visual artists also use certain compositional forms to emphasize symbolic concepts. For example, binary structures emphasize parallelism—virtually any **two shot** will suggest a couple, doubles, shared space **(4-29)**. Triadic compositions stress the dynamic interplay among three main elements **(4-24b)**. Circular compositions can suggest security, enclosure, the female principle **(4-13)**.

Design is generally fused with a thematic idea, at least in the best movies. In *Jules et Jim*, for example, Truffaut consistently used triangular designs, for the film

4-15. *Greed* (U.S.A., 1924), with Gibson Gowland and Jean Hersholt (right), directed by Erich von Stroheim.

Highly symmetrical designs are generally used when a director wishes to stress stability and harmony. In this photo, for example, the carefully balanced weights of the design reinforce these (temporary) qualities. The visual elements are neatly juxtaposed in units of twos, with the two beer-filled glasses forming the focal point. The main figures balance each other, as do the two converging brick walls, the two pairs of curtains, the two windows, the two people in each window, the shape of the picture above the men, and the shape of the resting dog below them. *(MGM)*

deals with a trio of characters whose relationships are constantly shifting yet always interrelated. The form of the images in this case is a symbolic representation of the romantic triangle of the dramatic content. These triangular designs dynamize the visuals, keeping them off balance, subject to change **(4-14)**. Generally, designs consisting of units of three, five, and seven tend to produce these effects. Designs comprising two, four, or six units seem more stable and balanced **(4-15)**.

SETTINGS

The visual impact of a movie depends on the director's organization of the mise en scène, but the framing of the film's visual materials is also deeply affected by the choice of setting. Settings are not merely backdrops for the action but symbolic extensions of the theme and characterization. They can convey an immense amount of information, whether they are specially constructed in a studio or filmed on location.

Epic films would be virtually impossible without the extreme long shots of vast expanses of land. Other genres, particularly those requiring a degree of stylization or deliberate unreality, have been associated with the studio: musicals, horror films, and

4-16. *October* (Russia 1928), directed by Sergei Eisenstein.
Eisenstein is best known for his approach to editing (see Chapter 6, "Editing") in which contrasting shots collide with each other to create an active response from the spectator. But he also applied the "montage" principle within individual shots, as in this image from his epic celebration of the Russian Revolution. The marked contrasts within the shot—between light and dark, high and low, foreground and background—enforce the idea of Lenin as the driving force of the revolution. *(Sovkino)*

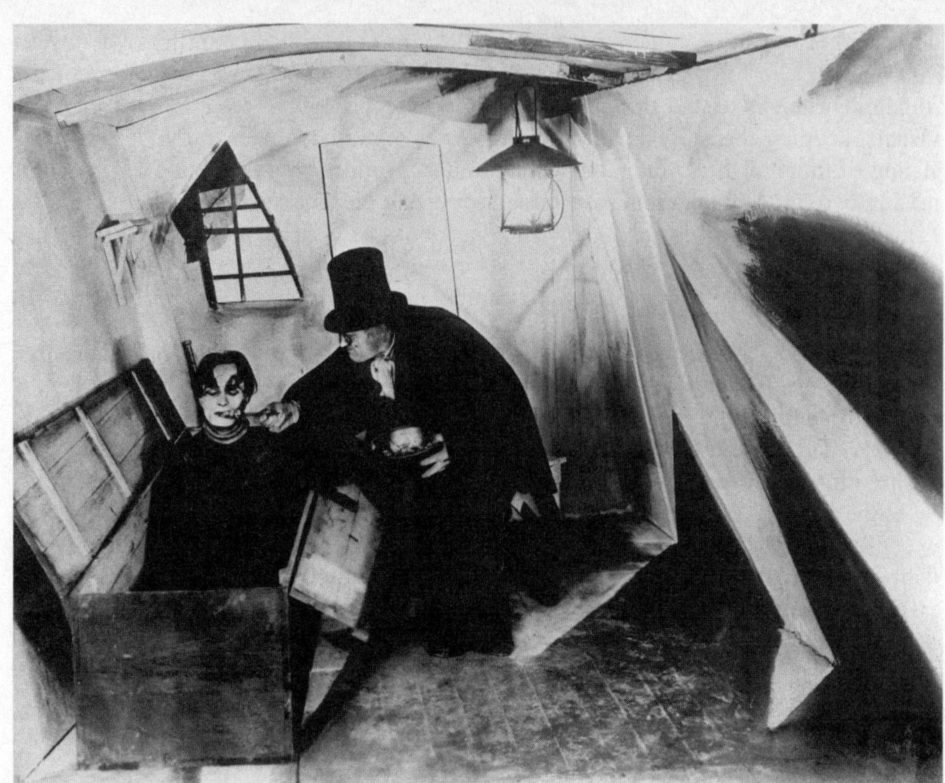

4-17. *The Cabinet of Dr. Caligari* (Germany, 1919), with Conrad Veidt and Werner Krauss (wearing hat), production design by Hermann Warm, Walter Röhrig, and Walter Reimann, directed by Robert Wiene. The German expressionist movement of the post–World War I era emphasized visual design above all. The movement's main contributions were in the live theatre, the graphic arts, and the cinema. The great stage director Max Reinhardt was a seminal influence. In his theory of design, Reinhardt advocated an ideal of "landscapes imbued with soul." The declared aim of most German expressionists was to eliminate nature for a state of absolute abstraction. It is a style steeped in anxiety and terror. The sets are deliberately artificial: flat, obviously painted, with no attempt to preserve the conventions of perspective and scale. They are meant to represent a state of mind, not a place. *(Museum of Modern Art)*

many period films. Such genres often stress a kind of magical, sealed-off universe, and images taken from real life tend to clash with these essentially claustrophobic qualities.

However, these are merely generalizations. Some westerns have been shot mostly indoors and some musicals have been photographed in actual locations. If a location is extravagantly beautiful, there is no reason why a romantic musical cannot exploit such a setting. The Paris locations of Vincente Minnelli's *Gigi* **(8-28a)** are a good example of how actual locations can enhance a stylized genre.

In set design, as in other aspects of movies, the terms *realism* and *formalism* are simply convenient critical labels. Most sets tend toward one style or the other, but few are pure examples. For instance, in *The Birth of a Nation* (1915), Griffith proudly proclaims that a number of his scenes are historical facsimiles of real places and events—like Ford's Theatre where Lincoln was assassinated, or the signing of the Emancipation Proclamation. These scenes are modelled on actual photographs of the period. Yet Griffith's facsimiles are created in a studio. Conversely, real locations can be exploited to create a somewhat artificial—formalistic—effect. For example, in shooting *October*, Eisenstein had the Winter Palace at his disposal for several months. Yet, the images in the movie are baroque: richly textured and formally complex. Although Eisenstein chose actual locations for their authenticity, they are never just picturesque backgrounds to the action. Each shot is carefully designed. Each exploits the inherent *form* of the setting, contributing significantly to the aesthetic impact of the sequence **(4-16)**.

Spectacle films usually require the most elaborate sets. One of the earliest films to use sets of this type was Griffith's *Intolerance.* The banquet scene for Belshazzar's feast alone cost a reputed $250 000 and employed more than four thousand extras. The story required the construction of a walled city so vast that for years it remained a standing monument—called "Griffith's Folly" by cynics in the trade. The set extended more than a kilometre in length. The court was flanked by enormous colonnades supporting pillars fifteen metres high, each holding up a huge statue of an erect elephant-god. The outer walls of the city were sixty metres high, yet were wide enough that two chariots were able to roar past each other on the road that perched on top.

Historical spectacle became a staple of Hollywood cinema, often as an excuse for sexual displays that would have been frowned on in more modern settings. Two opulent versions of *Cleopatra* (Cecil B. De Mille, 1934, with Claudette Colbert, and Joseph L. Mankiewicz, 1963, with Elizabeth Taylor) were notorious for their excess and extravagance, while the thrilling chariot races in the two versions of *Ben Hur* (Fred Niblo, 1925, with Ramon Navarro, and William Wyler, 1959, with Charlton Heston) provided more action-packed spectacle. More modern examples include blockbusters such as *Gladiator* (Ridley Scott, 2000) and *Alexander* (Oliver Stone, 2004), with the spectacular sets now enhanced by digital special effects.

Expressionistic sets are usually created in the studio, where the contaminations of reality cannot penetrate **(4-17)**. They appeal to our sense of the marvellous. For example, Federico Fellini's *Amarcord* is a stylized reminiscence of the director's youth in his hometown of Rimini. (The title, from the Romagnan dialect, means "I remember.") But Fellini shot the movie in a studio, not on location. He wanted to capture feelings, not facts. Throughout the film, the townspeople feel stifled by the provincial isolation of their community. They are filled with loneliness and long for something extraordinary to transform their lives. When they hear that a mammoth luxury liner, the *Rex*, will pass through the ocean waters not far beyond the town's shore, many of these wistful souls decide to row out to sea to greet the ship. Hundreds of them crowd into every available boat and stream away from the beach like fervent pilgrims on a quest. Then they wait. Evening settles, bringing with it a thick fog. Still they wait. In one boat Gradisca, the charming town sexpot, confides her dissatisfaction with her life to some sympathetic friends. At thirty she is still single, childless, and unfulfilled. Her "heart overflows with love," yet she has never found a "truly dedicated man." In the dark silence, she weeps softly over the prospect of a barren future. Midnight passes, and still the townspeople wait faithfully. Then, when most of the characters are sleeping in their fragile boats, they are awakened by a boy's shout: "It's here!" Like a graceful apparition, the light-bedecked *Rex* glides past in all its regal grandeur **(4-18)**. Nino Rota's rapturous music swells to a cres-

4-18. ***Amarcord*** **(Italy, 1974), art direction and costumes by Danilo Donati, cinematography by Giuseppe Rotunno, directed by Federico Fellini.**

For Fellini, who began his career as a realist, the studio became a place to create magic—along with his fellow magicians Donati and Rotunno. "To me and other directors like me," Fellini said, "cinema is a way of interpreting and remaking reality through fantasy and imagination. The use of the studio is an indispensable part of what we are doing." *(New World Pictures)*

cendo as the townspeople wave and shout joyously. Gradisca's eyes stream with tears of exhilaration and yearning while a blind accordionist says excitedly, "Tell me what it looks like!" Then, as mysteriously as it appeared, the phantom ship is swallowed by the fog and slips silently off into the night.

During the golden age of the Hollywood studio system, each of the **majors** had a characteristic visual style, determined in large part by the designers at each studio. Some were called production designers, others **art directors**, a few simply set designers. Their job was to determine the "look" of each film, and they worked closely with producers and directors to ensure that the sets, décor, costumes, and photographic style were coordinated to produce a unified effect. For example, MGM specialized in glamour, luxury, and opulent **production values**, and its art director, Cedric Gibbons, virtually stamped each film with "the Metro look" **(8-16)**. Because all the studios attempted to diversify their products as much as possible, however, their art directors had to be versatile. For instance, RKO's Van Nest Polglase supervised the design of such diverse movies as *King Kong* (Merian C. Cooper and Ernest Schoedsack, 1933), *Top Hat* (Mark Sandrich, 1935), *The Informer* (John Ford, 1935), and *Citizen Kane* (Orson Welles, 1941). Paramount's Hans Dreier began his

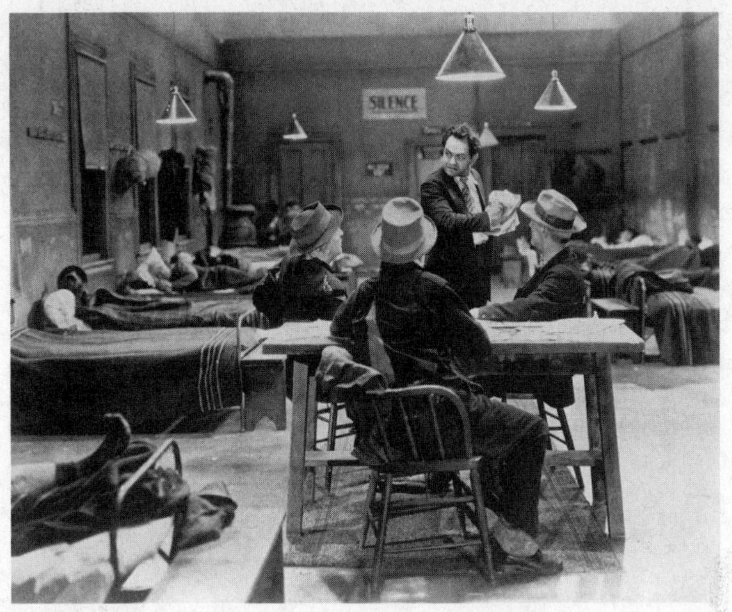

4-19. *Little Caesar* (U.S.A., 1930), with Edward G. Robinson (standing), art direction by Anton Grot, directed by Mervyn LeRoy.

Grot was art director at Warner Brothers from 1927 to 1948. Unlike his counterparts Gibbons, Dreier, and Polglase, however, Grot often took an active hand in designing the studio's major films. His earliest work is somewhat in the German expressionist tradition, but he soon became one of the most versatile of artists. He designed films like the gritty and realistic *Little Caesar*, as well as the Busby Berkeley musical *Gold Diggers of 1933*, with its surrealistic, dreamlike sets. *(Warner Brothers)*

career at Germany's famous UFA studio. He was usually at his best creating a sense of mystery and romantic fantasy, as in the films of Josef von Sternberg. Dreier also designed the superb art deco sets for Ernst Lubitsch's *Trouble in Paradise* (1932). Warner Brothers' art director, Anton Grot, was a specialist in grubby, realistic locales **(4-19)**. The studio claimed that its films were "Torn from Today's Headlines!" to quote from its publicity blurbs. Warner Brothers favoured topical genres with an emphasis on working-class life: gangster films, urban melodramas, and proletarian musicals. Like his counterparts at other studios, however, Grot could work in a variety of styles and genres. For example, he designed the enchanting sets for the 1935 adaptation of Shakespeare's *A Midsummer Night's Dream* (Max Reinhardt and William Dieterle).

Certain types of locales were in such constant demand that the studios constructed permanent **back-lot** sets, which were used in film after film: a turn-of-the-twentieth-century street, a European square, an urban slum, and so on. Of course these were suitably altered with new furnishings to make them look different each time they were used. The studio with the largest number of back lots was MGM, although Warner, Paramount, and Twentieth Century Fox also boasted a considerable number of them. Not all standing sets were located close to the studio. It was cheaper to construct some outside the environs of Los Angeles, where real estate values were

4-20. ***How Green Was My Valley*** **(U.S.A., 1941), art direction by Nathan Juran and Richard Day, directed by John Ford.**

The art directors at Twentieth Century Fox specialized in realistic sets, like this turn-of-the-century Welsh mining village, which covered thirty-five hectares and was built in a California valley. Elaborate sets like these were not dismantled after production, for with suitable alterations they could be converted into other locations. For example, two years after Ford's film, this set was transformed into a Nazi-occupied Norwegian village for *The Moon Is Down* (Irving Pichel). *(Twentieth Century Fox)*

at a premium. If a movie called for a huge realistic set—like the Welsh mining village for *How Green Was My Valley*—it was often built far from the studio **(4-20)**. Similarly, most of the studios owned western frontier towns, ranches, and midwestern-type farms, which were located outside Los Angeles.

What matters most in a setting is how it embodies the essence of the story materials and the artistic vision of the filmmaker. As the French designer Robert Mallet-Stevens noted, "A film set, in order to be a good set, must act. Whether realistic or expressionistic, modern or ancient, it must play its part. The set must present the character before he has even appeared. It must indicate his social position, his tastes, his habits, his lifestyle, his personality. The sets must be intimately linked with the action."

Settings can also be used to suggest a sense of progression in the characters. For example, in Fellini's *La Strada* (1954), one of his most realistic movies, the protagonist and his simple-minded assistant are shown as reasonably happy, travelling together from town to town with their tacky theatrical act. After he

4-21. *Blade Runner* (U.S.A., 1982), with Harrison Ford, directed by Ridley Scott.

A hybrid of science fiction, *film noir*, detective thriller, bounty-hunter western, and love story, *Blade Runner* is also eclectic in its visual style, a collaborative effort that includes the contributions of art director David Snyder, production designer Lawrence G. Paul, special visual effects designer Douglas Trumbull, and cinematographer Jordan Cronenweth. The story is set in Los Angeles in the year 2019. Nature has gone berserk, deluging the teeming city with an almost constant downpour. Smoke, fog, and steam add to the fumigated congestion. It is a city of dreadful night, punctuated by neon signs in Day-Glo colours, cheap Orientalized billboards, and a profusion of advertising come-ons. Hunks of long-discarded machinery litter the landscape. The sound track throbs with eerie sounds, echoes, pounding pistons, and the noises of flying vehicles shuttling through the poisonous atmosphere. It is a city choking on its own technology.
(Warner Bros.)

abandons her, he heads for the mountains. Gradually, the landscape changes: Trees are stripped of their foliage, snow and dirty slush cover the ground, the sky is a murky grey. The changing setting is a gauge of the protagonist's spiritual condition: Nature itself seems to grieve after the helpless assistant is left alone to die.

A film can fragment a set into a series of shots, now emphasizing one aspect of a room, later another, depending on the needs of the director in finding appropriate visual analogues for thematic and psychological ideas. In Joseph Losey's *The Servant*, a stairway is used as a major thematic symbol. The film deals with a servant's gradual control over his master **(11-7)**. Losey uses the stairway as a kind of psychological battlefield where the relative positions of the two men on the stairs give the audience a sense of who is winning the battle. Losey also uses the rails on the stairway to suggest prison bars: The master of the house is often photographed from behind these bars.

Even the furniture of a room can be exploited for psychological and thematic reasons. In one of his classes, Eisenstein once discussed at length the significance of a table for a set. The class exercise centred on an adaptation of Honoré de Balzac's novel *Le Père Goriot*. The scene is set at a dinner table that Balzac described as circular. But Eisenstein convincingly argued that a round table is wrong cinematically, for it implies equality, with each person linked in a circle. To convey the stratified class structure of the boarding house, Eisenstein suggested the use of a long rectangular table, with the haughty mistress of the house at the head, the favoured tenants close to her sides, and the lowly Goriot alone near the base of the table.

Such attention to detail often distinguishes a master of film from a mere technician, who settles for only a general effect. The setting of a movie can even take over as the central interest **(4-21)**. In *2001: A Space Odyssey*, Stanley Kubrick spends most of his time lovingly photographing the instruments of a spaceship, various space stations, and the enormous expanses of outer space itself **(4-4)**. The few people in the movie seem almost incidental and certainly far less interesting than the real centre of concern—the setting.

A systematic analysis of a set involves a consideration of the following eight characteristics:

1. *Exterior or interior.* If the set is an exterior, how does nature function as a symbolic analogue to the mood, theme, or characterization?
2. *Style.* Is the set realistic and lifelike, or is it stylized and deliberately distorted? Is it in a particular style, such as colonial American, art deco, or sleek contemporary?
3. *Studio or location.* If the set is an actual location, why was it chosen? What does it say about the characters?
4. *Period.* What era does the set represent?
5. *Class.* What is the apparent income level of the owners?
6. *Size.* How large is the set? Rich people tend to take up more space than the poor, who are usually crowded in their living area.
7. *Decoration.* How is the set furnished? Are there any status symbols, oddities of taste, and so forth?
8. *Symbolic function.* What kind of overall image does the set and its furnishings project?

TERRITORIAL SPACE

Since most movie images deal with the illusion of volume and depth, the film director must keep these considerations in mind while creating the visuals. It is one thing to construct a pleasing arrangement of shapes, lines, colours, and textures; but movie images, in feature films at least, must also tell a story in time, a story that generally involves human beings and their problems. Unlike notes of music, then, forms in film are not usually pure—they refer specifically to objects in reality.

Directors generally emphasize volume in their images precisely because they want to avoid an abstract, flat look in their compositions. In most cases, filmmakers compose on three visual planes: the midground, the foreground, and the background. Not only does this technique suggest a sense of depth, but it can also radically alter the dominant contrast of an image, serving as a kind of qualifying characteristic,

4-22. *A History of Violence* (U.S.A., 2005), with Ashton Holmes and Viggo Mortensen, directed by David Cronenberg.

A teenage son confronts his father—a man he admires, respects, and loves—because the father has been lying to his family and community, pretending to be someone he is not. The confrontation is territorial as well as vocal, for the youth invades his father's personal space, challenging his dad to tell him the truth about his past. *(New Line Cinema)*

either subtle or conspicuous. For example, a figure is often placed in the midground of a composition. Whatever is placed in the foreground will comment on the figure in some way (see **4-12**). Some foliage, for instance, is likely to suggest a naturalness and blending with the environment. A gauzy curtain in the foreground can suggest mystery, eroticism, and femininity. The cross-hatching of a window frame can suggest self-division. And so on, with as many foreground qualifiers as the director and cinematographer can think of. These same principles apply to backgrounds, although objects placed in these areas tend to yield in dominance to midground and foreground ranges **(4-24b).**

One of the most elementary, yet crucial, decisions the film director makes is what shot to use vis-à-vis the materials photographed. That is, how much detail should be included within the frame? How close should the camera get to the subject? Which is another way of asking how close *we* should get to the subject, since the viewer's eye tends to identify with the camera's lens. These are not minor problems; the amount of space included within the frame can radically affect our response to the photographed materials. With any given subject, the filmmaker can use a variety of shots, each of which includes or excludes a given amount of surrounding space. But how much space is just right in a shot? What is too much or too little?

4-23a. *The Blue Angel* (Germany, 1930), with Marlene Dietrich (left foreground), directed by Josef von Sternberg. *(Janus Films)*

Density of texture refers to the amount of visual detail in a picture. How much information does the filmmaker pack into the image and why? Most movies are moderately textured, depending on the amount of light thrown on the subject matter. Some images are stark, whereas others are densely textured. The degree of density is often a symbolic analogue of the quality of life in the world of the film. The cheap cabaret setting of *The Blue Angel* is chaotic and packed, swirling in smoke and cluttered with tawdry ornaments. The atmosphere seems almost suffocating. The stark futuristic world of *THX 1138* is sterile and empty.

4-23b. *THX 1138* (U.S.A., 1971), with Robert Duvall and Donald Pleasence, directed by George Lucas. *(Warner Bros.)*

Space is a medium of communication, and the way we respond to objects and people within a given area is a constant source of information in life as well as movies. In virtually any social situation, we receive and give signals relating to our use of space and those people who share it. Most of us are not particularly conscious of this medium, but we instinctively become alerted whenever we feel that certain social conventions about space are being violated. For example, when people enter a movie theatre, they tend to seat themselves at appropriate intervals from each other. But what is appropriate? And who or what defines it? Why do we feel threatened when someone takes a seat next to us in a nearly empty theatre? After all, the seat is not ours, and the other person has paid for the privilege of sitting wherever he or she wants. Is it paranoid to feel anxiety in such a situation, or is it a normal instinctive response?

Several psychologists and anthropologists—including Konrad Lorenz, Robert Sommer, and Edward T. Hall—have explored these and related questions. Their findings are especially revealing in terms of how space is used in cinema. In his study *On Aggression*, for example, Lorenz discusses how most animals—including humans—are territorial. That is, they lay claim to a given area and defend it from outsiders. This territory is a kind of personal haven of safety and is regarded by the organism as an extension of itself. When living creatures are too tightly packed into a given space, the result can be stress, tension, and anxiety. In many cases, when this territorial imperative is violated, the intrusion can provoke aggressive and violent behaviour, and sometimes a battle for dominance ensues over control of the territory.

Territories also have a spatial hierarchy of power. That is, the most dominant organism of a community is literally given more space, whereas the less dominant are crowded together. The amount of space an organism occupies is generally proportional to the degree of control it enjoys within a given territory. These spatial principles can be seen in many human communities as well. A classroom, for example, is usually divided into a teaching area and a student seating area, but the proportion of space allotted to the authority figure is greater than that allotted to each of those being instructed. The spatial structure of virtually any kind of territory used by humans betrays a discernible concept of authority. No matter how egalitarian we like to think we are, most of us conform to these spatial conventions. When a distinguished person enters a crowded room, for example, most people instinctively make room for him or her. In fact, they are giving that person far more room than they themselves occupy.

But what has all this got to do with movies? A great deal, for space is one of the principal means of communication in film. The way that people are arranged in space can tell us a lot about their social and psychological relationships. In film, dominant characters are usually given more space to occupy than others—unless the film deals with the loss of power or the social insignificance of a character. The amount of space taken up by a character in a movie does not necessarily relate to that person's actual social dominance but rather it relates to his or her dramatic importance. Authoritarian figures like kings generally occupy a larger amount of space than peasants; but if a film is primarily about peasants, they will dominate spatially. In short, dominance is defined contextually in film, not necessarily the way it is perceived in real life.

4-24a. ***La Grande illusion*** **[*Grand Illusion*] (France, 1937), with (centre to right) Erich von Stroheim, Pierre Fresnay, and Jean Gabin, directed by Jean Renoir.**

Tight and loose framing derive their symbolic significance from the dramatic context: They are not intrinsically meaningful. In Renoir's film set in a German prison camp during World War I, for example, the tight frame, in effect, becomes a symbolic prison, a useful technique in films that deal with entrapment, confinement, or literal imprisonment. *(Janus Films)*

4-24b. ***Igby Goes Down*** **(U.S.A., 2002), with Ryan Phillippe, Susan Sarandon, and Jeff Goldblum, written and directed by Burr Steers.**

There is not much love lost between an alienated son (Phillippe) and his mother's boyfriend (Goldblum). The seating arrangement is revealing. The triangular composition is weighted with the mother and her boyfriend sharing the same territory. The son is isolated on the left, an afterthought. *(United Artists)*

4-25. ***Sons of the Desert*** **(U.S.A., 1933), with Stan Laurel and Oliver Hardy, directed by William Seiter.**

Whenever Stan does something really dumb, which usually results in a loss of dignity for his partner, Ollie turns to the camera—to us—trying to restrain his exasperation, appealing to our sympathy as fellow superior beings. Only we can truly appreciate the profound depths of his patience. The dim-witted Stanley, totally puzzled as usual, is standing in a quarter-turn position, absorbed by other matters entirely, wondering how he will defend himself against Ollie's inevitable another-fine-mess accusation. *(MGM)*

The movie frame is also a kind of territory, though a temporary one, existing only for the duration of the shot. The way space is shared within the frame is one of the major tools of the director, who can define, adjust, and redefine human relationships by exploiting spatial conventions. Furthermore, once a relationship has been established, the director can go on to other matters simply by changing the camera **setup**. The mise en scène can express shifting psychological and social nuances with a single shot—by exploiting the space between characters, the depth planes within the images, the intrinsically weighted areas of the frame, and the direction the characters are facing.

An actor can be photographed in any of five basic positions, each conveying different psychological undertones: (1) full front—facing the camera; (2) the quarter turn; (3) profile—looking off frame left or right; (4) the three-quarter turn; and (5) back to camera. Because the viewer identifies with the camera's point of view, the positioning of the actor vis-à-vis the camera will determine many of our reactions. The more we see of the actor's face, the greater our sense of privileged intimacy; the less we see, the more mysterious and inaccessible the character will seem.

The full-front position is the most intimate—the character is looking in our direction, inviting our complicity. In most cases, of course, actors ignore the camera—ignore us—yet our privileged position allows us to observe them when their defences are down, their vulnerabilities exposed. On those rare occasions when a character acknowledges our presence by addressing the camera, the sense of intimacy is vastly increased, for in effect we agree to become his or her chosen confidants. One of the greatest masters of this technique was Oliver Hardy, whose famous slow burn was a direct plea for sympathy and understanding **(4-25)**.

The quarter turn is the favoured position of most filmmakers, as it provides a high degree of intimacy but with less emotional involvement than the full-front position. The profile position is more remote. The character seems unaware of being

4-26. *Sahara* (U.S.A., 2005), with Penélope Cruz and Matthew McConaughey, directed by Breck Eisner.
The profile position catches characters unaware as they look off frame left or right. We are allowed unimpeded freedom to stare, to analyze. Less intimate than the full-front or quarter-turn position, the profile view is also less emotionally involving. We view the characters from a detached, neutral perspective. *(Paramount Pictures)*

observed, lost in his or her own thoughts **(4-26)**. The three-quarter turn is more anonymous. This position is useful for conveying a character's unfriendly or antisocial feelings, since in effect the character is partially turning his or her back on us, rejecting our interest **(4-27)**. When a character has his or her back to the camera, we can only guess what is taking place internally. This position is often used to suggest a character's alienation from the world. It is useful in conveying a sense of concealment, mystery. We want to see more **(4-28)**.

The amount of open space within the territory of the frame can be exploited for symbolic purposes. Generally, the closer the shot, the more confined the photographed figures appear to be. Such shots are usually said to have **tight framing**. Conversely, the longer shots with **loose framing** tend to suggest freedom. Prison films often use tightly framed close-ups and medium shots because the frame functions as a kind of symbolic prison. In *Un Condamné à mort s'est échappé* [*A Condemned Man Escapes*] (1956), for example, Robert Bresson begins the movie with a close-up of the hero's hands, which are bound by a pair of handcuffs. Throughout the film, the prisoner makes elaborate preparations to escape, and Bresson preserves the tight framing to emphasize the sense of claustrophobia that the hero finds unendurable. This spatial tension is not released until the end of the movie when the protagonist disappears into the freedom of the darkness outside the prison walls. His triumphant escape is photographed in a loosely framed long shot—the only one in the film—which also symbolizes his sense of spiritual release. Framing and spatial metaphors of this kind are common in films dealing with the theme of confinement—either literal, as in *La Grande illusion* **(4-24a)**, or psychological, as in *Red Desert* **(4-28)**.

Often a director can suggest ideas of entrapment by exploiting perfectly neutral objects and lines on the set. In such cases, the formal characteristics of these literal

4-27. ***All or Nothing*** **(Britain, 2002), with Timothy Spall (extreme right) in three-quarter-turn position), directed by Mike Leigh.**

The three-quarter-turn position is a virtual rejection of the camera, a refusal to cooperate with our desire to see more. This type of staging tends to make us feel like voyeurs prying into the private lives of the characters. In this family dinner scene, the actors's body language and Leigh's mise en scène embody a sense of profound alienation. Each character seems to be imprisoned in his or her own space cubicle: They look buried alive. *(United Artists)*

objects tend to close in on a figure, at least when viewed on the flat screen. Michelangelo Antonioni is a master of this technique. In *Red Desert*, for example, the heroine (Monica Vitti) describes a mental breakdown suffered by a friend she once knew. The audience suspects she is speaking of her own breakdown, however, for the surface of the image implies constriction: While she talks, she is riveted to one position, her figure framed by the lines of a doorway behind her, suggesting a coffin-like enclosure. When figures are framed within a frame in this manner, a sense of confinement is usually emphasized.

Territorial space within a frame can be manipulated with considerable psychological complexity. When a figure leaves the frame, for example, the camera can adjust to this sudden vacuum in the composition by **panning** slightly to make allowances for a new balance of weights. Or the camera can remain stationary, thus suggesting a sense of loss symbolized by the empty space that the character formerly occupied. Hostility and suspicion between two characters can be conveyed by keeping them at the edges of the composition, with a maximum of space between them **(4-29d)**, or by having an intrusive character force his or her physical presence into the other character's territory, which is temporarily defined by the confines of the frame.

4-28. *Red Desert* (Italy, 1964), with Carlo Chionetti, Monica Vitti, and Richard Harris (back to camera), directed by Michelangelo Antonioni.

When characters turn their backs to the camera, they seem to reject us outright or to be totally unaware of our existence. We long to see and analyze their facial expressions, but we are not permitted this privilege. The character remains an enigma. Antonioni is one of the masters of mise en scène, expressing complex interrelationships with a minimum of dialogue. The protagonist in this film (Vitti) is just recovering from an emotional breakdown. She is still anxious and fearful, even of her husband (Chionetti). In this shot she seems trapped, like a wounded and exhausted animal, between her husband and his business associate. Note how the violent splashes of red paint on the walls suggest a haemorrhaging effect. *(Rizzoli Film)*

PROXEMIC PATTERNS

Spatial conventions vary from culture to culture, as anthropologist Edward T. Hall has demonstrated in such studies as *The Hidden Dimension* and *The Silent Language*. Hall discovered that **proxemic patterns**—the relationships of organisms within a given space—can be influenced by external considerations. Noise, danger, and lack of light tend to make people move closer together. Climate is another factor that affects spatial relations: People in northern countries tend to use more space than those in warmer climates. Taking these cultural and contextual considerations into account, Hall subdivides the way people use space into four major proxemic patterns: (1) intimate, (2) personal, (3) social, and (4) public distances.

Intimate distances range from skin contact to about half a metre away. This is the distance of physical involvement—of love, comfort, and tenderness between individuals. With strangers, such distances would be regarded as intrusive—most people would react with suspicion and hostility if someone they did not know very well invaded their space. In many cultures, maintaining an intimate distance in public is considered bad taste.

Personal distances range roughly from half a metre to about a metre away. Individuals can touch if necessary, since they are literally an arm's length apart. These distances tend to be reserved for friends and acquaintances rather than for lovers or members of a family. Personal distances preserve the privacy between individuals, yet these ranges do not necessarily suggest exclusion, as intimate distances usually do.

Social distances range from one metre to about four metres away. These are the distances usually reserved for impersonal business and casual social gatherings. It is a friendly range in most cases, yet somewhat more formal than the personal distance. Ordinarily, social distances are necessary when there are more than three members of a group. In some cases, it would be considered rude for two individuals to preserve an intimate or personal distance within a social situation. Such behaviour might be interpreted as standoffish.

Public distances extend from four metres to eight metres and more away. This range tends to be formal and rather detached. Displays of emotion are considered bad form at these distances. Important public figures are generally seen in the public range, and because a considerable amount of space is involved, people generally must exaggerate their gestures and raise their voices to be understood clearly.

Most people adjust to proxemic patterns instinctively. We do not usually say to ourselves, "This person is invading my intimate space" when a stranger happens to stand half a metre away from us. However, unless we are in a combative mood, we tend to involuntarily step away in such circumstances. Obviously, social context is also a determining factor in proxemic patterns. In a crowded subway car, for example, virtually everyone is in an intimate range, yet we generally preserve a public attitude by not speaking to the person whose body is literally pressed against our own.

Proxemic patterns are perfectly obvious to anyone who has bothered to observe the way people obey certain spatial conventions in actual life. But in movies, these patterns are also related to the shots and their distance ranges. Although shots are not always defined by the literal space between the camera and the object photographed, in terms of psychological effect, shots tend to suggest physical distances.

Usually filmmakers have a number of options concerning what kind of shot to use to convey the action of a scene. What determines their choice—though usually instinctively rather than consciously—is the emotional impact of the different proxemic ranges. Each proxemic pattern has an approximate camera equivalent. The intimate distances, for example, can be likened to the close and extreme close shot ranges. The personal distance is approximately a medium close range. The social distances correspond to the medium and full shot ranges. And the public distances are roughly within the long and extreme long shot ranges. Because our eyes identify with the camera's lens, in effect we are placed within these ranges vis-à-vis the subject matter. When we are offered a close-up of a character, for example, in a sense we feel that we are in an intimate relationship with that character. In some instances, this technique can bind us to the character, forcing us to care about him or her and to identify with his or her problems. If the character is a villain, the close-up can produce an emotional revulsion in us; in effect, a threatening character seems to be invading our space.

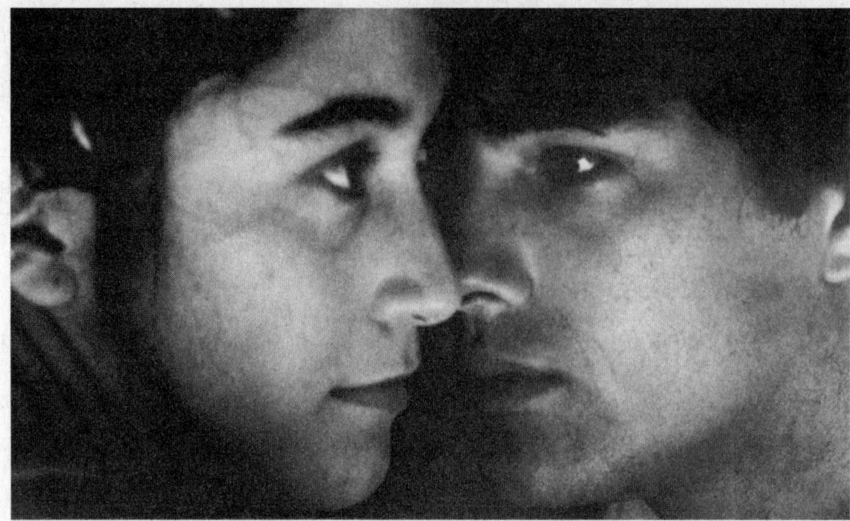

4-29a. *Like Water for Chocolate* (Mexico, 1992), with Lumi Cavazos and Marco Leonardi, directed by Alfonso Arau. *(Miramax Films)*

Although each of these photos portrays a conversation between a man and a woman, each is staged at a different proxemic range, suggesting totally different undertones. The intimate proxemics of *Like Water for Chocolate* are charged with erotic energy: The characters are literally flesh to flesh. In *Garden State*, the characters are strongly attracted to each other, but they remain at a more discreet personal proxemic range, with each respecting the other's space. The characters in *Your Friends & Neighbors* are more wary, especially the woman, who seems to find her blowhard date extremely resistible. The characters in *Zabriskie Point* are barely on speaking terms. The social proxemic range between them implies a lot of suspicion and reserve. Psychologically, they are miles apart. Each of these shots contains similar subject matter, but the real content of each is defined by its form—in this case, the proxemic ranges between the actors.

4-29b. *Garden State* (U.S.A., 2004), with Natalie Portman and Zach Braff, written and directed by Braff. *(Twentieth Century Fox)*

4-29c. ***Your Friends & Neighbors*** **(U.S.A., 1998), with Ben Stiller and Catherine Keener, directed by Neil LaBute.** *(Gramercy Pictures)*

4-29d. ***Zabriskie Point*** **(U.S.A., 1970), with Rod Taylor and Daria Halprin, directed by Michelangelo Antonioni.** *(MGM)*

In general, the greater the distance between the camera and the subject, the more emotionally neutral we remain. Public proxemic ranges tend to encourage a certain detachment. Conversely, the closer we are to a character, the more we feel that we are in proximity to him or her, and hence the greater our emotional involvement. "Long shot for comedy, close-up for tragedy" was one of Chaplin's most famous

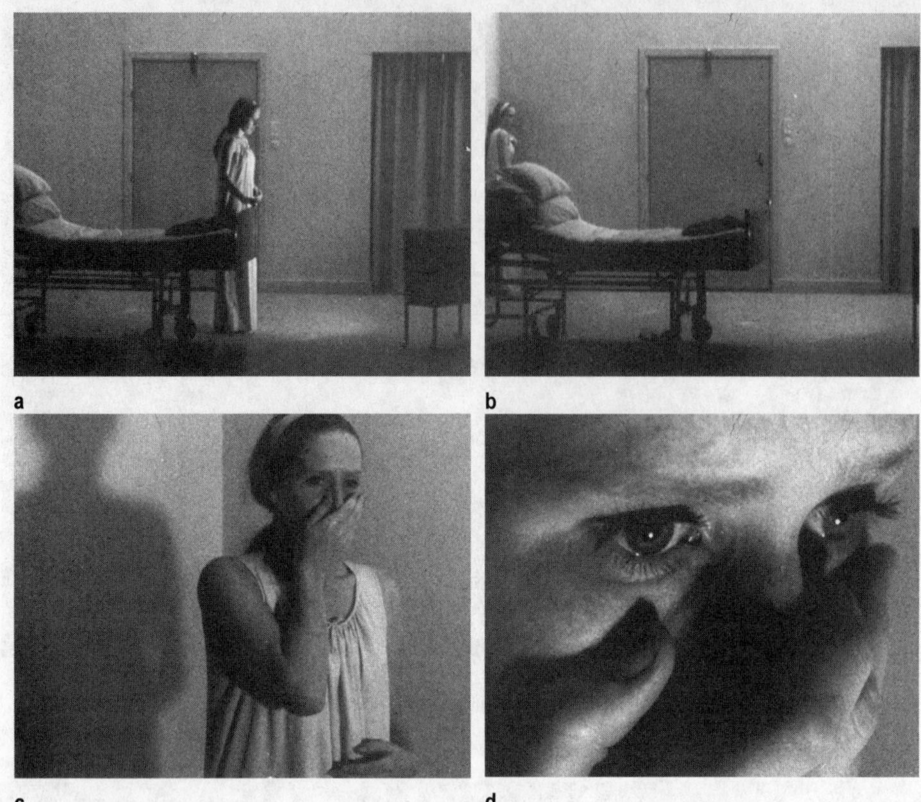

4-30. *Persona* (Sweden, 1966), with Liv Ullmann, directed by Ingmar Bergman.

Throughout this scene, which contains no dialogue, Bergman uses space to communicate his ideas—space within the frame and the space implied between the camera (us) and the subject. The character is in a hospital room watching the news on television **(a)**. Suddenly, she sees a horrifying scene of a Buddhist monk setting himself on fire to protest against the war in Vietnam. She retreats to the corner of the room, to the very edge of the frame **(b)**. Bergman then cuts to a closer shot **(c)**, intensifying our emotional involvement. The full horror of her reaction is conveyed by the extreme close-up **(d)**, bringing us into an intimate proximity with her.
(United Artists)

pronouncements. The proxemic principles are sound, for when we are close to an action—a person slipping on a banana peel, for example—it is seldom funny, because we are concerned for the person's safety. If we see the same event from a greater distance, however, it often strikes us as comical. Chaplin used close-ups sparingly for this very reason. As long as Charlie remains in long shots, we tend to be amused by his antics and absurd predicaments **(4-31a)**. In scenes of greater emotional impact, however, Chaplin resorted to closer shots, and their effect is often devastating on the audience. We suddenly realize that the situation we have been laughing at is no longer funny.

4-31a. *The Gold Rush* (U.S.A., 1925), with Charles Chaplin and Georgia Hale, directed by Chaplin.

Each of these scenes involves a fear of rejection by a woman Charlie holds in awe. The scene from *The Gold Rush* is predominantly comical. The tramp has belted his baggy pants with a piece of rope, but he does not realize it is also a dog's leash, and while dancing with the saloon girl, Charlie is yanked to the floor by the jittery dog at the other end of the rope. Because the camera remains relatively distant from the action, we tend to be more objective and detached and to laugh at his futile attempts to preserve his dignity. On the other hand, the famous final shot from *City Lights* is not funny at all and produces a powerful emotional effect. Because the camera is in close, we get close to the situation. The proxemic distance between the camera and the subject forces us to identify more with his feelings, which we cannot ignore at this range. *(RBC Films)*

4-31b. *City Lights* (U.S.A., 1931), with Charles Chaplin, directed by Chaplin.

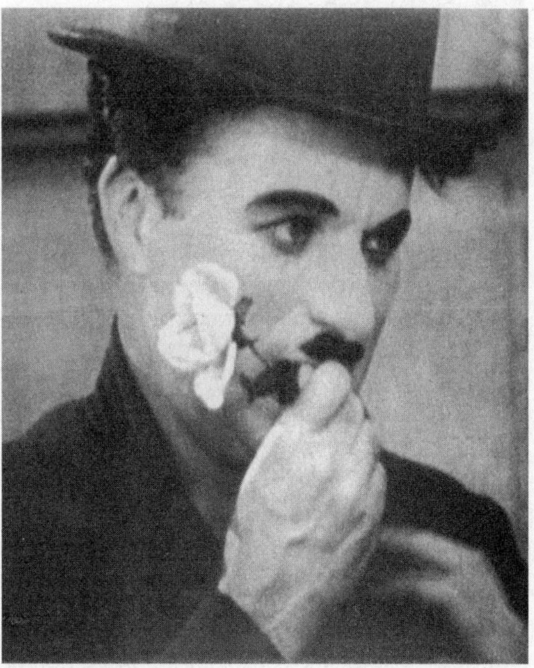

Perhaps the most famous instance of the power of Chaplin's close-ups is found at the conclusion of *City Lights*. Charlie has fallen in love with an impoverished flower vendor who is blind. She believes him to be an eccentric millionaire, and out of vanity he allows her to continue in this delusion. By engaging in a series of monumental labours—love has reduced him to work—he manages to scrape together enough money for her to receive an operation that will restore her sight. But he is dragged off to jail before she can thank him properly for the money. The final scene takes place several months later. The young woman can now see and owns her own modest flower shop. Charlie is released from prison, and dishevelled and dispirited, he meanders past her shop window. She sees him gazing at her wistfully and jokes to an assistant that she has apparently made a new conquest. Out of pity she goes out to the street and offers him a flower and a small coin. Instantly, she recognizes his touch. Hardly able to believe her eyes, she can only stammer, "You?" In a series of alternating close-ups, their embarrassment is unbearably prolonged **(4-31b)**. Clearly he is not the idol of her romantic fantasies, and he is painfully aware of her disappointment. Finally, he stares at her with an expression of shocking emotional nakedness. The film ends on this image of sublime vulnerability.

The choice of a shot is generally determined by practical considerations. Usually, the director selects the shot that most clearly conveys the dramatic action of a scene. If there is a conflict between the effect of certain proxemic ranges and the clarity needed to convey what is going on, most filmmakers will opt for clarity and gain their emotional impact through some other means. But many times shot choice is not determined by purely functional considerations.

OPEN AND CLOSED FORMS

The concepts of **open** and **closed forms** are generally used by art historians and critics, but these terms can also be useful in film analysis. Like most theoretical constructs, they are best used in a relative rather than absolute sense. No movie is completely open or completely closed in form; it only tends toward these polarities. Like other critical terms, these should be applied only when they are relevant and helpful in understanding what actually exists in a movie.

Open and closed forms convey two distinct attitudes about reality. Each has its own stylistic and technical characteristics. The two terms are loosely related to the concepts of realism and formalism. In general, realist filmmakers tend to use open forms, whereas formalists lean toward closed.

In terms of visual design, open form emphasizes informal, unobtrusive compositions. Often such images seem to have no discernible structure and suggest a random form of organization. Objects and figures seem to have been found rather than deliberately arranged **(4-32)**. Closed form emphasizes a more stylized design. Although such images can suggest a superficial realism, seldom do they have that accidental, discovered look that typifies open forms. Objects and figures are more precisely placed within the frame, and the balance of weights is elaborately worked out.

Open forms stress apparently simple techniques, because with these unselfconscious methods the filmmaker is able to emphasize the immediate, the familiar, the intimate aspects of reality. Sometimes, such images are photographed in only partially controlled situations, and these **aleatory techniques** can produce a

4-32. *The Garden of the Finzi-Continis* (Italy, 1970), with Dominique Sanda (centre), directed by Vittorio De Sica.

Realist directors are more likely to prefer open forms, which tend to suggest fragments of a larger external reality. Design and composition are generally informal. Influenced by the aesthetic of the documentary, open-form images seem to have been discovered rather than arranged. Excessive balance and calculated symmetry are avoided in favour of an intimate and spontaneous effect. Still photos in open form are seldom picturesque or obviously artful. Instead, they suggest a frozen instant of truth—a snapshot wrested from the fluctuations of time. *(Cinema 5)*

sense of spontaneity and directness that would be difficult to capture in a rigidly controlled context **(4-33)**. Closed forms are more likely to emphasize the unfamiliar. The images are rich in textural contrasts and compelling visual effects. Because the mise en scène is more precisely controlled and stylized, these images often have a deliberate artificiality—a sense of visual improbability, of being removed from reality. Closed forms also tend to be more densely saturated with visual information; richness of form takes precedence over considerations of surface realism. If a conflict should arise, formal beauty is sacrificed for truth in open forms; in closed forms, however, literal truth is sacrificed for beauty.

Compositions in open and closed forms exploit the frame differently. In open-form images, the frame tends to be deemphasized. It suggests a window, a temporary masking, and implies that more important information lies outside the edges of the composition **(4-33)**. Space is continuous in these shots, and to emphasize its continuity outside the frame, directors often favour panning their camera across the locale. The shot seems inadequate, too narrow in its confines to contain the copiousness of

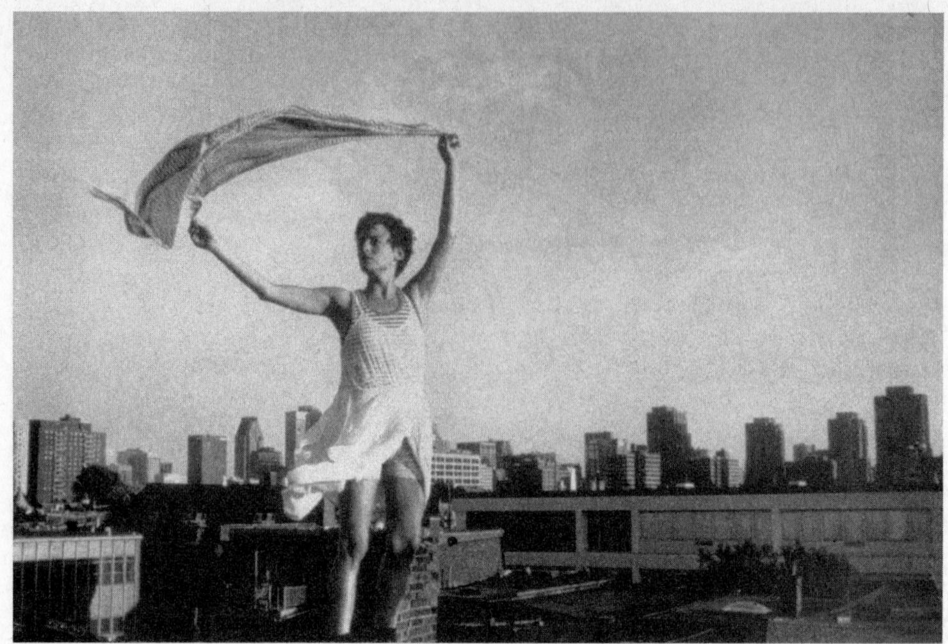

4-33. *Eldorado* (Canada, 1995), with Pascale Bussières, directed by Charles Binamé.

Open forms make us aware that reality extends beyond the film's frame. In *Eldorado*, the images are often filmed with a handheld camera to suggest the instability of the lives of the six young Montrealers whose stories intersect in its loosely constructed narrative. The rooftop setting of this shot captures both the exhilaration and the precarious balance of a character who wanders aimlessly through the city. *(Alliance Communications)*

the subject matter. Like many of the paintings of Edgar Degas (who usually favoured open forms), objects and even figures are arbitrarily cut off by the frame to reinforce the continuity of the subject matter beyond the formal edges of the composition. In closed forms, the shot represents a miniature proscenium arch, with all the necessary information carefully structured within the confines of the frame. Space seems enclosed and self-contained rather than continuous. Elements outside the frame are irrelevant, at least in terms of the formal properties of the individual shot, which is isolated from its context in space and time **(4-34)**.

In open-form movies, the dramatic action generally leads the camera. In *Traffic* (2000), for example, Steven Soderbergh emphasized the fluidity of the camera as it dutifully follows the actors wherever they go, seemingly placed at their disposal. Such films suggest that chance plays an important role in determining visual effects. Needless to say, it is not what actually happens on a set that is important but what seems to be happening on the screen. In fact, many of the simplest effects in an open-form movie are achieved after much painstaking labour and manipulation.

In closed-form films, the camera often anticipates the dramatic action (**anticipatory camera**). Objects and actors are visually blocked out within the confines of a predetermined camera setup. **Anticipatory setups** tend to imply fatality or determinism, for in effect the camera seems to know what will happen even before it occurs. In the films of Fritz Lang, for example, the camera often seems to be waiting in an

4-34. *Training Day* (U.S.A., 2001), with Ethan Hawke, directed by Antoine Fuqua.

Why is this shot threatening? Mostly because of the slightly high angle and the closed form, imprisoning the Hawke character between the two pairs of tattooed arms and the foreground table with its clutter. In closed form, the frame is a self-sufficient miniature universe with all the formal elements held in careful balance. Though there may be more information outside the frame (like the bodies attached to the arms), for the duration of any given shot this information is visually irrelevant. Closed forms are often used in scenes dealing with entrapment or confinement. *(Warner Bros.)*

empty room: The door opens, the characters enter, and the action then begins. In some of Hitchcock's movies, a character is seen at the edge of the composition, and the camera seems to be placed in a disadvantageous position, too far removed from where the action is apparently going to occur. But then the character decides to return to that area where the camera has been waiting. When such setups are used, the audience also tends to anticipate actions. Instinctively, we expect something or someone to fill in the visual vacuum of the shot. Philosophically, open forms tend to suggest freedom of choice, a multiplicity of options open to the characters. Closed forms, conversely, tend to imply destiny and the futility of the will: The characters do not seem to make the important decisions, the camera does—and in advance.

Open and closed forms are most effective in movies where these techniques are appropriate to the subject matter. A prison film using mostly open forms is not likely to be emotionally convincing. Most movies use both open and closed forms, depending on the specific dramatic context. Renoir's *La Grande illusion*, for example, uses closed forms for the prison camp scenes and open forms after two of the prisoners escape.

A systematic mise en scène analysis of any given shot includes the following fifteen elements:

1. *Dominance.* Where is our eye attracted first? Why?
2. *Lighting key.* Is it high key? low key? high contrast? some combination of these?
3. *Shot and camera proxemics.* What type of shot? How far away is the camera from the action?

4. *Angle.* Are we (and the camera) looking up at or down on the subject? Or is the camera neutral (eye level)?
5. *Colour values.* What is the dominant colour? Are there contrasting foils? Is there colour symbolism?
6. *Lens/filter/stock.* How do these distort or comment on the photographed materials?
7. *Subsidiary contrasts.* What are the main eye-stops after the dominant has been taken in?
8. *Density.* How much visual information is packed into the image? Is the texture stark, moderate, or highly detailed?
9. *Composition.* How is the two-dimensional space segmented and organized? What is the underlying design?
10. *Form.* Is it open or closed? Does the image suggest a window that arbitrarily isolates a fragment of the scene? Or is it a proscenium arch, in which the visual elements are carefully arranged and held in balance?
11. *Framing.* Is it tight or loose? Do the characters have no room to move around, or can they move freely without impediments?
12. *Depth.* On how many planes is the image composed? Does the background or foreground comment in any way on the midground?
13. *Character placement.* What part of the framed space do the characters occupy? centre? top? bottom? edges? Why?
14. *Staging positions.* Which way do the characters look vis-à-vis the camera?
15. *Character proxemics.* How much space is there between the characters?

These visual principles, with appropriate modifications, can be applied to any image analysis. Of course, while we are actually watching a movie, most of us do not have the time or inclination to explore all fifteen elements of mise en scène in each shot. Nonetheless, by applying these principles to a still photo, we can train our eyes to "read" a movie image with more critical sophistication.

For example, the image from *M* **(4-35)** is a good instance of how form (mise en scène) is actually content. The shot takes place near the end of the movie. A psychotic child-killer (Peter Lorre) has been hunted down by the members of the underworld. These "normal" criminals have taken him to an abandoned warehouse where they intend to prosecute him for his heinous crimes and in doing so take the police heat off themselves. In this scene, the killer is confronted by a witness who holds an incriminating piece of evidence—a balloon. The components of the shot include the following elements:

1. *Dominance.* The balloon, the brightest object in the frame. When the photo is turned upside down and converted to a pattern of abstract shapes, its dominance is more readily discernible.
2. *Lighting key.* The light is murky low key, with high-contrast spotlights on the balloon and the four main figures.
3. *Shot and camera proxemics.* The shot is slightly more distant than a full shot. The camera proxemic range is social, perhaps about three metres from the dominant.

4-35. *M* (Germany, 1931), with Peter Lorre (extreme right), directed by Fritz Lang. *(Janus Films)*

4. *Angle.* The angle is slightly high, suggesting an air of fatality.
5. *Colour values.* The movie is in black and white.
6. *Lens/filter/stock.* A standard lens is used, with no apparent filter. Standard slow stock is used.
7. *Subsidiary contrasts.* The figures of the killer, the witness, and the two criminals in the upper left are in subsidiary contrast.
8. *Density.* The shot has a high degree of density, especially considering the low-key lighting. Such details as the texture of the brick walls, the creases in the clothing, and the expressive faces of the actors are highlighted.
9. *Composition.* The image is divided into three general areas—left, centre, and right—suggesting instability and tension.
10. *Form.* Definitely closed: The frame suggests a constricting cell, with no exit for the prisoner.
11. *Framing.* Tight: The killer is trapped in the same territory with his threatening accusers.
12. *Depth.* The image is composed on three depth planes: the two figures in the foreground, the two figures on the stairs in the midground, and the brick wall of the background.
13. *Character placement.* The accusers and balloon tower above the killer, sealing off any avenue of escape, while he cowers below at the extreme right edge, almost falling into the symbolic blackness outside the frame.

14. *Staging position.* The accusers stand in a quarter-turn position, implying a greater intimacy with us than the main character, who is in the profile position and totally unaware of anything but his own terror.
15. *Character proxemics.* Proxemics are personal between the foreground characters, the killer's immediate problem, and intimate between the men on the stairs, who function as a double threat. The range between the two pairs is social.

A filmmaker has literally hundreds of different ways to convey meanings. Like the painter or still photographer, the movie director can emphasize visual dominants. In a scene portraying violence, for example, he or she can use diagonal and zigzagging lines, aggressive colours, close-ups, extreme angles, harsh lighting contrasts, unbalanced compositions, large shapes, and so on. Unlike most other visual artists, the filmmaker can also suggest violence through movement, either of the subject itself, the camera, or both. The film artist can suggest violence through editing, by having one shot collide with another in a kaleidoscopic explosion of different perspectives. Furthermore, through the use of the soundtrack, violence can be conveyed by loud or rapid dialogue, harsh sound effects, or strident music. Precisely because there are so many ways to convey a given effect, the filmmaker will vary the emphasis, sometimes stressing image, sometimes movement, other times sound. Occasionally, especially in climactic scenes, all three are used at the same time.

FURTHER READING

Barnwell, Jane, *Production Design: Architects of the Screen* (London: Wallflower Press, 2004). Historical overview of the role of the production designer.

Belton, John, *Widescreen Cinema* (Cambridge, Mass.: Harvard University Press, 1992). Examines the changing shape of the screen in the 1950s.

Bruzzi, Stella, *Undressing Cinema: Clothing and Identity in the Movies* (London: Routledge, 1997). Stimulating essays on the role of fashion in cinema.

Dyer, Richard, *The Matter of Images: Essays on Representations* (London: Routledge, 1993). The ideological implications of images.

Elsaesser, Thomas, ed., *Early Cinema: Space, Frame, Narrative* (London: British Film Institute, 1990). Essays on visual representation and storytelling in early cinema.

Gibbs, John, *Mise-en-scène: Film Style and Interpretation* (London: Wallflower Press, 2002). Close readings of visual style in a range of movies.

Pidduck, Julianne. *Contemporary Costume Film: Space, Place and the Past* (London: British Film Institute, 2004). Ideological analysis of costume in recent period films.

Rothman, William, *The "I" of the Camera: Essays in Film Criticism, History, and Aesthetics* (Cambridge, Mass.: Cambridge University Press, 1988). Close readings of major films with an emphasis on visual style.

Street, Sarah, *Costume and Cinema: Dress Codes in Popular Film* (London: Wallflower Press, 2001). Case studies of selected films.

Thomas, Deborah. *Reading Hollywood: Spaces and Meanings in American Film* (London: Wallflower Press, 2001). Discusses the relations of space and narrative in selected films.

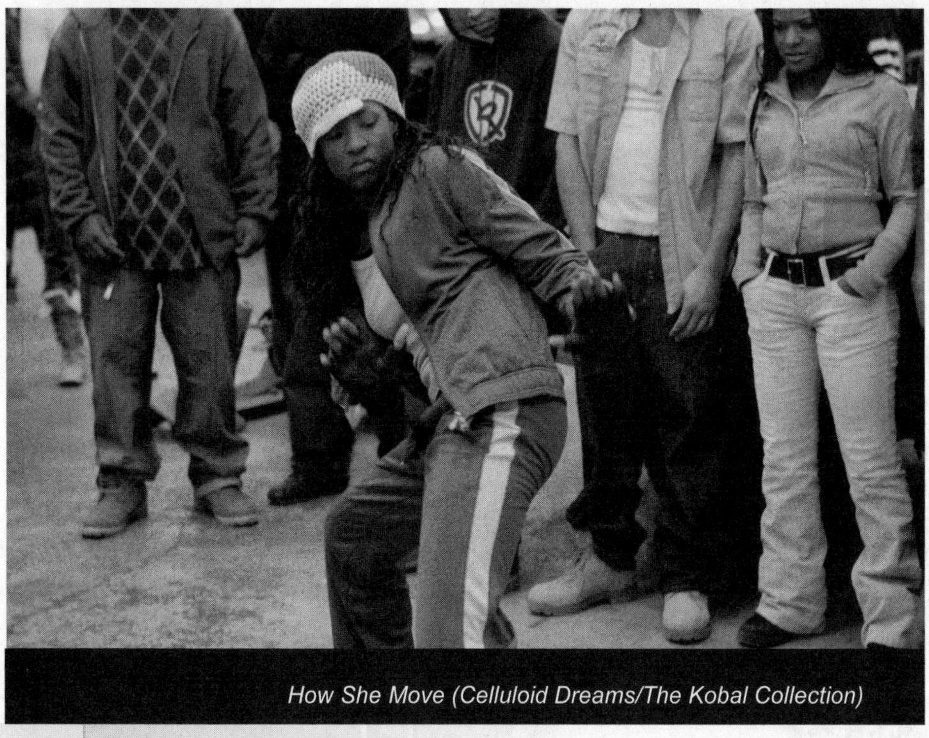

How She Move (Celluloid Dreams/The Kobal Collection)

MOVEMENT

5

The opening of a door, a hand, or an eye can bring about a climax as thrilling as a crash of locomotives on the screen.

— RICHARD DYER MACCANN

OVERVIEW

How movement has meaning. Different types of movement: realistic, pantomime, mime. Dance and choreography: the art of motion. The psychology of movement: lateral motions, left or right, up or down, toward or away from the camera. Movement in relation to shots and angles. Movement and film genres: comedies, action films, dance movies, animation, and musicals. Movement as metaphor: kinetic symbolism. The moving camera: kineticizing space. Dolly shots versus editing: the implications of each. Stasis versus dynamism: tripods or tracks? The mercurial instability of the handheld camera. Lyricism: cranes and other flying forms. Faux movement: zoom shots. Mechanical distortions of motion: animation, fast motion, slow motion, reverse motion, and freeze frames.

Movies, *motion pictures*, *moving pictures*—all these phrases suggest the central importance of motion in the art of film. *Cinema* derives from the Greek word for "movement," as do the words *kinetic*, *kinesthesia*, and *choreography*—terms usually associated with the art of dance. Yet, oddly enough, filmgoers and critics give surprisingly little consideration to movement per se as a medium of communication, as a language system. Like the image itself, motion is usually thought of in terms of gross subject matter. We tend to remember "what happens" only in a general sense. If we were to describe a sequence from a ballet in such vague terms, our discussion would certainly strike the sophisticated dance enthusiast as naive. Yet cinematic sequences—which can be choreographed with just as much or even greater complexity—are seldom appreciated for their **kinetic** richness and beauty.

KINETICS

Like images, motion can be literal and concrete or highly stylized and lyrical. In the kinetic arts—pantomime, ballet, modern dance—we find a wide variety of movements, ranging from the realistic to the formally abstract. This stylistic spectrum can also be seen in movies. For example, a naturalistic actor like Spencer Tracy used only realistic movements, the same sort that could be observed in actual life. Tracy moves so simply in his films that he hardly seems to be acting. Pantomimists are more stylized in their movements. Charlie Chaplin, for example, tended to use motion in a more balletic, more symbolical way. A swaggering gait and a twirling cane symbolized Charlie's (usually fleeting) arrogance and conceit.

Even more stylized are the movements of performers in a musical. In this **genre**, characters express their most intense emotions through song and dance **(5-1)**. A dance number is seldom meant to be taken literally: It is a stylized **convention** that we accept as a symbolic expression of certain feelings and ideas. In *Singin' in the Rain* (1952), for example, Gene Kelly does an elaborate dance routine in a downpour. He twirls around lampposts, splashes through puddles like a happy idiot, and leaps ecstatically through pelting rain—literally nothing can dampen the exhilaration of his love. A wide gamut of emotions is expressed in this sequence, with each kinetic variation symbolizing the character's feelings about his girl. She can make him feel dreamy, childlike, erotically stimulated, brave and forthright, dopey and moonstruck, and finally wild with joy. In some kinds of action genres, physical contests are stylized in a similar manner. Samurai and kung fu films, for example, often feature elaborately choreographed sequences **(5-16)**.

5-1. An American in Paris (U.S.A., 1951), with Gene Kelly and Leslie Caron, choreography by Kelly, score by George Gershwin, directed by Vincente Minnelli.

Kelly worked in a broad range of dancing styles—tap, ballroom, modern, and ballet. He was usually at his best in muscular, gymnastic styles, with an emphasis on virile trajectories and bravura leaps. But he was also charming in nonchalant styles, to which he usually added a characteristic swagger. He often incorporated lengthy ballet sequences in his movies, generally a dream sequence or a fantasy (see also **5-17**). Kelly's dancing is sexy, with an emphasis on pelvic movements, tensed loins, twisting torsos, and close-to-the-floor gyrations. He usually wore close-fitting clothes to emphasize his well-muscled body. He also allowed his personality to shine through, breaking the formality of the choreography with a cocky grin or an ecstatic smile. *(MGM)*

Ballet and mime are even more abstract and stylized. A great mime artist like Marcel Marceau was concerned with expressing not so much literal ideas (which is more properly the province of pantomime) as the essence of ideas, stripped of superfluities. A twisted torso can suggest an ancient tree, bent elbows its crooked branches, fluttering fingers the rippling of its leaves. In ballet, movements can be so stylized that we cannot always assign a discernible content to them, though the narrative context generally provides us with at least a vague sense of what the movements are supposed to represent. On this level of abstraction, however, movements acquire self-justifying characteristics. They are **lyrical**; that is, we respond to them more for their own beauty than for their function as symbolic expressions of ideas.

In dance, movements are defined by the space that encloses the choreography—a three-dimensional stage. In film, the **frame** performs a similar function. However, with each **setup** change, the cinematic "stage" is redefined. The intrinsic meanings

5-2a. *Temptress Moon* (China / Hong Kong, 1996), with Gong Li (white dress), directed by Chen Kaige.
Stasis and motion—two different worldviews. The image from *Temptress Moon* portrays a static world of frozen possibilities, where women are expected to be subservient, silent, and still. The world of professional football portrayed in *Any Given Sunday* is a breathless blur of motion, where the whirling camera is hardly able to keep the (mostly male) characters in focus. *(Miramax Films)*

5-2b. *Any Given Sunday* (U.S.A., 1999), with Al Pacino, directed by Oliver Stone. *(Warner Bros.)*

associated with various portions of the frame are closely related to the significance of certain kinds of movements. For example, with vertical movements, an upward motion seems soaring and free because it conforms to the eye's natural tendency to move upward over a composition. Movements in this direction often suggest aspiration, joy, power, and authority—ideas associated with the upper portions of the frame. Downward movements suggest the opposite ideas: depression, grief, weakness, insignificance, death, and so on.

Because the Western eye tends to read a picture from left to right, physical movement in this direction seems psychologically natural, whereas movement from the right to left often seems inexplicably tense and uncomfortable. The filmmaker can exploit these psychological phenomena to reinforce the dramatic ideas. Frequently, protagonists travel toward the right of the screen, whereas villains move toward the left. In John Huston's *The Red Badge of Courage* (1951), the hero moves from right to left when he runs away from a battle in fear. Later, when he courageously joins an infantry charge, his movements are from left to right.

Movement can be directed toward or away from the camera. Because we identify with the camera, the effect of such movements is somewhat like a character moving

5-3. *Zero Patience* (Canada, 1993), with Charles Azulay, David Gale, and Howard Rosenstein, directed by John Greyson.

The energy and spectacle of classic Hollywood musicals drew their audiences into a utopian world where they could forget their everyday problems. *Zero Patience* is a musical about AIDS. Greyson's witty and provocative film uses musical conventions to draw attention to the myths about AIDS and the cultural attitudes that lie behind them. Sir Richard Burton, a Victorian explorer now unaccountably working in a Toronto museum, investigates the life of the so-called Patient Zero, a French-Canadian flight attendant who supposedly brought the epidemic to North America. The film also depicts the suffering of an AIDS victim, a former friend of Zero, but its use of fantasy and artifice allows it to place the individual experience in its historical and cultural context. *(John Greyson)*

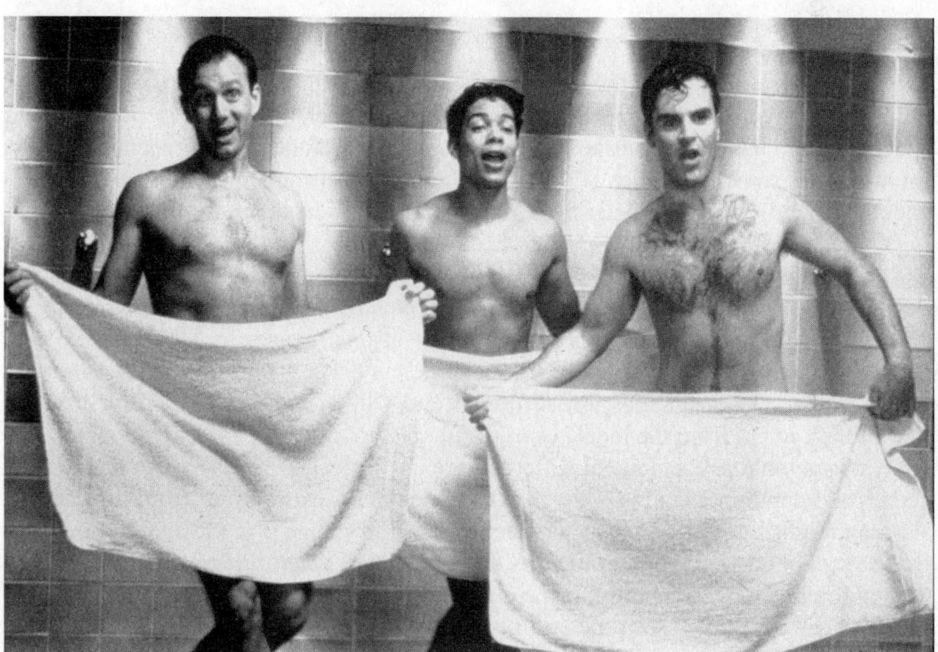

5-4. *Deux secondes* [*Two Seconds*] (Canada, 1998), with Charlotte Laurier, directed by Manon Briand.
A downhill bike racer (Laurier) hesitates for two seconds at the beginning of a race and loses her place on the team. Briand uses fast motion, slow motion, and freeze frames to capture the character's experience of the relativity of time as she adjusts to her new life as a courier in Montreal. In this shot, her forward momentum toward the camera expresses her determination and vitality, while the traffic that surrounds her suggests her vulnerability in the confined urban space.
(France Film)

toward or away from us. If the character is a villain, walking toward the camera can seem aggressive, hostile, and threatening, for in effect he or she is invading our space. If the character is attractive, movement toward the camera seems friendly, inviting, and sometimes even seductive. In either case, movement toward the audience is generally strong and assertive, suggesting confidence on the part of the moving character **(5-4)**.

Movement away from the camera tends to imply opposite meanings. Intensity is decreased and the character seems to grow remote as he or she withdraws from us. Audiences feel safer when villains move away in this manner and increase the protective distance between them and us. In some contexts, such movements can seem weak, fearful, and suspicious. Most movies end with a withdrawal of some sort, either of the camera from the locale or of the characters from the camera.

Considerable psychological differences exist between lateral movements on the screen and depth movements—that is, movements toward or away from the camera. A script might simply call for a character to move from one place to another, but how the director chooses to photograph this movement will determine much of its psychological implications. Generally, if the character moves from one side of the screen to the other, he or she will seem determined and efficient, a person of action. Unless the camera is at **extreme-long-shot** range, these movements are necessarily photographed in brief **takes**—shots lasting only a few seconds. Lateral movements tend to emphasize speed and efficiency, so they are often used in action movies **(5-5)**.

Conversely, when a character moves in or out of the depth of a scene, the effect is often one of slowness. Unless the camera is at close range or an extreme **wide-angle lens** is used, movements toward or away from the camera take longer to photograph than lateral movements. With a **telephoto lens**, such movements can seem hopelessly dragged out. Furthermore, when depth movement is photographed in an uninterrupted lengthy take, the audience tends to anticipate the conclusion of the movement, thus intensifying the sense of tedium while we wait for the character to arrive at his or her destination. Especially when a character's physical goal is apparent—the length of a long corridor, for example—audiences generally grow restless if they are forced to view the entire movement **(6-12)**.

Most classical filmmakers would photograph the action in several different setups, thus compressing the time and space from the inception of the movement to its conclusion. Classical filmmakers also tend to stage movement diagonally, to create a more dynamic trajectory of motion.

The distance and **angle** from which movement is photographed determine much of its meaning. Generally, the longer and higher the shot, the slower the movement tends to appear. If movement is recorded from close and low angles, it seems more intense, speeded up. A director can photograph the same subject—a running man, for example—in two different setups and produce opposite meanings. If the man is photographed in an extreme long shot from a high angle, he will seem ineffectual. If he is photographed from a low angle in a **medium shot**, he will seem a dynamo of energy. Although the subject matter in each setup is identical, the true content of each shot is its form.

Even film critics (who should know better) are often ignorant of these perceptual differences, thinking of movement only in terms of story and gross physical action. The result has been a good deal of naive theorizing on what is "intrinsically cinematic." The more movement is perceived as extravagant in real life, they argue, the more "filmic" it becomes. **Epic** events and exterior locations are presumed to be fundamentally more suited to the medium than intimate, restricted, or interior subjects. Such views are based on a misunderstanding of movement in film. True, we can use the terms *epic* and *psychological* in describing the general emphasis of a movie. Even on this general level, however, arguments about intrinsically cinematic subjects are usually crude. No sensible person would claim that Tolstoy's *War and Peace* is intrinsically more novelistic than Dostoyevsky's *Crime and Punishment*, although we may refer to one as an epic and the other as a psychological novel. In a similar vein, only a naive viewer would claim that Michelangelo's Sistine Chapel frescoes are intrinsically more visual than a Vermeer painting of a domestic scene. It is the treatment that counts, not the material per se.

Movement in film is a subtle issue, for it is necessarily dependent on the kind of shot used. The cinematic close-up can convey as much movement as the most sweeping vistas in an extreme long shot. In fact, in terms of the area covered on the screen's surface, there is actually more movement in a close-up showing tears running down a person's face than there is in an extreme long shot of a parachutist drifting twenty metres **(5-6)**.

Epic and psychological movies use movement in different ways, with emphasis on different shots. Epic movies usually depend on the longer shots for their effects,

5-5. *Run Lola Run* (Germany, 1998), with Franka Potente, directed by Tom Tykwer.
Our emotional response to movement can be strongly affected by whether it is staged from the depth of the shot toward the camera, as in **(a)**, or whether the desperate protagonist is photographed running laterally **(b)** from right to left (or vice-versa) in the frame. The in-depth movement seems slower, more frustrating, because it takes a long time to run from the distant "rear" of the scene to where the camera is patiently waiting. The lateral movement seems more decisive and powerful, because moving from one side of the frame to the other takes only a few split seconds. *(Sony Pictures Classic)*

a

b

whereas psychological films tend to use the closer shots. Epics are concerned with a sense of sweep and breadth, psychological movies with depth and detail. Epics often emphasize events, psychological films the implications of events. One stresses action, the other reaction.

Two filmmakers can approach the same story and produce totally different results. *Hamlet* is a good example. Laurence Olivier's 1948 film version of this play is essentially an epic, with emphasis on the longer shots. Franco Zeffirelli's version is primarily a psychological study, dominated by close and medium shots. Olivier's movie emphasizes setting. There are many **long shots**, especially of the brooding castle of Elsinore. Much is made of Hamlet's interaction with this moody locale. We are informed at the beginning of the film that the story is about "a man who could not make up his mind." The long shots are used to emphasize this interpretation visually. Most of them are **loosely framed**, suggesting that Hamlet (played by Olivier) has considerable freedom of movement, freedom to act. But he refuses to use this freedom, preferring to sulk in dark corners, paralyzed with indecision. When he does move, the motion is generally recorded from long distances, thus reinforcing the impotence of the protagonist in relationship to his environment.

Zeffirelli's *Hamlet* (with Mel Gibson) is photographed mostly in **tightly framed** close and medium shots **(5-7)**. Unlike Olivier's indecisive Hamlet, Gibson's is impulsive and rash, a man who often acts before he thinks. Imprisoned by the confining close shots, the tortured hero virtually spills off the edges of the frame into oblivion. The unstable handheld camera can barely keep up with him as he lunges hyperkinetically from place to place. If the same movements were photographed from a long-shot range, of course, the character would seem to move more normally.

If there is a great deal of movement in the closer shots, its effect on the screen will be exaggerated. For this reason, filmmakers tend to use these ranges for relatively static scenes. The animation of two people talking and gesturing, for example, has enough movement to prevent most medium shots from appearing static.

Close-ups are even subtler in their recording of movement. Robert Bresson and Carl Dreyer often highlighted subtle movements by photographing an expressive face in close-up. In fact, these two filmmakers referred to the human face as a spiritual "landscape." In Dreyer's *La Passion de Jeanne d'Arc* [*The Passion of Joan of Arc*] (1927), for instance, one of the most powerful scenes is a close shot of Jeanne as a tear slowly trickles down her face. Expanded thousands of times by the close-up, the path of the tear represents a cataclysmic movement on the screen, far more powerful than the cavalry charges and clashing armies of routine epic films.

Certain emotions and ideas—like joy, love, hatred—are so prevalent in cinema that filmmakers are constantly searching for new methods of presentation, methods that transform the familiar into something fresh and unexpected. For example, death scenes are common in movies. But because of their frequency, they are often presented tritely. Of course, death remains a universal concern, one that can still move audiences if handled with any degree of originality and imagination.

One method of avoiding staleness is to convey emotions through kinetic symbolism. Like the choreographer, the filmmaker can exploit the meanings inherent in certain types of movements. Even so-called abstract motions tend to suggest ideas and feelings. Some movements strike us as soft and yielding, for example, whereas others seem harsh and aggressive. Curved and swaying motions are generally graceful and "feminine." Those that are straight and direct strike us as intense, stimulating, and

5-6a. *The Stunt Man* (U.S.A., 1980), directed by Richard Rush. *(Twentieth Century Fox)*

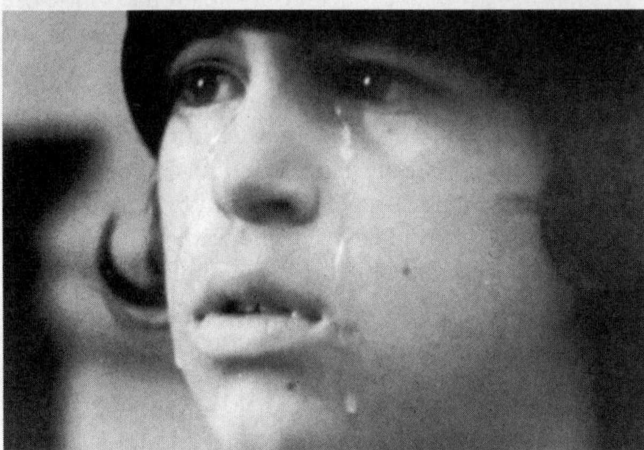

5-6b. *L'Enfant sauvage* [*The Wild Child*] (France, 1969), with Jean-Pierre Cargol, directed by François Truffaut. *(United Artists)*

Unlike movement in dance or the live theatre, cinematic movement is always relative. Only gross movements are likely to be perceived in an extreme long shot, whereas the flicker of an eye can rivet our attention in a close-up. In these photos, for example, the path of the boy's tear covers more screen space than the pilot's fall from the sky.

powerful. Furthermore, unlike the choreographer, the filmmaker can exploit these symbolic movements even without having people perform them.

If a dancer were to convey a sense of grief at the loss of a loved one, his or her movements would probably be implosive, withdrawn, with an emphasis on slow, solemn, downward movements. A film director might use this same kinetic principle but in a totally different physical context. For instance, in Walter Lang's *The King and I* (1956), we realize that the seriously ailing king (Yul Brynner) has died when we see a close-up of his hand slowly slipping toward the bottom of the frame, disappearing finally off the lower edge into darkness.

In Sergei Eisenstein's *Old and New* (1929) [also known as *The General Line*], a valuable stud bull dies, and its death has disastrous consequences for the agricultural commune that has purchased the animal. These consequences are expressed through two parallel shots emphasizing the same kinetic symbolism. First Eisenstein shows us an extreme close-up of the dying bull's eye as it slowly closes. The mournful lowering of the eyelid is magnified many times by the closeness of the shot. Eisenstein then cuts to a shot of the sun setting on the horizon, its streaming shafts of light slowly retracting as the sun sinks below the earth's rim. Trivial as a bull's death

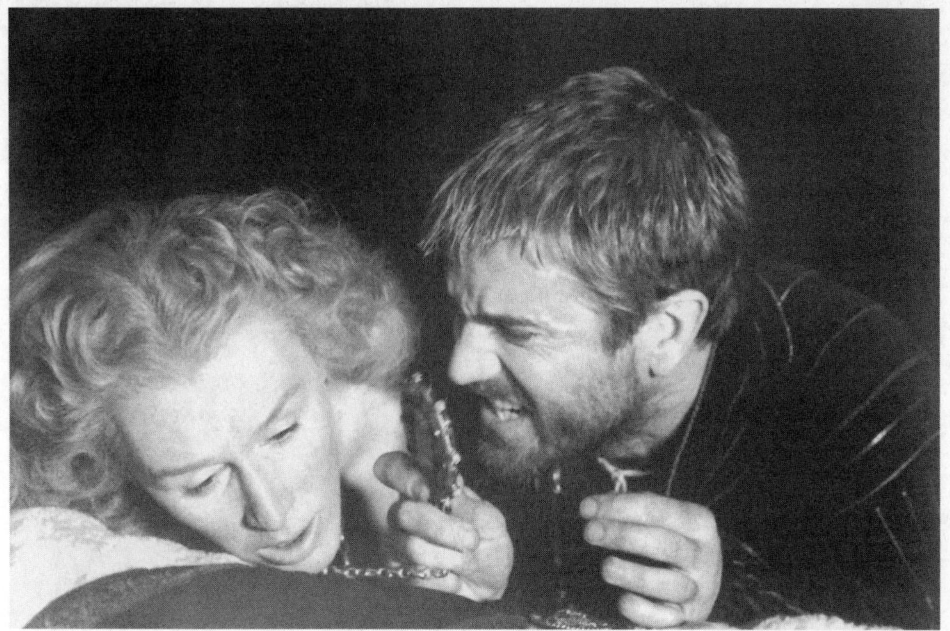

5-7. *Hamlet* (U.S.A. / Britain / France, 1990), with Glenn Close and Mel Gibson, directed by Franco Zeffirelli.

When the camera is close to the action, as in this photo, even small gestures seem magnified and highly kinetic. Gibson's portrayal of Shakespeare's tragic hero is volatile, exploding with energy—a far cry from the contemplative and indecisive Hamlet made famous in Laurence Olivier's film. *(Icon Distribution, Inc.)*

might seem, to the hardworking members of the commune it suggests an almost cosmic significance. Their hopes for a better future die with the animal.

Of course, context is everything in movies. The kind of symbolism in *Old and New* would seem obtrusive in a more realistic movie. However, the same kinetic principle can be used in almost any kind of context. In Norman Jewison's *In the Heat of the Night* (1967), for example, a police officer (Sidney Poitier) must inform a woman (Lee Grant) that her husband has been brutally murdered. When she hears the news, the woman shields her body with her arms in a kind of shrivelling, implosive gesture. In effect, she withdraws into herself, her body withering as the news sinks in. She will not permit even the sympathetic officer to touch or comfort her in any way.

In Mel Gibson's *Braveheart* (1995), the beheading of the rebel hero (played by Gibson) exploits downward movements in several ways. As the executioner's axe sweeps down toward the hero's neck, we see a close-up of Princess Isabelle (Sophie Marceau), a tear slowly rolling down her face. Just as the axe strikes the hero's neck, we see a handkerchief (a memento of his dead wife's love) fall from his hand to the ground in slow motion—a poetic symbol of his release from life.

In each of these instances, the filmmakers—Lang, Eisenstein, Jewison, and Gibson—were faced with a similar problem: how to present a death scene with freshness and originality. Each director solved the problem by exploiting similar movements: a

5-8. ***X2: X-men United*** **(U.S.A., 2003), with Hugh Jackman (flying), directed by Bryan Singer.**

Movement in film is closely related to mise en scène. The top of many images is associated with power and control, the bottom with vulnerability. In this shot from the sci-fi fantasy based on some Stan Lee comic book characters, Wolverine (Jackman) is at full fury when a school for gifted children comes under siege. He attacks from above, a position of maximum supremacy over those below. *(Twentieth Century Fox)*

slow, contracting, downward motion—the same kind of movement that a dancer would use literally on a stage.

Kinetic symbolism can be used to suggest other ideas and emotions as well. For example, ecstasy and joy are often expressed by expansive motions, fear by a variety of tentative or trembling movements. Eroticism can be conveyed with undulating motions. In Akira Kurosawa's *Rashomon* (1950), for example, the provocative sexuality of a woman is suggested by the sinuous motions of her silk veil—a movement so graceful and tantalizing that the protagonist (Toshiro Mifune) is unable to resist her erotic allure. In cultures that discourage expressions of overt sexuality, sexual ideas are often expressed through these symbolic methods.

Every art form has its rebels, and cinema is no exception. Because movement is almost universally regarded as basic to film art, several directors have experimented with the idea of stasis. In effect, these filmmakers are deliberately working against the nature of their medium, stripping it of all but the most essential motions. Such filmmakers as Bresson, Dreyer, and Yasujiro Ozu have been described as **minimalists** because their kinetic techniques are so austere and restrained. When virtually nothing seems to be moving in an image, even the slightest motion can take on enormous significance. In many cases, this stasis is exploited for symbolic purposes: Lack of motion can suggest spiritual or psychological paralysis, as in the movies of Michelangelo Antonioni, for example.

THE MOVING CAMERA

Before the 1920s, filmmakers tended to confine movements to the subject being photographed. Relatively few moved their cameras during a shot and, when they did, it was usually to keep a moving figure within the frame. In the 1920s such German filmmakers as F.W. Murnau and E.A. Dupont moved the camera within the shot not only for physical reasons but for psychological and thematic reasons as well. The German experiments permitted later filmmakers to use the mobile camera to communicate subtleties previously considered impossible. True, editing—that is, moving the camera *between shots*—is faster, cheaper, and less distracting, but cutting is also abrupt, disconnected, and unpredictable compared to the fluid lyricism of a moving camera.

A major problem of the moving camera involves time. Films that use this technique extensively tend to seem slow moving, since moving in or out of a scene is more time-consuming than a straight cut. A director must decide whether moving the camera is worth the film time involved and whether the movement warrants the additional technical and budgetary complications. If a filmmaker decides to move the camera, he or she must then decide how. Should it be mounted on a vehicle or

5-9. *Frantic* (U.S.A., 1988), with Harrison Ford, directed by Roman Polanski.

Filmmakers often exploit "negative space" to anticipate action that has not yet occurred. In this photo, for example, the camera seems to be waiting for something to fill in the empty space on the right. The unsuspecting protagonist does not know that he will soon be threatened by a careening auto that will almost run him down. But we have already been forewarned of the impending action by Polanski's framing. Anticipatory setups like these are especially common in thrillers. They are a kind of warning to the viewer to be prepared: Art as well as nature abhors a vacuum. *(Warner Bros.)*

5-10. *Yojimbo* (Japan, 1961), directed by Akira Kurosawa.

Kurosawa's movies are rich in symbolic kinetic techniques. He often creates dramatic tensions by juxtaposing static visual elements with a small but dynamic whirlpool of motion. In this scene, for example, the greatly outnumbered protagonist (Toshiro Mifune) prepares to do battle with a group of vicious hoodlums. In static visual terms, the samurai hero seems trapped by the enclosing walls and the human wall of thugs that block off his space. But surrounding the protagonist is a furious whipping wind (the dominant contrast of the shot), which symbolizes his fury and physical power. *(Janus Films)*

5-11. *The French Connection* (U.S.A., 1971), directed by William Friedkin.

Expansive outward movements and sunburst effects are generally associated with explosive emotions, like joy or terror. In this shot, however, the symbolism is more complex. The scene occurs at the climax of a furious chase sequence in which the protagonist (Gene Hackman, with gun) finally triumphs over a vicious killer by shooting him—just as he seems on the verge of eluding the dogged police officer once again. This kinetic outburst on the screen symbolizes not only the bullet exploding in the victim's body, but a joyous climax for the protagonist after his humiliating and dangerous pursuit. The kinetic "ecstasy of death" also releases the dramatic tension that has built up in the audience during the chase sequence: In effect, we are seduced into sharing the protagonist's joy in the kill. *(Twentieth Century Fox)*

a

b

5-12. *The Hunted* (U.S.A., 2002), with Tommy Lee Jones and Benicio Del Toro, directed by William Friedkin.

The closer and tighter the shot, the more motion dominates. In longer, more loosely framed shots, movement tends to recede in importance, usually in direct proportion to the distance of the kinetic action from the camera. Even the slightest alterations in framing can affect our reactions. The two shots here imply subtle differences. In the more loosely framed medium-full shot **(a)** Del Toro is dominated by Jones, who controls the left and centre of the mise en scène. Del Toro is backed into the right side of the screen. Jones's control over his adversary is reinforced by the amount of space allowed for his movements. The control of the visual elements within the frame becomes a spatial metaphor for Jones's (temporary) control over Del Toro. In the more desperate, tightly framed medium shot **(b)**, Del Toro has regained control. He dominates nearly two-thirds of the space within the frame, and Jones is trapped in the lower left corner of the screen. We know who is winning in each of these shots by seeing how much movement the characters can command within the confines of the frame. *(Dimension Films)*

simply moved around the axis of a stationary tripod? Each major type of camera movement implies different meanings, some obvious, others subtle. There are seven basic moving camera shots: (1) pans, (2) tilts, (3) dolly shots, (4) handheld shots, (5) crane shots, (6) zoom shots, and (7) aerial shots.

Panning shots—those movements of the camera that scan a scene horizontally—are taken from a stationary axis point, with the camera mounted on a tripod. Such shots are time-consuming because the camera's movement must ordinarily be smooth and slow to permit the images to be recorded clearly. Pans are also unnatural in a sense, for when the human eye pans a scene, it jumps from one point to another, skipping over the intervals between points. The most common use of a pan is to keep the subject within frame. If a person moves from one position to another, the camera moves horizontally to keep the person in the centre of the composition. Pans in extreme long shots are often found in epic films where an audience can experience the vastness of a locale. But pans can be just as effective at medium and close ranges. The so-called **reaction shot**, for instance, is a movement of the camera away from the central attraction—usually a speaker—to capture the reaction of an onlooker or listener. In such cases, the pan preserves the cause-and-effect relationship between the two subjects and emphasizes the solidarity and connectedness of people.

The **swish pan** (also known as a **flash pan** and a **zip pan**) is a variation of this technique and is mainly used for transitions between shots—as a substitute cut. The swish pan involves a whirling of the camera at a speed so rapid that only blurred images are recorded. Although they actually take more time than cuts, swish pans connect one scene to another with a greater sense of simultaneity than cuts can suggest. For this reason, flash pans are often used to connect events at different locales that might otherwise appear remote from each other.

Pan shots tend to emphasize the unity of space and the connectedness of people and objects within that space. Precisely because we expect a panning shot to emphasize the literal contiguity of people sharing the same space, these shots can surprise us when their realistic integrity is violated. In Robert Benton's *Places in the Heart* (1984), for example, the final shot of the movie connects the world of the living with the dead. The film is a celebration of the simple Christian values that bind a small Texas community together during the troubled times of the 1930s Depression. The final shot takes place in a church. The camera begins to pan the congregation in a long, sweeping motion down each row of pews. Interspersed among the surviving characters are several that we know to be dead, including a murderer and his victim, worshipping side by side. Though the rest of the movie is realistically presented, this final shot leaps to a symbolic level, suggesting that the unified spirit of the community includes all its members, deceased as well as living.

Tilt shots are vertical movements of the camera around a stationary horizontal axis. Many of the principles that apply to pans also apply to tilts: They can be used to keep subjects within frame, to emphasize spatial and psychological interrelationships, to suggest simultaneity, and to emphasize cause-and-effect relationships. Tilts, like pans, can also be used subjectively in point-of-view shots: The camera can simulate a character's looking up or down a scene, for instance. Since a tilt is a change in angle, it is often used to suggest a psychological shift within a character. When an eye-level camera tilts downward, for example, the person photographed suddenly appears more vulnerable.

5-13. *Cabaret* (U.S.A., 1972), with Joel Grey, choreographed and directed by Bob Fosse.
A former dancer, Fosse was the foremost stage choreographer-director of his generation, winning many Tony Awards for his Broadway musicals. He also directed a half dozen or so movies, including this musical, set in Germany during the rise of Nazism. Fosse's dancers are rarely elegant or lyrical. Rather, they are more likely to scrunch their shoulders, hunch up their backs, or thrust out their pelvises. Fosse also loved glitzy/tacky costumes—usually accompanied by hats, which were integrated into his dance numbers. He was also the most witty of choreographers, with his dancers snapping their fingers in unison, mincing to a percussive beat like cartoon characters, or locking their knees and pointing their toes inward. Above all, Fosse's dance numbers are sexy—not the wholesome athletic sex appeal of a Gene Kelly choreography, but something funkier, more raffish, and down-and-dirty. His mature style is highly cinematic, not merely an objective recording of a stage choreography. In *Cabaret*, for example, he **intercuts** shots from the musical numbers with shots of the dramatic action and vice versa. In some numbers, he cuts to an avalanche of colliding shots to create a choreography that could not exist in the literal space of a theatrical stage. *(Allied Artists)*

Dolly shots, sometimes called **trucking shots** or **tracking shots**, are taken from a moving vehicle (dolly). The vehicle literally moves in, out, or alongside a moving figure or object while the action is being photographed. Tracks are sometimes laid on the set to permit the vehicle to move smoothly—hence the term *tracking shot*. If these shots involve long distances, the tracks have to be laid or withdrawn while the camera is moving in or out. Today, any vehicular movement of the camera can be called a dolly shot. The camera can be mounted on a car, a train, even a bicycle.

Tracking is a useful technique in point-of-view shots to capture a sense of movement into or out of a scene. If a filmmaker wants to emphasize the *destination* of a character's movement, the director is more likely to use a straight cut between the initiation of the movement and its conclusion. If the experience of the movement itself is important, the director is more likely to dolly. Thus, if a character is searching for something, the time-consuming point-of-view dolly helps to elongate the suspense of the search. Similarly, the **pull-back dolly** can be used to surprise the character (and audience) with a revelation **(5-14, 5-15)**. By moving back, the camera reveals something startling, something previously off screen.

A common function of tracking shots is to provide an ironic contrast with dialogue. In Jack Clayton's *The Pumpkin Eater* (1964), a distraught wife (Anne Bancroft) returns to an ex-husband's house, where she has an adulterous liaison with him. As the two lie in bed, she asks him whether he was upset over their divorce and whether he has missed her. He assures her that he was not upset, but while their voices continue on the soundtrack, the camera belies his words by slowly dollying through his living room, revealing pictures and mementos of the ex-wife. The shot is a kind of direct communication between the director and audience, bypassing the characters. These techniques are deliberate authorial intrusions (see also **5-21**). They are favoured by filmmakers who view their characters with skepticism or irony—Ernst Lubitsch and Alfred Hitchcock, for example.

One common use of dolly shots is to emphasize psychological rather than literal revelations. By slowly tracking in on a character, the filmmaker is getting close to something crucial. The movement acts as a signal to the audience, suggesting, in effect, that we are about to witness something important. A cut to a close-up would

5-14. *Forrest Gump* (U.S.A., 1994), with Tom Hanks, directed by Robert Zemeckis.

Reverse dolly shots such as this one are more unsettling than conventional tracking shots. When we dolly into a scene, we can usually see where we're headed: to a geographical goal of some sort. But when the camera moves in reverse, sweeping backwards as it keeps the running protagonist in frame, we have no sense of a final destination, just the urgent, desperate need to flee. *(Paramount Pictures)*

5-15. *Gone With the Wind* (U.S.A., 1939), with Vivien Leigh (left, in front of boiling cauldron), directed by Victor Fleming.

The pull-back dolly or crane shot begins with a close view of a subject, then withdraws to reveal the larger context. The contrast between the close and distant views can be funny, shocking, or sadly ironic. In this famous scene, the camera begins with a close shot of the heroine (Leigh), then slowly pulls back, revealing the wounded bodies of hundreds of soldiers, and stopping finally at a distant long-shot range, in front of a high flagpole with a tattered Confederate flag blowing in the wind like a shredded remnant. *(MGM)*

tend to emphasize the rapidity of the discovery, but slow dolly shots suggest a more gradual revelation.

A stationary camera tends to convey a sense of stability and order, unless there is a great deal of movement within the frame. The moving camera—by its very instability—can create ideas of vitality, flux, and sometimes disorder. Orson Welles exploited the mobile camera to suggest the leading character's dynamic energy in *Othello* (1951). Early in the movie, the confident Moor is often photographed in travelling shots. In the ramparts scene, he and Iago walk with military briskness as the camera moves with them at an equally energetic pace. When Iago tells him of his suspicions, the camera slows down, then comes to a halt. Once Othello's mind has been poisoned, he is photographed mostly from stationary setups. Not only has his confident energy drained away, but a spiritual paralysis has also invaded his soul. In the final shots of the movie, he barely moves, even within the still frame. This paralysis motif is completed when Othello kills himself.

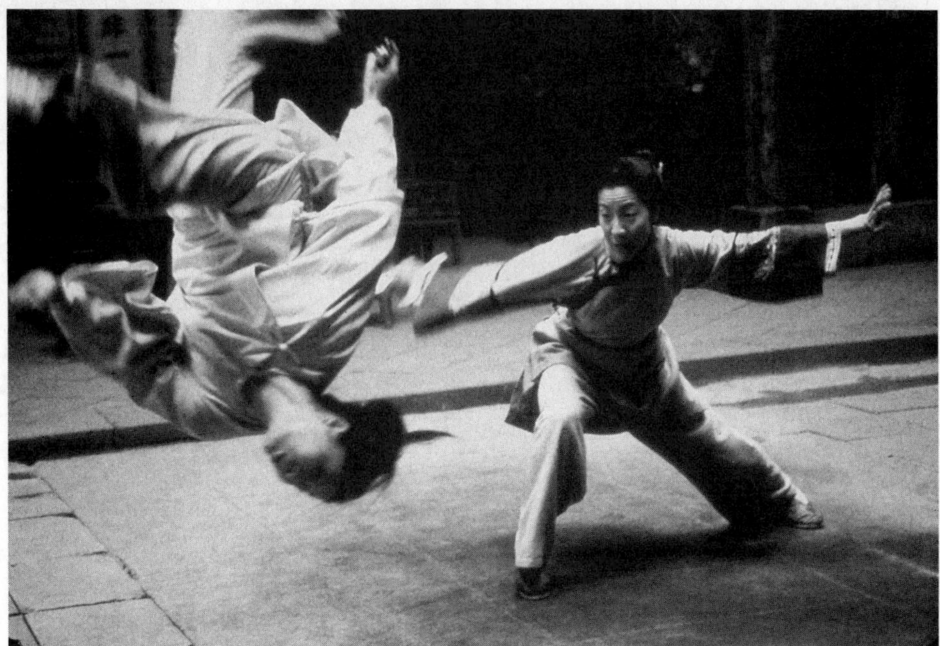

5-16. *Crouching Tiger, Hidden Dragon* (Hong Kong/Taiwan/U.S.A., 2000), with Michelle Yeoh (on ground), choreography by Yuen Wo Ping, directed by Ang Lee.

Action and adventure films are among the most kinetic of genres, stressing physical movement above all other qualities. The foremost martial arts choreographer in the world, Yuen Wo Ping makes frequent use of special effects in his choreographies, lending his action sequences a dreamy, surrealistic extravagance. His style is a blending of traditional Hong Kong martial arts, acrobatics, special effects, Chinese opera, and Hollywood dance musicals. His warrior/dancers frequently "vault"—fly or swoop up walls, slither up tall trees, or flit across rooftops like graceful flying creatures. Like Gene Kelly, Yuen Wo Ping frequently incorporates camera movement into his choreographies. He also likes to use women in his action sequences, fusing the erotic with the acrobatic. *(Sony Pictures Classics)*

When the camera literally follows a character, the audience assumes that it will discover something along the way. A journey, after all, usually has a destination. But travelling shots are often symbolic rather than literal. In Federico Fellini's *81/2* (1963), for example, the moving camera is used to suggest a variety of thematic ideas. The protagonist, Guido (Marcello Mastroianni), is a film director who is trying to put together a movie near a bizarre health spa. Everywhere he turns, he is confronted by memories, fantasies, and realities more fantastic than anything he can imagine. But he is paralyzed by indecision. What, if anything, from all this copious flux will he select for his movie? Throughout the film, the camera wanders restlessly, prowling over the fantastic locale, compulsively hoarding images of faces, textures, and shapes. Guido absorbs them all, but he is unable to detach them from their contexts to form a meaningful artistic structure.

The film's tracking shots function on several levels. They are used to suggest Guido's increasingly desperate search for a theme, a story, or a cinematic structure of some kind. They are also analogues of Guido's passive receptivity. He is like a walk-

5-17. *Singin' in the Rain* (U.S.A., 1952), with Gene Kelly and Cyd Charisse, choreographed by Kelly, directed by Kelly and Stanley Donen.

Cyd Charisse, tall, elegant, and gorgeous, was the foremost female dancer during MGM's golden age of musicals, the 1950s. Trained in ballet rather than tap, she was usually at her best in classy numbers such as this balletic dream sequence. However, she could also convey a sizzling eroticism in such torrid dance numbers as those from *It's Always Fair Weather* (Kelly and Donen, 1955) and *The Band Wagon* (Vincente Minnelli, 1953). Stage choreography is always viewed from a stationary position. Film choreography can be more complex. In movies, the camera can be choreographed as well as the dancers. Kelly's choreography often features lyrical crane shots in which the camera's swirling motions are dreamily counterpointed by the motions of the dancers, a virtual *pas de trois*. *(MGM)*

ing recording machine, seeking out and storing image upon image for their own sakes. The tracking shots, in conjunction with the movement of people, processions, and traffic, are also analogues for the unbroken flow of experiences that compose Guido's reality—a reality he finally refuses to simplify for the sake of producing a tidy little movie. But where Guido fails, Fellini succeeds triumphantly. The final sequence of the film (which takes place in Guido's imagination) emphasizes the continuity and coherence of *all* his experiences. The characters from his life—including those of Guido's past and fantasies—join hands and dance joyously around a circus ring, a ritual celebration of the limitlessness of the artistic imagination. The ring is a visual symbol of Fellini's conception of life's infinite flow, which has no beginning or end.

Many film theorists have discussed the capacity of cinema to convert space into time, and time into space. The amount of time it takes to photograph a concrete

5-18a. *Strictly Ballroom* (Australia, 1992), with Tara Morice and Paul Mercurio, directed by Baz Luhrmann. *(Miramax Films)*

"Dance is the activity where the sexual connection is most explicit," Michael Malone has pointed out, "which is why movies use it to symbolize sex and why skillful dancing is an invariable movie clue to erotic sophistication, a prerequisite for the lover." Eroticism underlies virtually all dances centred on the couple, whether the style is a sizzling flamenco with bodies literally pressed together as in *Strictly Ballroom*, or a formalized 1820 English dance as in *Vanity Fair* which still allows for some body-on-body contact as well as flirtatious smiles and smouldering eyes. In each, the male courts his partner with sinuously seductive urgency.

5-18b. *Vanity Fair* (Britain, 2004), with Jonathan Rhys Meyers and Reese Witherspoon, directed by Mira Nair. *(Focus Features)*

object can be the main purpose of a shot, especially a travelling shot. The acknowledged master of these types of dolly shots was Max Ophüls. In such movies as *Letter From an Unknown Woman* (1948) and *Madame De . . .* (1953), the heroines throw themselves into imprudent but glorious love affairs. The camera tracks relentlessly as the women become more and more irrevocably involved with their lovers. As critic Andrew Sarris pointed out, Ophüls uses his dolly shots as metaphors of time's cruel prodigality. His world is one of tragic flux and instability in which love is destined to run its eventually bitter course. These lengthy tracking shots preserve the continuity of time by preserving the continuity of space. No time is given for pause and reflection "between shots" in these films. The casual viewer may overlook this symbolic technique because the dolly shots are to some degree functional: They follow characters in their daily round of activities. But a stationary camera would be just as functional (not to mention less expensive), for the characters could move toward or away from a fixed setup.

Handheld shots are generally less lyrical, more noticeable than vehicular shots. Handheld cameras, which are usually mounted with a harness on the cinematographer's shoulder, were perfected in the 1950s to allow camera operators to move into or out of scenes with greater flexibility and speed. Originally used by documentarists to permit them to shoot in nearly every kind of **location**, these cameras were quickly adopted by many fiction film directors as well. Handheld shots are often jumpy and

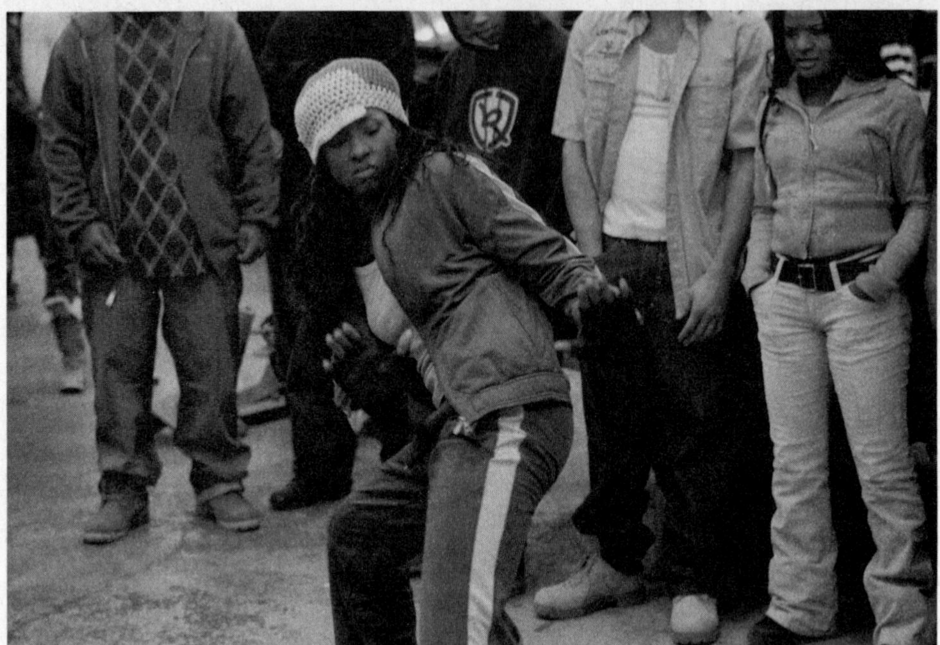

5-19. ***How She Move*** **(Canada, 2007), with Rutina Wesley, directed by Ian Iqbal Rashid.**

Dance can be erotic and seductive, but there is often an element of power and competition in the most formal of dances, with the woman usually expected to be the less assertive partner. In this movie, Raya (Wesley) must prove herself the equal of the men in a step-dancing team. The plot is conventional with a utopian ending, in which her team triumphs in the big contest in Detroit and Raya wins a scholarship that will allow her to escape from the impoverished Toronto neighbourhood where her family lives. But it is the dancing (supported by the cinematography and mise en scène) that provides the real appeal in the film, the energetic and skillful choreography contrasting with the stasis of the run-down social environment. *(Celluloid Dreams/The Kobal Collection)*

ragged. The camera's rocking is hard to ignore, for the screen exaggerates these movements, especially if the shots are taken from close ranges. For this reason, filmmakers often use the handheld camera for point-of-view shots. In Mike Nichols's *The Graduate* (1967), for example, a handheld shot is used to simulate the hero's attempts to manoeuvre through a crowded room of people. However, most cinematographers can manipulate a lightweight camera as steadily as a dolly if the situation requires, and the advent of **digital** video cameras makes elaborate handheld shots easy to achieve. The kinetic effect of the chase sequence across the ice in Zacharias Kunuk's *Atanarjuat: The Fast Runner* depends on the flexibility of the digital camera (as revealed in the production shots included in the final credits) **(10-27)**.

Crane shots are essentially airborne dolly shots. A crane is a kind of mechanical arm, often more than six metres long. In many respects, it resembles the cranes used by the telephone company to repair lines. It can lift a cinematographer and camera in or out of a scene. It can move in virtually any direction: up, down, diagonally, in, out, or any combination of these. Because of this flexibility, a crane shot can suggest a number of complex ideas. It can move from high, long distances to low, close ones, as it does in Hitchcock's *Notorious* (1946), where the camera sweeps from an

5-20. *The Blair Witch Project* (U.S.A., 1999), with Heather Donahue, directed by Dan Myrick and Eduardo Sanchez.

A rocking, turbulently roiling camera can produce a sense of nausea in some people, almost like seasickness aboard a violently swaying boat on rough waters. This low-budget thriller was shot with an unstable handheld camera, to suggest an on-the-spot documentary recording of events while they are actually taking place. The film is a good example of how budgetary liabilities can be converted into aesthetic virtues. The story centres on three college students who go to an isolated forest to explore a local myth about witchcraft. They plan to videotape the entire project. There was no set to build, no lights to set up, no costumes to sew, and no costly special effects to drain the budget. The cast consisted of only three nonprofessional actors. The movie cost $35 000 and grossed an astonishing $150 million. *(Artisan Entertainment)*

extreme high-angle long shot of a ballroom to an extreme close-up of the hand of the heroine (Ingrid Bergman) clasping a small key.

The Steadicam is a camera-stabilizing device that was perfected in the 1970s. It allows cinematographers to move smoothly through a set or location without shaking and eliminates the need for such expensive devices as cranes or dollies. Perhaps the most impressive early use of the Steadicam was in Stanley Kubrick's horror classic *The Shining* (1980), in which the camera was able to follow a young boy's tricycle as he peddled down eerily empty hotel corridors.

Zoom shots usually do not involve the actual movement of the camera, but on the screen their effect is very much like an extremely fast tracking or crane shot. The zoom is a combination of lenses, which are continuously variable, permitting the camera to change from close wide-angle distances to extreme telephoto positions (and vice versa) almost simultaneously. The effect of the zoom is a breathtaking sense of being plunged into a scene, or an equally jolting sense of being plucked out of it. In crowded locations, zoom lenses can be useful for photographing from long distances, away from the curious eyes of passersby.

5-21. ***Gangs of New York*** **(U.S.A., 2001), with Daniel Day-Lewis and Leonardo DiCaprio, directed by Martin Scorsese.**

Scorsese often complicates his shooting schedule by using a moving camera instead of simply cutting. Editing to separate shots is faster, easier, and cheaper. So why move the camera at all? In some cases the director wants to connect a series of images to suggest a subtle process of association. For example, in this period film set during the American Civil War era, we see the two main characters conducting their money business at the waterfront. In one continuous shot, the camera pans and we see Irish immigrants disembarking from a ship, at which point they are signed up to go into battle (they get automatic U.S. citizenship for doing so) and are then rerouted to a nearby troop ship, where the ship's cargo is also being loaded: coffins. The camera movement is making a political statement. *(Miramax Films)*

There are certain psychological differences between zoom shots and those involving an actual moving camera. Dolly and crane shots tend to give the viewer a sense of entering into or withdrawing from a set: Furniture and people seem to stream by the sides of the screen, as the camera penetrates a three-dimensional space. Zoom lenses foreshorten people and flatten space. The edges of the image simply disappear on all sides. The effect is one of sudden magnification. Instead of feeling as though we are entering a scene, we feel as though a small portion of it has been thrust toward us. In shots of brief duration, these differences are not significant, but in lengthier shots, the psychological differences can be pronounced.

Aerial shots, usually taken from a helicopter, are really variations of the crane shot. Like a crane, the helicopter can move in virtually any direction. When a crane is impractical—usually on exterior locations—an aerial shot can duplicate the effect. The helicopter shot can be much more extravagant, of course, and for this reason is occasionally used to suggest a swooping sense of freedom. In *Apocalypse Now* (1979), Francis Ford Coppola used aerial shots to produce a godlike sense of inexorability, as swirling American helicopters annihilate a Vietnamese village. The sequence is a kinetic tour de force, suffusing the action with a sense of exhilaration—and horror. Virtually every shot in this virtuoso edited sequence contains a forward rush, a sense of being swept up by events that are out of control.

MECHANICAL DISTORTIONS OF MOVEMENT

Movement in film is not a literal phenomenon but an optical illusion. Present-day cameras record movement at twenty-four frames per second (fps). That is, in each second, twenty-four separate still pictures are photographed. When the film is shown

5-22. *Ballet Mécanique* (France, 1924), directed by Fernand Léger.

Best known for his cubist paintings, Léger was also an avant-garde filmmaker. One of the first to explore abstraction in cinema, he created many striking kinetic effects by animating and choreographing ordinary objects like crockery, dishes, and machine gears. *(Museum of Modern Art)*

5-23. *The Little Mermaid* (U.S.A., 1989), directed by John Musker and Ron Clements.

Beginning with the "Silly Symphonies" of the early 1930s, the field of animation was dominated for many years by Walt Disney. Disney produced the first feature-length animated film, *Snow White and the Seven Dwarfs*, in 1937, and went on to build a vast organization that eventually branched out into television and theme parks. After Disney's death in 1966, the organization continued his tradition of animation, blending realism and fantasy in modern retellings of well-known fairy stories. *(Walt Disney Pictures)*

in a projector at the same speed, the human eyes mixes these still photographs instantaneously, giving the illusion of movement. This phenomenon is called the *persistence of vision.* By simply manipulating the timing mechanism of the camera or projector, a filmmaker can distort movement on the screen. Even at the turn of the twentieth century, Georges Méliès was experimenting with various kinds of trick photography, and although most of these experiments were just clever stunts, subsequent directors have used these discoveries with artistic results. Five basic distortions of this kind exist: (1) animation, (2) fast motion, (3) slow motion, (4) reverse motion, and (5) freeze frames.

There are two fundamental differences between **animation** and live-action movies. In animation sequences, each frame is photographed separately, rather than continuously at the rate of twenty-four frames per second. Another difference is that animation, as the word implies, does not ordinarily involve the photographing of subjects that move by themselves. The subjects photographed are generally drawings or static objects. Thus, in an animated movie, thousands of frames are separately photographed. Each frame differs from its neighbour only to an infinitesimal degree. When a sequence of these frames is projected at twenty-four fps, the illusion is that the drawings or objects are moving and, hence, are "animated."

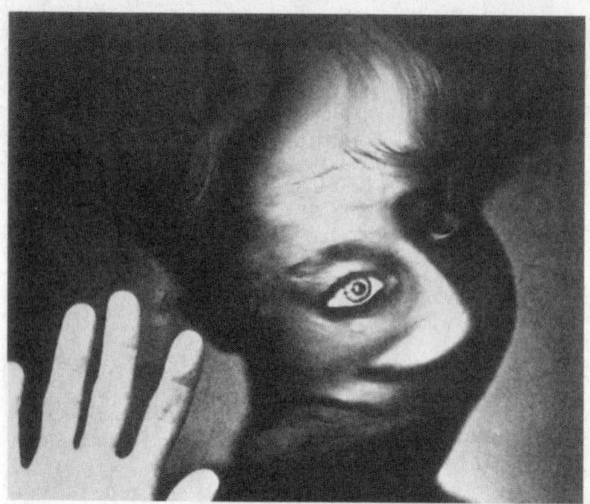

5-24a. *Photocopy Cha Cha* (U.S.A., 1991), by Chel White, included in The 23rd International Tournée of Animation. *(Expanded Entertainment)*

5-24c. *Tim Burton's Corpse Bride* (U.S.A., 2005), directed by Mike Johnson and Tim Burton. *(Warner Bros.)*

5-24b. *Can Film* (Bulgaria, 1992), by Zlatin Radev, included in The Fourth Animation Celebration. *(Expanded Entertainment)*

A number of commentators have referred to the contemporary animation scene as a golden age, encompassing a broad spectrum of styles and techniques from all over the world. *Photocopy Cha Cha* **(5-24a)** is the first animated movie created on a copy machine, by one of the most innovative of all animation artists. Unconventional artists love to create hybrid works, like *Can Film* **(5-24b)**, which combines stewed tomato cans with clay animation. Tim Burton's distinctive animated style employs stop-action techniques to bring the puppets and settings to life. *Corpse Bride* **(5-24c)** features characters who are only about 20 inches high in miniature sets. Stop-action animation is a technique that harks back to Méliès's time in the late nineteenth century.

For every second of screen time, twenty-four separate drawings usually have to be photographed. Thus, in an average ninety-minute feature, more than 129 600 drawings are necessary. Furthermore, some animators use transparent plastic sheets (called **cels**), which they layer over each other to give the illusion of depth to their drawings. Some single frames consist of as many as three or four layers of cels. Most animated films are short precisely because of the overwhelming difficulty of producing all the necessary drawings for a longer movie. Before the advent of computers, feature-length animated movies were produced in assembly-line fashion, with dozens of artists drawing thousands of separate frames.

Technically, animated films can be as complex as live-action movies. The same techniques can be used in both forms: panning and tracking, zooms, angles, various lenses, editing, dissolves, and so on. The only difference is that animators *draw* these

5-25. *Blinkity Blank* (Canada, 1955), directed by Norman McLaren.

Whereas animation in the Disney tradition combines fantasy with lifelike drawings, many of McLaren's animated films feature purely abstract patterns created without a camera. In this ingenious six-minute film, the designs were scratched directly onto the celluloid and accompanied by both instrumental music and sounds "drawn" on the soundtrack. *(National Film Board of Canada)*

elements into their images. Furthermore, animators can also use many painting techniques and tools: different kinds of paints, pens, pencils, pastels, washes, acrylics, and so on.

A popular misconception about animated movies is that they are intended primarily for the entertainment of children—perhaps because Walt Disney dominated the field for so many years. However, Disney's early *Silly Symphonies* and Mickey Mouse cartoons, with their grotesque and violent images clearly addressed to adult audiences, were much less sentimental than his later feature films. Animated films often deal with serious issues that live-action movies cannot or will not tackle. For example, George Orwell's *Animal Farm*, a satiric fable about totalitarianism, was adapted in 1955 by the animation team of Halas and Batchelor. More recently, the Japanese genre of *anime* has achieved a cult following with its stylized fantasies, often involving graphic violence and sexuality, that nevertheless address important tensions and concerns in a nation still recovering from the trauma of World War II.

Norman McLaren's 1953 antiwar animated film *Neighbours* ran into censorship problems because of its graphic depiction of the violent struggle of two men over a flower that grows on the boundary between their gardens. In films like *Neighbours* and *A Chairy Tale* (1957, co-directed with Claude Jutra), McLaren used a technique called **pixillation**, which involves photographing live actors frame by frame, a method sometimes called **stop-motion photography**. When the sequence is pro-

5-26. *Who Framed Roger Rabbit* (U.S.A., 1988), with Bob Hoskins and Roger Rabbit, directed by Robert Zemeckis.

Robert Zemeckis is a modern pioneer in the field of animation. In *Who Framed Roger Rabbit,* he combined live action characters with animated characters within the same frame with no disjunctions in style. *(The Walt Disney Company and Amblin Entertainment)*

jected onto the screen, the actors move in abrupt, jerky motions, suggesting a primitive cartoon figure. McLaren also made animated films without a camera by drawing directly on the celluloid **(5-25)**. He made these films for the National Film Board of Canada, where he arrived in 1941 ostensibly to provide maps and diagrams for documentaries. His innovative work earned the NFB an international reputation as a producer of animated films, and many other celebrated animators have since worked at the Board, including Arthur Lipsett, Co Hoedeman, and Frédéric Back.

Computers have now made possible the creation of animated features like *Toy Story* and *Shrek* that combine McLaren's idea of producing moving images without a camera with the realism for which the Disney films were famous (**Colour Plate 13**). Other filmmakers have combined animation and theatrical film techniques within the same frame. In recent years, computer animation often heightens the realism of special effects, as in the fusion of digital dinosaurs and live action in Steven Spielberg's *Jurassic Park* (1993). In his 2003 feature *Nothing*, Canadian filmmaker Vincenzo Natali used digital technology to create a fable in which two men gradually "wish away" the environment that oppresses them and eventually parts of each other's bodies, until they end up as disembodied heads bouncing around a white void **(10-18)**. The film thus plays with the question of "where is here?" that haunts discussions of Canadian identity (see Chapter 10, "Canadian Cinema") as well as the postmodern concept of hyperreality (see Chapter 11, "Theory").

Long before the introduction of digital imagery, mechanical distortions were used to manipulate the impression of movement in much the same way that the animator controls the world that he or she creates. **Fast motion** is achieved by having

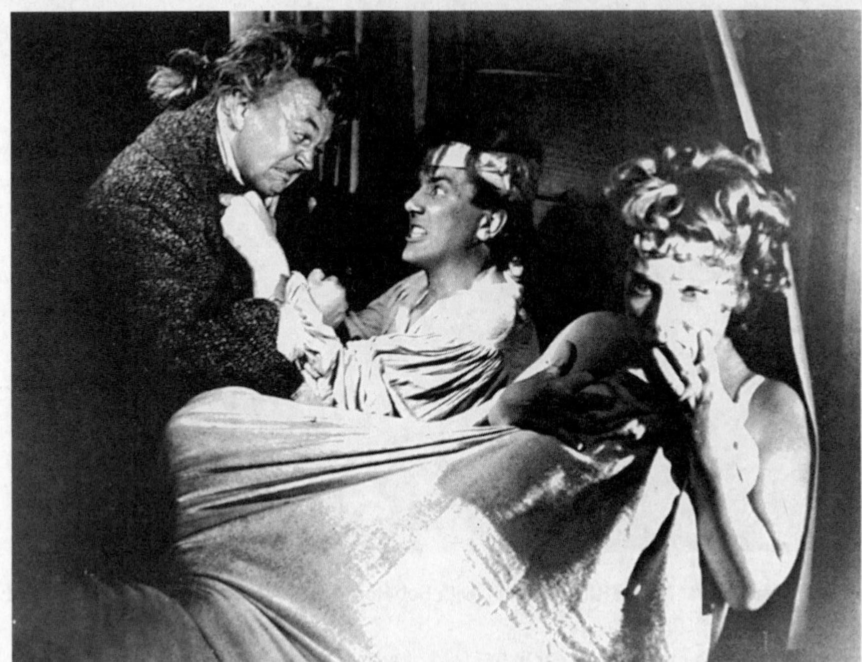

5-27. ***Tom Jones*** **(Britain, 1963), with George Cooper, Albert Finney, and Joyce Redman, directed by Tony Richardson.**

Richardson uses fast motion in this movie when he wishes to emphasize the machinelike behaviour of the characters—especially of the randy hero (Finney) whose sex drive often overpowers his judgment. In the famous Upton Inn mix-up (pictured), Tom is rudely interrupted in his nocturnal amours by the hot-tempered Mr. Fitzpatrick. The sequence is shot in fast motion to heighten the comedy: The drunken Fitzpatrick flails at our besieged hero as his terrified paramour screams for her life, thus waking all the inhabitants of the inn, including Sophie Western, the only woman Tom truly loves. *(The Samuel Goldwyn Company)*

events photographed at a slower rate than twenty-four fps. Ordinarily, the subject photographed moves at a normal pace. When the sequence is projected at twenty-four fps, the effect is one of acceleration. This technique is sometimes used to intensify the natural speed of a scene—one showing galloping horses, for example, or cars speeding past the camera. Early silent comedies were photographed before the standardization of cameras and projectors at twenty-four fps, and therefore movement in these films is often distorted by present-day film projectors (although the correct speed can now be captured on DVD). Even at sixteen or twenty fps, however, some of these early directors used fast motion for comic effects. Without the use of acceleration, the comedies of Mack Sennett would lose much of their loony vitality.

According to French aesthetician Henri Bergson, when people act mechanically rather than flexibly, comedy is the result. People, unlike machines, can think, feel, and act reasonably. A person's intelligence is measured by his or her ability to be flexible. When behaviour becomes machinelike and inflexible, we find it laughable. One aspect of machinelike behaviour is speed: When a person's movements are speeded up on film, he or she seems inhuman, ridiculous. Dignity is difficult in fast motion, for acceleration robs us of our humanity. The Upton Inn mix-up in Tony

5-28. ***The Last of the Mohicans*** **(U.S.A., 1992), with Daniel Day-Lewis, directed by Michael Mann.**

Slow motion, of course, prolongs time—sometimes unbearably, as in this shot. The hero is racing to the rescue of the woman he loves, who is under attack during a sudden Indian ambush. A weapon in each hand, photographed at the aggressive full-front position, with the foreground and background an irrelevant blur, Hawkeye (Day-Lewis) is totally focused on his enemy, but the slow-motion photography seems to hold him back—as an agonizing eternity passes. *(Twentieth Century Fox)*

Richardson's *Tom Jones* is funny precisely because the fast motion captures the machinelike predictability of all the characters: Tom flies from Mrs. Waters's bed, Mr. Fitzpatrick flies off the handle, Squire Western screams for his daughter, and the servants scream for their lives **(5-27)**.

Slow motion is achieved by photographing events at a faster rate than twenty-four fps and projecting the filmstrip at the standard speed. Slow motion tends to ritualize and solemnize movement **(5-28)**. Even the most commonplace actions take on a choreographic gracefulness in slow motion **(5-29)**. Whereas speed tends to be the natural rhythm of comedy, slow, dignified movements tend to be associated with tragedy. In *The Pawnbroker* (1965), Sidney Lumet uses slow motion in a flashback sequence, showing the protagonist as a young man on an idyllic country outing with his family. The scenes are lyrical and otherworldly—too perfect to last.

When violent scenes are photographed in slow motion, the effect is paradoxically beautiful. In *The Wild Bunch* (1969), Sam Peckinpah used slow motion to photograph the grisliest scenes of horror—flesh tearing, blood spattering, horses toppling, an almost endless variety. By aestheticizing these scenes of ugliness, Peckinpah demonstrates why the men are so addicted to a life of violence when it seems so profitless. Violence becomes almost an aesthetic credo, somewhat as it is portrayed in the fiction of Ernest Hemingway.

Reverse motion simply involves photographing an action with the film running reversed. When projected on the screen, the events run backward. Since Méliès's time, reverse motion has rarely progressed much beyond the gag stage. In *The Knack* (1965), Richard Lester used reverse motion as a comic choreographic retake for a quick laugh when an egg "returns" to its shell. One of the most expressive uses of reverse motion—combined with slow motion—is in Jean Cocteau's *Orphée* (1949). The protagonist has taken a journey into Hell to regain his lost wife. He makes a serious blunder while there and expresses a wish to return to his original point of decision to correct his mistake. Magically, he is whisked into the past before our eyes, as the previous sequence unfurls backwards in slow motion—to the physical setting

5-29. *Hair* (U.S.A., 1979), choreography by Twyla Tharp, directed by Milos Forman.
Slow motion etherealizes movement, lending it a dreamy, otherworldly grace. Throughout this musical, slow motion is used in the dance numbers to emphasize the individuality rather than the uniformity of the dancers. Twyla Tharp's choreography is organic to the story, which deals with the freewheeling lifestyle of some 1960s hippies. The dance numbers are loose and spontaneous, with each dancer doing his or her own thing—like jiggling links in a chain. *(United Artists)*

where the fateful decision was made. The reverse motion in this sequence is a good instance of how space can be temporalized and time spatialized in cinema.

A **freeze frame** suspends all movement on the screen. A single image is selected and reprinted for as many frames as is necessary to suggest the halting of motion. By interrupting a sequence with a freeze shot, the director calls attention to an image—offering it, as it were, for our delectation. Sometimes, the image is a fleeting moment of poignance that is over in a fraction of a second, as in the final shot of François Truffaut's *Les Quatre cent coups* [*The 400 Blows*] (1959). Directors also use freeze frames for comic purposes. In *Tom Jones*, Richardson freezes the shot of Tom dangling on a noose while the off-screen narrator urbanely explains to the audience that generic conventions require a last-minute rescue, which then promptly occurs.

In other instances, the freeze frame can be used for thematic purposes. The final image of Richardson's *The Loneliness of the Long Distance Runner* (1962) is frozen to emphasize the permanence of the protagonist's entrapment at the end of the film. Freeze frames are ideal metaphors for dealing with time, for in effect the frozen image permits no change. Near the end of *True Grit* (1969), for example, Henry Hathaway froze a shot of the protagonist (John Wayne) and his horse leaping over a fence. By halting the shot at the crest of the leap, Hathaway creates a metaphor of timeless grandeur: The image suggests a heroic equestrian statue, immune from the

5-30. *Viridiana* (Mexico / Spain, 1961), directed by Luis Buñuel.

This notorious freeze-frame parody of Leonardo's painting of the Last Supper is only one example of Buñuel's savage assaults on the Church, sentimental liberalism, and middle-class morality. His sardonic wit is often shocking and blasphemous. For example, the context of this freeze frame is a drunken orgy of beggars who pose for a group photo to the accompaniment of Handel's *Messiah*. A woman reeling in boozy stupor "snaps" the picture not with a camera but with her genitals. This raucous gesture throws the "disciples" into paroxysms of laughter. Though a nonbeliever, Buñuel was able to infuse a sense of scandal into these sacrilegious jokes. "Thank God I am still an atheist," he once sighed. *(Audio-Brandon Films)*

ravages of time and decay. Of course, the total absence of movement is often associated with death, and Hathaway's freeze frame also implies this idea. Perhaps a more explicit metaphor of death can be seen in the conclusion of George Roy Hill's *Butch Cassidy and the Sundance Kid* (1969), where the two heroes (Paul Newman and Robert Redford) are "frozen" just before they are shot to death. Like Hathaway's freeze frame, Hill's suggests an ultimate triumph over death.

Movement in film is not simply a matter of "what happens." The director has dozens of ways to convey motion, and what differentiates a great director from a merely competent one is not so much a matter of what happens, but how things happen—how suggestive and resonant the movements are in a given dramatic context, or how effectively the form of the movement embodies its content.

FURTHER READING

Bordwell, David, *Planet Hong Kong* (Cambridge: Harvard University Press, 2000). The use of movement in Hong Kong action genres.

Dobson, Terence, *The Film Work of Norman McLaren* (Eastleigh: John Libbey Publishing, 2006). Thorough study of the career of the Canadian animator.

Esther, Leslie, *Hollywood Flatlands: Animation, Critical Theory and the Avant-Garde* (London: Verso, 2004). Links between the European avant-garde and the U.S. cartoon industry.

Geuens, Jean-Pierre, "Visuality and Power: The Work of the Steadicam," *Film Quarterly* 47, no. 2 (Winter 1993–94): 8–17. The differences between Steadicam and earlier uses of the moving camera.

Johnson, Kenneth, "The Point of View of the Wandering Camera," *Cinema Journal* 32, no. 2 (Winter 1993): 49–56. The relations of camera movement and narration.

Napier, Susan J., *Anime: from Akira to Princess Mononoke: Experiencing Contemporary Japanese Animation* (New York: Palgrave, 2001). Critical and theoretical discussion of popular Japanese animation.

Pramaggiore, Maria, "Performance and Persona in the U.S. Avant-Garde: The Case of Maya Deren," *Cinema Journal* 36, no. 2 (1997): 17–40. Study of an avant-garde filmmaker who blended documentary and dance.

Robinson, Chris, *Canadian Animation: Looking for a Place to Happen* (Eastleigh: John Libbey Publishing, 2008). Interviews with leading Canadian animators.

Schrader, Paul, *Transcendental Style in Film: Ozu, Bresson, Dreyer* (Berkeley: University of California Press, 1972). Provocative argument about the use of stasis in the work of three directors.

Wells, Paul, *Understanding Animation* (London: Routledge, 1998). Comprehensive introduction to animated film.

Thirty-Two Short Films About Glenn Gould (The Samuel Goldwyn Company)

EDITING

The foundation of film art is editing.

—V.I. Pudovkin

OVERVIEW

Real time versus reel time: the problem of continuity. Cutting to continuity: condensing unobtrusively. D.W. Griffith and the development of classical cutting: editing for emphasis and nuance. The problem of time. Subjective editing: thematic montage and the Soviet school. Pudovkin and Eisenstein: two early masters of thematic cutting. The famous Odessa Steps sequence of *Battleship Potemkin*. The countertradition: the realism of André Bazin. How editing lies. When not to cut and why. Real time and space and how to preserve them. The realist arsenal: sound, deep focus, sequence shots, widescreen.

So far, we have been concerned with cinematic communication as it relates to the single shot, the basic unit of construction in movies. However, shots in film tend to acquire meaning when they are juxtaposed with other shots and structured into an edited sequence. Physically, **editing** is simply joining one strip of film (shot) with another. Shots are joined into **scenes** and **sequences**. On the most mechanical level, editing eliminates unnecessary time and space. Through the association of ideas, editing connects one shot with another, one scene with another, and so on. Simple as this may now seem, the conventions of editing represent what critic Terry Ramsaye referred to as the "syntax" of cinema, its grammatical language. Like linguistic syntax, the syntax of editing must be learned.

CONTINUITY

In the earliest years of cinema, the late 1890s, movies were short, consisting of brief events photographed in long shot in a single take. The duration of the shot and the event were equal. Soon filmmakers began to tell stories—requiring more than a single shot. Scholars have traced the development of narrative to filmmakers in France, Britain, and the United States.

By the early twentieth century, filmmakers had already devised a functional style of editing we now call **cutting to continuity**. This type of cutting is a technique used in most fiction films even today, if only for exposition scenes. Essentially, this style of editing is a kind of shorthand, consisting of time-honoured conventions. Continuity cutting tries to preserve the fluidity of an event without literally showing all of it.

For example, a continuous shot of a woman leaving work and going home might take forty-five minutes. Cutting to continuity condenses the action into five brief shots, each of which leads by association to the next. (1) She enters a corridor as she closes the door to her office. (2) She leaves the office building. (3) She enters and starts her car. (4) She drives her car along a highway. (5) Her car turns into her driveway at home. The entire forty-five minute action might take ten seconds of screen time, yet nothing essential is left out. It is unobtrusive condensation.

To keep the action logical and continuous, an edited sequence of this sort cannot have confusing breaks. Often, all the movement is carried out in the same direction on the screen to avoid confusion. For example, if the woman moves from right to left in one shot and her movements are from left to right in the other shots, we might think that she is returning to her office. Cause-and-effect relationships must be clearly set forth. If the woman slams on her brakes, the director is generally obliged to offer us a shot of what prompted the driver to stop so suddenly.

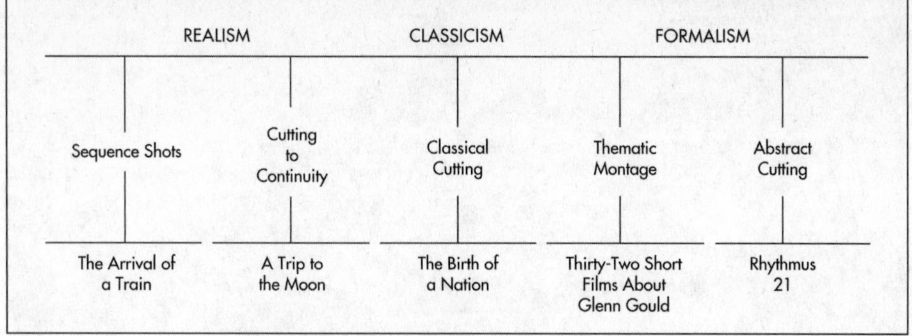

6-1. Editing styles can be classified according to how intrusive or interpretive the cutting is. The least manipulative style is found in a **sequence shot**, which contains no editing. **Cutting to continuity** merely condenses the time and space of a completed action. **Classical cutting** interprets an action by emphasizing certain details over others. **Thematic montage** argues a thesis—the shots are connected in a relatively subjective manner. Abstract cutting is a purely formalistic style of editing, totally divorced from any recognizable subject matter.

The continuity of actual space and time is fragmented as smoothly as possible in this type of editing. Unless the audience has a clear sense of a continuous action, an editing transition can be disorienting. To make their transitions smooth, filmmakers generally use **establishing shots** at the beginning of their stories or at the beginning of any new scene within the narrative.

Once the location is established, filmmakers can cut to closer shots of the action. If the events require a considerable number of cuts, the filmmaker might cut back to a **reestablishing shot**—a return to the opening long shot. In this way, the viewer is reminded of the spatial context of the closer shots. "Between" these various shots, time and space can be expanded or contracted with considerable subtlety.

By 1908, when D. W. Griffith began his career, filmmakers had already learned how to tell stories, thanks to the technique of cutting to continuity. But the stories were simple and crude compared with those in more sophisticated narrative media such as literature and drama. Nonetheless, movie storytellers already knew that by breaking up an action into different shots, the event could be contracted or expanded, depending on the number of shots. In other words, the shot, not the scene, was the basic unit of film construction.

Before Griffith, movies were usually photographed in stationary long shot—roughly the position of a close observer in the live theatre. Because film time does not depend on the duration of the literal event, Griffith and other filmmakers of this era introduced a more subjective time, one determined by the duration of the shots (and the elapsed time implied between them), not by the actual occurrence.

D.W. GRIFFITH AND CLASSICAL CUTTING

The basic elements of editing syntax were already in place when Griffith entered the field, but he more than any other individual moulded these elements into a language of power and subtlety. Film scholars have called this language **classical cutting**. Griffith has been called the Father of Film because he consolidated and expanded

6-2. *L'Arrivée d'un train* [*The Arrival of a Train*] (France, 1895), directed by Louis and Auguste Lumière. Their brief *actualités* (as the Lumière brothers called them) anticipate the documentary movement and depicted events that unfolded in the few minutes before the film in the camera ran out. *(Museum of Modern Art)*

many of the techniques invented by his predecessors. By 1915, the year of *The Birth of a Nation* **(6-4)**, classical cutting was already an editing style of great sophistication and expressiveness. Griffith had seized on the principle of the association of ideas in the concept of editing and expanded it in a variety of ways.

Classical cutting involves editing for dramatic intensity and emotional emphasis rather than for purely physical reasons. By using the close-up within the scene, Griffith managed to achieve a dramatic impact that was unprecedented. Close-ups had been used earlier, but Griffith was the first to use them for psychological reasons rather than for physical reasons alone. Audiences were now permitted to see the smallest details of an actor's face. No longer were performers required to flail their arms and tear their hair. The slightest arch of an eyebrow could convey a multitude of subtleties.

By splitting the action into a series of fragmentary shots, Griffith achieved not only a greater sense of detail, but also a far greater degree of control over his audience's reactions. In carefully selecting and juxtaposing long, medium, and close shots, he constantly shifted the spectator's point of view within a scene—expanding here, excluding there, emphasizing, consolidating, connecting, contrasting, paralleling, and so on. The possibilities were far ranging. The space and time continuum of

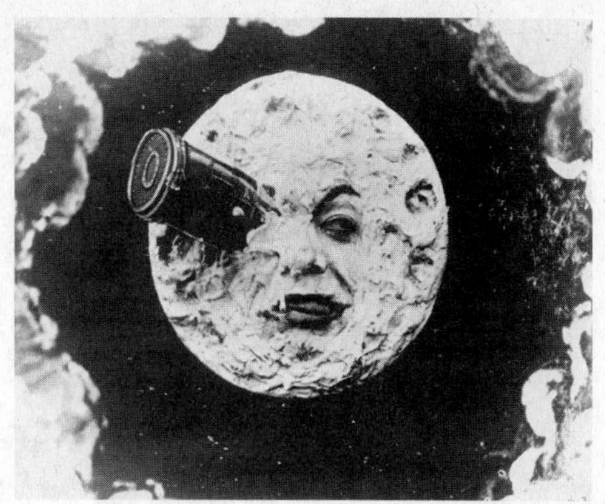

6-3. *Le Voyage dans la lune* [*A Trip to the Moon*] (France, 1902), directed by Georges Méliès.

Around 1900, in the United States, Britain, and France, filmmakers began to tell stories. Méliès was one of the first to devise the style of cutting to continuity. The narrative segments are connected by a fade—the diminishing of the light at the conclusion of a scene. The next scene then fades in, often in a different location and at a different time, though usually with the same characters. Méliès advertised these films as stories in "arranged scenes." *(Museum of Modern Art)*

the real scene was radically altered. It was replaced by a subjective continuity—the association of ideas implicit in the connected shots.

In its most refined form, classical cutting presents a series of psychologically connected shots. For example, if four characters are seated in a room, a director might cut from one speaker to a second with a dialogue exchange, then cut to a **reaction shot** of one of the listeners, then to a **two shot** of the original speakers, and finally to a close-up of the fourth person. The sequence of shots represents a kind of psychological cause-and-effect pattern. In other words, the breakup of shots is justified on the basis of dramatic rather than literal necessity. The scene could be photographed just as functionally in a single shot, with the camera at long-shot range. This type of setup is known as a **sequence shot**. Classical cutting is more nuanced and more intrusive. It breaks down the unity of space, analyzes its components, and refocuses our attention to a series of details. The action is mental and emotional rather than literal **(6-7)**.

During the golden years of the American studio system—roughly the 1930s and 1940s—directors were often urged (or forced) to adopt the **master shot** technique of shooting. An entire scene was filmed in long shot without cuts; this take contained all the dramatic variables and hence served as the basic or "master" shot for the scene. The action was then repeated a number of times, with the camera photographing medium shots and close-ups of the principles in the scene. When all this footage was gathered together, the editor had a number of choices in constructing a story continuity. Often disagreements arose over the proper sequence of shots. Usually, the director was permitted a **first cut**—that is, the sequence of shots representing his or her interpretation of the materials. Under this system, the studios usually had the right to a **final cut**. Many directors disliked master shot techniques precisely because, with so much footage available, a producer could construct a radically different continuity.

Master shots are still used by many directors. Without a master, editors often complain of inadequate footage—that the available shots will not cut smoothly. In complex battle scenes, most directors are likely to shoot many **cover shots**—that is, general shots that can be used to reestablish a sequence if the other shots will not cut. In *The Birth of a Nation*, Griffith used multiple cameras to photograph many of the battle scenes, a technique also used by Akira Kurosawa in some sequences of *The Seven Samurai* (1954).

Griffith and other classical filmmakers developed a variety of editing conventions that they thought made the cutting "invisible," or at least unobtrusive. One of these

6-4. *The Birth of a Nation* (U.S.A., 1915), directed by D. W. Griffith.

Griffith's greatest gift to cinema was classical cutting—a style of editing that still characterizes most of the fiction films around the world. Classical cutting allows filmmakers to inflect their narratives, to add nuances and emphasis. It also subjectivizes time. For example, in this famous last-minute rescue finale, Griffith cross-cuts to four different groups. Despite the sense of speed suggested by the brevity of the shots, the sequence actually expands time. Griffith used 255 separate shots for about twenty minutes of screen time. *(Museum of Modern Art)*

techniques is the eyeline match. We see character A look off frame left. Cut to a shot—from his point of view—of character B. We assume B is to A's left: cause and effect.

Another convention of classical cutting is matching action. Character A is seated but begins to rise. Cut to another shot of character A concluding the rising action and then moving away. The idea is to keep the action fluid, to mask the cut with a smooth linkage that is not noticed because the motion of the character takes precedence. The continuity of the movement conceals the suture.

The so-called 180° rule is still observed by filmmakers, though even during the big-studio era there was nothing sacred about it. (For example, John Ford loved violating the 180° rule. He loved violating almost any rule.) This convention involves mise en scène as well as editing. The purpose is to stabilize the space of the playing area so that the spectator is not confused or disoriented. An imaginary "axis of action" line is drawn through the middle of a scene, viewed from the bird's-eye angle **(6-8)**. Character A is on the left; character B is on the right. If the director wanted a two shot, he or she would use camera 1. If we then go to a close-up of A (camera 2),

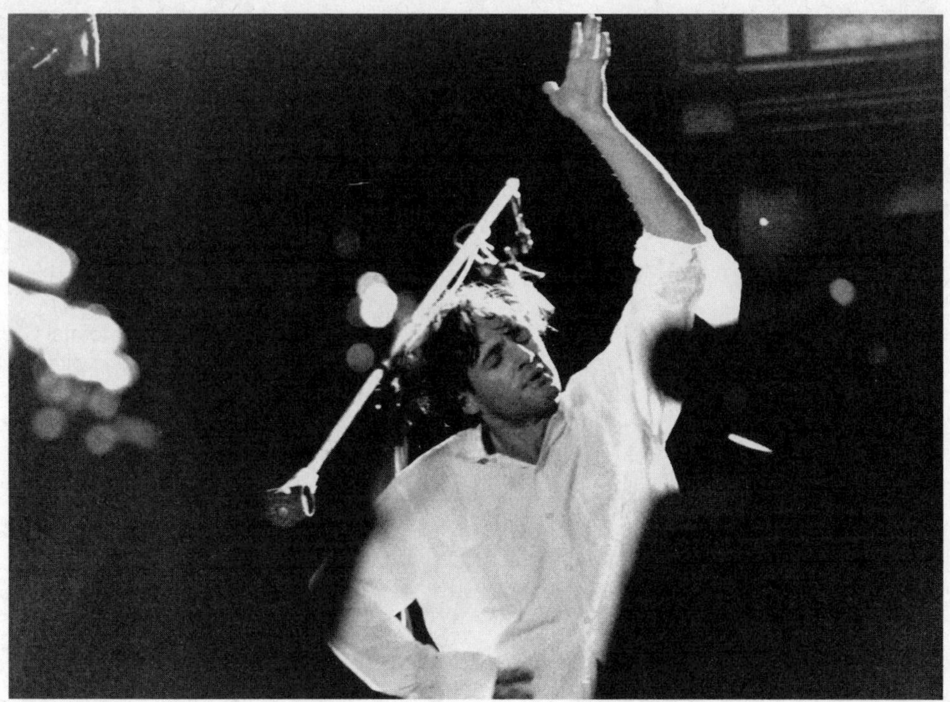

6-5. *Thirty-Two Short Films About Glenn Gould* (Canada, 1994), with Colm Feore, directed by François Girard.

This movie combines elements from documentary filmmaking, fiction films, and the avant-garde. Its editing style is radically subjective. The movie features documentary footage of the late Glenn Gould, a controversial and eccentric Canadian pianist considered to be one of the great musicians of the twentieth century. There are also many re-created scenes with Feore playing the quirky and obsessive artist. The movie's structure is not a straightforward narrative, but a series of fragments, loosely based on the thirty-two-part *Goldberg Variations* of Johann Sebastian Bach—one of Gould's most celebrated virtuoso performances. The film is structured around ideas rather than a linear story, and for this reason, thematic montage is its style of editing. *(The Samuel Goldwyn Company)*

the camera must stay on the same side of the 180° line to keep the same background—a continuity aid for the spectator. Similarly, a close-up of character B (camera 3) would be shot on the same side of the axis of action.

In **shot/reverse shot** exchanges—common for dialogue sequences—the director takes care to fix the placement of the characters from shot to shot. If character A is on the left and character B is on the right in the first shot, they must remain that way in the **reverse angle** taken from over the shoulder of character B. Usually the reverse angle is not literally 180° opposite, but we agree to accept it as such. Violations of this rule may lead us to question the reality of what we are seeing. In *Stay* (Marc Forster, 2005), for example, a conversation between a psychiatrist and his patient consists of alternating profile shots of each man in which they both occupy the same area on the left side of the wide screen. The effect suggests the two characters may be different aspects of one personality, a suggestion that the film's ending will both confirm and amplify.

6-6. ***Rhythmus 21*** **(Germany, 1921), directed by Hans Richter.**

In avant-garde cinema, subject matter is often suppressed or exploited primarily as abstract data. The continuity between shots has nothing to do with a story but is determined by purely subjective or formal considerations. Along with many other European abstract artists of his generation, Richter was a champion of the "absolute film," which consists solely of nonrepresentational forms and designs. *(Museum of Modern Art)*

Classical filmmakers were also expected to observe the 30° rule which required that the camera position must be moved at least 30° between shots. Otherwise, there will not be enough difference in the camera angle for the spectator to recognize that the second shot is a new one, creating the impression that the camera has jumped. The term **jump cut** thus refers to a violation of this rule, although it is often used to describe any disruption in the cutting continuity. True jump cuts are rarely used in Hollywood cinema. Ridley Scott uses them at the beginning of *Matchstick Men* (2003), along with other forms of discontinuity editing, **oblique angles**, and **fast motion**, to introduce the extreme nervous disorder from which the con man played by Nicholas Cage suffers. The effect also involves us in his skewed perception of events so that we are as surprised as he is when he realizes that he has himself become the victim of an elaborate con game.

Griffith also perfected the conventions of the chase—still very much with us. Many of his movies ended with a chase and last-minute rescue sequence. Most of them feature **parallel editing**—the alternation of shots of one scene with another at a different location. By **cross-cutting** back and forth between the two (or three or four) scenes, Griffith conveyed the idea of simultaneous time. For example, near the end of *The Birth of a Nation*, Griffith cross-cuts among four groups. In juxtaposing shots

6-7. ***Fat City*** **(U.S.A., 1972), directed by John Huston.**

Classical cutting involves editing for dramatic emphasis, to highlight details that might otherwise be overlooked. In Huston's fight scene, for example, the entire boxing match could have been presented in a single setup **(a)**, though such a presentation would probably strike us as unexciting. Instead, Huston breaks up his shots according to the psychological actions and reactions of the fighter protagonist (Stacy Keach), **(b)**, his manager (Nicholas Colasanto), **(c)**, and two friends in the auditorium (Jeff Bridges and Candy Clark), **(d)**. *(Columbia Pictures)*

from these separate scenes, he manages to intensify the suspense by reducing the duration of the shots as the sequence reaches its climax. The sequence itself lasts twenty minutes of film time, but the psychological effect of the cross-cutting (the shots average about five seconds each) suggests speed and tension. Generally, the greater the number of cuts within a scene, the greater its sense of speed. To avoid the risk of monotony during this sequence, Griffith changed his setups many times. There are extreme long, long, medium, and close shots, varied angles, lighting contrasts, even a moving camera (it was mounted on a truck).

If the continuity of a sequence is reasonably logical, the fragmentation of space presents no great difficulties. But the problem of time is more complex. Its treatment in film is more subjective than the treatment of space. Movies can compress years into two hours of projection time. They can also stretch a split second into many minutes. Most films condense time. There are only a handful that attempt to make

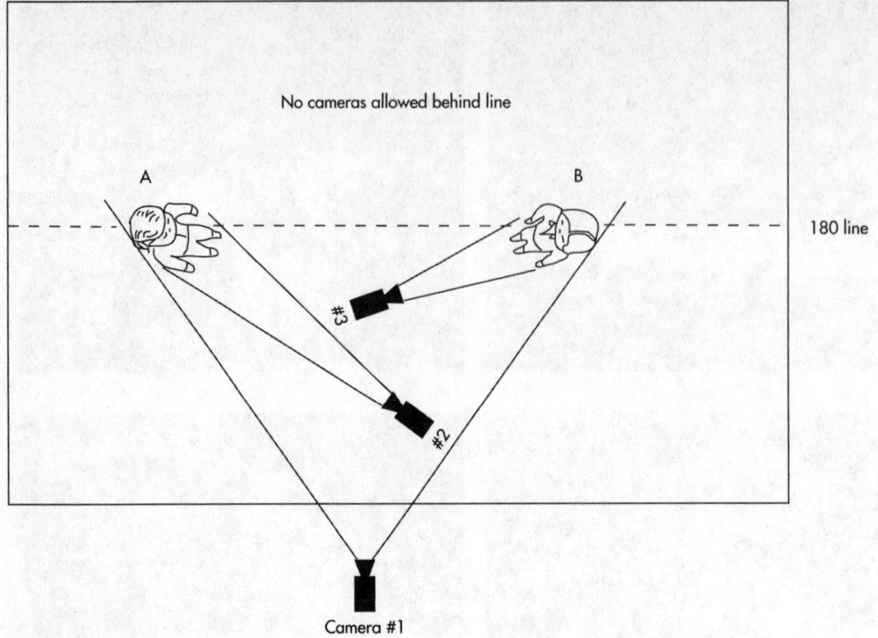

6-8. Bird's-eye view of 180° rule.

screen time conform to real time: Agnès Varda's *Cléo de 5 à 7* [*Cleo from Five to Seven*] (1961) and Fred Zinnemann's *High Noon* **(6-10)** are perhaps the best-known examples. Even these movies cheat by compressing time in the expository opening sequences and expanding it in the climactic scenes. In actual practice, time exists in a kind of limbo: As long as the audience is absorbed by the screen action, time is what the film says it is. The problem, then, is to absorb the viewer.

On the most mechanical level, screen time is determined by the physical length of the filmstrip containing the shot. This length is governed generally by the complexity of the subject matter. Usually, long shots are more densely saturated with visual information than close-ups and need to be held longer on the screen. Raymond Spottiswoode, an early film theorist, claimed that a cut must be made at the peak of the "content curve"—that is, the point in a shot at which the audience has been able to assimilate most of its information. Cutting after the peak of the content curve produces boredom and a sense of dragging time. Cutting before the peak does not give the audience time to assimilate the visual action. An image with a complex mise en scène requires more time to assimilate than a simple one. Once an image has been established, however, a return to it during the sequence can be considerably shorter, because it works as a reminder.

But the sensitive treatment of time in editing is largely an instinctive matter that defies mechanical rules **(6-11)**. The best-edited sequences are determined by mood as well as subject matter. Griffith, for example, generally edited love scenes in long lyrical takes, with relatively few setups. His chase and battle scenes are composed of brief shots jammed together. Paradoxically, the love scenes actually compress real time, whereas the rapidly cut sequences elongate it.

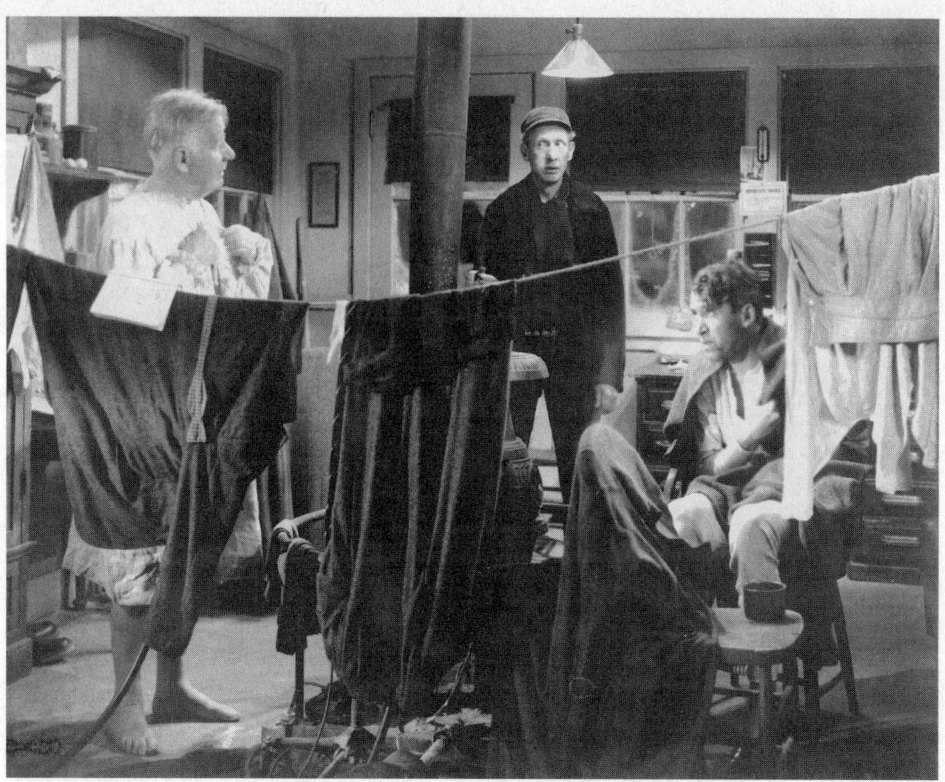

6-9. ***It's a Wonderful Life*** **(U.S.A., 1946), with James Stewart, directed by Frank Capra.**
Capra was a master of classical editing. His cutting style was fast, light, and seamless. But he never displayed his editing virtuosity for its own sake. Like every other technique in classical cinema, editing is subordinated to the needs of the characters in action. In this and other scenes, Capra includes a "reactive character" who guides the viewer's response to the action. This character represents a kind of norm, the way an average person would respond to a given situation. In this scene, for example, Capra's fantasy takes a whimsical turn. The forlorn hero (Stewart) listens to his guardian angel (Henry Travers, left) explain why he is not a very *distinguished* angel (he has yet to earn his wings). A casual bystander (Tom Fadden, centre) happens to overhear and is totally spooked by their conversation. Capra is able to punctuate the comedy of the scene by cutting to this character's response whenever the angel says something weird. *(RKO)*

There are no fixed rules concerning rhythm in films. Some editors cut according to musical rhythms (see **7-10**). The march of soldiers, for example, could be edited to the beat of a military tune, as can be seen in several marching sequences in King Vidor's *The Big Parade* (1925). This technique is also common with American avant-garde filmmakers, who feature rock music soundtracks or cut according to a mathematical or structural formula. In some cases, a director will cut before the peak of the content curve, especially in highly suspenseful sequences. In several movies, Alfred Hitchcock teases the audience by not providing enough time to assimilate all the meanings of a shot. Violent scenes are conventionally cut in a highly fragmented manner. Conversely, Michelangelo Antonioni usually cuts long after the content curve has peaked. In *La Notte* (1961), for example, the rhythm is languorous and

6-10. ***High Noon*** **(U.S.A., 1952), with Gary Cooper and Lloyd Bridges, directed by Fred Zinnemann.**
Almost all movies compress time, condensing many months or even years into a running time of roughly two hours, the average length of most films. Zinnemann's movie is a rare example of a literal adherence to the unities of time, place, and action, for the entire story takes place in a breathless eighty-four minutes—the film's running time. *(United Artists)*

even monotonous: The director attempts to create a sense of weariness in the audience, paralleling that of the characters (see also **6-12**).

Tact is another editing principle that is difficult to generalize about, because it too depends on content. People do not like to have the obvious pointed out, whether in real life or while watching a movie. Like personal tact, directorial tact is a matter of restraint, taste, and respect for the intelligence of others. Insecure directors often present us with emotionally gratuitous shots, falling over themselves to make sure we will not miss the point.

Griffith's most radical experiments in editing are found in his 1916 epic *Intolerance*, in which he tried to refute the charges of racism against *The Birth of a Nation*. This movie was the first fiction film to explore the idea of **thematic montage**. Both the film and the technique exerted an enormous influence on movie directors of the 1920s, especially in the Soviet Union. Thematic montage stresses the association of ideas, irrespective of the continuity of time and space.

Intolerance is unified by the themes of bigotry and persecution. Rather than tell one story, Griffith **intercut** four. One takes place in ancient Babylon. The second deals with the crucifixion of Jesus. The third concerns the massacre of the Huguenots by the Catholic royalists in sixteenth-century France. The last story takes place in America in 1916 and deals with a battle between labour and management.

The four stories are developed not separately but in parallel fashion. Scenes of one period are intercut with scenes of another. At the conclusion of the movie, Griffith features suspenseful chase sequences in the first and last stories; a brutal scene of slaughter in the French story; and a slow, tragic climax in the killing of Jesus. The concluding sequence contains literally hundreds of shots, juxtaposing images that are separated by great spans of time and distance. All these different time periods and locations are unified by the central theme of intolerance. The continuity is no longer physical, or even psychological, but conceptual—that is, thematic.

Intolerance was not a commercial success, but its influence was immense. The filmmakers of the Soviet Union were dazzled by Griffith's movie and based their own theories of montage on his practices in this film. A great many directors have profited from Griffith's experiments in the subjective treatment of time. In *Kamouraska*, for example, Claude Jutra exploits the art of editing to produce a series

6-11. *The Deer Hunter* (U.S.A., 1978), directed by Michael Cimino.

Editing is an art as well as a craft. Like all art, it often defies mechanical formulations, taking on a life of its own. For example, when sneak preview audiences were asked for their reactions to this three-hour-long movie, most viewers responded enthusiastically but felt that the hour-long wedding sequence at the opening could have been cut down. In terms of its plot, nothing much "happens" in this sequence. Its purpose is primarily lyrical—a loving celebration of the social rituals that bind the community together. The story content of the sequence could be condensed to a few minutes of screen time—which is exactly what its makers did. When the shortened version was shown to audiences, reactions were negative. Cimino and his editor, Peter Zinner, restored the cut footage. The long wedding sequence is necessary not for its story content so much as for its experiential value. It provides the movie with a sense of balance. The community solidarity of the sequence is what the characters fight for in the subsequent battle footage of the film. *(Universal Pictures)*

of parallels that are thematically rather than chronologically related **(6-13)**. He uses a kind of subliminal editing, in which some shots are held on the screen for only a fraction of a second. The central character is a middle-aged woman in nineteenth-century Quebec who conspired with her lover to murder her first husband; years later she watches over the death-bed of her second husband, whom she married to regain a respectable position in society. She tries to repress the memories of these earlier experiences, but they force their way into her consciousness. Jutra suggests this psychological process by intercutting a few frames of the memory shots during a scene that is occurring in the present. A present-tense event detonates the protagonist's memory of something similar from her past. As past contends with present, the flickering memory shots endure longer, until a **flashback** sequence eventually becomes dominant, and the present is suspended for a moment. With only a few exceptions, however, it was not until the 1960s that such unorthodox editing practices became widespread.

Filmmakers can interrupt the present with shots not only of the past but of the future as well. In Sydney Pollack's *They Shoot Horses, Don't They?* (1969) short **flashforwards** of a courtroom scene are interspersed throughout the present-tense story. The flashforwards suggest predestination: Like the dance contest of the story proper, the future is rigged, and personal effort is equated with self-deception. Flashforwards are also used in Alain Resnais's *La Guerre est finie* [*The War is Over*] (1966) and Joseph Losey's *The Go-Between* (1970). They even occur within flashbacks in *Kamouraska*, when the younger Elisabeth appears to foresee events that her older self is remembering.

Griffith also restructured time and place by using fantasy inserts. In *Intolerance*, for example, a young woman on the verge of murdering her unfaithful boyfriend imagines a scene where she is apprehended by the police. Flashbacks, flashforwards, and cutaways to fantasies allow filmmakers to develop ideas thematically rather than chronologically, freeing them to explore the subjective nature of time. The very flexibility of time in movies makes the theme of temporality an ideal subject for the medium.

Like William Faulkner, Marcel Proust, and other novelists, filmmakers have succeeded in cracking the tyranny of mechanically measured time. One of the most complex instances of the restructuring of time is found in Stanley Donen's *Two for the Road* (1966). The story deals with the development and gradual disintegration of a love relationship. It unfolds in a series of mixed flashbacks; that is, the flashbacks are not in chronological sequence, nor are they completed in any one scene. Rather, they are jumbled and fragmented, somewhat in the manner of a Faulkner novel. To complicate matters, most of the flashbacks take place on the road, during various trips the couple has taken in the past. If each time period of the film were designated with the letters A, B, C, D, and E, its temporal structure might be charted as follows: E (present), A (most distant past), B, C, D, B, A, E, C, D, B . . . ending with E. The audience gradually learns to identify each period through various continuity clues: the heroine's hairstyles, the modes of transportation, the particular crisis during each trip, and so on. In several recent movies, the editing involves not the fragmentation of time but the juxtaposition of alternative ways in which a character's life could develop. *Blind Chance* (Krzysztof Kieslowski, 1981), *Run Lola Run* (Tom Tykwer, 1998), and *Sliding Doors* (Peter Howitt, 1998), all operate in the conditional tense, depicting not what happens, has happened, or will happen but what might happen if ....

6-12. *L'Avventura* (Italy, 1960), with Monica Vitti, directed by Michelangelo Antonioni.

Psychological films often use movements in and out of the depth of an image, especially to create a sense of tediousness and exhaustion. Shots of this sort require **anticipatory setups** that reinforce these qualities, for we see the destination of a character's movement long before it is completed. Here, the heroine's search for her lover in the corridors of a hotel suggests the futility of her love affair. The endless succession of doors, fixtures, and hallways implies, among other things, the repetition of the frustration she is now experiencing. Much of the meaning of shots such as these lies in their duration: Space is used to suggest time. Needless to say, Antonioni's movies are among the slowest paced of the contemporary cinema: Long after the viewer has had time to absorb the visual information of a shot, it continues on the screen. When this film was originally shown at the Cannes Film Festival, an audience of hostile critics kept shouting "Cut! Cut!" at the screen. The shots were so lengthy and the pace so slow that viewers assumed the director was inept at editing. But like many of Antonioni's works, *L'Avventura* is about spiritual erosion, and the movie's slow rhythm is organically related to this theme. *(Janus Films)*

6-13. *Kamouraska* (Canada, 1973), with Richard Jordan and Geneviève Bujold, directed by Claude Jutra. The film opens with Elisabeth (Bujold) looking out of a window at a dark and stormy night. Suddenly there is a cut to a white, snow-covered landscape with a young man speeding toward the camera on a horse-drawn sleigh. This image quickly disappears, but we soon realize that it is a flashback or, rather, Elisabeth's subjective memory of the American doctor (Jordan) who was her lover in the past. The flashbacks gradually become longer, and we see her as a young woman attracted to the dashing squire of Kamouraska, who takes her off to his isolated manor, where she discovers that he is not the romantic figure she has imagined. *(Les Productions Pierre Lamy Ltée)*

From its crude beginnings, Griffith expanded the art of editing to include a wide variety of functions: locale changes, time lapses, shot variety, emphasis of psychological and physical details, overviews, symbolic inserts, parallels and contrasts, associations, point-of-view shifts, simultaneity, and the repetition of **motifs**.

Griffith's method of editing was also more economical. Related shots could be bunched together in the shooting schedule, regardless of their positions (or "time" and "place") in the finished film. Especially in later years, in the era of high-salaried stars, directors could shoot all the stars' sequences in a brief period and out of cinematic continuity. Less expensive details (extreme long shots, minor actors, close-ups of objects, etc.) could be shot at a more convenient time. Later, the shots would be arranged in their proper sequence on the editor's cutting bench.

SOVIET MONTAGE AND THE FORMALIST TRADITION

Griffith was a practical artist, concerned with communicating ideas and emotions in the most effective manner possible. In the 1920s, the Soviet filmmakers expanded Griffith's associational principles and established the theoretical premises for thematic editing, or **montage** as they called it (from the French *monter*, "to assemble"). V.I. Pudovkin wrote the first important theoretical treatises on what he called constructive editing. Most of his statements are explanations of Griffith's practices, but he differed with the American (whom he praised lavishly) on several points. Griffith's use of the close-up, Pudovkin claimed, is too limited. The close-up is used simply as a clarification of the long shot, which carries most of the meaning, and in effect the close-up is merely an interruption, offering no meanings of its own. Pudovkin insisted that each shot should make a new point. Through the juxtaposition of shots, new meanings can be created. The meanings, then, are in the juxtapositions, not in one shot alone.

Filmmakers in the Soviet Union were strongly influenced by the psychological theories of Ivan Pavlov, whose experiments in the association of ideas served as a basis for the editing experiments of Lev Kuleshov, Pudovkin's mentor. Kuleshov believed that ideas in cinema are created by linking together fragmentary details to produce a unified action. These details can be totally unrelated in real life. For example, he linked together a shot of Moscow's Red Square with a shot of Washington's White House, close-ups of two men climbing stairs with another close-up of two

6-14. *Flashdance* (U.S.A., 1983), with Jennifer Beals, directed by Adrian Lyne.

Editing is often used to deceive—to conceal rather than reveal. For example, the dance numbers in this film were performed by a double, a professional dancer whose identity is cunningly concealed by the artful lighting and the discreetly distanced camera. The dance shots were intercut with closer shots of Jennifer Beals, wearing the same costume and moving to the same music. With the musical number providing the continuity, these intercut shots create the illusion of a continuous movement, with Beals featured throughout. These editing techniques are also commonly used in such scenes as sword fights, dangerous stunts, and many other activities requiring specialized skills. *(Paramount Pictures)*

hands shaking. Projected as a continuous scene, the linked shots suggest that the two men are in the same place at the same time.

According to Pudovkin, Kuleshov conducted another famous experiment that provided a theoretical foundation for the use of nonprofessional actors in movies. Kuleshov and many of his colleagues believed that traditional acting skills were quite unnecessary in cinema. He used a close-up of an actor wearing a neutral expression. First, he connected the shot of the actor with a close-up shot of a bowl of soup. Then he joined the close-up of the actor with a shot of a coffin containing a female corpse. Finally, he linked the actor's neutral expression with a shot of a little girl playing. When these combinations were shown to audiences, they exclaimed at the actor's expressiveness in portraying hunger, deep sorrow, and paternal pride. In each case, the meaning was conveyed by juxtaposing two shots, not by one alone. Actors can be used as raw material, as objects juxtaposed with other objects. The emotion is produced not by the actor's performance, but by the associations created by the juxtapositions. In a sense, the *viewer* creates the emotional meanings, once the filmmaker has linked the appropriate objects.

For Kuleshov and Pudovkin, a sequence was not filmed, it was constructed. Using far more close-ups than Griffith, Pudovkin built a scene from many separate shots, all juxtaposed for a unified effect. The environment of the scene is the source of the images. Long shots are rare. Instead, a barrage of close-ups (often of objects) provides the audience with the necessary associations to link the meaning. These juxtapositions can suggest emotional and psychological states, even abstract ideas.

The Soviet theorists of this generation were criticized on several counts. This technique detracts from a scene's sense of realism, some critics complained, for the continuity of actual time and place is totally restructured. But Pudovkin and the other Soviet formalists claimed that realism captured in long shot is *too* near reality: It is theatrical rather than cinematic. Movies must capture the meaning, not merely the surface, of reality, which is filled with irrelevancies. Only by juxtaposing close-ups of objects, textures, symbols, and other selected details can a filmmaker convey *expressively* the idea underlying the undifferentiated jumble of real life.

Some critics also believe that this manipulative style of editing guides the spectator too much—the choices are already made. The audience must sit back passively and accept the inevitable associations presented on the screen. Political considerations are involved here, for the Soviets tended to link film with propaganda. Propaganda does not encourage free and balanced evaluations.

Like many Soviet formalists, Sergei Eisenstein was interested in exploring general principles that could be applied to a variety of apparently different forms of creative activity. He believed that these artistic principles were organically related to the basic nature of all human activity, and ultimately to the nature of the universe itself. Only the barest outline of his complex theories can be offered here. Like the ancient Greek philosopher Heraclitus, Eisenstein believed that the essence of existence is constant change. He believed that nature's eternal fluctuation is **dialectical**—the result of the conflict and synthesis of opposites. What appears to be stationary or unified in nature is only temporary, for all phenomena are in various states of becoming. Only energy is permanent, and energy is constantly in a state of transition to other forms. Every opposite contains the seed of its own destruction in time, Eisenstein believed, and this conflict of opposites is the mother of motion and change.

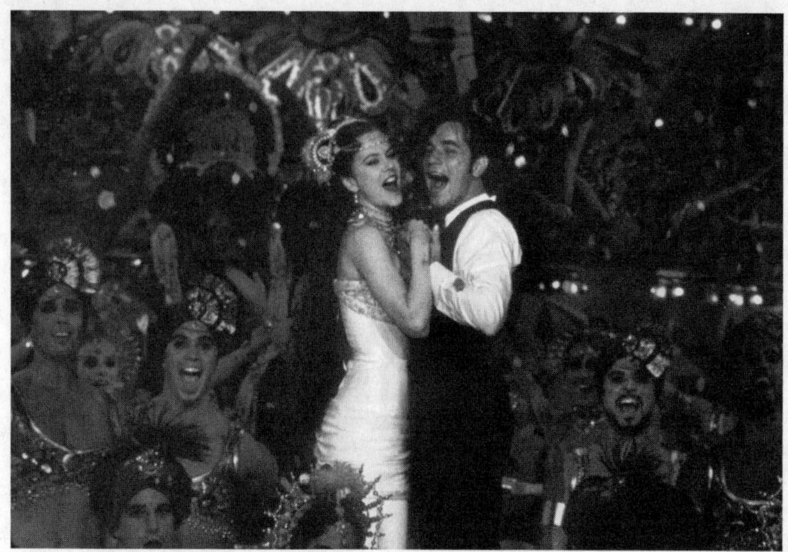

6-15. *Moulin Rouge* (U.S.A., 2001), with Nicole Kidman and Ewan McGregor, directed by Baz Luhrmann. The musical numbers of this period film are edited in volcanic explosions of split-second shots. In a sense, Baz Luhrmann's editing style is a throwback to the kaleidoscopic choreography of Busby Berkeley (**1-1b**) in the big studio era. Both directors make the musical numbers **reflexive**, as much about themselves as about the performers or the music. Full of deliberate anachronisms, this film's stylized depiction of nineteenth-century Paris evokes the beginning of the modern era. The pace and shock of the editing—drawing on Soviet montage cinema via the contemporary music video—capture the bustle and turmoil within which the central romance is acted out. *(Twentieth Century Fox)*

From this perspective, the function of all artists is to capture this dynamic collision of opposites, to incorporate dialectical conflicts not only in the subject matter of art but in its techniques and forms as well. Conflict is universal in all the arts, according to Eisenstein, and therefore all art aspires to motion. Potentially, at least, cinema is the most comprehensive of the arts because it can incorporate the visual conflicts of painting and photography, the kinetic conflicts of dance, the tonal conflicts of music, the verbal conflicts of language, and the character and action conflicts of fiction and drama.

Eisenstein placed special emphasis on the art of editing. Like Kuleshov and Pudovkin, he believed that montage was the foundation of film art. He agreed with them that each shot of a sequence ought to be incomplete, contributory rather than self-contained. However, Eisenstein criticized the concept of linked shots for being mechanical and inorganic. He believed that editing ought to be dialectical: The conflict of two shots (thesis and antithesis) produces a wholly new idea (synthesis). Thus, in film terms, the conflict between shot A and shot B is not AB (Kuleshov and Pudovkin), but a qualitatively new factor—C (Eisenstein). Transitions between shots should not be flowing, as Pudovkin suggested, but sharp, jolting, even violent. For Eisenstein, editing produces harsh collisions, not subtle linkages. A smooth transition, he claimed, was an opportunity lost.

6-16. ***Lifeboat*** **(U.S.A., 1944), with Tallulah Bankhead (centre), directed by Alfred Hitchcock.**
Hitchcock was one of Pudovkin's most articulate champions. "Cinema is form," Hitchcock insisted. "The screen ought to speak its own language, freshly coined, and it can't do that unless it treats an acted scene as a piece of raw material which must be broken up, taken to bits, before it can be woven into an expressive visual pattern." He referred to the piecing together of fragmentary shots as "pure cinema," like individual notes of music that combine to produce a melody. In this movie, he confined himself entirely to nine characters adrift at sea in a small boat. In other words, this photo contains the raw material for every shot in the film. Formalists insist that the artistry lies not in the materials per se, but in the way they are taken apart and reconstructed expressively. *(Twentieth Century Fox)*

Editing, for Eisenstein, was an almost mystical process. He likened it to the growth of organic cells. If each shot represents a developing cell, the cinematic cut is like the rupturing of the cell when it splits into two. Editing is done at the point that a shot "bursts"—that is, when its tensions have reached their maximum expansion. The rhythm of editing in a movie should be like the explosions of an internal combustion engine, claimed Eisenstein, a master of dynamic rhythms whose films are almost mesmerizing in this respect: Shots of contrasting volumes, durations, shapes, designs, and lighting intensities collide against one another like objects in a torrential river plunging toward their inevitable destination **(6-17)**.

The differences between Pudovkin and Eisenstein may seem academic. In actual practice, however, the two approaches produced sharply contrasting results. Pudovkin's movies are essentially in the classical mould. The shots tend to be additive and are directed toward an overall emotional effect, which is guided by the story. In Eisenstein's movies, the jolting images represent a series of essentially intellectual thrusts and parries, directed toward an ideological argument. The directors' narrative structures also differed. Pudovkin's stories did not differ much from the kind Griffith used; however; Eisenstein's stories were much more loosely structured, usually a series of documentary-like episodes used as convenient vehicles for exploring ideas.

When Pudovkin wanted to express an emotion, he conveyed it in terms of physical images—objective correlatives—taken from the actual locale. Thus, in the opening sequences of *The End of St Petersburg* (1927), the sense of anguished drudgery is conveyed through a series of shots showing details of a cart mired in the mud; close-ups of the wheel, the mud, hands coaxing the wheel, straining faces, the muscles of an arm pulling the wheel, and so on. Eisenstein, on the other hand, wanted film to be totally free of literal continuity and context. Pudovkin's correlatives, he felt, were too restricted by realism.

Eisenstein wanted movies to be as flexible as novels, especially to make figurative comparisons without respect to time and place. Movies should include images that are thematically or metaphorically relevant, Eisenstein claimed, regardless of whether they can be found in the locale or not. Even in his first feature, *Strike* (1925), Eisenstein intercut shots of workmen being machine-gunned with images of oxen being slaughtered. The oxen are not literally part of the story but are intercut purely for metaphorical purposes. A famous sequence from *Battleship Potemkin* links three shots of stone lions: one asleep, a second aroused and on the verge of rising, and a third on its feet and ready to pounce. Eisenstein considered the sequence an embodiment of a metaphor: "The very stones roar."

Ingenious as these metaphorical comparisons can be, the major problem with this kind of editing is its tendency to be obvious—or impenetrably obscure. Eisenstein saw no difficulty in overcoming the space and time differences between film and literature. But the two media use metaphors in different ways. We have no difficulty in understanding what is meant by the comparison "he's timid as a sheep," or even the more abstract metaphor, "whorish time undoes us all." Both statements exist outside of time and place. The simile is not set in a pasture, nor is the metaphor set in a brothel. Such comparisons are not meant to be understood literally, of course. In movies, figurative devices of this kind are more difficult. Editing can produce a number of figurative comparisons, but they don't work in quite the same way that they do in literature. Eisenstein's theories of collision montage have been explored primarily in avant-garde cinema, music videos, and TV commercials. Most fiction filmmakers have found them too intrusive.

ANDRÉ BAZIN AND THE TRADITION OF REALISM

André Bazin was not a filmmaker, but he was influential as both a critic and a theorist. For several years in the 1950s, he was the editor of the influential French journal *Cahiers du cinéma*, in which he set forth an aesthetic of film that was in sharp opposition to such formalists as Pudovkin and Eisenstein. Bazin was untainted by dogmatism. Although he emphasized the realistic nature of cinema, he was generous in his praise of movies that exploited editing effectively. Throughout his writings, however, Bazin maintained that montage was merely one of many techniques a director could use in making movies. Furthermore, he believed that in many cases, editing could actually destroy the effectiveness of a scene **(6-18)**.

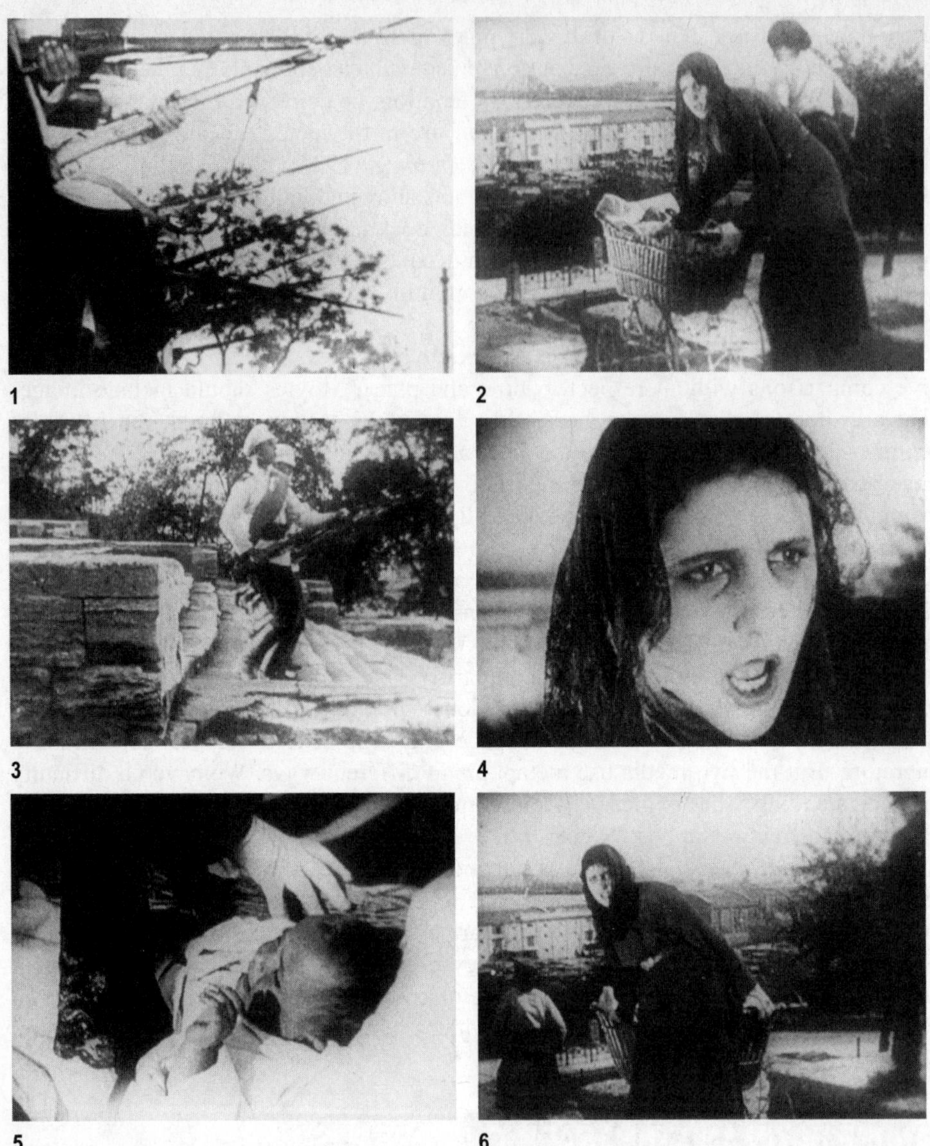

6-17. A portion of the Odessa Steps sequence from *Battleship Potemkin* (Russia, 1925), directed by Sergei Eisenstein.

This sequence, based on an actual massacre during the failed revolution of 1905, is the one most often used to demonstrate the possibilities of montage editing. Its full impact can be experienced only by viewing the sequence in its entirety with a musical accompaniment, either the original music composed by Edmund Meisel or music taken from Dmitri Shostakovich's *Symphony No. 11*, inspired by the same events. This brief extract gives some idea of the graphic conflicts between and within shots. *(Audio-Brandon Films)*

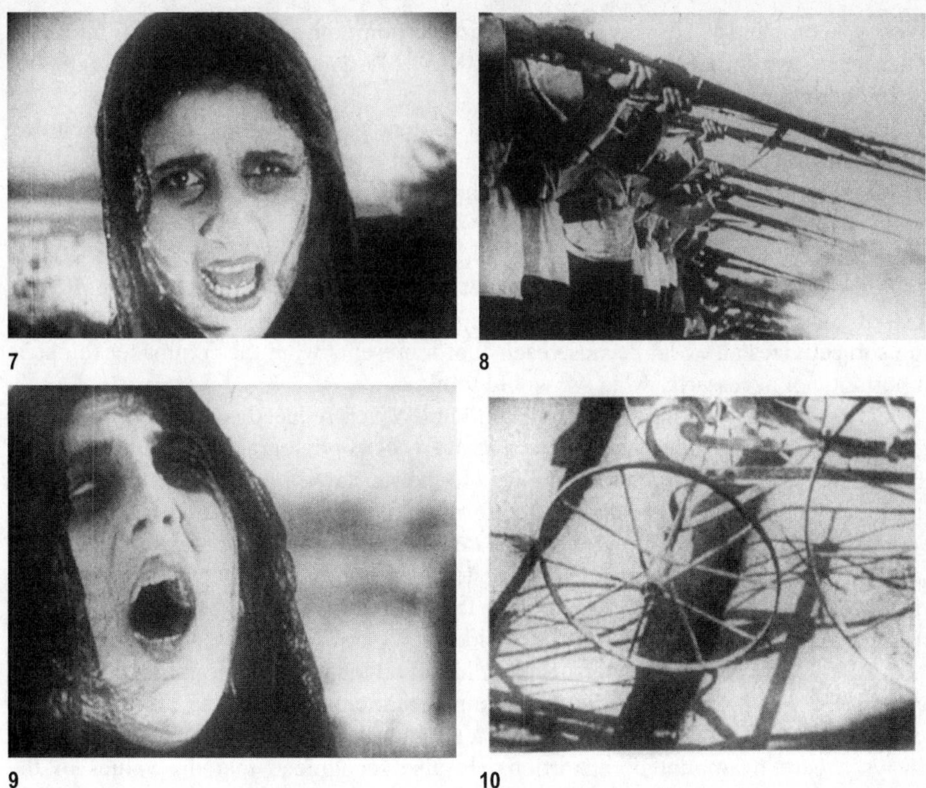
7 8 9 10

Bazin's realist aesthetic was based on his belief that photography, television, and cinema, unlike the traditional arts, produce images of reality automatically, with a minimum of human interference. This technological objectivity connects the moving image with the observable physical world. A novelist or a painter must represent reality by re-presenting it in another medium—through language or colour pigments. The filmmaker's image, in contrast, is essentially an objective recording of what actually exists. No other art, Bazin felt, can be as comprehensive in the presentation of the physical world. No other art can be as realistic, in the most elementary sense of the word.

Bazin's aesthetic had a moral as well as a technological bias. He was influenced by the philosophical movement called Personalism. This school of thought emphasized the individualistic and pluralistic nature of truth. The essence of reality, Bazin believed, lies in its ambiguity. To capture this ambiguity, the filmmaker must be modest and self-effacing, a patient observer willing to follow where reality leads. The film artists whom Bazin admired most—Robert Flaherty, Jean Renoir, and Vittorio De Sica, for example—are those whose movies reflect a sense of wonder before the ambiguous mysteries of reality.

Bazin believed that the distortions involved in using formalist techniques—especially thematic editing—often violate the complexities of reality. Montage seeks to superimpose a definite ideological meaning on the infinite variability of actual life. Formalists tend to be too egocentric and manipulative, he felt. They are concerned with imposing their view of reality, rather than allowing reality to exist in its awesome complexity. He was one of the first to point out that such great filmmakers as Charlie Chaplin, Kenji Mizoguchi, and F.W. Murnau preserve the ambiguities of reality by minimizing editing.

Bazin even viewed classical cutting as potentially corrupting. Classical cutting breaks down a unified scene into a certain number of closer shots that correspond implicitly to a mental process. But the technique encourages us to follow the organization of shots without our being conscious of its arbitrariness. "The editor who cuts for us makes in our stead the choice which we would make in real life," Bazin pointed out. "Without thinking, we accept his analysis because it conforms to the laws of attention, but we are deprived of a privilege." He believed that classical cutting subjectivizes an event because each shot represents what the filmmaker thinks is important, not necessarily what we would think.

One of Bazin's favourite directors, William Wyler, reduced editing to a minimum in many of his films, substituting the use of **deep-focus** photography and lengthy takes. "His perfect clarity contributes enormously to the spectator's reassurance and leaves to him the means to observe, to choose and form an opinion," Bazin said of Wyler's austere cutting style. In such movies as *The Little Foxes* (1941), *The Best Years of Our Lives* (1946), and *The Heiress* (1949), Wyler achieved an unparalleled neutrality and transparency. It would be naive to confuse this neutrality with an absence of art, Bazin insisted, for all of Wyler's effort tends to hide itself (see **3-12b**).

Unlike some of his followers, Bazin did not advocate a simple-minded theory of realism. He was perfectly aware, for example, that cinema—like all art—involves a certain amount of selectivity, organization, and interpretation. In short, there is always a certain amount of distortion. He also recognized that the values of the filmmaker inevitably influence the manner in which reality is perceived. These distortions are not only inevitable, but also in most cases desirable. For Bazin, the best films were those in which the artist's personal vision is held in delicate balance with the objective nature of the medium. Certain aspects of reality must be sacrificed for the sake of artistic coherence, then, but Bazin felt that abstraction and artifice ought to be kept to a minimum. The materials should be allowed to speak for themselves. Bazinian realism is not mere newsreel objectivity—even if there were such a thing. He believed that reality must be heightened somewhat in cinema, that the director must reveal the poetic implications of ordinary people, events, and places. By poeticizing the commonplace, cinema is neither a totally objective recording of the physical world nor a symbolic abstraction of it. Rather, cinema occupies a middle position between the sprawl of raw life and the artificially re-created worlds of the traditional arts.

Bazin wrote many articles overtly or implicitly criticizing the art of editing, or at least pointing out its limitations. If the essence of a scene is based on the idea of division, separation, or isolation, montage can be an effective technique in conveying these ideas. But if the essence of a scene demands the simultaneous presence of two or more related elements, the filmmaker ought to preserve the continuity of real time and space **(6-20)**. He or she can do this by including all the dramatic variables within the same frame—that is, by exploiting the resources of the long shot, the lengthy take, deep focus, and **widescreen**. The filmmaker can also preserve actual time and space by panning, craning, tilting, or tracking rather than cutting.

6-18. *Safety Last* (U.S.A., 1923), with Harold Lloyd, directed by Fred Newmeyer and Sam Taylor.

In direct opposition to Pudovkin, Bazin believed that when the essence of a scene lies in the simultaneous presence of two or more elements, editing is ruled out. Such scenes gain their emotional impact through the unity of space, not through the juxtaposition of separate shots. In this famous sequence, for example, Lloyd's comedy of thrills is made more comic and more thrilling by the scene's realistic presentation: The dangling hero and the street below are kept in the same frame. Actually, the distance between the two is exaggerated by the cunning placement of the camera, and there was always at least a platform about three stories below him—"but who wants to fall three stories?" Lloyd asked. *(Museum of Modern Art)*

John Huston's *The African Queen* (1951) contains a shot illustrating Bazin's principle. In attempting to take their boat downriver to a large lake, the two protagonists (Humphrey Bogart and Katharine Hepburn) get sidetracked on a tributary of the main river. The tributary dwindles down to a stream and finally trickles into a tangle of reeds and mud, where the dilapidated boat gets hopelessly mired. The exhausted travellers resign themselves to a slow death in the suffocating reeds, and eventually fall asleep on the floor of the boat. The camera then moves upward, over the reeds, to reveal—just a few hundred metres away—the lake. The irony of the scene is conveyed by the continuous movement of the camera, which preserves the physical proximity of the boat, the intervening reeds, and the lake. If Huston had cut to three separate shots, we would not understand these spatial interrelationships, and therefore the irony would be sacrificed.

Bazin pointed out that in the evolution of movies, virtually every technical innovation pushed the medium closer to a realistic ideal: in the late 1920s, sound; in the 1930s and 1940s, colour and deep-focus photography; in the 1950s, widescreen. In short, it is usually technology rather than critics and theorists that alters technique. For example, when *The Jazz Singer* ushered in the talkie revolution in 1927 **(7-1)**, sound eclipsed virtually every advance made in the art of editing since Griffith's day. With the coming of sound, films *had* to be more realistically edited, whether their directors wanted them so or not. Microphones were placed on the set itself, and sound had to be recorded while the scene was being photographed. Usually the microphones were hidden—in a vase of flowers, a wall sconce, and so on. Thus, in the earliest sound movies, not only

6-19a. ***Le Chagrin et la pitié* [*The Sorrow and the Pity*] (France / Switzerland / Germany, 1970), directed by Marcel Ophüls.**

Even in the world of documentary films, editing styles can range from ultrarealistic to ultraformalistic. Like most **cinéma-vérité** documentarists, Marcel Ophüls keeps editing to an absolute minimum. Implicit in the art of editing is artifice—that is, the manipulation of formal elements to produce a seductive aesthetic effect. Many documentarists believe that an edited analysis of a scene shapes and aestheticizes it—compromising its authenticity. A selected sequence of shots, however factually based, extrapolates one person's truth from an event and, in so doing, infuses it with an ideology. An unedited presentation, on the other hand, preserves a multiplicity of truths. *(Cinema 5)*

6-19b. ***Looking for Richard* (U.S.A., 1996), with Al Pacino, directed by Pacino.**

The editing style of this documentary is subjective and personal. The movie itself is almost like an intimate diary by a famous actor exploring one of his most celebrated stage roles, Shakespeare's fascinating disciple of evil, Richard III. Pacino's voice-over connects many of the shots, which include interviews with other actors, historical artifacts, views of Shakespeare's Globe Theatre, and snippets of scenes from the play in rehearsal and performance. The movie is like a dazzling lecture/presentation by someone who is both an artist and an educator. *(Twentieth Century Fox)*

was the camera restricted, but the actors were as well. If they strayed too far from the microphone, the dialogue could not be recorded properly.

The effects on editing in these early talkies were disastrous. **Synchronous sound** anchored the images, so whole scenes were played with no cuts—a return to the "primitive" sequence shot. Most of the dramatic values were aural. Even commonplace sequences fascinated audiences. If someone entered a room, the camera recorded the fact, whether or not it was dramatically important, and millions of spectators thrilled to the sound of the door opening and slamming shut. Critics and filmmakers despaired:

6-20. *Goin' Down the Road* (Canada, 1970), with Doug McGrath (left) and Paul Bradley, directed by Don Shebib.

After Joey (Bradley) and Pete (McGrath) arrive in Toronto from Nova Scotia, their efforts to find well-paying jobs are thwarted by their lack of skills. Shebib films many of the sequences in long takes, giving the film a sense of authenticity, as if it were a **direct cinema** documentary (see Chapter 9, "Nonfiction Films"). As Bazin would have appreciated, the pressures on their relationship are vividly conveyed by keeping the two men and their surroundings in the same frame. *(Evdon Films)*

The days of the recorded stage play had apparently returned. Later, these problems were solved by the invention of the **blimp**, a soundproof camera housing that permits the camera to move with relative ease, and by the practice of **dubbing** sound after the shooting is completed (see Chapter 7, "Sound"). But sound also provided some distinct advantages. In fact, Bazin believed that it represented a giant leap in the evolution toward a totally realistic medium. Spoken dialogue and sound effects heightened the sense of reality. Acting styles became more sophisticated because of sound. No longer did performers have to exaggerate visually to compensate for the absence of voices. Talkies also permitted filmmakers to tell their stories more economically, without the intrusive titles that interspersed the visuals of silent movies. Tedious expository scenes could also be dispensed with. A few lines of dialogue easily conveyed what an audience needed to know about the premise of the story.

The use of deep-focus photography also exerted a modifying influence on editing practices. Before the 1930s, most cameras photographed interiors on one focal plane at a time. These cameras could capture a sharp image of an object from virtually any distance, but unless an enormous number of extra lights were set up, other elements of the picture that were not at the same distance from the camera remained blurred, out of focus. One justification for editing, then, was purely technical: clarity of image.

The aesthetic qualities of deep-focus photography permitted composition in depth: Whole scenes could be shot in one setup, with no sacrifice of detail, for every distance appeared with equal clarity on the screen. For this reason, the technique is sometimes thought to be more theatrical than cinematic, for the effects are achieved primarily through a spatially unified mise en scène rather than a fragmented juxtaposition of shots.

Bazin liked the objectivity and tact of deep focus. Details within a shot can be presented more democratically, as it were, without the special attention that a close-up inevitably confers. Thus, realist critics like Bazin felt that audiences would be more creative—less passive—in understanding the relationships between people and things. Unified space also preserves the ambiguity of life. Audiences are not led to an inevitable conclusion but are forced to evaluate, sort out, and eliminate "irrelevancies" on their own.

In 1945, immediately following World War II, a movement called **neorealism** sprang up in Italy and gradually influenced directors all over the world. Spearheaded by Roberto Rossellini and Vittorio De Sica, two of Bazin's favourite filmmakers, neorealism deemphasized editing. The directors favoured deep-focus photography, long shots, lengthy takes, and an austere restraint in the use of close-ups. Rossellini's *Paisan* (1946) features a sequence shot that was much admired by realist critics. An American GI talks to a young Sicilian woman about his family, his life, and his dreams. Neither character understands the other's language, but they try to communicate in spite of this considerable obstacle. By refusing to condense time by using separate shots, Rossellini emphasizes the awkward pauses and hesitations between the two characters. Through its preservation of real time, the lengthy take forces us to experience the increasing, then relaxing, tensions that exist between them. An interruption of time by using a cut would have dissipated these tensions.

When asked why he deemphasized editing, Rossellini replied: "Things are there, why manipulate them?" This statement might well serve as Bazin's theoretical credo.

6-21. *Utamaro and His Five Women* (Japan, 1955), directed by Kenji Mizoguchi.

Bazin and his disciples were enthusiastic champions of the films of Mizoguchi. The Japanese master favoured the use of lengthy takes rather than editing. He generally cut within a continuous take only when there was a sharp psychological shift within the scene. Used sparingly in this way, the cut acquires a greater dramatic impact than can be found in more conventionally edited movies. *(New Yorker Films)*

6-22. *Clerks* (U.S.A., 1994), with Jeff Anderson and Brian O'Halloran, written, edited, and directed by Kevin Smith.

Sometimes economics dictates style, as with this witty low-budget feature. Everyone worked for free. Smith shot the movie in the same convenience store he worked at (for $5 an hour) during the day. He also used lengthy takes in a number of scenes. The actors were required to memorize pages of dialogue (often very funny) so that the entire sequence could be shot without a cut. Smith did not need to worry about such costly decisions as where to put the camera with each new cut, or how to light each new shot, or whether he could afford to rent editing equipment to cut the sequence properly. Lengthy takes require one setup: The lights and camera usually remain stationary for the duration of the scene. The movie's final cost: a piddling $27 575. He charged it. It went on to win awards at the Sundance and Cannes film festivals. *(Miramax Films)*

He deeply admired Rossellini's openness to multiple interpretations, his refusal to diminish reality by making it serve an a priori thesis. "Neorealism by definition rejects analysis, whether political, moral, psychological, logical, or social, of the characters and their actions," Bazin pointed out. "It looks on reality as a whole, not incomprehensible, certainly, but inescapably one."

Sequence shots tend to produce (often unconsciously) a sense of mounting anxiety in the viewer. We expect setups to change during a scene. When they do not, we often grow restless, hardly conscious of what is producing our uneasiness. Jim Jarmusch's bizarre comedy *Stranger Than Paradise* uses sequence shots throughout **(6-23)**. The camera inexorably waits at a predetermined location. The young characters enter the scene and play out their tawdry, comic lives, complete with boring stretches of silence, glazed expressions of torpor, and random tics. Finally, they leave. Or they just sit there. The camera sits with them. **Fade** out.

Like many technological innovations, widescreen provoked a wail of protest from many critics and directors. The new screen shape would destroy the close-up, many feared, especially of the human face. There simply was too much space to fill,

6-23. ***Stranger Than Paradise*** **(U.S.A., 1984), directed by Jim Jarmusch.**
Each scene in this movie is a sequence shot—a lengthy take without cuts. Far from being "primitive," the sequence-shot technique produces a sophisticated, wry effect, bizarre and funny. In this scene, the two protagonists (John Lurie and Richard Edson) eat yet another goulash dinner while Lurie berates his stout, outspoken aunt (Cecillia Stark) for still speaking Hungarian after years of living in the United States. The scene's comic rhythms are accented by the staging. The bickering relatives must bend forward to see each other, while the visitor, caught in the crossfire, tries unsuccessfully to stay neutral. *(Samuel Goldwyn)*

even in long shots, others complained. Audiences would never be able to assimilate all the action, for they would not know where to look. It was suitable only for horizontal compositions, some argued, useful for epic films, but too spacious for interior scenes and small subjects. Editing would be further minimized, the formalists complained, for there would be no need to cut to something if everything was already there, arranged in a long, horizontal series.

At first, the most effective widescreen films were, in fact, westerns and historical extravaganzas. But before long, directors began to use the new screen with more sensitivity. Like deep-focus photography, the wide screen meant that they had to be more conscious of their mise en scène. More relevant details had to be included within the frame, even at its edges. Filmmakers discovered that the most expressive parts of a person's face were the eyes and mouth, and consequently close-ups that chopped off the tops and bottoms of actors' faces were not as disastrous as had been predicted.

Not surprisingly, the realist critics were the first to reconsider the advantages of widescreen. Here was yet another step away from the distorting effects of editing, Bazin pointed out. As with deep focus, widescreen helped to preserve spatial and temporal continuity. Close-ups containing two or more people could now be photo-

6-24. *Le Fabuleux destin d'Amélie Poulain* [*Amélie*] (France, 2001), with Audrey Tautou, directed by Jean-Pierre Jeunet.

The more cutting a film contains, the faster the tempo will seem, which in turn produces more energy and excitement. Jeunet's movie is like a whimsical fairy tale that whizzes past us breathlessly, its editing style sparkling with effervescence. The main character (Tautou) is a shy Parisian waitress who lives in the picturesque—and digitally enhanced—neighbourhood of Montmartre. The exuberant tone of the movie is mostly due to the playful editing, but the special effects also contribute. For example, when Amélie first sees the love of her life, her heart visibly glows beneath her blouse. When her heart is broken, she digitally melts into a puddle on the ground. *(Miramax Films)*

graphed in one setup without suggesting inequality, as deep focus often did in its variety of depth planes. Nor were the relations between people and things fragmented as they were with edited sequences. It was also more realistic because the wide screen enveloped the viewer in a sense of an experience—a cinematic counterpart to the eye's peripheral vision. All the same advantages that had been applied to sound and deep focus were now applied to widescreen: its greater fidelity to real time and space; its detail, complexity, and density; its more objective presentation; its more coherent continuity; its greater ambiguity; and its encouragement of creative audience participation.

Ironically, several of Bazin's *protégés* were responsible for a return to more flamboyant editing techniques in the following decades. The French **New Wave** filmmakers shared Bazin's interests in neorealism and personal cinema, but their main enthusiasms were for Hollywood directors. However, their own films, made with lightweight equipment first developed for documentary production, broke all the rules of continuity editing and classical cinema. Godard's first feature *À bout de souffle* [*Breathless*] (1959), for example, drew on the crime genre, with Jean-Paul Belmondo masquerading as Humphrey Bogart, but hardly looks like a classical genre film. Its fragmentary style, including jump cuts, violations of the 180° rule, and direct address to the audience, emphasized discontinuity. Since these filmmakers insisted that *what* a movie says is inextricably bound up with *how* it is said, their films imply a world in which the stability and coherence of the classical style has been relegated to the past. The advent of digital video, and the use of video and computers in the editing process on many recent films, may well lead to new forms of editing **(6–24)**. Music videos accentuate the emphasis on rhythm and shock effects in the montage tradition, while digital cameras make possible a more intimate engagement with reality than even Bazin envisaged.

In assessing these new developments, as well as more traditional approaches, the questions we ought to ask ourselves about a movie's editing style include: How much cutting is there and why? Are the shots highly fragmented or relatively lengthy? What is the point of the cutting in each scene? to clarify? to stimulate? to lyricize? to create suspense? to explore an idea or emotion in depth? Does the cutting seem manipulative, or are we left to interpret the images on our own? What kind of rhythm does the editing establish within each scene? Is the personality of the director apparent in the cutting, or is the presentation of shots relatively objective and functional? Is editing a major language system of the movie, or does the director relegate cutting to a relatively minor function?

FURTHER READING (AND VIEWING)

Andrew, Dudley, *André Bazin* (New York: Oxford University Press, 1978). Biography with close attention to Bazin's ideas on realism.

Apple, Wendy, *The Cutting Edge: The Magic of Movie Editing* (2005). Documentary including interviews with many editors and well-chosen examples of editing techniques.

Gillespie, David C., *Early Soviet Cinema: Innovation, Ideology and Propaganda* (London: Wallflower Press, 2000). Introduction to the aesthetics of Soviet cinema in the 1920s.

Gunning, Tom, *D.W. Griffith and the Origins of American Narrative Film: The Early Years at Biograph* (Urbana: University of Illinois Press, 1991). Historical analysis of Griffith's innovations.

LoBrutto, Vincent, ed. *Selected Takes: Film Editors on Film Editing* (New York: Praeger, 1991). Insightful interviews on the aesthetics and practice of editing.

Oldham, Gabriella, ed. *First Cut: Conversations with Film Editors* (Berkeley: University of California Press, 1992). Interviews with twenty-three award-winning film editors.

Orpen, Valerie, *Film Editing: The Art of the Expressive* (London: Wallflower Press, 2003). Editing as an expressive strategy in sound films.

Taylor, Richard, ed. *The Eisenstein Reader* (London: British Film Institute, 1998). New translations of key essays.

Sargeant, Amy, *Vsevolod Pudovkin: Classic Films of the Soviet Avant-Garde* (London: I.B. Tauris, 2000). Thoughtful study of Pudovkin's theory and films.

Vernallis, Carol, *Experiencing Music Video: Aesthetics and Cultural Context* (New York: Columbia University Press, 2004). Music video as a multimedia artistic genre and cultural form.

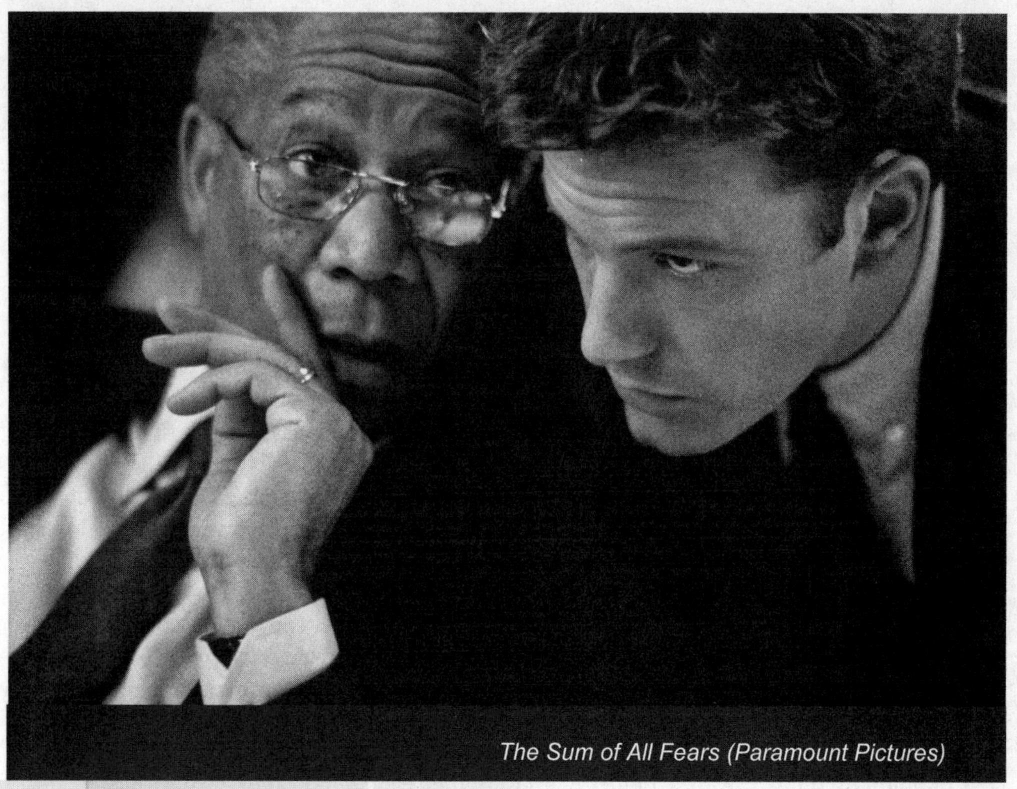

The Sum of All Fears (Paramount Pictures)

SOUND

7

Cinematic sound is that which does not simply add to, but multiplies, two or three times, the effect of the image.

—AKIRA KUROSAWA

OVERVIEW

Classifications of sound. Synchronous and nonsynchronous, diegetic and nondiegetic. The talkie revolution. Early experiments with sound. Sound montage. Sound effects: pitch, volume, tempo. Off-screen sounds. Sound symbolism. The uses of silence. Functions of music: descriptive, establishing mood, foreshadowing, irony. Musical motifs. Musicals: realistic and formalistic. Melodrama: music plus drama; women's films. Spoken language: vocal emphasis and rhythm; dialects and accents. Sound-image relations. Monologue and dialogue. Subtitling and dubbing foreign-language movies.

Sound in movies is classified in three ways: as sound effects (or noise), as music, and as speech. These elements can be used independently or in any combination. They may be **synchronous** or **nonsynchronous**, and **diegetic** or **nondiegetic**. These sets of terms are often used interchangeably but, strictly speaking, the first pair refer to the recording of sound during the production process and the second to the relations of the sound to the fictional world of the film. Synchronous sound is recorded at the same time as the images, while nonsynchronous sound is recorded at a different time and dubbed onto the image. If the sound is synchronized ("in sync") with the image, it may be difficult to tell whether it was recorded on the spot or added later. Nonsynchronous sound is most noticeable when post-synced dialogue does not match lip movements, which is usually the case when films are dubbed into a foreign language, but formalist directors sometimes use nonsynchronous sound purposefully in counterpoint with the images.

Diegetic sound has its source within the world depicted in the film (for example, dialogue or music from a radio), while nondiegetic sound comes from outside this world (voice-over commentary, background music). Even if the sound source is off screen, it is diegetic sound if we can imagine its source as part of the environment (street noise, dialogue overheard through a window). It should be noted that the source of the sound may be ambiguous as, for example, when a sequence begins with what appears to be background (nondiegetic) music that cuts out when a character turns off the radio. Formalist directors may use this ambiguity to create dreamlike effects that disturb our sense of everyday reality.

HISTORICAL BACKGROUND

In 1927, when *The Jazz Singer* ushered in the talkie era **(7-1)**, many critics felt that sound would deal a deathblow to the art of movies. But the setbacks were temporary, and today sound is one of the richest sources of meaning in film art. Actually, there never was a silent period, for virtually all movies before 1927 were accompanied by some kind of music. In the large city theatres, full orchestras provided atmospheric background to the visuals. In small towns, a piano was often used for the same purpose. In many theatres, the "Mighty Wurlitzer" organ, with its bellowing pipes, was the standard musical accompaniment. Music was played for practical as well as artistic reasons, for these sounds muffled the noises of the patrons who were occasionally rowdy, particularly when entering the theatre.

Most of the early talkies were visually dull. The equipment of the time required the simultaneous recording of sound and image: The camera was restricted to one position, the actors could not move far from the microphone, and editing was

7-1. *The Jazz Singer* (U.S.A., 1927), with Al Jolson, directed by Alan Crosland.

There had been a number of experiments in synchronous sound prior to this film, but they failed to create much of a stir with the public. Significantly, Warner Brothers managed to break the sound barrier with a new genre, the musical. Actually, even this movie was mostly silent. Only Jolson's musical numbers and a few snatches of dialogue were in sync sound. *(Warner Bros.)*

restricted to its most minimal function—primarily scene changes. The major source of meaning was in the sound, especially in the dialogue. The images tended merely to illustrate the soundtrack. Before long, adventurous directors began experimenting. The camera was housed in a soundproof **blimp**, thus permitting the camera to move in and out of a scene silently. Soon, several microphones, all on separate channels, were placed on the set. Overhead sound **booms** were devised to follow an actor on a set, so his or her voice was always within range, even when the actor moved around.

Despite these technical advances, formalist directors remained hostile to the use of synchronous sound. Sergei Eisenstein was especially wary of dialogue, and he predicted an onslaught of "highly cultured dramas" that would force cinema back to its stagy beginnings. Synchronous sound, he believed, would destroy the flexibility of editing and thus kill the very soul of film art. Synchronous sound did, in fact, require a more literal continuity, especially in dialogue sequences. Eisenstein's metaphoric cutting, with its leaps in time and space, would not make much sense if realistic sound had to be provided with each image. Indeed, Alfred Hitchcock pointed out that the most cinematic sequences are essentially silent. Chase scenes, for example, require only some general sound effects to preserve their continuity.

7-2. *Scarface* (U.S.A., 1932), with Paul Muni (centre), directed by Howard Hawks.
After the introduction of talkies, American movies—which had always been among the fastest in the world—got even faster. The films of such 1930s masters as Howard Hawks and Frank Capra emphasized speed by having the dialogue delivered 30 to 40% faster than normal. This breathless sense of urgency was especially effective in gangster films, which were immensely popular during the Depression era. In his classic essay, "The Gangster as Tragic Hero," Robert Warshow hit on why the gangster struck such a responsive chord in audiences and why he has held our imagination ever since: "The gangster is the man of the city, with the city's language and knowledge, with its queer and dishonest skills and its terrible daring, carrying his life in his hands like a placard, like a club.... It is not the real city, but that dangerous and sad city of the imagination which is so much more important, which is the modern world." *(United Artists)*

Most of the talented directors of the early sound era favoured nonsynchronous sound. The Frenchman René Clair believed that sound should be used selectively, not indiscriminately. The ear, he believed, is just as selective as the eye, and sound can be edited in the same way that images can. Even dialogue sequences need not be totally synchronous, Clair believed. Conversation can act as a continuity device, freeing the camera to explore contrasting information—a technique especially favoured by ironists like Hitchcock and Ernst Lubitsch.

Clair made several musicals illustrating his theories. In *Le Million* (1931), for example, music and song often replace dialogue. Language is juxtaposed ironically with nonsynchronous images. Many of the scenes were photographed without sound and later dubbed when the montage sequences were completed. These charming musicals are never immobilized by the stagy confinement that ruined most sound films

7-3. *She Done Him Wrong* (U.S.A., 1933), with Mae West, directed by Lowell Sherman.

Tone of voice can be far more communicative than words in revealing a person's thoughts. This is why most sophisticated moviegoers prefer written subtitles to dubbing in foreign language movies. Mae West was an expert in conveying sexual innuendoes through tone of voice—so much so, in fact, that censors insisted on monitoring her scenes during production for fear that the apparently neutral dialogue in her screenplays would be delivered in a "salacious" manner. America responded enthusiastically to Mae's insolence and snappy wisecracks. In this film she is at her outspoken best: cool, lecherous, cynical. In her opening scene, she saucily proclaims herself to be "one of the finest women who ever walked the streets." *(Paramount Pictures)*

of this era. The dubbing technique of Clair, though ahead of its time, eventually became a major approach in sound film production.

Several other directors also experimented with sound in these early years. Hitchcock's *Blackmail* (1929) started out as a silent film, but some sound sequences were added after shooting began. A British actress had to speak the lines of the Czech leading lady off-camera as the star mouthed them, but the inventive director quickly took advantage of the new possibilities provided by sound. In one remarkable sequence, Alice, a young woman who has just stabbed a man who tried to rape her, sits at breakfast with her family, while a gossiping neighbour chatters on about the local killing. Alice tunes out the irritating voice that becomes a blur on the soundtrack, except for the word "knife" that repeatedly startles her, until she jumps and drops the bread knife she is handing to her father.

The increased realism brought on by sound inevitably forced acting styles to become more natural, for performers no longer needed to compensate visually for the lack of dialogue. In silent cinema, directors had to use titles to communicate nonvisual information: dialogue, exposition, abstract ideas, and so on. In some films, these interruptions nearly ruined the delicate rhythm of the visuals. Carl Dreyer's *La Passion de Jeanne d'Arc* [*The Passion of Joan of Arc*] (1927), for example, has frequent interjections of explanatory titles and dialogue taken from the trial records, but sets up a

7-4. *The Silence* (Iran, 1999), with Tahmineh Normatova, written and directed by Mohsen Makhmalbaf. This gentle fable centres on the interior world of an impoverished blind boy (pictured) who works as a tuner of musical instruments. He is constantly distracted by the seductive lure of a pretty voice, or an intriguing piece of music hovering above the hum of everyday life. He is also obsessed with the first four notes of Beethoven's Fifth Symphony. The movie lyricizes the boy's ability to live in his imagination, to feel rapturous joy at the sounds enveloping him. *(New Yorker Films)*

powerful tension between the words we read and the visceral effect of the close-ups of Jeanne and her judges. Other directors avoided titles by dramatizing visually as much as possible. This practice led to many visual clichés. Early in the story, for example, the villain might be identified as such by a scene that showed him kicking a dog, or a heroine could be recognized by the halo-effect lighting around her head, and so forth.

Coming from the world of radio, Orson Welles was an important innovator in the field of sound. In *The Magnificent Ambersons* (1942), he perfected the technique of sound montage, in which the dialogue of one character overlaps with that of another, or several others. The effect is almost musical, for the language is exploited not necessarily for the literal information it may convey, but as pure sound orchestrated in terms of emotional tonalities. One of the most brilliant episodes using this technique is the leave-taking scene at the final Amberson ball. The scene is shot in deep focus with expressionistic lighting contrasts throwing most of the characters into silhouette. The dialogue of one group of characters gently overlaps with that of another, which in turn overlaps with a third group. The effect is hauntingly poetic, despite the relative simplicity of the words themselves. Each person or couple is characterized by a particular sound texture: The young people speak rapidly in a normal to loud volume, a middle-aged couple whispers intimately and slowly. The shouts of various other family members punctuate these dialogue sequences in sudden outbursts. The entire scene seems choreographed, both visually and aurally: Silhouetted figures stream in and out of the frame like graceful phantoms, their words floating and undulating in the

7-5. *The Sum of All Fears* (U.S.A., 2002), with Morgan Freeman and Ben Affleck, directed by Phil Alden Robinson.

Generally speaking, the volume of sound must correlate with the image that accompanies it. In this photo, for example, Freeman whispers confidentially to Affleck, and the camera appropriately moves into a close two shot to preserve the intimacy of the communication. *(Paramount Pictures)*

shadows. The quarrels among the Amberson family are often recorded in a similar manner. Welles's actors don't wait patiently for cues: Accusations and recriminations are hurled simultaneously, as they are in life. The violent words, often irrational and disconnected, spew out in spontaneous eruptions of anger and frustration. As in many family quarrels, everyone shouts, but people only half listen. The extent of Welles's achievement becomes apparent when compared to the conventional ending added at the Studio's insistence, with its banal dialogue and flat delivery.

Sound montage can also create complex relations between the different kinds of sound and the visual track. A common device is to create overlaps at the beginnings and ends of sequences so that the sound from one sequence "bleeds" into another. In *Lonely Boy*, a documentary on Canadian pop singer Paul Anka, the filmmakers frequently manipulate sound-image relations to provide an unspoken commentary on their subject **(9-9)**. During a concert performance, they bring out the hysterical response of the fans by cutting out first the voice of the singer and then the noise of the screaming audience. At the end of the film, they underline—probably with a sense of irony—the human cost of fame by juxtaposing a shot of Anka huddled in his limousine with a reprise of the hit song that gives the film its title.

Sound montage is used in a highly flamboyant manner in Jean-Claude Lauzon's *Léolo* in which fragments of music from different traditions (sacred/profane, Eastern/Western) collide with one another and interact with different levels of narration to immerse us in the delirious fantasy world created by a Québécois boy who imagines that he is Italian **(10-24)**. The technology of sound may thus add to film's ability to reproduce reality, but it can also be used to suggest the "postmodern" experience of a bombardment of images and messages that threatens traditional notions of a coherent identity (see Chapter 11, "Theory").

SOUND EFFECTS

Although the function of sound effects is primarily atmospheric (background noise), they can also be precise sources of meaning in film. The pitch, volume, and tempo of sound effects can strongly affect our responses to any given noise. High-pitched sounds are generally strident and produce a sense of tension in the listener. Especially if these types of noises are prolonged, the shrillness can be totally unnerving. For this reason, high-pitched sounds (including music) are often used in suspense sequences, particularly just before and during the climax. Low-frequency sounds, in contrast, are heavy, full, and less tense. Often they are used to emphasize the dignity or solemnity of a scene, like the male humming chorus in Akira Kurosawa's *The Seven Samurai* (1954). Low-pitched sounds can also suggest anxiety and mystery: Frequently a suspense sequence begins with such sounds, which gradually increase in frequency as the scene moves toward its climax.

Sound volume works in much the same way. Loud sounds tend to be forceful, intense, and threatening, whereas quiet sounds strike us as delicate, hesitant, and often weak. These same principles apply to tempo. The faster the tempo of sound, the greater the tension produced in the listener. In the chase sequence of William Friedkin's *The French Connection* (1971), all these principles are used masterfully.

7-6. *The Exorcist* (U.S.A., 1973), directed by William Friedkin.
Sound in film is generally geared to space: When a severe discrepancy exists, the effect can be disorienting and even frightening. In this movie, the devil has possessed a young girl (Linda Blair). The sounds emanating from her small body echo loudly, creating a cavernous effect, as if the girl's slight figure had been spiritually expanded thousands of times to accommodate the demons that inhabit it. *(Warner Bros.)*

7-7. *The Others* (Spain / U.S.A., 2001), with Nicole Kidman, written and directed by Alejandro Amenábar. In genres like ghost stories, suspense thrillers, and tales of the supernatural, off-screen sounds can create a sense of terror lurking beyond the frame. In this eerie psychological thriller, for example, Amenábar is able to keep the source of terror off screen for most of the movie, tantalizing us with scary sounds, and forcing us to bond with the terrified mother (Kidman) who is trying to protect her two children in an isolated Victorian mansion. *(Dimension Films)*

As the chase reaches its climax, the screeching wheels of the pursuing car and the crashing sound of the runaway train grow louder, faster, and higher pitched.

Off-screen sounds bring off-screen space into play: The sound expands the image beyond the confines of the frame. Sound effects can evoke terror in suspense films and thrillers. We tend to fear what we cannot see, so directors will sometimes use off-screen sound effects to strike a note of anxiety. The sound of a creaking door in a darkened room can be more fearful than an image of someone stealing through the door. In Fritz Lang's *M* (1931), the child murderer is identified by a tune he whistles off screen. During the early portions of the movie, we never see him; we recognize him only by his sinister tune.

In several scenes of Hitchcock's *Psycho* (1960), Bernard Herrmann's score—consisting entirely of strings—suggests shrill bird noises. This motif is used as a form of characterization. A shy and appealing young man (Anthony Perkins) is associated with birds early on in the film. He stuffs birds as a hobby, and his own features are intense and rather hawk-like. During a brutal murder sequence, the soundtrack throbs with screeching bird music. The audience assumes the murderer is the boy's mother, but birds have been associated with him, not her. One of Hitchcock's recurrent themes is the transference of guilt. In this film, the transfer is rather complex. The youth has dug up his long-dead mother's body and literally stuffed it. Often he

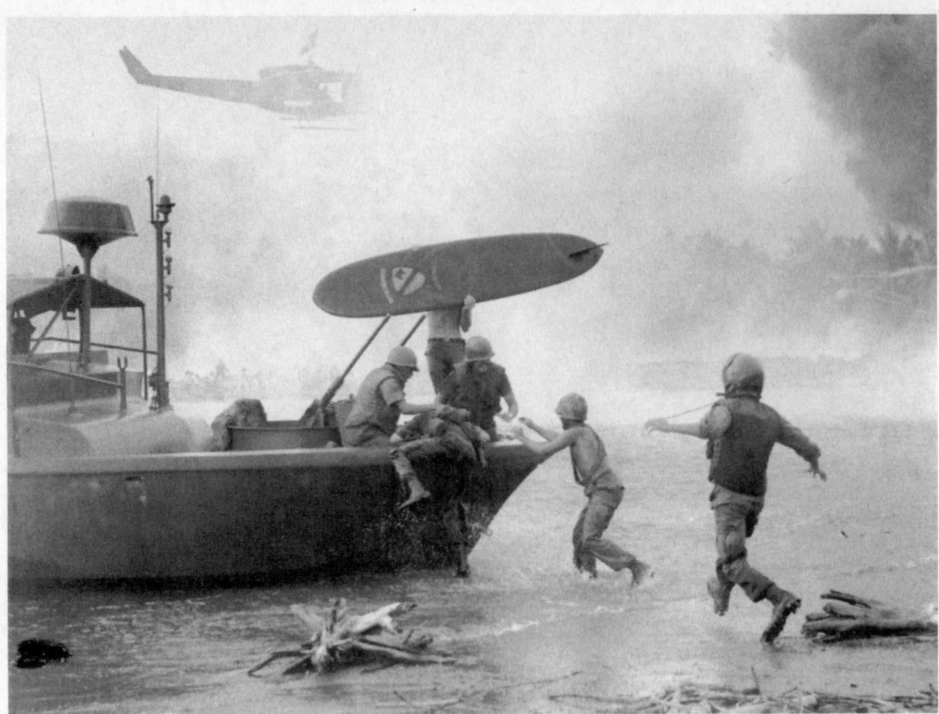

7-8. *Apocalypse Now* (U.S.A., 1979), directed by Francis Ford Coppola.

The sound mixing in Coppola's grotesque Vietnam epic is suffused with grotesque ironies. In this sequence, American helicopters hover and swirl like huge mechanized gods, dropping napalm bombs on a jungle village to the accompaniment of Wagner's inexorable "Ride of the Valkyries," which thunders on the sound track. As terrified peasants scurry for shelter, American soldiers prepare to go surfing in the poisonous fumes of battle. *(United Artists)*

dresses himself up in her clothing. Although we think we see the mother killing two victims, we have in fact seen the schizophrenic youth as his other self—his mother. The bird music offers an early clue to this psychological transference.

Because images tend to dominate sounds while we are actually experiencing a movie, many sound effects work on a subconscious level. In *Psycho*, the heroine (Janet Leigh) drives her car through a rainstorm. On the soundtrack, we hear her windshield wiper blades slashing furiously against the downpour. Later, when she is taking a shower in a motel, these sounds are repeated. The source of the water noise is apparent, but the slashing sounds seem to come from nowhere—until a demented killer crashes into the bathroom brandishing a knife.

Sound effects can also serve symbolic functions, which are usually determined by the dramatic context. In Luis Buñuel's *Belle de Jour* (1967), for example, the sounds of jingling bells are associated with the heroine's sexual fantasies. Other symbolic sound effects are more universally understood. In Ingmar Bergman's *Wild Strawberries* (1957), the protagonist, an elderly professor, has a nightmare. The **surrealistic** sequence is virtually silent except for the insistent sound of a heartbeat—a memento mori for the professor, a reminder that his life will soon end.

7-9. *The Pianist* (Poland / France / Britain / Germany, 2002), with Adrien Brody, directed by Roman Polanski. This movie is a biography of the distinguished pianist Wladyslaw Szpilman, a preeminent interpreter of the music of the Polish composer Chopin. A Jew, Szpilman survived the Nazi Holocaust in the 1940s. He managed to escape the Nazi roundup, but was separated from his family and hid out in the infamous Warsaw ghetto, where he barely survived disease and starvation. The soundtrack often features Chopin's piano music, lending the story a poetic, wistful melancholia. Polanski, himself a Polish Jew, was only a child during this period, but he too managed to elude capture by the Nazis and lived to tell about it. *(Focus Features)*

In reality, a considerable difference exists between hearing and listening. As Hitchcock demonstrates in *Blackmail*, our minds automatically filter out irrelevant sounds. While talking in a noisy city location, for example, we listen to the speaker, but we barely hear the sounds of traffic. The microphone is not so selective. Most movie soundtracks are cleaned up to rid them of such extraneous noises. A sequence might include selected city noises to suggest the urban locale, but once this context is established, outside sounds are diminished and sometimes even eliminated to permit us to hear the conversation clearly.

Since the 1960s, however, a number of directors have retained these noisy soundtracks in the name of greater realism. Influenced by the documentary school of **cinéma vérité**—which tends to avoid simulated or re-created sounds—directors like Jean-Luc Godard even allowed important dialogue to be partly washed out by on-location sounds. In *Masculin-Féminin* (1966), Godard's use of sound is especially bold. His insistence on natural noises—all of them as they were recorded during shooting—dismayed many critics, who complained of the "cacophonous din." The movie deals with violence and the lack of privacy, peace, and quiet. Simply by

7-10. ***Saturday Night Fever*** **(U.S.A., 1977), with Karen Lynn Gorney and John Travolta, directed by John Badham.**

A film's rhythm is often created through its musical score. In this famous dance musical, director Badham used the pulsating Bee Gees disco tune "Staying Alive" as a basis for both the staging and the editing rhythms. "Every time we shot a shot," Badham explained, "that music would be playing, so that all the movie that is on screen is in exact tempo to that [song]." The film triggered off a disco dance craze that swept the Western world in the late 1970s. *(Paramount Pictures)*

exploiting his soundtrack, Godard avoided the need to comment overtly on these themes—they are naggingly persistent in virtually every scene.

Like absolute stasis in a motion picture, silence in a sound film tends to call attention to itself. Any significant stretch of silence creates an eerie vacuum—a sense of something impending, about to burst. Arthur Penn exploited this phenomenon in the conclusion of *Bonnie and Clyde* (1967). The lovers stop on a country road to help a friend (actually an informer) with his truck, which has presumably broken down. Clumsily, he scrambles under the truck. There is a long moment of silence while the two lovers exchange puzzled, then anxious, glances. Suddenly, the sound track roars with the noise of machine guns as the lovers are brutally cut down by policemen hiding in the bushes. Silence is also used evocatively at the beginning of *Brokeback Mountain* (Ang Lee, 2005), when the two young men whose relationship the film will poignantly depict wait silently in a parking lot outside a locked building, their curiosity about each other (and ours about them) heightened by the long silence, punctuated only by the crunching of the gravel beneath their boots.

Like the **freeze frame**, total silence (with no ambient sound) can be used to symbolize death, because we tend to associate sound with the presence of ongoing life. Kurosawa uses this technique in *Ikiru* (1952), after a doctor informs the elderly protagonist that he is dying of cancer. Stupefied, the old man stumbles out on the street, and the soundtrack cuts out. When he is almost run over by a speeding car, the soundtrack suddenly roars with the noise of city traffic. The protagonist is yanked back into the world of the living.

MUSIC

Music is a highly abstract art, tending toward pure form. It is impossible to speak of the "subject matter" of a musical phrase. When merged with lyrics, music acquires a more concrete content because words, of course, have specific references. Both words and music convey meanings, but each in a different manner. With or without lyrics, music can be more specific when juxtaposed with film images. In fact, many musicians have complained that images tend to rob music of its ambiguity by anchoring musical tones to specific ideas and emotions. For example, few moviegoers can listen to Richard Strauss's *Thus Spake Zarathustra* without being reminded of Stanley Kubrick's *2001: A Space Odyssey* (1968).

Theories about film music are surprisingly varied. Pudovkin and Eisenstein insisted that music must never serve merely as accompaniment: It ought to retain its

7-11. *Do the Right Thing* (U.S.A., 1989), with Spike Lee and Danny Aiello, written and directed by Lee. Set in a predominantly African-American section of Brooklyn, this movie explores the tensions between the black community and the Italian-American proprietor (Aiello) of a pizza restaurant. The two cultures are characterized by their music as well as their lifestyles. The African-American characters listen to soul, gospel, and rap music, whereas the Italian-American characters typically prefer the ballads of Frank Sinatra. Spike Lee, who hails from a musical family himself, is painstakingly precise about his musical scores. *(Universal Pictures)*

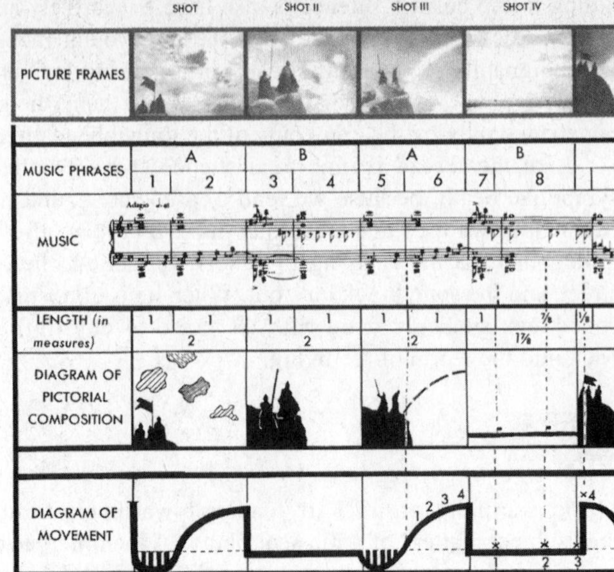

7-12. Audiovisual score from *Alexander Nevsky* (Russia, 1938), music by Sergei Prokofiev, directed by Sergei Eisenstein.

The composer need not always subordinate his or her talents to those of the film director. Here, two great Soviet artists aligned their contributions into a totally fused production in which the music corresponds to the movement of the images set in a row. Prokofiev avoided purely "representational" elements (mickeymousing). Instead, both composer and director concentrated sometimes on the images first, other times on the music. The result was what Eisenstein called "vertical montage," where the notes on the staff, moving from left to right, parallel the movements or major lines of the images which, set side by side, also "move" from left to right. Thus, if the lines in a series of images move from lower left to upper right, the notes of music would move in a similar direction on the musical staff. If the lines of a composition were jagged and uneven, the notes of music would also zigzag in a corresponding manner.

own integrity. The film critic Paul Rotha claimed that music must even be allowed to dominate the image on occasion. Some filmmakers insist on purely descriptive music—a practice referred to as **mickeymousing** (so called because of Disney's early experiments with music and animation). This type of score uses music as a literal equivalent to the image. If a character stealthily tiptoes from a room, for example, each step has a musical note to emphasize the suspense. Other directors believe that film music should not be too distinguished or it will detract from the images. Most imaginative directors reject this notion. For them, the music of even the greatest composers can be used in movies.

A filmmaker does not need to have technical expertise to use music effectively. As Aaron Copland pointed out, directors must know what they want from music *dramatically*: It is the composer's business to translate these dramatic needs into musical terms. Directors and composers work together in a variety of ways. Most composers begin working after they have seen the **rough cut** of a movie—that is, the major footage before the editor has tightened up the slackness between shots. Some composers do not begin until the film has been completed except for the music. Directors of musicals, on the other hand, usually work with the composer before shooting begins.

Beginning with the opening credits, music can serve as a kind of overture to suggest the mood or spirit of the film as a whole. John Addison's opening music in Tony Richardson's *Tom Jones* (1963) is a witty, rapidly executed harpsichord piece. The harpsichord itself is associated with the eighteenth century, the period of the film. The occasionally jazzy phrases in the tune suggest a sly twentieth-century overview—a musical equivalent of the blending of centuries found in the movie itself. Similarly, Michael Nyman's score for Jane Campion's *The Piano* (1993) evokes the nineteenth-century romantic piano concerto (and Nyman later arranged it as a concerto), in keeping with the film's period setting, but incorporates more modern elements that reinforce the film's feminist perspective on its Gothic narrative.

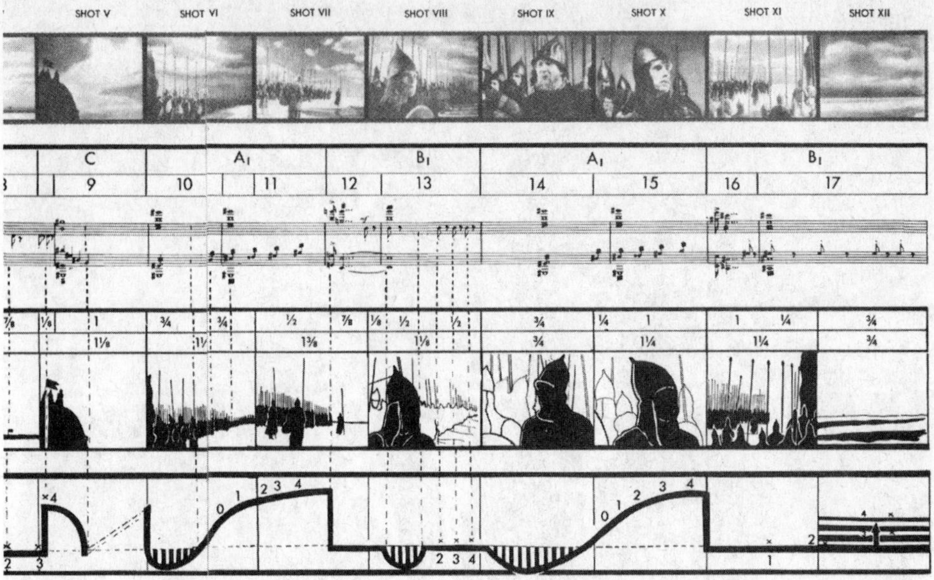

The function of music to establish the mood of a film is also well illustrated by the work of two Canadian composers. Mychael Danna's rhythmic scores, often incorporating non-Western instruments, are a vital component of Atom Egoyan's films that explore the tensions between tradition and technology, while Howard Shore's edgy music underlines the constant sense of paranoia in the films of David Cronenberg. Both composers have also worked extensively in Hollywood.

Certain kinds of music can suggest locales, classes, or ethnic groups. For example, John Ford's westerns feature simple folk tunes like "Red River Valley" or religious hymns like "Shall We Gather at the River," which are associated with the American frontier of the late nineteenth century. Richly nostalgic, these songs are often played on frontier instruments—a plaintive harmonica or a concertina. Similarly, many Italian movies feature lyrical, highly emotional melodies, reflecting the operatic heritage of that country. The greatest composer of this kind of film music was Nino Rota, who scored virtually all of Federico Fellini's films, as well as such distinguished works as Franco Zeffirelli's *Romeo and Juliet* (1968) and Francis Ford Coppola's *The Godfather* (1972).

7-13. *Amadeus* (U.S.A., 1984), with Tom Hulce (right), directed by Milos Forman.

Based on the celebrated play by Peter Shaffer, this film depicts the short and difficult life of Wolfgang Amadeus Mozart (Hulce) through the eyes of his rival Antonio Salieri (F. Murray Abraham). Salieri is tormented by the awareness of his own mediocrity as a composer, despite his pious life, while God allows the irrepressibly vulgar and irreligious Mozart to create music of overwhelming beauty and grace. In accordance with the legends surrounding Mozart's mysterious death, the film suggests that Salieri poisoned him to silence him, but the glorious music lives on and is generously incorporated into the film's soundtrack. *(New Yorker Films)*

Music can be used as foreshadowing, particularly when the dramatic context does not permit a director to prepare an audience for an event. Hitchcock, for example, often accompanied an apparently casual sequence with "anxious" music—a warning to the audience to be prepared. Sometimes these musical warnings are false alarms; other times they explode into frightening crescendos. Similarly, when actors are required to assume restrained or neutral expressions, music can suggest their internal—hidden—emotions. Bernard Herrmann's music functions in both ways in *Psycho*.

Music can also provide ironic contrast. In many cases, the predominant mood of a scene can be neutralized or even reversed with contrasting music. In *Bonnie and Clyde*, the robbery scenes are often accompanied by high-spirited banjo music. Jon Brion's schizoid score for *Punch-Drunk Love* (Paul Thomas Anderson, 2002) often conveys agitated emotions within a calm context. When the strung-out protagonist (Adam Sandler) is under pressure at his job, the musical score becomes aggressively percussive, with lots of weird electronic sounds. When he falls in love with a mysterious stranger (Emily Watson), the orchestral accompaniment is a Frenchified lyrical waltz, as romantic as a boat ride down the Seine. The music is full-bodied, lilting,

7-14. *Sleepless in Seattle* (U.S.A., 1993), with Tom Hanks, written and directed by Nora Ephron.

Ephron's romantic comedy combines the contemporary with the traditional. This double perspective is best illustrated by the songs on the soundtrack. Many of them are classic tunes of the 1940s, but sung by contemporary singers—such as "In the Wee Small Hours of the Morning" sung by Carly Simon, or "When I Fall in Love," a sweet duet sung by Celine Dion and Clive Griffin. Other standards: "As Time Goes By" sung by Jimmy Durante, "A Kiss to Build a Dream On" by Louis Armstrong, and "Stardust" crooned by the velvet-voiced Nat King Cole. The musical score of the movie became a huge best-selling album (produced by Sony Music). *(Tri-Star Pictures)*

rhapsodic—usually accompanying perfectly undramatic visuals, such as the couple just walking along the street.

Characterization can be suggested through musical motifs. In Fellini's *La Strada* (1954), the pure, sad simplicity of the heroine (Giulietta Masina) is captured by a melancholy tune she plays on a trumpet. This theme is varied and elaborated on in Nino Rota's delicate score, suggesting that even after her death her spiritual influence is still felt. Characterization can be even more precise when lyrics are added to music. In Peter Bogdanovich's *The Last Picture Show* (1971), for instance, pop tunes of the 1950s are used in association with specific characters. The bitchy Jacy (Cybill Shepherd) is linked to "Cold, Cold Heart," and her deceived boyfriend Duane (Jeff Bridges) is characterized by "A Fool Such as I."

In *American Graffiti* (1973), George Lucas uses pop tunes in a similar manner. Two young lovers who have just quarrelled are shown dancing at a sock hop to the tune of "Smoke Gets in Your Eyes." The line of the song "yet today my love has flown away" acquires particular poignancy for the girl because the boy has just told her that he intends to date others when he goes off to college. The lovers are reconciled at the end of the movie when he decides not to leave after all. On the soundtrack, "Only You" is appropriately intoned, its syrupy lyrics emphasizing the destiny of love. In many sequences in this film, the music comes from car radios—and is thus diegetic—but the actual source is often forgotten as the songs function as nondiegetic background music, often providing an ironic commentary on the action.

In Lauzon's *Léolo*, the bizarre story is accompanied by music taken from many different traditions, from Tibetan monks chanting to the Rolling Stones, from the plaintive songs of Jacques Brel to the gravelly voice of Tom Waits, with religious music often accompanying images of gross bodily functions. Jean-Marc Vallée's *C.R.A.Z.Y.* also uses a mixture of music to bring out the pressures at work in Quebec culture in the 1960s and 1970s (see **10-2**). At one point, the young boy who must

7-15. *Footlight Parade* (U.S.A., 1933), with Ruby Keeler, Joan Blondell, and (standing) James Cagney, directed by Lloyd Bacon.

Musicals were all the rage in the early talkie era, and each of the major Hollywood studios specialized in a house style. The musicals at Warner Brothers, for example, were typically proletarian, with emphasis on "ordinary" people and working-class values. This backstage musical is characteristically fast-paced and down-to-earth, although, as in most movies choreographed by Busby Berkeley, the realism is stunningly transcended in the final lavish production numbers, supposedly performed onstage but requiring the full resources of the film medium.
(Warner Bros.)

come to terms with his own sexuality imagines the choir performing the Stones' "Sympathy for the Devil" at Midnight Mass. He scandalizes his neighbourhood by lip-syncing to a David Bowie song, while his father's conservative attitudes and tastes are exemplified by his obsession with the country music of Patsy Cline.

Stanley Kubrick was a bold—and controversial—innovator in the use of film music. In *Dr. Strangelove* (1963), he sardonically juxtaposed Vera Lynn's sentimental World War II tune "We'll Meet Again" with images of a global nuclear holocaust—a grim reminder that we probably *won't* meet again after World War III. In *2001: A Space Odyssey*, images of a twenty-first-century rocket ship gliding through the blueness of space are accompanied by Johann Strauss's nineteenth-century "Blue Danube Waltz"—an aural foreshadowing of man's obsolete technology in the more advanced technological universe beyond Jupiter. In *A Clockwork Orange* (1971), Kubrick uses music as a distancing device, particularly in violent scenes. Musical incongruity undercuts the realism of an otherwise vicious gang fight that takes place to the accompaniment of Rossini's urbane and witty overture to *The Thieving Magpie*. A brutal attack and rape scene becomes a grotesque song-and-dance routine set to the tune of "Singin' in the Rain."

A frequent function of film music is to underline speech, especially dialogue. A common assumption about this kind of music is that it merely acts to prop up bad dialogue or poor acting. The hundreds of mediocre love scenes performed to quivering violins have perhaps prejudiced many viewers against this kind of musical accompaniment. However, some of the most gifted actors have benefited from it. In Laurence Olivier's *Hamlet* (1948), the composer William Walton worked out his score with painstaking precision. In the "To be or not to be" soliloquy, the music provides a counterpoint to Olivier's brilliantly modulated delivery, adding yet another dimension to this complex speech.

MUSICALS AND MELODRAMA

The soundtrack is, of course, a vital component of the musical, one of the most enduring and popular film genres. Musicals can be divided into the realistic and the formalistic according to the relations between their narratives and the musical numbers. Realistic musicals are generally backstage stories, in which the production numbers are presented as dramatically plausible. Such musicals usually justify a song or dance with a brief bit of dialogue—"Hey, kids, let's rehearse the barn number"—and the barn number is then presented to the audience **(7-15)**. A few realistic musicals are virtually dramas with music. In George Cukor's *A Star Is Born* (1954), for example, the narrative events would hold up without the musical numbers, as they did in the William Wellman's nonmusical version (1937), starring Janet Gaynor in the role that Judy Garland later made her own. Martin Scorsese's *New York, New York* **(7-16)** and Bob Fosse's *Cabaret* **(5-13)** are also dramas interspersed with music. The music in these films is often diegetic, produced by the characters in the film, although nondiegetic background music may well accompany the major production numbers.

Formalist musicals make no pretence at realism. Characters burst out in song and dance in the middle of a scene without easing into the number with a plausible pretext. This convention must be accepted as an aesthetic premise, otherwise the entire film will strike the viewer as absurd. Everything is heightened and stylized in such works—sets, costumes, acting, and so on. Most of Vincente Minnelli's musicals, including *An American in Paris* **(5-1)** and *The Band Wagon* **(7-17)**, are of this type.

Although musicals have been produced in several countries, the genre is most closely associated with American popular cinema, perhaps because it is so intimately related to the Hollywood studio system. In the 1930s, several major studios specialized in a particular type of musical. RKO produced the charming Fred Astaire–Ginger Rogers star vehicles (see **11-26**), while Paramount specialized in sophisticated "continental" musicals. At Warner Brothers, choreographer-director Busby Berkeley delighted audiences with his proletarian show-biz stories like *Gold Diggers of 1933* and *Dames* **(1-1b)**.

In the 1940s and 1950s, the musical was dominated by MGM, which had the finest musical directors under contract: Gene Kelly, Stanley Donen, and Minnelli. Indeed, this prosperous studio had a virtual monopoly on the musical personalities of the day, including Garland, Kelly, Frank Sinatra, Mickey Rooney, Ann Miller, Vera-Ellen, Leslie Caron, Donald O'Connor, Cyd Charisse, Howard Keel, Mario Lanza, Kathryn Grayson, and many others. Arthur Freed was the **producer** of most

7-16. *New York, New York* (U.S.A., 1977), with Liza Minnelli and Robert De Niro, music by John Kander and Fred Ebb, directed by Martin Scorsese.

A number of commentators have pointed out that the most enduring genres tend to evolve toward a revisionist phase—subjecting many of the genre's original values to skeptical scrutiny (see Chapter 2, "Story"). For example, most musicals of the big-studio era were essentially love stories and are concluded with the obligatory boy-wins-girl finale. Such revisionist musicals as *Cabaret* and *New York, New York*, however, end with the lovers going their separate ways, too absorbed by their own careers to submit to love's rituals of self-sacrifice. *(United Artists)*

7-17. *The Band Wagon* (U.S.A., 1953), with Fred Astaire, Nanette Fabray, and Jack Buchanan, music by Howard Dietz and Arthur Schwartz, directed by Vincente Minnelli.

Like Busby Berkeley's musical numbers, this song-and-dance routine, supposedly performed during the production of a stage musical also called *The Band Wagon*, would be difficult to pull off in the live theatre, for the three performers were required to strap false legs and feet onto their knees, their real legs bent behind them as they executed their song and dance. Although the story draws on the tradition of the backstage musical, many of the earlier numbers are in the formalist tradition, as when Astaire spontaneously bursts into an exuberant dance number in an entertainment arcade. *(MGM)*

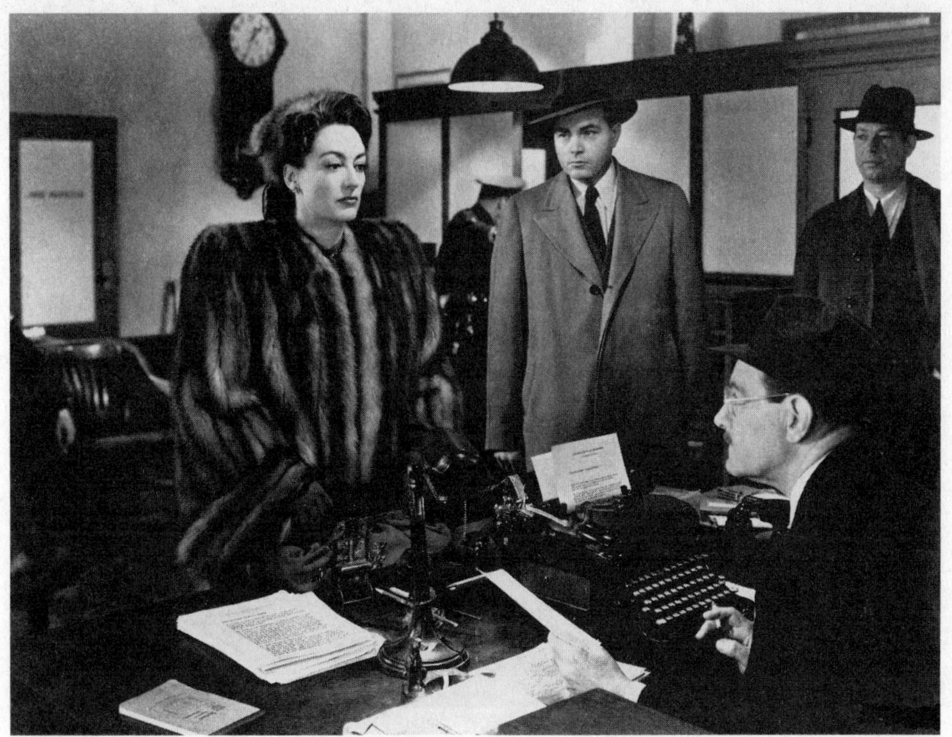

7-18. *Mildred Pierce* (U.S.A., 1945), with Joan Crawford, directed by Michael Curtiz.
Police are investigating a murder in which Mildred (Crawford) is implicated, and the visual style and hard-boiled dialogue define the movie as a *film noir*. The flashbacks, which take up most of the screen time, take us into the territory of "women's films," telling the story of Mildred's personal sacrifices to build up a business so that she can provide for her daughter who, predictably, does not appreciate her mother's efforts and causes her more suffering. At the end, Mildred is left desolate when the police discover that she has been trying to protect her daughter—the real murderer—but the ending does not cancel out Crawford's depiction of a confident and successful businesswoman. *(Warner Bros.)*

of MGM's important musicals, including the majority of Minnelli's films, as well as the stylish works of Donen (see **5-17**).

With the rise of rock music in the 1950s, the **classical** musical began to seem old-fashioned, although there were numerous attempts to adjust the old form to the new musical styles, most successfully in a succession of films starring Elvis Presley. In *A Hard Day's Night* (1964), Richard Lester used a frenetic and irreverent approach to match the youthful energy of the Beatles, pushing the genre in new directions that anticipated the music video. However, the classical musical was not dead, as shown by the enormous success of two movies starring Julie Andrews: *Mary Poppins* (Robert Stevenson, 1964) and *The Sound of Music* (Robert Wise, 1965). The following decades were dominated by the rock musical, but Bob Fosse directed three musicals, *Sweet Charity* (1969), *Cabaret*, and *All That Jazz* (1979), that integrated music, dance, and editing in ways that drew on the traditions of the genre even as the disturbing narratives called them into question. After these **revisionist** movies, the

7-19. *Dark Victory* (U.S.A., 1939), with Bette Davis and George Brent, directed by Edward Goulding. This highly emotional melodrama depicts the struggles of a fun-loving young woman (Davis) who is diagnosed with a brain tumour. She marries the doctor who operates on her (Brent), but he conceals from her that she has only six months to live. A fairly routine "tear-jerker" is transformed by the performance of the star, who was not a conventional beauty but whose **persona** conveyed a sense of independence and determination, both in her on-screen roles and in her dealings with the Studio bosses. *(Warner Bros.)*

musical lost momentum, but enjoyed a revival with the success of the nostalgic *Chicago* (Rob Marshall, 2002) and Baz Luhrmann's highly **reflexive** deconstruction of the genre in *Moulin Rouge* **(6-15)**.

The other major genre in which music has a primary function is melodrama. The term itself means music (*melos*) + drama, and it was originally applied to early forms of opera. In the nineteenth century, melodrama became an enormously popular theatrical form, in which music heightened the intense emotions generated by conflicts between characters who represented very clearly defined moral positions. Dialogue was simple and kept to a minimum, and the action often climaxed in visual tableaux, which functioned as virtual freeze frames that symbolized the struggle between good and evil.

This form carried over into silent cinema, which depended on situations that could be easily understood without verbal explanations. The heroine tied to the railroad tracks by the ruthless villain became a stock image for early attempts to generate suspense, and D.W. Griffith developed the language of melodrama into his stories of suffering heroines and last-minute rescues. More specifically, however, melo-

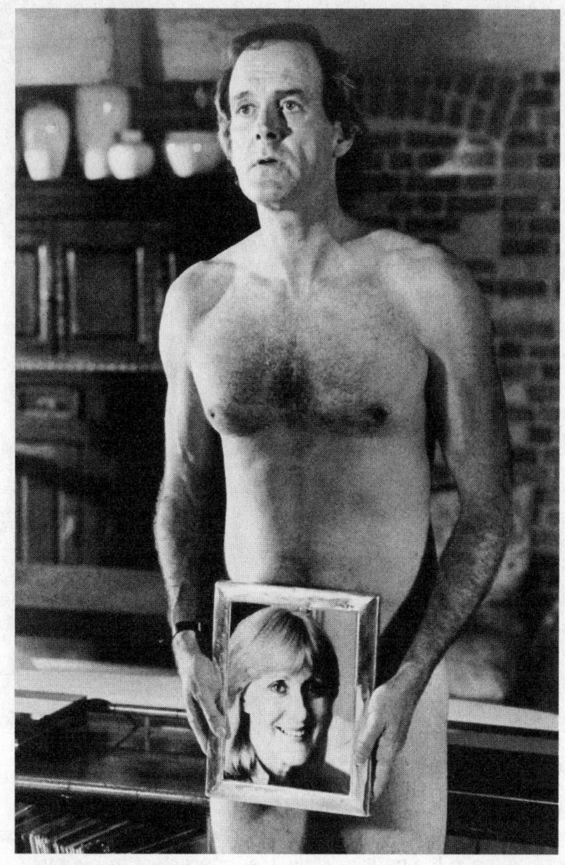

7-20. ***A Fish Called Wanda*** **(Britain / U.S.A., 1988), with John Cleese, directed by Charles Crichton.**

As a graduate of the legendary Monty Python's Flying Circus troupe, John Cleese is, of course, perfectly comfortable with truly tasteless slapstick comedy. But like many British comedians, he is also highly literate, and he wrote the screenplay for this movie and assisted the director (uncredited). His dialogue is fiendishly witty. And of course truly tasteless, too. *(MGM)*

drama in film studies often refers to the domestic melodramas or **women's films** that flourished in Hollywood between 1930 and 1960.

As well as his musicals, Minnelli directed some of the greatest Hollywood melodramas, including *The Cobweb* (1955) and *Home from the Hill* (1960), but the most celebrated examples of the genre are a series of films directed for Universal in the 1950s by Douglas Sirk. In films like *All That Heaven Allows* (1955) and *Imitation of Life* (1959), Sirk depicted families torn apart by the narrow moral attitudes that prevailed in his stylized depiction of American middle-class society. These "weepies" were commercially successful, but critics tended to despise their sentimentality and lack of subtlety. More recently, Sirk's films—and melodrama in general—have been rehabilitated by critics who point to the way in which the mise en scène often undercuts the apparent moral clarity of the dialogue and the narrative. Sirk is especially noted for creating tearful "happy endings" that are so excessive as to become unbelievable. Although domestic melodramas often focus on women as victims, they provided strong roles for a number of forceful female stars (Bette Davis, Joan Crawford, Lana Turner) (**7-18** and **7-19**).

Many later filmmakers have expressed great admiration for Sirk. In the 1970s, the German director Rainer Werner Fassbinder wrote an enthusiastic essay on his work (Sirk himself emigrated from Germany when Adolf Hitler came to power) and

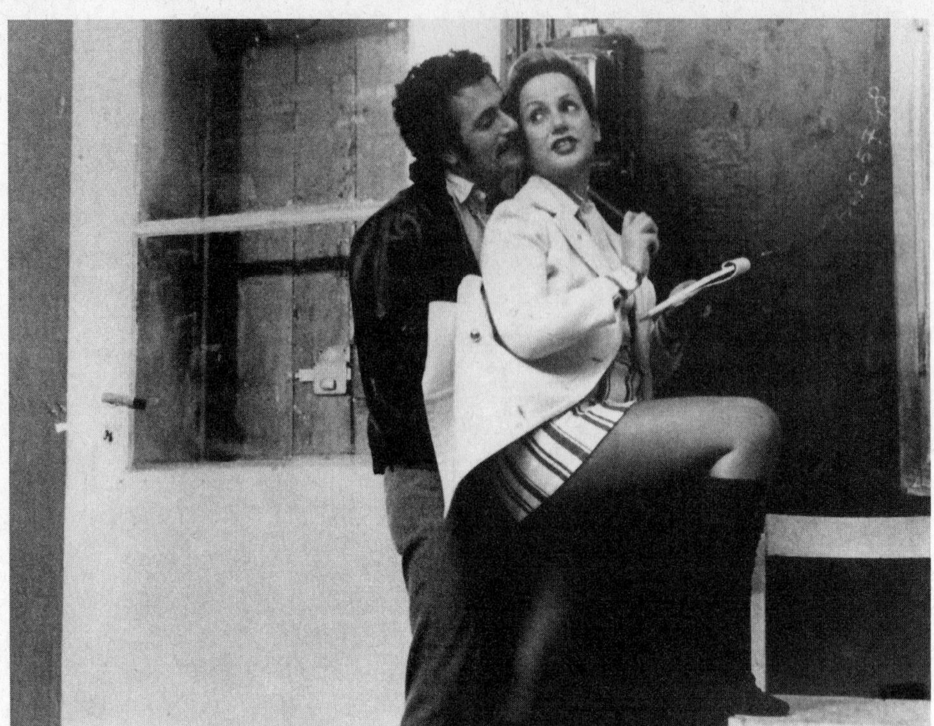

7-21. *All Screwed Up* (Italy, 1973), directed by Lina Wertmüller.

Wertmüller is acutely sensitive to the ideological implications of dialects. Much of her comedy is mined from the earthy idioms of working-class southerners in contrast to the standard (Tuscan) dialect spoken in the north of Italy. Her characters frequently swear or express themselves in coarse language, which is often very funny. Much of this comedy is lost in translation. *(New Line Cinema)*

remade *All That Heaven Allows* as *Fear Eats the Soul* (1974). In Sirk's version, a well-to-do widow causes a scandal when she falls in love with her gardener; Fassbinder depicts an affair between a middle-aged cleaning lady and a young Moroccan immigrant. *All That Heaven Allows* was also the inspiration in 2002 for Todd Haynes's *Far From Heaven*, which lovingly re-creates the visual style of the original but adds additional complications. The husband is not dead but is struggling to come to terms with his homosexual desires, and the gardener is black, introducing the racial issues that Sirk himself confronted in *Imitation of Life*.

SPEECH

In some respects, language in film can be more complex than it is in literature. In the first place, the words of a movie are spoken, not written, and the human voice is capable of far more nuances than is the cold printed page. The written word is a crude approximation of the connotative richness of speech. Thus, to take a simple example of no literary merit, the meaning of the words "I will see him tomorrow" seems obvi-

7-22. *Trainspotting* (Britain, 1996), with Jonny Lee Miller, Ewan McGregor, Kevin McKidd, and Ewen Bremner, directed by Danny Boyle.

Spoken language is steeped in ideology. It is an instant revealer of class, education, and cultural bias. In most countries, regional dialects are considered substandard—at any rate by those speaking the "official" (that is, ruling-class) dialect. In Britain in particular, dialects correlate closely with the class system. People in power usually speak the same "Establishment" dialect taught in the exclusive private schools that still educate most ruling-class Britons. On the other hand, the working-class Scottish dialect of the main characters in this movie clearly places them outside the spheres of power and prestige. They are unemployed, have no sense of a future, and behave in self-destructive ways, but their idiomatic language brings out their vitality and lost potential. *(Miramax Films)*

ous enough in written form. But an actor can emphasize one word over the others and thus change the meaning of the sentence completely. Here are a few possibilities:

- *I* will see him tomorrow. (Implying not you or anyone else.)
- I *will* see him tomorrow. (Implying and I don't care if you approve.)
- I will *see* him tomorrow. (Implying but that's all I'll do.)
- I will see *him* tomorrow. (Implying but not anyone else.)
- I will see him *tomorrow*. (Implying not today, or any other time.)

Of course, a novelist or poet could emphasize specific words by italicizing them, but writers do not generally underline words in every sentence. Actors, however, routinely go through their dialogue to see which words they should stress, which they can "throw away," and how to best achieve these effects—in every sentence. To a gifted actor, the written dialogue is a mere blueprint, an outline, compared with the complexities of spoken speech. A performer with an excellent voice—a Meryl Streep

7-23. *La Maudite galette* (Canada, 1972), with Marcel Sabourin, J. Léo Gagnon, and Luce Guilbeault, directed by Denys Arcand.

The French spoken in Quebec is quite different from the French spoken in France. The difference is at its most extreme in *joual*, a dialect used mainly by the urban working class, with its own vocabulary, idioms, and structures. Although the title of Arcand's comic *film noir* (virtually impossible to translate into English—"The Damned Dough" has been suggested) uses a colloquial phrase familiar to French audiences, the language spoken by the characters in their heavy Quebec accents would require subtitles if the film were shown in France. *(Cinak ltée)*

or a Kenneth Branagh—could wrench ten or twelve meanings from this simple sentence, let alone a Shakespearean soliloquy.

The effects of speech are often tied to the use of dialects and accents that convey social meanings. Dialects comprise the distinctive idioms, vocabulary, and pronunciation used by specific groups of speakers. Speech patterns deviating radically from the official dialect are generally regarded as substandard. These dialects can be used to subversive effect. For example, the comic art of Richard Pryor is steeped in the jivy idioms of America's black ghettos—best illustrated by his diabolically funny concert films. A number of European filmmakers have also exploited the expressive richness of dialects **(7-21)**.

A spoken language also involves many variations of accent—the way sounds are pronounced—which is often, but not always, associated with a dialect, and which also affects our response to the speakers. In Britain a standard "southern" accent, often called BBC English, was regarded as the correct way of speaking until the 1960s, when regional accents gained acceptance, partly because of the success of

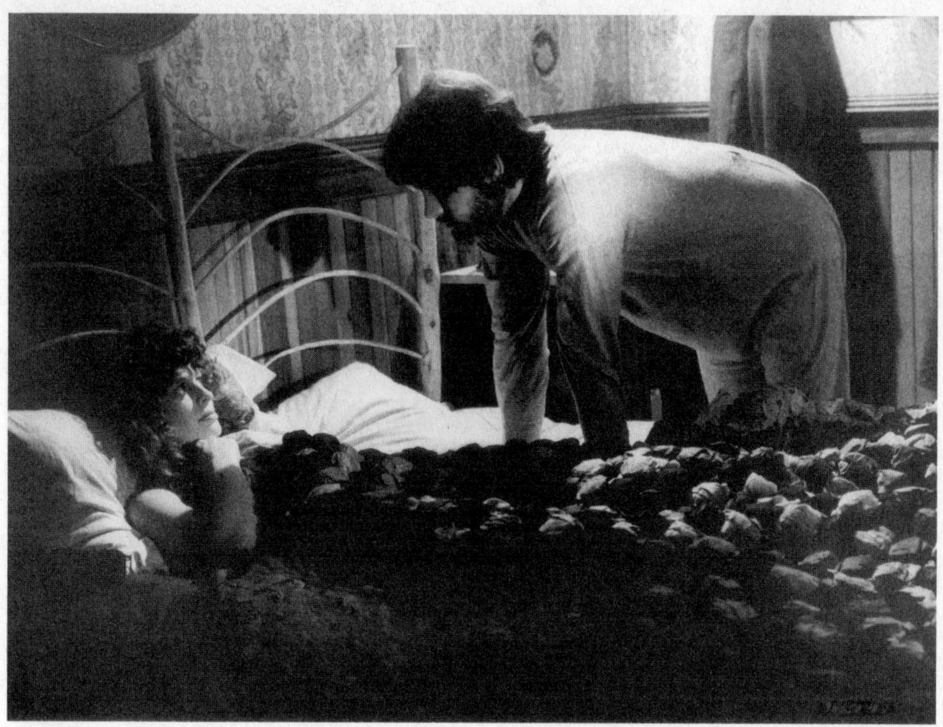

7-24. *McCabe & Mrs. Miller* (U.S.A., 1970), with Julie Christie and Warren Beatty, directed by Robert Altman.

"What I am after is essentially the subtext," Robert Altman has declared. "I want to get the quality of what's happening between people, not just the words. The words often don't matter, it's what they're really saying to each other without the words. Most of the dialogue, well, I don't even listen to it. As I get confident in what the actors are doing, I don't even listen to it. I find that actors know more about the characters they're playing than I do." *(Warner Bros.)*

films set in northern industrial cities and the popularity of rock groups like the Beatles and the Rolling Stones (see **7-22**). Canadian films also incorporate a rich variety of regional and ethnic accents, although characters with such accents rarely occupy positions of power or authority **(7-23)**.

Speech can also be enriched by a **subtext** that suggests implicit meanings *behind* the language **(7-24)**. For example, the following lines of dialogue might be contained in a script:

Woman: May I have a cigarette, please?
Man: Yes, of course. (Lights her cigarette.)
Woman: Thank you. You're very kind.
Man: Don't mention it.

As written, these four not very exciting lines seem simple enough and rather neutral emotionally. But, depending on the dramatic context, they can be exploited to suggest other ideas, totally independent of the apparent meaning of the words. If the

7-25. *Xala* (Senegal, 1975), directed by Ousmane Sembène.
Senegal, a former French colony, has a population of only four million, yet it has produced some of Africa's most important movies, most notably those of Sembène, the continent's best-known filmmaker. French and Wolof, the native language of Senegal, are both spoken in *Xala* (which roughly translates as "The Curse of Impotence"). The movie is an *exposé* of the nation's servile ruling class, whose members have eagerly embraced the culture of their white colonial predecessors. (At this lavish wedding reception, for example, several Frenchified Beautiful People wonder what the English translation is for "le weekend.") The cultural commentator Hernandez Arregui has observed, "Culture becomes bilingual not due to the use of two languages but because of the conjuncture of two cultural patterns of thinking. One is national, that of the people, and the other is estranging, that of the classes subordinated to outside forces. The admiration that the upper classes express for the United States or Europe is the highest expression of their subjection." *(New Yorker Films)*

woman were flirting with the man, for example, she would deliver the lines very differently than she would as an efficient businesswoman. If they detested one another, the lines would take on another significance. If the man were flirting with a hostile female, the lines would be delivered in yet another way, suggesting other meanings. In short, the meaning of the passage is provided by the actors, not the language, which is merely camouflage.

Any script meant to be spoken has a subtext, even one of great literary distinction. A good example from a classic text can be seen in Zeffirelli's *Romeo and Juliet*, in which Mercutio (John McEnery) is played not as the witty bon vivant who is intoxicated with his own talk, but as a neurotic young man with a shaky grasp of reality. This interpretation upset some traditionalists, but in the context of the movie, it

7-26. *The Usual Suspects* (U.S.A., 1995), with Kevin Pollak, Stephen Baldwin, Benicio Del Toro, Gabriel Byrne, and Kevin Spacey, directed by Bryan Singer.

Voice-overs are especially effective in presenting us with a contrast between what is said socially and what is thought privately. Almost always, the private voice-over contains the truth, the character's real feelings about a situation. *The Usual Suspects*, a quirky psychological crime thriller, is unusual in that the voice-over narrator is a compulsive liar and manipulator. Almost everything he tells us is a tissue of lies. And we fall for his story, at least until the final scene when we discover—surprise—we have been duped. *(Gramercy Pictures)*

reinforces the loving bond between Romeo and his best friend and helps justify Romeo's impulsive (and self-destructive) act of revenge later in the film after Tybalt kills Mercutio.

Some contemporary filmmakers deliberately neutralize their language, claiming that the subtext is what they are really after. Harold Pinter, the dramatist and screenwriter, is perhaps the most famous example of a contemporary writer who stresses the significance of the subtext. In *The Homecoming* (Peter Hall, 1973), a scene of extraordinary eroticism is conveyed through dialogue involving the request for a glass of water! Pinter claims that language is often a kind of "cross-talk," a way of concealing fears and anxieties. In some respects, this technique can be even more effective in film, where close-ups can convey the meanings behind words more subtly than an actor on a stage (see **11-7**). (For a further discussion of the concept of a subtext, see Chapter 8, "Acting.")

As an art of juxtaposition, movies can also extend the meanings of language by contrasting spoken words with images. The sentence "I will see him tomorrow" acquires still other meanings when the image shows the speaker smiling, for example, or frowning, or looking determined. All sorts of juxtapositions are possible. The sen-

7-27. *Badlands* (U.S.A., 1973), with Sissy Spacek, written and directed by Terrence Malick.

Not all voice-over narrators are omniscient. This movie is narrated by a bored and dimwitted teenager (Spacek) who talks in *True Romance* clichés and lacks any understanding of what has wrecked her life. *(Warner Bros.)*

tence could be delivered with a determined emphasis, but an image of a frightened face (or eye, or a twitching mouth) can modify the verbal determination or even cancel it out. The juxtaposed image could be a **reaction shot**—thus emphasizing the effect of the statement on the listener. Or the camera could photograph an important object, implying a connection among the speaker, the words, and the object. If the speaker is photographed in long shot, his or her juxtaposition with the environment could also change the meanings of the words. The same line spoken in close-up would emphasize yet different meanings.

Music and sound effects can also modify the meanings of words considerably. The same sentence spoken in an echo chamber will have different connotations from the sentence whispered intimately. If a clap of thunder coincided with the utterance of the sentence, the effect would be different from the chirping of birds or the whining of the wind. Because film is also a mechanical medium, the sentence could be modified by a deliberate distortion in the sound recording. In short, depending on the vocal emphasis, the visual emphasis, and the accompanying soundtrack, this simple sentence could have dozens of different meanings in film, some of them impossible to capture in written form.

Movies contain two types of speech: the monologue and dialogue. Monologues are often associated with documentaries, in which an off-screen commentator provides the audience with information to accompany the visuals (see Chapter 9, "Nonfiction Films"), but they have also been used in fiction films. This technique is especially useful in condensing events and time. Narrative monologues can be used omnisciently to provide an ironic contrast with the visuals. In *Tom Jones*, John Osborne's script features an off-screen narrator who is nearly as witty and urbane as Henry Fielding's, though necessarily less chatty. This narrator sets up the story, provides us with thumbnail sketches of the characters, connects many of the episodes with necessary transitions, and comments philosophically on the escapades of the incorrigible hero (see **5-27**).

Off-screen narration tends to give a movie a sense of objectivity and often an air of predestination. Many of the works of Billy Wilder are structured in flashbacks, with ironic monologues emphasizing fatality: The main interest is not what happened, but how and why. In *Double Indemnity* (1944), for example, the narrator is

7-28. *La Strada* (Italy, 1954), with Richard Basehart and Giulietta Masina, directed by Federico Fellini.

Virtually all Italian movies are dubbed after the footage has been photographed and sometimes even after it has been edited. Fellini selected his players according to their face, body type, or personality. Like many Italian filmmakers, he often used foreign actors, even in major roles. American actor Richard Basehart spoke his lines in English during this film's production. Once shooting was completed, Fellini hired an Italian actor with the same vocal quality to dub in the character's voice. *(Audio-Brandon Films)*

the fatally wounded hero, who admits his guilt at the opening of the film. As Wilder pointed out, "By identifying the criminals right off the bat—and identifying ourselves with them—we can concentrate on what follows: their efforts to escape, the net closing, closing."

The interior monologue is one of the filmmakers' most valuable tools, for with it they can convey what a character is thinking. The interior monologue is frequently used in adaptations of plays and novels. Before Olivier, most film soliloquies were delivered as they are on stage: The camera and microphone record a character literally talking to himself. Olivier's *Hamlet* introduced a more cinematic soliloquy. In the "To be or not to be" speech, several of the lines are not spoken but "thought"—via a voice-over soundtrack. Suddenly, at a crucial line, Olivier spews out the words in exasperation. By using the soundtrack, private ruminations and public speech can be combined in complex ways, with new and often more subtle emphases.

7-29. *Reservoir Dogs* (U.S.A., 1992), with Steve Buscemi and Harvey Keitel, written and directed by Quentin Tarantino.

This stylized gangster film features an almost steady torrent of foul language, as violent as the lives of the characters. In fact, eventually the swearing becomes grotesquely comical, adding to the movie's bizarre tone, which blends violence, cruelty, and pathos with black comedy. In a case like this, sanitized dialogue would be a form of aesthetic dishonesty, totally at odds with the movie's nasty edge of realism. *(Miramax Films)*

Movie dialogue does not have to conform to natural speech. If language is stylized, the director has several options for making it believable. Like Olivier, he or she can emphasize an intimate style of delivery—sometimes even having the actors whisper the lines. Orson Welles's Shakespearean films are characterized by a visual flamboyance: The expressionistic stylization of the images in *Othello* (1951) complements the artificiality of the language. Generally, if dialogue is nonrealistic, the images must be co-expressive: Sharp contrasts of style between language and visuals can produce jarring and often comic incongruities.

Foreign-language movies are shown either in dubbed versions or in their original language, with written subtitles. Both methods of translation have obvious limitations. Dubbed movies often have a hollow, tinny sound, and in most cases, the dubbing is performed by actors who are less gifted than the originals. Sound and image are difficult to match in dubbed films, especially in the closer ranges where the movements of the actors' lips are not synchronized with the sounds. Even bilingual actors who do their own dubbing are less nuanced when they are not speaking their native language. For example, Sophia Loren's performance in the English-language version of Vittorio De Sica's *Two Women* **(8-21)** is very good, but it lacks the vocal expressiveness of the original Italian. In English, Loren's classy pear-shaped tones are at odds with her role as an earthy peasant. Yet dubbing is a fine art in Italian cinema, where the dialogue is almost always post-synchronized and directors often use different actors to voice the characters than those who embody them on screen **(7-28)**.

Most experienced filmgoers prefer subtitles despite their being cumbersome. In the first place, some spectators are sufficiently conversant in foreign languages to understand most of the dialogue (especially in Europe, where virtually all educated people speak a second language). An actor's tone of voice is often more important than the dialogue per se, and subtitled movies allow us to hear these vocal nuances. In short, subtitles permit us to hear what the original artists said, not what some disinterested technician—however clever—decided we would settle for. Nevertheless, the problems involved in translating films have created major problems for the Canadian film industry whose already small domestic market is further divided by language. Popular French-language films may break box-office records in Quebec but rarely make an impact in the rest of Canada, where they are distributed (if they are distributed at all) in poorly dubbed versions.

The advantages of sound, then, make it indispensable to the film artist. As René Clair foresaw many years ago, sound permits a director more visual freedom, not less. Because speech can reveal a person's class, region, occupation, prejudices, and so on, the director doesn't need to waste time establishing these facts visually. A few lines of dialogue can convey all that is necessary, thus freeing the camera to go on to other matters. There are many instances where sound is the most economical and precise way of conveying information in film.

FURTHER READING

Altman, Rick, ed., *Sound Theory/Sound Practice* (London: Routledge, 1992). Essays on the history and theory of film sound.

Gomery, Douglas, *The Coming of Sound* (New York: Routledge, 2005). Historical reconsideration of the transition to sound film in Hollywood.

Inglis, Ian, ed., *Popular Music and Film* (London: Wallflower Press, 2003). Essays on a wide range of films and music.

Kalinak, Kathryn, *Settling the Score: Music and the Classical Hollywood Film* (Madison: University of Wisconsin Press, 1992). Historical, theoretical, and musical analysis.

Marshall, Bill, and Robynn Stilwell, eds., *Musicals: Hollywood and Beyond* (Exeter: Intellect, 2000). New approaches to the Hollywood musical and its influence on other national cinemas.

Mercer, John, and Martin Shingler, *Melodrama: Genre, Style, Sensibility* (London: Wallflower Press, 2004). Introduction to melodrama with critical analysis of key films.

Mundy, John, *Popular Music on Screen: From Hollywood Musical to Music Video* (Manchester: Manchester University Press, 1999). Historical and critical analysis of the relations between music and image in film and television.

Reay, Pauline, *Music in Film: Soundtracks and Synergy* (London: Wallflower Press, 2004). Study of the role of music in a broad range of films.

Smith, Susan, *The Musical: Race, Gender and Performance* (London: Wallflower Press, 2005). Critical analysis of key films with close attention to issues of race and gender.

Weis, Elisabeth, and John Belton, eds., *Film Sound: Theory and Practice* (New York: Columbia University Press, 1985). Anthology of major essays on sound by historians, critics, and filmmakers.

Taxi Driver (Columbia Pictures)

ACTING

8

In the cinema the actor must think and let his thoughts work upon his face. The objective nature of the medium will do the rest. A theatrical performance requires magnification, a cinema performance requires an inner life.

—CHARLES DULLIN

OVERVIEW

Acting classifications. The physical requirements of acting: face, voice, body. Shooting out of sequence. Film acting as a directorial language system. Acting in realist and formalist movies. The origins of the star system. Star personas: on-screen/off-screen. The mythology of stardom. The contract system and the Golden Age of the Hollywood studios. Stars as icons and commodities. Personality stars versus actor stars. Styles of acting: realism and expressionism. Silent-film acting. British acting traditions. The American Method school of acting: texts and subtexts. Improvisation. National styles. Canadian actors. Casting as characterization. Typecasting, casting against type. How casting determines thematic and iconographic meaning. Costumes and characterization. Costume and makeup as enhancements of the actor's body and face.

Film acting is a complex and variable art, and its players can be broken down into four categories:

1. *Extras*. These actors are used primarily to provide a sense of a crowd—as in "a cast of thousands." Players of this type are used as camera material, like a landscape or a set.
2. *Nonprofessional performers*. These are amateur players who are chosen not because of their acting ability, which can be negligible, but because of their authentic appearance or because their situation in life corresponds to that of the character.
3. *Trained professionals*. These performers are capable of playing a variety of roles in a variety of styles. The majority of actors fall into this category.
4. *Stars*. These are famous performers who are widely recognized by the public. Their drawing power is one of the main attractions of popular cinema. The **star system** was developed and has been dominated by the Hollywood studios, though it is hardly unique to movies. Virtually all the performing arts—opera, dance, live theatre, television, concert music—have exploited the box-office popularity of a charismatic performer.

SCREEN ACTING

The stage actor is physically present in the same space as the audience, whereas the film actor is absent, represented only by patterns of light, shade, and colours on the screen. Yet, while the stage actor may be a more substantial figure, his or her performance is ephemeral, changing from night to night and vanishing once the production ends its run (unless a particular performance has been recorded on film or video). The film actor may only appear on screen in an ephemeral form, but his or her performance is fixed forever. These differences have a major effect on both the actor's approach and the audience's response to the actor. On the one hand, the physical absence of the actor makes it easier for the spectator to project him- or herself onto the image on the screen; on the other hand, the properties of the film medium—the larger-than-life image, the darkened auditorium, the various aspects of film language discussed in the previous chapters—ensure that the bodies of the actors generate an intense (if illusory) impression of physical presence, of embodiment.

8-1. *Narcissus* (Canada, 1983), with Jean-Louis Morin and Sylvie Kinal, directed by Norman McLaren.

The beauty of the human form provides one of the main pleasures of cinema. Dance also celebrates this beauty: Choreography makes the most of the sensuous appeal of bodies in motion while creating an aesthetic framework that allows us to enjoy this appeal without feeling like voyeurs. McLaren's dance films are among the most sensuous cinematic treatments of physical beauty. In this film, the dancers perform against a black background, and McLaren uses techniques such as slow-motion, dissolves, and optical printing to tell the story of Narcissus (Morin) who rejects both female and male lovers and falls in love with his own reflected image. *(National Film Board of Canada)*

8.2. *Die Another Day* (Britain / U.S.A., 2001), with Halle Berry, directed by Lee Tamahori.

Almost since the inception of motion pictures, one of the main pleasures of moviegoing has been gazing at beautiful people and admiring their exquisitely toned bodies—not unlike how the ancient Greeks and Romans enjoyed looking at statues of goddesses or magnificent athletes. *(MGM)*

8-3. *The Gold Rush* (U.S.A., 1925), with Charles Chaplin and Mack Swain, directed by Chaplin.
Film actors must be especially conscious of body language and what it reveals about character. Silent actors were deprived of their voices, so they externalized their feelings and thoughts through gesture, movement, facial expression, and body language—all of which had to be heightened to compensate for their lack of speech. In this shot, for example, Big Jim McKay is puzzled by the scary rumbling and quaking of the cabin during a violent blizzard. The hung-over Charlie explains—through pantomime—that his queasy stomach is the culprit. *(RBC Films)*

The voyeuristic pleasure of looking at other people's bodies was fully exploited in the peep-shows that preceded the invention of motion picture projection, and many early movies offered risqué shots of semi-clad actors. As movies became more sophisticated, other pleasures emerged, but the spectacle of the actor's body remained an underlying factor in the appeal of the new mass medium (as censors were very much aware). Body shape and body language thus became vital components of film acting: The actor literally embodies the character.

Film acting was refined during the silent era through the expressive use of the close-up and the development of the principles of continuity editing (see Chapter 6, "Editing"). The actor now enjoyed an intimate relation to the spectator that was impossible in the theatre, and the face became a tool for engaging attention and expressing emotion. Through such devices as eyeline matches and **shot/reverse-shot** structures, the spectator was no longer simply looking at actors but also caught up in their acts of looking. The coming of sound introduced verbal language as one of the

8-4. *The Hours* (U.S.A., 2002), with Meryl Streep, directed by Stephen Daldry.

The cinematic close-up allows the film actor to concentrate totally on the truth of the moment—without the need to worry about projecting to the back row. Gestures and facial expressions can be exquisitely nuanced. The Hungarian theorist Béla Balázs believed that the movie close-up can isolate the human face from its surroundings and penetrate the soul: "What appears on the face and in facial expression is a spiritual experience," Balázs observed. *(Miramax Films)*

film actor's resources, reducing the reliance on body language but also enabling it to be used more subtly. Speech, of course, allowed filmmakers to use dialogue, much as in the theatre, to convey necessary information. For a while, the effect was to diminish visual invention as well as the possibilities of film acting. In the long run, however, the introduction of sound ensured that the actor's voice was as important as his or her body and face in attracting audiences: A distinctive and pleasing voice became a major, if intangible, aspect of star appeal. Conversely, the lack of a voice considered appropriate to the actor's appearance led to the decline of several stars of silent cinema (see Chapter 7, "Sound").

Because the shooting schedule of a movie is usually determined by economic considerations, the order of the shooting script is not always artistically logical. An actor may be required to perform the climactic scene first and low-keyed exposition shots later. The screen actor, then, does not "build" emotionally like the stage actor but must be capable of an intense degree of concentration, turning emotion on and off for very short periods. Because the shot is the basic building unit in film, the actor does not have to sustain a performance for very long—even in realistic movies in which the takes can run to two or three minutes. In a highly fragmented film—in which shots can last for less than a second—one can scarcely refer to the performer's contribution as acting at all: He or she simply *is*.

8-5. *Secrets & Lies* (Britain, 1996), with Brenda Blethyn (extreme right), written and directed by Mike Leigh.

Mike Leigh prefers to work with many of the same actors from film to film, much like a cinematic repertory company. They rehearse extensively, improvising much of their dialogue and reshaping the script with their insights and discoveries. The result of this artistic collaboration is a performance style of extraordinary intimacy, spontaneity, and humanity. In *Secrets & Lies*, a single mother (Blethyn) always manages to find the worst possible moment to embarrass or shock her family, as when she introduces them to her newly discovered daughter, who is black, at her other daughter's birthday party. Weepy, self-pitying, grotesquely funny, and desperately needy, she manages to repel us even while enlisting our compassion. With Leigh's actors, you do not notice the technique: just the raw emotions. *(October Films)*

In addition, a film actor is expected to play even the most intimate scenes with dozens of technicians on the set, working or observing. Because the camera distorts, actors are required to perform some scenes unnaturally. In an embrace, for example, lovers cannot really look each other in the eyes or they will appear cross-eyed on the screen. In **point-of-view shots**, actors must direct their lines at the camera rather than at another player. Much of the time, the performer has no idea where a shot might appear in the finished film, if indeed it appears at all, for many an actor's performance has been left on the cutting-room floor. In short, the discontinuity of time and space in cinema places the performer almost totally in the hands of the director.

Acting in cinema is thus almost totally dependent on the director's approach to the story materials. Generally, realist directors tend to place more emphasis on the actor's performance, attempting to minimize the effects of the fragmented conditions in which it is created by shooting chronologically as much as possible and using **long shots** and **long takes** to reduce the impression of directorial interference. Formalist

8-6. ***The New World*** **(U.S.A., 2005), with Colin Farrell and Q'orianka Kilcher, written and directed by Terrence Malick.**

Realism in movies is often more convincing precisely because of the player's lack of technical skill. This movie is based on the Pocahontas/Captain John Smith legend and the founding of the Jamestown colony in Virginia in 1607. Malick used the 14-year-old nonprofessional Kilcher to play the idealistic Pocahontas precisely because of her artless sincerity. She is totally devoid of theatrical mannerisms, and hence totally believable as an innocent in a garden of Eden—before the arrival of the white man and his European contaminations, both physical and spiritual. *(New Line Cinema)*

directors tend to rely more on the expressive use of editing and mise-en-scène rather than on the actors' skills.

Although many realist directors value the ability of professional actors to create complex characters, others stress the importance of ensemble acting, in which the individual performance is important only as it contributes to the effect of the interactions among the entire cast (see **8-5**). Still others do not use actors at all and prefer to work with nonprofessionals, who may lack the technique of professionals but have had personal experience of the situations depicted in the film or whose lack of professional experience lends their performance a naturalness appropriate to the role **(8-6)**.

Formalist directors may also use nonprofessional actors, as did the Soviet montage directors in many of their films. Even when they use professionals, they tend to value their visual appearance rather than their acting abilities. According to Alfred Hitchcock, "the best screen actor is the man who can do nothing extremely well." In his typically provocative manner, he was underscoring the familiar observation that actors are no more significant or expressive in cinema than the objects that surround them. The so-called Kuleshov experiment demonstrated that it was possible to convey emotions by editing together shots of various objects with the same close-up of an actor, who thus, in effect, does not act these emotions at all (see Chapter 6, "Editing").

8-7. Sequence from *Sabotage* (Britain, 1936), with Sylvia Sidney and Oscar Homolka, directed by Alfred Hitchcock.

Through the art of editing, a director can construct a highly emotional "performance" by juxtaposing shots of actors with shots of objects. In scenes such as these, the actor's contribution tends to be minimal: The effect is achieved through the linking of two or more shots. This associational process is the basis of Pudovkin's theory of constructive editing. *(Gaumont-British)*

d e f

j k l

p q r

v w x

Michelangelo Antonioni once stated that he uses his actors only as part of the composition—"like a tree, a wall, or a cloud." Many of the major themes of his films are conveyed through long shots where the juxtaposition of people and their settings suggests complex psychological and spiritual states. Perhaps more than any other director, Antonioni was sensitive to how meanings change, depending on the mise en scène. Similarly, the French director Robert Bresson believed that a film actor is not an interpretive artist but merely one of the "raw materials" of the mise en scène and the editing. He generally preferred to use nonprofessional actors in his movies because trained actors tend to want to convey emotions and ideas through performance, as in the live theatre. For Bresson, films should be made cinematically rather than theatrically, by "bypassing the will of those who appear in them, using not what they do, but what they are."

Some of Hitchcock's most stunning cinematic effects were achieved by minimizing the contributions of actors. During the production of *Sabotage*, Sylvia Sidney burst into tears on the set because she was not permitted to act in a crucial scene. The episode involved a murder in which the sympathetic heroine kills her brutish husband after learning that he has caused the death of her young brother. On stage, of course, the heroine's feelings and thoughts would be communicated by the actress's exaggerated facial expressions. But in real life, Hitchcock observed, people's faces don't necessarily reveal what they think or feel. The director preferred to convey these ideas and emotions through edited juxtapositions **(8-7)**.

The setting for the scene is a dinner table. The heroine looks at her husband, who is eating. Then a close-up shows a dish containing meat and vegetables with a knife and fork lying next to it; the wife's hands are seen behind the dish. Hitchcock then cuts to a medium shot of the wife thoughtfully slicing some meat. Next, a medium shot of the brother's empty chair. Close-up of the wife's hands with knife and fork. Close-up of a birdcage with canaries—a reminder to the heroine of her dead brother. Close-up of the wife's thoughtful face. Close-up of the knife and plate. Suddenly a close-up of the husband's suspicious face: He notices the connection between the knife and her thoughtful expression, for there is a camera **pan**, rather than a cut, back to the knife. He gets up next to her. Hitchcock quickly cuts to a close-up of her hand reaching for the knife. Cut to an extreme close-up of the knife entering his body. Cut to a two shot of their faces, his convulsed with pain, hers with fear. When Sylvia Sidney saw the finished product, she was delighted with the results. The entire scene, of course, required very little acting in the conventional sense of the term.

THE STAR SYSTEM

The star system has been the backbone of the American film industry, and many other national cinemas, since the second decade of the twentieth century. Stars are the creation of the public, its reigning favourites. Their influence in the fields of fashion, values, and public behaviour has been enormous. "The social history of a nation can be written in terms of its film stars," British critic Raymond Durgnat has observed. Alexander Walker, among others, has pointed out that Hollywood stars are the direct or indirect reflection of the needs, drives, and anxieties of American society, but they have achieved an international appeal: They are the food of dreams, allowing us to live out our deepest fantasies and obsessions. Like the ancient gods and goddesses, stars have been adored, envied, and venerated as mythic **icons**.

Before 1910, actors' names were almost never included in movie credits because producers feared the players would then demand higher salaries. But the public named their favourites anyway. Canadian-born Mary Pickford, for example, was first known by her character's name, "Little Mary." From the beginning, the public often fused a star's artistic **persona** with his or her private personality. In Pickford's case, as with many others, the two were radically dissimilar. She specialized in playing waggish juveniles—the bouncy, high-spirited, and sentimental young heroines of such popular hits as *Rebecca of Sunnybrook Farm* (1917) and *Pollyanna* (1920), in which her blonde curls were her trademark. In actuality, Pickford was clever and sophisticated and the most powerful woman in the American film industry of the silent era. "My career was planned," she insisted, "there was never anything accidental about it." By the time she was five, she was performing in live theatre. She began working with D.W. Griffith in 1909 and made seventy-five short films with him at Biograph before leaving the studio in 1912. Soon she was earning $40 000 per picture. By 1914 she was pulling in $150 000. She was neck and neck with Chaplin in the star salaries sweepstakes, and she collected from $300 000 to $500 000 per film between 1917 and 1919. In 1919 she helped form United Artists with Chaplin, Griffith, and Douglas Fairbanks (her husband) as partners. As an **independent producer**, she grossed as much as $1.2 million per film. Reputedly, she was the business brain behind United Artists. She also directed many of her own films, although never with official credit.

Unless the public is receptive to a given screen personality, audiences can be remarkably resistant to anyone else's notion of a star. For example, producer Samuel Goldwyn ballyhooed his Russian import, Anna Sten, without stinting on costs. But audiences stayed away from her movies in droves. "God makes the stars," the chastened Goldwyn finally concluded. "It's up to the producers to find them."

Throughout the silent era, stars grew giddy with their wealth and power. Intoxicated by the opulence of Hollywood's royalty, the public was eager to learn more about its favourites. Fan (short for fanatic) magazines sprang up by the dozens, and the burgeoning studios churned out a steady stream of publicity to feed this insatiable curiosity. Paramount's rival queens Gloria Swanson and Pola Negri vied with each other in the extravagance of their lifestyles. Both of them married many times, and each managed to snare at least one petty nobleman among her stable of rapt admirers. "I have gone through a long apprenticeship," Swanson said. "I have gone through enough of being nobody. I have decided that when I am a star I will be every inch and every moment the star. Everyone from the studio gateman to the highest executive will know it" **(8-8)**. The mythology of stardom often incorporated this rags-to-riches motif. The humble origins of many stars encouraged the public to believe that anyone—even ordinary people—could be "discovered" and make it to Hollywood, where all their dreams would come true.

The so-called golden age of the star system—roughly the 1930s and 1940s—coincided with the supremacy of the Hollywood studio system. Most of the stars during this period were under exclusive contract to the five major production companies: MGM, Warner Brothers, Paramount, Twentieth Century Fox, and RKO—known in the trade as the Big Five, or the **majors**. Throughout this period, the majors produced approximately 90 percent of the fiction films in America. They also ruled the international market: Between the two world wars, American movies dominated 80 percent of the world's screens and were more popular with foreign audiences than all but a few natively produced movies.

After the talkie revolution, the majors turned to live theatre for new stars. Such important newcomers as James Cagney, Bette Davis, Edward G. Robinson, Cary Grant, Mae West, and Katharine Hepburn became popular in part because of their distinctive manner of speaking—the "personality voices," as they were known in the trade. In their first years under studio contract, they were given maximum exposure. For example, Clark Gable appeared in fourteen movies in 1930, his first year at MGM. Each of his roles represented a different type, and the studio kept varying them until one clicked with the public. After a particularly popular performance, a star was usually locked into the same type of role—often under protest. Because the demand for stars was the most predictable economic variable in the business of

8-8. *Sunset Boulevard* (U.S.A., 1950), with Gloria Swanson, directed by Billy Wilder.

One of the great stars of the silent era, Swanson, retired from the movies in 1934. In this dark comedy based on the legends associated with her own star persona, she plays the role of Norma Desmond, who was once a silent film star but now lives on her memories: When she screens one of her films, we see Swanson at the height of her fame in *Queen Kelly* (Erich von Stroheim, 1928). The aging actress shoots her young lover when he abandons her and then cracks under the strain. She now believes that the newsreel cameramen covering her arrest are a film crew photographing her triumphant return and she indignantly rejects the term "comeback." *(Paramount Pictures)*

filmmaking, the studios used their stars as a guarantee of box-office success. In short, stars provided some measure of stability in a traditionally volatile industry. To this day, stars are referred to as "bankable" commodities—that is, insurance for large profits to investors.

The majors viewed their stars as valuable investments, and the build-up techniques developed by the studios involved much time, money, and energy. Promising neophytes served an apprenticeship as "starlets," a term reserved for females, although male newcomers were subjected to the same treatment. They were often assigned a new name, were taught how to talk, walk, and wear costumes. Frequently, their social schedules were arranged by the studio's publicity department to ensure maximum press exposure. Suitable "romances" were concocted to fuel the columns of the four hundred or more reporters and columnists who covered the

8-9. ***Erin Brockovich*** **(U.S.A., 2000), with Julia Roberts, directed by Steven Soderbergh.**

"Show me an actor with no personality, and I'll show you someone who isn't a star," Katharine Hepburn once observed. In contemporary cinema, Julia Roberts radiates personality. She is the only female star who consistently places among the top ten box office attractions in America. Beloved by the public for her spectacular good looks and captivating smile, she is an accomplished performer in straight dramatic roles. But she really shines in comedies, where her acting style is so spontaneous it hardly looks like she is working. *(Universal Studios)*

Hollywood beat during the studio era. A few zealous souls even agreed to marry studio-selected spouses in the hopes that such alliances would further their careers.

Though the studios often exploited stars, there were compensations. As a player's box-office power increased, so did his or her demands. Top stars had their names above the title of the film, and they often had script approval stipulated in their contracts. Some of them also insisted on director, producer, and co-star approval. Glamorous stars boasted their own camera operators who knew how to conceal physical defects and enhance their virtues. Many of them demanded their own clothes designers, hair stylists, and lavish dressing rooms. The biggest stars had movies especially tailored for them, thus guaranteeing maximum camera exposure.

And, of course, they were paid enormous sums of money. In 1939, for example, more than fifty stars earned more than $100 000. But the studios got much more. Mae West rescued Paramount from bankruptcy in the early 1930s. Later in the decade, Shirley Temple made more than $20 million for Twentieth Century Fox. Furthermore, although there were a few important exceptions, movies without stars generally failed at the box office. Serious stars used money and power to further their art, not just to gratify their vanity. Bette Davis was considered "difficult" during her stormy tenure at Warners, because she insisted on better scripts, more varied roles, more sensitive directors, and stronger co-stars (see **7-19**).

8-10. Publicity photo of Marilyn Monroe in *The Seven Year Itch* (U.S.A., 1955), directed by Billy Wilder. Marilyn Monroe has become a symbol of the personal tragedy that can befall a star. She was born (out of wedlock) to an emotionally unstable mother who spent most of her life in mental asylums. As a child, Norma Jean Baker was raised in a series of orphanages and foster homes. Even then—especially then—she dreamed of becoming a famous Hollywood star. She was raped at the age of eight, married to her first husband at sixteen. She used sex (like many before her) as a means to an end—stardom. In the late 1940s she had a few bit roles, mostly as sexy dumb blondes. Not until John Huston's *The Asphalt Jungle* (1950) did she create much of a stir. In that same year, Joseph Mankiewicz cast her in *All About Eve*, as "a graduate of the Copacabana School of Dramatic Art," as George Sanders dryly deadpans in the film. (Sanders claimed he knew Marilyn would one day become a star "because she desperately needed to be one.") After Twentieth Century Fox signed her to a contract, the studio was unsure what to do with her. She appeared in a series of third-rate studio projects, but despite their mediocrity, the public clamoured for more Marilyn. She rightly blamed Fox for mismanaging her career: "Only the public can make a star. It's the studios who try to make a system of it," she bitterly complained. At the peak of her popularity, she left Hollywood in disgust, to study at the Actors Studio. When she returned, she demanded more money and better roles—and got both. Joshua Logan, who directed her in *Bus Stop* (1956), said she was "as near genius as any actress I ever knew." Supremely photogenic, she gave herself entirely to the camera, allowing it to probe her deepest vulnerabilities. Laurence Olivier, her costar and director in *The Prince and the Showgirl* (1957), marvelled at her cunning way of fusing guilelessness with carnality—the mind and soul of a little girl wrapped in the body of a prostitute. Throughout her years as a top star, her private life was a shambles. "She was an unfortunate, doped-up woman most of the time," biographer Maurice Zolotow observed. Her failed marriages and love affairs were constantly in the headlines, and increasingly she turned to drugs and alcohol for solace. She was notorious for her irresponsibility, often not bothering to show up on set for days at a time, thus incurring enormous cost overruns. Because of her addiction to drugs and alcohol, even when she did show up she scarcely knew who—much less where—she was. She was found dead in 1962, from an overdose of barbiturates and alcohol. *(Twentieth Century Fox)*

8-11. *Rocky* (U.S.A., 1976), with Sylvester Stallone, directed by John Avildsen.

Personality stars frequently convey a ready-made ideology—a set of values that are associated with a given star because of his or her previous film roles. Stallone achieved instant stardom in this film about a poor boxer who rises to fame when he defeats the champion who views him as an easy opponent. The fight is held on July 4, and the plot embodies the American Dream, as did the off-screen story of Stallone, who wrote the screenplay and thereby escaped a life of poverty. There were four sequels, and the patriotic implications of his star persona were reinforced when he starred as a Vietnam veteran John Rambo, heroically rescuing prisoners of war, in *First Blood* (Ted Kotcheff, 1982) and its sequels. *(United Artists)*

Top stars attracted the loyalty of both men and women, although as sociologist Leo Handel pointed out, 65 percent of the fans preferred stars of their own gender. The studios received up to 32 million fan letters per year, 85 percent of them from young females. Major stars received about three thousand letters per week, and the volume of their mail was regarded as an accurate barometer of their popularity. The studios spent as much as $2 million a year processing these letters, most of which asked for autographed photos. Box-office appeal was also gauged by the number of fan clubs devoted to a star. The stars with the greatest number of clubs were Gable, Jean Harlow, and Joan Crawford—all of them under contract to MGM, "The Home of the Stars." Gable alone had seventy clubs, which partly accounted for his supremacy as the top male star of the 1930s.

The mythology of stardom usually emphasizes the glamour of movie stars, lifting them above the mundane concerns of ordinary mortals. Critic Parker Tyler observed that stars fulfill an ancient need, almost religious in nature: "Somehow their wealth, fame, and beauty, their apparently unlimited field of worldly pleasure—these conditions tinge them with the supernatural, render them immune to the bitterness of ordinary frustrations." Of course, this mythology also involves the tragic victims of stardom, like Marilyn Monroe and James Dean. The fact that many stars have died young—at the height of their physical beauty—only enhances their romantic image of immutable perfection **(8-10)**.

The realities behind the myths are considerably less romantic. For every actor who manages to scale the peaks of stardom, there are hundreds of thousands who fail, their hard work wasted, their sacrifices scoffed at, their dreams shattered. Stars must pay a high price for their wealth and fame. They must get used to being treated like commodities with a price tag. Even at the beginning of the star system, they were reduced to simplified types, virgins, vamps, swashbucklers, flappers, and so on. Over the years, a vast repertory of types evolved: the Latin lover, the he-man, the heiress, the good-bad girl, the cynical reporter, the career girl, and many others. Of course, all great stars are unique, even though they might fall under a well-known category. For example, the cheap blonde has long been one of America's favourite types, but such important stars as Mae West, Jean Harlow, and Marilyn Monroe were highly distinctive as individuals. A successful type was always imitated. In the mid-1920s, for example, the Swedish import Greta Garbo created a sophisticated and complex type, the femme fatale. Garbo inspired many imitations, including such important stars as Marlene Dietrich and Carole Lombard, who were first touted as "Garbo types," only with a sense of humour. In the 1950s, Sidney Poitier became the first black star to attract a wide following outside of his own race. In later years, several other black performers attained stardom, in part because Poitier had established the precedent.

At about the turn of the twentieth century, George Bernard Shaw wrote a famous essay comparing the two foremost stage stars of the day—Eleonora Duse and Sarah Bernhardt. Shaw's comparison is a useful springboard to a discussion of the different kinds of film stars. Bernhardt, Shaw wrote, was a bravura personality, and she managed to tailor each different role to fit this personality. This is what her fans both expected and desired. Her personal charm was larger than life, yet undeniably captivating. Her performances were filled with brilliant effects that had come to be associated with her personality over the years. Duse, on the other hand, possessed a quieter talent, less dazzling in its initial impact. She was totally different with each role, and her own personality never seemed to intrude on the character as conceived by the playwright. Hers was an invisible art: Her impersonations were so totally believable that the viewer was likely to forget they were impersonations. In effect, Shaw was pointing out the major distinctions between a personality star and an actor star.

Personality stars commonly refuse all parts that go against their type, especially if they are leading men or leading ladies. Performers like Tom Hanks would never play cruel or psychopathic roles, for example, because such parts would conflict with their sympathetic image. If a star is locked into his or her type, any significant departure can result in box-office disaster. For example, when Pickford tried to abandon her little-girl roles in the 1920s, her public stayed at home: They wanted to see Little Mary or nothing. She retired in disgust at the age of forty, just when most players are at the peak of their powers.

However, many stars prefer to remain in the same mould, playing variations on the same character type. John Wayne was the most popular star in film history. From 1949 to 1976 he was absent from the top ten only three times. "I play John Wayne in every part regardless of the character, and I've been doing okay, haven't I?" he once asked. In the public mind, he was the archetypal westerner, a man of action—and violence—rather than words. His persona is steeped in a distrust of sophistication and intellectuality. His name is virtually synonymous with masculinity—though his persona suggests more of the warrior than the lover. As he grew older, he also grew more human, developing his considerable talents as a comedian by mocking his own macho image. Wayne was fully aware of the enormous influence a star can wield in transmitting values, and in many of his films, he embodied a right-wing ideology that made him a hero to conservative Americans **(2-17)**.

As film theorist Richard Dyer has pointed out, stars are signifying entities. Any sensitive analysis of a film with a star in its cast must take into account that star's iconographical significance. Stars like Wayne, Arnold Schwarzenegger, and Susan Sarandon embody complex political associations simply by demonstrating the lifestyle of their politics and displaying those political beliefs as an aspect of their personas on and off screen.

8-12a. *Jerry Maguire* (U.S.A., 1996), with Tom Cruise and Cuba Gooding, Jr., directed by Cameron Crowe.

Most of the great stars become their own genres. That is, their films are tailored to highlight those qualities that made them stars in the first place. These traits are recycled and repackaged to give the public what it wants, and thereby make lots of money. Most of Tom Cruise's movies follow a similar generic pattern: He begins as a brash, confident youth, a bit cocky and full of himself. A great-looking guy, of course. But he is not as smart as he thinks he is, and is humbled by a conspicuous error in judgment. With the help of a supportive young woman who loves him, however, he sees the error of his ways and goes on to even greater success—only now without the swagger.
(TriStar Pictures)

8-12b. *Magnolia* (U.S.A., 1999), with Tom Cruise, directed by Paul Thomas Anderson.

In addition to being a savvy career manager, Cruise is also an ambitious artist, eager to test his limits, unafraid of taking calculated risks by playing against type. He has expanded his range considerably in such offbeat parts as those in *The Color of Money* (Martin Scorsese, 1986), *Born on the Fourth of July* (Oliver Stone, 1989), and *Interview with the Vampire* (Neil Jordan, 1994). In *Magnolia* he plays a strutting, woman-hating "self-empowerment" guru, so puffed up with his own irresistibility that when his pomposity is punctured, he collapses like a spent balloon. It is arguably his most brilliant performance—brazen, funny, and, finally, poignantly vulnerable.
(New Line Cinema)

8-13a. ***Charlie and the Chocolate Factory*** **(U.S.A., 2005), with Johnny Depp, directed by Tim Burton.**

Johnny Depp and Tim Burton have worked together on several films, including *Edward Scissorhands* (see **Colour Plate 11**), *Ed Wood* (1994), *Sleepy Hollow* (1999), and *Corpse Bride* (see **5-24c**). "Johnny is a great character actor," Burton has observed, "a character actor in the form of a leading man. He's not necessarily interested in his image but more in becoming a character and trying different things. He's willing to take risks. Each time I work with him he's something different." He is also one of the most admired actors of his generation. *(Warner Bros.)*

8-13b. ***Shakespeare in Love*** **(Britain, 1998), with Colin Firth and Judi Dench, directed by John Madden.**

Dame Judi Dench won a Best Supporting Actress Oscar for her performance as Queen Elizabeth I, even though she is on camera for only about seven minutes. But in those few minutes, she absolutely commands. Shrewd, sardonic, bawdy, and nobody's fool, this is one very tough dame. From Dench's performance, it is easy to believe that old Queen Bess was the greatest monarch in British history. *(Miramax Films)*

8-14. *Vertigo* (U.S.A., 1958), with James Stewart and Kim Novak, directed by Alfred Hitchcock.

Perhaps Hitchcock's greatest genius was how he managed to outwit the system while still succeeding brilliantly at the box office. For example, Hitchcock knew that a star in the leading role virtually guaranteed the commercial success of his pictures. But he liked to push his stars to the dark side—to explore neurotic, even psychotic undercurrents that often subverted the star's established iconography. Everyone loved Jimmy Stewart as the stammering, decent, all-American idealist, best typified by *It's a Wonderful Life* **(6-9)**. In *Vertigo*, Stewart's character is obsessed with a romantic idealization of a mysterious woman (Novak). He has convinced himself that he is desperately in love—ironically, with a woman who does not exist. Within the generic format of a detective thriller, Hitchcock is able to explore the obsessions, self- delusions, and desperate need that many people call love. *(Universal Pictures)*

The top box-office attractions tend to be personality stars. They stay on top by being themselves, by not trying to impersonate anyone. Gable insisted that all he did in front of the camera was "act natural." Similarly, Marilyn Monroe was always at her best when she played roles that exploited her indecisiveness, her vulnerability, and her pathetic eagerness to please.

Conversely, many stars have refused to be typecast and have attempted the widest array of roles possible. Such actor stars as Davis, Hepburn, Marlon Brando, and Robert De Niro have sometimes undertaken unpleasant character roles rather than conventional leads to expand their range, for variety and breadth have traditionally been the yardsticks by which great acting is measured.

Many stars fall somewhere between the two extremes, veering toward personality in some films, toward impersonation in others. Such gifted performers as James Stewart, Cary Grant, and Audrey Hepburn played wider variations of certain types of roles. Nonetheless, we could hardly imagine a star like Hepburn playing a woman of weak character or a coarse or stupid woman, so firmly entrenched was her image as an elegant and rather aristocratic female. Similarly, most people know what is meant by "the Clint Eastwood type."

The distinction between a professional actor and a star is not based on technical skill, but on mass popularity. By definition, a star must have enormous personal magnetism, a riveting quality that commands our attention. Few public personalities have inspired such deep and widespread affection as the great movie stars. Some are loved because they embody such traditional American values as plain speaking, integrity, and idealism: Gary Cooper and Tom Hanks are examples of this type. Others are identified with anti-establishment images and include such celebrated loners as Bogart, Eastwood, and Jack Nicholson. Players such as Cary Grant and Carole Lombard are so captivating in their charm that they are fun to watch in almost anything. And, of course, many of them are spectacularly good-looking: Names like Michelle Pfeiffer and Tom Cruise are virtually synonymous with godlike beauty.

Sophisticated filmmakers exploit the public's affection for its stars by creating ambiguous tensions among a role as written, as acted, and as directed. "Whenever the hero isn't portrayed by a star, the whole picture suffers," Hitchcock observed. "Audiences are far less concerned about the predicament of a character who's played by someone they don't know." When a star rather than a conventional actor plays a role, much of the characterization is automatically fixed by the casting, but what the director and star then choose to add to the written role is what constitutes its full dramatic meaning. Some directors have capitalized on the star system with great artistic effectiveness, particularly studio-era filmmakers **(8-14)**.

Perhaps the ultimate glory for a star is to become an icon in American popular mythology. Some stars are so universally known that one name alone is enough to evoke an entire complex of symbolic associations—"Marilyn" or "Elvis" for example. Unlike the character actor (however gifted), the star automatically suggests ideas and emotions that are deeply embedded in his or her persona. These undertones are determined not only by the star's previous roles, but often by his or her actual personality as well. Naturally, over many years, this symbolic information can begin to drain from public consciousness, but the iconography of a great star like Gary Cooper becomes part of a shared experience. As the French critic Edgar Morin has pointed out, when Cooper played a character, he automatically "gary-cooperized" it, infusing himself into the role and the role into himself. Because audiences felt a deep sense of identification with Coop and the values he symbolized, in a sense they were celebrating themselves—or at least their spiritual selves. The great originals are cultural archetypes, and their box-office popularity is an index of their success in synthesizing the aspirations of an era. As several cultural studies have shown, the persona of a star can bring together communal myths and symbols of considerable complexity and emotional richness.

STYLES OF ACTING

Acting styles differ radically, depending on period, genre, tone, national origins, and directorial emphasis. Such considerations are the principal means by which acting styles are classified. Even within a given category, however, generalizations are, at best, a loose set of expectations, not carved in stone. For example, the realist-formalist dialectic that has been used as a classification aid throughout this book can also be applied to the art of acting, but there are many variations and subdivisions. These terms are also subject to different interpretations from one period to the next. Lillian Gish was regarded as a great realistic actress in the silent era, but by today's standards, her performances look rather ethereal. In a parallel vein, the playing style of Klaus Kinski in such movies as *Aguirre, the Wrath of God* is stylized, but compared to an extreme form of expressionistic acting, such as that of Conrad Veidt in *The Cabinet of Dr. Caligari*, Kinski is relatively realistic **(4-17, 8-15)**.

During the relatively brief history of silent cinema, from the invention of movies in 1895 until the changeover to sound in the late 1920s, a wide variety of playing styles evolved, ranging from the detailed, underplayed realism of Gibson Gowland in *Greed* (see **4-15**), to the grand, ponderous style of such tragedians as Emil Jannings in *The Last Command* (Joseph von Sternberg, 1928). The great silent clowns like Chaplin, Buster Keaton, Harold Lloyd, Harry Langdon, and Stan Laurel and Oliver Hardy also developed highly personal styles that bear only a superficial resemblance to each other.

A popular misconception about the silent cinema is that all movies were photographed and projected at "silent speed"—sixteen frames per second (fps). In fact,

8-15. *Aguirre, the Wrath of God* (Germany, 1972), with Klaus Kinski, directed by Werner Herzog.

Expressionistic acting is generally associated with the German cinema—a cinema of directors, rarely actors. Stripped of individualizing details, this style of acting stresses a symbolic concept rather than a believable three-dimensional character. It is presentational rather than representational, a style of extremes rather than norms. Psychological complexity is replaced by a stylized thematic essence. For example, Kinski's portrayal of a Spanish conquistador is conceived in terms of a treacherous serpent. His Dantean features a frozen mask of ferocity, Aguirre can suddenly twist and coil like a cobra poised for a strike. *(New Yorker Films)*

8-16. *Grand Hotel* (U.S.A., 1932), with Greta Garbo, directed by Edmund Goulding.

MGM, "the Tiffany of studios," prided itself on its opulent and glossy production values. Garbo's languorous movements and luminous face fitted perfectly into the dreamy glamour of the studio settings, creating a mystique of aloofness and inscrutability. It was in this film that she uttered the line, "I want to be alone," and her character's words came to epitomize the star's persona: her refusal to reveal her private life and her decision to retire before age could undermine her romantic image. *(MGM)*

silent speed was highly variable, subject to easy manipulation because cameras were hand cranked. Even within a single film, not every scene was necessarily photographed at the same speed. Generally, comic scenes were undercranked to emphasize speed, whereas dramatic scenes were overcranked to slow down the action, usually twenty or twenty-two fps. Projected at sound speed (twenty-four fps)—or indeed at the so-called silent speed—the original rhythms of the performances are violated. This is why players in silent dramas can appear jerky and slightly ludicrous at twenty-four fps. In comedies, this distortion can enhance the humour, which is why the performances of the silent clowns have retained much of their original charm. Many silent films are now available on DVD, restored and projected at the correct speed, often with the original music score, so modern audiences can see these movies as the filmmakers intended, although the actual experience of viewing a silent film can only be reproduced in a large auditorium with live musical accompaniment.

The most popular and critically admired player of the silent cinema was Chaplin. The wide variety of comic skills he developed in his early years of vaudeville made him the most versatile of the clowns. In the area of pantomime, no one approached his inventiveness. Critics waxed eloquent on his balletic grace, and even the brilliant dancer Vaslav Nijinsky proclaimed Chaplin his equal. His ability to blend comedy with pathos was unmatched. George Bernard Shaw described Chaplin as "the only

8-17a. ***Yankee Doodle Dandy* (U.S.A., 1942), with James Cagney, directed by Michael Curtiz.**

Acting styles are determined in part by a player's energy level. High-voltage performers like Cagney usually project out to the audience, commanding our attention with a bravura style. Much of our pleasure in a Cagney performance is watching him "struttin' his stuff." He was a highly kinetic performer, expressing his character's emotions through movement. His dancing is exhilarating—cocky, sexy, and funny. Even in dramatic roles, he is seldom at rest—edgy, punctuating the air with his hand gestures, prancing on the balls of his feet. "Never settle back on your heels," was his credo. "Never relax. If you relax, the audience relaxes." Other high-energy performers include Harold Lloyd, Katharine Hepburn, Bette Davis, Gene Kelly, George C. Scott, Barbra Streisand, James Woods, Joe Pesci, and Richard Dreyfuss. *(Warner Bros.)*

8-17b. ***Belle de Jour* (France / Italy, 1967), with Catherine Deneuve (right), directed by Luis Buñuel.**

Low-key performers like Deneuve are sometimes said to work "small" or "close to the lens." Rather than projecting out to the audience, these performers allow the camera to tune *in* on their behaviour, which is seldom exaggerated for dramatic effect. Eyewitness accounts of Deneuve's acting usually stress how little she seems to be working. The subtleties are apparent only at very close range. Other players in this mode include Harry Langdon, Spencer Tracy, Henry Fonda, Marilyn Monroe, Montgomery Clift, Kevin Costner, Jack Nicholson, and Winona Ryder. Of course dramatic context is all-important in determining an actor's energy level. *(United Artists)*

8-18. ***Hamlet*** **(Britain, 1996), with Kenneth Branagh, directed by Branagh.**

Because of their national literary heritage, British actors are widely considered masters of period styles of acting. Branagh is one of the leading Shakespearian actors of his generation on stage and screen. He challenged comparison with Laurence Olivier by directing and playing the title characters in *Henry V* (1989) and *Hamlet*, as Olivier had done in the 1940s. Yet Branagh is also a great admirer of Hollywood cinema and often casts American actors in his films. Jack Lemmon and Charlton Heston both appear in his extremely long, full-text adaptation of *Hamlet*, whose romantic extravagance and visual spectacle evoke both the "golden age" of Hollywood and the great actor-managers of nineteenth-century British theatre. *(Castle Rock Entertainment/Columbia Pictures)*

genius developed in motion pictures," and Bertolt Brecht (see **11-14**) was a great admirer. After viewing Chaplin's powerful—and very funny—performance in *City Lights* (1931), the fastidious critic Alexander Woollcott, who otherwise loathed movies, said, "I would be prepared to defend the proposition that this darling of the mob is the foremost living artist."

Greta Garbo perfected a romantic style of acting that had its roots in the silent cinema and held sway throughout the 1930s **(8-16)**. "What, when drunk, one sees in other women, one sees in Garbo sober," said the British critic Kenneth Tynan. Almost invariably, MGM cast her as a woman with a mysterious past: the mistress, the courtesan, the "other woman"—the essence of the Eternal Female. Her face, in addition to being stunningly beautiful, could unite conflicting emotions, withholding and yielding simultaneously, like a succession of waves rippling across her features. Tall and slender, she moved gracefully, her collapsed shoulders suggesting the exhaustion of a wounded butterfly. She could also project a provocative bisexuality, as in *Queen Christina* (Rouben Mamoulian, 1933), in which, disguised as a man, her resolute strides and masculine attire provide a foil to her exquisite femininity.

The love goddess par excellence, Garbo was most famous for her love scenes, which epitomized her romantic style. She is often self-absorbed in these scenes, musing on a private irony that can even exclude the lover. Frequently, she looks away from him, allowing the camera—and us—to savour the poignancy of her conflict. She rarely expresses her feelings in words, for her art thrives on silence, on the unspeakable. Her love scenes are sometimes played in literal solitude, with objects serving as erotic fetishes. The way she touches a bouquet of flowers, a bedpost, a telephone—these allude to the missing lover, recalling a multitude of painful pleasures. She is often enraptured by her surroundings, "like Eve on the morning of creation," to use Tynan's memorable phrase. But she is also oppressed by the knowledge that such ecstasy cannot last; she arms herself against her fate with irony and stoicism. Garbo's performances are striking examples of how great acting can salvage bad scripts, and even bad direction. "Subtract Garbo from most of her movies and you are left with nothing," one critic noted.

The most important British film actors are also those most prominent in live theatre. Virtually every medium-sized British city has a resident drama company, where actors can learn their craft by playing a variety of roles from the classic repertory, especially the works of Shakespeare. As players improve, they rise through the ranks, attempting more complex roles. The best of them migrate to the larger cities, where the most prestigious theatre companies are found. The discipline that most British actors have acquired in this repertory system has made them the most versatile of players. The finest of them are regularly employed in the theatres of London, which is adjacent to the centres of film production in Britain. This centralization allows them to move from live theatre to film to television with a minimum of inconvenience.

British acting traditions tend to favour a mastery of externals, based on close observation. Virtually all players are trained in diction, movement, makeup, dialects, fencing, dancing, body control, and ensemble acting. For example, Laurence Olivier always built his characters from the outside in. He moulded his features like a sculptor or painter. "I do not search the character for parts that are already in me," he explained, "but go out and find the personality I feel the author created." Like most British actors of his generation, Olivier had a keen memory for details: "I hear remarks in the street or in a shop and I retain them. You must constantly observe: a

8-19. *On the Waterfront* (U.S.A., 1954), with Marlon Brando and Eva Marie Saint, directed by Elia Kazan. Kazan considered Brando as close to a genius as he ever encountered among actors—a view that was widely shared by others, especially other actors. Many regard his performance in this movie as his best—emotionally powerful, tender, poetic. It won him his first Academy Award (best actor) as well as the New York Film Critics' Award and the British Oscar as best foreign actor—his third year in a row. Kazan was often surprised by his gifted *protégé* because he came up with ideas so fresh and arrived at in so underground a fashion that they seemed virtually discovered on the spot. *(Columbia Pictures)*

8-20. ***The End of Summer*** **(Japan, 1961), directed by Yasujiro Ozu.**

A master of psychological nuances, Ozu believed that in the art of acting, less is more. He detested melodramatic excesses and demanded the utmost realism from his players, who frequently chafed at his criticism that they were "acting" too much. He avoided using stars and often cast against type so audiences would view the characters with no preconceptions. He usually chose his players according to their personality rather than their acting ability. Above all, Ozu explored the conflict between individual wishes and social necessity. His scenes are often staged in public settings, where politeness and social decorum require the stifling of personal disappointment. Ozu often instructed his players not to move, to express their feelings only with their eyes. Note how the two characters on the left are privately in worlds of their own, while still conforming superficially to the decorum of the occasion. *(New Yorker Films)*

walk, a limp, a run; how a head inclines to one side when listening; the twitch of an eyebrow; the hand that picks the nose when it thinks no one is looking; the moustache puller; the eyes that never look at you; the nose that sniffs long after the cold has gone."

Olivier kept his body in peak condition. Even as an old man, he continued running and lifting weights. When illness curbed these forms of exercises, he took to swimming. At the age of seventy-eight, he was still swimming eight hundred metres almost every morning. "To be fit should be one of the actor's first priorities," he insisted. "To exercise daily is of utmost importance. The body is an instrument which must be finely tuned and played as often as possible. The actor should be able to control it from the tip of his head to his little toe."

The post–World War II era tended to emphasize realistic styles of acting. In the early 1950s, a new interior style of acting, known as "the **Method**," was introduced to American movie audiences. It was commonly associated with director Elia Kazan.

8-21. ***Two Women*** **(Italy, 1960), with Sophia Loren, directed by Vittorio De Sica.**

One of the paradoxes of art is that the misfortunes of the characters are somehow transformed into something powerful, moving, and spiritually illuminating. This movie is set in war-torn Italy during World War II. The Loren character and her 13-year-old daughter are violently raped on a deserted road. It is a brutal coming-of-age for the girl, and for the mother a bitter realization that we cannot always protect our children, no matter how cautious we are. Like most of the great Italian neorealist films, *Two Women* does not offer any cheap comfort at the end. Only a sense of spiritual solidarity with two deeply wronged human beings. Loren's performance is devastating, transcendent. In addition to a Best Actress Academy Award, she also won the New York Film Critics' Award and the top acting prize at the Cannes Film Festival. *(Embassy Pictures)*

Kazan's *On the Waterfront* was a huge success and a virtual showcase for this style of performance **(8-19)**. It has since become the dominant style of acting in American cinema and live theatre. The Method was an offshoot of a system of training actors and rehearsing developed by Constantin Stanislavsky at the Moscow Art Theatre. Stanislavsky's ideas were widely adopted in New York theatre circles, especially by the Actors Studio in New York, which received much publicity during the 1950s because it had developed such well-known graduates as Marlon Brando, James Dean, Julie Harris, Paul Newman, and many others.

The central credo of Stanislavsky's system was, "You must live the part every moment you are playing it." He rejected the tradition of acting that emphasized externals. He believed that truth in acting can be achieved only by exploring a character's inner spirit, which must be fused with the actor's own emotions. One of the most important techniques he developed is *emotional recall*, in which an actor delves

8-22. *L'Amour en fuite* [*Love on the Run*] (France, 1979), with Jean-Pierre Léaud, directed by François Truffaut.

In 1959, when he was fifteen, Léaud established himself as one of the icons of the French New Wave in the role of Antoine Doinel in Truffaut's film about his own childhood, *Les Quatre cents coups.* Although Léaud made many films for other directors, his persona was almost that of Truffaut's alter ego. Truffaut went on to make a series of films about Antoine Doinel over twenty years, following the character and the actor as they both grew older. In this film, the last in the series, the director, in a typical New Wave **reflexive** gesture, posed Léaud/Doinel in front of a series of images from the earlier films. *(New World Pictures)*

into his or her own past to discover feelings that are analogous to those of the character. "In every part you do," Julie Harris explained, "there is some connection you can make with your own background or with some feeling you've had at one time or another." Stanislavsky's techniques were strongly psychoanalytical: By exploring their own subconscious, actors could trigger *real* emotions, which are recalled in every performance and transferred to the characters they are playing. He also devised techniques for helping actors focus their concentration on the "world" of the play—its concrete details and textures. In some form or another, these techniques are probably as old as the acting profession itself, but Stanislavsky was the first to systematize them with exercises and methods of analysis. Nor did he claim that inner truth and emotional sincerity are sufficient unto themselves. He insisted that actors need to master the externals as well, particularly for classic plays, which require a somewhat stylized manner of speaking, moving, and wearing costumes.

Stanislavsky was famous for his lengthy rehearsal periods, in which players were encouraged to improvise with their roles to discover the resonance of the text—the **subtext**. Kazan and other Method-oriented directors used this concept in directing movies: "The film director knows that beneath the surface of his screenplay there is a subtext, a calendar of intentions and feelings and inner events. What appears to be

8-23. *The Seduction of Mimi* (Italy, 1972), with Giancarlo Giannini and Elena Fiore, directed by Lina Wertmüller.

Farcical acting is one of the most difficult and misunderstood styles of performance. It requires an intense comic exaggeration and can easily become tiresome and mechanical if the farceur is not able to preserve the humanity of the character. Here, Giannini plays a typical ethnic stereotype—a sleazy, heavy-lidded lothario who, in an act of sexual revenge, embarks on a campaign to seduce the unlovely wife of the man who has cuckolded him. *(New Line Cinema)*

8-24. *The Act of the Heart* (Canada, 1970), with Geneviève Bujold, directed by Paul Almond.

Like many Canadian actors before her, Bujold went to Hollywood and became a star. Before she left, she made three films with Almond, who was then her husband, in which she played young women suffering from religious and sexual fears. The characters, like Bujold, are bilingual, linking their crises to tensions within Quebec culture. In *The Act of the Heart*, Martha (Bujold) falls in love with a priest (played by Donald Sutherland, who also left for Hollywood) and then, suddenly and shockingly, burns herself alive in a final act of the heart, apparently in protest against a world without love. *(Quest Film)*

happening, he soon learns, is rarely what is happening. The subtext is one of the film director's most valuable tools. It is what he directs." Spoken dialogue is secondary for Method players. To capture a character's "inner events," actors sometimes "throw away" their lines, choke on them, or even mumble. Throughout the 1950s, some critics ridiculed Method actors like Brando and Dean for mumbling their lines.

Stanislavsky disapproved of the star system and individual virtuosity. In his own productions, he insisted on ensemble playing, with genuine interactions among the actors and characters. Players were encouraged to analyze all the specifics of a scene: What does the character really *want*? What has happened before the immediate moment? What time of day is it? And so on. When presented with a role utterly foreign to their own experience, actors were urged to research the part so it would be understood in their guts as well as in their minds. Method actors are famous for their ability to bring out the emotional intensity of their characters. Method-oriented directors generally believe that a player must have a character's experience within him or her, and they go to considerable lengths to learn about the personal lives of their players to use such details for characterization.

In the 1960s, the French **New Wave** directors—especially Jean-Luc Godard and François Truffaut—popularized the technique of improvisation while their players were on camera. The resultant increase in realism was highly praised by critics. Of course, there was nothing new in the technique itself. Actors often improvised in the silent cinema, and it was the foundation of silent comedy. For example, Chaplin, Keaton, and Laurel and Hardy needed to know only the premise of a given scene. The comic details were improvised and later refined in the editing stage. The cumbersome technology of sound put an end to most of these practices. Method-trained actors use improvisation primarily as an exploratory rehearsal technique, but their performances are usually set when the camera begins to roll.

Godard and Truffaut, to capture a greater sense of discovery and surprise, would occasionally instruct their players to make up their dialogue while a scene was actually being photographed. The flexible technology introduced by *cinéma vérité* allowed these directors to capture an unprecedented degree of spontaneity. In Truffaut's *Les Quatre cent coups* [*The Four Hundred Blows*], for example, a prison psychologist interviews the youthful protagonist (Jean-Pierre Léaud) about his family life and sexual habits. Drawing heavily on his own experience, Léaud (who wasn't informed of the questions in advance) answers them with disarming frankness. Truffaut's camera is able to capture the boy's hesitations, his embarrassment, and his charming macho bravado (see **8-22**). In one form or another, improvisation has become a valuable technique in contemporary cinema. Such filmmakers as Robert Altman **(7-24)**, Rainer Werner Fassbinder, and Martin Scorsese have used it with brilliant results.

Genre and directorial emphasis influence acting styles significantly. For example, in such stylized genres as the samurai film, Toshiro Mifune is bold, strutting, and larger than life, as in Akira Kurosawa's *Yojimbo* **(5-10)**. In a realistic contemporary story like *High and Low* (1963, also directed by Kurosawa), Mifune's performance is all nuance and sobriety. For this reason, classifying acting styles according to national origins is also likely to be misleading, at least for those countries that have evolved a wide spectrum of styles, such as Japan, the United States, and Italy. For example, the Italians (and other Mediterranean peoples) are said to be theatrical by national temperament, acting out their feelings with animation, as opposed to the reserved deportment of the Swedes and other Northern Europeans.

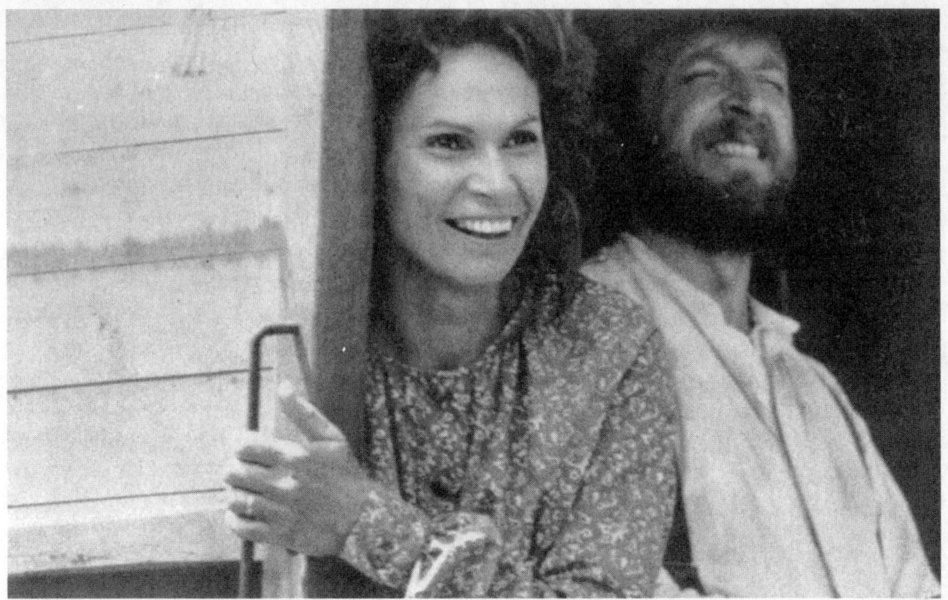

8-25. *J.A. Martin, photographe* (Canada, 1977), with Monique Mercure and Marcel Sabourin, directed by Jean Beaudin.

Mercure and Sabourin have been familiar figures in Quebec cinema for many years. In this film, which takes its cue from the formal portraits produced by the title character, a nineteenth-century photographer, they both give restrained, understated performances, but both are adept at a wide range of acting styles. Mercure has appeared in small-budget, documentary-influenced films like Claude Jutra's *À tout prendre* [*Take It All*] (1963), in popular soft-core pornographic romps like Claude Fournier's *Deux femmes en or* [*Two Women in Gold*] (1970), and in the ritualistic dramas of playwright Michel Tremblay. Her performance in *J.A. Martin* won the best actress award at the 1978 Cannes Film Festival. *(National Film Board of Canada)*

But within the Italian cinema, these generalizations are subject to considerable modification. Southern Italian characters tend to be acted in a manner that conforms to the volatile Latin stereotype, as can be seen in the movies of Lina Wertmüller **(8-23)**. Northern Italians, conversely, are usually played with more restraint and far less spontaneity, as the works of Antonioni demonstrate.

Canadian actors from Mary Pickford to Keanu Reeves and Jim Carrey have made major contributions to the Hollywood star system, but the Canadian national cinema lacks the resources to compete with the glamour and spectacle of major Hollywood productions (see Chapter 10, "Canadian Cinema"). Canada has also produced great character actors like Donald Sutherland and Christopher Plummer, but Canadian films do not usually work in the intense psychological mode associated with Method acting. In a nation that often questions its own identity, actors are often asked to portray characters who are searching for personal and cultural values that will give their lives meaning.

Like most national cinemas, Canadian cinema encompasses a wide variety of film production, perhaps even more varied than most, given the country's regional differences, its bilingual status, and its increasingly multicultural population. However, the documentary tradition had a major impact on the new Canadian cinema that emerged in the 1960s, following the example set by the French New Wave, and it encouraged the adoption of realist acting styles. These small-budget films used documentary techniques, and the actors were often required to improvise, as when director Don Owen created a powerful effect at the end of *Nobody Waved Good-bye* by not informing one of the actors of a major plot development (see **10-7**). The success of films like Don Shebib's *Goin' Down the Road* owed much to the ability of the professional actors to create the impression of nonprofessionals reacting spontaneously to unexpected situations **(6-20)**.

The commercial pressures on the Canadian film industry mean that producers often cast American actors in the hope of attracting international audiences. In Quebec, co-production arrangements often call for the inclusion of French actors, with the result that audiences find the accents unsuited to the characters they are playing. Of course, as in all national cinemas, foreign actors are also used as a means of bringing out, through contrast, the distinctive characteristics of the domestic performers.

8-26. *Bicycle Thieves* (Italy, 1948), with Enzo Staiola and Lamberto Maggiorani, directed by Vittorio De Sica.

One of the most famous casting coups in film history is De Sica's selection of Maggiorani and Staiola as an impoverished labourer and his idolizing son. Both were nonprofessionals. Maggiorani actually was a labourer and had difficulty finding a factory job after this movie. When De Sica was trying to finance the film, one producer agreed to put up the money provided that the leading role was played by Cary Grant! De Sica could not imagine an elegant and graceful actor like Grant in the role, and the director wisely went elsewhere for his financing. *(Audio-Brandon Films)*

8-27. *Taxi Driver* (U.S.A., 1976), with Robert De Niro, directed by Martin Scorsese.
Scorsese first cast De Niro in *Mean Streets* (1973), and since then they have worked together many times, with the actor contributing powerfully to the director's vision of the edgy intensity of Italian-American culture. In this film, he plays the title character, a lonely Vietnam War vet who becomes a media hero when he shoots the pimp of a young prostitute. De Niro's mesmerizing performance draws us into his perception of the nightmare city through which he travels, leaving us very uncertain how to respond to the bloody violence of the ending and his naive acceptance of his no doubt temporary fame. *(Columbia Pictures)*

In these circumstances, Canadian actors have to be versatile, working in television as well as film and in very different genres and production circumstances. French-language production in Quebec, for the small and big screen, attracts large audiences, and many actors have achieved star status. In English Canada, there is less public interest, but television exposure did allow Paul Gross to direct and star in *Men With Brooms*, an attempt to create a more commercial form of Canadian cinema **(10-3)**. Many young Canadian actors—including Sarah Polley, Molly Parker, Pascale Bussières, Bruce Greenwood, and Callum Keith Rennie—work mainly in Canada but have developed international reputations.

CASTING

Casting a movie is almost an art in itself. Most stage and screen performers are classified according to role categories: leading men, leading ladies, character actors, juveniles, villains, light comedians, tragedians, ingénues, singing actors, dancing actors, and so on. Typing conventions are rarely violated. For example, even though homely people obviously fall in love, romantic roles are usually performed by attractive players. Similarly, audiences are not likely to be persuaded by a player with an all-American persona (like Tom Hanks) cast in European roles. Nor is one likely to accept a performer like Klaus Kinski as the boy next door, unless one lives in a very weird neighbourhood. Of course, a player's range is all-important in determining his or her type. Some, like Nicole Kidman, have extremely broad ranges, whereas others, like Woody Allen, are confined to variations of the same type.

Typecasting was almost invariable in the silent cinema. In part, this was because characters tended toward allegorical types rather than individuals and often were even identified with a label: "The Man," "The Wife," "The Mother," "The Vamp," and so on. Blonde players were usually cast in parts emphasizing purity, earthy brunettes in erotic roles. Sergei Eisenstein insisted that players ought to be cast strictly to type and was inclined to favour nonprofessionals because of their greater authenticity. Eisenstein's concept of "typage" depended on the actor's appearance rather than his or her "real life" background, whereas realist directors ask nonprofessional

8-28a. *Gigi* (U.S.A., 1958), with Maurice Chevalier, Leslie Caron, and Louis Jourdan; directed by Vincente Minnelli.

A traditional distinction in acting styles is presentational versus representational. A *presentational style* openly acknowledges the audience. A character sometimes even addresses us directly, establishing an intimate rapport that excludes the other characters. The Chevalier character in this famous Lerner and Loewe musical is presentational. Note how he seems to act as an intermediary between the world of the movie (Paris, 1900) and the world of the audience. *(MGM)*

actors to "play themselves": If the character is a factory worker, then the actor should also be a factory worker **(8-26)**.

But trained actors tend to resent being typed and often attempt to broaden their range. Humphrey Bogart is a good example. For years he was stereotyped as a tough, cynical gangster, until 1941 when he joined forces with director John Huston, who cast him as the hard-boiled detective Sam Spade in *The Maltese Falcon* **(2-3)**. Huston weaned him even further from his type in *The Treasure of the Sierra Madre* (1948), in which Bogart played a crafty paranoid, the prospector Fred C. Dobbs. The actor totally reversed his image in *The African Queen* (1951), in which he played Charlie Allnut, a lovable and funny drunk whose vulnerability endeared him to audiences and won Bogart an Academy Award for best actor. But in *Beat the Devil* (1954), Huston's celebrated casting instincts deserted him when he used Bogart in a role beyond his powers—as a sophisticated adventurer stranded with a shabby assortment of rogues and loons. The witty tongue-in-cheek dialogue fell flat in Bogart's self-conscious performance. A polished player like Cary Grant could have acted the part with much greater believability and grace.

"Casting is characterization," Hitchcock pointed out. Once a role has been cast, especially with a personality star, the essence of the fictional character is already established. In a sense, stars are more "real" than other characters, which is why many people refer to a character by the actor's name rather than by the name of the person in the story. After working with Hitchcock on the script of *Strangers on a Train* (1951), the novelist Raymond Chandler ridiculed the director's method of characterization. "His idea of character is rather primitive," Chandler complained

8-28b. *North Country* (U.S.A., 2005), with Richard Jenkins, Charlize Theron, and Sissy Spacek, directed by Niki Caro.

A *representational style* is generally more realistic and self-contained. The characters inhabit their own separate world and never acknowledge the presence of an audience or a camera. We are allowed to act as voyeurs and eavesdrop on their conversations, but actors always perform as though no one is watching or listening. As this shot of a family crisis in *North Country* suggests, a representational style can seem invasive, prying into a private moment. *(Warner Bros.)*

8-29. *The Leopard* (Italy, 1963), art direction by Mario Garbuglia, costumes by Piero Tosi, directed by Luchino Visconti.

Visconti had the unusual distinction of being both a Marxist and an aristocrat (he was the Duke of Modrone). A master of the period film, he was exceptionally sensitive to the symbolic significance of costumes and *décor*. They are part of Visconti's political statement. For example, the clutter, texture, and florid patterns of the Victorian furnishings in this movie suggest a stifling, hothouse artificiality, sealed off from nature. The costumes, impeccably accurate to period, are elegant, constricting, and totally without utility. They were meant to be. Idle people of independent income—that is, income derived from the labour of others—rarely concern themselves with utility in clothing. *(Twentieth Century Fox)*

("Nice Young Man," "Society Girl," "Frightened Woman," and so on). Like many literary types, Chandler believed that characterization must be created through language. He was insensitive to the other options available to a filmmaker. For example, Hitchcock was a cunning exploiter of the star system—a technique that has nothing to do with language. For his leading ladies, for instance, he favoured elegant blondes with an understated sexuality and rather aristocratic, ladylike manners—in short, the Society Girl type. But there are great individual differences between such heroines as Joan Fontaine, Ingrid Bergman, and Grace Kelly, to mention only three of Hitchcock's famous blondes.

Hitchcock's casting is often meant to deceive. His villains were usually actors of enormous personal charm—like James Mason in *North by Northwest* (1959). Hitchcock counted on the audience's good will toward an established star, permitting his "heroes" to behave in ways that can only be described as morally dubious. In *Rear Window* **(11-9)**, for example, James Stewart is literally a voyeur, yet we find it difficult to condemn such a wholesome type as Jimmy Stewart, the all-American boy. Audiences also assume that a star will remain in the movie until the final reel, at which point it is permissible—though seldom advisable—to kill him or her off. But in *Psycho* (1960), the Janet Leigh character is brutally murdered in the first third of the film—a shocking violation of convention that jolts audiences out of their complacency. Sometimes Hitchcock cast awkward, self-conscious actors in roles requiring a note of evasive anxiety, like Farley Granger in *Rope* (1948) and *Strangers on a Train*. In cases such as these, bad acting is precisely what is called for—it is part of the characterization.

Many filmmakers believe that casting is so integral to character, they do not even begin work on a script until they know who will play the major roles. Yasujiro Ozu confessed, "I could no more write, not knowing who the actor was going to be, than an artist could paint, not knowing what colour he was using." Billy Wilder always tailored his dialogue to fit the personality of his players. When Montgomery Clift backed out of playing the lead in *Sunset Boulevard* (1950), Wilder rewrote the part to fit William Holden, who brought totally different character nuances to the role.

A change in the cast can profoundly alter the impact and meanings of a film even without changes in dialogue. In Atom Egoyan's *The Sweet Hereafter* (1997), internationally known Canadian actor Donald Sutherland was originally cast as the lawyer who arrives in a small British Columbia community to persuade bereaved families to take legal action after their children have died in a school bus accident. Sutherland, who usually brings a nervous intensity to his performances, withdrew at the last moment, and Egoyan turned to British actor Ian Holm, whose restrained performance gives the role a powerful ambiguity that enhances the emotional impact of the film.

COSTUMES AND MAKEUP

The effect of an actor's performance depends heavily on the work of costume designers and makeup artists. Costumes and makeup are not merely frills added to enhance an illusion, but are also aspects of character and theme. Their style can reveal class, self-image, and even psychological states. Depending on their cut, texture, and bulk, certain costumes can suggest agitation, fastidiousness, delicacy, and so on. A close-up of a fabric can suggest information independent even of the wearer. One of the directors most sensitive to the meanings of costumes was Sergei Eisenstein. In his *Alexander Nevsky* (1938), the invading German hordes are made terrifying primarily through their costumes. The soldier's helmets, for example, conceal their eyes: Two sinister slits are cut into the fronts of the metal helmets. Their inhumanity is further emphasized by the animal claws and horns the officers have at the top of their helmets as insignia. The highly ornate armour they wear suggests their decadence and machine-like impersonality. An evil churchman is costumed in a black monk's habit: The sinister hood throws most of his hawk-like features into darkness. In contrast, Nevsky and the Russian peasants are costumed in loose, flowing garments. Even their armour reflects a warm, humane quality. Their helmets are shaped like Russian church onion domes and permit most of the features of the face to be seen. Their chain mail reminds the viewer of the fishing nets of the

8-30. *Kandahar* (Iran, 2001), written and directed by Mohsen Makhmalbaf.

An Afghan-born Canadian journalist returns to her ravaged homeland to prevent her sister from committing suicide. Travelling undercover—literally—she manages to enter Afghanistan, which is ruled by the Taliban, the Islamic fundamentalists who opposed the emancipation of women. Wearing the burqa that covers a woman from head to toe, the journalist surveys the degradation of women everywhere. It is risky even for women to be seen reading a book (pictured), and the dress code here expresses the fears as well as the confinement inherent to their situation. *(Avatar Films)*

earlier portions of the movie, where the peasants are shown happiest at their work repairing their fishing nets.

Colour symbolism is used by Franco Zeffirelli in *Romeo and Juliet* (1968). Juliet's family, the Capulets, are characterized as aggressive parvenus: Their colours are appropriately hot: reds, yellows, and oranges. Romeo's family, conversely, is older and perhaps more established, but in obvious decline. They are costumed in blues, deep greens, and purples. These two colour schemes are echoed in the liveries of the servants of each house, which helps the audience identify the combatants in the brawling scenes. The colour of the costumes can also be used to suggest change and transition. The first view of Juliet, for example, shows her in a vibrant red dress. After she marries Romeo, her colours are in the cool blue spectrum. Line as well as colour can be used to suggest psychological qualities. Verticals, for example, tend to emphasize stateliness and dignity (Lady Montague); horizontal lines tend to emphasize earthiness and comicality (Juliet's nurse).

Perhaps the most famous costume in film history is Chaplin's tramp outfit. The costume is an indication of both class and character, conveying the complex mixture of vanity and dash that makes Charlie so appealing. The moustache, derby hat, and cane all suggest the fastidious dandy. The cane is used to give the impression of self-importance as Charlie swaggers confidently before a hostile world. But the baggy trousers several sizes too large, the oversized shoes, the too-tight coat—all these sug-

8-31. ***Titanic*** **(U.S.A., 1997), with Kate Winslet and Leonardo Di Caprio, written and directed by James Cameron.**

As the "unsinkable" ocean liner slowly surrenders to the frigid waters of the Atlantic, the scenes get darker, colder, and more desperate. The colours, so richly luxurious in the earlier scenes, begin to fade with the light as they are swallowed by the enveloping waters. But the young lovers, radiating humanity with their warm fleshtones and halo lighting, cling to each other like a beacon of hope in the final stages of the wounded ship's watery descent. They are like the doomed, tragic lovers of a nineteenth-century romantic novel. (*Twentieth Century Fox/Paramount Pictures*)

gest Charlie's insignificance and poverty. Chaplin's view of humanity is symbolized by that costume: vain, absurd, and—finally—poignantly vulnerable.

In most cases, especially period films, costumes are designed for the performers who will be wearing them. The costumer must always be conscious of the actor's body type—whether he or she is thin, overweight, tall, short—to compensate for any deficiency. If a performer is famous for a given trait—Dietrich's legs, Monroe's bosom, Schwarzenegger's chest—the costumer will often design the actor's clothes to highlight these attractions. Even in period films, the costumer has a wide array of styles to choose from, and his or her choice will often be determined by what the actor looks best in within the parameters defined by the milieu of the story.

During the Hollywood studio era, powerful stars often insisted on costumes and makeup that heightened their natural endowments, regardless of period accuracy. The studio bosses, who wanted their stars to look as glamorous as possible by suggesting a "contemporary look," encouraged this practice. The results are usually jarring and incongruous. In John Ford's western *My Darling Clementine* (1946), which is set in a rough frontier community, actress Linda Darnell, one of Twentieth Century Fox's biggest stars, was allowed to wear glamorous star makeup and a 1940s-style hairdo, even though the character she was playing was a cheap Mexican "saloon girl"—a coy period euphemism for a prostitute. She looks as though she just stepped out of a Max Factor salon after receiving the Deluxe Treatment.

In realistic contemporary stories, costumes are often bought off the rack rather than individually designed. This is especially true in stories dealing with ordinary people, people who buy their clothes in department stores. When the characters are lower class or poor, costumers often purchase used clothing. For example, in *On the Waterfront*, which deals with dockworkers and other working-class characters, the costumes are frayed and torn. Costumer Anna Hill Johnstone bought them in used-clothing stores in the neighbourhood adjoining the waterfront area.

8-32. Publicity photo for *Batman Forever* (U.S.A., 1995), with Val Kilmer and Chris O'Donnell, directed by Joel Schumacher.

A costume's silhouette refers to its outline, how much of the body is revealed or obscured by the outer form of the garment. The more formfitting the silhouette, the more erotic the costume—assuming, of course, that the wearer is in good shape. In these costumes, the male musculature is stylized and embossed into the rubberized suits. They weighed over forty pounds each and were intensely uncomfortable and hot under the studio lights. The actual bodies of Kilmer and O'Donnell, though perfectly respectable, are not quite so statuesque: The suits were designed to add muscles here and there and to flatten a few inconvenient protuberances. But there is no question that the costumes make them look good—powerful, sexy, pumped up for action. *(DC Comics and Warner Bros.)*

If costume design complements the actor's expressive use of body language, makeup is an aid to facial expression. Even the most delicate changes in makeup can be perceived in cinema. Mia Farrow's pale green face in *Rosemary's Baby* (Roman Polanski, 1968), for example, was used to suggest the progressive corruption of her body while she was pregnant with the devil's child. Similarly, the ghoulish makeup of the actors in Fellini's *Satyricon* (1969) suggests the degeneracy and death-in-life aspect of the Roman population of the period. In *The Graduate* (Mike Nichols, 1967), Anne Bancroft is almost chalk white in the scene where she is betrayed by her lover.

In *The New World* (2005), Terrence Malick uses makeup to set up a conflict between different attitudes to nature and society **(8-6)**. During most of the film, the lack of adornment of the English soldiers and settlers in their isolated fort contrasts with the painted faces of many of the Native Americans, who use colours drawn from nature to express their closeness to the land that they are about to lose. Then, when Pocahontas is taken to the English court, both groups are contrasted with the elaborate, artificial makeup of the courtiers who live in large country houses with ornate cultivated gardens.

Makeup is an important aspect of the glamour image in cinema. Conventionally, female stars enhance their appearance with cosmetics, and their images have often been used to sell glamour products to the women who admire them. Male stars also use makeup, although usually more discreetly, since the use of cosmetics violates conventional codes of masculinity. Some makeup is necessary to stand up to the glare of film lighting, but directors who want a starkly realist effect use natural lighting as much as possible and ask their actors to use little or no makeup.

Character actors and actor stars are less concerned with glamour than with makeup as a means of concealing their own features and constructing a distinctive look for their characters. Brando and Olivier represent different acting traditions, but they were equally likely to wear false noses, wigs, and distorting cosmetics. Because Orson Welles was known primarily for playing strong domineering roles, he resorted to such tricks in makeup to maximize the differences between the roles. In her role as Virginia Woolf in *The Hours*, Nicole Kidman is almost unrecognizable. Nonprofessional players probably wear the least amount of makeup, for they are chosen precisely because of their physical appearance. Yet, even when they wear what appear to be their own clothes and no makeup, these choices become part of the meaning of their performance.

In analyzing the acting in a movie, we should consider what types of actors are featured and why: amateurs, professionals, or popular stars? How are the actors treated by the director: as camera material or artistic collaborators? Is the editing manipulative or are the actors allowed to perform without a lot of cuts? Does the film highlight the stars or does the director encourage ensemble playing? What about the star's iconography? Does he or she embody certain cultural values? What style of acting predominates? How realistic or stylized are the acting style and the costumes and makeup? Why were these actors cast? What do they bring with them to enhance their characters?

FURTHER READING

Butler, Jeremy G., ed., *Star Texts: Image and Performance in Film and Television* (Detroit: Wayne State University Press, 1991). Essays on a wide range of issues and actors.

Dyer, Richard, *Heavenly Bodies: Film Stars and Society*, 2nd edition (London: Routledge, 2004). Case studies of three major stars: Marilyn Monroe, Paul Robeson, and Judy Garland.

Fischer, Lucy, and Marcia Landy, eds., *Stars: The Film Reader* (New York: Routledge, 2004). Anthology of essays on stars and stardom in film and television.

Hollinger, Karen, *The Actress: Hollywood Acting and the Female Star* (New York: Routledge, 2006). Case studies of leading contemporary star actresses.

Klevan, Andrew, *Film Performance: From Achievement to Appreciation* (London: Wallflower Press, 2005). Close analysis of performance in a range of Hollywood films.

Lovell, Alan and Peter Krämer, eds., *Screen Acting* (London: Routledge, 1999). Essays on actors and acting in a range of national cinemas.

McCann, Graham, *Rebel Males: Clift, Brando and Dean* (London: Hamish Hamilton, 1991). Examines the careers and personas of three great male stars associated with the Method.

Naremore, James, *Acting in the Cinema* (Berkeley: University of California Press, 1988). Comprehensive overview of performance styles.

Tucker, Patrick, *Secrets of Screen Acting*, 2nd edition (New York: Routledge, 2003). Technical analysis of the actor's craft.

Wojcik, Pamela Robinson, *Movie Acting: The Film Reader* (New York: Routledge, 2004). Classic essays and contemporary scholarship on all aspects of film acting.

My Winnipeg (Buffalo Gal/Everyday Pictures/The Kobal Collection)

9 NONFICTION FILMS

You photograph the natural life, but you also, by your juxtaposition of detail, create an interpretation of it.

—John Grierson

OVERVIEW

Documentary as evidence and interpretation. The stages of documentary film history. The emergence of the classical documentary: Flaherty and Grierson. The early years of the National Film Board (NFB) of Canada. *Cinéma vérité* and direct cinema. Censorship and the problem of objectivity. The mock-documentary. Avant-garde cinema: visionary and structural films. Combining documentary and the avant-garde.

The term **nonfiction film** is most commonly applied to documentary cinema, but it has also been used to describe avant-garde films. These two filmmaking practices—**documentary** and **avant-garde**—are the major alternative modes to the fiction films we normally expect to find in local cinemas and with which this book is mostly concerned. Documentary realism and avant-garde formalism may seem to be opposite modes of filmmaking, but both started from a suspicion of the use of

9-1. *Hearts and Minds* (U.S.A., 1975), directed by Peter Davis.

The emotional impact of a documentary image usually derives from its truth rather than its beauty. Davis's indictment of America's devastation of Vietnam consists primarily of TV news footage. This photo shows some Vietnamese children running from an accidental bombing raid on their community, the clothes literally burned off their bodies by napalm. "First they bomb as much as they please," a Vietnamese observes, "then they film it." It was images such as this that eventually turned the majority of Americans against the war. Fernando Solanas and Octavio Getino, documentary filmmakers themselves, point out, "Every image that documents, bears witness to, refutes or deepens the truth of a situation is something more than a film image or purely artistic fact; it becomes something which the System finds indigestible." *(Warner Bros.)*

spectacle and narrative in fiction films to involve spectators in a world of fantasy and illusion. The distinction between fiction and nonfiction is not as easy to make as some filmmakers and theorists imply, and several recent filmmakers have begun to mix the modes in quite provocative ways.

THE DOCUMENTARY MODE

The documentary mode depends on the basic assumption that film images provide evidence of a state of affairs that exists, or once existed, in the world outside the film. Whereas fiction films usually involve us with the subjective viewpoints of the characters, even in stories based on actual events, documentaries rely on the camera's capacity for recording reality and provide what Andrew Higson calls a "public gaze" on the world. Many filmgoers assume that documentaries must be dry and boring, at best a useful source of information; and there are, of course, many unassuming instructional documentaries. However, no documentary is simply an objective representation of facts, and the key question for the great documentary filmmakers has been how to create a convincing interpretation of reality without distorting the evidence.

If fiction films create meanings through narrative structure—the relations of story and plot—documentaries are structured more like essays. The raw images provide the evidence that is then organized to develop an argument. This argument is constructed largely through the way in which the images are edited together and through the way in which the images relate to the soundtrack. In the course of film history, documentaries have evolved several different approaches to the relation of argument or interpretation to evidence or reality. These stages can be compared with the ways in which critics classify genre movies (see Chapter 2, "Story"), although there is no simple linear progression and considerable overlap among these stages:

1. *Formative.* In this stage, the idea of the documentary emerged and the basic issues and conventions were established. The formative stage is usually associated with films made by Robert Flaherty during the 1920s.
2. *Classical.* In this phase, the conventions were used and developed with an underlying confidence in their ability to express important truths about reality. This stage was most fully developed in the ideas and work of John Grierson during the 1930s.
3. *Revisionist.* During this stage, documentaries became less certain about their treatment of reality and began to question the conventions developed in the classical stage. In the 1950s and 1960s, this skeptical attitude was found in diverse movements, variously defined as ***cinéma vérité***, or **direct cinema**, that sprang up in many countries, especially in France, Britain, the United States, and Canada.
4. *Reflexive.* Documentary films from this stage increasingly draw attention to the conditions in which they are made, reflecting the sophistication of viewers in the television age and perhaps also a new sense that, in the age of digital technology, it is now possible to make fake documentary images perfectly convincing.

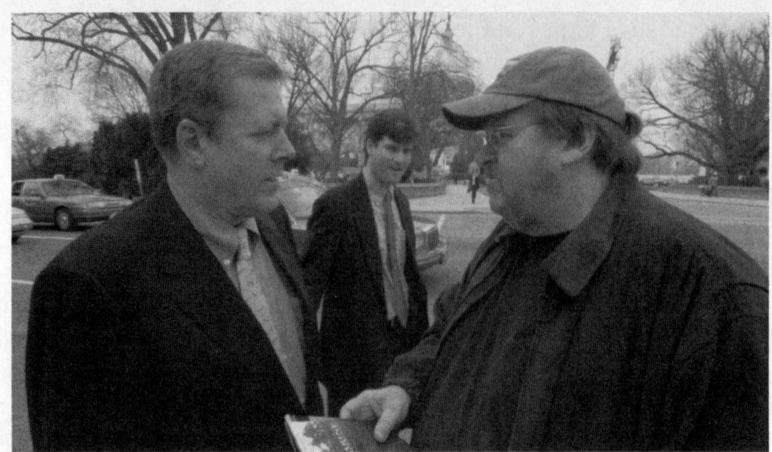

9–2. *Fahrenheit 9/11* (U.S.A., 2004), with Michael Moore (wearing cap), directed by Moore.
Like Moore's other controversial documentaries, *Fahrenheit 9/11* is frankly one-sided, in-your-face, and occasionally manipulative. It is also compassionate, insightful, and very funny. In this scene, for example, he corners a U.S. Representative and tries to get him to enlist his son to go fight in Iraq, a military engagement the Representative voted for in Congress. The filmmaker appears on screen throughout and presents himself as a no-nonsense, dogged pursuer of truth, an exposer of hypocrisy and absurdity, a very different truth claim from that made by classical documentary filmmakers. *(Lions Gate Films/IFC Films/Fellowship Adventure Group)*

These four stages suggest the range and complexity of the films and theory of the documentary. Although we will focus on developments in the United States and Canada since the 1950s, we need to look briefly at the conventions of the classical documentary, since these provide a model against which later filmmakers have defined their own practices. (Of course, many documentaries continue to be made using the classical approach.)

JOHN GRIERSON AND THE CLASSICAL DOCUMENTARY

The first films made and screened by the Lumière brothers in 1895 were brief segments of everyday life, often referred to as "actualities" **(6-2)**. Although fiction cinema soon emerged as the dominant mode, many newsreels, travelogues, and other nonfiction films continued to be made and shown in commercial cinemas. This period even saw the first controversies about the ethics of nonfiction filmmaking, when actual events were re-created in the studio and passed off as newsreel coverage. However, despite these forerunners, most historians agree that the first true documentary was the work of Robert Flaherty, an American explorer who used a camera to record his travels in the Canadian Arctic and who eventually released a feature film called *Nanook of the North* **(9-3)**.

The term "documentary" was first applied to film by John Grierson to describe Flaherty's second film, *Moana* (1925), made during a trip to Polynesia. Grierson was a Scottish sociologist who had visited the United States to study the social effects of the mass media, and he used Flaherty's films to argue his case that film should be

9-3. *Nanook of the North* (U.S.A., 1922), directed by Robert Flaherty.

Often regarded as the first documentary, this film also raised some of the basic problems of documentary ethics. Flaherty was quite prepared to alter the reality in front of his camera to capture what he saw as the *essential* reality of the way of life of Nanook and his family (the alterations extended to changing the Inuit's name from his commercially less viable given name of Allakaralliak). This way of life was fast disappearing, and Flaherty wanted to preserve it on film. Ironically, in doing so, he was helping to introduce the people to modern technology.

used for social purposes, not just for what he saw as the escapist fantasies of Hollywood cinema. He felt that Flaherty had shown the way, but had not yet gone far enough because he still organized his films around the exploits of an individual hero and tended to present a romantic view of exotic cultures.

Flaherty's attitude to the reality he depicted also raised problems. On the one hand, he stayed with the people he was filming for a considerable time to learn about their ways and to allow them to become comfortable in the camera's presence. The use of long takes and deep focus to preserve the duration and the space of the actual events added to the impression of authenticity, as critic André Bazin pointed out when he included Flaherty in his list of admired realist directors. On the other hand, Flaherty was quite prepared to interfere in the events to capture what he saw as the essence of reality. When Nanook was unable to find a seal to hunt, Flaherty had a dead seal flown in and filmed the hunter's epic struggle to land it. He also persuaded Moana, the subject of his second film, to undergo a painful tattooing ceremony that was no longer practised by his people.

Hollywood studios supported Flaherty's first two films, and distributors booked them into commercial cinemas, but the studio executives were dismayed by the high **shooting ratios** that his approach entailed. Ironically, Grierson came to share the Hollywood response when he invited Flaherty to work on *Industrial Britain* (1932), which Grierson eventually finished himself. He thought that Flaherty was too concerned with making his images beautiful and not concerned enough with the social purposes of a film intended to demonstrate the benefits of industrial development.

By this time, Grierson was not just writing about documentary; he was also putting his ideas into action. He directed only one film, *Drifters* (1929), about the North Sea fishing industry, in which he combined Flaherty's observational approach with a use of montage influenced by Soviet cinema. His major contribution to the future of the documentary was made as a producer whose enthusiasm could convince governments and industry of the value of sponsoring films that would make people more aware of social issues. He set up film units in Britain, first at the Empire Marketing Board in 1927 and then at the General Post Office in 1933, and he was also responsible for the establishment of the National Film Board (NFB) of Canada in 1939.

In his brief but highly influential definition, Grierson called documentary the "creative treatment of actuality." Although he often stressed the social objectives of documentary rather than its aesthetics, Grierson was well aware of the need for creative techniques to develop a convincing interpretation of actuality. Two of the most famous films produced by the GPO Film Unit—*Coalface* (1935) and *Night Mail* (1936)—included poetry by W.H. Auden and music by Benjamin Britten. More typically, however, Grierson's documentaries established the classical style in which the images are subservient to a verbal argument that has been scripted in advance. The commentary unifies the film and is spoken in a voice of authority. It is often referred to as a **voice-of-God commentary**, since the speaker is apparently omniscient and remains off screen. For reasons that did not have to be justified at the time, the voice is always male. These films correspond to what Bill Nichols calls the "expository mode"—documentaries that directly address the audience to advance an argument.

Grierson's approach has been criticized for three major reasons:

1. He wanted to bring about social change, but his reliance on government and industrial sponsorship often meant that social criticism gave way to propaganda and advertising.
2. He argued that documentary was opposed to the "illusions" of the Hollywood dream factory, but the classical style, like its fictional counterpart, depended on the spectator not being aware of the filmmaking process and also on the assumption that this process in no way affected the filmed events.
3. The emphasis on the commentary meant that people were not allowed to speak for themselves, which ran contrary to Grierson's theoretical stress on documentary as a force for democracy.

Despite these criticisms, Grierson's energetic championing of the documentary cause firmly established its importance and continues to influence discussion today.

Grierson did produce one film that allowed the people involved to speak about their situations. The film was *Housing Problems*, made to draw attention to living conditions in the urban slums of Britain and to promote the building of modern housing estates. It begins with a voice-of-God commentator who introduces the topic but then gives way to the voice of an expert, a local politician who describes

9-4. *Housing Problems* (Britain, 1935), directed by Arthur Elton and Edgar Anstey.

Evidence of slum conditions is provided not only by the camera, which shows wallpaper peeling off the walls, but also by the people who describe the experience of living in such conditions. We are asked to identify with the victims and then to welcome the solution provided by the modern housing estate seen at the end of the film.

examples of squalor and neglect. He remains off screen but speaks in a somewhat less polished style than the commentator. We are then shown some of the slum dwellers, who stand in their homes as they describe what it is like to live in them. The working-class accents and colourful idioms used by these speakers give their testimony a powerful authenticity, but the very fact that they are on screen diminishes their authority, especially since they seem uncomfortable in the glare of the lights required by the location shooting **(9-4)**.

Grierson later claimed that this film was the origin of *cinéma vérité*, but the framing of the slum dwellers' testimony by more official voices limits its impact. Since the film was sponsored by a gas company that would profit from the construction it was promoting, its social purpose co-exists with a public relations function. This is not necessarily a problem, but it does perhaps suggest why the film does not tackle such issues as the effects of relocation on the community. *Housing Problems* is an early indication that the question of who is speaking in a documentary is never an easy one, even when interviews and other strategies seem to allow people to speak for themselves.

A more typical example of the role of the commentary in the classical documentary is found in a film produced by Grierson at the National Film Board of Canada. *Alexis Tremblay, Habitant* (1943) was directed by Jane Marsh, one of several women

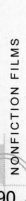

9-5. *Churchill's Island* (Canada, 1941), directed by Stuart Legg.
Legg, who was recruited by Grierson from the British documentary movement, was the master of the compilation film, editing archival footage to illustrate an argument forcefully delivered by a voice-of-God commentary. This film, released in the National Film Board's *World in Action* series, argued that Britain would win the war because of the determination of its people. It won the Academy Award for best short documentary in 1941. *(National Film Board of Canada)*

recruited to work at the film board during World War II, and was part of a project to promote awareness of the lives of people in different regions of the country. In this case, the film depicted a year in the life of a family in rural Quebec, but the English commentary, spoken by a male voice, effectively overrides the French voices of the film's subjects and the female voices of its makers.

Grierson's arrival in Canada coincided with the outbreak of war, and the early years of the NFB were devoted mainly to the production of documentaries in support of the war effort. These films were organized into two extended series, *Canada Carries On* and *World in Action*, and consisted mainly of archival footage (some of it captured from the enemy) selected to illustrate the argument put forward with great urgency by a voice-of-God commentator **(9-5)**. When Grierson resigned as commissioner in 1945, after being implicated in a spy scandal, the young Canadian filmmakers at the NFB were uncomfortable with applying his methods to the apparently less urgent, but more complicated, problems of the postwar period. Some attempted to expand the range of documentary by using dramatized reconstruction, but it was not until the 1950s that a new and distinctive approach emerged at the NFB.

CINÉMA VÉRITÉ AND DIRECT CINEMA

The documentary movement in general lost much of its momentum in the years after World War II, and it was only the development of lightweight equipment that led to a new approach in the 1950s. *Cinéma vérité* or direct cinema filmmakers insisted that their films should be shaped by what was found in the process of making them, not "scripted" in advance. The open-minded exploration of reality was to be shared by the spectator, whose response would no longer be guided by an authoritative commentary. Different versions of this new approach appeared at about the same time in several countries, most notably in Britain, France, the United States, and Canada.

In Britain, the Free Cinema movement, a loose-knit group of young filmmakers led by Lindsay Anderson, experimented with personal and poetic visions of the social environment. One of the most successful of these works is Karel Reisz's film about a working-class youth club, *We Are the Lambeth Boys* (1959). In France, the new developments were closely linked to the work of ethnographic filmmakers, who needed film equipment that could be transported easily to the remote locations where they recorded the rituals and customs of the cultures they were studying. The key figure was Jean Rouch, an anthropologist who worked extensively in Africa and whose highly influential version of *cinéma vérité* was very sensitive to the influence of both the ethnographer and the camera on the events being recorded.

In the United States, the new approach to documentary was more directly linked to the arrival of television. Because of its need to capture news stories quickly, efficiently, and with minimal crew, television journalism was responsible for the development of a new technology, which in turn led eventually to a new philosophy of truth in documentary cinema. The technology included lightweight 16 mm handheld cameras, flexible zoom lenses, fast film stocks, and portable tape recorders. This equipment was so easy to use that only two people—one at the camera, the other with the sound system—were required to bring in a news story.

The flexibility of this equipment permitted documentaries to redefine the concept of authenticity. This new aesthetic amounted to a rejection of planning and carefully detailed scripts. A script involves preconceptions about reality and tends to cancel out any sense of spontaneity or ambiguity. The American *cinéma vérité* filmmakers rejected such preconceptions as fictional: Reality is not being observed; rather, it is being arranged to conform to what the script says it is. The documentarist is superimposing a plot over the materials. Re-creations of any kind are no longer necessary because crew members can be present at an event and capture it while it is happening.

The concept of minimal interference with reality became the dominant preoccupation of the American school of *cinéma vérité*. The filmmaker must not control events in any way. Re-creations—even with the people and places actually involved—were unacceptable. Editing was kept to a minimum, for otherwise it could lead to a false impression of the sequence of events. Actual time and space were preserved whenever possible by using lengthy takes.

Cinéma vérité also uses **nondiegetic** sound minimally. These filmmakers were hostile to voice-of-God commentaries that interpret images for the spectators, relieving them of the necessity of analyzing for themselves. Some dispensed with voice-

9-6. *Law and Order* (U.S.A., 1969), directed by Frederick Wiseman.
Cinéma vérité prided itself on its objectivity and straightforward presentation. Of course, the documentarists realized that total neutrality is an impossible goal to achieve. Even Wiseman, among the most objective of documentarists, insists that his movies are a subjective interpretation of actual events, people, and places. He tries to be as "fair" as possible in presenting his materials. For example, he refuses to use off-screen narrators. The subjects of the film are allowed to speak for themselves, and the burden of interpretation is placed on the spectators, who must analyze the significance of the material on their own. *(Zipporah Films)*

over commentary entirely, and almost all eschewed the musical scores that sought to guide spectator response in most classical documentaries.

An alternative tradition of formalistic or subjective documentaries can be traced back to the Soviet filmmaker Dziga Vertov. Like most Soviet artists of the 1920s, Vertov was a propagandist. He believed that cinema should be a tool of the Revolution, a way of instructing workers about how to view events from an ideological perspective. "Art," he once wrote, "is not a mirror that reflects the historical struggle, but a weapon of that struggle."

Documentarists in this formalistic tradition tend to build their movies thematically, arranging and structuring the story materials to demonstrate a thesis, like the news stories on television's *60 Minutes*. In many cases, the sequence of shots and even entire scenes can be switched around with relatively little loss of sense or logic. The structure of the film is not based on chronology or narrative coherence, but on the filmmaker's argument (see also **9-1**).

Although the terms *cinéma vérité* and direct cinema are often used interchangeably, they have also been used to distinguish between two different attitudes to the question of truth in documentary cinema:

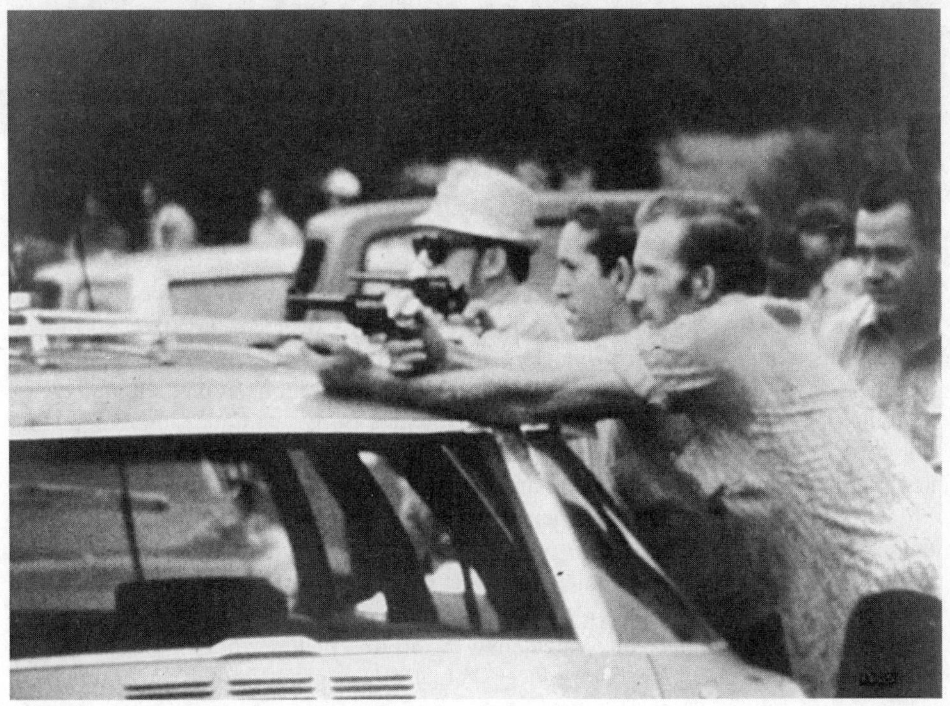

9-7. ***Harlan County, U.S.A.*** **(U.S.A., 1977), directed by Barbara Kopple.**

Cinéma vérité filmmakers in the United States have tended to seek out materials that are intrinsically dramatic, like crisis situations in which a conflict is about to reach its climax. For example, during the production of this documentary, which deals with a bitter coalminers' strike for decent working conditions, Kopple and her crew were repeatedly plunged into violence. In one sequence, they actually came under fire. The camera recorded it all. Implicit in the concept of documentary is the verb "to document"—to verify, to provide an irrefutable record of an event. In a nonfiction film, these privileged moments of truth generally take precedence over considerations of narrative. *(Museum of Modern Art)*

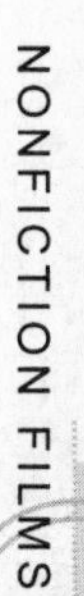

1. The filmmaker tries to avoid interfering with reality to provide evidence of the way things really are (Bill Nichols calls this approach the "observational mode").
2. The filmmaker accepts that the presence of crew and equipment must affect the reality being filmed, and the film becomes a record of this intervention in the way things are (Nichols's "interactive mode").

Unfortunately, the filmmakers and critics applied the terms inconsistently to each of these attitudes. In the United States they tended to refer to the first, the "fly-on-the-wall" approach, as direct cinema and to the second as *cinéma vérité*. In Canada, the emphasis was on exploring the possibilities of the more interactive approach, but the term most commonly used was direct cinema—and in Quebec *cinéma direct* or simply *le direct*.

A rather more useful distinction was made by Canadian filmmaker Michel Brault, whose innovative camerawork can be seen in many important Canadian and French documentaries. Brault distinguished between two kinds of direct cinema:

1. Films made with a telephoto lens, which enables actions to be filmed at a distance, often with a hidden camera.
2. Films made with a wide-angle lens, which enables the cinematographer to film people in intimate close-ups.

Of course, many films make use of both kinds of lens, and both can be used in the service of the two attitudes to documentary truth. The extreme alternatives of hidden camera (in which people are unaware they are being filmed) and "in-your-face" filmmaking (in which people are unable to hide their emotions at moments of crisis) are quite familiar to the modern television audience. Both techniques involve making public what had previously been regarded as private experiences, thus altering the accepted boundaries between public and private life.

These developments were especially important in Canada in the 1950s, when there was virtually no production of fiction films. Documentaries *were* the national cinema, and it was the development of direct cinema that would eventually lead to a distinctive Canadian approach to fiction films in the 1960s (see Chapter 10, "Canadian Cinema"). The movement had its origins in the work of Unit B at the NFB; under the leadership of producer Tom Daly, a group of young filmmakers,

9-8. *Corral* (Canada, 1954), directed by Colin Low.

At a fairly late stage in the editing, the filmmakers decided to dispense with commentary and to accompany the images of a round-up of wild horses with only a solo guitar piece. The result was a film that was, according to Quebec filmmaker Claude Jutra, "a precursor of all sorts of things to come." *(National Film Board of Canada)*

many of whom had worked with Norman McLaren in the animation department, started to make short documentaries. An emphasis on the precise editing of images for rhythmic effect was accompanied by a questioning tone far removed from the certainties of the classical documentary and from the crisis structures often used in American *cinéma vérité*.

Two of the earliest and most influential of these Unit B films were made in 1954. In Roman Kroitor's *Paul Tomkowicz: Street Railway Switchman*, a Polish immigrant is shown at work in the cold Winnipeg night, while the commentary consists of his own description of his feelings and experiences (the commentary was, in fact, rerecorded for intelligibility by a professional broadcaster). Colin Low's *Corral* was even more influential because it dispenses with commentary and simply depicts a cowboy rounding up horses to the accompaniment of a solo guitar **(9-8)**.

Many of the Unit B documentaries did include commentary, but only sparingly and with a much less authoritative tone of voice than classical documentaries. They were often made for television, and many new ideas were tried out in a Canadian Broadcasting Corporation (CBC) series called *The Candid Eye*. The first film shown in this series was *The Days Before Christmas* (1958), for which a group of filmmakers roamed Montreal to find images and sounds that would capture the spirit of the pre-Christmas season. Its perspective is rather ambiguous, as sequences that

9-9. *Lonely Boy* (Canada, 1961), directed by Wolf Koenig and Roman Kroitor.

One of the most famous of the Unit B films, *Lonely Boy* deals with the effect of fame on Paul Anka, the Canadian pop singer, as he performs in the United States. The title refers to one of Anka's biggest hits, but it also describes Anka's personal life as the film depicts it. He is alone among the frenzied fans, mainly young women, and very conscious of the need to maintain a positive image. The film is often reflexive about its own role in the media circus, most notably when Anka and the owner of a nightclub are asked to repeat an already very self-conscious embrace. *(National Film Board of Canada)*

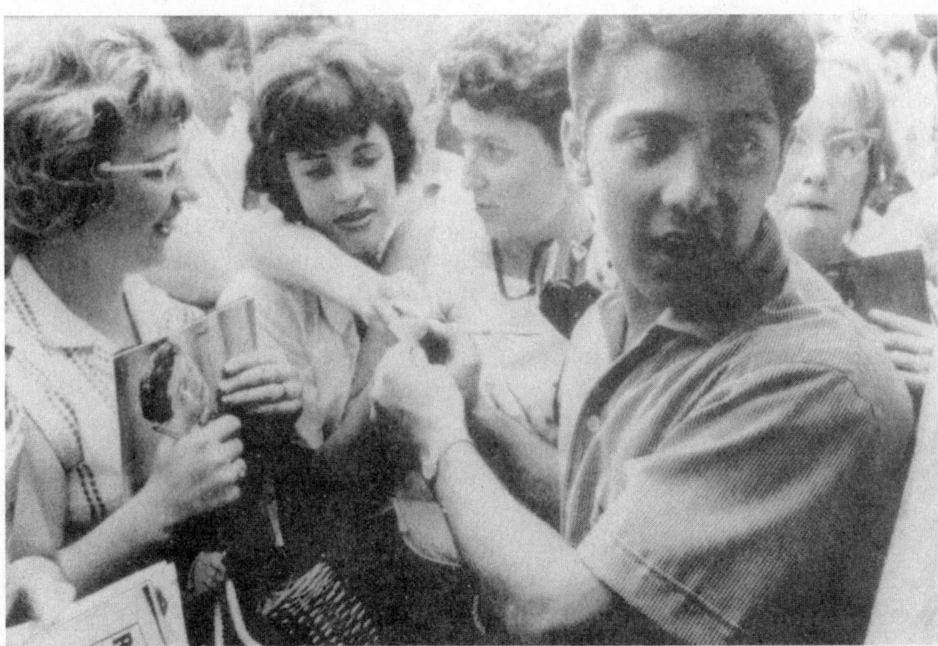

9-10. *Les Raquetteurs* [*The Snowshoers*] (Canada, 1958), directed by Gilles Groulx and Michel Brault. One of the first major works of the French-language unit at the NFB, this film was made on the initiative of the two filmmakers and almost consigned to the stock footage archive by producers who thought it insignificant. Brault's use of the wide-angle lens allowed him to mingle with the snowshoers at a convention in Sherbrooke, creating an affectionate if often ironic view of the events and initiating a series of direct cinema films about the collective rituals of ordinary people in Quebec. *(National Film Board of Canada)*

stress festive good humour are set against others showing lonely people or commercial exploitation. In one sequence, which had an enormous impact on the documentary film community, Wolf Koenig picked up a camera and followed a security guard walking from inside a store to his van, maintaining a close-up of the security guard's gun in its holster.

One of the camera operators on *The Days Before Christmas* was Michel Brault, who soon became a key figure in new developments at the French-language unit of the NFB and who was invited to France to work with Jean Rouch. The NFB moved its headquarters from Ottawa to Montreal in 1956, and French-language production increased to meet the needs of television. Brault was credited as co-director of two of the most important early films produced by the French-language unit, *Les Raquetteurs*, a short film in the wide-angle style on a snowshoers' convention, and *Pour la suite du monde*, a beautifully shot feature-length film about a rural community on the Île-aux-Coudres in the St Lawrence River **(9-10, 9-11)**.

Because direct cinema films were not scripted in advance, administrators at the NFB now had less control over production, and French-unit filmmakers could more easily deal with topics relating to Quebec's political and cultural concerns. They did, however, sometimes run into trouble after the films were completed. The most

9-11. *Pour la suite du monde* (Canada, 1963), directed by Pierre Perrault and Michel Brault. Perrault had already worked with the people of Île-aux-Coudres on radio programs that revealed his fascination with their language and speech. For this feature-length documentary, he persuaded the community to revive the long-abandoned practice of catching beluga whales with poles planted in the river bed. The film alternates close-ups of the inhabitants discussing the project and beautiful long shots of the men at work. As the French title (which might be translated as *For Generations to Come*) suggests, the film explores the value of traditional culture in the modern world, but much of the point of the film was lost in *Moontrap*, the English-language version, which adds a commentary and eliminates most of the sequences in which the islanders speak for themselves. The NFB finally released a subtitled video edition, entitled *Of Whales, The Moon and Men*, in 1999, and a DVD with subtitles has now appeared under the original title. *(National Film Board of Canada)*

notorious case concerned Denys Arcand's *On est au coton* (1970); the title, an untranslatable pun on a colloquial phrase meaning "We're fed up," implies a parallel between Quebec's status in Canada and working conditions in the textile industry, the actual topic of the film. After complaints from the industry, the NFB withdrew the film from circulation on the grounds that it was not sufficiently objective. Since all the workers shown in the film were francophone and many of the bosses anglophone, this act of censorship was seen to be politically motivated, and many bootlegged video copies were circulated among students and activists.

The vexed problem of documentary objectivity was not confined to Quebec, and it has been an ongoing issue in the relations between documentary filmmakers and the CBC. Allan King's *Warrendale* was produced for the CBC but not shown, ostensibly because of the language used by some of the emotionally disturbed children at the treatment centre that gives the film its title. The decision was probably also influenced by the film's intense involvement with the children, who are often shot in

9-12. *Warrendale* (Canada, 1966), directed by Allan King.

As a documentary on a controversial method of treating emotionally disturbed children through holding and touching, *Warrendale* seeks to convey the spirit of this treatment to the spectator through its close-up involvement with its subjects. The film focuses on the children's reactions to the death of a cook, which occurred during the shooting. Some critics objected to what they saw as the film's voyeuristic invasion of private space and its refusal to explain the issues, precisely the kinds of objection made to the treatment at Warrendale. *(Allan King Associates)*

close-up, and its refusal to provide "objective" information about the controversial methods used at the centre **(9-12)**. King also created controversy with his next film, *A Married Couple* (1968), in which he and his crew virtually moved into a couple's home and observed their stormy relationship, giving rise to uncomfortable questions about whether it had in fact provoked the arguments that eventually led to the breakup of the marriage.

The CBC also refused to show the films of Michael Rubbo, who was born in Australia but became one of the most innovative of the NFB documentary filmmakers. Rubbo appears on screen and provides the commentary in most of his films, which have sometimes been called "diary films" (**9-13**). Since they depend on Rubbo's personal response to his subjects, the CBC insisted that they did not meet its standards of objectivity. Indeed, these films issue a direct challenge to the concept of objectivity as they constantly remind us of the filmmaker's limited perspective. *Sad Song of Yellow Skin* (1970) opens with Rubbo ruminating on how his arrival in Vietnam changed his sense of the film he wanted to make, and *Waiting for Fidel* (1974) depicts his visit to Cuba for an interview with Fidel Castro that never takes place.

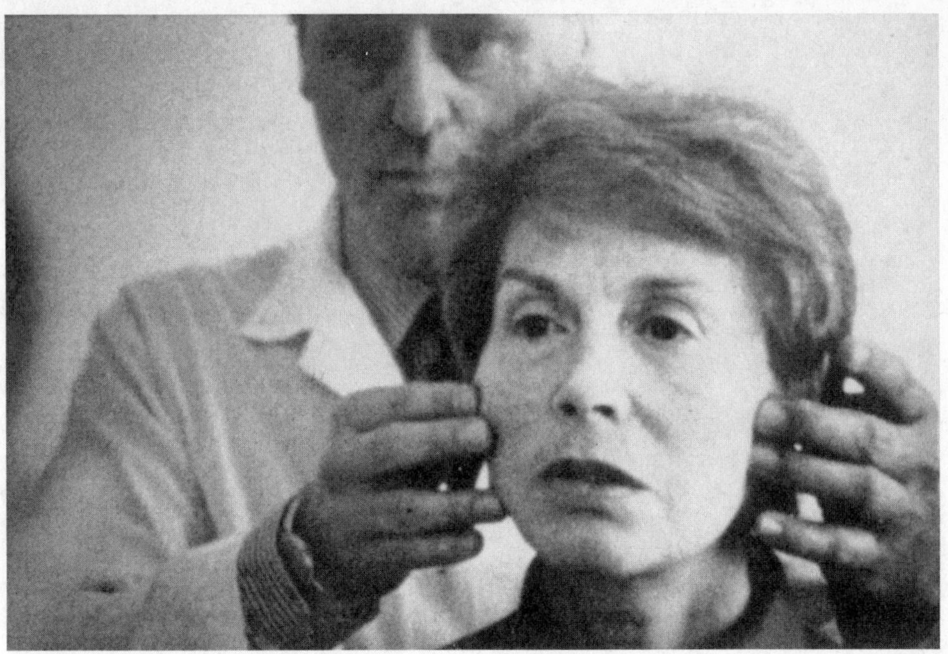

9-13. *Daisy: The Story of a Facelift* (Canada, 1982), directed by Michael Rubbo.

Rubbo has said that his main interest is in "character," a focus more usually associated with fiction films, but Rubbo argues that documentary is more interesting because the situations are "lived by a real person." He becomes a character in his own films, but his point of view is difficult to pin down. In *Daisy*, he uses the decision of a female colleague at the NFB to have a facelift as a springboard for a personal investigation into the role of appearances in our everyday lives. *(National Film Board of Canada)*

The issue of objectivity is one of the most vital in contemporary documentary practice. It has long been a key part of the professional codes of television journalism, not just at the CBC, and it is a basic principle of the classical style of documentary. Filmmakers like Rubbo and, more recently, Ross McElwee and Michael Moore in the United States **(9-2)** remind us that their perspective is personal even though the issues with which they deal exist independently and are not entirely within their control. Feminist critics and filmmakers have also challenged the standard of objectivity, arguing that it promotes an attitude to reality that excludes or devalues women's concerns.

Through her work as a producer and director at the NFB, Anne Claire Poirier sought to evolve new forms that can respond to these concerns. Her film on rape, *Mourir à tue-tête* [*Scream from Silence*], uses both fictional and documentary techniques to create a powerful emotional experience grounded in identification with the rape victim and an awareness of the way women have been oppressed throughout history and in different cultures **(11-15)**. Bonnie Sherr Klein's *Not a Love Story* did not resort to fiction but was designed to provoke feelings of outrage through its juxtaposition of women's personal responses to the pornography industry with the actual products of that industry **(9-14)**.

Poirier and Klein rely on the emotional impact of images of rape and pornography to convince spectators of the truth of their case, and the filmmakers were accused of

9-14. *Not a Love Story* (Canada, 1981), directed by Bonnie Sherr Klein.
Studio D, a women's film unit established at the NFB in 1974, produced many documentaries that explore contentious issues from a feminist perspective. Like Rubbo, Klein (right) appears in her own film, along with stripper Lindalee Tracey, as they investigate the pornography industry. But unlike Rubbo, there is no doubt about Klein's point of view, as the film clearly endorses the perspective of those interviewees who argue that pornography should be censored because it leads to the degradation and abuse of women. Ironically, the pornographic images used by the film as evidence to support its argument led to the film being banned by the Ontario and Saskatchewan censor boards. *(National Film Board of Canada)*

exploiting the degraded sexual imagery that they deplored. Both films are intensely personal, even though Poirier appears in her film only by proxy in fictional sequences in which a director (played by the actress Monique Miller) works with her editor (Micheline Lanctôt) on a film about rape. In these films, the personal involvement of the filmmaker is not just a matter of acknowledging that all viewpoints are personal but of acting on the feminist principle that the "personal is political."

In the case of Alanis Obomsawin, an Abenaki singer and activist as well as filmmaker, personal involvement stems from a sense of solidarity with the cause of Aboriginal peoples. Although her work has been supported for many years by the NFB, the CBC remains uncomfortable with films whose committed stance implies the need to redress past misrepresentations. The standard of objectivity was again raised when the CBC demanded cuts to *Kanehsatake: 270 Years of Resistance*, Obomsawin's feature-length documentary on the Oka crisis. The full version was aired only after an impassioned public debate **(9-15)**.

These controversies make us aware that documentaries cannot be objective, and those that claim to be are more likely to manipulate audiences than those (in the reflexive mode) that acknowledge the viewpoints of their makers. The clear-cut

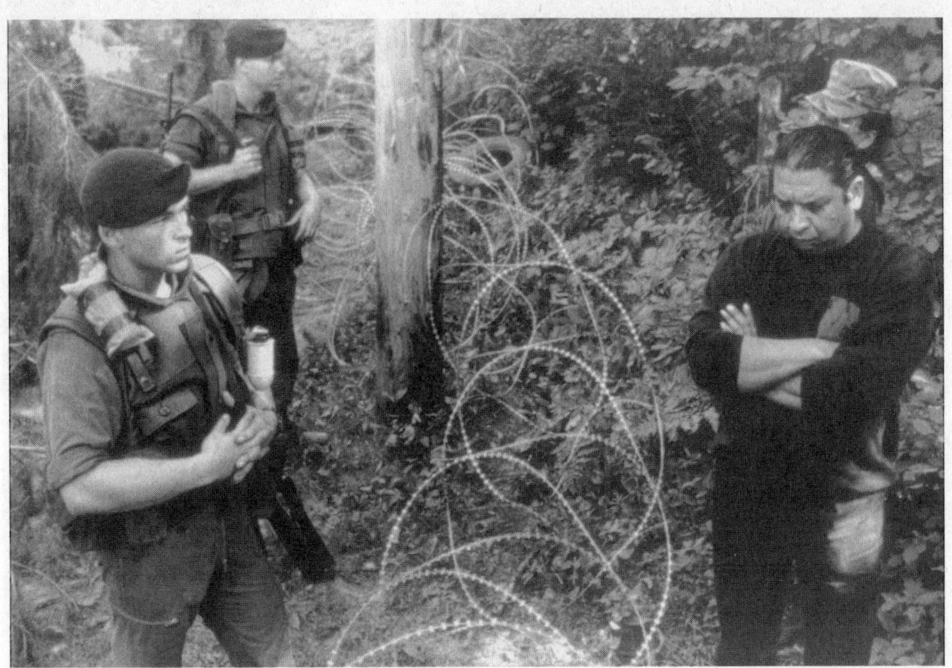

9-15. *Kanehsatake: 270 Years of Resistance* (Canada, 1993), directed by Alanis Obomsawin.

During the summer of 1990, a group of Mohawks occupied land in Oka, Quebec, that was sacred to their people but that the local authorities wished to use to expand a golf course. The result was a tense stand-off that involved the Quebec and federal governments and affected negotiations on a new constitution. Obomsawin and her crew spent most of the siege behind the barricades. As the film's title suggests, the confrontation at Oka is depicted not as an isolated incident but as the outcome of a long process in which Aboriginal peoples have been ignored and misrepresented. *(National Film Board of Canada)*

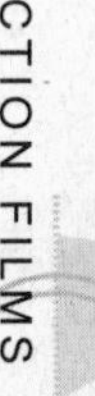

distinction between fiction and nonfiction can no longer be taken for granted. Fiction films like *JFK* **(11-3)** and *Schindler's List* **(3-16d)** borrow documentary techniques, such as the handheld camera, to give their stories a sense of objectivity and authenticity. Meanwhile, documentaries have tended to incorporate elements of fiction or performance, as in the hybrid category of the **docudrama**, which is notoriously difficult to define but which usually involves some form of re-enactment using actors instead of the original subjects.

In docudramas, the use of actors often results in complaints that the film is not factual or accurate and concerns that viewers might not be able to distinguish the fiction from the more conventional documentary elements. Contemporary audiences are probably more astute than this argument suggests, but, at some level, docudramas do claim to document actuality. With the advent of digital imagery and reality television, the boundaries between documentary and fiction have become even more fragile. The documentary claim to objectivity, already called into question by filmmakers such as Rubbo and Moore or in reflexive documentaries such as *The Falls* **(9-16)**, has become the target of numerous **mock-documentaries** (or **mockumentaries**). These are fiction films that masquerade as documentaries, drawing attention to the

9-16. *The Falls* (Canada, 1991), directed by Kevin McMahon.

As a female commentator muses on the different ways in which Niagara Falls has been "framed" in the course of history, the camera frames the Falls and the surrounding area in images that invite us to see them in new ways. Meanwhile, interviews with local informants reveal the contradictory realities of present-day Niagara Falls as tourist site, power source, and chemical waste dump. The film asks us to reflect on the ways in which documentary conventions construct the "truths" they often claim to reflect. *(Still courtesy of Primitive Features Inc.)*

subjectivity and manipulation that have always haunted the documentary idea. In some cases, such as *David Holzman's Diary* (Jim McBride, 1967) and *The Blair Witch Project* **(5-20)**, the imitation was so convincing that many in the audience were taken in and responded to the films as documentaries. In others, such as Woody Allen's *Zelig* (1983) and Rob Reiner's *This is Spinal Tap* (1984), the films gradually incorporate bizarre elements that undermine the documentary framework. Several recent Canadian mockumentaries, including *Le Moitié gauche du frigo* [*The Left Side of the Fridge*] (Philippe Falardeau, 2000), *FUBAR* **(9-17)**, and *The Delicate Art of Parking* (Trent Carlson, 2003), depict direct cinema filmmakers whose projects fail because of their own increasing involvement in the filmmaking process.

AVANT-GARDE CINEMA

Whereas documentary has usually been defined in opposition to fiction, the **avant-garde** has tended to define itself in opposition to films that rely on narrative, at least on the coherent narrative structures of the classical style. Avant-garde films either do not tell stories at all or tell stories that are highly personal and simulate the

9-17. *FUBAR* (Canada, 2002), with Dave Lawrence (left) and Paul J. Spence, directed by Michael Dowse. A (fictional) film director sets out to make a documentary on heavy metal "headbanger" culture by observing the lives of two friends in Calgary, Terry (Lawrence) and Dean (Spence). The comic tone of this mockumentary is disturbed when Terry is diagnosed with testicular cancer and again when the director dies in a swimming accident. However, the supposed documentary subjects respond with their usual irreverent humour. The film is preceded by a caption, apparently provided by the distributor, apologizing to those who took part thinking it was a true documentary, thus alerting viewers to its fictionality, but the style remains "documentary" throughout. *(Courtesy of the Everettt Collection and Canadian Press)*

fragmented patterns of inner thought. The objective is not to make statements about the world outside the film, but to explore the formal properties of film as a medium and the ways in which these properties can be used to evoke the inner experience of the artists and spectators.

With few exceptions, avant-garde films are not written out in advance. In part, this is because the same artist usually shoots and edits the footage and is therefore able to control the material at these stages of the filmmaking process. Many avant-garde filmmakers also value chance and spontaneity in their movies, and to exploit these elements they avoid the inflexibility of a script.

Maya Deren, an American avant-garde filmmaker of the 1940s, differentiated her kind of movie (which she called "personal" or "poetic") from mainstream commercial films primarily in terms of structure. Like a lyric poem, personal films are "vertical" investigations of a theme or situation. The filmmaker is concerned not so much with what is happening as with what a situation feels like or what it means. The film artist is concerned with probing the depths and meanings of a given moment.

According to Deren, fiction movies are like novels and plays, in that they are essentially "horizontal" in their development. Narrative filmmakers use linear structures that must progress from situation to situation, from feeling to feeling. Fiction directors do not have much time to explore the implications of a given idea or emotion, for they must keep the plot moving.

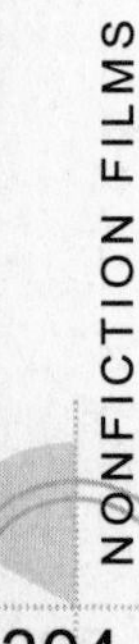

9-18. *Wavelength* (Canada, 1967), directed by Michael Snow.
Snow has been called "the most significant experimental filmmaker in the world." He is also a painter, sculptor, and musician. He has described *Wavelength* as "a continuous zoom, which takes forty-five minutes to go from its widest field to its smallest and final field." The zoom across a loft in New York, where Snow was living at the time, is accompanied by an electronic noise that rises in pitch as the wavelengths are continually shortened. We are occasionally distracted from these formal effects by fragments of narrative that add a touch of black humour to the film's meditation on the cinematic experience of space and time. *(Michael Snow)*

Other avant-garde filmmakers disdain any kind of recognizable subject matter. Hans Richter and other early avant-garde artists in Europe totally rejected narrative. Richter was a champion of the "absolute film," which consists solely of abstract shapes and designs (see **6-6**). Insisting that movies should have nothing to do with acting, stories, or literary themes, Richter believed that film—like music and abstract painting—should be concerned with pure, nonrepresentational forms.

Richter began his experiments in abstraction in Germany in the early 1920s. An influential avant-garde movement also sprang up in France during the 1920s. The French filmmakers used recognizable but distorted images that suggested reality filtered through subjective vision, or impressions, of the filmmaker. This approach provided the basis for the impressionist films of Jean Epstein (*La Chute de la maison Usher* [*The Fall of the House of Usher*], 1928) and Germaine Dulac (*La Souriante Madame Beudet* [*The Smiling Madame Beudet*], 1923) as well as more shocking surrealist films, including *Un Chien andalou* (Luis Buñuel and Salvador Dali, 1928), which begins with a notorious sequence showing a razor blade slicing through an eyeball.

These French films deeply influenced later American avant-garde filmmakers such as Deren and Stan Brakhage who belonged to what P. Adams Sitney has called

9-19. *Gambling, Gods and LSD* (Canada, 2002), directed by Peter Mettler.

A demanding work, made over several years and distilled from a first cut that was fifty-five hours long, Mettler's film received support from mainstream producers and a wider release than most avant-garde films. Its rambling structure allows the filmmaker to investigate a number of manifestations of the desire for transcendence within different cultures. Despite the often exotic images of geographical and cultural difference, the journey gradually brought Mettler to realize that "everything I looked at contained the things I had seen before." *(Grimthorpe Film Inc.)*

a tradition of "visionary film." The more abstract tradition reemerged strongly in the 1960s in a movement known as **structural film**. For the structural filmmakers, the form or shape of the film is a rigorous demonstration of a specific element of film language and its relation to the spectator's perceptual experience. "Flicker films," for example, depend on the flickering of light as the frames of film move through the projector, an effect of which we are normally unaware but that becomes the central focus of these films (see **3-17**).

Structural films need not be entirely abstract: One of the most famous, *Wavelength*), made by Canadian artist Michael Snow, consists of a forty-five-minute zoom shot across a room and into a photograph of breaking waves on the opposite wall **(9-18)**. A few events occur during the zoom, but they remain marginal and never add up to a coherent narrative.

The structural approach has had a major impact on Canadian avant-garde filmmaking, encompassing the distinctive films of Joyce Wieland, David Rimmer, and Bruce Elder. In recent years, however, the avant-garde, in Canada and elsewhere, has moved away from exploring the specific qualities of film as a medium toward more hybrid forms that explore the implications of the diverse media images that have become part of our everyday experience, especially as they affect perception and identity. As with recent developments in documentary, the effect is to break

9-20. *My Winnipeg* (Canada, 2007), directed by Guy Maddin.

Horses frozen in the Red River after escaping from a stable fire are one of the amazing images that Maddin dredges up from the imaginary past in his tribute to the city of his birth. Actors play Maddin and his family in a film that he calls "a documentary about home, and our attitudes about home and nostalgia and memory." As with several of his recent films, Maddin also breaks down the idea of film as a finished product by narrating the movie live at selected screenings. *(Buffalo Gal/Everyday Pictures/The Kobal Collection)*

down distinctions that had previously been taken for granted: Thus, *The Falls* can be described as an avant-garde documentary whose mixture of philosophy and humour makes it accessible to mainstream film and television audiences (**9-16**; see also **6-5**).

The Swiss-Canadian filmmaker Peter Mettler also combines avant-garde techniques with the documentary tradition. In *Picture of Light* (1994), about his journey to northern Manitoba to film the Northern Lights, and *Gambling, Gods and LSD* (**9-19**), a three-hour record of his travels in Canada, the United States, Switzerland, and India, Mettler creates documentaries that are as much concerned with the processes of perception as with what is perceived. An even more radical challenge to traditional conceptions of documentary is found in *My Winnipeg*, Guy Maddin's delirious autobiographical tribute to his native city (**9-20**). In this film, local myths combine with the filmmaker's dream life to create a fantastic world that completely undermines any sense of objective reality.

As these films suggest, documentary and avant-garde practices are both undergoing major changes that transcend the differences between them and the differences between both and mainstream fiction films. The cinematic traditions of nonfiction filmmaking are being challenged and developed in new ways that respond to the interests and needs of increasingly media-literate audiences.

FURTHER READING

Black, Joel, *The Reality Effect: Film Culture and the Graphic Imperative* (New York: Routledge, 2002). Provocative discussion of the blurred boundaries between documentary and fiction in contemporary culture.

Corner, John, *The Art of Record: A Critical Introduction to Documentary* (Manchester: Manchester University Press, 1996). Thorough and accessible.

Evans, Gary, *In the National Interest: A Chronicle of the National Film Board of Canada from 1949–1989* (Toronto: University of Toronto Press, 1991). Valuable historical survey.

Grant, Barry Keith, and Jeannette Sloniowski, eds., *Documenting the Documentary: Close Readings of Documentary Film and Video* (Detroit: Wayne State University, 1998). Anthology of new critical essays on major documentaries.

Jones, D.B., *The Best Butler in the Business: Tom Daly of the National Film Board* (Toronto: University of Toronto Press, 1996). Biography that provides fascinating insights into the workings of the NFB.

Leach, Jim, and Jeannette Sloniowski, eds., *Candid Eyes: Essays on Canadian Documentaries* (Toronto: University of Toronto Press, 2003). Close readings of key films.

MacDonald, Scott, *Avant-Garde Film: Motion Studies* (Cambridge: Cambridge University Press, 1993). Critical analysis of selected films.

Nichols, Bill, *Introduction to Documentary* (Bloomington: Indiana University Press, 2001). Useful survey based on the author's long engagement with the field.

Roscoe, Jane, and Craig Hight, *Faking It: Mock-documentary and the Subversion of Factuality* (Manchester: Manchester University Press, 2001. Thorough study of fiction texts masquerading as documentaries.

Sitney, P. Adams, *Visionary Film: The American Avant-Garde* (New York: Oxford University Press, 1974). Major pioneering critical survey.

Away from Her (The Film Farm/Foundry Films Inc./The Kobal Collection)

10 CANADIAN CINEMA

I'm talking about Canada as a state of mind, as the space you inhabit not just with your body but with your head.

—MARGARET ATWOOD

OVERVIEW

Arguments for and against national cinemas. Subsidies and quotas. Films as expressions of national identity. Canadian films as unfamiliar experiences. English-language and French-language production: two national cinemas or one? The four stages of Canadian film history. Early Canadian feature films. The Canadian Cooperation Project. Direct cinema feature films. The creation of the Canadian Film Development Corporation. Cultural versus economic objectives. Canadian genre films. The Capital Cost Allowance Act. Films that conceal their Canadian origins. Telefilm Canada. Canadian auteurs. Multiculturalism and diasporic cinema. National cinema in the age of globalization.

Hollywood films continue to dominate the world's screens. The glamour of the star system and high production values have enormous appeal for international audiences. Few national cinemas can match this appeal, and their films must compete with Hollywood's vast economic resources to be seen even by local audiences. Most Hollywood films have publicity budgets that equal or exceed their production budgets, and the publicity spills over international borders by means of modern communications media. Hollywood has also invested in the distribution systems of many countries and has been able to exert considerable influence on governments seeking to protect national film industries. With the growth of a global media marketplace, the pressures on national cinemas become even more complex, and many critics argue that it is no longer relevant—or perhaps even possible—to discuss films in their national contexts.

NATIONAL CINEMA

When D.W. Griffith visited Toronto in 1925, he was the most famous filmmaker in the world. His films had done much to shape the classical paradigm that gave Hollywood cinema its enormous international appeal. Canada had no film industry of its own, but Griffith told his Canadian hosts, "You should have your own films and exchange them with other countries." Twenty years later, the federal government asked John Grierson, as commissioner of the National Film Board (NFB), to advise on film policy. Not surprisingly, in view of his strong commitment to the documentary mode, Grierson's advice was very different from that of Griffith: He argued against government measures to encourage feature-film production in Canada. "What is the difference," he asked, "whether a film comes from Hollywood or Timbuktu or Saskatchewan as long as it is about the life of man as it is lived and dreamed in common everywhere?"

Hollywood films have an apparently universal appeal and set the norms against which other national cinemas have had to define themselves. Most of these national cinemas—India and Japan are the major exceptions—have small domestic markets that cannot support a commercial film industry without some form of government aid. Virtually every nation in the world has shared Griffith's view and has taken steps to protect its domestic film industry. There are two basic approaches, and most nations have used a combination of the two:

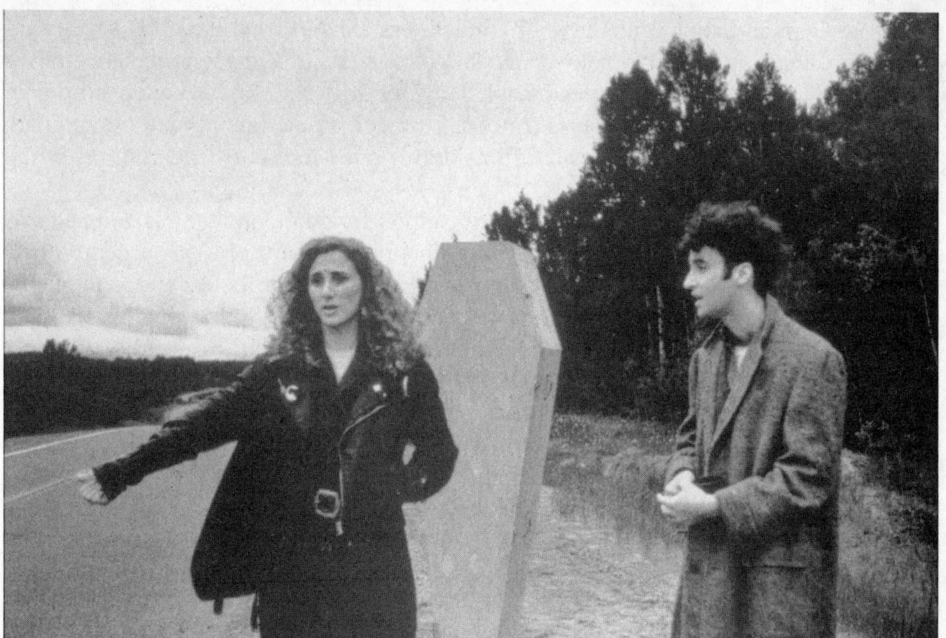

10-1. *Highway 61* (1991), with Valerie Buhagiar and Don McKellar, directed by Bruce McDonald. National identities do not exist in reality; they are myths—fictions that draw on reality but are necessarily selective. They can harden into stereotypes and can affect the behaviour of real people. Bruce McDonald's road film plays with, and disrupts, stereotypes of Canadian and American identity. Its Canadian hero, Pokey Jones (McKellar), a timid barber and part-time trumpet player, finds himself accompanying a gun-toting American (Buhagiar) down the legendary highway between Thunder Bay and New Orleans, pursued by a character who seems to be the Devil. *(Shadow Shows)*

1. Subsidies or tax incentives, which support production either through the investment of public money or by encouraging investment by private individuals.
2. Quotas, which target the distribution and exhibition of films by requiring that cinemas devote a certain percentage of screen time to domestic films, thus increasing the likelihood that these films will retrieve their production costs at the box office.

Both methods have been used successfully, but both have potential drawbacks. Subsidies can result in a national cinema whose films remain largely unseen because commercial screens are occupied by the latest Hollywood productions. Quotas may resolve this problem, but they can encourage the production of cheaply made films that nobody wants to see.

The issues are not just political or economic. As Margaret Atwood has argued, a nation is not just a political entity but also "a state of mind," and film critics have often explored the ways in which films interact with discourses of national identity. State intervention can lead to overt propaganda, as in the case of Leni Riefenstahl's *Triumph of the Will* (1935), commissioned by Adolf Hitler to publicize the Nazi view of a true German national identity. In a much less sinister way, the NFB was established in Canada in 1939 "to help Canadians in all parts of Canada to understand the ways of living and the problems of Canadians in other parts." More interesting than these conscious attempts to express (or construct) a national identity are the indirect, and often inadvertent, ways in which films draw on the traditions and cultures of the nations in which they are made.

In discussions of national cinemas, critics look for common features and patterns of meaning that seem to express a sense of national identity, just as a genre critic might find evidence in westerns of deep-rooted assumptions about gender and community that have shaped American history. The risk involved in this kind of approach is that it can obscure the diversity of the national cinema, and it can lead to attempts to prescribe what films should be made rather than to describe or interpret the films that have been made. An adequate theory of national cinema cannot end up arguing that, for example, certain Canadian films are not really Canadian because they do not conform to a preconceived idea of the national identity.

The first major work of film criticism to focus on national identity was Siegfried Kracauer's *From Caligari to Hitler: A Psychological History of the German Film*, first published in 1948. Through close readings of German films, Kracauer argued that recurring plot structures and visual motifs reveal a fear of disorder and a desire for a strong authority figure, thus explaining why the Nazis had succeeded in mobilizing popular support. This book has been both influential and contentious, with its critics pointing to the circular argument it employs: The so-called national identity explains the films, while the films become evidence of the existence of this identity.

Yet there certainly are national myths that grow out of people's shared experience of history and geography and are then circulated and developed in the national culture. We are all influenced by these myths, whether or not we feel a close attachment to them, and they affect the choices made by both filmmakers and filmgoers. Because films can create such powerful effects of identification, a national cinema offers especially valuable insights into the working of these myths of national identity. In the case of Canadian cinema, the myths have tended to focus on a perceived lack of an identity capable of encompassing the diverse regions and cultural traditions that make up the nation. Questions about how the nation is represented in Canadian cinema have often been framed in terms of the relations between identity and a sense of place, a preoccupation that was supported by Northrop Frye's account of the "Canadian sensibility." Frye argued that Canadians are "less perplexed by the question 'Who am I?' than by some such riddle as 'Where is here?'"

In recent years, discussions of national cinema have been complicated by political, economic, and technological changes that have deeply affected our understanding of national identity. On the one hand, the power of nation states has been challenged by the emergence of multinational corporations and by new alliances among nations, such as the European Union and the North American Free Trade Agreement. On the other hand, nations have been faced with internal pressures from minority groups demanding independence, as exemplified in Canada by the aspirations of the separatist movement in Quebec.

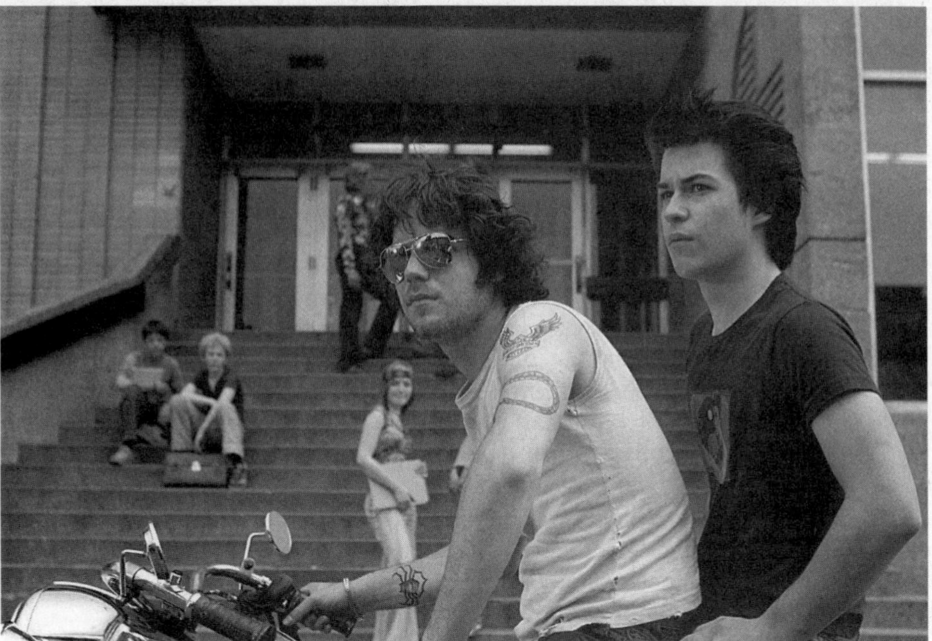

10-2. *C.R.A.Z.Y.* (2005), with Marc-André Grondin and Pierre-Luc Brillant, directed by Jean-Marc Vallée. Zac (Grondin) is the fourth of five sons whose first initials provide the acronym in the title of this box-office hit that has also gained recognition outside Quebec. The title also alludes to Patsy Cline's poignant song "Crazy." Cline is his father's favourite singer, but the song ironically evokes Zac's confusions as he grows up in a conflicted family during the 1960s and 1970s, the time of both the sexual revolution and social change in Quebec. With a religious mother who thinks he has "special" powers, Zac wants nothing more than to be "normal," which means living up to his father's code of masculinity. He refuses to acknowledge that he may be gay, and even pays his older brother Raymond (Brillant) to pick him up from school on his motorcycle to impress his classmates with his masculine credentials. *(Courtesy of the Everett Collection and Canadian Press)*

As a result of these developments, there has been a trend toward international coproductions in which investment from several nations allows films to be made with production values close to those that audiences have come to expect from Hollywood films. Despite some successes, the pressure to use actors from each participating nation means that this approach often results in films that lack a clear cultural identity. Movies produced through the European Union's fund to encourage coproductions have been called, disparagingly, "Europudding films. Yet the emergence of this new global image culture has also provided outlets for low-budget film and video productions from nations or groups that previously lacked the resources to tell their own stories.

The political and technological challenges to the myths, and even the existence, of nation states, have left many countries in the world facing a crisis of national identity with which Canadians have long been familiar. In this volatile situation, Canadian cinema provides an especially relevant example of the issues at stake in approaching film through the study of national cinemas.

According to Canadian filmmaker Patricia Rozema, "films are to society what dreams are to the individual." However, few Canadians seem to feel that their dreams are reflected in Canadian films. Most Canadian films enjoy only short runs at cinemas in Montreal, Toronto, and Vancouver, and they are rarely distributed at all in the rest of the country. When Canadians do see the products of their own national cinema, they often respond as if these were foreign films with unfamiliar conventions and cultural values. In Canadian video stores, Canadian films are often found in the "international" section.

To discover how and why this situation exists, we need to examine the economic and political aspects of the problem as well as the kinds of films that have been made. Economic factors obviously affect the choices made by filmmakers, but Canadian films exhibit distinctive formal qualities that cannot be accounted for only in economic terms. Nor should it be assumed that all Canadian films exhibit the same qualities. We are dealing with a much larger number of films than most Canadians would assume and with a great variety of styles. Any attempt to define the national cinema must deal in tendencies rather than in fixed categories.

10-3. *Men With Brooms* (2002), with (left to right) Paul Gross, Peter Outerbridge, Jed Rees, and James Allodi, directed by Gross.

When their former coach dies, four curlers reunite and, despite their extremely complicated personal lives, win the Golden Broom tournament against all odds, using a curling rock containing the coach's ashes. Gross, the popular star of the American television series *Due South*, was determined to make a commercial movie with winners rather than the losers familiar in many Canadian films (although these characters are very much in this tradition until their final improbable triumph). Alliance Atlantis provided a $1 million promotional budget, modest by Hollywood standards but unprecedented for a Canadian movie. *(Serendipity Point Films)*

Although a national cinema consists of all films produced within the national boundaries, most discussions focus on the feature films that tell the stories and develop the **iconography** that embody national myths. It is in the production of these films that the national cinema comes up most directly against Hollywood's cultural and economic power. Canada's geographical situation has made it especially vulnerable to this power, and Hollywood has historically insisted on treating Canada as part of its domestic market.

In Canada, films are produced in both official languages, and the language barrier divides what is already a relatively small domestic market. French-language production, centred primarily in Quebec, is clearly distinguished from Hollywood cinema by linguistic difference, but anglophone filmmakers have to define themselves in relation to a dominant cinema that speaks the same language. In addition, English-language production is more geographically dispersed, with large centres in Toronto and Vancouver and production companies in almost every region of the country.

Some critics have argued that Canada's bilingual cinema is a product of two cultures so distinct that we should really be speaking of two national cinemas, an argument that clearly parallels the political claims of Quebec separatists. The only

10-4. *Away from Her* (2006), with Julie Christie and Gordon Pinsent, directed by Sarah Polley.

Polley acted in Atom Egoyan's *Exotica* and *The Sweet Hereafter* (see **Colour Plate 16**) and went on to achieve an international reputation, working in Hollywood and Europe as well as in Canada. In her debut as a feature-film director, based on a short story by Canadian author Alice Munro, she shares Egoyan's preoccupation with the instability of memory, placed in the context of the contemporary concern with the ravages of Alzheimer's disease. As Fiona's memory deteriorates, she loses all sense of her identity, and her husband struggles to come to terms with his loss, haunted by his memories of their shared past. *(The Film Farm/Foundry Films Inc./The Kobal Collection)*

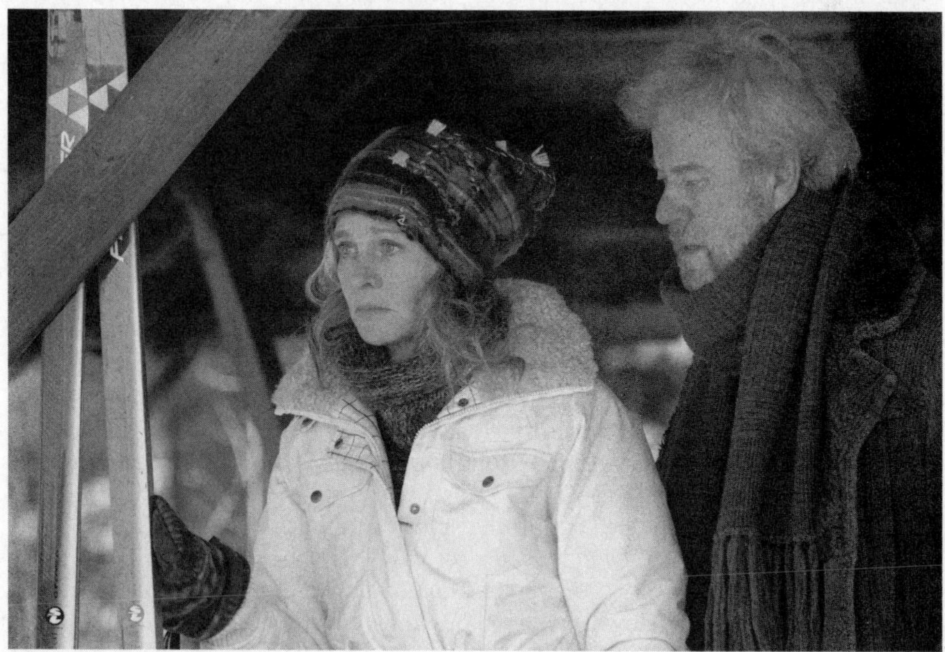

way to judge the validity of such a claim is to examine the history of Canadian cinema in both languages, discussing the specific qualities of the films in the context of the policies and institutions that have attempted to build a national cinema. For our purposes, this history can be divided into four stages:

1. What might be called the prehistory of Canadian cinema, during which there was little feature-film production in Canada.
2. A period beginning in the early 1960s, when the production of many small-budget films resulted in the establishment of the Canadian Film Development Corporation (CFDC) to invest in feature-film production.
3. A period roughly from 1974 to 1984 in which the CFDC, with the help of the Capital Cost Allowance Act, emphasized commercial goals and the need for films that could compete in the international market.
4. The period since 1984, when the CFDC changed its name to Telefilm Canada and encouraged the development of smaller-budget films that have established several Canadian filmmakers as major figures in world cinema.

We will look at each of these stages in turn.

THE FORMATIVE YEARS

The first film screenings in Canada took place shortly after the Lumière brothers had perfected their invention in 1895, but Canada was a large, sparsely populated country that lacked the resources to sustain its own film industry. Before Griffith's visit in 1925, there had been some sporadic feature-film production, beginning with *Evangeline* (1913), based on the poem by American poet Henry Wadsworth Longfellow, which deals with the expulsion of the French-speaking Acadians from Nova Scotia. Made by the Canadian Bioscope Company in Halifax, the film was directed by two Americans and had a largely American cast. A few more films followed, often produced under very difficult circumstances. The most notable of these were *Back to God's Country* (David M. Hartford, 1919) **(10-5)**, *Carry on Sergeant!* (Bruce Bairnsfather, 1928), and *The Viking* (George Melford, 1931).

The coming of sound added to the costs of filmmaking and virtually wiped out the production of feature films in Canada for the next forty years. Two short-lived bursts of activity only highlighted the difficulties of Canada's situation:

1. When Britain introduced a quota system in 1927, Hollywood immediately took advantage of a loophole in the legislation that allowed films made in the British Empire to be counted as British films. The studios established branch-plant operations in British Columbia where they made so-called "quota quickies" on very low budgets simply to fulfill the quota requirements. These films did at least provide some experience for Canadian filmmakers and were often better than their reputation suggests, but the loophole was closed in 1938, and this production boom came to an end.
2. After World War II, which cut off the supply of French-language films to Quebec, two domestic studios produced a series of very popular feature film. These films had the support of the Catholic Church and were usually set in traditional rural communities. However, they often dwelled on cruelty and perverse

10-5. *Back to God's Country* (1919), with Nell Shipman, directed by David M. Hartford.

Nell Shipman, who wrote, produced, and starred in the film, poses with a bear, one of the wild animals with whom the protagonist Dolores lives in harmony in an idyllic landscape ("God's country"). When the action moves to the "Great White North," an otherwise savage dog, Wapi, befriends Dolores and helps her save her husband from the villains. Although Shipman was born in Canada, *Back to God's Country*, shot on location in Alberta, was her only Canadian film, and the crew and cast were mainly imported from Hollywood. Her pioneering work has provoked much interest among feminist film historians.

behaviour, pointing to serious tensions in Quebec culture at this time **(10-6)**. The arrival of television in the early 1950s soon led to the closure of the Quebec studios.

When the Church and the conservative Union Nationale government gave their blessing to these Quebec productions, their intention was not just to provide wholesome local alternatives to Hollywood films, but also to counter the influence of the National Film Board. Under Grierson's guidance, NFB documentaries promoted a "pan-Canadian" viewpoint, stressing common concerns rather than regional differences and advocating the benefits of technological progress. These attitudes alarmed the authorities in Quebec, who wanted to preserve a traditional culture based on closeness to the land, but the NFB's perspective was shared by many younger people who were beginning the movement known as the Quiet Revolution, which would lead to a period of rapid change in Quebec.

When Grierson left Canada in 1945, he had already delivered his advice on the development of a national film policy. He urged the government to put pressure on Hollywood to live up to its "international obligations" and ensure that "a due

10-6. *La Petite Aurore, l'enfant martyre* [*Little Aurore's Tragedy*] (1951), with Lucie Mitchell and Yvonne Laflamme, directed by Jean-Yves Bigras.

Based on a successful play from the 1920s, this film was enormously popular with Quebec audiences. It relentlessly depicts the abuse of Aurore (Laflamme) by her stepmother, Marie-Louise (Mitchell). Although she knows that Marie-Louise poisoned her mother, Aurore suffers in silence until she dies, despite the well-meaning efforts of the village priest. Some critics have suggested that the film provoked such intense identification because Aurore's plight reflected that of the people of Quebec before the Quiet Revolution.

proportion of their films are devoted to Canada." The government duly entered into negotiations with the Hollywood studios, and the result was the Canadian Cooperation Project, which came into effect in 1948. In return for the government's agreement not to introduce a quota system, the studios promised to ensure that Canada was mentioned as often as possible in Hollywood films, to promote the tourist industry.

It seems likely that this agreement was responsible for a reference to Canada in the Howard Hawks western *Red River* (1948). When a group of cowboys become lost, they fear that they will end up driving their cattle "across the icebergs in Canada." In addition to such rather questionable attempts to promote tourism, Hollywood did agree to make a few films set in Canada, the most distinguished of which was *I Confess*, Alfred Hitchcock's thriller made in Quebec City in 1952. The agreement remained in effect until 1958.

THE DIRECT CINEMA TRADITION

The ending of the Canadian Cooperation Project coincided with the international triumph of the French New Wave. Using techniques and equipment originally developed for documentary filmmaking, François Truffaut, Jean-Luc Godard, and their colleagues showed a cheerful disregard for the rules of classical cinema and Hollywood production values. Their low-budget productions changed the economics of filmmaking and inspired young filmmakers in many countries to create or revive national cinemas. Several Canadian filmmakers rose to the challenge, and the early 1960s saw the production of many films made in difficult circumstances on shoestring budgets.

The young French filmmakers had paved the way for their own films by their work as film critics. Their Canadian counterparts were deeply influenced by the documentary tradition, and many of them had been involved in the development of **direct cinema** at the NFB in the 1950s. Whereas the French films often paid homage to Hollywood **auteurs**, the Canadians could not share this enthusiasm. From a documentary perspective, Hollywood films had always been viewed with suspicion as mass-produced escapist fantasies. For Canadian filmmakers, Hollywood was too close for comfort, the source of popular films with which the domestic output would inevitably be compared. Hollywood was also associated with the new consumer culture, which many Canadians saw as a sign of "Americanization." These early Canadian films explore all these issues, but—like the NFB's direct cinema documentaries (see Chapter 9, "Nonfiction Films")—they tend to raise questions rather than offer solutions.

The French New Wave had the advantage of belonging to an established national cinema and quickly achieved international recognition, but the Canadian filmmakers were faced with the task of creating a national cinema virtually from scratch, at least as far as fiction films were concerned. This was a question not only of the lack of producers and production facilities but also of finding an audience. Canadian cinemas were controlled by the Hollywood studios, and the spectators who did see these new Canadian films were often puzzled by the unfamiliar experience they offered.

There were some promising signs. A major breakthrough occurred in 1964 when two films, made under remarkably similar circumstances in Toronto and Montreal, were released. Both were, somewhat reluctantly, produced by the NFB despite its continuing commitment to documentaries. In Toronto, Don Owen used the budget for a half-hour documentary on juvenile delinquency to make *Nobody Waved Goodbye*, a largely improvised feature film on the same subject **(10-7)**. Meanwhile, in Montreal, Gilles Groulx managed to get approval to make a fiction film, *Le Chat dans le sac*, in which he sought to "eliminate the boundaries between documentary and fiction" **(10-8)**.

These two movies are often regarded as the founding films of a Canadian tradition of direct cinema fiction films, and critics have been divided over the implications of their similarities and differences. Groulx's film is more analytic and formalist in its style, in the manner of Godard's earlier films, while Owen's more observational and sometimes lyrical approach suggests the influence of Truffaut. Yet both films tell remarkably similar stories about adolescent males who rebel against the inadequate values of adult society.

10-7. *Nobody Waved Good-bye* (1964), with Julie Biggs and Peter Kastner (right), directed by Don Owen. Much of the enduring freshness of this film stems from its spirit of improvisation in both the dialogue and the filming of the action. At the end of the film, when Julie tells Peter that she is pregnant, Kastner had no idea what Biggs would be saying, and the look of surprise on his face is not acted. In the sequence illustrated, Peter plays chess with a French-Canadian youth (the actor was uncredited). He rejects the idea of a collective identity, which he thinks exists in Quebec, but he is not able to explain what his own values are. The sequence ends as his opponent says, "Your move, Peter." *(National Film Board of Canada)*

In *Nobody Waved Good-bye*, Peter is just finishing high school and engages in a self-destructive rebellion against the materialist values that his parents try to impose on him. In *Le Chat dans le sac*, Claude is trying to establish himself as a journalist and is more aware of the political context of his rebellion, reflecting the shift from a French-Canadian to a more confident Québécois identity associated with the Quiet Revolution. Yet even Claude is unable to translate this awareness into meaningful action, and declares, "I am Québécois; therefore I am searching."

Both films leave their heroes facing uncertain futures. Peter ends up alone on the road to nowhere in a stolen car after his girlfriend has just told him she is pregnant. Claude moves out of the city in an effort to simplify his life, effectively ending his complicated relationship with Barbara, a Jewish anglophone actress. He ends up standing in the snow, gazing at the distant figure of a young woman skating—an ambiguous ending that suggests the temptation to substitute an idealized image, associated with Quebec's rural past, for the messy reality of the modern urban world.

The breakup of a couple is also central to *À tout prendre* [*The Way it Goes*], Claude Jutra's first feature film, released in 1963, but virtually forgotten in the excitement generated by the two films of the following year **(3-18)**. In this case, the

10-8. *Le Chat dans le sac* [*The Cat in the Bag*] (1964), with Barbara Ulrich and Claude Godbout, directed by Gilles Groulx.

As in *Nobody Waved Good-bye*, the two main characters in this film share first names with the actors who portray them. The close relationship between actors and characters suggests that these fiction films could almost be seen as documentaries about actors who have experienced similar situations in their own lives. *(National Film Board of Canada)*

situation is more complicated, because Johanne is black and Claude (played by Jutra himself) is an adolescent (in spirit, at least) who belatedly discovers that he is gay. The film's realist conventions are frequently punctured by brief fantasy sequences that signal Jutra's doubts about the direct cinema approach and anticipate future developments in Canadian cinema.

The personal identity crisis of the male adolescent in all of these films can be seen as a metaphor for a country seeking to find terms on which it can develop a truly independent national identity. Other films in the same vein include Larry Kent's *Sweet Substitute* (1964) from Vancouver, David Secter's *Winter Kept Us Warm* (1965) from Toronto, and Pierre Patry's *Trouble-fête* [*Trouble Maker*] (1964) from Montreal. Two prolific Quebec directors also began their very different careers at this time. Gilles Carle made *La Vie heureuse de Léopold Z* [*The Merry World of Léopold Z*] (1965) at the NFB and went on to become a successful and often controversial director of films exploring the relations between sexuality and identity **(10-9)**. Jean Pierre Lefebvre's *Le Révolutionnaire* (1965) was produced independently and was quickly followed by a series of low-budget personal films in which politics, lyricism, and humour are provokingly blended **(10-10)**. Unlike their English-Canadian counterparts, these Quebec filmmakers enjoyed long careers in which their personal visions moved a long way from the direct cinema tradition.

10-9. *La Mort d'un bûcheron* [*Death of a Lumberjack*] (1972), with Carole Laure, directed by Gilles Carle.

The absent father is a recurring motif in Quebec literature and films, a reminder of pioneer times when men had to leave home to seek work, often in lumber camps. In Carle's film, Marie Chapdelaine (Laure)—named after the heroine of a classic Quebec novel—sets out in search of her father who disappeared in mysterious circumstances while working in a lumber camp. She frequently finds herself in situations where she becomes the object of men's gazes, as when she gets a job singing in a bar, and the film creates an uneasy tension between our condemnation of the male characters and the voyeurism we are invited to share. *(Les Films Gilles Carle, Inc.)*

Filmed on location and with a great deal of improvisation on the part of actors and crew, the direct cinema films tended to rely on long takes and jump cuts, making no attempt to emulate the production values and smooth continuity of Hollywood cinema. Their loose narrative structures, fragmentary presentation, and handheld shots reflected the uncertainty and insecurity of their protagonists. They preferred open, and often downbeat, endings to the closed and happy endings of most Hollywood films.

Many of these qualities disturbed Canadian critics and audiences. Yet, although none of the direct cinema films was a huge box-office success, together they aroused enough public interest—at a time when the Montreal Expo of 1967 provoked reflection on a Canadian cultural identity—to encourage the federal government to enact legislation in support of a national cinema. The Canadian Film Development Corporation (CDFC) was established in 1968 with a mandate "to foster and promote the development of a feature film industry in Canada." From the beginning, the CFDC was faced with two major problems:

10-10. *Les Maudits Sauvages* [*Those Damned Savages*] (1971), with Pierre Dufresne, directed by Jean Pierre Lefebvre.

In the opening sequence of Lefebvre's "almost historical film," Thomas Hébert (Dufresne) is seen trading with Aboriginal people in the year 1670. As he travels back from their camp, power lines and other signs of modernity begin to creep into the frame. At first, this seems like a terrible mistake, but then Hébert arrives in twentieth-century Montreal, and the film proceeds to use its anachronisms to explore the continuities and discontinuities over three centuries of Quebec history. *(Cinak Ltée)*

1. Should its primary objective be cultural or economic? Should it support distinctively and visibly Canadian films (like the direct cinema films), or should it focus on films with high production values and "international" appeal?
2. How could it ensure that the films in which it invested were actually shown in cinemas, when the government, under pressure from the Hollywood studios, would not introduce a quota system?

These problems are obviously interconnected and suggest more general questions that apply to all national cinemas: Are cultural and economic goals necessarily opposed? Does attention to local circumstances detract from the creation of films that will appeal to audiences in other countries?

The direct cinema filmmakers and their supporters insisted that the answer to both these questions should be "no." They argued that a national cinema must be rooted in the reality of the nation and, in Canada's case at least, the reality of the various regions that make up the nation. Only films with a distinct cultural identity can deal with issues in ways that will allow audiences elsewhere to relate them to their own cultural environment. If Canadian films tended to stress feelings of doubt and instability, then that was because Canada had not yet achieved unity and a clear sense of national identity (or, in Quebec, because the Quiet Revolution was not really over and because the question of independence was still unresolved). If their films were rarely popular, they blamed a distribution system that ensured the expectations of Canadian audiences were shaped by Hollywood films.

The CFDC wavered between support for this line of argument and a desire to invest in films with more immediate prospects of commercial success. Yet there were some signs that the insistence on cultural specificity might eventually pay off. The direct cinema movement was encouraged by the critical and commercial success of Don Shebib's *Goin' Down the Road*, a film about two young men from Cape Breton who come to Toronto in search of jobs, prove to be ill-equipped to handle the complications of life in the big city, and end up driving west in search of something better **(6-20)**. A little later, Jutra's *Mon oncle Antoine*, supported not by the CFDC but by the NFB, was hailed by several reviewers as "the great Canadian film," and it has since been repeatedly voted the best film ever made in Quebec and in Canada (see Chapter 12, "Writing about Film").

The focus on young men who are unable or unwilling to assume the responsibilities of adult life led critic Robert Fothergill to write an article in 1973 in which he argued that Canadian cinema was populated by cowards, bullies, and clowns. He attributed this crisis in masculine identity to the pressures of trying to live up to the potent images of American popular culture. Yet some of these films featured female protagonists, also usually adolescent. Clarke Mackey's *The Only Thing You Know* (1971) places its heroine in a situation very much like that of Peter in *Nobody Waved Good-bye*, with subtly different effects that could be attributed to the gender difference. Paul Almond made a trilogy of English-language films in Quebec—*Isabel* (1968), *The Act of the Heart* **(8-24)**, and *Journey* (1972)—all starring Geneviève Bujold, whose bilingualism suggested that the troubled characters she played in some way represented Canada's divided culture.

Almond's films gain their power from an unresolved tension between fantasy and reality. The first Canadian feature films by female directors also challenged the documentary tradition through their depiction of their protagonists' inner lives. In Sylvia Spring's *Madeleine Is . . .* (1970), filmed in Vancouver, a young woman finds herself caught between two men—her counter-culture boyfriend, who is revealed to be a bully, and an introverted youth who embodies the figure of a clown from her dreams. Mireille Dansereau's *La Vie rêvée*, deals with two young women who work for a film company where the males in authority treat females as objects **(10-11)**. Both films end with the women breaking free of their dependence on men, and both introduce fantasy sequences that are sometimes difficult to distinguish from reality.

All these films reflect a culture searching for norms of its own that could provide a basis for personal and national identity. In cinema, the established norms had come from Hollywood and were often used to point to the deficiencies of Canadian films. But the "failure" to be "normal" is not necessarily negative, for either the filmmakers or their characters: It implies the possibility of a different culture and different ways of seeing (see also **10-2**). A refusal to be normal would later become an even more overt marker of Canadianness in comedies such as *Outrageous!* **(10-12)** and *Perfectly Normal* (Yves Simoneau, 1990), an ironic title for a movie in which an inept brewery worker and part-time hockey player opens an Italian restaurant and overcomes his inhibitions by singing grand opera to his customers. The incongruities

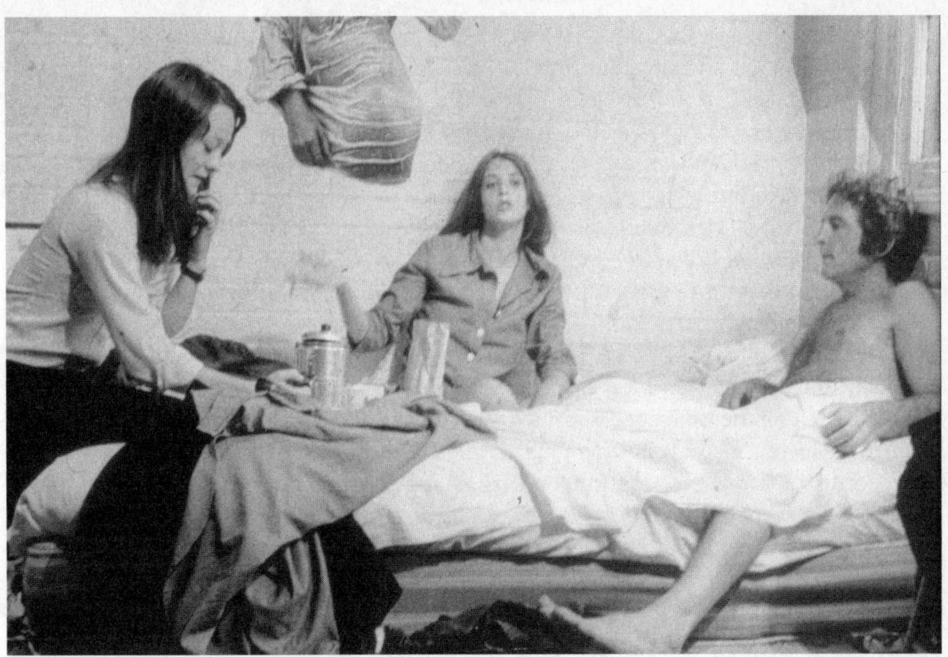

10-11. *La Vie rêvée* [*Dream Life*] (1972), with Véronique Le Flaguais (left), Liliane Lemaître-Auger, and Jean-François Guité, directed by Mireille Dansereau.

Shot in super-16 mm and produced by a cooperative, this film focuses on two women employed by a commercial film company, contrasting their working lives with their fantasy lives. As Dansereau put it, in this film "the dreams are true and as real as reality." Jean-Jacques (Guité) becomes the object of their fantasies, as an imagined perfect lover, but when Isabelle (Lemaître-Auger) seduces him, he proves to be impotent. The film ends as the women tear from their walls the advertising images that have colonized their minds. *(ACPAV)*

in these films paved the way for the current reputation for "weirdness" in Canadian cinema, a far cry from its realist beginnings.

Although the direct cinema tradition continues to be a significant factor in Canadian cinema, its influence is out of all proportion to the relatively small number of films that it produced. The myth that Canadian films are predominantly in the documentary-realist style has obscured the many films that adopt more commercial strategies as well as the rich tradition of the "fantastic" or "Gothic" to which some of the films already mentioned belong in varying degrees. It also underestimates the extent to which many of the direct cinema films, drawing on a tendency apparent in many of the NFB documentaries, call into question the realist tradition by calling attention to the difficulties involved in adequately representing reality.

CANADIAN GENRE FILMS

While the direct cinema films were incorporated into a critical canon for the national cinema, few of them were commercially successful. Recognizing the popular appeal of genre films, many Canadian filmmakers sought to adapt American genres to the Canadian situation. Among the first of these were two important English-Canadian examples released in 1973: Peter Pearson's *Paperback Hero*, in which a minor-league hockey player poses as the marshal of a small town in Saskatchewan **(10-13)**, and Don Shebib's *Between Friends*, which deals with an abortive armed robbery in a northern Ontario mining town. In both films, the American dream is betrayed by the Canadian context. Meanwhile, in Quebec, Denys Arcand directed a series of crime films—*La Maudite galette* **(7-23)**, *Réjeanne Padovani* (1973), and *Gina* (1974)—in which political corruption and violent crime act as metaphors for the tensions created by the independence debate and several terrorist bombings.

These, and other films like them, inflect the codes of American genres in distinctive ways that depend on their Canadian settings, although once again few achieved the goal of commercial success. Two other genre-based approaches proved more controversial but also attracted much larger audiences. In Quebec, a series of soft-core pornographic films was initiated by Denis Héroux's *Valérie* (1968), in which the heroine escapes from a convent, becomes a prostitute, and finally chooses to settle down with a painter and his young son. This film, which exploited new, liberal attitudes to sexuality, was a huge box-office success and inspired many imitators.

10-12. *Outrageous!* (1977), with Allan Moyle (left), Craig Russell, and Hollis McLaren, directed by Richard Benner.

Based on short stories by Margaret Gibson, this engaging film deals with the relationship between a flamboyant female impersonator (Russell) and a timid schizophrenic (McLaren). Their crises of personal and sexual identity typify the resistance to being "normal" found in many Canadian films. They are both victims of "straight" society in Toronto, and the film's happy ending is made possible only when they move to New York. The film was commercially successful but its sequel, *Too Outrageous!* (1987), was less so, perhaps because of the dark shadow cast over it by the impact of AIDS in the intervening decade. *(Bill Marshall)*

10-13. *Paperback Hero* (1973), with Keir Dullea, directed by Peter Pearson.

In Pearson's Canadian western, the fantasies of Rick Dillon (Dullea) are never seen from his point of view, and his attempt to act like Matt Dillon, the hero of the TV series *Gunsmoke*, seems rather pathetic. Canadian reality constantly fails to match up to the American dream. In the final shoot-out, "Marshal" Dillon confronts the town's sheriff, but the tension evaporates as a farmer drives his tractor down the street and calmly wishes him "Good day." Although he is a bully and a clown, Dillon has a vitality lacking in most of the other characters in the film.
(BBS Productions, Inc.)

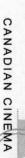

Héroux's production company, Cinépix, became identified with attempts to build a commercial cinema in Quebec based on the appeal of sex and violence.

The other controversial commercial success of these times was achieved by David Cronenberg, who became a key figure in the development of the modern horror film. His first feature film, known both as *Shivers* and *The Parasite Murders* (1975), was made with the support of the CFDC and sparked a debate over whether public money should have been invested in a lurid story of sexual parasites that prey on the inhabitants of an apartment building. It proved to be the beginning of Cronenberg's career as a filmmaker whose "body horror" films address anxieties about the effects of modern technology on the human body.

Whether Cronenberg's films explored or exploited these anxieties became a subject for debate, as did the question of their significance in relation to Canadian national cinema. They have often been discussed as American genre films, but some critics see thematic similarities with the direct cinema films, especially their concern with issues of identity and their open endings. Their obsessive treatment of the relations between biology and technology has certainly influenced many Canadian directors whose films deal with similar issues outside the horror-film framework.

Unlike several other Canadian filmmakers, Cronenberg did not leave the country to pursue commercial success, but his films rarely drew attention to their Canadian settings. *The Dead Zone* (1983) is explicitly set in the United States, although filmed in Canadian locations. Cronenberg's remake of the classic horror film *The Fly* (1986) was filmed in Canada with two young Hollywood stars (Jeff Goldblum and Geena Davis) but it never identifies the city in which it takes place, even though the 1958 original, filmed in Hollywood, was explicitly set in Montreal, perhaps in deference to the Canadian Cooperation Project. Although *Videodrome*, whose plot depends on cross-border television signals, has an explicitly Canadian setting **(10-14)**, the undistinguished cities of films like *Scanners* (1980) and *Dead Ringers* (1988) suggest that technology, based on the use of reason to control nature, has created an ordered and uniform environment that, among other things, eradicates distinctive national characteristics.

These varied attempts to create popular genre films led the CFDC to place more emphasis on the economic than on the cultural aspect of its mandate. This tendency was encouraged by the enactment in 1974 of the Capital Cost Allowance Act (CCA), which allowed investments in Canadian films to be claimed as a 100 percent tax

10-14. *Videodrome* (1981), with James Woods, directed by David Cronenberg.

The horror film has always drawn on fears of sexuality and death, but Cronenberg's "body horror" films combine these fears with contemporary concerns about the impact of technology on the body. In this film, Max Renn (Woods), the owner of an independent Canadian television station, is first fascinated by video images of sex and violence received by satellite from an unknown source, and then finds that his body has developed a video slot for tapes that can be used by a sinister corporation to program his actions. *(Copyright © 1981 by Universal City Studios, Inc. Courtesy of Universal Studios Publishing Rights. All Rights Reserved.)*

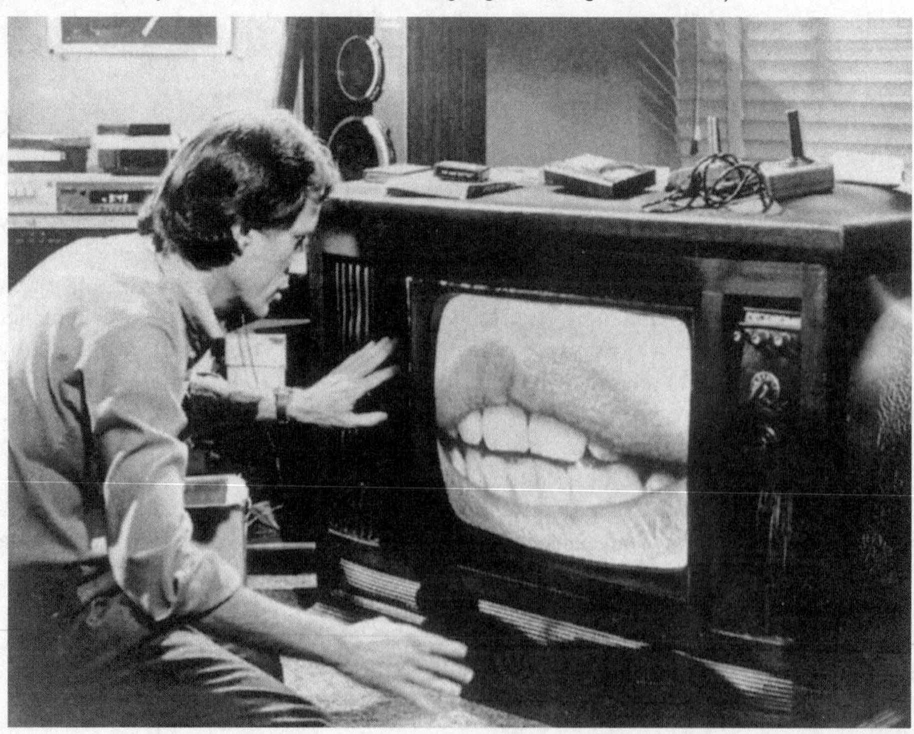

10-15. ***Pouvoir intime* [*Blind Trust*] (1986), with Marie Tifo and Pierre Curzi, directed by Yves Simoneau.** Like all good heist films, this one begins with the careful planning of the robbery, but a guard's upset stomach disrupts the plans, setting in motion a series of events that result in a final, bloody massacre. The use of English on the security van links the plot to the politics of language in Quebec, but also points to the betrayal of trust by the shady political figures who set up the robbery. At the end, two survivors meet in a ruined church to share the money, an ironic comment on Quebec's own betrayal of its past. *(Les Films Vision 4)*

shelter. Although there was an immediate increase in production activity, the need to attract investors who might be unfamiliar with Canadian cinema meant that many films were made with imported "stars" (usually young or aging Hollywood actors) and crew. Many films were never released, because even these supposedly commercial films could not resolve the distribution problem and, in any case, they had already fulfilled their function of providing tax relief for the investors. Although the complex regulations ensured that lawyers made profits, the Canadian direct cinema filmmakers were virtually excluded from these "boom" years.

Many of the films produced under the CCA were Canadian in name only; they masqueraded as Hollywood films, going to great lengths to conceal such identifying features as car licence plates. They were either set in some unidentified "nowhere" or their Canadian locations stood in for American settings. One of the more commercially successful films of this period was *The Changeling* (1979), a horror film voted "best film" at the Canadian Film Awards, which had a British director (Peter Medak) and an American star (George C. Scott), and whose locations in Ontario and Vancouver were labelled in the film as northern New York State and Seattle. The biggest box-office hit was *Porky's* (Bob Clark, 1981), an adolescent sex comedy set in Florida in the 1950s, whose cast included a few Canadian actors. On a more positive note, the CCA also supported *The Grey Fox* (Phillip Borsos, 1982), an ironic and

10-16. *Bon Cop, Bad Cop* (1998), with Colm Feore and Patrick Huard, directed by Erik Canuel. The plot of this popular crime film draws on Canada's linguistic divisions and the national obsession with hockey. Two cops, one from Toronto, the other from Montreal, investigate the murder of a man whose body is found beside the highway, lying across the sign indicating the boundary between Ontario and Quebec. The serial killer leaves clues that point to a vendetta against hockey officials whose business interests have weakened the Canadian teams. The film itself is bilingual, and the differences between the uptight English-Canadian cop and his much more casual Québécois counterpart correspond to stereotypes of the national identity, adapting similar antagonistic relations between partners in Hollywood crime films. *(Park Ex Inc. Pictures)*

moving western about an aging American train robber who tries to settle down in Canada.

Despite a few successes, there was general agreement that the CCA had failed to achieve its economic goals and certainly worked against the cultural distinctiveness of Canadian cinema. The Act was quietly allowed to lapse in the early 1980s. Canadian filmmakers continued to make genre films, however. In the 1980s, two films used the crime genre to reflect on the cultural and political tensions in Quebec, as Arcand had done in the 1970s. They appeared at a time when the rejection of "sovereignty-association" in the 1980 referendum marked a setback for the independence movement, provoking a political climate of doubt and disillusionment. In Yves Simoneau's *Pouvoir intime*, two government officials hire a gang of criminals to rob a security van in an attempt to retrieve a compromising document **(10-15)**. Jean-Claude Lauzon's *Un Zoo la nuit* [*Night Zoo*] (1987) begins as a violent story about an ex-convict harassed by corrupt police officers, but gradually shifts its focus to his reconciliation with his dying father, culminating in an absurd but strangely moving sequence in which the son tries to fulfill his father's desire to go on a moose hunt by taking him to a zoo, where he has to make do with shooting an elephant.

10-17. *Passchendaele* (Canada, 2008), with Paul Gross, directed by Gross.

In the opening battle sequence during World War I, Michael bayonets a German soldier in the head. The plot then jumps forward several months to show him convalescing in a hospital in Calgary, where he reveals that he received a medal but was so disgusted by his action that he went absent without leave. He falls in love with a nurse, and they have a whirlwind romance in idyllic Alberta landscapes before he returns to the wasteland of the trenches. In the final sequence, he tries to rescue her brother from no-man's land, and the action builds to an emotional climax that some critics rejected as unrealistic but that has a symbolic function as a broad anti-war statement. *(© Alliance Films/Courtesy Everett Collection/Canadian Press)*

In contemporary Canadian cinema, genre films still make a significant contribution to the film industry. Many are routine straight-to-DVD productions, but higher-profile films such as *Ginger Snaps* **(2-27)**, *Bon Cop, Bad Cop* **(10-16),** and Paul Gross's powerful war film *Passchendaele* **(10-17)** continue to provoke debate about whether the generic formats are appropriate in a Canadian context. Two Canadian films set during the Rwandan genocide of 1994—*Un Dimanche à Kigali/One Sunday in Kigali* (Robert Favreau, 2006) and *Shake Hands with the Devil* **(11-4)**—deal with Canadians caught up in the horrific events in Africa, inflecting the conventions of the political thriller and raising questions about Canada's role in an increasingly globalized cultural environment that places pressures on traditional ideas of nations as well as genres.

There has also been a movement towards **reflexive** genre films in which the ironic deployment of genre conventions relates the traditional Canadian question of "where is here" to a more global sense of identity crisis in world of electronic media and eroding national boundaries. Andrew Currie's zombie film *Fido* (2006) parodies genre conventions and 1950s Cold War propaganda to create a **pastiche** of affluent suburban life in which zombies are treated as pets and humans behave like zombies

10-18. ***Nothing*** **(2003), with David Hewlett (left) and Andrew Miller, directed by Vincenzo Natali.**

Following up on the success of *Cube* (1997), in which a disparate group of people find themselves mysteriously trapped in the featureless rooms of a giant cube-shaped structure, Natali created an ironic science-fiction movie that begins in a city clearly identified as present-day Toronto, albeit in a stylized version that evokes the distortions of German expressionism (see **4-17**). Dave (Hewlett) and Andrew (Miller) cannot function in the urban environment and take refuge in their ramshackle home beneath a network of highways. The cluttered **mise en scène** gradually disappears as they wish away the contents of the house and then the house itself, until they find themselves alone in a vast empty space. Northrop Frye's Canadian question of "Where is here?" takes on new meaning in a global culture increasingly filled with virtual and digital imagery.

(49th Parallel/Alliance Atlantis/The Kobal Collection/L. Pief Weyman)

(Colour plate 14). Other recent films have built on Don McKellar's ironic dampening down of science-fiction conventions in *Last Night* **(2-26)** to create a distinctive Canadian subgenre. Gary Burns's *A Problem with Fear* (2003) draws us into the world of a young man whose paranoid fears of his urban environment are fed and heightened by a security firm's advertising campaign. In Vincenzo Natali's *Nothing*, two similarly dysfunctional males find they can wish away each other's possessions and even body parts until they find themselves reduced to bodiless heads in a pure white emptiness **(10-18).**

CANADIAN CINEMA SINCE TELEFILM

In 1984, the CFDC changed its name to Telefilm Canada, in recognition of the increasing importance of television as a medium in its own right, and as a means of resolving the distribution problems that had always plagued Canadian cinema.

Canadian content requirements (in effect, a quota system) had long been a condition of broadcasting licences in Canada, and television became an increasingly important outlet for Canadian filmmakers. With the introduction of pay-TV and specialty satellite channels, the demand for program material increased enormously, not just in Canada but also worldwide, and the growing home video market also proved to be a significant source of revenue. In the years that followed, genre films remained an important part of the increasingly diverse output of the Canadian film industry; but Canada also became known for more personal "art" films that took an innovative approach to film language and explored controversial themes, often related to questions of sexuality and identity. Many of these films premiered at international festivals, and they were often more appreciated abroad than in Canada.

One of the first, and most spectacular, successes of this new approach was Patricia Rozema's first feature film, *I've Heard the Mermaids Singing* **(10-19)**. It was produced on a budget of $350 000, raised with great difficulty from numerous sources (including Telefilm), but it went on to gross more than $6 million worldwide. The film's appeal depends largely on its central character, Polly, a touchingly inept "person Friday" who becomes infatuated with the female art gallery curator for

10-19. *I've Heard the Mermaids Singing* (1987), with Sheila McCarthy, directed by Patricia Rozema.

The film begins when Polly turns on the video camera she has stolen from the art gallery where she works. She addresses it directly but places herself slightly off-centre, suggesting that she cannot see herself as the centre of even her own story. Verbally, Polly's clumsy attempts to explain herself contrast with the articulate but sterile language of the art world, just as her photographs of everyday reality (pinned to the wall behind her) contrast with the sublime painting she finds in the curator's house (and which is represented only by the bright glowing light that it emits). *(Patricia Rozema)*

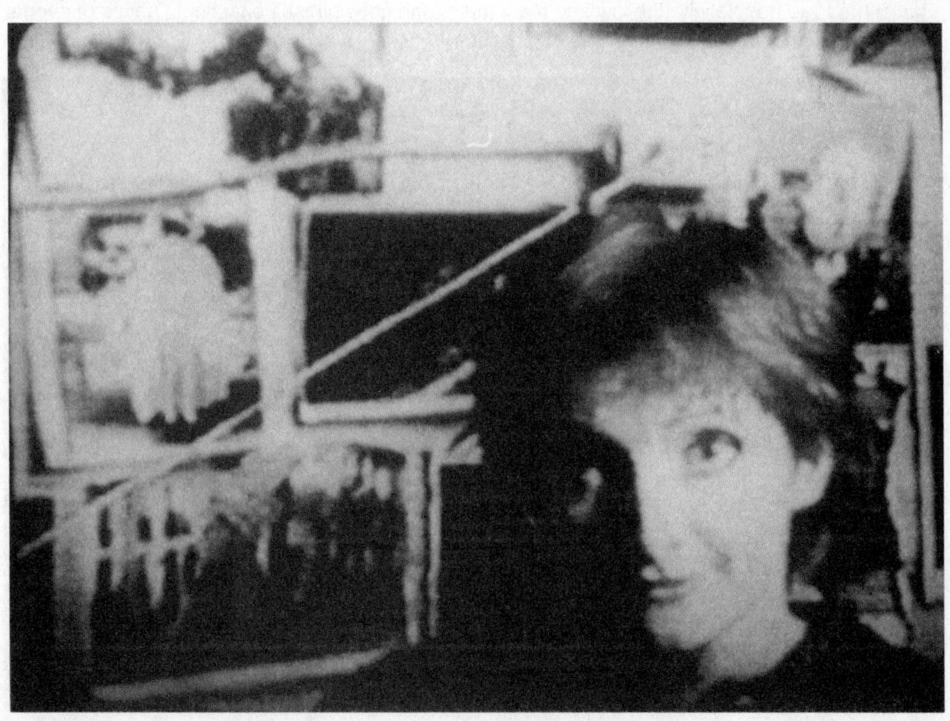

whom she works. The way the story is told gives the film its unusual flavour, as it weaves together video images of Polly's narration, flashbacks that illustrate her account of events, and fantasy sequences in which she defies gravity by flying above the city and walking on water.

After working in documentary and television during the CCA years, Denys Arcand made a triumphant return to feature filmmaking with *Le Déclin de l'empire américain*, in which a group of women work out at a health spa and then enjoy an elaborate meal cooked by their male friends **(4-13)**. The film's gender reversals and its sexual frankness brought Arcand an invitation to direct an English-language remake in Hollywood (a project that eventually came to nothing). For the Quebec audience, an even more remarkable feature is that these characters are historians, but their witty conversation is marked by the virtual absence of any reference to Quebec's past or future, although, in a lecture in a pre-credits sequence, one professor effectively dismisses the prospects for independence.

Arcand, who studied history at university, achieved another success with *Jésus de Montréal*, in which an actor, attempting to modernize a traditional play, investigates the historical truth behind the story of Christ **(10-20)**. The play's new version of the story restores the emotional power of Christ's message for many who see it, but it is rejected by church authorities and hilariously misinterpreted by the critics

10-20. *Jésus de Montréal* [*Jesus of Montreal*] (1989), with Johanne-Marie Tremblay (left), Lothaire Bluteau, and Catherine Wilkening, directed by Denys Arcand.

Following up on the international success of *The Decline of the American Empire*, which focused on the material pleasures of eating and sex, Arcand took on Quebec's spiritual state in this film. Daniel Coulombe (Bluteau) plays Jesus in a contemporary version of the Passion Play presented on Mount Royal. In his attempt to create a version of Jesus relevant to life in the modern city, Daniel runs into trouble with the law and the church, and finds himself enacting a series of events in his own life that uncannily mirror the original story. *(Max Films Inc.)*

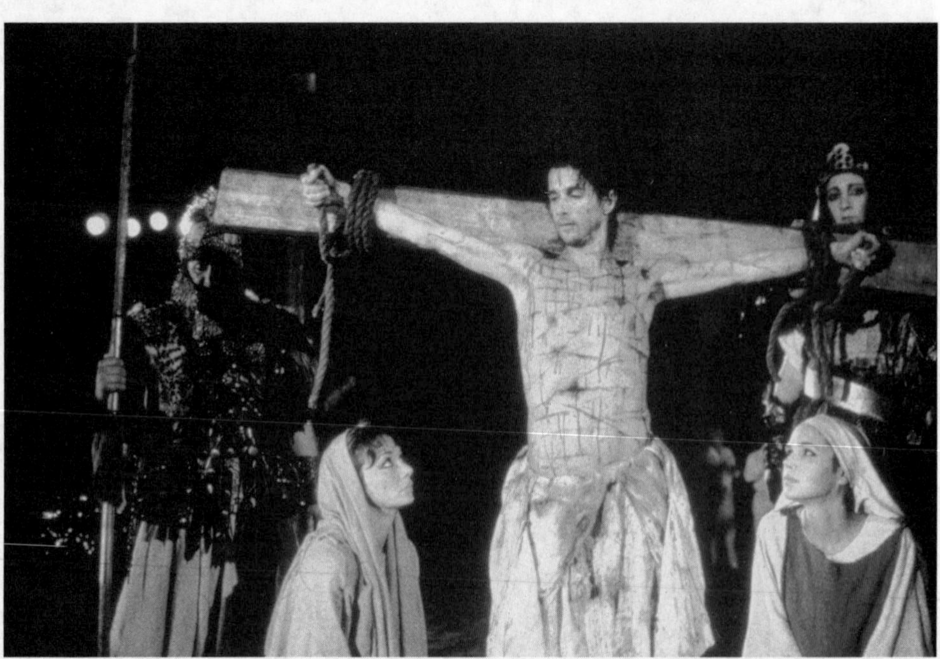

who constitute the "church" of modern media. The film becomes an exploration of the relations between acting and truth, even as it depicts the exploitation of actors by a culture in which advertising and pornography are the major outlets for their talents.

The new policies at Telefilm also contributed to the emergence of Atom Egoyan as the most prolific and influential of a new generation of English-Canadian filmmakers. Egoyan's films are centrally concerned with the ways in which we use images in an effort to fix our identities. In many of these films, he contrasts the permanence and intensity of film images with grainy video images that can be more easily used for storing memories but that are also subject to instant erasure. In *Next of Kin* (1984), *Family Viewing* **(4-9)**, and *Calendar* (1993), Egoyan draws on his own Armenian background to develop ironic and moving stories about the erosion of ethnic roots in modern urban environments. All these films, as well as *Speaking Parts* **(3-21)**, *The Adjuster* (1991), *Exotica* **(11-13)** and *The Sweet Hereafter* (**Colour Plate 16**) also explore the ways in which technology and media images affect people's sexual experience and fantasy lives.

The revival of English-Canadian cinema during this period also revealed the continued vitality of regional filmmaking. Two early successes were Anne Wheeler's *Loyalties* from Alberta and Sandy Wilson's *My American Cousin* from British Columbia **(11-18)**, both released in 1985. Both films work within the realist tradition, but two other regional directors made important contributions to the movement away

10-21. *Life Classes* (1986), with Jacinta Cormier, directed by William MacGillivray.

MacGillivray's films are understated but deceptively complex character studies that explore the ways in which identity is shaped by environment and, increasingly in the modern world, by the media. *Life Classes* deals with a single mother who seeks her own independence and identity as an artist at a time when the electronic communications media are transforming both the remote Cape Breton community, in which she lives, and the values traditionally associated with high art. *(Picture Plant Ltd./David Middleton)*

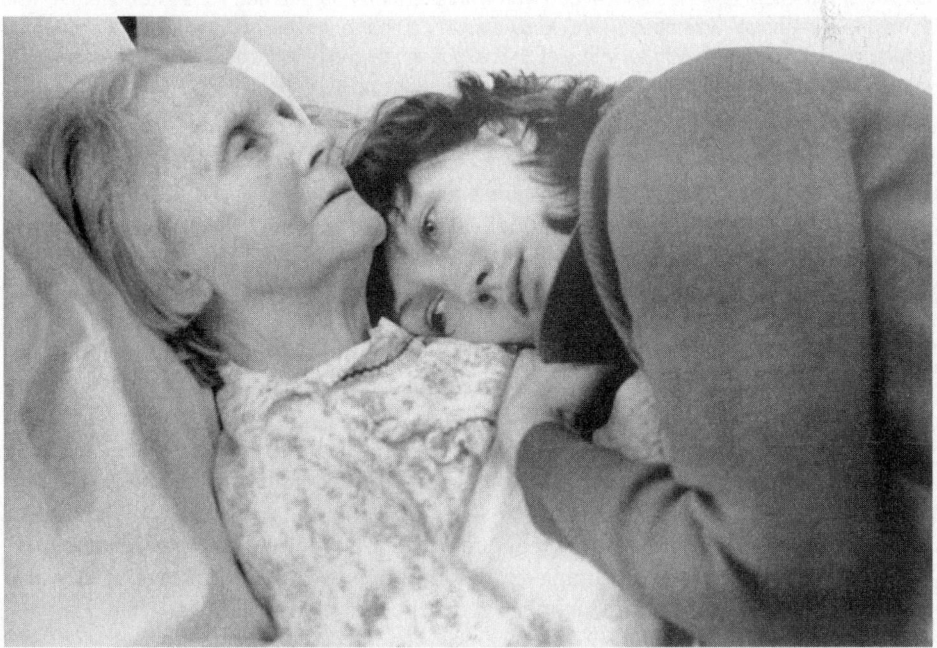

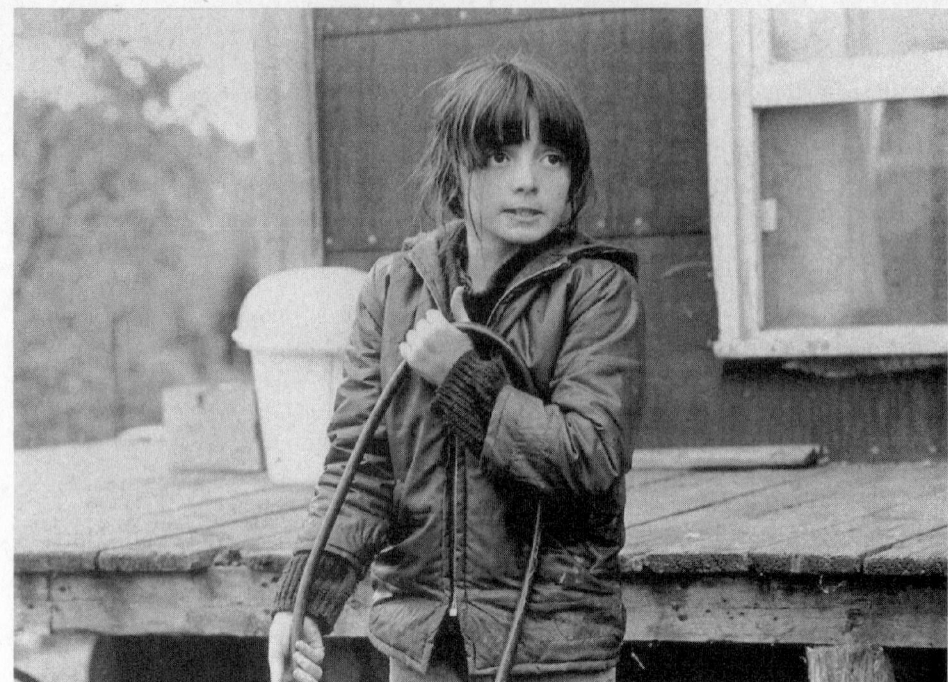

10-22. *Les Bons débarras* [*Good Riddance*] (1979), with Charlotte Laurier, directed by Francis Mankiewicz.

At a time when Quebec filmmakers were under strong pressure to make their films in English, Mankiewicz enjoyed great acclaim for this film, whose roots are firmly planted in Quebec's francophone culture. It centres on the ruthless efforts of Manon (Laurier) to keep her mother's love to herself. In the Quebec tradition, there is no father, but Manon is jealous of her retarded uncle, who lives with them, and of the local cop who wants to marry her mother. Réjean Ducharme, who wrote the screenplay, was already well known as the author of novels and plays about children who pursue their desires with an intensity that exposes the compromises and inhibitions of the adult world. Mankiewicz and his actors perfectly catch the spirit of the writer's vision.
(Les Productions Prisma)

from this tradition. The films of William MacGillivray, based in Nova Scotia, quietly undermine their realist surfaces through a reflexive concern with the way images work in our culture **(10-21)**; and, in Manitoba, Guy Maddin has made a series of films that create their own bizarre worlds, rejecting any form of realism **(1-28, 9-20)**.

Although realist films and genre films continued to be made, the new policies encouraged the development of a Canadian "art cinema" that quickly built an international reputation. The distinction between popular cinema and art cinema is in many ways an artificial one, and one that is becoming increasingly difficult to maintain in the contemporary media environment, but the latter has become associated with the idea of film as personal expression. Emphasis is placed on the filmmaker as auteur (see Chapter 11, "Theory"), although it should be noted that the *Cahiers du cinéma* critics who originated the auteur theory felt that it applied to their favourite Hollywood directors as well as to filmmakers with more personal control over their work. The new approach at Telefilm emphasized exposure at international film festivals,

10-23. ***Au Clair de la lune* [*Moonshine Bowling*] (1982), with Guy L'Écuyer (left) and Michel Côté, directed by André Forcier.**

Forcier's darkly comic vision owes much to the long surrealist tradition in Quebec culture. His characters tend to live in fantasy worlds, but the boundaries between fantasy and reality are very difficult to define, as they are in the very different films of David Cronenberg. This film develops its surreal vision around the friendship between two homeless men: Albert (L'Écuyer), a former bowling champion, and François (Côté), an albino from "Albinia" who dreams of returning to his own imaginary country. *(Bernard Lalonde)*

although many films still did not secure widespread distribution even after achieving success on the festival circuit. Since art cinema privileged films in languages other than English, Quebec fit more easily into this category; and indeed, the developments at Telefilm were anticipated in Quebec, where modest productions dealing with the intimate lives of troubled characters became an alternative to both genre films and films that overtly engaged with ongoing political debates (see **8-25** and **10-22**).

In Quebec, there has been a rich surrealist tradition that also explores the boundaries between fantasy and reality. This tradition is very apparent in the films of André Forcier **(10-23, Colour Plate 10)**, who was once known as the "enfant terrible of Quebec cinema." The term has also been applied to Jean-Claude Lauzon, whose delirious reimagining of his own childhood in *Léolo* provoked considerable controversy. In this film, Léo, a French-Canadian boy, understandably rejects his abject working-class family and lives instead in a dream world in which he imagines his father as an Italian. His visions of a sun-drenched Sicilian landscape contrast with the dark Montreal slum in which he lives and imply that the Italian community has cultural roots that Quebec now lacks. Although Léo finally succumbs to the mental illness that afflicts his family, the film celebrates the power of the imagination to transcend cultural limitations, largely through its "mosaic" style, mixing a few

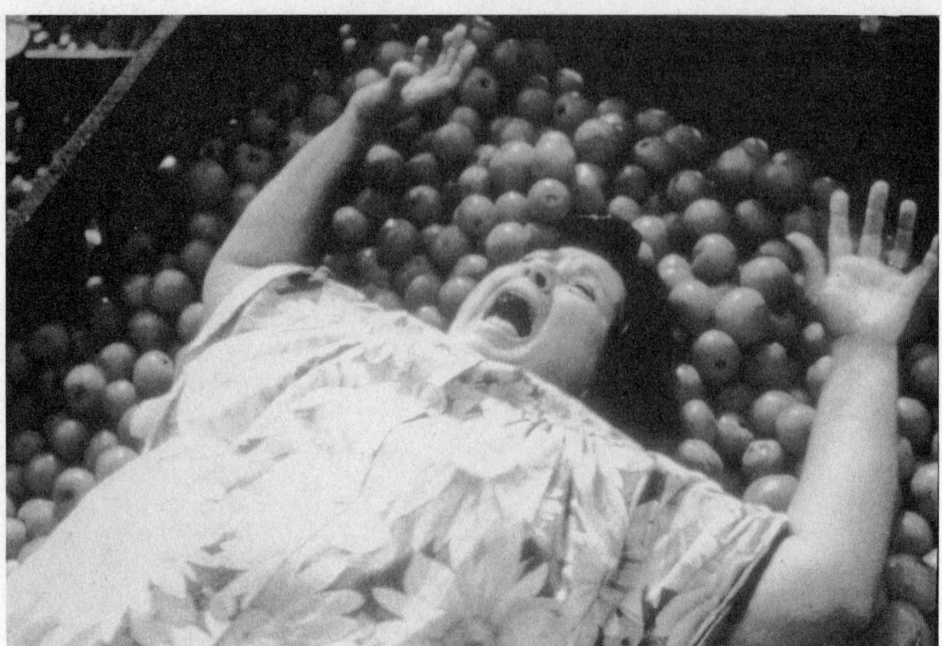

10-24. *Léolo* (1992), with Ginette Reno, directed by Jean-Claude Lauzon.

In his dream life, Léo Lozeau imagines that he is an Italian, Léolo Lozone, conceived when his mother (Reno) fell into a pile of tomatoes contaminated with the semen of a masturbating Sicilian farm worker. Lauzon, who had an abrasive personality that often got him into trouble with the Quebec media, based the film on his memories of his own childhood, heavily filtered through his vivid imagination. Lauzon died when his small plane crashed in 1997. For a fascinating account of his life and films, see Louis Bélanger's feature-length documentary *Lauzon/Lozone* (2002). *(Alliance Communications)*

allusions to Quebec culture with a jumble of quotations that range from the chanting of Tibetan monks to the music of Tom Waits. Many critics in Quebec found the film offensive, but the real scandal of *Léolo* is that the "normal" world is even more absurd than Léo's fantasies **(10-24)**.

TOWARD A POST-NATIONAL CINEMA?

In the twenty-first century, the traditions of Canadian cinema have been challenged and broadened even further to take in response to the multicultural dimension of Canadian society as well as the impact of cultural globalization and new technologies. These changes complicate earlier debates around the relations between English and French, between realism and formalism, and between cultural and economic objectives.

The late twentieth century was marked, in Canada as in many other nations, by the growth of communities formed by migrants and exiles from countries affected by war, oppression, famine, and poverty. An official "policy of multiculturalism within a bilingual framework," announced in 1971 by the government of Pierre Trudeau, was intended to promote "national unity . . . founded on confidence in one's own individual identity." The NFB responded by producing numerous documentary and fiction films on various ethnic and racial groups, but these films, which tended to stress social problems and efforts to overcome them, have been described by critic Cameron Bailey as a "cinema of duty." However, a series of films made by members of these groups has encouraged what critic Peter Harcourt has called a movement from "the dual cinema of the past to a cinema of cultural diversity."

A number of influential films from the 1990s engaged with the hybrid identities emerging from the diasporic communities. Srinivas Krishna's *Masala*, for example, is a flamboyant satire on an official policy that sees the culture of ethnic communities as folklore to be preserved in museum conditions **(10-25)**. As the director and in the role of the film's disaffected hero, Krishna is also critical of the Indian community, which goes along with this patronizing attitude. By mixing together many genres and stereotypes, Krishna suggests that we live in a world full of cultural contradictions in which it is no longer possible to believe that stories can make sense of the world. Other examples of **diasporic cinema** include Deepa Mehta's *Sam and Me* (1990), a gently comic film about a young Indian immigrant who gets a job caring for an old Jewish man whose family is unable to control him; Mina Shum's *Double Happiness*

10-25. *Masala* (1991), with Saeed Jaffrey (centre) and Les Porter, directed by Srinivas Krishna.

Krishna insists that his films are not part of the traditions of Canadian cinema. "That kind of nation-state way of dividing culture is irrelevant to my personal experience," he says. Just as a "masala" in Indian cooking is a mixture of spices that combine to create a distinctive flavour, *Masala* is a montage of different styles, including musical numbers in the style of popular Indian (Bollywood) movies, to expose the pressures of living in a multicultural society as they affect different generations of the community. Although it satirizes official multiculturalism, as embodied by the pompous Minister (Porter), the film suggests that, in an increasingly globalized culture, identities are becoming mixtures of diverse traditions and influences. *(Divani Films)*

10-26. *Bollywood/Hollywood* (2002), with Lisa Ray, directed by Deepa Mehta.

Mehta's Indian films ran into violent opposition because of their critique of fundamentalist religious oppression. Her response was this colourful satire on intolerance and prejudice, whose title playfully relegates Canada—the film is set in Toronto—to the slash separating the traditions of popular Indian musicals and Hollywood melodrama that collide with each other in the film. Lisa Ray was born in Toronto but could not find enough work to pursue her acting career in Canada. She went to India, where she achieved superstar status as a model and then began to make movies. *(Mongrel Media)*

(1994), a wry comedy about the dilemmas of an aspiring actress who lives at home in Vancouver with her Chinese family; and Clement Virgo's mystical film noir *Rude*, set in Toronto's Jamaican community **(2-4)**. For such diasporic filmmakers, the question "Where is here?" is translated into the closely related one of "Where is home?"

The situation in Quebec has been rather different because the Québécois identity that emerged from the Quiet Revolution was so tied to the French language and to Quebec's history that immigrants and ethnic communities seemed to be excluded by definition. There was concern that immigration would lead to an erosion of this identity, and the "ethnic vote" became a contentious issue in the 1995 referendum in which the independence option was narrowly defeated. The rapid growth of the Italian community, in particular, caused an anxiety reflected in Lauzon's *Un Zoo la nuit*, in which the father's apartment is being gradually taken over by an expanding Italian restaurant. The relations between the Italian community in Quebec and the French majority were explored from the Italian perspective in the films of Paul Tana, who was born in Italy (see **4-11**). In more recent productions, the influence of the diasporic communities on Quebec culture is beginning to be explored in ways that are more open to new forms of identity.

Another challenge to the traditional concept of national cinema is provided by the recent work of Deepa Mehta. She returned to her native India to make *Fire* (1997), which sparked a major scandal there because of its depiction of the oppression of women in Indian families, and of the lesbian relationship that develops between its two main characters. *Earth* (1999), dealing with the violent partition of India at the end of British colonial rule, proved equally controversial and, when religious riots interrupted the shooting of *Water* (2005), the third film in her Indian trilogy, Mehta returned to Canada to make *Bollywood/Hollywood*, a light-hearted and optimistic celebration of the hybrid forms of identity that form within diasporic cultures **(10-26)**.

As well as incorporating influences from other cultural traditions, Canadian cinema is now also beginning to respond to the experience of Aboriginal peoples, who have been subjected to a kind of internal diaspora. The making of *Atanarjuat: The Fast Runner*, the first feature film in the Inuktitut language, became possible only after its producers had challenged the funding practices at Telefilm, whose budget was divided between English- and French-language productions **(10-27)**. Using digital video cameras, the filmmakers drew on the skills of indigenous artists to create the costumes and props needed to present a legendary story of the distant past.

The cultural traditions in *Atanarjuat* and its depiction of elemental struggle in the vast Arctic landscape are especially attractive in a world in which new developments in communications technology and politics are constantly changing our cultural environment. After the success of this first film, its makers followed up with *The Journals of Knud Rasmussen* (2006), which, despite its title, depicts an encounter between an Inuit community and Danish explorers in the 1920s from the Inuit point

10-27. *Atanarjuat: The Fast Runner* (2000), with Natar Ungalaaq, directed by Zacharias Kunuk.

The remarkable images of the hero running naked across the ice to escape his enemies are part of a story that has been handed down from generation to generation. Kunuk was the first of his family to live in a permanent settlement (Igloolik), and he used the latest digital technology to re-create the traditions of oral storytelling. *(Igloolik Isuma Productions Inc.)*

of view. In Quebec, *Ce qui'l faut pour vivre/The Necessities of Life* (Benoît Pilon, 2008), starring the lead actor from *Atanarjuat*, deals with the culture shock experienced by an Inuit man isolated in a Quebec hospital in the 1950s. That neither of these historical films made the same impact as what one critic called the "unmistakably authentic myth" in the first film, points to the tension between the desire for authenticity and the more common experience of hybrid identities that is central to Canadian cinema. Of course, this tension is not unique to Canada and is very much part of the "postmodern condition" (see Chapter 11, "Theory").

The portrayal of characters who feel detached from their environment and are searching for a sense of cultural identity has a long history in Canadian cinema, going back at least to the direct cinema films. In more recent films, however, the search often involves an immersion in imaginary worlds and sexual experimentation. As a result, Canadian cinema has gained a reputation for "weird sex" and grotesque imagery. In particular, recent Canadian movies have extended the traditional Canadian concern with problems of identity to encompass an exploration of the relations of fantasy, memory, and technology. Although the influence of the direct cinema tradition is still apparent, there has been a marked emphasis on fantastic, bizarre, and extreme images and stories. As a result, Canadian films have often faced censorship problems at home and abroad: The British attempt to ban Cronenberg's *Crash* is just one of the most notorious examples **(Colour Plate 12)**. Of course, the pleasure of watching car crashes is a staple of Hollywood cinema, and the perversity shown in films like *Crash* is that they raise disturbing questions about activities that are culturally accepted as "normal."

Although his interest in imaginary obsessions and distortions once made him seem a marginal figure in the context of the national cinema, Cronenberg now seems absolutely central. In his films of the 1990s, he moved away from the horror film genre but not from his concern with bodies and minds in the grip of irrational forces: Bill Lee's drug-induced hallucinations in *Naked Lunch* (1991); René Gallimard's refusal to admit to himself in *M. Butterfly* (1993) that the Chinese actress he loves is really a man; and the characters' obsessive desire to repeat the contact of metal and flesh in *Crash*. In *eXistenZ*, Cronenberg playfully explores the erasure of the distinction between image and reality as his characters find themselves caught inside the simulated worlds of a bizarre game system **(2-7)**.

The main character in David Wellington's *I Love a Man in Uniform* also escapes into a world of his own imagining. He is an actor who gets a part in a television cop show and starts to wear his uniform on the streets, gradually losing the ability to distinguish fiction from reality **(10-28)**. In some ways, this film resembles *Paperback Hero* **(10-13)**, whose protagonist also masquerades as an authoritative male figure from an American genre; the difference is that Wellington draws us into his character's obsessions, so that we often share his disorientation.

The cop show is a parody of the Americanized crime series often seen on Canadian television and set in anonymous North American cities. Yet, the "real" police do not notice any difference from their own uniforms when the actor wears his costume on the streets of Toronto. The film thus plays on the sense of placelessness that became a characteristic of English-Canadian cinema during the CCA years. Originally a device designed (usually in vain) to secure commercial success, the anonymous location was also employed by other directors, including Egoyan, to suggest the alienation of the characters from their environment. Although Quebec films are

10-28. *I Love a Man in Uniform* (1993), with Tom McCamus, directed by David Wellington.

As in *Jesus of Montreal*, the protagonist in this film is an actor who identifies with his role, with tragic results. As in *Paperback Hero*, the protagonist is a Canadian who adopts the masculine style of an American genre hero. Henry (McCamus) is torn between his desire to be an actor and the security of his job in a bank. When he gets a role in a TV cop show, made in Canada but made to look American, he finds that his fictional uniform gains him acceptance by real cops on the city streets. The city is clearly Toronto, but it comes to seem as anonymous and unreal as the location of the TV show. *(Miracle Pictures)*

usually more culturally specific than most of their English-Canadian counterparts, some films, including *Léolo*, give the impression that Quebec's failure to become a "nation" portends its geographical disappearance. Denis Villeneuve's *Maelström* sets its story of a modern woman's crisis of identity in present-day Montreal, but the specific location is contradicted by the use of a grotesque fish as the narrator and by the inclusion of captions in Norwegian and even a specially composed cantata in the same language **(2-6)**.

In complete opposition to this development, filmmakers in Quebec have produced a number of enormously popular comedies, notably *Les Boys* (Louis Saia, 1997) and *C't à ton tour Laura Cadieux* [*It's Your Turn Laura Cadieux*] (Denise Filiatrault, 1998) and their sequels, whose huge popularity depended on the playful celebration of specific Québécois stereotypes previously seen as demeaning. There have also been some attempts to replicate this success by English-Canadian filmmakers (see **10-3**). There has also been a series of popular Quebec heritage films that revive traditional versions of the francophone cultural identity. *Un Homme et son péché* [*Séraphin: Heart of Stone*] (Charles Binamé, 2002), a colourful historical melodrama about a miser oppressing young lovers in a remote community, was a remake of one of the most successful films of the period after World War II, and the historical events that inspired *La Petite Aurore* **(10-6)** were also retold in *Aurore* (Luc Dionne, 2005). Some of these films were enormously popular, outdrawing Hollywood blockbusters in Quebec, but critics were not impressed, complaining that Telefilm's funding policies encouraged formula filmmaking rather than auteur cinema. Yet Quebec still produces an impressive number of accomplished art films, including Denys Arcand's *Les Invasions barbares* [*The Barbarian Invasions*] (2003)—a belated sequel to *The Decline of the American Empire*—which won the award for best screenplay at the Cannes Film Festival and the Academy Award for best foreign-language film.

The question of "Where is here?" still resonates strongly in English-Canadian cinema. The films of Gary Burns, for example, depict a modern urban environment in which traditional landmarks have been replaced by anonymous office blocks and suburbs. His *waydowntown* is set in a Calgary shopping mall full of generic stores that could be found anywhere in North America **(10-29)**, and his documentary *Radiant City* (2006) offers a vision of suburban sprawl that was also filmed in Calgary, even if this is not apparent until the end. And the city that threatens the paranoid pro-

10-29. *waydowntown* (2000), with Jennifer Clement, directed by Gary Burns.

Four office workers make a bet on who can avoid going outdoors longest. Filmed in Calgary's Plus 15 system of buildings connected by indoor walkways, the actual location is apparent from a few passing indications, but the glass and concrete architecture of the office buildings and shopping mall could be in any modern city. As in many recent Canadian movies, the lack of specific landmarks expresses the characters' sense of detachment from their environment, but the film also treats the situation playfully through the main character's fantasies about a super-hero protecting the city. Here the confinement leads to hallucinations, and even those workers not in on the bet find themselves venting their frustrations in public. *(Lot 47 Films/Courtesy of the Everett Collection and Canadian Press)*

tagonist of *A Problem With Fear* is a hybrid made up of Calgary's city centre and Montreal's metro system.

The sense that globalization is eroding already insecure national identities is apparent not only in the hybrid identities explored in diasporic cinema and in films set in anonymous urban landscapes, but also in those films that seek to reassert older forms of identity (see **10-30**). It is increasingly clear that discussions of national cinemas—and the development of national film and media policy—must take the global context into account. The situation is even further complicated by elaborate coproductions like *The Red Violin* **(10-31)** and by the exchange of filmmakers among national cinemas. Are Deepa Mehta's Indian films to be seen as Canadian? Egoyan, Rozema and Cronenberg have all made films in Britain that explore themes and use **motifs** familiar from their earlier, Canadian-made films. Egoyan and Cronenberg have also both made films set wholly in the United States: Egoyan's *Where the Truth Lies* (2005) is a Canadian production filmed in Canada and Britain as well as the United States, while Cronenberg's *A History of Violence* (2005) is officially a U.S. production but filmed entirely in Canada. These films need to be judged on their own merits as auteur films, but their relation to the national cinema remains an open question.

10-30. *One Week* (2008), with Joshua Jackson, directed by Michael McGowan.

In complete opposition to films such as *Nothing* (**10-18**) and *waydowntown* (**10-29**), *One Week* foregrounds and celebrates its Canadian settings. After being diagnosed with cancer, Ben (Jackson) decides to take a journey across Canada on his motorcycle, a trip on which he encounters Canadian landmarks (the giant nickel in Sudbury), **icons** (the Stanley Cup in a Manitoba ice rink), an array of eccentric characters, the wide open landscapes of the prairies, and the splendour of the Rockie Mountains. The playful tone, despite the serious topic, is an affirmation of life as well as Canadian culture. *(Mulmer Feed Co./The Kobal Collection)*

10-31. ***The Red Violin*** **(1998), with Carlo Cecchi and Irene Grazioli, directed by François Girard.**
The phenomenon of globalization has had a major impact on national cinemas. This visually and aurally beautiful film was officially a Canada-Italy-U.S.A.-Britain coproduction, with a Québécois director who collaborated on the screenplay with the English-Canadian filmmaker and actor Don McKellar (see **2-26** and **10-1**). It traces the history of a violin made in seventeenth-century Italy and includes segments filmed in Italy, Austria, Britain, and China, with international actors speaking the appropriate languages. The present-day sequences that frame the film take place in Montreal, where the violin is up for auction, but most of the dialogue is in English rather than French, and the main focus is on an expert called in by the auction company, played by Hollywood star Samuel L. Jackson. *(Rhombus Media)*

It is still too early to predict how the balance between global communications and local needs will be determined, but it is certain that Canadian cinema will continue to operate within a fragile and evolving national context as it seeks to define its place in the postmodern media environment.

FURTHER READING

Armatage, Kay, et al., eds., *Gendering the Nation: Canadian Women's Cinema* (Toronto: University of Toronto Press, 1999). Collection of historical and critical essays.

Beard, William, and Jerry White, eds., *North of Everything: English-Canadian Cinema Since 1980* (Edmonton: University of Alberta Press, 2002). Wide-ranging collection of essays.

Dorland, Michael, *So Close to the State/s: The Emergence of Canadian Feature Film Policy* (Toronto: University of Toronto Press, 1998). Provocative analysis based on archival research.

Leach, Jim. *Film in Canada* (Toronto: Oxford University Press, 2005). Comprehensive examination of Canadian cinema in its political and cultural contexts.

Magder, Ted, *Canada's Hollywood: The Canadian State and Feature Films* (Toronto: University of Toronto Press, 1993). Thoughtful study of national film policy.

Marshall, Bill, *Quebec National Cinema* (Montreal: McGill-Queen's University Press, 2001). Theoretical analysis of Quebec cinema and its cultural and political contexts.

Melnyk, George. *One Hundred Years of Canadian Cinema* (Toronto: University of Toronto Press, 2004). Historical perspective on the evolution of Canadian cinema.

Monk, Katherine, *Weird Sex and Snowshoes and Other Canadian Film Phenomena* (Vancouver: Raincoast Books, 2001). Enthusiastic and thoughtful overview by a lively film reviewer.

Morris, Peter, *Embattled Shadows: A History of Canadian Cinema 1895–1939* (Montreal: McGill-Queen's University Press, 1978). Key work on Canadian film history.

Wise, Wyndham, ed., *Take One's Essential Guide to Canadian Film* (Toronto: University of Toronto Press, 2001). Useful reference work.

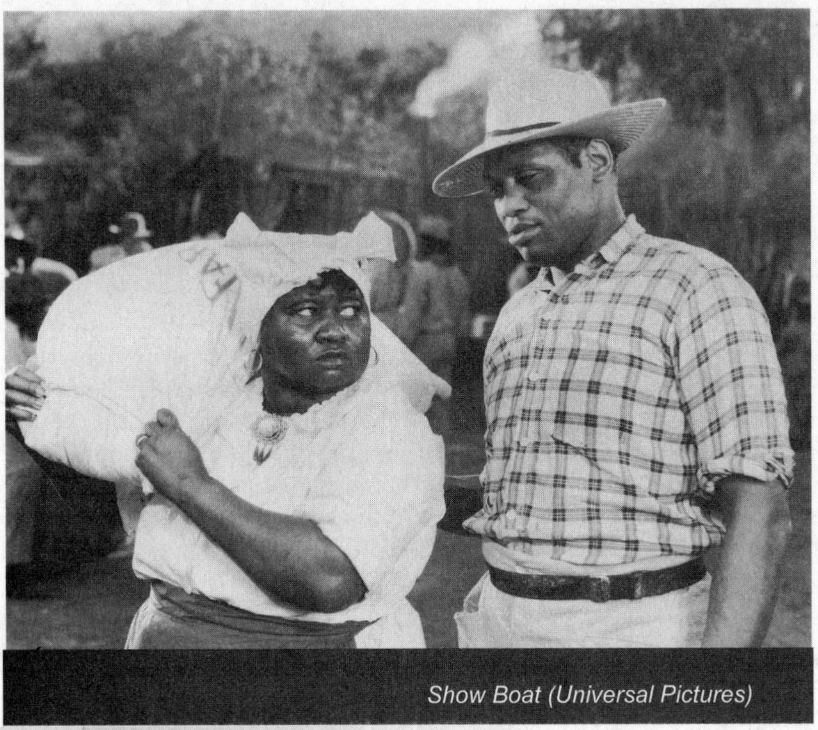

Show Boat (Universal Pictures)

THEORY

11

The apparently simple act of spectating . . . involves theories of representation, of human nature, of morality, of the nature of reality, of the conditions for human happiness, etc. Similarly, for the filmmaker, however self-consciously intuitive the approach, there is inevitably a comparable set of theories underlying the production of a film. For the critic, or for anyone engaged in a discussion of cinema, judgements also involve theories. . . . Those claiming to stand outside theory are simply unaware of the theory they are using.

— Robert Lapsley and Michael Westlake

OVERVIEW

The function and goals of film theory. Theories of realism: Bazin and Italian neorealism; Zavattini and the rejection of plot; Kracauer and the redemption of reality. Formalist film theories: Arnheim on perception; montage theory. The auteur theory. *Cahiers du cinéma* and personal vision; Hollywood auteurs and genre; Sarris's pantheon. Structuralism and semiology: Saussure on signs and codes; Peirce on symbolic, iconic, and indexical signs; Metz on cinematic signs and codes; Lévi-Strauss on binary structures. Ideology and culture: Lacan and psychoanalytic theory; Althusser on ideology; British Cultural Studies and hegemony; Mulvey and the male gaze; gay liberation and queer theory; race and ethnicity. Post-theory: cognitive, historical, and reception theory. Postmodern theory: cyborg bodies, fragmented identities, pastiche, and intertextuality.

Most theories of film are concerned with the wider context of the medium—its social, political, and philosophical implications. Theorists have also explored the essential nature of cinema—what differentiates it from other art forms, what its basic properties are. A theory is an intellectual grid, a set of aesthetic generalizations, not eternal verities. Some theories are more useful than others in understanding specific movies. No single theory can explain them all. For this reason, recent developments in the field have stressed an eclectic approach, synthesizing a variety of theoretical strategies.

THEORIES OF REALISM

Most theories of **realism** emphasize the documentary aspects of film art. Movies are evaluated primarily in terms of how accurately they reflect external reality. The camera is regarded as essentially a recording mechanism rather than an expressive medium in its own right. The subject matter is paramount in the cinema of realism, technique its discreetly transparent handmaiden. As we have seen in the case of André Bazin (Chapter 6, "Editing"), most theories of realism have a moral and ethical bias and are often rooted in the values of Islamic, Christian, or Marxist humanism.

Realist theorists believe that cinema is essentially an extension of photography and shares with it a pronounced affinity for recording the visible world around us. Unlike other art forms, photography and cinema tend to leave the raw materials of reality more or less intact. There is a minimum of interference and manipulation on the artist's part, for film is not an art of invention so much as an art of "being there."

Bazin's theory of realism owed much to the Italian neorealist movement, which was inaugurated by Roberto Rossellini's *Rome, Open City* **(11-1)**. The movie deals with the collaboration of Catholics and Communists in fighting the Nazi occupation of Rome shortly before the American army liberated the city. Technically, the film is rather crude. Good quality film stock was impossible to obtain, so Rossellini had to use inferior newsreel stock. Nevertheless, the technical flaws and the resultant grainy images convey a sense of journalistic immediacy and authenticity. (Many neorealists began their careers as journalists, and Rossellini himself began as a documentarist.) Virtually all the movie was shot at actual locations, and in many exterior shots, no additional lights were used. With the exception of the principal players, the actors

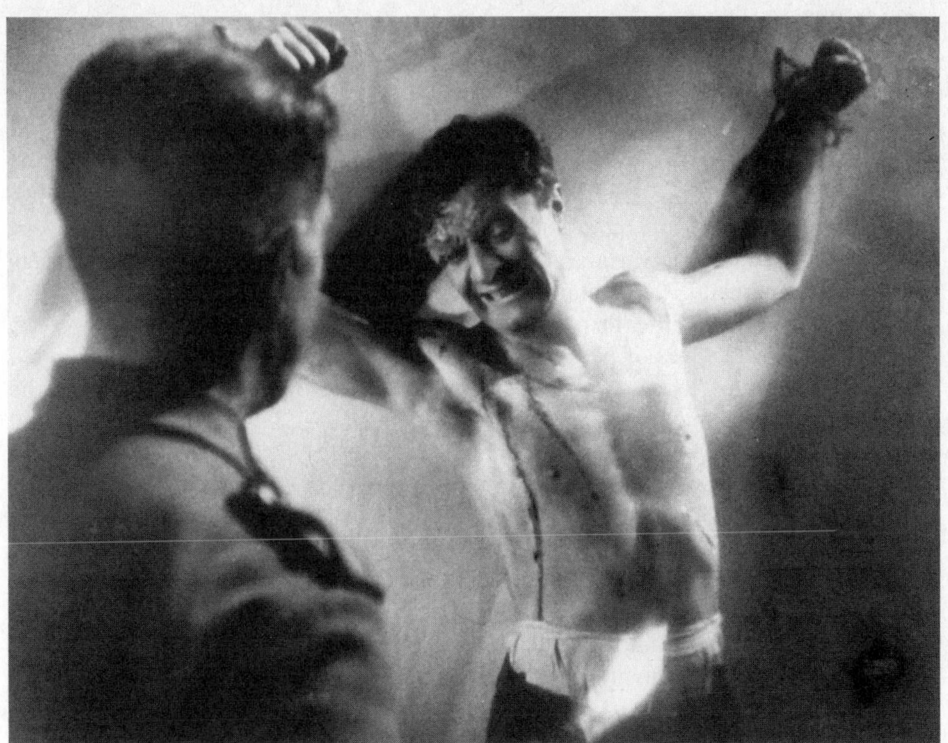

11-1. *Rome, Open City* (Italy, 1945), with Marcello Pagliero, directed by Roberto Rossellini.

The torture scenes of this famous Resistance film were so realistic that they were cut out of some prints. In this episode, a Nazi SS officer applies a blowtorch to the body of a Communist partisan in an effort to force him to reveal the names of his comrades in the underground. The crucifixion allusion is deliberate, even though the character is a nonbeliever. It parallels the death of another partisan, a Catholic priest, who is executed by a military firing squad. André Bazin was a champion of Italian neorealism, applauding its moral fervour even more than its technical restraint. "Is not neorealism primarily a kind of humanism, and only secondarily a style of filmmaking?" he asked. *(Pathé Contemporary Films)*

were nonprofessionals. The structure of the movie is episodic—a series of vignettes showing the reactions of Roman citizens to the German occupation.

Rome, Open City is saturated with a sense of unrelenting honesty. "This is the way things are," Rossellini is said to have declared after the film premiered. The statement became the motto of the neorealist movement. The film provided a rallying point for an entire generation of Italian filmmakers whose creative talents had been stifled by the repressive Fascist regime of the prewar era. Within the next few years, an astonishing series of movies followed that catapulted the Italians into the front ranks of international cinema. The major filmmakers of the movement were Rossellini, Luchino Visconti, and Vittorio De Sica and his frequent scriptwriter, Cesare Zavattini.

There are considerable differences between these men and even between their early and later works. Furthermore, **neorealism** implied a style as well as an ideology. Rossellini emphasized the ethical dimension: "For me, Neorealism [was] above all a moral position from which to look at the world. It then became an aesthetic position, but at the beginning it was moral." De Sica, Zavattini, and Visconti also stressed morality as the touchstone of neorealism.

The five main ideological characteristics of the movement can be summarized as follows: (1) a new democratic spirit, with emphasis on the value of ordinary people such as labourers, peasants, and factory workers; (2) a compassionate point of view and a refusal to make facile moral judgments; (3) a preoccupation with Italy's Fascist past and its aftermath of wartime devastation, poverty, unemployment, prostitution, and the black market; (4) a blending of Christian and Marxist humanism; and (5) an emphasis on emotions rather than abstract ideas.

The stylistic features of neorealism include (1) an avoidance of neatly plotted stories in favour of loose, episodic structures that evolve organically from the situations of the characters; (2) a documentary visual style; (3) the use of actual locations—usually exteriors—rather than studio sets; (4) the use of nonprofessional actors, sometimes even for principal roles; (5) an avoidance of literary dialogue in favour of conversational speech, including dialects; and (6) an avoidance of artifice in the editing, camerawork, and lighting in favour of a simple "styleless" style.

Realists have shown a persistent hostility toward plot and neatly structured stories. For example, Zavattini, more than any single individual, defined the ordinary and the everyday as the main business of cinema (see **1-9** and **8-26**). Spectacular events and extraordinary characters should be avoided at all costs, he believed. He

11-2. *A Taste of Cherry* (Iran, 1998), with Homayoun Ershadi, written and directed by Abbas Kiarostami. As a movement, Italian neorealism was pretty much over by the mid-1950s, but as a style and an attitude toward reality, its influence spread to many other countries. At the end of the twentieth century, *A Taste of Cherry* demonstrated to the world that neorealism was alive and thriving in Iran. Shot on actual locations with a nonprofessional cast, the movie poetically validates the sacredness of life, from an Islamic-humanist perspective. The plot is episodic and loosely structured, allowing maximum space to explore philosophical and religious themes, but in a simple, unpretentious way. *(Zeitgeist Films)*

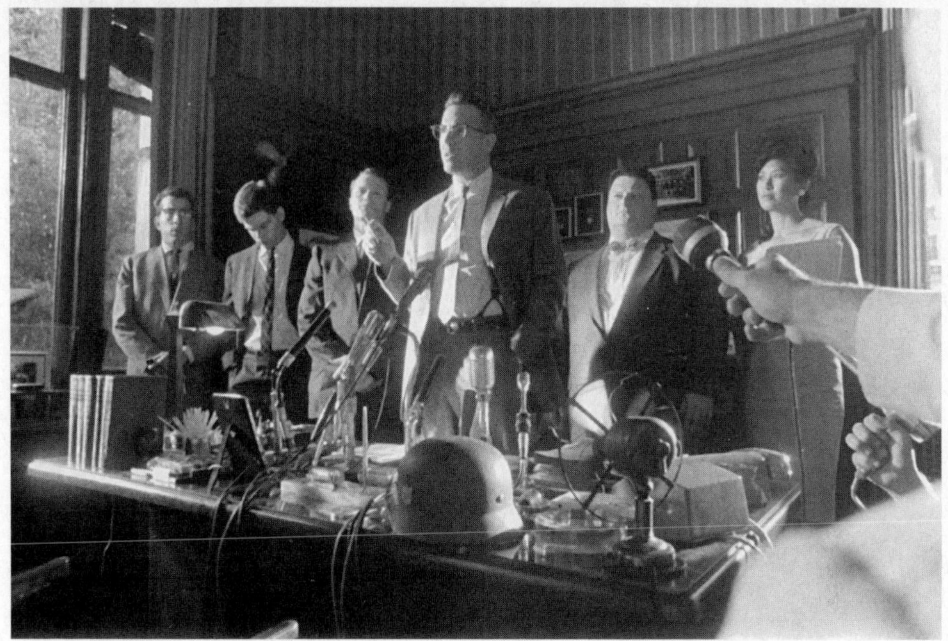

11-3. *JFK* (U.S.A., 1991), with Kevin Costner (centre), written and directed by Oliver Stone.
Theories of realism often portray the filmmaker as an observer who should remain politically neutral. Stone uses many realist techniques in his account of the investigation of the assassination of John Kennedy by New Orleans District Attorney Jim Garrison (Costner), including the insertion of newsreel footage and handheld camera shots. But he does not try to be objective. By casting an attractive star as Garrison and involving us in his frustrated efforts to uncover the truth, the film supports the hypothesis of a political conspiracy and a cover-up in high places. Many critics found Stone's approach irresponsible but, whether or not they admit it, all historical accounts are selective attempts to make sense of the past. We often find films "unrealistic" if they do not accord with our own vision of the world. *(Warner Bros.)*

claimed that his ideal movie would consist of ninety consecutive minutes from a person's actual life. There should be no barriers between reality and the spectator, no directorial virtuosity to "deform" the integrity of life as it is. The artistry should be invisible, the materials "found" rather than shaped or manipulated.

Suspicious of conventional plot structures, Zavattini dismissed them as dead formulas. He insisted on the dramatic superiority of life as ordinary people experience it. Filmmakers should be concerned with the "excavation" of reality. Instead of plots, they should emphasize facts and all their "echoes and reverberations." According to Zavattini, filmmaking is not a matter of "inventing fables" that are superimposed over the factual materials of life, but of searching unrelentingly to uncover the dramatic implications of these facts. The purpose of cinema is to explore the "dailiness" of events, to reveal certain details that had always been there but had never been noticed.

In his book *Theory of Film: The Redemption of Physical Reality* (1960), Siegfried Kracauer also attacks plot as an enemy of realism. According to Kracauer, cinema is characterized by several natural affinities. First, it tends to favour "unstaged

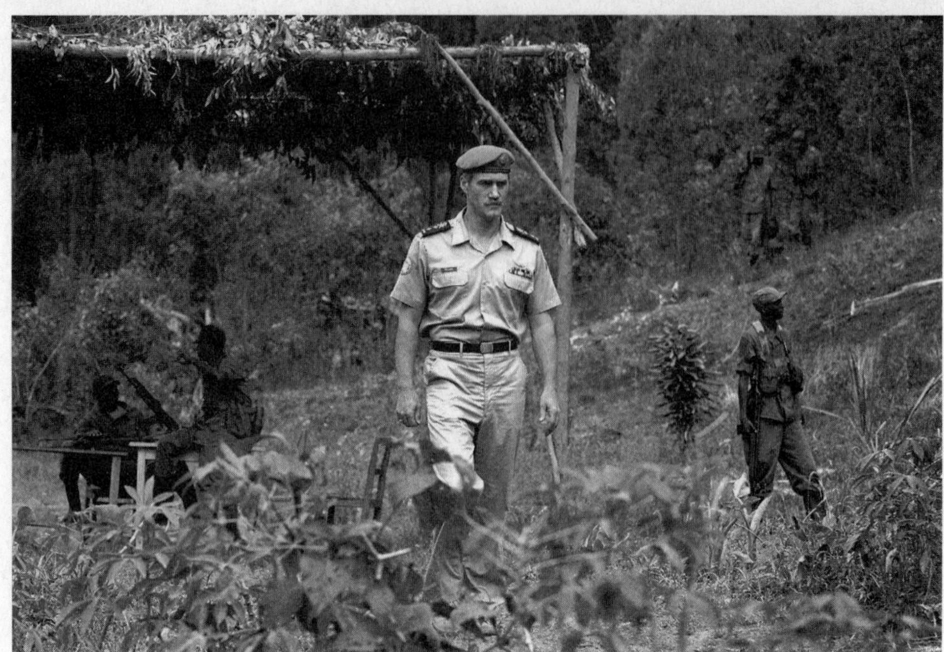

11-4. *Shake Hands With the Devil* (Canada, 2007), with Roy Dupuis, directed by Roger Spottiswoode. In this film, Roméo Dallaire, the Canadian general in charge of the United Nations troops in Rwanda in 1994, is ordered to remain politically neutral during the massacre of Tutsis by the Hutu majority. The film itself provides a powerful realist depiction of the events, framed by sequences in which Dallaire (Dupuis) attempts to exorcise his memories with the help of a psychiatrist and in which figures from the past appear around him. Controversially, the UN policies that prevented its troops from intervening to prevent the massacre are not explained, but the effect is leave viewers asking the same questions with which Dallaire was faced at the time. *(© Seville Pictures/Courtesy Everett Collection/Canadian Press)*

reality"—that is, the most appropriate subject matter gives the illusion of having been found rather than arranged. Second, film tends to stress the random, the fortuitous. Kracauer is fond of the phrase "nature caught in the act," meaning that film is best suited to recording events and objects that might be overlooked in life. Realistic cinema is a cinema of "found moments" and poignant revelations of humanity. The third affinity is indeterminacy: The best movies suggest endlessness. They imply a slice of life, a fragment of a larger reality rather than a self-contained whole. By refusing to tie up all the loose ends at the conclusion of the movie, the filmmaker can suggest the limitlessness of reality.

Kracauer is hostile toward movies that demonstrate a "formative tendency," such as historical films and fantasies. He regards such films as moving away from the basic concerns of the medium, and he also dismisses most literary and dramatic adaptations because he believes that literature is ultimately concerned with "interior realities," what people are thinking and feeling, whereas movies explore surfaces, exterior reality. He regards all stylistic self-consciousness as "uncinematic," because instead of emphasizing the subject matter, the filmmaker calls attention to *how* it is presented.

11-5. *Italian for Beginners* (Denmark, 2002), written and directed by Lone Scherfig.

In 1995, a group of Danish filmmakers banded together under the name Dogme 95 and issued a list of strict rules that they would observe in their films. The most famous of these directors are Lars von Trier (*Breaking the Waves*, 1996) and Thomas Vinterberg (*The Celebration*, 1998). Some of these rules: Only real locations can be used as sets; props also have to be found on the location; sound must always be **diegetic**; the camera must be handheld; no flashbacks, no dream or fantasy sequences; the director must not be credited. Very few of the filmmakers have been able to obey all these draconian injunctions. This movie was shot on video, on location, and with only diegetic music, but it is basically a quirky comedy about a group of lonely people who use an Italian class to search for romantic partners. *(Miramax Films)*

FORMALIST FILM THEORIES

Formalist film theorists believe that the art of cinema is possible precisely because a movie is unlike everyday reality. The filmmaker exploits the limitations of the medium—its two-dimensionality, its confining frame, its fragmented time-space continuum—to produce a world that resembles the real world only in a superficial sense. The real world is merely a repository of raw material that needs to be shaped and heightened to be effective as art. Film art is not a reproduction of reality, but a translation of observed characteristics into the *forms* of the medium.

Rudolf Arnheim, a Gestalt psychologist, put forth an important theory of cinematic formalism in his book *Film as Art*, which was originally published in German in 1933. Arnheim's book is primarily concerned with the perception of experience. His theory is based on the different modes of perception of the camera on the one hand and the human eye on the other. Anticipating some of the theories of the Canadian communications specialist Marshall McLuhan, Arnheim insists that the camera's image of a bowl of fruit, for instance, is fundamentally different from our perception of the fruit bowl in actual life. Formalist theorists celebrate these differences, believing that what makes photography fall short of perfect reproduction is also what makes cinema an art, not just a species of xerography.

Formalists have pointed out many instances where the camera's image of reality and what the human eye sees diverge. For example, film directors must choose from which viewpoint to photograph a scene. They do not necessarily choose the clearest view, for often this does not emphasize the major characteristics of the scene, its expressive essence. In life, we perceive objects in depth and can penetrate the space that surrounds most things. In movies, space is an illusion, since the screen has only two dimensions, permitting the director to manipulate objects and perspectives in the

11-6. *Ugetsu Monogatari* (Japan, 1953), with Masayuki Mori and Machiko Kyo, directed by Kenji Mizoguchi. Realist critics and theorists tend to underestimate the flexibility of an audience's response to nonrealistic movies. To be sure, it is easier for a filmmaker to create the illusion of reality if the story deals with everyday events, for the world of the movie and the actual world are essentially the same. On the other hand, a gifted artist can make even fantasy materials "realistic." A movie like *Ugetsu Monogatari* (*Tales of the Pale and Silvery Moon after the Rain*), which is set in the remote past and features spirits and demons, presents us with a self-contained magical universe which we are able to enter by temporarily forgetting the outside world of reality. In so doing, we share the experience of the potter (Mori) in the film, who is seduced by a beautiful ghost (Kyo) away from the reality of his family and a country devastated by civil war into an enchanting fantasy world. *(Janus Films)*

11-7. *The Servant* (Britain, 1963), with Wendy Craig, Dirk Bogarde (foreground), and James Fox, directed by Joseph Losey.

A scene can be photographed in literally hundreds of different ways, but the formalist selects the camera setup that best captures its symbolic or psychological implications. In this shot, for example, a young woman (Craig) suddenly realizes the enormous power that a valet (Bogarde) wields over her weak fiancé (Fox). She is isolated on the left, half plunged in darkness. A curtained doorway separates her from her lover, who is so stupefied with drugs he scarcely knows where he is, much less what is really going on. The servant coolly turns his back on them, the camera's low angle further emphasizing his effortless control over his "master." *(Landau Distributing)*

mise en scène. For example, important objects can be placed where they are most likely to be noticed first. Unimportant objects can be relegated to inferior positions, at the edges or rear of the image.

In real life, space and time are experienced as continuous phenomena. Through editing, filmmakers can chop up space and time and rearrange them in a more meaningful manner. Like other artists, the film director selects certain expressive details from the chaotic plenitude of physical reality. By juxtaposing these space and time fragments, the filmmaker creates connections that do not exist in raw nature. This, of course, was the basic position of the Soviet **montage** theorists (see Chapter 6, "Editing").

Formalists are always concerned with patterns, with methods of restructuring reality into aesthetically appealing designs. Patterns can be expressed visually, through the photography and mise en scène, or aurally, in stylized dialogue, symbolic sound

11-8. ***La Règle du jeu* [*The Rules of the Game*] (France, 1939), directed by Jean Renoir.**

Although the auteur theory was most noted for paying serious attention to Hollywood directors working within the studio system, André Bazin and the *Cahiers du cinéma* critics also admired independent European filmmakers like Renoir. Throughout his long career (which began in the 1920s), Renoir pursued his personal vision with an uncompromising tenacity. He worked in Hollywood during World War II but returned to France and made his last film there in 1970. His films are noted for combining a realist aesthetic with an awareness of the theatrical artifice that can be found even in everyday life. He also refuses to judge his characters: "Everyone has his reasons," as Octave (played by the director himself) comments in this comedy of manners set in an enclosed aristocratic milieu doomed to extinction by the political crises in the outside world. Renoir believed that a director's work consisted of just one ongoing film, and in 1974 he dedicated his autobiography to the New Wave filmmakers. *(Janus Films)*

effects, and musical motifs. Camera movements are often kinetic patterns superimposed on the visual materials, commenting on them in some heightened manner.

THE AUTEUR THEORY

In the mid-1950s, the French journal *Cahiers du cinéma* revolutionized film criticism with its concept of *la politique des auteurs* (see also Chapter 1, "Medium"). This committed policy of authors was put forth by the pugnacious young critic François Truffaut. The **auteur theory** became the focal point of a critical controversy that eventually spread to Britain and North America. Before long, the theory became a militant rallying cry for critics writing for such lively journals as *Movie* in Britain

11-9. ***Rear Window*** **(U.S.A., 1954), with Grace Kelly and James Stewart, directed by Alfred Hitchcock.**

Andrew Sarris used the auteur theory as an evaluative tool. At the top of his list were "Pantheon Directors," like Hitchcock, whose "personal style" creates "inner meaning." Hitchcock's films are bound up with feelings of guilt, often associated with voyeurism, which some critics attribute to his Catholic upbringing. In *Rear Window*, a photographer (Stewart), confined to a wheelchair as the result of an accident, spies on his neighbours and uncovers a murder. When the murderer realizes that he is being watched, Hitchcock builds up the suspense for which he was celebrated, but he also makes us uneasily aware that the photographer is merely doing what we do every time we watch a movie. Nobody is innocent in a Hitchcock film—not even the spectator. *(Paramount Pictures)*

and *Film Culture* in the United States. Although a number of writers rejected the theory as simplistic, auteurism dominated film criticism throughout the 1960s.

Truffaut, Godard, and their critical colleagues proposed that the greatest movies are dominated by the personal vision of the director. A filmmaker's "signature" can be perceived through an examination of his or her total output, which is characterized by a unity of theme and style. Movies ought to be judged on the basis of *how*, not *what*. Like other formalists, the auteur critics claimed that what makes a good film is not the subject matter as such, but its stylistic treatment. The director dominates the treatment, provided he or she is a strong director, an auteur.

The American auteurs whom these critics praised worked within the studio system. What the auteurists especially admired was how gifted directors could circumvent studio interference and even hackneyed scripts through their technical expertise. The subject matter of Hitchcock's thrillers or Ford's westerns was not significantly different from that of others working in these genres. Yet both auteurs managed to create great films, precisely because the real meanings were conveyed through the mise en scène, the editing, and all the other formal devices at the director's disposal.

The sheer breadth of their knowledge of film history permitted these critics to reevaluate the major works of a wide variety of directors. In many instances, they completely reversed previous critical judgments. Before long, personality cults developed around the most popular directors, mostly filmmakers who had been virtually ignored by the critical establishment of the previous generation: Hitchcock, Ford, Howard Hawks, Fritz Lang, and many others. The auteur critics were often dogmatic in their dislikes as well as their likes. Bazin expressed alarm at their negativism. To praise a bad movie, he felt, was unfortunate; but to condemn a good one was a serious failing. He especially disliked their tendency to hero worship, which led to superficial a priori judgments. Movies by admired directors were indiscriminately praised, whereas those by directors out of fashion were automatically condemned.

The principal spokesperson for the auteur theory in the United States was Andrew Sarris, the influential critic of the *Village Voice*. More knowledgeable about the complexities of the star and studio system than his French counterparts, Sarris nonetheless defended their basic argument, especially the principle of tension between an artist's personal vision and the genre assignments that these directors were given by their Hollywood bosses.

The auteur theory suffers from several limitations. On the one hand, some excellent films have been made by directors whose other work seems undistinguished and impersonal. Michael Curtiz, for example, is not usually regarded as an auteur, and the success of *Casablanca* is often cited as a major obstacle to the auteur theory (see **1-11**). On the other hand, determined critics can find recurring themes, motifs, and stylistic tendencies in the most unlikely directors. By stressing the value of personal vision, the auteur theory encourages critics to develop their own subjective responses to films and downplays the generic, industrial, social, and political contexts, which have a major impact on the style and content of all movies.

Despite its shortcomings and excesses, the auteur theory had a liberating effect on film criticism, establishing the director as the key figure at least in the art of cinema, if not always in the industry. By the 1970s, the major battle had been won. Virtually all serious discussions of movies were at least partly couched in terms of the director's personal vision. To this day, the concept of directorial dominance remains firmly established, and it is now often used by the film industry itself in publicity campaigns.

STRUCTURALISM AND SEMIOLOGY

Despite its persistence, the auteur theory came under attack in the 1970s from film scholars who demanded more rigorous methods. The new theorists were less concerned with expressing their enthusiasm for the films of their favourite directors and more interested in discovering the underlying principles of film language. **Structuralism** and **semiology** were attempts to introduce a more scientific approach that would allow for more systematic and detailed analyses of movies. Borrowing their ideas from such diverse disciplines as linguistics, anthropology, psychology, and philosophy, these two theories first concentrated on the development of a more precise analytical terminology.

In film, semiology is the study of *how* movies signify. It draws on concepts developed in the study of verbal language by Ferdinand de Saussure, who founded the study of structural linguistics at the beginning of the twentieth century. Saussure argued that language consists of **signs** that are organized by **codes**, and that meaning comes from the relations between the signs rather than from their reference to the world outside the language system. A sign consists of a signifier (the letters T-R-E-E or a picture of a tree, for example) and a signified (a mental image that is created in

11-10. *Blonde Venus* (U.S.A., 1932), with Marlene Dietrich, directed by Josef von Sternberg.

Semiologists believe that treating the **shot** as the basic unit of meaning in film is too general and inclusive to be of much use in a systematic analysis of a movie. Every cinematic shot draws on dozens of signifying codes that are hierarchically structured. Using what they call the "principle of pertinence," semiologists decode cinematic discourse by first establishing what the dominant signs are, then analyzing the subsidiary codes. This methodology is similar to a detailed analysis of mise en scène, only in addition to spatial, textural, and photographic codes, semiologists would also explore other relevant signs—kinetic, linguistic, musical, rhythmic, etc. In this shot, a semiologist would explore the symbolic significance of such major signs as Dietrich's white suit. Why a masculine suit? Why white? What does the *papier-mâché* dragon signify? The distorted perspective lines of the set? The "shady ladies" behind the archways? The symbolism of stage and audience? The tight framing and closed form of the image? The protagonist's worldly song? Within the dramatic context, semiologists would also explore the rhythms of the editing and camera movements, the symbolism of the kinetic motions of the performer, and so on. A complex shot can contain a hundred different signs, each with its own precise symbolic significance. *(Paramount Pictures)*

the mind when we read the letters or look at the picture), and Saussure stressed the arbitrary nature of the sign.

In his book *Signs and Meaning in the Cinema* (first published in 1969), British theorist Peter Wollen suggested that the work of the American philosopher Charles Sanders Peirce, who was working independently at about the same time as Saussure, was more relevant to the study of film than the Saussure's. Peirce preferred the term *semiotics*, which implies a rather less systematic approach, and he defined three different kinds of signs distinguished by their relations to what they signify. A **symbol** (a word, for example) is purely arbitrary, since there is no necessary reason why these letters should signify that meaning, but an **icon** (such as a portrait painting) represents its object by resemblance, and an **index** is a sign that has a direct connection to what it represents (for instance, smoke is a sign of fire). These categories are not exclusive, and most signs incorporate elements of more than one kind. Film is a highly complex sign system that is indexical because of its photographic basis (the image is created by light falling on the sensitive film stock), but the visual images are **iconic** because they resemble the real world. Films also incorporate the **symbolic** signs of verbal language.

French theorist Christian Metz was at the forefront of applying Saussure's ideas to the study of film language. Using many of the concepts and much of the terminology of structural linguistics, Metz and others developed a theory of cinematic communication founded on the concept of signs or codes. They argued that a film is a complex network of signs that we decipher based on our knowledge of cinematic and cultural codes **(11-10)**.

In earlier discussions of film, the shot was generally accepted as the basic unit of construction. Semiotic theorists rejected this unit as too vague and inclusive. They insisted on a more precise concept. Accordingly, they suggested that the sign be adopted as the minimal unit of signification. A single shot from a movie generally contains dozens of signs, forming an intricate hierarchy of counterpoised meanings. In a sense, this book, and especially the earlier chapters, can be viewed as a classification of signs, although necessarily more limited in scope than the type of identification and classification envisioned by Metz and other semiologists.

As Metz pointed out, semiology is concerned with the systematic classification of types of codes used in cinema; structuralism is the study of how various codes function to create the structures through which we make sense of the world. As applied to film studies, structuralism is strongly eclectic and often combines the techniques of semiology with other theoretical perspectives, such as auteurism, genre studies, ideology, stylistic analyses, and so on. For example, Colin McArthur's *Underworld USA* (1972) is a structuralist analysis of gangster and crime films and the style known as *film noir*.

Structuralists and semiologists have been fascinated by the concept of a deep structure—an underlying network of symbolic meaning that is related to a movie's surface structure but is also somewhat independent of it. This deep structure can be analyzed from several perspectives, including Freudian psychoanalysis, Marxist economics, Jungian concepts of the collective unconscious, and the theory of structural anthropology popularized by Claude Lévi-Strauss.

The methods of Lévi-Strauss are based on an examination of regional myths, which he believed express certain underlying structures of thought in codified form. These myths exist in variant forms and usually contain the same or similar binary structures—pairs of opposites. By collapsing the surface (narrative) structure of myths, their symbolic motifs can be analyzed in a more systematic and meaningful manner. These polarities are usually found in dialectical conflict: Depending on the culture analyzed, they can be agricultural (for example, water vs. drought), sexual (male vs. female), conceptual (cooked vs. raw), generational (youth vs. age), and so

11-11. *An Autumn Afternoon* (Japan, 1962), with Chishu Ryu (right), directed by Yasujiro Ozu.

Ozu's films deal with the impact of modernity on Japanese life. Their structures can be described in terms of a series of binary oppositions: Japanese/Western, feudal/democratic, past/future, society/individual, and so on. Unlike Akira Kurosawa, for example, Ozu was a conservative and thus privileged the first item in each binary. But he was also an ironist, well aware of the gap between reality and the ideal. In this film, his final work, the protagonist (Ryu) is a gentle, aging widower who lives with his unmarried daughter. His loneliness is assuaged by a few drinking buddies who spend much of their free time at the local bar. After hearing of the marriage of a friend's daughter, the widower decides that it is time for his daughter to move on as well. He arranges a marriage with a decent young man recommended by friends. The movie ends on a bittersweet note as the father muses contentedly on the success of his arrangements. He also realizes that he is getting old—and that he is alone. *(New Yorker Films)*

on. Because these myths are expressed in symbolic codes, their full meanings are often hidden even from their creators.

These structural techniques can be used to analyze a national cinema, a genre, or a specific movie. For example, the conflict between "traditional" and "modern" values can be seen in virtually all Japanese movies, and in Japanese society in general **(11-11)**. Similarly, Jim Kitses, Peter Wollen, and others have pointed out how westerns are often vehicles for exploring clashes of value between East and West, "civilization" and "wilderness," in American culture (see Chapter 2, "Story"). They explain that by clustering the thematic motifs around a "master antimony" (a controlling or dominant code), one can analyze a western according to its deep structure rather than its plot, which, as is typical in genre films, is often conventionalized (and less meaningful) in genre films. Such critics have demonstrated how each cultural polarity symbolizes a complex of positive and negative traits:

According to structuralist theory, the key to such a list of binary oppositions is that the meanings produced by the genre are to be found in the *relations* between the terms. In principle, genres (and cultures) generate value systems in which the terms on one side of the list are positive and are defined by contrast with their negative counterparts. In practice, things are rarely that simple: The western hero is thus usually a rugged figure, identified with the wilderness, who nevertheless paves the way for civilization by standing up against anarchic outlaws and savage Indians. Individual films must work within the structures that define the genre but may exploit the instability of the relations among the terms to create distinctive effects.

West	***East***	***West***	***East***
Wilderness	Civilization	Masculine	Feminine
Individual	Community	Pragmatism	Idealism
Self-interest	Social welfare	Agrarian	Industrial
Freedom	Restriction	Purity	Corruption
Anarchy	Law and order	Tradition	Change
Savagery	Refinement	Past	Future
Private honour	Institutional justice	Experience	Knowledge
Paganism	Christianity	American	European
Nature	Culture		

IDEOLOGY AND CULTURE

Semiology (or semiotics) and structuralism are essentially formalist theories, centrally concerned with *how* meaning is created. During the 1960s, at a time when established social structures were being widely challenged, theorists began to be more concerned with *why* certain structures had become dominant and in whose interests they worked. Film studies turned to psychoanalytic theory in an attempt to explain the social impact of the medium.

In particular, film theorists turned to the work of French psychoanalyst Jacques Lacan. Lacan's dense and purposefully obscure verbal style meant that few theorists read his original works, but they were attracted to his theory of the imaginary and symbolic dimensions of human experience. According to Lacan, the human infant becomes aware of itself as a separate individual during the "mirror phase," when it sees its reflection and experiences a jubilant—but imaginary—sense of freedom and power. When the child learns to speak, it enters the realm of the symbolic order, governed by rules that limit individual freedom and thus make social life possible. The imaginary and symbolic continue to function in adult life, and their relations determine the development and quality of the individual's psychic life. In his book *The Imaginary Signifier* (1977), Metz combined semiology and psychoanalysis, arguing that classical cinema is so effective because it provides the spectator with a sense of mastery over the world, like that of the infant in front of the mirror. It does so by inviting us to identify with the camera and by concealing the work that went into creating the film.

Lacan's ideas were also taken up by political philosopher Louis Althusser, who put forward a theory of ideology that had a major influence on the social activists of

11-12. *Dances With Wolves* (U.S.A., 1990), with Kevin Costner (left), directed by Costner.

In an attempt to redress the treatment of Native Americans in the traditional western, Costner plays a U.S. army officer who lives with the Lakota Sioux and discovers that their culture is morally superior to his own. His education occupies the first part of the film, but the dramatic climax occurs when he helps the Sioux to fight their enemies, the savage Pawnee tribe. The film thus scrambles, but does not completely reverse, the structural oppositions on which the genre was founded, reflecting the tensions and anxieties in contemporary North American society that have led to a new interest in "Native spirituality." *(Orion Pictures)*

the late 1960s. In his interpretation of the writings of Karl Marx, Althusser defined ideology not just as a body of ideas but also as the representation of "the imaginary relationship of individuals to their real conditions of existence." From this perspective, ideology works beneath the level of the conscious mind and persuades us to accept the values of our culture as if they were produced by nature. Beginning even before we are born, the workings of ideology provide us with "subject positions" through which we view the world and construct our identities. We may assume that these identities are personal and private, but they are actually shaped by social institutions and the mass media. Films "interpellate" or "hail" us and, by responding, we accept our assigned subject positions and the "dominant ideology" on which the existing social order depends.

The events of May 1968, in which French students took to the streets and almost toppled the government, led many filmmakers, most notably Jean-Luc Godard, to think about the political implications of their work. During the 1960s, Godard's films gradually became more formally challenging and politically radical. For several years after 1968, he made his films as an anonymous member of the Dziga Vertov

11-13. *Exotica* (Canada, 1994), directed by Atom Egoyan.

At the Exotica nightclub, patrons can look, but are strictly forbidden to touch. Mirrors abound in this film and are often used for surveillance purposes. The owner of the club has a two-way mirror so that she can watch over the dancers and clients, and a similar mirror appears in the opening sequence, in which customs officers spy on passengers at an airport. These mirrors remind us that we are voyeurs watching the film, but they also suggest a society in which the imaginary and symbolic dimensions of human experience, as described by Jacques Lacan, have become difficult to distinguish. The film is populated by lonely characters for whom looking is a substitute for touching and obsession a way of coping with broken relationships. *(Ego Film Arts/Johnnie Eisen)*

Cooperative, named after the Soviet documentary filmmaker (see Chapter 9, "Nonfiction Films"). The former champion of the auteur theory thus protested against the idea of film as the expression of an individual artist and advocated the need for collective political action.

Godard's new direction received support from the editors of *Cahiers du cinéma*, who had also turned against the journal's earlier commitment to the auteur theory. During the 1970s, these ideas became increasingly influential in film studies, despite many complaints about the high degree of abstraction and the jargon used by many theorists. The British film journal *Screen* published many important essays in this tradition, including translations from the French and new work by its own contributors.

Filmmakers and theorists influenced by Althusser were especially suspicious of classical narrative cinema with its stress on **continuity editing**. They argued for new kinds of cinema that would call attention to the means by which the images were produced. Whereas classical narrative cinema aims to create an illusion of reality and encourages the spectator to identify with the main character, the new forms require an

11-14. *Les Ordres* [*Orders*] (Canada, 1974), with Jean Lapointe, directed by Michel Brault.

Brault's film has been called "a perfect application of the theories of Brecht to the cinema." Bertolt Brecht, the great German dramatist, influenced Louis Althusser and many film theorists, because of his insistence that spectators should not be drawn into the theatrical illusion. By constantly reminding us that we are watching a play, Brechtian drama draws attention to ideological processes normally taken for granted. *Les Ordres* deals with the events of October 1970, when the Front de libération du Québec kidnapped a British diplomat and a Quebec cabinet minister, and the federal government responded by invoking the War Measures Act. Brault uses Brechtian "distancing" devices, such as having the actors introduce themselves and the roles they will play, but, even so, he came under attack for not providing a political analysis of the events. Instead, he evokes the nightmare experience of the innocent victims who were arrested by police acting on orders from above. *(Les Productions Prisma)*

active and critically detached audience. The models to which these theorists pointed included the Soviet montage school of the 1920s and various **avant-garde** traditions.

The key idea was that old forms could not convey new ideas. However, most audiences tended to reject these new kinds of film as unfamiliar and unpleasant. The theorists, of course, attributed this negative response to the ideological processes through which classical narrative cinema became the norm against which all other films were judged. As we have seen, a similar argument was put forward in Canada to explain why Canadian audiences preferred Hollywood films over the work of Canadian filmmakers (see Chapter 10, "Canadian Cinema"). Nevertheless, the effect was that radical filmmakers produced films that did not communicate with the masses in whose interests they were supposedly made.

This kind of analysis has other problems. It attributes enormous power to ideology and often implies that it is virtually impossible to escape from its clutches, even if the theorists have somehow managed to do so. Unlike Lacan, whose theory posits the unstable but necessary interaction of the imaginary and symbolic in psychic proc-

11-15. *Mourir à tue-tête* [*Scream from Silence*] (Canada, 1978), directed by Anne Claire Poirier.

This film opens with a long and graphic rape scene depicted from the point of view of the victim. It then reveals that this scene is actually part of a film about an actual case of rape and being made by a (fictional) director and an editor who discuss the implications of their film. The brutal effect of the opening is contextualized by several documentary sequences—including a ritual clitoridectomy in Africa and the shaving of women's heads in France after World War II—that imply rape is the product of systematic male violence. The film also includes symbolic sequences like the one shown here: An anonymous group of rape victims addresses a male judge, who remains an off-screen voice (of God?), drawing attention to the indifference of the legal system. All these devices are designed to disrupt the imaginary pleasures of film viewing and to promote a symbolic understanding of the traumatic real event shown at the beginning. *(National Film Board of Canada)*

esses, Althusser and his followers stressed the need for symbolic knowledge, insisting that film spectators are passive victims of the imaginary illusions conjured up by mainstream cinema. The goal of film theory became, as Metz put it, "to disengage the cinema from the imaginary and to win it for the symbolic" (see **11-14**).

At the same time as this version of ideological analysis came to dominate film theory, an alternative approach emerged from the work of Stuart Hall and the British Cultural Studies movement, which challenged the idea that audiences are "cultural dopes" at the mercy of an all-powerful ideological apparatus. This work draws on semiotic and ideological approaches but suggests that the processes of encoding and decoding cultural texts allow for a range of different responses. The stress is on what people do with texts rather than on what texts do to people. Instead of ideology, theorists within this tradition tend to speak of *hegemony*, a term used by the Italian Marxist thinker Antonio Gramsci, who insisted that the dominant social class needs to win the consent of other classes to maintain its power. In this dynamic process,

11-16. *High Hopes* (Britain, 1988), with Ruth Sheen, Edna Dore, and Philip Davis, directed by Mike Leigh.

In several articles published in *Screen* in the 1970s, Colin MacCabe denounced the "classic realist text" as a vehicle of ideology. Realist films, he argued, create an illusion of reality that prevents them from analyzing and criticizing the causes of social injustice. The rehabilitation of realism in British cinema came with a series of films by Leigh and Ken Loach that attacked the state of British society after the cutbacks in social services instituted by the government of Margaret Thatcher in the 1980s. In this film, Leigh depicts an eccentric couple (Sheen and Davis) who try to keep alive the political hopes associated with the 1960s in a world of greed, pretension, and conspicuous consumption. *(Skouras Pictures)*

audiences are neither completely controlled by the film industry nor completely free to make their own choices and construct their own meanings.

Contemporary cultural studies have encouraged film theorists to become more interested in broader issues of culture and technology. Like the films themselves, film theory has been deeply influenced by the major social movements of the past decades, including feminism, the gay liberation movement, and the politics of race and ethnicity. While historians have explored the unequal conditions in which women, gays, and racial and ethnic minorities have worked in the film industry, theorists have focused on the ways in which members of these groups are represented (or not represented) on screen.

Until recently, female directors and producers were rare in every major national cinema, and even today men far outnumber women in these positions of power. Feminist critics have drawn attention to the neglected work of female filmmakers, while theorists have explored the images of women in the one area of filmmaking in which they have been conspicuous: as actors and the characters they embody. In an enormously influential essay, first published in *Screen* in 1975, Laura Mulvey argued

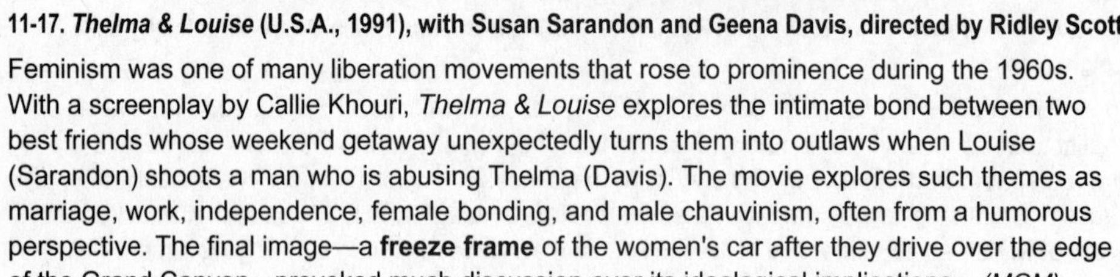

11-17. *Thelma & Louise* (U.S.A., 1991), with Susan Sarandon and Geena Davis, directed by Ridley Scott. Feminism was one of many liberation movements that rose to prominence during the 1960s. With a screenplay by Callie Khouri, *Thelma & Louise* explores the intimate bond between two best friends whose weekend getaway unexpectedly turns them into outlaws when Louise (Sarandon) shoots a man who is abusing Thelma (Davis). The movie explores such themes as marriage, work, independence, female bonding, and male chauvinism, often from a humorous perspective. The final image—a **freeze frame** of the women's car after they drive over the edge of the Grand Canyon—provoked much discussion over its ideological implications. *(MGM)*

that classical narrative cinema assumes a "male gaze" of which women are the object. According to Mulvey, the male hero typically drives the film's action, while female characters exist only in relation to his desire—and that of the male spectator. Women connote "to-be-looked-at-ness."

Later theorists, and Mulvey herself, questioned the psychoanalytic and ideological framework of her thesis. Although many films do conform to her model, critics have pointed to genres that address women's desires, such as the domestic melodrama or "women's film" of the 1940s and 1950s (see Chapter 7, "Sound"). Theorists have also suggested that popular films do not always enforce traditional gender roles but often offer fantasies of escaping from these roles.

Although feminist theory focused attention on representations of gender, most of the discussion, until recently, dealt with ideological constructions of femininity. As gender roles have gradually changed in society, however, traditional ideas of masculinity, once taken for granted, have been called into question. Theorists have begun to explore the different ways in which films have represented male identities, analyzing for example the ideological meanings of such masculine icons as Sylvester Stallone **(8-11)** and Arnold Schwarzenegger in the context of the feminist movement.

11-18. *My American Cousin* (Canada, 1984), with John Wildman and Margaret Langrick, directed by Sandy Wilson.

Feminist critics have examined film history to draw attention to the contributions of women filmmakers. There have been few women directors or producers, a situation that is slowly changing in many countries. Women made major contributions to the revival of Canadian cinema in the 1980s and 1990s, one of the first being Sandy Wilson's small-budget autobiographical film, set in British Columbia in the 1950s, about a teenager's infatuation with her rebellious American cousin. *(Fineline Productions)*

Feminist theories also called into question the heterosexual norms that governed the depiction of sexuality in mainstream films. The gay liberation movement challenged these norms and the culture that created them. The film industry had always operated within a dominant ideology that prevented the overt expression of homosexual desire. Gay filmmakers in Hollywood and elsewhere had to conceal their sexual orientation, and gay characters could appear in films only in highly coded or negatively stereotyped ways.

Although gay characters now appear more frequently in Hollywood films, and even in network television series, critics and theorists continue to debate whether these representations succeed in breaking with dominant ideological conceptions. The depiction of a young woman discovering her lesbian identity in *Lianna* (John Sayles, 1983) or a gay lawyer dying of AIDS in *Philadelphia* (Jonathan Demme, 1993) broke new ground for Hollywood cinema, but some critics argued that the good intentions were confounded by narrative structures that reaffirmed heterosexuality as the norm. Outside Hollywood, filmmakers like Rainer Werner Fassbinder and Derek Jarman dedicated careers to examining contemporary society

11-19. *La Femme de l'hôtel* [*A Woman in Transit*] (Canada, 1984), with (from left to right) Louise Marleau, Paule Baillargeon, and Marthe Turgeon, directed by Léa Pool.

Pool's highly personal films deal with characters—usually, but not always, women—who feel out of place and who are unsure of their sexual identities. In this film, Baillargeon plays a filmmaker who has just returned to Montreal after a long absence, and encounters a woman (Marleau) who has left home and is wandering through the city. She brings this woman together with the actress (Turgeon) who is to play the main character in her film, and the three women develop a friendship in which they seem to form one composite character. *(ACPAV)*

from a gay perspective. In Canada, important work in this direction has come from John Greyson **(5-3)** and Thom Fitzgerald **(11-20)**.

Gay filmmakers have adopted a variety of styles, although many have been associated with a **camp** sensibility that involves the theatrical exaggeration and mockery of conventional stereotypes. Recently, **queer theory** has explored and celebrated films and filmmakers whose work expresses forms of subjectivity and sexuality that deviate from the established norms. Originally, a pejorative term used against homosexuals, "queer" was adopted by theorists to undermine the binary oppositions on which most thinking about sexuality depends. Sexual orientation is thus not an either/or proposition in which heterosexuality is the norm, but rather an unstable and complex process within which individuals pursue their, sometimes unacknowledged, desires. Queer theorists have also interpreted mainstream films "against the grain" to show how the codes of heterosexual romance are often subverted by subtexts that allow for more perverse readings.

Alongside the new ways of thinking about gender and sexuality associated with the feminist and gay liberation movements, attitudes toward race and ethnicity have also changed. Film theorists have explored the implications for the medium of what Cornel West has called "the new cultural politics of difference," which seeks to break

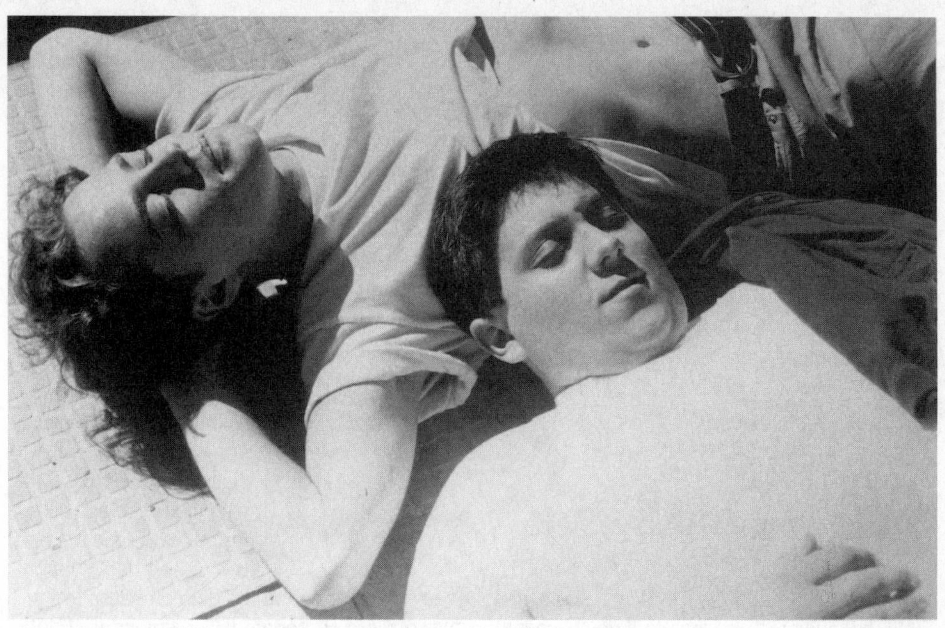

11-20. *The Hanging Garden* (Canada, 1997), with Troy Veinoftte and Joel S. Keller, directed by Thom Fitzgerald.

An overweight adolescent (Veinotte) awakens to an awareness of his homosexuality and then hangs himself in the garden in which his father abused him as a child. At least this is what appears to happen in a film whose realism often becomes surrealist; we have already seen William (played by a different actor) return to his rural Nova Scotia home from the city where he has lost weight and become secure and comfortable with his sexual identity. As the director puts it, the film shows that "no matter how much you hate your life and yourself in the current moment, it is possible to become the person you want to be." *(Alliance Atlantis)*

down the binary oppositions that **structuralists** identified as vital to the dominant ideology and classical narrative cinema. Instead of oppositions, such as us/them, white/black, in which one term is always preferred, the new approach advocates hybrid identities and hybrid forms to express a range of different possibilities (see **10-25** and **10-26**).

Black film historians have chronicled the sad, shameful treatment of black people in American movies—a mean-spirited reflection of their treatment in American society as a whole **(11-21)**. For the first fifty years of American cinema, black characters were usually relegated to demeaning stereotypes. The title of Donald Bogle's 1989 history of blacks in American films says it all: *Toms, Coons, Mulattoes, Mammies & Bucks*. More recently, some critics have begun to analyze how some performers were able to transcend these stereotypes and certain movies (especially musicals) were able to critique them.

When movies began to address issues of race and ethnicity, they often dramatized the tensions between the dominant ideology and the cultural values of a minority community. For example, in Australian cinema, several movies dealt with the clash between the predominantly white, Anglo-Saxon power structure and the

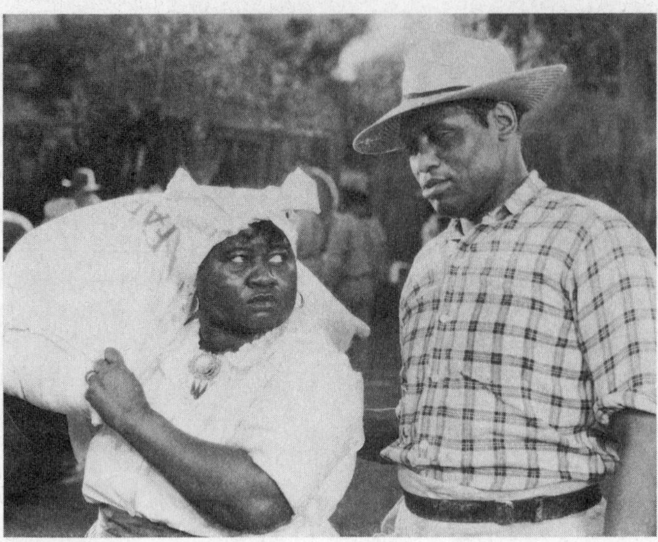

11–21. *Show Boat* (U.S.A., 1936), with Hattie McDaniel and Paul Robeson, directed by James Whale. Throughout the big studio era, African-American performers were almost invariably stereotyped as mammies, maids, Uncle Toms or sinister "bucks." Hattie McDaniel was usually cast as a Mammy, but within that narrow range, she was superb, especially in comic roles. She was the first black performer ever to win an Oscar—as best supporting actress in *Gone With the Wind*. She was not even invited to attend the gala premiere in Atlanta, because in 1939, parades down Peachtree Street were segregated. The legendary Paul Robeson was treated even more shabbily. His famous rendition of "Ol' Man River" in *Show Boat* was considered his signature song for decades. But Robeson became increasingly critical of the racism in America and was drawn to left-wing politics, rendering him a controversial figure during the "Red Scare" of the post–World War II era. In 1950 the U.S. State Department revoked his passport, preventing him from working abroad. Long before the Civil Rights Movement of the 1960s, Paul Robeson was admired as a symbol of black pride and outstanding achievement in the face of fierce hostility. *(Universal Pictures)*

dark-skinned Aboriginal peoples, who have a long heritage of oppression and exploitation, as in *The Chant of Jimmie Blacksmith* **(11-22)**.

In contemporary cinema, black directors have made their mark in Hollywood, and filmmakers from other ethnic groups have made successful films in many countries, offering a new perspective on old problems, but also celebrating their cultural traditions and exploring the new identities emerging within contemporary popular culture. No black filmmaker has provoked more controversy than Spike Lee. Much of his criticism has been directed at people of his own race. In *Do the Right Thing*, Lee explores the smouldering tensions between black ghetto dwellers and an Italian-American family who owns a pizzeria in an inner-city neighbourhood **(7-11)**. In *Jungle Fever* (1991), Lee dramatizes the problems of an interracial couple. The story ends with the lovers calling it quits—defeated by the prejudices of their own communities as well as their personal failings.

The values and characteristics of the dominant groups in society are not normally regarded as ethnic, while the different values of so-called ethnic groups have often been represented in the media through negative stereotypes. It is often difficult for filmmakers to avoid confirming these stereotypes even if they set out to oppose them. Thus, John Smith's National Film Board film *Sitting in Limbo* (1986), which deals with the problems of teenagers in Montreal's Caribbean community, runs the risk of reinforcing stereotypes because of its focus on a pregnant black woman and her unemployed boyfriend.

11-22. *The Chant of Jimmie Blacksmith* (Australia, 1978), with Angela Punch and Tommy Lewis, directed by Fred Schepisi.

This film is based on an actual series of events that took place around 1900. Jimmie Blacksmith (Lewis), half white and half Aborigine, is rescued from a life of misery by a Caucasian missionary couple. They raise him to be docile and respectful, to admire all that is white and despise all that is black. The Reverend Mrs. even advises the youth to marry a white farm girl and produce children, who in turn will produce children who would be "scarcely black at all." The roots of racism, Schepisi demonstrates, are both economic and sexual. Whites exploit Jimmie and other Aborigines as cheap labour and fear them as sexual threats. *(New Yorker Films)*

Members of ethnic groups have historically been faced with the choice of assimilating into the mainstream of society or attempting to conserve the group's cultural heritage. Canada's policy of multiculturalism was designed to offer a third option, in which ethnic groups could participate in the national culture while retaining their distinct identities. Although this policy had some unforeseen effects, it anticipated recent changes caused by increased mobility and the spread of electronic media in the modern world.

After his critically acclaimed first feature *Masala* (see **10-25**), dealing with the East Indian community in Canada, Srinivas Krishna broadened his scope to tackle many of these issues in his next film. The title character in *Lulu* is a Vietnamese woman who was introduced to her white Canadian husband on a videotape made in a Hong Kong refugee camp **(Colour Plate 5)**. Other characters include an Asian expelled from Uganda by Idi Amin, the husband's Caribbean friend, and a Chilean refugee making a video documentary about the experience of ethnic minorities. The movie deals with the emergence of hybrid identities in what the husband calls a "mixed neighbourhood," and with the role of the media in this process. It draws on ethnic and gender stereotypes but constantly unsettles the assumptions on which they

11-23. *Boyz N the Hood* (U.S.A., 1991), with Cuba Gooding Jr., Larry Fishburne, and Ice Cube, written and directed by John Singleton.

Black filmmakers in the United States often use a realistic style to depict the authentic textures of everyday life. *Boys N the Hood* is a powerful coming-of-age drama set in the mean streets of the black ghettos of Los Angeles. Director John Singleton made this debut film on a small budget when he was only twenty-two years old. He was the youngest director in history to be nominated for an Academy Award in directing. *(Columbia Pictures)*

are based. The film proved a critical and commercial failure, perhaps because of the tacit assumption that diasporic filmmakers should restrict their attention to those groups to which they belong.

POST-THEORY

In 1996 David Bordwell and Noël Carroll published a large collection of essays entitled *Post-Theory: Reconstructing Film Studies*. The book was an attack on the dominance of structuralist-psychoanalytic theory, which the editors called "Grand Theory." By the time the book appeared, however, the field of film theory had already become much more diverse, and theorists drew on different theoretical frameworks as required to investigate specific issues and problems. Three of the most important lines of inquiry have involved the use of cognitive psychology, archival research, and reception theory.

Bordwell himself has been especially interested in cognitive models of spectatorship that stress the conscious activity involved in responding to a film, as opposed to psychoanalytic theories, which insist that film viewing is most profoundly shaped by the unconscious. This interest is an extension of Bordwell's early work, which drew

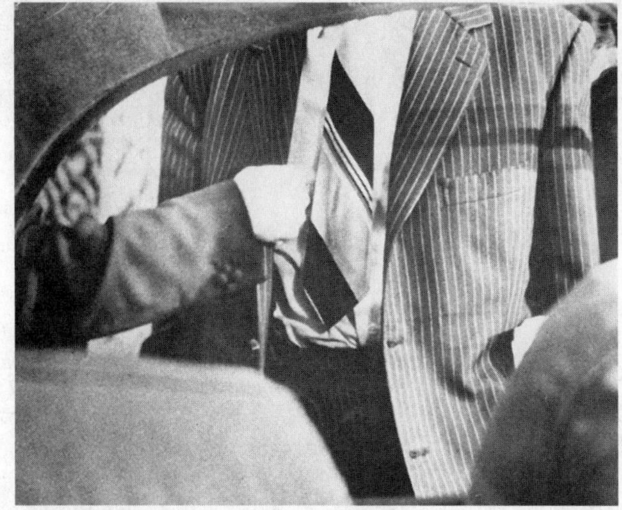

11-24. *Pickpocket* (France, 1959), directed by Robert Bresson.

"Every film trains its spectator," writes David Bordwell. In classical cinema, this can be done very easily at the outset by cues that establish the ways in which the film will use the devices of film language already familiar to the spectator. In Bresson's minimalist films, a scarcity of cues disorients the spectator and often makes it difficult to interpret the action. In the sequences depicting the pickpocket at work, the editing juxtaposes close-ups of his hands with shots of his impassive face, making it difficult for us to interpret his feelings, but also to be sure of exactly how the shots relate to each other. By the end of the film, we have been trained, if we do not reject the experience, in a way of seeing that resists our attempts to read meaning into the characters and events depicted. *(New Yorker Films)*

on the ideas of a group of theorists, often referred to as the Russian formalists, who influenced the Soviet montage filmmakers of the 1920s. The formalists argued that works of art make us aware of their formal procedures and make it possible for us to view familiar events or experiences in new ways. In the case of movies, spectators compare images and sounds to their previous experience of similar films with the help of cues provided by the filmmakers **(11-24)**.

Cognitive psychology deals with the activities of the mind involved in perception and comprehension. From this perspective, even quite conventional films require an active response from their audiences, a marked contrast from the passive spectators manipulated by ideology associated with psychoanalytic theory. Our creative activity enables us to recognize the schemas and templates that we need to decipher images and to construct a film's story from its plot (see Chapter 2, "Story"). Film theorists interested in these processes typically focus on short segments of movies to demonstrate how the mind processes information as a film unfolds.

The new film historians also tend to work in close-up rather than long shot. Broad historical surveys continue to appear, integrating technological, economic, and social factors into discussions of major films from world cinema. A recent example of this approach is *Film History: An Introduction* by Bordwell and Kristin Thompson. Such works are vital for understanding the development of the medium, but they are inevitably highly selective even when they run, as they often do, to several hundred pages. The new interest in history among film scholars is centrally concerned with questions about the processes of selection, and with analyzing the evidence that the "broad brush" approach leaves out. In *Film History: Theory and Practice*, Robert C. Allen and Douglas Gomery outline the main theoretical debates around the writing of film history.

11-25. Publicity photo of cinematographer Billy Bitzer, perched in front of a moving railroad engine with his famous "Biograph camera," circa 1908.

The moving camera (in the full sense of the term) was a major "attraction" in early cinema. Years before this photo was taken, filmmakers had mounted cameras on trains to create spectacular travelogues, and exhibitors sometimes showed such films in simulated railroad coaches that vibrated as the scenery rushed past the windows. The excitement of railroads was soon integrated into the plot structures of the emerging classical cinema. Bitzer worked for D.W. Griffith, who often exploited the speed and glamour of the steam engine for his last-minute-rescue sequences, as in *The Lonedale Operator* (1911) and *Intolerance* (1916). The narrative (and comic) possibilities of locomotion were fully exploited by Buster Keaton in *The General* (1927). *(Kino on Video)*

Historians may choose to focus on a particular period. The discovery and restoration of many early films has allowed historians to correct earlier assumptions about the origins of the medium and to challenge evolutionary approaches that referred to a "primitive" phase, which paved the way for the classical paradigm. Tom Gunning's work on early cinema as a "cinema of attractions" has proved especially fruitful **(11-24)**. He argues that early films were exhibitionist rather than voyeuristic, appealing to the spectator's visual curiosity by offering a succession of spectacular sights, rather like the varied attractions in a fairground. Gunning claimed that this tradition was quite distinct from the emphasis on plot and character in classical cinema and suggested that it persisted in certain forms of avant-garde filmmaking. Some critics have taken up the idea of the cinema of attractions and applied it to developments in contemporary Hollywood where action films, like the James Bond and Indiana Jones

11-26. ***Follow the Fleet*** **(U.S.A., 1936), with Ginger Rogers and Fred Astaire, directed by Mark Sandrich.**

In her book *Star Gazing: Hollywood Cinema and Female Spectatorship*, Jackie Stacey draws on letters and questionnaires from more than three hundred respondents to investigate the appeal of Hollywood stars to women in Britain in the 1940s and 1950s. By comparing these women's memories of filmgoing to statistics about the makeup of cinema audiences, Stacey argues that there was a greater range of responses than earlier feminist theory had allowed. One of the letter writers compared her intense experience of the movies to the "high young people get now by doing drugs." "It wasn't Ginger Rogers dancing with Fred Astaire," she wrote, "it was me." *(RKO)*

series, offer loosely constructed narratives as a vehicle for a series of spectacular chases and explosions.

Film historians have also investigated the industrial organization within which films are made and shown. A good deal of work has been done on the Hollywood studio system, which was an attempt on the part of a handful of large corporations—MGM, Paramount, Warner Brothers, and so on—to monopolize the production of fiction films and hence maximize their profits. For about three decades—roughly from 1925 to 1955—the major studios succeeded, producing about 90 percent of the fiction films in the United States, largely because the companies practised **vertical integration**; that is, they controlled all three phases of the industry: (1) production—the Hollywood studios; (2) distribution—financial headquarters in New York; and (3) exhibition—the large chains of big-city first-run theatres owned by the company. As well as investigating the creation, functioning, and eventual decline of this vast economic machine, historians have also been concerned with regional and local aspects of the film business. Gregory Waller's painstaking study of "movies and commercial entertainment" in Lexington, Kentucky is just one example of this kind of work.

Film historians have also focused on issues of government policy and the institutions involved in regulating and supporting film production, distribution, and exhibition. In his book *So Close to the State/s*, Michael Dorland uses a vast range of archival papers to uncover the backroom debates that went on in Canada during the long period leading up to the establishment of the Canadian Film Development Corporation (see Chapter 10, "Canadian Cinema").

Archival research is also a component of much recent work in **reception theory**. This term covers a wide range of activities, all aimed at finding out more about how actual audiences respond to movies as opposed to the implied reader that critics extrapolate from the text or to the ideological subject of psychoanalytic film theory. Evidence about viewing habits during the Hollywood studio era can be found in the fan magazines that flourished at the time, and many theorists are interested in contemporary fan culture. Henry Jenkins, for example, has stressed the ways in which fans actively engage with texts and often rework them in their own creative variations (a process that has been greatly facilitated by the Internet). Other researchers have used interviews and questionnaires to discover audience reaction to specific films, a practice that requires a good deal of care in securing the cooperation of the informants and in interpreting their answers **(11-26)**.

By naming their book *Post-Theory*, Bordwell and Carroll wanted to draw attention to the need for more empirical approaches to film study, of which the cognitive, historical, and reception theories discussed above are among the most prominent examples. The title plays on the proliferation of "posts" in contemporary cultural theory. We have had post-structuralism, post-colonialism, post-industrialism, post-feminism, and, of course, postmodernism, which often claims to encompass all the others. This terminology points to the fragmentation of the field of theory that

11-27. *Austin Powers: The Spy who Shagged Me* (U.S.A., 1999), with Mike Myers and Heather Graham, directed by Jay Roach.

In full postmodern mode, the Austin Powers movies are full of allusions and cultural in-jokes. The abject figure of Myers's secret agent mocks the fantasy of the handsome and sexually potent hero in the James Bond movies, but this film also draws on the time-travel paradoxes of the *Terminator* movies and the therapeutic discourses of TV talk shows. As a **parody** of cultural texts that already include a strong element of self-mockery, the film immerses us in a media culture that refers only to itself rather than to anything that might be considered the real world outside. *(New Line Cinema)*

11-28. *Multiplicity* (U.S.A., 1996), with (from left to right) Michael Keaton, Michael Keaton, Michael Keaton, and Michael Keaton, directed by Harold Ramis.

In this zany comedy, Keaton plays a man who cannot keep pace with the demands of his job and find time to spend with his family. His life becomes even more complicated when he tries to solve the problem by cloning himself and must prevent others from seeing his multiple selves. Each clone has a different personality, but the film works as a satire on contemporary society, which encourages people to be themselves, but also expects them to conform to prescribed roles. The possibility of cloning human beings has still not been realized, but Hollywood's technology can generate multiple images of the same actor with complete realism (or is this hyperrealism?). *(Columbia Pictures)*

occurred at the same time as the fragmentation of the mass audience with which earlier film theory was so concerned.

An anxiety about the effects of mass culture was a distinguishing feature of modernism, a term that refers to a set of theories and aesthetic practices developed in response to modernity (the industrial society that created the conditions for the emergence of mass media, including film). Modernists tended to deplore the new popular forms and the "standardization" that they entailed. They rejected realism and narrative, since these forms now dominated mass culture, and admired complex and difficult works of art that demanded an active response from the audience. In contrast, postmodernism stresses aesthetic *play*, rather than the *work* of art, and involves the breakdown of the clear-cut opposition between high and popular culture on which modernism depended. So many divergent explanations of postmodernism exist that it is difficult to define it succinctly, but essentially it involves a response to postmodernity (the so-called post-industrial era saturated with media messages and images). Television and related electronic media are perhaps more suited to the postmodern era than movies, but the cultural changes have had a major impact on films and film theory.

11-29. *Le Confessionnal* [*The Confessional*] (Canada / Britain / France, 1995), directed by Robert Lepage. In his first film, Lepage, who had established his reputation as an avant-garde theatre director, tells the story of a young man who returns to Quebec from China to attend his father's funeral. He finds that his brother is missing and begins to uncover family secrets. Flashbacks take us back to 1952, when Alfred Hitchcock was filming *I Confess* in Quebec City as a contribution to the Canadian Cooperation Project (see Chapter 10, "Canadian Cinema"). Lepage re-creates the premiere of Hitchcock's film at the end of his own film. In sequences set in the past, the glamour of Hollywood is set in opposition to the parochial society of Quebec before the Quiet Revolution (which Hitchcock exploited in his film), and both are contrasted with the global culture of the present, of which the film itself, as a multinational coproduction, is an example. *(Cinémaginaire Inc.)*

Two French cultural theorists have provided most of the key elements of postmodern theory. Jean-François Lyotard, in his 1979 study of the "postmodern condition," commissioned by the Quebec government, attributed the changes in contemporary culture to the decline of the Grand Narratives of modernity, especially the idea of scientific progress. These narratives claimed a universal validity, but they had lost their authority and given way to what Lyotard calls "language games." The postmodern individual must construct (or perform) his or her own identity within the multiple and competing discourses of contemporary society. According to Jean Baudrillard, however, postmodernity is also marked by an even more fundamental loss, the loss of our contact with nature or the real. He refers to this state as hyper-reality, a condition in which images no longer signify the real but simply refer us to other images. Thus, he argues that *Schindler's List* (1993) did not restore the memory of the Holocaust, as Steven Spielberg had hoped, but created a simulation of it, drawing on the well-known photos and artifacts that were then swallowed up into his fiction.

The most well known English-language exponent of postmodern theory is Fredric Jameson. He writes from a Marxist perspective and defines postmodernism as "the cultural logic of late capitalism." A shift has occurred, he argues, so that people are no longer identified by what they produce but by what they consume. Identity has become a matter of images and, in general, postmodernism stresses the importance of surface appearances rather than what may or may not lie beneath them. It is a culture marked by what Jameson calls "the waning of affect," hence the need for films to escalate images of violence and sexuality to provoke a reaction from the audience. Another postmodern symptom, according to Jameson, is the loss of a sense of history: Although the media bombard us with the signs and images of history, we are no longer able to situate them in a causal sequence. He points to the popularity of the nostalgia film as the sign of a frustrated desire for a more meaningful relation with the past: The *Back to the Future* series (Robert Zemeckis, 1985–1990) thus becomes the paradigmatic product of postmodern cinema.

Following up on the ideas of Marshall McLuhan, who especially influenced Baudrillard, postmodern theorists explore the relations between culture and technology, and this issue becomes a theme in many contemporary films. Donna Haraway's influential "cyborg manifesto" pointed to the many ways in which we now spend our everyday lives "plugged in" to technological devices that extend our minds and senses, so that the boundaries between human and machine, and between inside and outside are increasingly difficult to define. This situation is explored in the work of filmmakers such as David Cronenberg and Atom Egoyan, and it permeates many recent Hollywood action films, including *RoboCop* (Paul Verhoeven, 1987), *Total Recall* (Verhoeven, 1990), *Blade Runner* **(4-21)**, the *Terminator* films (James Cameron, 1984, 1991), and *The Matrix Trilogy* **(3-20)**.

The postmodern condition is often described in terms of "information overload," as media images constantly surround us in our everyday lives. Families remain an important part of most people's experience, and those opposed to the trends in contemporary society often speak in the name of "family values"; however, many of the traditional functions of the family have been taken over by the media. Different versions of postmodernism bemoan the fragmentation of identity or celebrate the possibilities offered by hybrid forms of identity (see **2-6** and **10-26**). With the collapse of traditional binary oppositions, there is a sense that people have multiple selves that are constantly shifting in diverse and rapidly changing cultural environments **(11-28)**. In typical postmodern fashion, it is difficult to separate the personal aspects of these developments from the economic and technological forces that produce and exploit them.

According to Jameson, these cultural conditions result in distinctive postmodern forms that rely heavily on **pastiche**. Pastiche involves the recycling of past styles but with a slight ironic distance. For Jameson, this is an impoverished cultural form, but pastiche can be used creatively. Jane Campion's *The Piano* (1993), for example, uses the narrative structure and iconography of the Gothic melodrama but filters these through a contemporary feminist consciousness. Michael Nyman's pastiche romantic score for the film works in a similar way. A related feature of postmodernism is **intertextuality**, which means that films constantly refer to other films and texts, drawing on the cultural memory bank and challenging the viewer to recognize the significance of the allusion **(11-29)**. In one rather obvious, but highly relevant, example of this practice, the hero in *The Matrix* (Andy and Larry Wachowski, 1999) hides his computer discs in a fake (or simulated) copy of Baudrillard's book *Simulacra and Simulation*.

Pastiche and intertextuality are by no means new phenomena, but their prevalence in postmodern texts implies that originality is no longer possible because everything has been done before. All that can be done is to play with the codes and combine things in new ways. From this perspective, the auteur theory, with its emphasis on the director's personal vision, was definitely modernist but, since everything is grist to the postmodern mill, auteurism is alive and well in film studies (out of nostalgia for lost originality, a postmodernist would say) and in distributors' publicity campaigns (*The Piano*, for example, was marketed as "a Jane Campion film").

As technological developments produce a new global culture that overflows national boundaries, the **diasporic** condition is now experienced by people who have not literally migrated. It is a restless culture in which films are increasingly influenced by the compressed narratives of television advertising and music videos, and by the viewing habits of people used to channel surfing and menu clicking. Popular cinema has responded to these developments either by adapting to them or by resisting them. The challenge for film theory will be to find ways to describe and respond to these broad cultural processes, in which filmmaking is inextricably involved as an art and as an industry, while also pursuing the more precisely defined questions about the medium raised by the cognitivists, film historians, reception theorists, and others.

FURTHER READING

Allen, Robert C., and Douglas Gomery, *Film History: Theory and Practice* (New York: Alfred A. Knopf, 1985). A provocative study of the problems of writing film history.

Bordwell, David, and Noël Carroll, eds., *Post-Theory: Reconstructing Film Studies* (Madison: University of Wisconsin Press, 1996). A variety of new approaches to film theory.

Braudy, Leo, and Marshall Cohen, eds., *Film Theory and Criticism: Introductory Readings* (6th ed.) (New York: Oxford University Press, 2004). An excellent collection of articles from a variety of perspectives.

Chaudhuri, Shohini, *Feminist Film Theorists* (London: Routledge, 2006). Lucid introduction to the ideas of several key theorists.

Connor, Steven, *Postmodernist Culture: An Introduction to Theories of the Contemporary* (2nd ed.) (Oxford: Blackwell, 1997). Lucid survey with a chapter on postmodern TV, video, and film.

Dickinson, Peter, *Screening Gender, Framing Genre: Canadian Literature into Film* (Toronto: Toronto University Press, 2007). Theoretical study of adaptation.

Lapsley, Robert, and Michael Westlake, *Film Theory: An Introduction* (2nd ed.) (Manchester: Manchester University Press, 2005). Thorough survey of the field.

McGowan, Todd, and Sheila Kunkle, eds., *Lacan and Contemporary Film* (New York: Other Press, 2004). New approaches to psychoanalytic theory and its application to contemporary cinema.

Smith, Murray, *Engaging Characters: Fiction, Emotion, and the Cinema* (Oxford: Clarendon Press, 1995). Cognitive theory of spectatorship.

Stam, Robert, and Toby Miller, eds., *Film and Theory: An Anthology* (Oxford: Blackwell, 2000). An exhaustive collection of major theoretical work.

Citizen Kane (RKO)

WRITING ABOUT MOVIES

12

I don't make a distinction between directing and criticism.

—JEAN-LUC GODARD

OVERVIEW

Kinds of writing about movies: reviews, critical essays, theory. Preparing the essay. Writing: introduction, argument, analysis, conclusion. Constructing an argument. Analyzing a movie. Final editing.

The previous chapters have provided an introduction to the basic elements of film language as well as to some of the ways in which critics have approached film analysis. This chapter will provide some guidelines for writing critical essays about movies in the context of an introductory film course. These guidelines should not be seen as rigid rules; just as there are many kinds of movie, there are many ways to write a good essay. However, it is best to know the common strategies and conventions before thinking about how they can be modified or broken.

The main emphasis here will be on an assignment in which students are required to write about a single film—a common assignment in introductory courses, although the basic principles also apply to more advanced and extensive topics. In order to make these instructions as concrete as possible, we will relate these principles of writing to two specific movies: *Citizen Kane* (Orson Welles, 1941) and *Mon oncle Antoine* (Claude Jutra, 1971). Welles's film has often been cited as one of the greatest films ever made, while critics have repeatedly selected Jutra's film as the best Canadian film, but the main reason for choosing them is not their celebrity: As well as being easily accessible, they are rich texts that provide the opportunity to relate questions of writing to the issues of film language, style, and meaning discussed in the preceding chapters.

It is unlikely that students in an introductory course would be asked to write critical essays on these classic, and much discussed, films. The following guidelines provide pointers to strategies that can be applied to other films that may be chosen by the instructor or by the student.

KINDS OF WRITING ABOUT MOVIES

There are basically three different types of writing about movies: reviews, critical essays, and theory. The main focus in this chapter will be on the critical essay, since this is what is most usually required in introductory film courses. As a first step, however, it is useful to distinguish critical writing from the other types, although there are no firm boundary lines and much writing on film includes elements of more than one type.

A reviewer writes for readers who have not seen the film in question and are seeking an informed opinion about whether it is worth seeing. Reviewing is thus largely concerned with value judgments—with whether, in the writer's opinion, a film is good or bad. A review thus offers a subjective response to a film (although some reviewers write as if their word were law) and should provide enough information for the reader to understand the criteria by which the film is being judged. Reviewers must be aware of the readership of the journal or newspaper in which their work will be published but will not normally expect a specialized background in film studies. Reviews in film journals tend to be longer and more detailed than those in daily newspapers, and they may adopt the more rigorous and formal style of a critical essay.

12-1. Promotional poster for *Citizen Kane*.

The promotional campaign for *Citizen Kane* stressed Welles's box-office appeal as the film's star and the "boy wonder" whose controversial reputation as a director for theatre and radio included the infamous radio adaptation of H.G. Wells's *The War of the Worlds* that caused panic across the U.S. in 1938. True to form, the film itself caused a major controversy when it came under attack from William Randolph Hearst, who claimed (correctly) that he was the model for Charles Foster Kane and refused to allow any publicity for the film in his newspaper chain. The studio capitalized on Welles's reputation, but the campaign also revealed anxiety about its impact on the film's commercial prospects. Posters and lobby displays exaggerated the love angle, presumably to appeal to women patrons: "I hate him!" proclaims Kane's second wife. "I love him!" counters his first. (Neither statement is in the movie, of course). *(RKO)*

A theorist uses films as examples to explore and test hypotheses about film language or about the cultural, philosophical, or political implications of certain kinds of filmmaking. Theorists usually assume their readers will be familiar with a wide range

Mon oncle Antoine
Réalisé par Claude Jutra
Produit par Marc Beaudet

12-2. Promotional poster for *Mon oncle Antoine*. Although the National Film Board was mainly interested in documentaries, it did produce several fiction films in the late 1960s and early 1970s. The most successful of these was *Mon oncle Antoine*, the story of a boy growing up among the asbestos mines in a rural Quebec community before the Quiet Revolution (see Chapter 10, "Canadian Cinema") and based on the childhood experiences of the screenwriter Clément Perron. When the film was finished, NFB executives were not impressed and delayed its release. It was eventually shown to great acclaim at a number of international film festivals, an achievement that the NFB emphasized in its publicity campaign. Images of the wintry landscape highlight the film's visual appeal as well as the harsh conditions in which "an adolescent discovers the adult universe." *(National Film Board of Canada)*

of films and will often expect them to be well versed in earlier film theory and other relevant disciplines. In some cases, a theorist may hardly refer to specific films at all, but the most convincing theoretical arguments are usually supported by examples drawn from a film or body of films. Theory can be descriptive or prescriptive: A genre theorist, for example, might simply describe the range of conventions as they appear over time in the history of the genre, but another might argue that certain ways of using the conventions are "truer" to the genre than others.

Critical essays occupy a middle ground, usually assuming that the reader has seen the films under discussion but is less familiar with them than the writer. This means that the critic has to strike a delicate balance: Plot summary should be avoided, but enough information about the narrative should be included so that the reader can understand how specific sequences and images fit into the film's overall structure. One common misconception is that being "critical" implies a negative value judgment; rather, the critical attitude is one that asks questions about how a film creates the effects and meanings the critic discovers in it. Although value judgments are ultimately important, the first task of a critic is to analyze a film on its own terms, to look for the cues that tell us how the film wants us to respond.

What this means is that, in adopting the role of the critic in an essay assignment, your task is analysis—not evaluation. Whether or not you enjoyed a particular film is not at issue in most assignments, although it is certainly easier to write about a movie you respect than one you detest. More important are questions about film form, meaning, and structure, and your interpretation of the relationships among these things. The expected writing style in a critical essay also occupies a middle ground between the colloquial style adopted in some reviews and the specialized vocabulary that theorists often find unavoidable.

Most critical essays in film journals and edited collections involve research into the film's background, its social and historical context, other related films, and so on. Although students will eventually learn to do this kind of research, the emphasis in many introductory courses is on the important skill of textual analysis drawing on evidence found in viewing the film. One common first assignment in such courses is a sequence analysis, in which students are asked to identify the shots in a short segment of a film, how they are organized through editing, and how they function within the overall structure of the film. A critical essay dealing with an entire film is really just an extension of this assignment. In the case of famous films such as *Citizen Kane* and *Mon oncle Antoine*, it is difficult to ignore all the surrounding information about their production and their contributions to film history (some of which is summarized in the captions to the photos in this chapter), but for the purpose of the guidelines in this chapter, they will be treated as if they were new and relatively unknown movies.

PREPARING TO WRITE

The process of writing a good film essay has much in common with making a good movie. Film is, of course, a collaborative medium, whereas in the case of an essay, you alone are responsible for the content; but the stages of pre-production (writing the script, organizing the resources), production (shooting the film), and post-production (editing) can be compared to the work of preparing, writing, and editing an essay.

Preparing an essay is a much less elaborate process than the pre-production of a film, but it is equally important. The first thing to do is to make certain you understand the assignment and the particular requirements of the instructor. The guidelines offered in this chapter should not override the specific instructions you receive in the course.

Viewing the film or films is the obvious next step. To produce a good essay usually requires you to view the film more than once and to take notes, either during or immediately after the viewing. You need to analyze your responses to the film and think about *how* the film encouraged these responses, using the elements of film language discussed in the earlier chapters of this book. This process should allow you to develop a topic for the essay, a particular question about an aspect of the film you want to explore. This should become the primary focus as you move to the writing stage and should be used to prepare a plan of the structure of the essay (see **12-6** and **12-7**).

As part of the preparation stage, make sure you are aware of the expectations regarding the use of secondary sources in the assignment. In a film essay, the primary sources are the films you discuss; secondary sources are other writings that you use to support your own argument. If the assignment is one that requires close textual analysis, you may not be encouraged to use secondary sources, in which case the essay should consist of your own interpretation of the film, supported by analysis of the film itself. If you do make use of secondary sources, be sure to acknowledge them. Whenever you quote or paraphrase someone else's words or ideas, this should be acknowledged by endnotes or in-text citations with page numbers, using a standard reference format (such as APA or MLA). As well, a bibliography should be included at the end of your essay (for an example of correct formatting, see the Works Cited/Further Reading section at the end of this chapter). All quotations should be clearly indicated by the use of quotation marks. You do not need to provide references for basic film terms but, if you do draw on definitions taken from

12-3. *Citizen Kane.*

Citizen Kane begins with the end—the death of its protagonist when he is about seventy-five. In his final moments of life, the old man holds a small crystal ball containing a miniature scene that flurries with artificial snow when shaken. With his last dying breath, he utters the word "Rosebud." Then the glass ball crashes to the floor, splintering into a thousand fragments. The plot of the movie is structured like a search—for the meaning of this final utterance. *(RKO)*

books, you must acknowledge this. Failure to acknowledge your sources constitutes plagiarism, a serious form of academic misconduct. It is permissible, however, to quote the dialogue from a film without providing references.

WRITING THE ESSAY

Many of the expectations of a critical essay about a film also apply to any form of writing. There are basic rules of format that should be followed (again, you should ensure that you are aware of any specific instructions for the assignment). Normally, you should print the essay, double-spaced, leaving ample margins for the marker's comments. Film and book titles should be *italicized* whenever they occur in an essay. You may underline them, if you wish, but this is a relic from the days of typewriters when underlining indicated to a publisher that the words should be italicized in the final copy. In any case, be consistent. If you refer to articles or chapters in books, their titles should not be italicized but placed within quotation marks; the titles of journals or books should be in italics. Your first mention of a film must include the director's name and the release date (unless some other convention is required).

It is best to avoid using the first person ("I") unless you are making a critical point about your own experience of the film. There is no need to preface sentences

12-4. *Mon oncle Antoine*, with Jean Duceppe and Jacques Gagnon, directed by Claude Jutra.

Originally the film was to have been called *Silent Night* (in English), a reference to both the Christmas setting and what Jutra called "Quebec's night which lasted so long." The film centres on Benoît (Gagnon), an adolescent boy who lives at the village store with his Uncle Antoine (Duceppe). He observes his elders and sees how they have been ground down by the conditions in which they live, especially his uncle, who also runs an undertaking business despite his fear of the bodies. The film's apparently nostalgic **tone** is belied by Benoît's critical perspective and by his own fears of death and sexuality. In this sequence, he is shocked by his uncle's hearty appetite when they arrive at an isolated farmhouse to collect the corpse of a boy of Benoît's age who has just died, and his disgust is portrayed through distorted close-ups of Antoine's mouth as he eats and drinks. From the youth's perspective, his uncle is callous and unfeeling, but the food is part of the ritual of rural life, in which mourning for the dead does not exclude a practical concern for the needs of the living. *(National Film Board of Canada)*

with "I think," because it is assumed that the essay presents your views, using evidence from the film to convince the reader rather than relying on an assertion of your opinion. Also you should avoid the second person ("you"): Addressing a reader directly when giving instructions, as in these guidelines (or in a marker's comments on an essay), is acceptable because it makes the communication more personal, but, in a critical essay, it gives the impression of assuming that everyone shares your response to the film (inviting the reader to disagree).

Provide your essay with a title that will explain its purpose. As we have seen, a film title cues audiences to the kind of movie they can expect to see (see Chapter 1, "Medium"), and it is often a good idea to think about why the filmmakers chose the title they did: Why did Welles emphasize that Kane is a "citizen"; why did Jutra use the first person ("my") and focus attention on Benoît's uncle? Similarly, an essay should have a title that prepares the reader for what is to follow. Finding a good title

Claude Jutra's *Mon oncle Antoine* (1971) is set, as the opening caption tells us, "not so long ago" in a small town in the asbestos-mining region of Quebec. It offers what may at first seem to be a nostalgic view of the past, but, as the film progresses, we come to see that the situation is much less attractive than it might seem. Our perspective is closely tied to that of Benoît, a teenage boy adopted by Antoine and Cécile, who own the general store that is at the centre of the life of the community. This essay will analyze the use of point-of-view shots to show how the film involves us with his adolescent fears of sexuality and death as well as his growing disillusionment with adult society, especially with his "uncle" who turns out to be far from the authority figure he seems to be.

12-5. Sample introductory paragraph.

This paragraph might introduce an essay on *Mon oncle Antoine* (see **12-7**). A research essay, more appropriate to an upper-level course, would use secondary sources to discuss the relationship between Benoît's personal experience and the social changes associated with the Quiet Revolution, which is often traced back to strike action by asbestos miners in the 1940s. The essay envisaged here would draw its evidence entirely from the film.

is also an effective way of starting to organize your ideas. Simply putting "Film Studies Term Paper" on the title page is no help to you or to the reader. Titles such as "Film as the Narration of Space: *Citizen Kane*" or "Double Vision: *Mon oncle Antoine* and the Cinema of Fable," as in two essays listed in the "Further Reading" section, not only specify the films the essays deal with but also indicate what the central focus of their arguments will be. As in these cases, a subtitle, separated from the title by a colon, is a common way of drawing attention to what will be studied and how the essay will be organized, although a subtitle is not always necessary.

The essay title gestures toward the topic and the basic argument, and these should be briefly fleshed out in the introductory paragraph. Normally, an introduction begins by explaining the research question you want to answer in the essay and ends with a thesis statement indicating the steps you will take to develop your argument in the body of the essay (see **12-5**). As in classical narrative cinema, the opening poses a question, and your task is to ensure that the reader—like the viewer—has a clear sense of the different stages of your investigation.

In a short essay on a single film, there is usually no need for section headings, but each paragraph should develop a distinct idea and be understood as a step on a journey taking your reader through your argument and evidence. Organizing your ideas into paragraphs is important: You should avoid one-sentence paragraphs that would disrupt the continuity of your argument; on the other hand, very long paragraphs become difficult to follow, and you should find ways of breaking the argument into smaller units if you find the paragraphs taking up more than a page.

Title:	THE PRIVATE LIFE OF A PUBLIC CITIZEN: *CITIZEN KANE*
1. Intro:	Film depicts rise to power and loss of all Kane gained
Opening:	Death of Kane and newsreel, from private to public
Thesis statement:	Kane seeks power to compensate for lack of love
2. Plot and story:	Fragmented narrative stresses difficulty of knowing inner life "No Trespassing" sign
3. Loss of mother:	Use of space to emphasize separation of mother and son She places his future over her love for him
4. First wife:	Breakfast scene: editing and breakdown of relationship His immersion in work; her social snobbery
5. Second wife:	Opera sequences: Kane uses Susan to overcome shame Suicide attempt: Kane admits defeat
6. Xanadu:	Huge spaces reflect power but also isolation and loss of control
7. Possessions:	Kane's mania for "collecting" (associated with two wives) collection becomes "junk" after his death (Rosebud hidden there)
8. Conclusion:	film depicts Kane as public figure undermined by private needs Does Rosebud explain Kane?

12-6. Sample plan for an essay on *Citizen Kane*.

This is a plan for an essay that explores a particular theme, in this case the relationship of public and private life, and demonstrates the significance of this theme by drawing attention to the ways in which it is developed through the use of film language (including, in this case, narrative structure, mise en scène, and editing).

The body of the essay should consist of an argument grounded in evidence based on analysis of the film. Do not try to write about everything. If you choose to focus on a theme (such as "masculinity" or "the search for identity"), make sure that you deal with *how* the film conveys its attitude to the theme. If you choose to focus on technique, make sure that you show how the film's style (the use of editing or colour, for example) contributes to its meanings. Always try to be as precise as possible: Avoid vague words such as "interesting," "significant," and "effective." You need to demonstrate *why* what you are describing is interesting and *how* it is relevant to the overall argument. It is also important to be precise about the film techniques you are discussing: For example, do not write "the camera shifts" if you are describing a cut from one shot to the next, or "the camera cuts," as if the camera were editing the film.

Analysis involves focus and selection. You must develop your points by connecting the sequences, images, and details with which you choose to deal in order to construct an organized presentation which will convince the reader that your interpretation is consistent and plausible (the reader does not have to agree with you). You are concerned with effects, not intentions. Do not speculate on what a filmmaker intended to do, especially if you think the film does not succeed in achieving what was intended. You may want to discuss the expectations created by the audience's

Title:	THE BENOÎT PERSPECTIVE: POINT OF VIEW IN *MON ONCLE ANTOINE*
1. Intro:	Film set "not so long ago" Traditional life of village beside asbestos mine
Thesis statement:	Film uses Benoît's POV to critique adult society
2. Society:	English-speaking boss (throwing Christmas presents) Christmas and church (Benoît spies on priest) General store (community: everyone knows everyone else's business)
3. Death and sexuality:	Benoît views body at wake Spies on Alexandrine trying on girdle
4. Male role models:	Jos (cannot settle down) Antoine (patriarch: gets drunk and breaks down) Fernand (easygoing, seduces aunt)
5. POV shots at farmhouse: Benoît observes Antoine eating, boy's body	
6. Journey home: Antoine's confession, Fernand and aunt found together	
7. Ending: Benoît views family around coffin (cf. unveiling of manger scene)	
8. Conclusion:	Essay has shown how film uses Benoît to expose failings of adults Ending leaves us to ask if he is trapped or will break out

12-7. Sample plan for an essay on *Mon oncle Antoine*.

This is a plan for an essay that begins from an issue of film language (**point-of-view shots**) and then shows how this technique contributes to the film's meaning (exposing the hypocrisy and repression of traditional society).

cultural knowledge (of the film's genre or stars, for example), but your main focus should be on the cues provided in the film text.

Providing a satisfactory ending to an essay is often as difficult as finding one for a movie. But while the ending of a movie may leave the viewer uncertain about whether the initial question has been fully answered (as is the case with both films discussed here), the conclusion of an essay should convince the reader that the goals set out in the introduction have been achieved. It is often a good idea to refer back to the introduction, without using exactly the same words you used there. The conclusion should not introduce any new evidence, although it may suggest possibilities for further research (see **12-8**).

CONSTRUCTING AN ARGUMENT

The argument in a film essay illustrates the essential unity of form and content, as discussed in Chapter 1, "Medium." A convincing critical essay will present an interpretation of its meaning (content) grounded in close critical analysis of the techniques that express this meaning (form). *Citizen Kane* would be a very different film if Welles had chosen to depict Kane's story in linear fashion using the conventional

As this essay has shown, the film depicts Charles Foster Kane as a complex man whose drive to power and subsequent loss of all he gained can be traced back to his traumatic separation from his mother. However, the film's "jigsaw puzzle" narrative raises questions about how much we can really know about another person's inner life. Although we see Kane's life through the testimony of numerous people who came into contact with him, and Welles uses a barrage of realist and expressionist techniques, *Citizen Kane* still leaves the viewer to decide whether the final revelation explains everything about Kane's character—or nothing at all. The film is an energetic demonstration of the power of cinema but also of the mysteries of human psychology.

12-8. Sample conclusion.
This paragraph might serve as a conclusion to an essay on *Citizen Kane* (see 12-6). It refers back to the initial question posed in the introduction and summarizes the view of the film that has emerged from the argument and analysis in the body of the essay.

techniques of **classical cinema**. Jutra could have made *Mon oncle Antoine* as a nostalgic coming-of-age story or as a darkly satirical depiction of Quebec's past, but instead the frequent shifts in tone keep viewers off-balance and encourage them to think of how the depiction of the past relates to the present (see **12-4**). It is the critic's job to show how the film creates unity—which may mean thinking about the relevance of elements that at first do not seem to belong. The topics discussed in the previous chapters can be used as an aid to finding the organizing principle for an essay.

Citizen Kane and *Mon oncle Antoine* both lend themselves to discussions organized around their relations to the realist and formalist traditions. As David Bordwell has suggested, *Citizen Kane* is a film that celebrates "the two founts of cinema—the fantasy of Méliès and the reportage of Lumière." André Bazin used the film to illustrate his arguments about realism and drew attention to the extensive use of long takes and deep-focus compositions, but other critics have shown that, far from respecting real space and time, many of the shots discussed by Bazin were actually created through special effects. The lighting and editing techniques also often draw on the formalist tradition, and the film certainly does not conform to the idea, shared in different ways by Bazin and classical filmmakers, that style should not call attention to itself. The often jarring combination of realism and formalism occurs at all levels of the film's style and helps to express the tensions that emerge in the film about the interpretation of the life of Charles Foster Kane.

Similarly, for some critics, *Mon oncle Antoine* belongs to the Canadian tradition of fiction films drawing on the techniques of documentary cinema (see Chapter 10, "Canadian Cinema"), but others have stressed the extent to which Jutra departs from this tradition. For example, U.S. critic Herman Weinberg regretted "the implementation of an imposed 'story'" and thought that the film would have worked even better as a "straight documentary on the Québécois." On the other hand, Bruce Elder, an

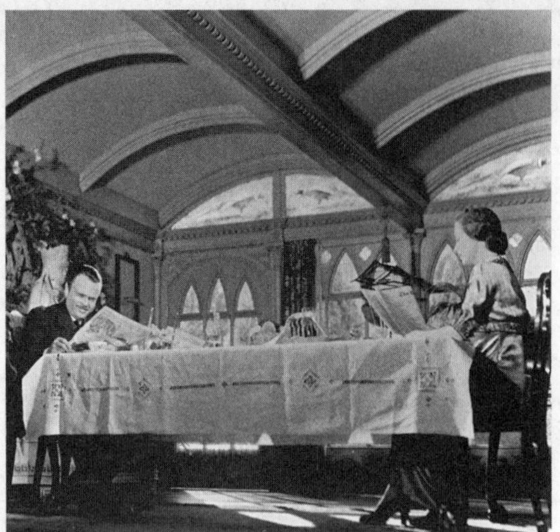

12-9. *Citizen Kane*, with Orson Welles and Ruth Warrick.

A critical analysis would examine how this bravura sequence expresses the growing estrangement between Kane and his first wife. Welles combines a variety of formal devices to create his vision. A rapid **montage** of breakfast scenes, linked by **swish pans**, compresses several years of marriage into a few minutes of screen time. The dialogue records the disagreements that destroy their marriage, and Welles reinforces the effect through the use of space in the **mise en scène**: The physical closeness of the newly married couple gives way to an increasing separation until they sit at either end of a long table with nothing to say to each other. As in many other shots in the film, the **low angle** emphasizes the ceiling, adding to the sense of claustrophobia. The effect of the sequence is also complicated by the fact that it is part of the section narrated by Jed Leland, Kane's former friend and colleague, who cannot have witnessed these scenes himself. *(RKO)*

English-Canadian filmmaker and critic, insisted that *Mon oncle Antoine* owed little to the documentary tradition and stressed "the importance of narrative in the film."

Any argument dealing with the films in terms of their realist and formalist tendencies would need to address how the formal elements work in the context of the overall narrative structures. In both films, one of the central themes is the importance of childhood experiences in shaping adult life, but the formal expression of this theme results in two very different films.

Welles's film begins with the death of an old newspaper tycoon, whose last word is "Rosebud" **(12-3)** and then constructs the story of his life in a series of flashbacks from the point of view of people who knew him. Only at the end do we learn the significance of his dying utterance, but critics have been deeply divided over whether this revelation explains Kane's subsequent life, or whether it shows the folly of believing that one word can explain a man's life. As Dudley Andrew suggests in his book *Film in the Aura of Art*, "The more we search, the more paths we find we must take and the less certain we become of what we see."

Whereas Kane's childhood occupies only one sequence in the narrative in *Citizen Kane*, *Mon oncle Antoine* is entirely focused on the coming of age of Benoît and leaves it up to the viewer to imagine the effects of his experiences on his adult life. The action takes place around Christmas, and a major event in village life occurs when the community gathers to witness the unveiling of the crèche in the store window. At the end, this image is darkly parodied as Benoît peers through the window of a farmhouse, observing the family of an adolescent boy gathered around the coffin, which fell from the sleigh on which Antoine and Benoît were taking it to the village **(12-17)**. Again, critics have been divided over whether the film suggests that nothing will ever change or whether it ends with the hope that Benoît's critical gaze will inspire him to break

Our involvement with Benoît's look reaches a high degree of intensity when he and Antoine travel to the Poulin house to collect the body of the son who has suddenly died on Christmas Eve. This is the first time that Benoît has accompanied his uncle on such an errand, and his eyes are drawn irresistibly, as represented by another zoom shot, to the half-open door of the dead boy's room. His anxiety emerges most vividly through his evident disgust at the sight of Antoine eating the food that the grieving mother has provided. However, his emotional response is conveyed by the use of a fish-eye lens that distorts Antoine's appearance; when viewed "normally," Antoine's behaviour does not seem so inappropriate. He hugs the wife when he arrives and tells her he has tried to contact her husband. Her provision of food and his acceptance of it, after a long and cold journey, are expected behaviour in a traditional peasant culture in which mourning for the dead does not exclude a practical concern with the needs of the living. If this is the case, the distortion reflects Benoît's alienation from this culture as he grapples with his own fears and desires.

12-10. Sample analysis.

This paragraph corresponds to # 5 in the plan for an essay on *Mon oncle Antoine* (**12-7**, see also **12-4**). It follows from a paragraph discussing Benoît's critical observation of the various men in the film who might function as a father figure for him. It is part of an argument that emphasizes the way in which the film involves the viewer with the boy's point of view but does not require an uncritical identification with him. Note: The writer uses technical terms by referring to zoom shots and a fish-eye lens, as described in Chapter 5 ("Movement") and Chapter 3 ("Photography"), but does not need to define them or provide sources.

with that past. The director himself appeared uncertain: In one interview he suggested that Benoît's future seems "hopeless" because there is "no opening available to him," but in another he expressed his belief that the boy would "exorcise" his past and would "learn to live, not all alone, but collectively."

The following list suggests some of the ways in which the topics discussed in this book could be applied in constructing an argument for a critical essay on *Citizen Kane* or *Mon oncle Antoine*:

1. *Story*. The **plot** in *Citizen Kane* divides the **story** into a series of overlapping flashbacks, in which some of the events are seen more than once, linked by the investigations of a news reporter trying to unravel the mystery of Kane's dying word. The focus is thus not on what happened but on the problem of interpretation: piecing together the meaning of what happened based on competing versions of the events. In *Mon oncle Antoine*, the plot is much simpler, taking place over a short period of time, but gradually revealing past events that shaped the characters' present lives: the fact that Benoît is an orphan, for example, or the terrible revelation on the night of the storm that Antoine is afraid of the dead and

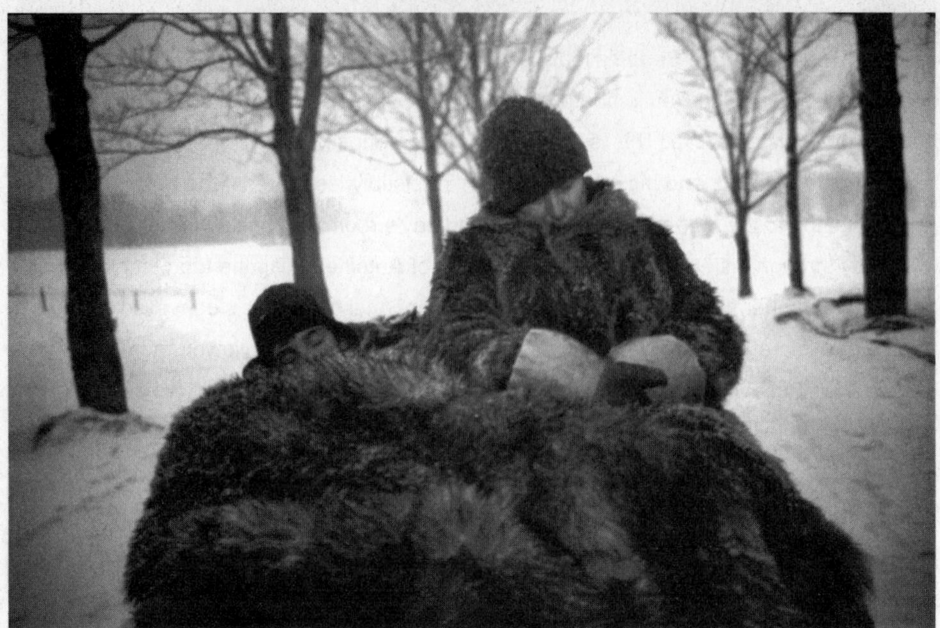

12-11. *Mon oncle Antoine*, with Jacques Gagnon and Jean Duceppe.

As well as running the village store, Antoine is the local undertaker. On Christmas Eve, he receives a message that the son of a farming family has died, and he and Benoît set out through the snow-covered landscape to pick up the body in a horse-drawn sleigh. The events of this night will shatter the adolescent's confidence in the patriarchal figure of his guardian.

has been prevented by his wife from moving to the United States. It is also important that, in a film so focused on Benoît's gaze on the community, the opening sequences place more emphasis on Jos, a farmer who also works at the local mine and whose frustrations cause him to abandon his family to work as a lumberjack. This opening cues us to focus less on the events depicted than on the alternative male models for adult life suggested by Antoine, Jos, and Fernand, the store manager (played by Jutra himself), who Benoît discovers in bed with Antoine's wife when he returns from his terrifying trip to Jos's farm.

2. *Photography*. One of the most notable features of *Citizen Kane* is the deep-focus cinematography created by Gregg Toland. Bazin argued that this technique allows the viewer's eye to scan the image for relevant information much as it would in an actual situation, thereby encouraging a more active response than the continuity editing of classical cinema. Yet Welles's shots, often using unusual angles, call much more attention to themselves than the deep-focus shots Toland contributed to the films of William Wyler (see **3-12b**). The cinematographer on *Mon oncle Antoine* was Michel Brault, who had gained an international reputation for his use of the handheld camera in direct cinema documentaries (see **9-10** and **9-11**) and for his pioneering work with available light. His locating shooting creates a strong sense of physical presence that often makes us forget the film's period setting, but the frequent **zoom shots**, also derived from his documentary practice, create a distancing effect that disturbs some viewers.

12-12. Citizen Kane, with Dorothy Comingore.

Citizen Kane demonstrates that virtually every kind of visual has its aural counterpart. This montage sequence showing the tour that Kane has arranged to show off his second wife as an opera singer is reinforced by an aural montage of Susan Alexander's shrieking arias, orchestral music, popping flashbulbs, and the sounds of newspaper presses rolling. The pounding sounds are machinelike and inexorable, battering their sacrificial victim until she is stupefied by terror and exhaustion. *(RKO)*

3. *Mise en scène*. Welles's theatrical experience clearly influenced his approach to cinematic space. The images are often composed in depth, with important information in the foreground, midground, and background (**12-14**). The **proxemic patterns** among the characters are choreographed to suggest their shifting power relationships. Welles often exaggerates the depth to create a dynamic tension, as in the shot in which a glass and spoon dominate the foreground, while Susan Alexander, Kane's mistress, who has taken an overdose, lies on a bed in the middle ground, and the door through which Kane will burst to save her is seen in the far distance. In the sequences set in Xanadu, the palatial mansion to which Kane withdraws with Susan after the failure of her operatic career, the characters are dwarfed by the massive architecture. Spatial relationships are also important in *Mon oncle Antoine*, although they rarely seem to be as purposefully arranged as in Welles's film. The opening establishes the space of the village surrounded by countryside scarred by asbestos mines, and the viewer is encouraged to adopt a critical view similar to that which Benoît brings to bear on his community. For example, when Benoît and his uncle arrive at the farm, the eldest daughter takes the boy's coat, while a picture of the Virgin Mary on the calendar behind her suggests the traditional role of women to which she is expected to conform.

12-13. *Mon oncle Antoine*.

At the end of the film, Benoît returns to the farmhouse with Fernand, his uncle's assistant (played by Jutra himself) in search of the coffin that fell from the sled on the journey back to the village through a snowstorm. The picturesque image of the sleigh arriving in the morning light, in the calm after the storm, contrasts with the grim circumstances and the traumatic effect of the previous night's experience on the already disillusioned young man. *(National Film Board of Canada)*

4. *Movement*. The moving camera in *Citizen Kane* is usually associated with vitality and youth, paralleling the contrast between the energetic movements of Kane and his friends as young men and the lumbering slowness of Kane in his lonely old age and the stasis of the equally unfulfilled old men the reporter interviews. Movement is also associated with youth in *Mon oncle Antoine*, as when Benoît dances across the pews in church after being released from his duties as an altar boy and, more disastrously, when, after swigging from his uncle's gin bottle, he whips the horse into a gallop, which results in the coffin falling from the sleigh. Stillness is associated with death, as in the funeral wake that Benoît attends at the beginning and in the final tableau of the grieving family.
5. *Editing*. If deep-focus cinematography creates a sense of real space in *Citizen Kane*, several montage sequences condense time into a rapid succession of fragmentary scenes, just as the narrative presents us with fragments of Kane's life at different times (see **12-9**). As with so many aspects of the film's style, the editing draws attention to itself, unlike in *Mon oncle Antoine*, in which the editing is usually unobtrusive. At the beginning, however, the narration jumps around from the mine, to a funeral parlour, to a bar, and to a farm, with little sense of how these locations fit together, encouraging the viewer to think in terms of relationships rather than focus too heavily on the ongoing action.

12-14. ***Citizen Kane,*** **with Harry Shannon, Buddy Swan (in window), George Coulouris, and Agnes Moorehead.**

In this deep-focus composition, the young Charlie Kane plays in the snow in the far background, while his mother sits with a lawyer in the foreground, signing the document that will separate her from her son, and his father looks on impotently in the middle ground. *(RKO)*

6. *Sound.* As might be expected, given Welles's background in radio, sound is as complex in *Citizen Kane* as the visual imagery. Speech is at the core of the film, as the articulate characters pour forth a torrent of words in a futile attempt to pin down Kane's character or to reveal the meaning of a single word, "Rosebud." Bernard Herrmann's music becomes part of a rich web of sound, emphasizing the energy of the young Kane and the brooding loneliness of his old age. The distinction between music and noise breaks down in the sequences involving Susan's rehearsals and performances, in which her shrill voice makes clear to everyone except Kane that she cannot sing (**12-12**). As might be expected, Jean Cousineau's music in *Mon oncle Antoine* is much less prominent, although the ominous drumbeats that sound as Benoît approaches the window at the end of the movie work much like the swelling music Herrmann wrote to accompany the camera moving across the piles of junk in Xanadu after Kane's death, just before it reveals the meaning of his final word. One of the most obvious uses of sound in Jutra's film are the few English words that reveal the gulf between the francophone characters and the economic order outside the

village, most notably apparent in the language of the foreman who takes Jos to task in the opening sequence.

7. *Acting*. The meanings associated with different styles of acting are often difficult to analyze, although an argument may be built around the star personas that actors bring from their previous films. There are no real stars in *Citizen Kane* or *Mon oncle Antoine*, but both directors do appear on screen. Kane was Welles's first film role, but he brought with him a reputation as an actor as well as director on stage and radio, and many of the supporting cast were members of the Mercury Theatre Company that he had founded. He is so obviously at the centre of the film, on screen as well as behind the camera, that critics have often suggested that the brash newspaper tycoon had much in common with the man who created him. Fernand, the role played by Jutra in *Mon oncle Antoine*, is a minor character, but viewers in Quebec knew Jutra from television appearances and his central role in his first feature, *À tout prendre* (**3-18**); they would have been aware that it was the film's director playing this unassuming character who nevertheless quietly directs many of the other characters (even though he is finally seen to be as compromised as Antoine). Unless you are making a point about the casting of a particular actor, it is important that you refer to the characters in a film by their names rather than those of the actors who play them.
8. *Theory*. Theory is unlikely to play a major role in a critical essay, but it can provide a starting point for developing an argument. The tension between realism and formalism in both films has already been mentioned, and both could also lend themselves to feminist arguments regarding the treatment of gender roles (questions of masculinity and authority are central, in different ways, to the depiction of Kane and Benoît). *Mon oncle Antoine* might be discussed in terms of its representation of Quebec or Canada, using the debates about national cinema outlined in Chapter 10, "Canadian Cinema."

In constructing an argument, it is important to be selective: You cannot say everything in a single essay, and the essay would become hopelessly diffuse if you tried. The crucial point is to ask how the filmmakers' choices affect the meanings and impact of their films: *How* does form become content?

PRESENTING THE EVIDENCE

Analysis involves referring to specific elements of the film that support your argument. It is important to avoid straining the evidence. Except in cases where a film presents itself as an allegory, there is no abstract meaning that can simply be read off the images in a movie. Similarly, any analysis of the ideological effects of a movie needs to be sensitive to the context in which the characters and plot developments are embedded. Although an essay can never reproduce for the reader the experience of viewing a movie, you should try to respect the form of the film: Pay attention to the specific characteristics that differentiate it from other movies. For example, an essay on *Citizen Kane* that simply ignored the fragmented way in which it tells its story would miss an important aspect of its meaning and effect.

In other words, you should keep an open mind. It may well be that the process of closely analyzing the film will lead you to adjust your argument. You need to keep the context in mind at all times, but you also need to be selective. Do not provide a long

12-15. *Mon oncle Antoine*, with Monique Mercure.

The arrival of the glamorous wife of a local dignitary in the village store coincides with an explosion at the nearby mine, a comic sound effect that suggests just how conscious she is of her impact on the stunned customers. *(National Film Board of Canada)*

plot summary, but explain only those elements that are relevant to your argument, in sufficient detail to carry your argument. Always use the present tense when discussing the events depicted and the techniques used in a film (as in the caption to **12-15**).

It is always a good idea to look for things that stand out in a movie, that do not seem to fit with the rest: Rather than being a sign of the filmmakers' incompetence, these details can often be the key to uncovering elements of meaning that remain implicit elsewhere in the movie. At the same time, it is usually a good strategy to focus on sequences that are especially important to your sense of how the film constructs its meanings.

The sequence in which Kane's mother sends her son away (**12-14**) is likely to be an important one in the discussion of *Citizen Kane* from a number of different perspectives. To provide a narrative context for the analysis of this sequence, it would be necessary to explain that Mrs. Kane runs a boarding house and has inherited the deed to a supposedly worthless gold mine from one of her lodgers. After gold is discovered there, she uses her newfound wealth to send her son to boarding school, apparently to remove him from the clutches of his weak but abusive father. It might also be worth mentioning that the sequence occurs in that part of the narrative illustrating the version of events the reporter discovers in the unpublished memoirs of

Thatcher, the lawyer who will become Kane's guardian, the white of the manuscript paper dissolving into the snow in which the boy is playing at the beginning of the sequence. The most striking shot in this sequence is a **long take** of the inside of the house from which the boy can be seen playing in the distant background through the window. As he plays, Thatcher and his mother are determining his future in the foreground, while his father mutters a few feeble protests behind them. The mise en scène is compartmentalized into twos, with the wall serving as the vertical dividing line. Kane senior and young Charles are grouped to the left in the upper portion of the frame; Thatcher and the severe Mrs. Kane dominate the right lower half, their pens poised to sign the contract that will soon separate Charles from his parents. Ironically, Mrs. Kane is motivated by love and self-sacrifice, but her decision apparently has a lasting impact on her son, whose success as a newspaper tycoon is achieved at the cost of two failed marriages. The sled with which he is playing, and which he uses to knock Thatcher over at the end of the sequence, will become important in hindsight at the end of the film as a reminder of this moment when Kane's boyhood ended abruptly and his mother disappeared from his life.

Much more could be written about this sequence and its function in the movie as a whole. Indeed, as Bazin suggested, *Citizen Kane* invites this kind of attention from its viewers, creating complex images over which the eye can wander, linking the different levels of action and the visual imagery to the accompanying soundtrack. In some ways, it is more difficult to write about apparently simpler films in which the cinematic language does not call so much attention to itself. On the other hand, the kind of active reading that Welles's film virtually demands can be rewarding when applied to films that do not seem to require it.

One of the few sequences in *Mon oncle Antoine* not directly tied to Benoît's perspective illustrates the ways in which analysis can trace the complex meanings that emerge from apparently small events. After a number of sequences have established the centrality of Antoine's store to the communal life of the village, Alexandrine, the notary's wife, makes a dramatic entrance (**12-15**). As she throws open the door, the sun streams in from behind her, and an explosion booms out. Since the use of explosives at the mine is a daily occurrence at this time, it is highly possible she has timed her entry to create a sensation, and the assembled customers respond in dumbstruck awe to the glamorous wife of a local dignitary. Her arrival also provides the punch line for a running gag involving a barrel of nails, standing in the middle of the floor, over which several characters have already stumbled. Fernand has just persuaded Maurice, another boy who works in the store, to move it, and he is carrying it as the woman comes in. He is so stunned that he turns and automatically steps over the place where the barrel once stood. This joke suggests the way in which habit can control behaviour, as it does in the comforting but restrictive communal life of the village. The sequence also prepares for the next: As Maurice and Benoît spy on Alexandrine trying on her new corset, they are interrupted by Carmen, another store employee—who falls over the barrel, which Maurice has put down in order to watch. This experience seems to inspire Benoît's erotic interest in Carmen, and they have a fumbling encounter among the coffins. The linkage of sexuality and death culminates in a feverish dream that Benoît has after he and Antoine return from the farm without the dead boy's coffin. In this dream, Alexandine replaces the boy's body in the coffin and bounces up and down in her corset, smiling invitingly at Benoît. The moments when Benoît's feelings push beyond the limits of realism, as in this dream sequence and the meal at the farmhouse (**12-4**), are few in number, but they are very important in shaping our response to his less obviously distorted observation of the world around him.

The endings of both films manage to create a sense of finality while still leaving much to the viewer's imagination. Since endings are crucial in establishing our final impressions of a movie, it is often a good idea to pay some attention to them in an essay (in the context of your argument, of course).

An analysis of the ending of *Citizen Kane* would discuss the use of dissolves and crane shots as the camera pulls away from the reporter admitting defeat (**12-16)** to move across the piles of junk stored in Xanadu, treasured possessions when Kane was alive, to the furnace where workers are burning them in a furnace. The movement creates a god-like perspective, making us aware of the narrator who has been guiding our responses throughout, even when we were sharing the points of view of the reporter and his interviewees. Although some spectators find this ending, which reveals the meaning of Kane's dying word, a disappointing outcome for such a complex narrative, others feel it is a powerful final image that connects with many of the film's motifs.

12-16. *Citizen Kane*, with William Alland and Paul Stewart.

Near the end of the movie, Thompson (Alland) admits defeat. He never does find out what Rosebud means, and he describes his investigation as "playing with a jigsaw puzzle," while the camera cranes back and up, revealing thousands of crates of artwork, memorabilia, and personal effects—the fragmented artifacts of a person's life. "I don't think any word can explain a man's life," Thompson continues. "No, I guess Rosebud is just a piece in a jigsaw puzzle, a missing piece." *(RKO)*

12-17. *Mon oncle Antoine,* with Lionel Villeneuve and Hélène Loiselle.
Jos Poulin (Villeneuve) and his wife (Loiselle) stand grief-stricken among their surviving children around the coffin of their oldest child. Although the film does not show the scene, Jos has presumably made the grim discovery on his way home from the lumber camp—on the same road where the boy's coffin fell from Antoine's sleigh. *(National Film Board of Canada)*

The movie leaves us wondering whether it has explained who Kane was, revealed the emptiness behind his bravado, or simply shown that we can never fully understand another human being. After all, the first "sign" in the film is a "No Trespassing" warning.

At the end of *Mon oncle Antoine*, having failed to find the coffin, Fernand and Benoît arrive at the farmhouse (**12-13**), and the final sequence underlines our complicity with Benoît's look and invites us to consider the implications of what he sees. A long shot shows him following Fernand towards the house, and there is a cut to a shot in which the camera, apparently handheld, moves unsteadily forward. The instability of the moving camera and the sound of drumbeats on the soundtrack evoke the pressures weighing on Benoît, whose point of view the shot clearly represents, as he approaches the front window of the house. Three shots from inside, showing Benoît peering through the window, alternate with two shots of what he sees: the family gathered around the open coffin (**12-17**). The final shot of Benoît's face at the window freezes and forms a background for the unrolling of the credits. The **freeze-frame** ending, like the famous close-up of Antoine's face as he turns back from the sea at the end of François Truffaut's *Les Quatre cent coups* (see Chapter 5, "Movement"), functions as a challenge to the spectator to respond to the questions that have troubled the adolescent throughout the film. In both cases, the effect of the final image is difficult to decipher because of the virtual silence of the protagonist during the last part of the film. What is read into the final image will thus be largely a projection of the spectator's response to the entire film.

FINISHING THE ESSAY

The final stages in preparing your essay are not quite so elaborate as putting together the final cut of a movie and preparing its release. Yet, just as most film directors will not be satisfied during the post-production process until the final version of the movie represents their vision as fully as possible, it is important to ensure that your instructor receives your best possible effort. Re-read the assignment to be certain you have not overlooked anything. Then re-read the essay, proofreading for errors, but also making sure that the argument flows smoothly. If you are unsure of your writing skills, it is often a good idea to read the essay aloud. Then print a clean copy, and make sure you keep a back-up copy in case the original goes astray.

If you feel that you need more help with your writing, most universities and colleges have centres that offer support in essay writing and basic writing skills. You might also consult the websites listed at the front of this book.

WORKS CITED/FURTHER READING

Andrew, Dudley, *Film in the Aura of Art* (Princeton: Princeton University Press, 1984).

Bazin, André, *Orson Welles: A Critical View*, trans. Jonathan Rosenbaum (New York: Harper and Row, 1978).

Bordwell, David, "Citizen Kane," *Film Comment* 7, no. 2 (Summer 1971): 38–47.

Corrigan, Timothy, *A Short Guide to Writing About Film*, 6th ed. (New York: Longman, 2006).

Jaffe, Ira S., "Film as the Narration of Space: *Citizen Kane*," *Literature/Film Quarterly* 7, no. 2 (1979): 99–111.

Leach, Jim, *Claude Jutra Filmmaker* (Montreal: McGill-Queen's University Press, 1999).

— "Double Vision: *Mon oncle Antoine* and the Cinema of Fable," in *Canada's Best Features: Critical Essays on 15 Canadian Films*, ed. Gene Walz (Amsterdam: Rodopi, 2002): 27–49.

McKee, Alan, *Textual Analysis* (London: Sage, 2003).

Mulvey, Laura, *Citizen Kane* (London: British Film Institute, 1992).

Naremore, James, *The Magic World of Orson Welles* (New York: Oxford University Press, 1978).

Glossary

(C)	predominantly critical terms	(T)	predominantly technical terms
(I)	predominantly industry terms	(G)	terms in general usage

A

adaptation (G). A film based on a work in another medium, usually a novel or a play. Adaptations may be loose, faithful, or literal, depending on the extent of the changes made to the source material.

aerial shot (T). Essentially a variation of the *crane shot*, though restricted to exterior locations. Usually taken from a helicopter.

aleatory techniques (C). Techniques of filmmaking that depend on the element of chance. Images are not planned out in advance, but must be composed on the spot by the camera operator. Usually used in documentary situations.

allegory (C). A symbolic technique in which stylized characters and situations represent rather obvious ideas, such as Justice, Death, Religion, Society, and so on.

allusion (C). A reference to an event, person, or work of art, usually well known.

angle (G). The camera's angle of view relative to the subject being photographed. A high-angle shot is photographed from above, a low angle from below the subject.

animation (G). A form of filmmaking characterized by photographing inanimate objects, individual drawings or computer images, with each *frame* differing minutely from its predecessor. When such images are projected, the result is that the objects or drawings appear to move, and hence seem "animated."

anticipatory camera, anticipatory setup (C). The placement of the camera in such a manner as to anticipate the movement of an action before it occurs. Such setups often suggest predestination.

archetype, archetypal (C). An original model or type after which similar things are patterned. Archetypes can be well-known story patterns, universal experiences, or personality types. Myths, fairy tales, *genres*, and cultural heroes are generally archetypal, as are the basic cycles of life and nature.

art director (G). The individual responsible for designing and overseeing the construction of sets for a movie, and sometimes its interior decoration and overall visual style.

aspect ratio (T). The ratio between the horizontal and vertical dimensions of the screen.

auteur theory (C). A theory of film popularized by the critics of the French journal *Cahiers du cinéma* in the 1950s. The theory emphasizes the director as the major creator of film art, stamping the material with his or her own personal vision, style, and thematic obsessions.

available light (G). That light which actually exists on location, either natural (the sun) or artificial (house lamps). When available light is used in interior locations, generally a sensitive *fast film stock* must also be used.

avant-garde (C). From the French, meaning "in the front ranks." Unconventionally daring, progressive, or experimental in style. Those artists whose works are characterized by innovation (often controversial) are also referred to as "the avant-garde."

B

backlighting (G). Lighting for a shot that derives from the rear of the set, thus throwing the foreground figures into semidarkness or silhouette.

back-lot (I). During the studio era, standing exterior sets of such common locales as a turn-of-the-century city block, a frontier town, a European village, and so on.

bird's-eye view, bird's-eye shot (G). A shot in which the camera photographs a scene from directly overhead.

blimp (T). A soundproof camera housing that muffles the noise of the camera's motor so sound can be clearly recorded on the set.

boom, mike boom (T). An overhead telescoping pole that carries a microphone, permitting the *synchronous* recording of sound without restricting the movement of the actors.

C

camp, campy (C). An artistic sensibility typified by comic mockery, especially of the straight world and conventional morality. Campy movies are often ludicrously theatrical, stylistically gaudy, and gleefully subversive.

canted shot (T). See *oblique angle*.

cels, *also* cells (T). Transparent plastic sheets that are superimposed in layers by animators to give the illusion of depth and volume to their drawings.

cinematographer, *also* director of photography (G). The artist or technician responsible for the lighting of a shot and the quality of the photography.

cinéma vérité (C). A method of documentary filming using *aleatory* methods that do not interfere with the way events take place in reality. Such movies are made with a minimum of equipment, usually a handheld camera and portable sound apparatus.

classical (C). Adhering to the established norms of film style (as in *classical cinema*) or of a particular *genre* or mode of filmmaking (as in the classical musical, classical documentary).

classical cinema, classical paradigm (C). A vague but convenient term used to designate the style of mainstream fiction films edited according to conventions of *classical cutting* and structured by a narrative with a clearly defined conflict, complications that intensify to a rising climax, and a resolution that emphasizes formal closure.

classical cutting (C). A style of editing in which a sequence of shots is determined by a scene's dramatic and emotional emphasis rather than by physical action alone.

closed forms (C). A visual style that inclines toward self-conscious designs and carefully harmonized compositions. The *frame* is exploited to suggest a self-sufficient universe that encloses all the necessary visual information, usually in an aesthetically appealing manner.

close-up, close shot (G). A detailed view of a person or object. A close-up of an actor usually includes only his or her head.

code (C). In semiology, an organized system within which signs are related to each other and gain their meaning. Most films make use of multiple codes interacting in complex ways.

continuity (T). The kind of logic implied between edited shots, their principle of coherence. *Cutting to continuity* (or *continuity editing*) emphasizes smooth transitions between shots, in which time and space are unobtrusively condensed.

convention (C). A frequently used technique or device accepted by the audience as appropriate to a particular genre or style, e.g., that the hero in a western wears a white hat and the villain a black one, or that people burst into song in a musical. When a convention wears out it becomes a cliché.

coverage, covering shots, cover shots (T). Extra shots of a scene that can be used to bridge transitions in case the planned footage fails to edit as planned. Usually *long shots* that preserve the overall continuity of a scene.

crane shot (T). A shot taken from a special device called a crane, which resembles a huge mechanical arm. The crane carries the camera and the *cinematographer* and can move in virtually any direction.

cross-cutting (G). The alternating of shots from two sequences, often in different locales, suggesting that they are taking place at the same time.

cutting to continuity (T). A type of *editing* in which the shots are arranged to preserve the fluidity of the action without showing all of it. An unobtrusive condensation of a continuous action.

D

day-for-night shooting (T). Scenes that are filmed in daytime with special *filters* to suggest nighttime settings in the movie image.

deep-focus (T). A technique of photography that permits all distance planes to remain clearly in focus, from close-up ranges to infinity.

dialectical, dialectics (C). An analytical methodology, derived from Hegel and Marx, that juxtaposes pairs of opposites—a thesis and antithesis—to arrive at a synthesis of ideas.

diasporic cinema (C). Films made by members of communities founded by exiles or immigrants displaced from their homelands. These films interact with the traditions of the national cinemas in which they are made but often share themes, motifs, and actors with films made by the same diasporic groups elsewhere.

diegesis, diegetic (C). The fictional world presented in a film and its properties. Diegetic sound is thus sound that has an established source within the diegesis.

digital (G). Refers to the electronic coding of information for use in a computer. Digital effects create clearer and more manipulable sounds and images than previous analogue techniques. Widely used for animation, special effects, and increasingly to film whole movies.

direct cinema (C). A term often used as a synonym for *cinéma vérité*. In France and Canada, especially, it is used to designate an approach to documentary that stresses the relationship between filmmakers and their subjects. It is also applied to fiction films that use the equipment and techniques developed for documentary in the 1950s.

dissolve, lap dissolve (T). The slow fading out of one shot and the gradual fading in of its successor, with a superimposition of images, usually at the midpoint.

docudrama (C). A rather vague term often applied to various kinds of fictional reconstruction of actual events.

documentary (G). A nonfiction film that represents actuality, depicting people and situations that exist, or once existed, in the real world. Documentaries often claim, or imply, an objective viewpoint, but they inevitably select and shape (and sometimes fabricate) the reality they depict.

dolly shot, tracking shot, trucking shot (T). A shot taken from a moving vehicle. Originally tracks were laid on the set to permit a smoother movement of the camera.

dominant contrast, dominant (C). That area of the film image that compels the viewer's most immediate attention, usually because of a prominent visual contrast.

double exposure (T). The superimposition of two literally unrelated images on film. See also *multiple exposure*.

dubbing (T). The addition of sound after the visuals have been photographed. Dubbing can be either *synchronous* with an image or *nonsynchronous*. Foreign-language movies are often dubbed by actors who lip-sync (i.e. they try to match the new words to the lip movements of the original actors).

E

editing (G). The joining of one shot (strip of film) with another.

epic (C). A film *genre* characterized by bold and sweeping themes, usually in heroic proportions. The protagonist is often an ideal representative of a culture—national, religious, or regional. The tone of most epics is dignified, the treatment larger than life.

establishing shot (T). Usually an *extreme long* or *long shot* offered at the beginning of a scene, providing the viewer with the context of the subsequent closer shots.

expressionism, expressionist, expressionistic (C). A formalist style of filmmaking emphasizing extreme distortion, *lyricism*, and artistic self-expression at the expense of objectivity. Used more specifically to describe a movement in German cinema after World War I.

extreme close-up, extreme close-shot (G). A minutely detailed view of an object or person. An extreme close-up of an actor generally includes only his or her eyes or mouth.

extreme long shot (G). A panoramic view of an exterior location, photographed from a great distance, often as far as four hundred metres away.

eye-level shot (T). The placement of the camera approximately one and a half to two metres from the ground, corresponding to the height of an observer on the scene.

F

fade (T). The fade-out is the snuffing of an image from normal brightness to a black screen. A *fade-in* is the opposite.

fast motion (T). Shots of a subject photographed at a slower rate than twenty-four fps, which, when projected at the standard rate, conveys motion that is jerky and slightly comical, seemingly out of control.

fast stock, fast film (T). Film stock that is highly sensitive to light and generally produces a grainy image.

film noir (C). Originally a French term—literally, "black cinema"—referring to a kind of urban American crime film that sprang up during and after World War II. Stylistically, *noir* emphasizes *low-key* and *high-contrast* lighting, complex compositions, and a strong atmosphere of dread and paranoia.

filters (T). Pieces of glass and plastic placed in front of the camera lens that distort the quality of light entering the camera and hence the movie image.

final cut, release print (I). The completed movie as it will be released to the public.

first cut, rough cut (I). The initial version of a movie, often constructed by the director and usually much longer than the *final cut*.

flashback (G). An editing technique that interrupts the present action by a shot or series of shots representing the past.

flashforward (G). An editing technique that interrupts the present action by a shot or series of shots representing the future.

focus (T). The degree of acceptable sharpness in a film image. "Out of focus" means the images are blurred and lack acceptable linear definition.

formalism, formalist, formalistic (C). Applied to styles of filmmaking in which aesthetic forms take precedence over the subject matter as content. Time and space as ordinarily perceived are often distorted. Emphasis is on the essential, symbolic characteristics of objects and people, not necessarily on their superficial appearance. Formalists are often *lyrical*, self-consciously heightening their style to call attention to it as a value for its own sake.

formative (C). Applied to the early stages of a *genre* or mode of filmmaking in which the *classical* norms have not yet become fully established. Sometimes referred to as the "primitive" phase.

frame (T). The dividing line between the edges of the screen image and the enclosing darkness of the theatre. Can also refer to a single photograph from the filmstrip.

freeze frame, freeze shot (T). A shot composed of a single *frame* that is reprinted a number of times on the filmstrip; when projected, it gives the illusion of a still photograph.

full shot (T). A type of *long shot* that includes the human body in full, with the head near the top of the *frame* and the feet near the bottom.

G

genre (C). A recognizable type of movie, characterized by certain pre-established conventions. Some common American genres are westerns, thrillers, sci-fi movies, etc. A ready-made narrative form.

H

handheld shot (G). A shot taken with a moving camera that is held by the camera person and thus rather shaky compared to shots taken using a tripod or dolly. Often used in fiction films to suggest documentary footage in an uncontrolled setting.

high-angle shot (T). A shot in which the subject is photographed from above.

high contrast (T). A style of lighting emphasizing harsh shafts and dramatic streaks of lights and darks. Often used in thrillers and melodramas.

high key (T). A style of lighting emphasizing bright, even illumination, with few conspicuous shadows. Used mostly in comedies, musicals, and light entertainment films.

homage (C). A direct or indirect reference within a movie to another movie, filmmaker, or cinematic style. A respectful and affectionate tribute.

I

icon, iconic (C). In film and cultural studies, a person or an image that has acquired a widely understood cultural significance. In semiology, a sign that resembles what it signifies (e.g. a painting of a tree).

iconography (C). The use of a well-known cultural symbol or complex of symbols in an artistic representation. In movies, iconography can involve a star's *persona*, the preestablished conventions of a genre (like the shootout in a western), the use of *archetypal* characters and situations, and such stylistic features as lighting, settings, costuming, props, and so on.

independent producer (G). A producer not affiliated with a studio or large commercial firm. Many stars and directors have been independent producers to ensure their artistic control.

index, indexical (C). In semiology, a sign that has an actual link to what it signifies (e.g., smoke as a sign of fire).

intercutting (T). See *cross-cutting*.

intertextuality (C). The creation of meaning through references and allusions within a film to other films and cultural texts.

intrinsic interest (C). An unobtrusive area of the film image that nonetheless compels our most immediate attention because of its dramatic or contextual importance.

iris (T). A *masking* device that blacks out portions of the screen, permitting only a part of the image to be seen. Usually the iris is circular or oval in shape and can be expanded or contracted.

J

jump cut (T). An abrupt transition between shots in which the second shot is taken from an angle only slightly different from that of the first so that characters or objects seem to "jump." The same effect can be created by the removal (deliberate or accidental) of frames from the middle of a single take.

K

key light (T). The main source of illumination for a shot.

kinetic (C). Pertaining to motion and movement.

L

lens (T). A ground or moulded piece of glass, plastic, or other transparent material through which light rays are refracted so they converge or diverge to form the photographic image within the camera.

location (G). A place where a film or part of a film is shot (as opposed to a studio).

long shot (G). A shot taken from a distance that includes a full view of the subject and some of the surrounding area.

long take (C). A single shot of lengthy duration.

loose framing (C). Usually in longer shots. The *mise en scène* is so spaciously distributed within the confines of the framed image that the people photographed have considerable freedom of movement.

low-angle shot (T). A shot in which the subject is photographed from below.

low key (T). A style of lighting that emphasizes diffused shadows and atmospheric pools of light. Often used in mysteries and thrillers.

lyrical (C). A stylistic exuberance and subjectivity, emphasizing the sensuous beauty of the medium and producing an intense outpouring of emotion.

M

majors (I). The principal production studios of the golden age of the Hollywood studio system—roughly the 1930s and 1940s—MGM, Warner Brothers, RKO, Paramount Pictures, and Twentieth Century Fox.

masking (T). A technique whereby a portion of the movie image is blocked out, thus temporarily altering the dimensions of the screen's *aspect ratio.*

master shot (T). An uninterrupted shot, usually taken from a *long-* or *full-shot* range, that contains an entire scene. The closer shots are photographed later, and an *edited* sequence, composed of a variety of shots, is constructed on the editor's bench.

matte shot (T). A process of combining two separate shots on one print, resulting in an image that looks as though it had been photographed normally. Used mostly for special effects, such as combining a human figure with animation, like giant dinosaurs.

medium shot (G). A relatively close shot, revealing the human figure from the knees or waist up.

metaphor (C). An implied comparison between two otherwise unlike elements, meaningful in a figurative rather than literal sense.

Method acting (C). A style of performance derived from the Russian stage director Stanislavsky, which has been the dominant acting style in the United States since the 1950s. Method actors emphasize psychological intensity, extensive rehearsals to explore a character, emotional believability rather than technical mastery, and "living" a role internally rather than merely imitating the external behaviour of a character.

metteur en scène (C). The artist or technician who creates the *mise en scène*—that is, the director. In *auteur theory*, a director who acts as a technician rather than as an artist expressing a personal vision.

mickeymousing (T). A type of film music that is purely descriptive and attempts to mimic the visual action with musical equivalents. Often used in cartoons.

miniatures, model, or miniature shots (T). Small-scale models photographed to give the illusion that they are full-scale objects. For example, ships sinking at sea, giant dinosaurs, airplanes colliding, etc.

minimalism (C). A style of filmmaking characterized by austerity and restraint, in which cinematic elements are reduced to the barest minimum of information.

mise en scène (C). The arrangement of visual weights and movements within a given space. Cinematic mise en scène encompasses both the staging of the action and the way that it is photographed.

mock-documentary, mockumentary (C). A fiction film that presents itself as if it were a documentary, usually with the intent of parodying the documentary's claims to objectivity and authority.

montage (T). An editing technique that stresses the dynamic relations between shots, often associated with the Soviet filmmakers of the 1920s and seen as an alternative to continuity editing. In Europe montage is often used as a synonym for editing.

montage sequence (T). A transitional sequence of rapidly edited images, used to suggest the lapse of time or the passing of events. Often uses *dissolves* and *multiple exposures*.

motif (C). Any unobtrusive technique, object, or thematic idea systematically repeated throughout a film.

multiple exposures (T). A special effect that permits the superimposition of many images simultaneously.

N

neorealism (C). An Italian film movement that produced its best works between 1945 and 1955. Strongly *realistic* in its techniques, neorealism emphasized documentary aspects of film art, stressing loose episodic plots, ordinary events and characters, natural lighting, actual location settings, nonprofessional actors, a preoccupation with poverty and social problems, and an emphasis on humanistic and democratic ideals.

New Wave, Nouvelle vague (C). A group of young French directors who came to prominence during the late 1950s.

nondiegetic (C). Refers to a sound or image that has no source in the fictional world of the film (background music, symbolic inserts, etc.).

nonfiction film (C). Often used as a synonym for *documentary*, but may also refer to any kind of film that does not depend on involving the viewer with an imaginary world.

nonsynchronous sound (T). Sound that is not recorded simultaneously with the image, or sound that is detached from its source in the film image.

O

oblique angle shot (T). A shot photographed by a camera that is not set up horizontally. When the image is projected on the screen, the subject itself seems to be tilted on a diagonal.

omniscient point of view (C). An all-knowing narration that provides the spectator with all the necessary information.

open forms (C). Used primarily by *realist* filmmakers, these techniques are likely to be unobtrusive, with an emphasis on informal compositions and apparently haphazard designs. The *frame* is exploited to suggest a temporary masking, a window that arbitrarily cuts off part of the action.

optical printer (T). A machine used to create special effects in movies. Today many of these effects are created with *digital* technology.

overexposure (T). Too much light enters the aperture of a camera lens, bleaching out the image. Useful for fantasy and nightmare scenes.

P

pan, panning, panning shot (T). Short for panorama, this is a revolving horizontal movement of the camera from left to right or vice versa.

parallel editing (T). See *cross-cutting*.

parody (C). A humorous imitation of another film or style of filmmaking. Often associated with *reflexive* genre films, but parodies began to appear very early in film history.

pastiche (C). The imitation and/or combination of earlier styles without the mockery of *parody* but often with a twist that acknowledges the present context. Often associated with postmodernism.

persona (C). From the Latin, "mask." An actor's public image, based on previous roles, and often incorporating elements from his or her actual personality as well.

pixillation, stop-motion photography (T). An *animation* technique involving the photographing of live actors frame by frame. When the sequence is projected at the standard speed of twenty-four fps, the actors move abruptly and jerkily, like cartoon figures.

plot (C). The arrangement of *story* events in the order in which they appear in the film. For example, events that occurred in the past might be introduced at any point through *flashbacks* or dialogue.

point-of-view shot, pov shot (T). Any shot that is taken from the vantage point of a character in the film, showing what the character sees.

producer (G). An ambiguous term referring to the individual or company that controls the financing of a film, and often the way it is made. The producer may be concerned solely with business matters, or with putting together a package deal (such as script, stars, and director), or function as an expeditor, smoothing over problems during production.

production values (I). The box-office appeal of the physical mounting of a film, such as sets, costumes, props, etc.

property (I). Anything with a profit-making potential in movies, though generally used to describe a story of some kind: a screenplay, novel, short story, etc.

proxemic patterns (C). The spatial relationships among characters within the *mise en scène* and the apparent distance of the camera from the subject photographed.

pull-back dolly (T). Withdrawing the camera from a scene to reveal an object or character that was previously out of *frame*.

Q

queer theory (C). A way of reading films (and other cultural texts) that challenges conventional notions of sexuality and subjectivity in which heterosexuality is assumed as the norm.

R

rack focusing, selective focusing (T). The blurring of focal planes in sequence, forcing the viewer's eyes to travel with those areas of an image that remain in sharp focus.

reaction shot (T). A cut to a shot of a character's reaction to the contents of the preceding shot.

realism (G). A range of styles of filmmaking that attempt to represent reality as it is commonly perceived, with emphasis on authentic locations and details, *long shots*, *lengthy takes*, and a minimum of distorting techniques.

reception theory (C). A term applied to a variety of approaches that study the meanings audiences take from films rather than relying on critics' readings of film texts.

reestablishing shot (T). A return to an initial *establishing shot* within a scene, acting as a reminder of the physical context of the closer shots.

reflexive (C). Making apparent the processes by which a film is made. Applied to *avant-garde* cinema and a phase of genres or modes in which films play self-consciously with conventions and film history (sometimes in the form of *parody*).

reverse angle shot (T). A shot taken from an angle 180° opposed to the previous shot. That is, the camera is placed opposite its previous position.

reverse motion (T). A series of images are photographed with the film reversed. When projected normally, the effect is to suggest backward movement—an egg "returning" to its shell, for example.

revisionist (C). Applied to a phase of genres or modes that follows the *classical* phase, in which the established norms are subject to critical questioning.

rough cut (T). The crudely edited footage of a movie before the editor has tightened up the slackness between shots. A kind of rough draft.

S

scene (G). An imprecise unit of film, composed of a number of interrelated *shots*, in which the action takes place in continuous time in one location or set (or in more than one place if cross-cutting is used to depict simultaneous events).

screwball comedy (C). A film *genre*, introduced in the 1930s in the United States, characterized by zany lovers, often from different social classes. The plots are often absurdly improbable and have a tendency to veer out of control. These movies usually feature slapstick comedy scenes, aggressive and charming heroines, and an assortment of outlandish secondary characters.

script, screenplay, scenario (G). A written description of a movie's dialogue and action, which occasionally includes camera directions.

selective focusing (T). See *rack focusing*.

semiology, semiotics (C). The study of the processes of signification, through signs and codes, in films and other cultural texts.

sequence (G). A significant segment of a film's overall structure usually containing a completed line of action. Often used synonymously with *scene* but may include more than one location or set and is not necessarily continuous in time.

sequence shot (C). A single lengthy shot, usually involving complex staging and camera movements.

set (G). A place, constructed in a studio, where a film or part of a film is shot.

setup (T). (1) The positioning of the camera and lights for a specific shot. (2) The opening section of a narrative.

shooting ratio (I). The amount of film stock used in photographing a movie in relation to what is included in the finished product. A shooting ratio of 20:1 means that twenty feet of film were shot for every one used in the *final cut*.

short lens. See *wide-angle lens*.

shot (G). In production, those images that are recorded continuously from the time the camera starts to the time it stops, in other words, a take. In the completed movie, an uninterrupted piece of film between edits.

shot/reverse shot (T). Two or more shots edited together, often depicting a conversation and using over-the-shoulder compositions. One of the basic techniques of classical cinema.

sign (C). In semiology, a unit in a language system or code, consisting of a signifier (a word or an image, for example) and a signified (the meaning we attach to that word or image).

slow motion (T). Shots of a subject photographed at a faster rate than twenty-four fps, which, when projected at the standard rate, produce a dreamy, dance-like slowness of action.

slow stock, slow film (T). Film stocks that are relatively insensitive to light and produce crisp images and a sharpness of detail. When used in interior settings, these stocks generally require considerable artificial illumination.

soft focus (T). The blurring out of focus of all except one desired distance range. Can also refer to a glamourizing technique that softens the sharpness of definition so facial wrinkles can be smoothed over and even eliminated.

star (G). A film actor or actress of great popularity.

star system (G). The technique of exploiting the charisma of popular performers to enhance the box-office appeal of films. The star system was developed in America and has been the backbone of the American film industry since the mid-1910s.

stock (T). Unexposed film. There are many types of movie stocks, including those highly sensitive to light (*fast stocks*) and those relatively insensitive to light (*slow stocks*).

stop-motion photography (T). See *pixillation.*

story (C). All the events that we see, hear about, or infer in a fiction film in the order in which they are supposed to have happened. The filmmaker constructs the *plot* from these events; the spectator reconstructs the story on the basis of the information supplied by the plot.

structural film (C). An avant-garde movement that explores the physical properties of the film medium.

structuralism, structuralist (C). A philosophical approach that finds meaning in the relations between elements in a text rather than in the elements themselves.

studio (G). A large corporation specializing in the production of movies, such as Paramount, Warner Brothers, and so on; any physical facility equipped for the production of films.

subsidiary contrast (C). A subordinated element of the film image, complementing or contrasting with the *dominant contrast.*

subtext (C). A term used to signify the dramatic implications beneath the language of a play or movie.

surrealism, surrealistic (C). An *avant-garde* movement in the arts stressing Freudian and Marxist ideas, unconscious elements, irrationalism, and the symbolic association of ideas. Surrealist movies were produced roughly from 1924 to 1931, primarily in France, though there are surrealistic elements in the works of many directors.

swish pan, also flash or zip pan (T). A horizontal movement of the camera at such a rapid rate that the subject photographed blurs on the screen.

symbol, symbolic (C). A figurative device in which an object, event, or cinematic technique has significance beyond its literal meaning. In semiology, a sign that has an arbitrary relation to what it signifies.

synchronous sound (T). The agreement or correspondence between image and sound, which are recorded simultaneously, or seem so in the finished print.

T

take (T). One version of a specific shot. The final shot is often selected from a number of possible takes.

telephoto lens, long lens (T). A lens that acts as a telescope, magnifying the size of objects at a great distance. A side effect is its tendency to flatten perspective.

thematic montage (C). A type of *editing* propounded by the Soviet filmmaker Eisenstein, in which separate shots are linked together not by their literal continuity in reality but by symbolic association. A shot of a preening braggart might be linked to a shot of a toy peacock, for example. Most commonly used in documentaries, in which shots are connected in accordance to the filmmaker's thesis.

three shot (T). A *medium shot*, featuring three actors.

tight framing (C). Usually in close shots. The *mise en scène* is so carefully balanced and harmonized that the people photographed have little or no freedom of movement.

tilt, tilt shot (T). A vertical *panning shot* in which the camera moves on its axis up or down.

tone (G). The manner of presentation and the general atmosphere of a movie.

tracking shot, trucking shot. See *dolly shot.*

two shot (T). A *medium shot* featuring two actors.

V

vertical integration (I). A system in which the production, distribution, and exhibition of movies are all controlled by the same corporation. In America the practice was declared illegal in the late 1940s but restored in the 1980s.

viewfinder (T). An eyepiece on the camera that defines the playing area and the *framing* of the action to be photographed.

voice-of-God commentary (C). In documentary, the text spoken by an unseen, authoritative, and apparently all-knowing (male) commentator.

voice-over (T). A *nonsynchronous* spoken commentary in a movie, often used to convey a character's thoughts or memories.

W

wide-angle lens (T). A lens that permits the camera to photograph a wider area than a normal lens. A side effect is its tendency to exaggerate perspective. Also used for *deep-focus* photography.

widescreen (G). A movie image that has an *aspect ratio* wider than the standard Academy ration of 1.33:1 (i.e. one third wider than its height) or the now standard ratio of 1.85:1. Most widescreen films now have a ratio of 2.45:1.

women's films (G). A film *genre*, often referred to as domestic melodrama, that focuses on the problems of women, such as career versus family conflicts.

Z

zoom lens, zoom shot (T). A lens of variable focal length that permits the cinematographer to change from *wide-angle* to *telephoto shots* (and vice versa) in one continuous movement, often plunging the viewer in or out of a scene rapidly.

[illegible]

[illegible]

[illegible]

[illegible]

[illegible]

[illegible]

[illegible]

[illegible]

[illegible]

[illegible]

[illegible]

[illegible]

[illegible]

[illegible]

[illegible]

[illegible]

[illegible]

Index

INDEX

E

F

H

I

J

K

L

N

T

X

Y

Z